Trans-Siberian Railway

A CLASSIC OVERLAND ROUTE

Simon Richmond
Mara Vorhees

LONELY PLANET PUBLICATIONS

Melbourne | Oakland | London | Paris

THE TRANS-SIBERIAN RAIL ROUTES

RAIL ROUTES

Trans-Siberian
Trans-Mongolian
Trans-Manchurian
Baikal-Amur Mainline
Ural
Other

0   500   1000km
0   300   600mi

ARCTIC

NORTH SEA

BRITAIN

NORWAY

Oslo

SWEDEN

DENMARK
Copenhagen

Stockholm

Baltic Sea

POLAND

Warsaw

RUSSIA

BELARUS

Minsk

Kyiv

UKRAINE

Tallinn   Helsinki

Riga

ESTONIA

LATVIA

LITHUANIA

Vilnius

Smolensk

St Petersburg

Lake Ladoga

Norwegian Sea

FINLAND

White Sea

BARENTS SEA

Murmansk

Arkhangelsk

Svalbard

Zemlya Frantsa-Iosifa

Novaya Zemlya

KARA SEA

Dixon

Yamal Peninsula

Amderma

Vorkuta

Salekhard

Gydansky Peninsula

Ob Gulf

ARCTIC

Dudinka

Norilsk

Igarka

Siberian Lowland

MOSCOW

Yaroslavl

Suzdal

Vladimir

Nizhny Novgorod

Vyatka (Kirov)

Kazan

Perm

Nizhniy Tagil

RUSSIA

URAL MOUNTAINS

Khanty-Mansiysk

Syzran

Samara

Saratov

Yekaterinburg

Tobolsk

Chelyabinsk

Magnitogorsk

Petropavl (Petropavlovsk)

Omsk

Tomsk

Mariinsk

Novosibirsk

Volgograd

Orsk

Astrakhan

Sea of Azov

Rostov-on-Don

Elbrus (5642m)

CAUCASUS MTS

BLACK SEA

Grozny

GEORGIA

Tbilisi

ARMENIA

Yerevan

AZERBAIJAN

Baku

CASPIAN SEA

Astana

Karaganda

Semey (Semipalatinsk)

Balkhash

Aktogay

Lake Balkhash

ALTAY MOUNTAINS

Belukha (4506m)

KAZAKHSTAN

Aral Sea

Nukus

Tashauz

TURANIAN PLATEAU

UZBEKISTAN

Syr Darya

TURKMENISTAN

Ashkabad

Bukhara

ZAGROS MOUNTAINS

Tehran

IRAN

Tashkent

Bishkek

KYRGYZSTAN

Almaty

Urumqi

Dushanbe

TAJIKISTAN

AFGHANISTAN

Kabul

CHINA

Tarim Basin

Trans-Siberian Railway
1st edition – June 2002

Published by
Lonely Planet Publications Pty Ltd ABN. 36 005 607 983
90 Maribyrnong St, Footscray, Victoria 3011, Australia

Lonely Planet Offices
Australia Locked Bag 1, Footscray, Victoria 3011
USA 150 Linden St, Oakland, CA 94607
UK 10a Spring Place, London NW5 3BH
France 1 rue du Dahomey, 75011 Paris

Photographs
Many of the images in this guide are available for licensing from
Lonely Planet Images.
w www.lonelyplanetimages.com

Front cover photograph
The Trans-Siberian express weaves through a Russian winter landscape.
(Martin Moos)
Trans-Siberian title page
Open your eyes with Lonely Planet's guide to the journey.
(Patrick Horton)
Trans-Mongolian title page
'Welcome to Mongolia', downtown Ulaan Baatar. (Olivier Cirendini)
Trans-Manchurian title page
See the Great Wall up close as you travel between Manchuria and
Beijing. (Diana Mayfield)

ISBN 1 86450 335 1

Printed by The Bookmaker International Ltd
Printed in China

Contents – Text

Contents – Maps

MAP INDEX

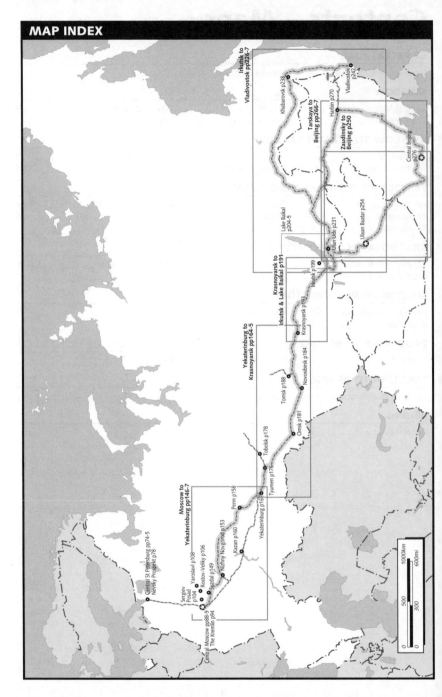

1000km

500

600mi

300

The Authors

Simon Richmond

Classic rail-journey enthusiast Simon Richmond clocked up his first Trans-Siberian trip from Vladivostok in 1997, during which he was attacked by dogs, robbed on the train and got so plastered at Lake Baikal that it's a wonder he ever found his way back to Irkutsk let alone Moscow. None of this put the award-winning writer off returning to Russia to coordinate this guide, travelling entirely by train from London to Vladivostok, and then by boat to Japan – just because you can. Co-author of Lonely Planet's *Istanbul to Kathmandu* route guide, *South Africa*, *Cape Town, Central Asia*, *Walking in Australia* and the *Out to Eat* guides to London and Sydney, Simon also writes for several other guidebook publishers, magazines and newspapers.

Mara Vorhees

Mara was born in St Clair Shores, Michigan. Her fascination with world cultures and her penchant for good deeds led her into the field of international development, and she set out to assist Russia in its economic transition. (She claims no responsibility for the outcome.) Having travelled extensively in Scandinavia, the Baltic region and the former Soviet Union, she is now trying to work her way to warmer climes. Mara currently lives in Somerville, Massachusetts, with her husband and her cat. When not railing around the world, she works at the Center for International Development at Harvard University.

FROM THE AUTHORS

Simon Richmond

I'll start by thanking Andrew Humphreys for getting the ball rolling on this guide so long ago, and to Mark Griffiths, Liz Filleul and Brigitte Ellemore at LP for keeping it on track since. My co-author Mara did a splendid job, too.

For help with research along the railroad many thanks to the following: Steve Caron, Molly Graves, Valudya Kovalev and Barnaby Thompson in St Petersburg; Sergey Frolov, David Arkley and colleagues at the British Embassy, Leonid Ragozin and Masha Makeeva, Kevin O'Flynn, Neil McGowan and Jan Passoff in Moscow; Evgeny Zakablukovsky in Nizhny Novgorod; Olga and Konstantin Brylakov in Yekaterinburg; Igor Sinyepalnikov and Viacheslav Novitsky in Tobolsk; Dan Gotham in Novosibirsk; Youry Nemirovsky and colleagues in Irkutsk; Rashit Yahin in Severobaikalsk; Valera Bukrova, Dmitri Boldetsov and Sergey Sigachyov in Khabarovsk; and Alex Hamilton and Eugene Degtyarev in Vladivostok.

Cheers to all those fellow travellers, past and present, who chipped in with their experiences including Judith Alexander,

Dean Arthur (and Barnaby), Jan Dodd, Anne and Julian Epps, Hayden Glass, Caroline Guilleminot, Stephen Hammond, Brett & Betty Hyland, Patrick Horton, Markus Lageder, Adam Levy and Melissa McVeigh.

Finally, the biggest thanks of all goes to the fascinating range of Russians I met along the way, who always make a journey through Russia so memorable. In particular, Leonid Zakharia and his family extended the hand of friendship when I needed it most – *bolshoya spasibo*.

Mara Vorhees

Thanks first of all to my co-author Simon Richmond for his friendly cooperation on and efficient coordination of this title. I am also grateful to Liz Filleul for the opportunity to work on this project. I owe a huge debt of gratitude to Caroline Liou, Bradley Mayhew, Suzanne Possehl and other LP authors, without whose prior research my job would have been 10 times tougher.

For helpful hints and hospitality along the Trans-Manchurian and Trans-Mongolian, I am grateful to Chris Stanley and Andy Jones (Monkey Business) and Dang Kai in Beijing; Zhao Yang (CITS) in Harbin; Gan Batbold (UB Tour) and Graham Taylor (Karakorum Expeditions) in Ulaan Baatar; and Lena & Valeri Vysotin in Irkutsk. I also appreciate the assistance of Yong Zhang and Anatoly & Olga Kukarin back in Boston. Thanks also for advice and anecdotes from fellow travellers Maggie and Jerry Gross, Jimmy Nagle, Daniel and Sioned Williams and Edward Gowan.

Finally, for hours of entertainment on the train and encouragement at the writer's desk, thanks to Jerry Easter, whose unbounded interest and unconditional support are my greatest inspiration.

This Book

This first edition of *The Trans-Siberian Railway* was written by Simon Richmond (coordinating author) and Mara Vorhees. Material has been used from a number of other Lonely Planet guidebooks: *Russia, Ukraine & Belarus*; *Moscow*; *St Petersburg*; *China*; *Beijing*; *Mongolia*.

FROM THE PUBLISHER

This first edition of *Trans-Siberian Railway* was produced in Lonely Planet's Melbourne office. It was edited and proofed by Yvonne Byron, with assistance from Will Gourlay and Helen Yeates. Adrian Persoglia coordinated the mapping, with assistance from Gus Balbontin, Katie Butterworth, Csanad Csutoros, Huw Fowles, Cris Gibcus, Anna Judd, Sally Morgan, Ray Thomson and Celia Wood. Anna laid out the Nature Guide, Csanad prepared the climate charts and Lachlan Ross provided country map expertise.

Thanks also to Maria Vallianos for designing the cover, Matt King for coordinating the illustrations, Barbara Dombrowski and Gerard Walker for coordinating the photographic images, Mark Germanchis for his Quark support, and Quentin Frayne who grappled with multiple fonts to produce the Language chapter and Glossary. Mick Weldon (MW), Trudi Canavan (TC) and Sarah Jolly (SJ) drew the illustrations. We are also grateful to Jim Jenkin and Valentina Kremenchutskaya for their advice on the vagaries of Cyrillic, which could not have been overcome without the assistance of Chris Lee Ack and his font masters. Nick Stebbing helped with the Chinese script. Guidance from Adriana Mammarella about the design of a route guide was invaluable in planning. Nikki Anderson advised us of our copyright responsibilities and Melena McKaskill prepared many contracts at short notice to ensure that we complied. Thanks also to seniors Liz Filleul (editing), who was ably assisted by Susie Ashworth during layout, and Mark Griffiths (design) for their valuable assistance and expert checking.

Acknowledgments

Lonely Planet gratefully acknowledges permission from the following to reprint material.

Northwestern University Press for an extract from the translation by G Mikkelson & M Winchell of *Siberia, Siberia* by Valentin Rasputin.

Ger magazine, Mongolia for an edited extract of an article about the Naadam festival by N Enkhbayar, published in the January 2000 issue.

Dean Arthur of the British School of Bahrain for his item on Barnaby the Bear.

Foreword

ABOUT LONELY PLANET GUIDEBOOKS

The story begins with a classic travel adventure: Tony and Maureen Wheeler's 1972 journey across Europe and Asia to Australia. There was no useful information about the overland trail then, so Tony and Maureen published the first Lonely Planet guidebook to meet a growing need.

From a kitchen table, Lonely Planet has grown to become the largest independent travel publisher in the world, with offices in Melbourne (Australia), Oakland (USA), London (UK) and Paris (France).

Today Lonely Planet guidebooks cover the globe. There is an ever-growing list of books and information in a variety of media. Some things haven't changed. The main aim is still to make it possible for adventurous travellers to get out there – to explore and better understand the world.

At Lonely Planet we believe travellers can make a positive contribution to the countries they visit – if they respect their host communities and spend their money wisely. Since 1986 a percentage of the income from each book has been donated to aid projects and human rights campaigns, and, more recently, to wildlife conservation.

Although inclusion in a guidebook usually implies a recommendation we cannot list every good place. Exclusion does not necessarily imply criticism. In fact there are a number of reasons why we might exclude a place – sometimes it is simply inappropriate to encourage an influx of travellers.

UPDATES & READER FEEDBACK

Things change – prices go up, schedules change, good places go bad and bad places go bankrupt. Nothing stays the same. So, if you find things better or worse, recently opened or long-since closed, please tell us and help make the next edition even more accurate and useful.

Lonely Planet thoroughly updates each guidebook as often as possible – usually every two years, although for some destinations the gap can be longer. Between editions, up-to-date information is available in our free, quarterly *Planet Talk* newsletter and monthly email bulletin *Comet*. The *Upgrades* section of our website (W www.lonelyplanet.com) is also regularly updated by Lonely Planet authors, and the site's *Scoop* section covers news and current affairs relevant to travellers. Lastly, the *Thorn Tree* bulletin board and *Postcards* section carry unverified, but fascinating, reports from travellers.

Tell us about it! We genuinely value your feedback. A well-travelled team at Lonely Planet reads and acknowledges every email and letter we receive and ensures that every morsel of information finds its way to the relevant authors, editors and cartographers.

Everyone who writes to us will find their name listed in the next edition of the appropriate guidebook, and will receive the latest issue of *Comet* or *Planet Talk*. The very best contributions will be rewarded with a free guidebook.

We may edit, reproduce and incorporate your comments in Lonely Planet products such as guidebooks, websites and digital products, so let us know if you don't want your comments reproduced or your name acknowledged.

How to contact Lonely Planet:
Online: e talk2us@lonelyplanet.com.au, W www.lonelyplanet.com
Australia: Locked Bag 1, Footscray, Victoria 3011
UK: 10a Spring Place, London NW5 3BH
USA: 150 Linden St, Oakland, CA 94607

Introduction

It is time, high time!
Alexander III, 1886

With these words the tsar gave the thumbs up to arguably one of the wonders of the modern world – the Trans-Siberian Railway. Spanning mighty rivers and running through mountains, dense forests, murky swamps and vast steppes, coated with deep snow for the better part of the year and baking hot in summer, the Trans-Siberian Railway's construction is an engineering achievement with little parallel. The 9289km journey from Moscow to the Pacific Coast, taking seven days, is also the longest single-service rail trip in the world. As Eric Newby famously quipped 'The Trans-Siberian is *the* big train ride. All the rest are peanuts'.

Don't look for it on a timetable though. The term 'Trans-Siberian Railway' is used generically for three main services and some of the numerous other trains that run along the route, physically linking the extremes of the largest country on earth.

The classic Trans-Siberian service, the *Rossiya*, runs alternate days from Moscow's Yaroslavl Station across a third of the globe to Vladivostok, Russia's decrepit but visually appealing Far Eastern gateway. Along the way it memorably skirts Lake Baikal, the beautiful body of water that appears, as if out of nowhere, in the middle of the Siberian *taiga*.

Veering off the main line after Ulan Ude in eastern Siberia is the Trans-Mongolian service. Russian gingerbread cottages and forests give way to the endless steppe and sky of Mongolia – a view broken only by an occasional horseman or *ger*. Onward the train trundles to Beijing, past the spectacular Great Wall of China. With such attractions en route, it's hardly surprising that this is the most popular of the Trans-Siberian trips, one to be recommended whichever direction you choose to travel.

Finally, the weekly Trans-Manchurian service, which leaves the main line at Tarskaya, east of Chita, follows a route to Beijing through Harbin. Home of an amazing Ice Lantern Festival, Harbin is one of the many places along the route where the centuries-old mingling of cultures and history is still visible in the lively cross-border trade and many graceful architectural remnants of an earlier age.

Some want to experience these epic train trips nonstop, savouring the slowly evolving landscapes and on-board life as if on an overland cruise. There's merit in this, but we think you'd be crazy not to want to break your journey at least once. Russia is now more open to travellers than at any time in the past, and the possibilities for exploration are practically limitless. The Trans-Siberian route gives access to cities such as Yekaterinburg and Krasnoyarsk, off limits for decades, but fascinating to visit today. Or you may choose to soak up the old Siberian atmosphere of more off-the-beaten-track gems such as Tomsk or Tobolsk. Pollution and neglect are all too apparent, but there are still vast expanses of pristine wilderness – particularly in Siberia – providing ample opportunities for outdoor activities like trekking and white-water rafting.

Designed for everyday transport, travel on these working trains ain't glamorous, but it's rarely dull, not least because of the chance you'll have to interact with fellow passengers. Russians are among some of the kindest people you could wish to meet, ever ready to share their provisions and time. We won't kid you that travel in this part of the world isn't still a challenge, but you're certain to also find the boundless stoicism of Russians in the face of day-to-day trials inspiring.

Perhaps more than anything else in a jet-set world, where the rules of international travel seem to be in continuous and dangerous flux, the Trans-Siberian route – little changed in nearly a century of operation – harks back to a more leisurely, romantic age. So go ahead and buy that ticket: it's time, high time, to be travelling along the Trans-Siberian Railway.

Facts for the Visitor

HIGHLIGHTS
Gateway Cities
Russia's awe-inspiring capital **Moscow** is where all Trans-Siberian trips begin (or end), but consider visiting **St Petersburg**, too. Both cities are fascinating, with contrasting histories and atmospheres. As well as fabulous palaces, museums and theatres they have excellent restaurants, great nightlife and a reasonable range of accommodation options to choose from.

Terminus of the Trans-Siberian route, **Vladivostok** ('Lord of the East') is one of the most geographically impressive cities in Russia. Its seedy charms and buzzing mercantile atmosphere lend it a raffish appeal and the local tour companies offer plenty of adventurous outdoor activities.

Goal of both the Trans-Mongolian and Trans-Manchurian routes, **Beijing**, may not be typical China, but its role in history – as well as its present-day progress and politics – make it a fascinating place (not to mention the architectural achievements and delectable dining!). A trip to Beijing is not complete, of course, without experiencing first-hand the 'greatness' of the Great Wall.

The Mongolian capital of **Ulaan Baatar** is neither as cosmopolitan nor as exciting. This urban centre, however, is an intriguing anomaly set in traditional, nomadic Mongolia. It is also a gateway to the expansive Mongolian countryside. Within hours of the city, travellers can ride horseback across the sprawling steppe, pick wildflowers amid the forested hills and drink the local favourite of *airag* (fermented mare's milk) with nomadic families.

Along The Way
Nizhny Novgorod, Russia's third-largest city, occupies a prime position on the mighty Volga. From here you can take a day cruise along the river to the beautiful monastery at **Makarevo**.

On the edge of Siberia, **Yekaterinburg** is one of the most pleasant and historic cities to visit in Russia. Brush up on the grizzly details of the deaths of the Romanovs, then take a trip into the Ural Mountains to villages that seem hardly changed from the times of the tsars.

As a contrast to many of the stops along the railroad route, the modern metropolis of **Novosibirsk** offers big-city diversions such as good restaurants and a lively nightlife. Train enthusiasts will not want to miss the West Siberian Railway Museum here.

Moving into eastern Siberia, **Krasnoyarsk** is also a worthwhile stop, particularly for the chance to cruise up the Yenisey, another of Russia's great rivers. The city has one of the best-designed regional museums on the Trans-Siberian route and great hiking in the Stolby Nature Reserve.

Irkutsk, at one time hailed as the 'Paris of Siberia', is a charming place to spend a bit of time either side of a trip to **Lake Baikal**.

If you are not heading on to Mongolia or China, consider pausing at **Ulan Ude**, the somewhat surreal capital of the Buryatia Republic. It has an excellent open-air ethnographic museum and is also close to the Ivolginsk *Datsan*, the Siberian centre of Buddhism.

Stretching along the banks of the Amur River, **Khabarovsk** retains interesting architectural vestiges of its past and has a definite laid-back atmosphere. The major gateway to the Russian Far East, it's also the place to organise trips to more remote locations.

Side Trips
If you have more time, a side trip to one of the 'Golden Ring' historic towns around Moscow is recommended. The best example is **Suzdal**, a living picture book of traditional Russian country life.

Consider detouring from Tyumen to visit the old Siberian capital of **Tobolsk** and its handsome kremlin. **Tomsk** is an overlooked jewel just off the Trans-Siberian route, north of Taiga, packed with fine examples of traditional Siberian architecture.

Lake Baikal's pure blue waters and cliff-adorned shores are a must-see for anyone riding the Trans-Siberian. Fortunately, it is nearly impossible to miss, even if you don't get off the train! The best views are not from the train, however. There are some great opportunities for hiking and exploring around the lake and it's a wonderful place to meet some true *Sibiryaki* and get a taste of the Siberian lifestyle.

PLANNING
When to Go

The Trans-Siberian tourist season runs from May to the end of September, with mid-July to early September being the busiest time for foreign visitors as well as Russians coming and going on their annual holidays. Tickets for all trains during this time should be booked well ahead if possible – particularly for the Moscow-Beijing routes.

Although July and August are the warmest months in Siberia (with temperatures rising as high as 40°C), they can also be the dampest months in parts of European Russia, with as many as one rainy day in three. You may find May and June preferable or September and the first half of October, when autumn brings stunning colours as the leaves turn, particularly in Russia's Far East.

Winter nights are long and freezing, but if you're prepared for it this time of the year can also be fantastic. The theatres open, the furs and vodka come out and the snow makes everything picturesque. Train-ticket prices are the same year-round, but you're likely to find travel agency packages sold at a discount in winter.

Least liked everywhere are the first snows and the spring thaw, which turn everything to mud and slush.

What Kind of Trip?

Independent vs Group Tour Independent travel in Russia, China and Mongolia can be a lot of fun, although you shouldn't expect it to be necessarily cheap or, indeed, easy to organise. Away from the major cities your odds of meeting anyone who speaks English are slim, so it will help you get more from your experiences if you are able to speak and read some Russian and, on the Trans-Mongolian and Trans-Manchurian routes, Chinese. With limited language skills, everything you attempt will possibly be more costly and more difficult. However, it's far from impossible and if you really want to meet locals and have a flexible itinerary this is the way to go.

To smooth the way somewhat it's a good idea to consider using a specialist travel agency to arrange your visa and make some of your train and accommodation bookings along the way. Most will be happy to work on any itinerary to create your own individual package tour. It's also possible to arrange

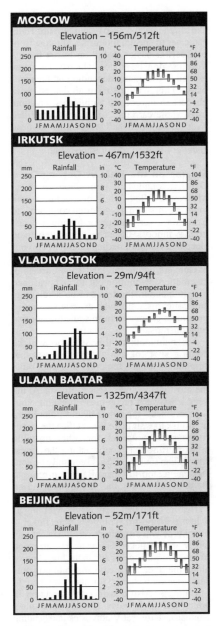

guides and transfers through an agency and the prices can sometimes be better than you'd be able to negotiate yourself with or without language skills.

On group tours everything is taken care of and all you need do is pay and turn up. Tours can cater to special interests and range from backpacker basics to full-on tsarist luxury. You'll seldom be alone – which can be curse as well as a blessing depending on the company. This will also cut down on your chances of interacting with locals: on some trips whole carriages of the train are filled with foreign tourists. Opportunities to head off the beaten track or alter the itinerary are also very limited, if not impossible.

Staying on the Train vs Getting On & Off

Aficionados of going nonstop from Moscow to Vladivostok or Beijing – both journeys of seven days – often compare it to being on a sea voyage or having a beach holiday indoors. It's a chance to catch up on sleep and reading, perhaps sharpen up your card-playing and chess skills with fellow passengers, while the landscape unreels in cinematic slow motion outside. Approached in this manner, the trip can be a relaxing, and deliciously slobbish experience, not to mention a chance to form some memorable relationships.

For many others this scenario will be nothing short of a nightmare. Besides, it completely misses the point that the Trans-Siberian route allows you access to some of the most interesting places in Russia. At the very least we'd recommend breaking your journey once – the most obvious point being in Irkutsk to visit Lake Baikal. See the Highlights section earlier for other possible stops in Russia. If you're taking the Trans-Mongolian route you'd also certainly be considering a stop in Ulaan Baatar en route to Beijing, while on the Trans-Manchurian route a pause in Harbin is a possibility.

Bear in mind that there is no such thing as a hop-on, hop-off Trans-Siberian ticket – every time you disembark you'll have to buy a new onward ticket. This can all be arranged in advance with agents and in the bigger cities along the route it's pretty simple to do yourself – see each chapter for hints on where to buy tickets. Also consider the direction in which you might travel. If you want to meet Russians, starting at Vladivostok and heading west is recommended since far fewer foreign travellers take this route than the popular eastbound services from Moscow or westbound from Beijing.

Maps

Good maps of most Russian cities of any size do exist, but they can be hard to find. Rail enthusiasts might want to search out the cumbersome *Atlas Skhem Zheleznikh Dorog Gosudarskv-uchastnikov CNG, Latvii, Litvy, Estonii*, the most comprehensive rail atlas to the former Soviet Union; you should be able to buy it in Moscow.

RIS Publications' bilingual wall map of Russia is a useful overseas source, as are the CIS map from the German publisher Hallwag and *Hildebrand's Travel Map CIS*.

Depending on the extent of your visit, useful maps that cover both China and Mongolia include *China & Far East* (1:6,000,000) by Hallway, *China* (1:5,000,000) by Kümmerly & Frey, and *China* (1:6,000,000) by Cartographia. If you are travelling independently in the countryside, however, you will need to pick up some more-detailed maps in Ulaan Baatar and Beijing. The best map for jeep travel inside Mongolia is the *Road Map of Mongolia* (1:2,500,000), published in 1999. The best source in Beijing for top-quality, English-language maps is the Friendship Store or the Foreign Language Bookstore.

What to Bring

Among the travelling essentials for this trip are:

- toilet paper
- a plug for the toilet sink
- a short length of hose that you can fit to the toilet tap to create a makeshift shower
- soft, slip-on footwear like thongs (flip-flops) or Chinese cloth sandals
- loose, comfortable clothes, such as a tracksuit
- in summer, strong insect repellent
- a small torch
- a mug and spoon
- a bottle opener and corkscrew (or a Swiss army knife)
- compass (for hiking)
- sunglasses, sunscreen and lip salve
- a travel alarm clock

Everything else, including Western toiletries and most medicines, are readily available in the cities and towns along the route, so you should only pack extra if there's an item you absolutely have to have. For crucial health-related items, see the boxed text 'Medical Kit Check List' under Health later in this chapter.

Extra clothes can also be bought along the way. It goes without saying that you'll need plenty of warm and waterproof layers during winter, particularly in Siberia. For summer, though, when most Trans-Siberian trips are undertaken, you can comfortably get away with a light wardrobe plus a raincoat. Except for some posh restaurants in Moscow and St Petersburg, casual dress is fine. You'll need something modest for visiting churches and mosques – men shouldn't wear shorts and women should don a head scarf.

Boiling water is always available from a *samovar* (hot-water urn) at the end of each carriage. Sheets and blankets are also provided (you'll usually pay a small fee of around US$1 for the sheets) and carriages are kept warm so you won't need a sleeping bag. If you've forgotten a mug and teaspoon, the provodnitsas (female train attendants – see the boxed text 'A Tour Guide's Tale') always have some you can borrow, along with sachets of appalling instant coffee, tea bags, sugar and creamer, for which you'll have to pay a few roubles.

How many books, games and other distractions you take along depends on whether you're travelling alone or with companions. Many people mention *War & Peace* as the *de rigueur* long-distance read, but few actually get around to finishing it, distracted as they are by life on the train. A couple of light paperbacks are a better bet. Cards and chess are a good idea, particularly for breaking the ice with non-English speakers.

Baggage Space In *Journey Into Russia*, Laurens Van Der Post commented that:

In Europe and America people travel in a train fully aware that it belongs either to a state or company and that their ticket grants them only temporary occupation and certain restricted rights. In Russia people just take them over.

Russians have the knack of making themselves very much at home on trains – which often means that they'll be travelling with plenty of luggage. Some juggling of the available space in a four berth compartment will become inevitable.

There's a luggage bin underneath each of the lower berths (50cm wide, 40cm high, 110cm long) and also enough space beside the bin to squeeze in another medium-sized

A Tour Guide's Tale

I worked as a tour guide in the European summer of 1997. My guests came from all over the world and their expectations varied as widely as their ages.

The first lesson I learnt was that being creative was the key to making a tour successful, not just to keep my groups happy, motivated and inspired, but also to provide them with the little extras that make any tour that little bit more memorable. The Trans-Siberian journey is as much about the train journey itself as it is about sightseeing.

The provodnitsas and provodniks (female and male train attendants – they're generally female though) hold all the power. They know it and exploit it and as a traveller you have to respect it! For certain legs of the journey you are on the train for days at a time, so it pays to organise with your attendant to make sure the facilities are available at all times. On one trip, the Western-style toilet was permanently closed as the provodnitsa had packed the space with all the goods, plants and produce she could find to send home. The only alternative was the standard squat toilet, which is not that easy to navigate on a fast-moving train – especially if you are a bit older.

It is extremely important that you also get the attendant to tell you when the train is about to depart as there is no warning. With this in mind, it's good to always keep your passport and money on you in case you get left behind. One of my passengers was so involved in his train-side purchasing at a small Siberian town that he failed to hear the attendant call everyone back on the train. He was waiting near the last carriage, dressed in his pyjamas with no passport and little money. Needless to say that when the train began to depart, he ran very fast!

Not all attendants were equally helpful, but if you want to get the most out of the train experience, a sense of humour, good sign language skills and a huge smile go a long way.
Melissa McVeigh

canvas bag. Above the doorway there's a coffin-like space that measures 160cm long, 67cm wide and 30cm high, which at a push, kick and shove will accommodate a couple of rucksacks.

There are no baggage restrictions travelling from the Moscow end, but in Beijing there's an enforced 35kg allowance. Passengers with excess baggage are supposed to present it (along with passport, ticket and customs entry declaration) the day before departure at the Luggage Shipment Office (☎ 5183 1479), which is outside the Beijing main train station at the right corner. The excess is charged at about $20 per 10kg, with a maximum excess of 40kg allowed. Bicycles require a box.

TRAIN BOOKINGS
Routes & Trains

For the first four days' travel from Moscow, the main Trans-Siberian, Trans-Manchurian and Trans-Mongolian services all follow the same route through the Urals and into western Siberia, over the Yenisey River and on to Irkutsk in eastern Siberia.

On the fifth day, after rounding the southern tip of Lake Baikal, the Trans-Mongolian train branches off, heading south for the Mongolian border 250km away. The Trans-Manchurian stays with the main line for 12 hours past Lake Baikal, before it too peels off, heading south-east for Zabaikalsk on the Chinese border, some 368km distant. For full details of the routes see the descriptions at the start of each chapter.

The regular long-distance service is a fast train *(skoryy poezd)*, which rarely gets up enough speed to merit being called 'fast', but is indeed much quicker than the frequently stopping passenger trains *(passazhirskiy poezd)* found mainly on routes of 1000km or less.

The top-end trains are called *firmennye poezdy* and often have names (eg, *Rossiya*). These generally have cleaner and more upper-class carriages, polite(er) attendants, more convenient arrival/departure times and a reasonable (or at least functioning) restaurant car. Sometimes the ticket prices will also include your linen as well as a packed breakfast.

Every carriage has a timetable (in Cyrillic) posted in the corridor, which notes how long the train will stop at each station. These timetables, however, are not set in stone, so always ask the provodnitsa when getting off the train how long you're going to be at a station. Usually, stops last from two to five minutes, but at least twice a day the train

stops for 15 or 20 minutes, allowing time to get off, stretch your legs and stock up on food from platform sellers.

Moscow to Vladivostok The No 1/2 *Rossiya* train is the top Moscow-Vladivostok firmennye service. If you're planning to stop off at Irkutsk, also consider using the No 9/10 *Baikal*, reputed to be one of the best trains in Russia in terms of carriage standards and service. We've even heard of proper showers having recently been installed on this train – please report back if you find them!

Other good services that can be usefully included in a Moscow to Vladivostok itinerary include: the No 15/16 *Ural* between Moscow and Yekaterinburg; No 25/25 *Sibiryak* between Moscow and Novosibirsk; No 7/8 *Sibir* between Novosibirsk and Vladivostok; No 55/56 *Yenisey* between Moscow and Krasnoyarsk; and No 5/6 *Okean* between Khabarovsk and Vladivostok.

Moscow to Beijing The more popular of the two options running between Moscow and Beijing is the No 3/4 Trans-Mongolian service, a Chinese train that travels via Ulaan Baatar and the only one to offer deluxe carriages (see Classes of Travel section).

If you're planning to stop off in Irkutsk, there's also the daily No 264/263 service to Ulaan Baatar.

The weekly No 19/20 Trans-Manchurian service is a Russian train and takes half a day longer to reach Beijing, but in doing so it avoids the need for a Mongolian visa.

Classes of Travel

Other than in the deluxe class on the Chinese train, there are no showers in any category. All compartments are air-conditioned in summer and heated in winter – that's why the windows are locked shut (although sometimes you'll be able to open them). There's also a speaker above the window through which the provodnitsa gets to inflict her taste in music on you – a knob allows you to switch this off.

Note that no account is taken of sex when allocating a cabin, so a single woman might find herself sharing with three men. If you don't feel comfortable, ask the provodnitsa if she can engineer a swap – it's often possible.

There's no need to bring a sleeping bag; fresh linen is provided, usually for a fee of

Reading a Train Timetable

Russian train timetables vary from place to place but generally list: a destination; train number; category of train; frequency of service; and time of departure and arrival – in *Moscow* time unless otherwise noted (see the following information on arrival and departure times).

Trains in smaller city stations generally begin somewhere else, so you'll see a starting point and a destination on the timetable. For example, when catching a train from Omsk to Irkutsk, the timetable may list Moscow as an origination point and Irkutsk as the destination. The following are a few key points to look out for.

Number
Номер (Nomer). The higher the number of a train, the slower it is; anything over 900 is likely to be a mail train.

Category
Скорый, Пассажирский, Почтовый-багажный, Пригородный *(Skory, Passazhirsky, Pochtovy-bagazhny, Prigorodny)*, and various abbreviations thereof, are train categories and refer, respectively, to fast, passenger, post-cargo and suburban trains. There may also be the name of the train, usually in Russian quotation marks, eg, Россия *('Rossiya')*.

Frequency
Ежедневно *(yezhednevno,* daily); чётные *(chyotnye,* even dates); нечётные *(nechyotnye,* odd dates); отменён *(otmenyon,* cancelled). All of these, as well, can appear in various abbreviations. Days of the week are listed usually as numbers (where 1 is Monday and 7 Sunday) or as abbreviations of the name of the day (Пон, Вт, Ср, Чт, Пт, Сб, and Вск are, respectively, Monday to Sunday).

On some trains, frequency depends on the time of year, in which case details are usually given in hard-to-decipher, abbreviated, small print: eg, '27/VI–31/VIII Ч; 1/IX–25/VI 2,5' means that from 27 June to 31 August the train runs on even dates, while from 1 September to 25 June it runs on Tuesday and Friday.

Arrival & Departure Times
Most train times are given in a 24-hour time format, and almost always in Moscow time (Московское время, *Moskovskoe vremya*). But suburban trains are usually marked in local time (местное время, *mestnoe vremya*). From here it gets tricky (as though the rest wasn't), so don't confuse the following:

время отправления *(vremya otpravlenia)*, which means time of departure
время отправления с начального пункта *(vremya otpravlenia s nachalnogo punkta)*, the time of departure from the train's starting point
время прибытия *(vremya pribytia)*, the time of arrival at the station you're in
время прибытия на конечный пункт *(vremya pribytia na konechny punkt)*, the time of arrival at the destination
время в пути *(vremya v puti)*, the duration of the journey

Corresponding trains running in opposite directions on the same route may appear on the same line of the timetable. In this case you may find route entries like время отправления с конечного пункта *(vremya otpravlenia s konechnogo punkta)* or the time the return train leaves its station of origin.

Distance
You may sometimes see the растояние *(rastoyanie)* – distance in kilometres from the point of departure – on the timetable as well. These are rarely accurate and usually refer to the kilometre distance used to calculate the fare.

Tracking your Progress

Small black-and-white painted kilometre posts on the southern side of the line mark the distance to and from Moscow, although these are sometimes difficult to spot because they're so close to the track – or just not there at all. In between each kilometre marker are smaller posts counting down roughly every 100m. The distances on train timetables don't always correspond to these marker posts.

around $1 paid to the provodnitsa. On some trains the linen charge is included in the ticket price. There are also warm blankets.

If you want true luxury, you'll need to shell out for the trips offered by companies such as Mir Corporation in the USA and GW Travel in the UK (see the Travel Agencies & Organised Tours section of the Getting There & Away chapter), which use private rail cars that are complete with plush compartments and showers.

Deluxe 1st class These are only available on the No 3/4 Trans-Mongolian train. These two-berth compartments are roomy, have wood-panelling, are carpeted and also have a sofa. A shower cubicle is shared with the adjacent compartment.

1st class/SV On the Russian trains these are the same size as 2nd class, but have only two berths so there's more room and more privacy, for double the cost. Some 1st-class compartments now have TVs on which it's possible to watch videos supplied by the provodnitsa for a small fee (there's nothing to stop you bringing your own). You could even unplug the TV and plug in your computer. These carriages have the edge in that there are only half as many people queuing to use the toilet every morning.

On the Chinese train, 1st-class *myagky* has softer beds but hardly any more space than 2nd class and is not worth the considerably higher fare.

2nd class/kupeyny or kupe This class is the standard accommodation on all long-distance, Trans-Siberian-related trains. These carriages are divided into nine enclosed compartments, each with four reasonably comfortable berths, a fold-down table and

just enough room between the bunks for occupants to turn around.

In every carriage there's also one half-sized compartment with just two berths. This is usually occupied by the provodnitsas or reserved for railway employees, but there's a slim chance that you may end up in it, particularly if you do a deal directly with a provodnitsa for a train ticket (see the Ticket Costs section later in this chapter).

3rd class/platskartny This class is not available on the Trans-Manchurian or Trans-Mongolian trains, but common to most other services offered in Russia. It's essentially a dorm carriage sleeping 54. The carriage is not compartmentalised, and the bunks are arranged in blocks of four down one side of the corridor and in twos on the other, with the lower bunk on this side converting to a table during the day.

Privacy is out of the question. The scene often resembles a refugee camp, with clothing strung between bunks, a great swapping of bread, fish and jars of tea, and even babies sitting on potties while their snot-nosed siblings tear up and down the corridor. That said, many travellers (women in particular) find this a better option than being cooped up with three possibly drunken Russian men. It's also a great way to meet ordinary Russians. Platskartny tickets cost half to two-thirds the price of a 2nd-class berth.

If you do travel platskartny, it's worth requesting specific numbered seats when booking your ticket – the prime ones are 52 to 39, which are the doubles with the bunk that converts to a table. The ones to avoid are 1 to 4, 33 to 38 and 53 and 54, at each end of the carriage, close by the samovar and toilets where people are constantly coming and going.

4th class/obshchiy For shorter legs of the journey – say from Taiga to Tomsk – you'll be looking at catching an *elektrichka* (also called *prigorodny poezd*), a local train that has only unreserved bench-type seating. It's cheap, but it certainly ain't comfortable. This said, it has been known for people to follow the Trans-Siberian route using *elektrichka* all the way. One bohemian Russian character, Anton Krotov, has made his name doing so (see the boxed text 'Budget Trans-Siberian Travel the Scientific Way' later in this chapter).

Ticket Costs

Foreigners and Russians pay the same for train tickets. These prices have been rising each year, but still, on a per-kilometre basis, a Trans-Siberian ticket remains one of the world's travel bargains. See the Getting There & Away sections of the destination chapters for more about how and where to buy tickets.

The following prices (in US$) are from the 2001 season – prices have since risen by

How to Read your Ticket

When buying a ticket in Russia you'll always be asked for your passport so that its number and your name can be printed on your ticket. The ticket and passport will be matched up by the provodnitsa before you're allowed on the train – so make sure the ticket seller gets these details correct.

Most tickets are printed by computer and come with a duplicate. Shortly after you've boarded the train the provodnitsa will come around and collect the tickets; sometimes she will take both copies and give you one back just before your final destination, sometimes she will leave you with the copy. It's a good idea to hang on to these tickets, especially if you're hopping on and off trains, since they provide evidence of how long you've been in a particular place if you're stopped by police.

Sometimes tickets are also sold with a chit for insurance in the event of a fatal accident (this is a small payment, usually less than $1), and an advance payment for linen, again around $1. Following is a guide for deciphering the rest of what your Russian train ticket is about:

1 Train number
2 Train type
3 Departure date – day and month
4 Departure time – always Moscow time for long-distance trains
5 Carriage number and class: Л = 2-bed SV, M = 4-bed SV, K = Kupe, П = Platskartny, O = Obshchiy
6 Supplement for class of ticket above platskartny
7 Cost for platskartny ticket
8 Number of people travelling on ticket
9 Type of passenger: полный (polny, adult); детский (detsky, child); студенческий (studenchesky, student)
10 From/to
11 Bed number
12 Passport number and name
13 Total cost of ticket
14 Tax and service fee
15 Arrival date
16 Arrival time – always Moscow time for long-distance trains

The Original Monkey Business

If you were wondering how the long-running China-based travel agency Monkey Business (see Travel Agencies & Organised Tours in the Getting There & Away chapter) got its name, we can let you in on just one of the legends of the Trans-Siberian – it all revolves around how to save money on buying international tickets.

If you look at the table in the Ticket Costs section you'll see that it's actually cheaper to buy a ticket to Ulaan Baatar from Moscow than it is to Irkutsk, despite the fact that the former is another 1084km farther from Moscow. The reason for this is an anomaly in the pricing of international tickets. Back in the days of the Soviet Union it meant that canny travel agencies like Monkey Business could bulk buy dirt-cheap tickets on the Trans-Mongolian and Trans-Manchurian routes, sell them on to customers and turn a tidy profit.

These days the differences in prices are getting smaller (and are hardly worth bothering with for anything less than 1st-class tickets). Agencies have also told us that this discrepancy is likely to end soon. Besides it's technically against the rules to buy a ticket to Ulaan Baatar from Moscow and get off at Irkutsk (not to mention that you'd be limiting yourself to the two international services per week rather than the stacks of daily trains that pass through Irkutsk). But then again, if you were to do this, there's nobody checking that you have got back on the train.

should cost so that you don't pay well over the odds.

route	SV	Kupe	Platskartny
Moscow to Vladivostok	$342	$157	$72
Moscow to Beijing	$267 (deluxe)	$148	n/a
Moscow to Ulaan Baatar	$176 (deluxe)	$113	n/a
Moscow to Irkutsk	$273	$123	$62
Irkutsk to Vladivostok	$236	$108	$50
Irkutsk to Ulaan Baatar	$58	$33	n/a
Ulaan Baatar to Beijing	$109	$56	n/a

For all trips within Russia children under five can travel free if they share a berth with an adult, otherwise children under 10 pay half fare for their own berth. On the Trans-Mongolian and Trans-Manchurian services, kids under four travel free if they share a berth, while those under 12 pay around 75% of the full fare for their own berth.

The price of the train ticket is only one expense. The other major dents in your budget are going to be the cost of getting to the train's departure point and then home again at the end of the ride (see the Getting There & Away chapter), and accommodation costs at stops along the way (see the Costs section later in this chapter). Considering these extra expenses, some of the packages that are offered by travel agencies can turn out to be good deals.

around 30%. If you are buying your ticket through an agency (see Travel Agencies & Organised Tours in the Getting There & Away chapter) expect to pay a premium. Note however, that if you're planning a hop-on, hop-off Trans-Sib tour (say Moscow, Yekaterinburg, Krasnoyarsk, Irkutsk, Ulaan Baatar, Beijing) some agents *may* be able to get you a better deal than if you were to buy these tickets separately yourself in Russia. Also see the boxed text 'The Original Monkey Business' for how to save some money on international tickets.

If you find it difficult to get the ticket you want at the station or through an agent, it might be possible to do a deal directly with a provodnitsa – you'll need some Russian language skills for this and it's a good idea to have a rough idea of what the ticket

RESPONSIBLE TOURISM

Siberians, as closely as they live with nature, don't always respect it. In fact many tend to regard nature as their worst enemy, and survival is a matter of taking everything they can gather, shoot or cut. Littering and poaching are everyday pastimes.

As a responsible traveller you're probably going to be appalled by the mess some Siberian comrades leave in the forests and at how readily rubbish is chucked out of the train windows. Accept that you're not going to change how all Russians live, but realise that you might be able to make a small impression by your own thoughtful behaviour.

One important way you can help the local people is to buy food and souvenirs from vendors along the way – this is often the only income those *babushkas* (literally 'grandmothers') on the train platforms might have. Don't, however, buy goods that are made from endangered species.

TOURIST OFFICES
Russia
Tourist offices, like those you might be used to in the West, largely don't exist in Russia (St Petersburg is an exception and even that's not great). Instead you're dependent for information on hotel staff, administrators and travel firms. If you're not paying to use their services, or if the people are in an unhelpful mood (it can happen), then you might not get very far with any questions.

Outside of Russia, the best source of information is travel agencies specialising in Russian travel (see the Travel Agencies & Organised Tours section in the Getting There & Away chapter).

China
The China International Tourist Service (CITS) is known outside of China and Hong Kong as the China National Tourist Office (CNTO). There are offices in:

Australia (☎ 02-9299 4057, fax 9290 1958,
 W www.cnto.org.au) 44 Market St, 19th
 floor, Sydney NSW 2000
Canada (☎ 16-599 6636, fax 599 6382)
 480 University Ave Suite 806, Toronto,
 Ontario M5 GIV2
France (☎ 01 56 59 10 10, fax 01 53 75 32 88)
 15 Rue de Berri, Paris 75008
Germany (☎ 069-520 135, fax 528 490)
 Ilkenhansstr 6, D-60433 Frankfurt am Main
Hong Kong (☎ 2732 5888, fax 2721 7154)
 New Mandarin Plaza, 12th floor, Tower A,
 14 Science Museum Rd, Tsimshatsui East
Japan
 Tokyo:(☎ 03-3591 8686, fax 3591 6886)
 China National Tourism Administration, Air
 China Building 2-5-2, Toranomon, Minato-ku
 Osaka: (☎ 06-6635 3280, fax 6635 3281)
 China National Tourism Administration,
 4F OCAT Building, 1-4-1 Minatomachi,
 Naniwa-ku
Singapore (☎ 337 2220, fax 338 0007)
 7 Temasek Blvd, No 12-02A Suntec Tower
 One, 038987 Singapore
UK (☎ 020-7935 9787, fax 7487 5842)
 4 Glentworth St, London NW1
USA (W www.cnto.org)
 Los Angeles: (☎ 818-545 7507, fax 545 7506)

333 West Broadway, Suite 201,
 Glendale CA 91204
 New York: (☎ 212-760 8218, fax 760 8809)
 Empire State Bldg, Suite 6413, 350 Fifth
 Ave, New York NY 10118

Mongolia
Juulchin, once the Mongolian national tourist agency, has been privatised. It is still the largest Mongolian travel agency with offices around the world.

China (☎ 8610-6512 6688, fax 6525 4339,
 e julnpek@public.bta.net.cn) Beijing
 International Hotel, 9 Jianguo Mennei Ave,
 Beijing
Germany (☎ 030-440 57646, fax 440 57645,
 e juulchin@aol.com), Chausseestrasse 84,
 D-10115 Berlin
Japan (☎ 03-3486 7351, fax 3486 7440,
 e mjt-tyo@mvj.biglobe.ne.jp) Daini Kawana
 Bldg, 3rd floor, 14-6 Sibuya 2 Chome,
 Shibuya Ku, Tokyo
USA (☎ 609-419 4416, fax 275 3827) 707 Alexander Rd, Suite 208, Princeton NJ 08540

VISAS & DOCUMENTS
You'll certainly need to have a Russian visa of some sort, and also perhaps Chinese and Mongolian visas, depending on the route you choose. It's best to obtain all visas in your home country before setting out. Some tour companies can arrange your visas as part of their Trans-Siberian package. Bear in mind, if you're also travelling through Belarus, Ukraine, the Baltic countries or Central Asia, you may need visas for some of those countries.

Russia
All foreigners visiting Russia need visas. You must complete a visa application form and send it along with three identical passport photos (signed on the back), the visa-processing fee, your passport and a visa invitation or accommodation vouchers of some sort to the embassy or consulate. The visa invitation/accommodation vouchers are supposed to confirm accommodation for every night you'll be in Russia, though in practice it isn't necessary to have booked and paid for all this in advance.

The cost depends on several factors:

• type of visa – see the following section
• your nationality

- where you're applying for the visa – costs vary from country to country and are also affected by exchange rates
- how quickly the visa is processed – the faster you need it, the more expensive it will be

As a very rough guide, reckon on around $40 for a single-entry tourist visa and $50 for a business visa; both are processed in 15 working days. On top of this you'll have the fee for the visa invitation (again anything from $20 to $50 or more), but this might be waived if you're booking accommodation.

Visas come in two forms: either a sticker in your passport or a separate piece of paper listing entry/exit dates, your passport number, any children travelling with you and visa type. It's an exit permit too, so look after it since if you lose it (or overstay) leaving the country can be harder than getting in.

Types of Visa For a Trans-Siberian trip you will typically need a tourist visa (valid for up to one month) or a business visa (valid for up to three months). Tourist visas are best for organised trips when you know exactly what you're doing and when, where and for how long you'll be doing it.

The business visa is best for independent travellers who want to make up an itinerary as they go. It's supported by a Russian company, eliminating the need for pre-arranged hotel confirmations. Many travel companies (see the Travel Agencies & Organised Tours section of the Getting There & Away chapter) can arrange the business invitation needed for such a visa for a fee – usually not an outrageous amount.

Most Russian embassies will only issue transit visas for up to 72 hours (which won't get you very far) except for the one in Beijing, which issues 10-day transit visas that allow time to make the trip to Moscow, stay one night and then leave the country. If you want to stay more than one night in Russia you'll need a tourist visa. Given Russian bureaucracy it's safer to have one of these anyway.

Registration & Extensions *All* Russian visas must be registered with OVIR (Otdel Viz i Registratsii; Department of Visas & Registration) within three business days of your arrival in Russia and then again at any place you stay after that for more than three days. Be highly suspicious of any company that tells you this isn't the case.

The company or organisation that invites you to Russia is responsible for your registration. You can't take a visa that was issued on the invitation of, say, the HI Hostel in St Petersburg and have it registered in Moscow by the Travellers Guest House. If you run into problems, the simplest option is to spend a night at one of the major hotels, which will register your visa for you right at the front desk. There may be a fee of $5 to $10.

If you're caught with a visa that's not registered you can expect to be fined – anything up to $500.

Extending any visa is hugely difficult and the extension, if granted, will usually be for a short time only. If it's possible that you'll be in Russia for over a month it will be safer, less time consuming and certainly less costly to apply for a business visa instead of a tourist visa that you'll need to have extended.

To minimise any bureaucratic problems along the way bring with you every piece of paper you gave to and received from the embassy, any vouchers from your tour company and anything else on fancy letterhead that has been stamped.

China

All foreigners need a visa for the People's Republic of China (PRC). Your passport should have at least six months validity and one empty page. Submit your passport, a covering letter, an application, one passport photo and a money order for the appropriate fee. Processing should take four working days for a walk-in application; by mail requires more time and usually a higher fee.

Be aware that you must submit these documents to the consulate whose jurisdiction includes the state or city where you reside. Exact requirements and fees vary depending on where you apply, so be sure to check the details with your nearest Chinese consulate.

A standard visa is valid for one entry and a 30-day stay in China. A double entry is fairly straightforward. You can also get a transit visa, which is good for seven days. Requirements are more stringent for multiple entries or for longer stays in China.

Visa extensions are the domain of the Public Security Bureau's (PSB) Foreign Affairs Branch. In Beijing, PSB (☎ 6404 7799) is at

2 Andingmen Dongdajie, 300m east of the Lama Temple. The penalty for overstaying your visa is Y500 per day!

Mongolia

Most nationalities need a visa to enter Mongolia, with the following exceptions: Polish, for stays up to 90 days; Israeli, Malaysian and now American, up to 30 days; and Hong Kong and Singaporean, up to 14 days. To obtain a Mongolian visa, your passport must have six months validity. In theory, it's possible to obtain a Mongolian visa at the Ulaan Baatar airport if you have a letter of invitation and two passport photos.

Standard tourist visas are valid for 30 days and cost $25. Processing the application usually takes three to five days. For double the price, the visa is supposed to be ready within 24 hours. For longer than 30 days, you must obtain an invitation from a travel agency or 'sponsoring organisation'. If you are not leaving the train in Ulaan Baatar, or you are getting off only for a very short stay, you may obtain a transit visa – good for 48 or 72 hours – for $15.

For visa extensions, go to the Ministry of External Relations on Peace Ave (grey building just south of Sükhbaatar Square) between 9.30am and noon Monday to Friday. Enter through the southern door at the back of the building. The extension is $15 for seven days and requires a passport photo. Some guesthouses will handle visa extensions for a small fee. Note that transit visas cannot be extended.

If you intend to stay in Mongolia for more than 30 days, you must register with the Police Registration Office (☎ 327 182), officially known as the Citizens Registration and Information Bureau. The Police Registration Office is about 1km north of the corner of Ikh Toiruu and Krkhuugiin Gudamj on the right-hand side of the road. Look for the sign that reads 'Government Council for Foreign Citizens Issui'. Before you leave the country, you should return to the office to 'close' your registration.

Visas for Other Countries

Of the other countries that you're likely to pass through on an overland trip before, after or during your Trans-Siberian travels, the ones for which most people will need visas are Belarus and Kazakhstan. Contact the embassies of these countries in your home country (or along the route if there isn't one near where you live) for the latest details.

Lost or Stolen Documents

In order to facilitate replacement of your documents it is imperative that you make and carry photocopies of them, especially your Russian visa (see Copies later in this section for further hints). Without this photocopy, replacing a lost or stolen visa can be a nightmare.

Your embassy or consulate in Russia can replace a lost or stolen passport, but if you lose your visa you must go to the local visa office, OVIR. A Russian travel agent, your hotel service bureau or the youth hostels can help with this, including reporting the loss to the police. Again, both procedures are much easier if you've stashed away a few passport-sized photos, your visa number and photocopies of your visa and your passport's personal information and validity pages.

Travel Insurance

Make sure that you have adequate health insurance. A travel insurance policy to cover theft, loss and medical problems is a wise idea. Make certain that it covers medical evacuation back to your home country from any part of Russia where you are likely to travel.

In order to get a Russian visa, citizens of Austria, Belgium, Estonia, Finland, France, Germany, Greece, Israel, Italy, Luxembourg, the Netherlands, Portugal and Spain are also supposed to have health insurance with a company that has an agreement with the Russian company Ingosstrakh/Rosso. Check with your embassy for the latest details.

Youth, Student & Seniors Cards

Full-time students and people aged under 26 or over 59 years tend to get a substantial discount on admissions to museums etc. Always try flashing your ID before paying.

For about $6, full-time students can get an ISIC from student agencies worldwide. If you're not a student but you are under 26, ask a student agency at home for an ISIC International Youth Travel Card.

Railways in the UK and The American Association for Retired People issue identification cards for seniors. Similar organisations exist in other Western countries.

Copies

All important documents (passport data page and visa page, credit cards, travel insurance policy, air/bus/train tickets, driving licence etc) should be photocopied before you depart. Leave one copy with someone at home and keep another with you, separate from the originals. Also take some spare passport photos. After you have entered Russia, try to get a photocopy of your customs declaration *(deklaratsia)* if you've been issued with one. All these will be very useful if your original documents go astray.

You can also store your vital travel documents in Lonely Planet's free online Travel Vault, in case you lose the photocopies or can't be bothered with them. Your password-protected Travel Vault is accessible online anywhere in the world – create it at W www .ekno.lonelyplanet.com.

EMBASSIES & CONSULATES

It's important to realise what your own embassy – the embassy of the country of which you are a citizen – can and can't do to help you if you get into trouble.

Generally speaking, it won't be much help if the trouble you're in is remotely your own fault. You are bound by the laws of the country you are in, and your embassy will not be sympathetic if you end up in jail after committing a crime locally, even if such actions are legal in your own country.

In genuine emergencies you might get some assistance, but only if other channels have been exhausted. For example, if you need to get home urgently, a free ticket is exceedingly unlikely – the embassy would expect you to have insurance. If you have all your money and documents stolen, the embassy might assist with getting a new passport, but a loan for onward travel is out of the question.

If you're planning to head off the beaten track, or just want to be safe, it's prudent to register with your embassy so it has your name, passport and address details and an idea of your travel itinerary in case anything does go wrong. This can be done over the phone or by email.

Embassies & Consulates Abroad

For a complete list of Russian embassies and consulates have a look at the Web site u www.russianembassy.net; for China try

W www.travelchinaguide.com/embassy/em bassy_list.htm; and for Mongolia W www .extmin.mn/embadd.htm.

Australia
China
> *Embassy:* (☎ 02-6273 4780 or 6273 4783, fax 6273 4878, W www.chinaembassy.org.au) 15 Coronation Drive, Yarralumla, ACT 2600

Mongolia
> *Honorary Consulate:* (☎/fax 02-9966 1922, e monconoz@yahoo.com) Level 10, 80 Mount St, North Sydney, NSW 2060

Russia
> *Embassy:* (☎ 02-6295 9033/9474, fax 6295 1847, e rusemb@dynamite.com.au) 78 Canberra Ave, Griffith, ACT 2603
> *Consulate:* (☎ 02-9326 1188, fax 9327 5065, e russcon@ozemail.com.au) 7–9 Fullerton St, Woollahra, NSW 2025

Canada
China
> *Embassy:* (☎ 613-789 3434, fax 613-789 1911, W www.chinaembassycanada.org) 515 St Patrick St, Ottawa, Ontario K1N 5H3

Mongolia
> *Embassy:* (☎ 613-569 3830, fax 569 3916, W www.mongolembassy.org) 151 Slater St, Suite 503, Ottawa, Ontario K1P 5H3

Russia
> *Embassy:* (☎ 613-235 4341, fax 236 6342, e rusemb@intranet.ca) 285 Charlotte St, Ottawa, Ontario K1N 8L5
> *Consular section:* (☎ 613-336 7220, fax 238 6158) 52 Range Rd, Ottawa K1N 8J5
> *Consulate:* (☎ 514-843 5901, fax 842 2012, e consulat@dsuper.net) 3685 Ave de Musée, Montreal, Quebec H3G 2EI

France
China
> *Embassy:* (☎ 01 47 36 02 58, W www .amb-chine.fr) 9 ave Victor Cresson, 92130 Issy-les-Moulineaux

Mongolia
> *Embassy:* (☎ 01 46 05 23 18, fax 01 46 05 30 16, e 106513.2672@compuserve.com) Ambassade de Mongolie, 5 ave Robert Schumann, 92100 Boulogne-Billancourt

Russia
> *Embassy:* (☎ 1-45 04 05 50, fax 45 04 17 65, e rusembfr@club-internet.fr) 40–50 bvd Lannes, 75116 Paris
> *Consulate:* (☎ 91-77 15 15, fax 77 34 54, e consrus@aix.pacwan.net) 8 ave Ambrois Pare, 13008 Marseilles

Germany
China
> *Embassy:* (☎ 049-3027 5880, W www.chi na-botschaft.de) Markisches Ufer 54, Berlin

Mongolia
Embassy: (☎ 030-446 9320, fax 446 9321, [e] mongolbot@aol.com) Gotlandstrasse 12 D-10439 Berlin

Russia
Embassy: (☎ 030-220 2821 or 226 6320, fax 229 9397, [e] russembassyg@trionet.de) Unter den Linden 63–5, 10117 Berlin
Consular section: (☎ 030-229 9468, fax 229 0057)
Consulate: (☎ 0228-312 085, fax 312 164, [e] bonn@russische-botschaft.de) Waldstrasse 42, 53177 Bonn

Japan
China
Embassy: (☎ 03-3403 3389, fax 3403 3345, [w] www.china-embassy.or.jp) 3-4-33 Mono-Azabu, Minato-Ku, Tokyo

Mongolia
Embassy:(☎ 03-3469 2088, fax 3469 2216, [w] www.embassy-avenue.jp/mongolia /index.htm) 21–4 Kamiyama Cho Shibuya Ku, Tokyo 150

Russia
Embassy: (☎ 03-3583 4224, fax 3505 0593, [e] rosconsl@ma.kcom.ne.jp) 2-1-1 Azabudai, Minato-ku, Tokyo 106-0041
Consular section: (☎ 03-3583 4445, fax 3586 0407)
Consulate: (☎ 06-6848 3452, fax 848 3453, [e] ruscons@mb.kcom.ne.jp) 1-2-2 Nishi Mid-origaoka, Toyonaka-shi, Osaka-fu 560-0005

New Zealand
China
Embassy: (☎ 04-472 1382, fax 499 0419, [w] www.chinaembassy.org.nz) 2–6 Glenmore St, Kelburn, Wellington

Russia
Embassy: (☎ 04-476 6113, fax 476 3843, [e] eor@netlink.co.nz) 57 Messines Rd, Karori, Wellington

UK
China
Embassy: (☎ 020-7299 4024, [w] www .chinese-embassy.org.uk) 49–51 Portland Place, London W1N 5AG
Consular Section: (☎ 020-7631 1430, fax 7636 9756) 31 Portland Place, London W1B 1QD

Mongolia
Embassy: (☎ 020-7937 0150, fax 7937 0150, [e] embmong@aol.com) 7 Kensington Court, London W8 5DL

Russia
Embassy: (☎ 020-7229 3628, fax 7727 8625, [w] www.russialink.org.uk/embassy) 13 Kensington Palace Gardens, London W8 4QX

Consular Section: (☎ 020-7229 8027, visa information message ☎ 0891-171 271, fax 020-7229 3215) 5 Kensington Palace Gardens, London W8 4QS
Consulate: (☎ 0131-225 7121, fax 225 9587, [e] visa@edconsul.demon.co.uk) 58 Melville St, Edinburgh EH3 7HL

USA
China
Embassy: (☎ 202-328 2500, fax 328 2551, [w] www.china-embassy.org) 2300 Connect-icut Ave NW, Washington DC 20008
Consular Section: (☎ 202-338 6688, fax 558 9760) Room 110, 2201 Wisconsin Ave NW, Washington DC 20007

Mongolia
Embassy: (☎ 202-333 7117, fax 202-298 9227) 2833 M street NW, Washington DC 20007

Russia
Embassy: (☎ 202-298 5700/01, fax 628 0252) 2641 Wisconsin Ave, NW, Washington DC 20007
Consular Section: (☎ 202-939 8907, fax 939 8909, [e] waconsru@prodigy.net) 2641 Tunlaw Rd, Washington DC 20007
Consulates: (☎ 212-348 0926, fax 831 9162, [w] www.ruscon.org) 9 East 91 St, New York, NY 10128
(☎ 415-928 6878, fax 929 0306) 2790 Green St, San Francisco, CA 94123
(☎ 206-728 1910, fax 728 1871) 2323 Westin Bldg, 2001 Sixth Ave, Seattle, WA 98121-2617

Foreign Embassies & Consulates along the Route
Moscow The area code for the telephone numbers in the following list is ☎ 095. For a full list of embassies and locations check the Web site [w] www.themoscowtimes.ru /travel/facts/embassies.html.

Australia (☎ 956 60 70, fax 956 61 70, [w] www.australianembassy.ru) Kropotkinsky per 2
Belarus (☎ 924 70 31 or, for visa inquiries, ☎ 924 70 95) ul Maroseyka ul 17/6
Canada (☎ 956 66 66, fax 232 99 48) Starokonyushenny per 23
China (☎ 095-938 2006, fax 956 1169, [w] www.chinaembassy.ru) 6 ul Druzhby
France (☎ 937 15 00, fax 937 15 77, [w] www.ambafrance.ru) Bolshaya Yakimanka ul 45
Germany (☎ 937 95 00, fax 936 21 43, [w] www .germany.org.ru) ul Mosfilmovskaya 56
Consular Section: (☎ 933 43 11) Leninsky prosp 95A

Japan (☎ 291 85 00, fax 200 12 40) Kalashny
per 12
Kazakhstan (☎ 208 98 52, fax 208 26 50)
Chistoprudny bul 3A
Mongolia (☎ 290 6792, fax 291 6171,
Ⓔ mongolia@online.ru) ul Borisoglbsky per 11
New Zealand (☎ 956 35 79, fax 956 35 83,
Ⓦ www.nzembassy.msk.ru) Povarskaya ul 7
UK (☎ 956 72 00 fax 956 72 50, Ⓦ www
.britemb.msk.ru) Smolenskaya nab 10
USA (☎ 728 50 00, fax 728 50 90, Ⓦ www
.usembassy.state.gov/moscow) Novinsky
bul 19/23

St Petersburg The area code for St Petersburg is ☎ 812.

Canada (☎ 325 84 48 or 316 72 22, fax 316
72 22) Malodetskoselsky per 32
China (☎ 114 62 30) nab Kanala Griboedova 134
Finland (☎ 273 73 21) ul Chaykovskogo 71
France (☎ 312 11 30 or 311 85 11, fax 311 85
11) Naberzhnaya Reki Moyki 15
Germany (☎ 327 31 11) ul Furshtadtskaya 39
UK (☎ 325 60 36, fax 325 61 66)
pl Proletarskoy Diktatury 5
USA (☎ 275 17 01, fax 110-70-22)
ul Furshtadtskaya 15

Yekaterinburg

UK (☎ 3432-56 4931, fax 59 2901,
Ⓦ www.britain.sky.ru) Gogolya ul 15A
USA (☎ 3432-56 4619, fax 56 4515,
Ⓔ uscgyekat@gin.ru) Gogolya ul 15A

Irkutsk
Mongolia
Consulate: (☎ 3952-342 145, fax 342 143,
Ⓔ irconsul@angara.ru) ul Lapina 11

Ulan Ude
Mongolia
Consulate: (☎ 3012-220 499, fax 214 188,
Ⓔ mnc@burnet.ru) Hotel Baikal, ul Ebanova 12

Khabarovsk
China
Consulate: (☎ 4212-34 75 50, fax 32 83 90)
Lenin Stadium 1. Visa applications accepted
10.30am to 1pm Monday, Wednesday and Friday only. The cost is $30 for a single-entry visa
and processing takes a week. For a visa in two
days the cost is $45, in one day $60.
Japan
Consulate: (☎ 4212-32 69 07, fax 32 72 12,
Ⓔ consul@japan.khv.ru) ul Pushkina 38A

Vladivostok
South Korea
Consulate: (☎ 4232-22 77 29, fax 22 73 18)
ul Aleutskaya 45A

Japan
Consulate: (☎ 4232-26 74 81, fax 26 75 41)
ul Verkhneportovaya 46
USA
Consulate: (☎ 30 00 70, fax 26 02 48) ul
Pushkinaskaya 32

Beijing Most foreign embassies in Beijing
are in one of two main compounds, Jianguomenwai or Sanlitun.

Australia (☎ 6532 2331, fax 6532 6957)
21 Dongzhimenwai Dajie, Sanlitun
Canada (☎ 6532 3536, fax 6532 3507)
19 Dongzhimenwai Dajie, Sanlitun
France (☎ 6532 1331, fax 6532 5336)
3 Dongsan Jie, Sanlitun
Germany (☎ 6532 2161, fax 6532 5336)
17 Dongzhimenwai Dajie, Sanlitun
Ireland (☎ 6532 1908, fax 6532 2168)
3 Ritan Donglu, Jianguomenwai
Japan (☎ 6532 2361, fax 6532 4625)
7 Ritan Lu, Jianguomenwai
Mongolia (☎ 6532 1810 or 6532 1203, fax 6532
5045, Ⓔ monembbj@public3.bta.net.cn) No
2, Xiushui Beijie Jian Guo Men Wai Da Jie
Netherlands (☎ 6532 1131, fax 6532 4689)
4 Liangmahe Nanlu, Sanlitun
Russia (☎ 6532 1267, fax 6532 4853)
4 Dongzhimen Beijzhongjie, west of the
Sanlitun compound.
UK (☎ 6532 1961, fax 6532 1937,
Ⓦ www.britishembassy.org.cn) 11 Guanghua
Lu Jianguomenwai
USA (☎ 6532 3831, fax 6532 6057) 3 Xiushui
Beijie, Jianguomenwai

Ulaan Baatar For most nationalities, the
nearest embassy to Mongolia is Beijing. A
few countries, however, have representation
in Ulaan Baatar.

Canada
Consulate: (☎ 328 281, fax 328 289)
Diplomatic Services Corps Bldg, Suite 56
China
Embassy: (☎ 320 955, fax 311 943)
5 Zaluuchuudyn Örgön Chölöö
France
Embassy: (☎ 324 519, fax 329 644)
Diplomatic Services Corps Bldg, no 48
Germany
Embassy: (☎ 323 325, fax 323 905)
7 Negdsen Undestnii Gudamj
Japan
Embassy: (☎ 320 777, fax 313 332)
6 Marksyn Gudamj
Russia
Embassy: (☎ 326 037, fax 324 425)
6A Enkh Taivny Örgön Chölöö.

UK
 Embassy: (☎ 458 133, fax 358 036)
 30 Enkh Taivny Örgön Chölöö
USA
 Embassy: (☎ 329 095, fax 320 776,
 W www.us-mongolia.com) 59/1 Ikh Toiruu

CUSTOMS
Russia
Generally speaking, customs in airports is much stricter than at most border crossings.

You may be asked to fill out a declaration form *(deklaratsia)* when you enter the country; you must declare whether the currency and value of goods you are bringing in exceed $1500. If they do, you must have your form stamped by a customs official. Keep this form safely as you will be asked for it when you leave the country: this is to ensure that you're not taking out more than you brought in.

If you have bought any type of art (even paintings at a tourist art market) or antiques, you're most likely going to need special permission to take them out of the country. Keep all receipts, get photos made of the item and be prepared for a bureaucratic time with the local Ministry of Culture. Check with the Ministry at 7 Kitaygorodskiy proezd (☎ 364-5986) in Moscow, and at Malaya Morskaya 17 in St Petersburg for the latest details.

China
Customs procedures are no longer the quite traumatic affairs they used to be. The only regulation to pay close attention relates to the export of antiques. In short, anything made before 1949 requires a certificate and a red seal to clear customs; anything made before 1795 cannot be exported at all. You can obtain the proper certificate and seal from the Relics Bureau (☎ 6401 4608) at the Friendship Store, 17 Jianguomenwai Dajie, between 1.30pm and 4.30pm Monday and Friday only. China also has a strange Y300 limit on the value of herbal medication taken out of the country.

Mongolia
Again, customs procedures are fairly straightforward and the main issue for the foreign traveller is the export of antiques. Most shops in Ulaan Baatar will provide the proper receipt and documentation when you purchase an antique. Otherwise, you can obtain one from the Department of Culture (☎ 320 024) at the Ministry of Culture (behind the Ulaan Baatar Hotel). The penalty for exporting fossils is $100 to $150 or five years in jail.

When you enter the country, you must fill out a customs declaration form. Hang on to this form, which will be collected when you exit the country. You may also want to keep your receipts for currency exchange.

MONEY
There are no official facilities for exchanging money on the train itself, so you'll need to stock up at your major stops. There are usually exchange places at border-town train stations.

Russia
Currency The official currency is the rouble, which comes in denominations of 10, 50, 100 and 500 rouble notes. There are 100 kopecks in a rouble and these come in one, 10 and 50 kopeck coins.

In recent years the rouble has been much more stable since its devaluation in 1998 (rouble notes with loads of zeros are from before this time and no longer valid). Even so we've chosen to list Russian prices in this book in US$ (abbreviated to $). It's illegal to make purchases in any currency other than roubles. When you run into prices in dollars – or the favoured pseudonym, 'units' – in expensive restaurants and hotels you will still be presented with a final bill in roubles.

Exchange Rates Many prices in Russia track the exchange rate of the US dollar, so when the rouble loses value, prices rise to compensate.

country	unit		rouble
Australia	A$1	=	RR15.96
Canada	C$1	=	RR19.24
China	Y1	=	RR3.75
Euro	€1	=	RR26.81
Japan	¥100	=	RR23.05
Mongolia	T100	=	RR2.82
UK	UK£1	=	RR44.01
USA	US$1	=	RR30.97

Exchanging Money US dollars are by far the easiest currency to change – don't even bother bringing anything else, particularly travellers cheques and credit cards, which despite acceptance signs in banks can be fiendishly difficult or impossible to exchange or use. Cash or credit cards *may* work in ATMs – you probably won't have too much of a problem in big cities such as Moscow or St Petersburg, but don't count on them anywhere else. Generally, the best Russia-wide bank to hunt down for exchanging money is Sebrbank, the state savings bank.

Make sure your dollars are in pristine condition. Banks and exchanges do not accept tatty bills with rips or tears, and some won't accept any bills printed before 1990 regardless of how good their condition.

There is no advantage to exchanging money on the black market in Moscow and St Petersburg, but the farther east you head the lower (and less advantageous) the exchange rate will be at banks. This is where you might want to risk exchanging money on the street – you'll often be approached outside banks or post offices. Be very cautious, since it's easy to be ripped off in these circumstances. Agree on the rate and make sure the dealer counts out all the money before you hand over any of yours.

Costs Although it's possible to travel in Russia on very little (see the boxed text 'Budget Trans-Siberian Travel the Scientific Way'), for most visitors a reasonable budget would be around $50 a day.

Moscow and St Petersburg will be the two most expensive cities you'll encounter on a Trans-Siberian trip. With serious economising you could scrape by on $30 a day in Moscow, but if you visit museums, take excursions and indulge in the nightlife you're heading towards the $100-a-day mark. Prices are marginally lower in St Petersburg. The only bargain you'll share with the locals in either city is riding the metro ($0.15). For more about accommodation costs see the Accommodation section later in this chapter.

Heading into Siberia prices drop, but not significantly: you can still easily be up for $50 a night or more at a decent hotel in Yekaterinburg, Novosibirsk, Irkutsk, Khabarovsk and Vladivostok. It's possible to get away at under $5 per head when dining out, but in cities such as Khabarovsk or Vladivostok a good restaurant meal is at least $10.

Tipping & Bargaining Tipping is standard in the better restaurants – count on leaving 10% – whereas elsewhere 5% to 10% of the total is fine. Tipping your guide, if you have one, is an accepted practice. Generally about $5 to $10 is OK.

Prices in stores are usually firm, and although you could haggle over food prices in markets, for the $0.05 you're likely to save it's not worth bothering. For other goods in markets and souvenir stalls, you can make a counter bid that is somewhat lower than the price the merchant is asking, but Russia is not a place where you can expect protracted haggling.

China

Currency The basic unit of Chinese currency is the yuan (designated in this book by Y). Ten jiao make up one yuan. Ten fen make up one jiao, but these days fen are rare because they are worth next to nothing.

The Bank of China issues Renminbi (RMB), or 'people's money'. Paper notes are issued in denominations of one, two, five, 10, 50 and 100 yuan; one, two and five jiao; and one, two and five fen. The smallest notes are hardly worth the paper they are printed on. Coins are in denominations of one yuan; five jiao; and one, two and five fen.

Exchange Rates Exchange rates at the time of publication include:

country	unit		RMB
Australia	A$1	=	Y4.27
Canada	C$1	=	Y5.15
Euro	€1	=	Y7.17
Japan	¥100	=	Y6.17
Mongolia	T100	=	Y0.75
Russia	RR10	=	Y2.68
UK	UK£1	=	Y11.78
USA	US$1	=	Y8.29

Exchanging Money Foreign currency and travellers cheques can be changed at the airport, banks and most hotels. These institutions all offer the same official rate, though some hotels do add on a small commission. Some hotels only change money for their own guests. Most currencies are acceptable in China, although US dollars are still the easiest.

Besides the advantage of safety, travellers cheques are useful in China because the exchange rate is actually more favourable than

Budget Trans-Siberian Travel the Scientific Way

'When we disembarked at Port Vanino all we had was an old Soviet 10 kopeck coin. But I had warned Andrey that we would have enough money only for the journey there, so on the way back we would need to travel the scientific way.'

This is how charismatic Russian hitchhiker and author Anton Krotov starts telling about the return leg of his trip, in which he and his buddy Andrey Petrov crossed the whole of Russia from east to west on a tight budget without starving or begging in churches.

On the first leg they hitchhiked from Moscow to Magadan on the Pacific Ocean for an average of $2 a day for two. The money was earned in the course of the journey by selling Krotov's books as they went. In Magadan they got a lift on a cargo ship heading south to Port Vanino, from where it took them just two weeks to return home.

Krotov's 'scientific' method of travelling is based on the assumption that most people are kind and happy to give food and shelter to a traveller. You only need to find the key to their heart. How to do that is the subject of his 'scientific' books that are in fact hilarious accounts of Krotov's many odysseys not only in Russia, but also in India and South Africa, to where he hitchhiked all the way from Moscow.

According to Krotov, the main peculiarity of hitchhiking in Russia – where an uninterrupted highway from Europe to the Pacific is still only the wishful thinking of Soviet cartographers – is that one must seek to get a lift not only in cars, but also on cargo trains, barges and the occasional military plane. Lodging consists either of a tent, or resorting to the *vpiska* method developed by Soviet hippies (no joke, they really existed) back in the '70s. For this you need a notebook called a *ringushnik* (from the English to ring), in which you accumulate hundreds of phone numbers of the people 'in the system' that you copy from similar notebooks belonging to other travellers. When you come to a new town, you try all these numbers, and there is a fair chance that by your fifth or so call a kind soul will indeed offer you shelter and maybe even food.

Krotov's brainchild, the Academy of Free Travel, a clandestine establishment based in his own flat in northern Moscow (200 steps north from Rechnoy Vokzal metro station, as he describes the exact location), welcomes travellers who want to obtain or share experiences, but don't expect to be immediately greeted with open arms.

The bearded Krotov, now in his mid-20s, may at first seem gloomy and somewhat arrogant. His terrible hippy-like slang doesn't help either. The best first step towards getting acquainted with him is to phone and ask if he could sell you some of his books (so far available only in Russian) – they are dirt cheap and are indeed a mine of information. For those who can read Russian, you can find contact details at the academy's Web site (**W** www.avp.travel.ru), from where you can also download Krotov's books.

If Krotov and his friends decide you are cool enough (by their own mysterious criteria) you will be rewarded with heaps of ideas on low- or no-budget travelling and perhaps an opportunity of joining some of their projects, such as a round-the-world hitchhiking tour.

Leonid Ragozin & Masha Makeeva

the rate for cash. Be sure to use cheques from the leading institutions such as Citibank, American Express and Visa.

Beijing has several ATM machines that are compatible with Western banking networks. Most ATMs throughout China, however, only work within the Chinese banking system. Even in Beijing, machines are often out of order, so travellers should not rely on ATMs as their sole source of money.

Credit cards are becoming more acceptable, especially at major department stores, upmarket hotels and expensive restaurants. Some travel agencies accept plastic but they will tack a 4% to 5% service charge on to the bill.

Costs Costs in Beijing vary widely depending on the level of comfort expected. Once in Beijing, ascetics can survive on as little as $15 per day by staying in youth hostels, travelling by bicycle or bus, and eating from street stalls and cafes. Less-austere travellers can expect to spend $40 per day for a decent hotel room, moderately-priced meals and an occasional taxi ride. The range, of course, goes all the way up the scale to $300 for a five-star luxury hotel and accompanying fancy meals.

Tipping & Bargaining Tipping is neither required nor expected in China, except in the case of porters in upmarket hotels.

Bargaining, on the other hand, is certainly expected in smaller shops, street stalls and even hotels. Prices may come down significantly just by asking for a 'discount', especially during the off season.

Mongolia

Currency The currency of Mongolia is the tögrög, designated here as T. Banknotes are issued in denominations of one, three, five, 10, 20, 50, 100, 500, 1000, 5000 and 10,000 tögrög. The smallest bills are often lacking, especially in the countryside, so you may receive change in the form of sticks of chewing gum instead.

Mongolian law states that all transactions must be made in tögrög, with the exception of airlines and travel agencies that have special permits. In reality, many hotels and *ger* (traditional round felt tents) camps continue to accept US dollars. We have quoted accommodation costs in dollars.

Exchange Rates The following currencies are convertible in Ulaan Baatar:

country	unit		tögrög
Australia	A$1	=	T567
Canada	C$1	=	T684
China	Y1	=	T133
Euro	€1	=	T952
Japan	¥100	=	T819
Russia	RR10	=	T355
UK	UK£1	=	T1563
USA	US$1	=	T1100

Exchanging Money Foreign currency can be changed at several banks and countless licensed moneychangers in Ulaan Baatar. Moneychangers often offer better rates and accept a wider range of currency than the banks. In any case, the US dollar is still the easiest currency to exchange. Changing your money in the countryside is not straightforward: rates are not as good as in Ulaan

Baatar and currencies other than US dollars are not likely to be accepted. If you want to travel in the country, you're better off bringing all the tögrög you'll need.

Banks and hotels in Ulaan Baatar will change travellers cheques – but only those in US dollars and from major companies – into tögrög. They may charge a 1% commission. Travellers cheques are useless outside the capital city.

Credit cards are often accepted at top-end hotels, the expensive souvenir shops, airline offices and travel agencies. The Trade & Development Bank in Ulaan Baatar can arrange a US dollar cash advance on your Visa, MasterCard and American Express. Plastic is not accepted outside the capital.

Costs A thrifty traveller can get by in Ulaan Baatar for as little as $10 per day, assuming guesthouse lodging and public transportation. More comfortable lodging and Western meals will quickly increase this average to $40 to $50 per day. Travelling in the countryside will cost around $30 to $40 if you share your transportation and pitch a tent. All of these costs increase substantially – to as much as $100 per day – when travelling on an organised tour.

Tipping & Bargaining Tipping is still optional in Mongolia. If you round up the bill then your server will be satisfied. Nobody bargains in the government shops, but don't be afraid to negotiate for a fair price in the markets, at taxi stands and even in the hotels.

POST & COMMUNICATIONS
Post
If there is a mail car attached to the train, there will be a slot in the side into which you can drop letters. However, there's no guarantee that your mail will reach its destination, so it's best to post things from cities along the way or in post boxes at the stations.

Russia's main post offices are open 8am to 8pm or 9pm, with shorter hours on Saturday and Sunday; in big cities one office will possibly stay open 24 hours a day.

Outward post is slow but fairly reliable. Airmail letters take two to three weeks from Moscow and St Petersburg to the UK, longer from other cities, and three to four weeks to the USA or Australasia. A standard-sized airmail letter to any place abroad costs $0.25. In major cities you can usually find the services of at least one of the following express carriers: Fedex, UPS, DHL International and TNT Express Worldwide.

Incoming mail is unreliable and anything addressed to poste restante should be considered lost before it is sent. Should you decide to send mail to Russia or to receive it, note that addresses should be written in reverse order: Russia, postal code (if known), city, street address, name.

The Chinese postal system is efficient: airmail to Europe and North America takes about one week. It is possible to post your letters from most hotels, as well as at the post office. Packages, however, should be sent from the International Post Office. Officials there do inspect all parcels, so don't wrap and seal them until after inspection.

The International Post Office in Beijing is on Jianguomenwai Dajie not far from the Friendship Store. It's open 8am to 6pm, Monday to Friday. Mail should be addressed to you at Poste Restante, Beijing Main Post Office (you will need your passport and Y1.50 per letter to retrieve it).

In Mongolia international postal rates are relatively expensive, especially considering how slow the service is. International mail takes about two weeks to arrive in Europe or North America. Stamps are often available only in Ulaan Baatar.

The Central Post Office is on Peace Ave just off Sükhbaatar Square (open 24 hours). Bring your passport to retrieve mail addressed to you at Poste Restante, Central Post Office, Ulaan Baatar.

Telephone
Russia City codes are listed in this book under the relevant section heading. The telephone country code for Russia is ☎ 7.

To call internationally from a private phone, dial ☎ 8, wait for the second tone, then dial ☎ 10 plus the country and city codes, then the number. Omit any zeros from the city code (eg, to call Sydney the code would be ☎ 8 [tone] 10 61 2 and then the phone number). At the time of reasearch, the daytime telephone prices per minute were just over a $1 to Europe, $0.75 to the USA and Canada and $1.60 to Australasia.

Local calls made from hotels and restaurants are free. For pay phones it's easiest to buy a prepaid phonecard, generally available from kiosks. There are several types of cardphones, and not all are interchangeable. Cardphones can be used for local and domestic or international long-distance calls.

State-run, long-distance telephone offices are found everywhere, usually in the same building as or near a post office. In most you leave a deposit with an attendant and are assigned a private booth where you dial your number directly. After you finish, pay the attendant the outstanding balance or collect change from your deposit. Some cities also have privately run phone centres with more reliable satellite links to the outside world. Their rates tend to be more competitive.

Mobile (or cellular) phones are becoming increasingly popular with Russians who want to bypass the antiquated state system. In Moscow and St Petersburg they're as common as in most major Western cities. The coverage gets a lot patchier the farther east you head until you hit the major Far Eastern urban centres of Khabarovsk and Vladivostok. There are several different systems and you may be able to use your regular cellular phone while you are in Russia: check with your service provider for details.

China China's telephone system is undergoing a major overhaul but, for the most part, both domestic and international calls are possible with a minimum of fuss. Most hotel rooms have phones, from which local calls are free. Otherwise, the hotel probably has a phone in the lobby you may use, sometimes for a small fee. Local calls can also be made from public pay phones or from private phone booths.

You can place an international or long-distance call at the main telecommunications office. You pay a Y200 deposit beforehand, then your call is timed and the price is calculated after your call. Now, the cheapest way to make international phone calls from Beijing is to use the new Internet Phone (IP) cards. IP cards are available at Internet cafes and newsstands. The caller dials a local number, and then is prompted to enter an account number and a destination number. English service is usually available. Regular cardphones are also available in hotel lobbies and most telecommunications buildings, but their international rates are about double the IP rates.

The international access code in China is ☎ 00. Another option is to dial the direct-dial number (☎ 108), which connects the caller with a local operator, who then can assist with collect calls or credit-card calls. To place a call to China from outside the country, dial ☎ 86.

Mongolia The French company Alcatel is upgrading Mongolia's telecommunications system, so we can expect some great improvements in the future. At the moment, the system is adequate in Ulaan Baatar, where calling domestically or internationally is no problem. Outside the capital, however, telephone calls are not so straightforward.

Most telephone numbers in Ulaan Baatar and Erdenet have six digits. (If you are not successful at reaching a UB number that only has five digits, try adding a 3 or 4 to the front of the number.) Elsewhere in the country, where there are few telephones, numbers may have only three or four digits. Mobile phones are increasingly common. Mobile phone numbers are recognisable by their ☎ 9911 exchange and their eight digits. Domestic phone calls can usually be made from your hotel (free of charge) or from a public telephone (T100 per call).

International calls can be a more complicated process. If you have access to an IDD telephone, dial ☎ 00 plus your international country code. On a non-IDD phone, you should dial ☎ 106 for the international operator (who probably will not speak English). Otherwise, you can book a call from your local post office. You must pay an advance deposit, from which the total price will be deducted. You can also call internationally from the business centres or reception desks of top-end hotels, but they tend to be pricey. To call Mongolia from outside the country, dial ☎ 976. The city area code for Ulaan Baatar is ☎ 11.

Email & Internet Access

It's no problem finding Internet cafes across Russia – even the smallest towns have connections. The best place to start looking is the main post or telephone office – they often have the cheapest rates, too, of around $1 an hour or less for online access.

Similarly Internet cafes are easy to find in all tourist destinations, and even in some of the smaller towns, in China. Unfortunately, censorship is a reality. The Chinese government has blocked access to sites with 'dangerous' pornographic or political content, including those of most Western newspapers and universities.

Internet cafes are on every corner in Ulaan Baatar, but rare in the rest of the country. They usually charge between T1000 and T2000 per hour.

An easy option for sending and receiving mail on the road is to open a free eKno Web-based email account online at Ⓦ www.ekno .lonelyplanet.com. Other providers that offer services including Web-based free email accounts are Ⓦ hotmail.com, Ⓦ nettaxi.com and Ⓦ yahoo.com.

DIGITAL RESOURCES

On the World Wide Web you can research your trip, hunt down bargain air fares, book hotels or chat with locals and other travellers about the best places to visit (as well as to avoid). Lonely Planet's Web site (Ⓦ www .lonelyplanet.com) is a good place to start. Among many other things here you'll find summaries for most places on earth, postcards from other travellers and the Thorn Tree bulletin board, where you can ask questions before you go or dispense advice of your own.

Wherever possible we've listed helpful Web sites at the appropriate places in this book, eg, in the destination chapters you'll find sites for local information. The sites of most travel agents (see the Travel Agencies & Organised Tours section of the Getting There & Away chapter) can be useful for background research. Other sites for Trans-Siberian travellers to check out include:

Trans-Siberian

Ⓦ **www.transsib.ru/Eng** Far and away the best Trans-Siberian site, regularly updated with tons of useful information and a huge photo library. Also has a German-language version at Ⓦ www.trans-sib.de.

Ⓦ **www.washingtonpost.com/wp-srv/world /siberiadiary** The *Washington Post* journalist Robert G Kaiser and photographer Lucian Perkins crossed Siberia in August 2001 filing these fascinating stories along the way.

Ⓦ **herbert.groot.jebbink.nl/tsr** One man's entertaining account of his trip from Beijing to Moscow with photos.

Ⓦ **kbzd.irk.ru** A photographic essay of the historic Circumbaikal railway.

Ⓦ **www.parovoz.com/cgi-bin/rrr.cgi?lang=ENG** Brings together all Internet resources that have anything to do with Russian railways, subways and tramways – most sites it links to are in Cyrillic, though.

Ⓦ **www.whereishayden.org** Postings from a Kiwi's 2001 global tour, including thoughtful and fun accounts of Siberia from Vladivostok westward along the BAM.

Ⓦ **www.F8.com/FP/Russia** High-quality photojournalism on the Trans-Siberian route from 1995 but still good for background reading.

Russia

Ⓦ **www.departments.bucknell.edu/russian** Bucknell University in the USA runs this huge award-winning site with links to just about any topic on Russia you can imagine.

Ⓦ **www.kremlinkam.com** Entertaining site with live pictures from the capital that even manages to have fun with Lenin's tomb; it's good for a real-time weather check of Moscow.

Ⓦ **travel.state.gov/russia.html** Official US State Department information page on Russia, with the most up-to-date information on visas, safety issues, trouble spots and other practical matters.

Ⓦ **www.interknowledge.com/russia** Official site of the Russian National Tourist Office with information on Lake Baikal and the Arctic region.

Ⓦ **www.russianfareast.com** Predominantly concerned with business travellers and investment but provides a number of useful links for tourists.

Ⓦ **www.infoservices.com** *Traveller's Yellow Pages* for Moscow and St Petersburg.

Ⓦ **www.waytorussia.net** Useful site by students from Moscow University with links to travel agencies in Russia. You can also buy Trans-Siberian tickets through it and arrange visas.

Ⓦ **www.eki.ee/books/redbook/index1.shtml** This site comprises a comprehensive research study into the ethnic communities of the Russian Federation.

Ⓦ **www.mnh.si.edu/arctic/features/croads** Detailing the major ethnic groups in north-eastern Siberia is the Internet site of the National Museum of Natural History in Washington.

China

Ⓦ **www.chinadaily.com.cn** Site of *China Daily*, the online mouthpiece of the CCP.

Ⓦ **www.chinese-art.com** Features both traditional and contemporary Chinese art.

Ⓦ **www.cbw.com/tourism** Travel guide that is useful for discounts on flights and hotels.

Ⓦ **www.insidechina.com** News stories related to China, Hong Kong and Taiwan.

Ⓦ **china.muzi.com/index1.shtml** General and travel information and news about China.

Mongolia

Ⓦ **www.irex.org/publications-resources/re source-pages/mongolia.htm** An extensive list of links to practical information and scholarly studies about Mongolia.

Ⓦ **www.mongoliathisweek.mn** A subscription-only online English-language newspaper.

Ⓦ **www.mongoliatoday.com** A colourful online magazine on Mongolian culture.

Ⓦ **www.indiana.edu/~mongsoc** Excellent resources with links to other useful sites.

Ⓦ **www.mongols.com** An in-depth look at Mongolian history, politics and culture.

Ⓦ **www.un-mongolia.mn** Highlights various UN projects in Mongolia and features the cultural magazine *Ger*.

BOOKS

The 'Reading between the Lines' special section on literature from and about Siberia and Mongolia provides many recommendations for what's best to read about those regions in preparation for your adventure. Here we offer some other suggestions relevant to a Trans-Siberian trip.

Lonely Planet

Aside from this guidebook, Lonely Planet offers a host of books which may be useful, especially for anybody spending a significant amount of time in areas away from the railway routes.

For detailed information on each of the three countries covered by this guide see *Russia, Ukraine & Belarus*, *China* and *Mongolia*. The in-depth guides to *Beijing*, *Moscow* and *St Petersburg* are recommended for those staying in these cities for a while. The *Central Asia* guide is also useful for any travellers branching out along the Turk-Sib route, while *The Arctic* guide has full details for those planning excursions in Russia's far, far north.

Very handy, especially if you're travelling independently and don't speak the languages of the countries, are Lonely Planet's *Mandarin phrasebook*, *Mongolian phrasebook* and *Russian phrasebook*.

Guidebooks

Trekking in Russia & Central Asia by Frith Maier details many interesting hikes in Siberia, including the Circumbaikal railroad. For in-depth details on the BAM route see Athol Yates & Nicholas Zvegintzov's *Siberian BAM Guide* published by Trailblazer. *A Travel Guide to Jewish Russia & Ukraine* by Ben G Frank is an impressive work documenting Jewish culture and its effects on these lands.

In Search of Old Peking by LC Arlington & W Lewisohn is a classic guidebook with many details about the city. It's out of print, but may be found in libraries or second-hand bookshops. *Biking Beijing,* written by Diana Kingsbury, has a selection of self-guided tours around the thoroughfares and back alleys of the Chinese capital.

Travel

Although it was first published in the 1960s Laurens Van Der Post's *Journey Into Russia* still often rings true today, besides being a well-written, balanced and insightful account of the Soviet years. Italian journalist Tiziano Terzani's *Goodnight Mr Lenin* captures the death of communism and his efforts to return to Moscow from the Far East during that tumultuous time.

Mark Taplin's *Open Lands – Travels through Russia's Once Forbidden Places* is an easy and engrossing read covering some of the off-limit cities of the Trans-Siberian route, including Vladivostok and Nizhny Novgorod. Among the essays in celebrated Polish journalist Ryszard Kapusinski's volume *Imperium* is one on a Trans-Siberian trip he made in 1958.

The best cycling-across-Siberia book is *Between the Hammer and the Sickle* by Simon Vickers, although you'll have to hunt around for it since it's out of print. Likewise, Lesley Blanch's *Journey Into the Mind's Eye* is worth searching out. Its author's semi-autobiographical account of her romantic addiction to Russia is at times overly ripe, but she eventually gets to travel the Trans-Siberian route so longed for.

In *Wall to Wall: From Beijing to Berlin by Rail*, Mary Morris relates her personal experiences – not always positive – during a pre-Glasnost journey on the Trans-Mongolian.

Fully fictional, but fine reading for its chapters on the Trans-Mongolian trip and St Petersburg is David Mitchell's dazzling debut *Ghostwritten*.

Bartel Bull's *Around the Sacred Sea* is an interesting and nicely illustrated account of an epic horseback ride around Lake Baikal.

Wild East: The New Mongolia by Jill Lawless is a portrait of contemporary Mongolia by a Canadian journalist who lived there for two years.

History & Politics

If you can find it (again it's out of print), *To The Great Ocean* by Harmon Tupper is *the* book to read on the history of the Trans-Siberian Railway. *Railwaymen and Revolution: Russia, 1905* by Henry Reichman is an examination of the revolutionary movement among workers who built the Trans-Siberian.

The Princess of Siberia by Christine Sutherland is a biography of Maria Volkonskaya, who followed her husband into exile in Siberia. A more contemporary account of being banished to the Siberian Gulag is Eugenia Ginsburg's *Into the Whirlwind*.

As a more general account, *A History of Russia* by Nicholas Riasanovsky is one of the best single-volume versions of the whole Russian story through to the end of the Soviet Union. David Remnick's *Lenin's Tomb* and *Resurrection: The Struggle for a New Russia*, are both notable volumes by the *Washington Post*'s award-winning ex-Moscow correspondent.

China Remembers by Calum MacLeod and Zhang Lijia is an excellent collection of first-person essays by writers whose lives exemplify the major historical periods of the PRC. *Dragon Lady: The Life and Legend of the Last Empress of China* by Sterling & Peggy Seagrave is the definitive biography of Cixi, who ruled China in the late 19th century. *The Last Manchu*, written by K Tsai and edited by Paul Kramer, is an intimate account of the life of the Emperor Pui after his abdication in 1912. It is also the basis for the film *The Last Emperor*.

Probably the best book on contemporary Chinese history is Jung Chang's phenomenally successful *Wild Swans: Three Daughters of China*, a hefty but compelling read about three generations of women living in China in the 20th century.

NEWSPAPERS & MAGAZINES

On the train you'll sometimes come across the free glossy monthly magazine *Ekspress*. It's also common for deaf and dumb hawkers to sell newspapers, magazines and books along the carriages – a pile will be left in your compartment to leaf through. If you fancy brushing up on your Cyrillic skills go for one of the publications with the crossword puzzles that many Russians seem addicted to.

In Moscow the best source of English-language news is the daily *Moscow Times*, available free across the city; in St Petersburg, the same company's *St Petersburg Times* is an excellent free bi-weekly read. Top-end hotels in these cities usually have day-old copies of the *International Herald-Tribune*, the *Financial Times* and occasionally some of the British broadsheets, as well as weekly magazines, such as *Newsweek, The Economist* and *Time*. Elsewhere in Russia the pickings of English media are very slim, and most likely nonexistent.

China's most widely distributed English-language publication is the *China Daily*, a newspaper providing a strong dose of the government perspective on current events. Foreign news publications are often available in the Friendship Store and in upmarket hotels. Local rags geared to Beijing expats include the biweeklies *City Edition* and *Metro*. Tourist freebies like *Beijing Journal, This Month Beijing* and *Beijing Weekend* are available at many hotels. All of these have listings of restaurants, sports and cultural events in the city.

Mongolia has two English-language weekly newspapers, *The Mongol Messenger* and *The UB Post*. Both are good for local news and entertainment information. There are also seasonal tourist publications such as *Welcome to Mongolia* and *UB Guide*, but it is not clear if the information is actually updated from year to year.

RADIO & TV

Radio in Russia is broken into three bands, AM, UKV (the lower band of FM from

Russia's Railway Gazette

Although those in charge at the old Soviet mouthpiece *Izvestiya* might challenge it, Sergey Frolov, Editor-in-Chief of *Gudok*, the daily transport newspaper, claims his is the longest consistently published daily in Russia. *Gudok* – which means signal and also denotes the whistle sound of trains – has been in business since December 1917. The importance of a newspaper for the railway workers was instantly recognised by Lenin and the Bolsheviks who knew the only way they could gain a grip on such a huge country would be to control the railways.

Still partly owned by the Ministry of Railways and the trade union of railway workers, the broadsheet shifts around 167,000 copies Monday to Saturday with 70,000 on Sunday. Writers of the calibre of Mikhail Bugakov (author of *The Master and Margarita*) wrote for the paper in the 1920s and 1930s. In today's more competitive media market, *Gudok* takes a populist approach to its news coverage. You should be able to find it – only available in Cyrillic – on sale at stations across the country.

66MHz to 77MHz) and FM (100Mhz to 107MHz). Western-made FM radios usually won't go lower than 85MHz. The private Russian-language radio scene has come a long way and it's worth listening to hear some interesting contemporary music amid the cacophonous pop.

The clearest BBC World Service short-wave (SW) frequencies in the morning, late evening and at night are near 9410 MHz, 12,095 MHz (the best) and 15,070MHz – though the exact setting varies with location in Russia.

On TV the national channels include ORT and RTR (which generally run US-style talk shows, soap operas and badly dubbed films). Kultura (Culture) is heavy on the arts. Each region or territory also has its own TV channel – usually a mix of local news and yet more imported soaps. The one channel that you'll be able to watch without any language difficulties is Russian MTV. Top hotels have satellite TV offering CNN International, BBC World and the like.

Chinese domestic radio broadcasting is controlled by the Central People's Broadcasting Station. In Beijing, you can listen to

English-language broadcasts 12 hours a day on 'Easy FM' at 91.5 FM. Chinese Central Television also offers some English programs, including news, on CCTV 4. Most of this programming serves mainly as another outlet for government propaganda. Satellite TV is becoming increasingly prevalent, and some hotels and bars may even show American TV programming.

Mongolian radio is big on traditional folk music and oral epics, some classical music, and the ever-present Russian techno music. The BBC World Service is available in Ulaan Baatar at 103.1 FM. Ulaanbaatar TV and Mongol TB (not a disease) generally feature poorly dubbed Russian flicks, documentaries about nomads, and Mongolian sports (wrestling). A new missionary-owned station, Eagle TV, regularly shows NBA basketball, CNN news and BS evangelism.

PHOTOGRAPHY & VIDEO

As anywhere, use good judgment and discretion when taking photos of people. In Russia you also need to be particularly careful about photographing stations and any official-looking building or even vaguely military/security structure (see the boxed text 'Arrested in Siberia' in the Krasnoyarsk to Irkutsk & Lake Baikal chapter); if in doubt, don't snap!

Colour-print film is available almost everywhere in Russia and China, but slide film is very hard to come by outside the major cities.

In China slide film can be bought at the Friendship Store and at upmarket hotels, but it is very pricey. Many tourist attractions charge an extra fee for the privilege of photographing or videotaping at the site. Photographing monks or the interiors of temples is generally forbidden. If you are spotted taking photos of protests, you will almost certainly have your film confiscated and you may also be detained by the police.

In Ulaan Baatar, you can find print and Polaroid film in hotels and tourist shops, but it is usually overpriced. Slide film is rare indeed. Photography is prohibited inside monasteries and temples, although you can usually photograph the exterior buildings and grounds. In most museums you need to pay an extra fee (often outrageously high) to take photos or videos.

For tips on taking decent shots, Lonely Planet's *Travel Photography: A Guide to Taking Better Pictures* is written by internationally renowned travel photographer, Richard I'Anson.

The predominant video format in Russia and Mongolia is SECAM, a system not compatible with that used in most of Europe (France and Greece are among the exceptions) and Australia, or that used in the USA. China subscribes to the PAL broadcasting standard, which is the same as Australia, New Zealand, the UK and most of Europe.

TIME

No one on the train knew what time it was. Some people said the train travelled on Moscow time but operated on local time, if you can figure that out. But half the people were on Beijing time and one diplomat said he was on Tokyo time, which was the same for some reason as Ulaan Baatar time. Our Chinese porter changed his watch 15 minutes every few hours or so but this was a system of his own devising.

Mary Morris, *Wall to Wall*

One of the most disorienting aspects of a Trans-Siberian trip is working out what time it is. The important thing to remember is that all long-distance trains run on Moscow time – so check carefully when you buy a ticket exactly what time *locally* you should be at the station. Once inside the station and on the train all clocks are set to Moscow time.

In the route chapters we list the number of hours a stop is ahead of Moscow time and highlight when the time zone changes.

From the early hours of the last Sunday in September to the early hours of the last Sunday in March, Moscow and St Petersburg time is GMT/UTC plus three hours. From the last Sunday in March to the last Sunday in September, 'summer time' is in force and it's GMT/UTC plus four hours.

Most of European Russia is in the same time zone as Moscow and St Petersburg. The exception along the Trans-Siberian route is Perm, which is two hours ahead of Moscow. East of the Ural Mountains, Yekaterinburg is on Moscow time plus two hours, Irkutsk on Moscow time plus five hours and Vladivostok on Moscow time plus seven hours.

All of China is on Beijing's clock, which is eight hours ahead of GMT. Daylight-savings time was abandoned in 1992, so the

How to Have a Trans-Siberian Shower

One of the major gripes of a long-distance Trans-Siberian journey for many travellers is the lack of shower facilities. This said, the train toilets, with a sink and hole in the floor for drainage, do allow for various DIY options.

You're going to need some props. A universal plug is essential since there is never a plug for the basin. Soap is handy although this is often provided, as is a sponge or flannel (you'll be given a small towel as part of your linen supply). Some travellers also swear by a short piece of hose or plastic shower attachment that can be fixed onto the fiddly taps (to get the water to run you need to push up on the lever under the tap.

Note that in the summer it's rare to have hot water and it's not always guaranteed at other times either. You could always fill a bowl or large mug at the samovar and use it to warm your wash up!

time difference with Europe and the USA is reduced by one hour during the summer months.

Mongolia is divided into two time zones. Most of the country, including Ulaan Baatar, is GMT plus eight hours, so it is the same time zone as Beijing.

ELECTRICITY

Electrical power in China, Mongolia and Russia is 220V, 50Hz. Sockets in Russia and Mongolia are designed to accommodate two round prongs in the European style. Chinese plugs come in at least four designs: three-pronged angled pins as used in Australia; three-pronged round pins as in Hong Kong; two-pronged flat pins as in the USA; or two narrow round pins as in Europe.

WEIGHTS & MEASURES

Russia and Mongolia both follow the international metric system. Although China also officially subscribes to the metric system, ancient Chinese weights and measures persist. Fruit and vegetables are sold by the *jin*, which is 0.6kg (1.32lbs). Tea and herbal medicines are usually sold by the *lia*, which is 37.5g (1.32oz).

LAUNDRY

Coin-operated laundries of the kind found in the West are unheard of along the Trans-Siberian route. Almost all hotels in Russia, China and Mongolia offer a laundry service, though. Prices vary widely, so you may want to inquire about the cost ahead of time.

TOILETS

Toilets on the trains are the Western variety, although you'll notice when you lift the seat

that the bowl rim is also designed for those who would prefer to squat rather than sit. The provodnitsas generally do a good job of keeping the toilets reasonably clean, particularly on the more prestigious class of firmennye trains.

It is also important to remember that shortly before and after any major stops, and along any densely populated stretches of the line, the toilets will be locked. Sometimes the toilet next to the provodnitsa's compartment remains her own personal fiefdom and off limits too.

Public toilets in Russia are rare and, where they do exist, often are of the squat variety and poorly maintained. This can also be the case in restaurants (McDonald's is an honourable exception). Pay toilets are identified by the words платный туалет *(platny tualet)*. In any toilet Ж stands for women's *(zhenskiy)*, while M stands for men's *(muzhskoy)*.

In China and Mongolia, public toilets in hotels, ger camps and restaurants are usually European-style, moderately clean facilities (although there seems to be a shortage of intact toilet seats in Mongolia). On the other hand, public facilities in parks, stores and train stations usually require that you squat over a smelly hole.

Toilet paper is readily available in shops throughout Russia, China and Mongolia. It's rare though that paper will actually be available in the stalls of public toilets, or on the trains, so always bring a supply of toilet paper or tissue with you.

Plumbing systems in these countries often have problems digesting toilet paper. If there is a rubbish basket next to the toilet, this is where the paper should go.

HEALTH

Apart from the chief provodnitsa probably having a first-aid box, there is no medical assistance available on the train itself.

Public health in Russia is pretty appalling and, despite well-trained personnel, lack of funds often means the quality of medical care ain't great either. However, on the whole there are few health issues here for the traveller to be overly concerned about.

A specific local hazard in some Siberian and Russian Far East areas, from May to September, is tick-borne encephalitis, while Japanese encephalitis (caused by mosquito bites) is a danger in rural areas bordering Mongolia, China and North Korea. Trekkers, campers and others going to rural areas should consider immunisation.

Mongolia suffers from a serious lack of medical facilities and caregivers. In short, an ill person is better off in Ulaan Baatar than in the countryside, and better off in Beijing than in Ulaan Baatar. If you must obtain medical assistance in Mongolia, try to seek out a hospital or private clinic that caters to foreigners and be sure to bring a translator.

Predeparture Planning

Immunisations There are no official vaccination requirements for travel to any of the countries covered by this route guide, but some vaccinations are recommended for a healthy trip. If you plan to spend longer than three months in Russia you will have to provide a certificate of a recent AIDS test to get your visa.

Seek medical advice at least six weeks before travel. Discuss your requirements with your doctor: vaccinations you should consider include the following (for more details about the diseases themselves, see the individual disease entries later in this section).

Diphtheria & Tetanus Vaccinations for these two diseases are usually combined and are recommended for everyone. After the initial course of three injections (usually given in childhood), booster injections are necessary every 10 years.

Hepatitis A Vaccine for Hepatitis A (eg, Avaxim, Havrix 1440 or VAQTA) provides long-term immunity (possibly for more than 10 years) after an initial injection and a booster at six to 12 months. Alternatively, an injection of gamma globulin can provide short-term protection against hepatitis A – for two to six months, depending on the dose given. It is not a vaccine but a ready-made antibody collected from blood donations. It is reasonably effective and, unlike the vaccine, it is protective immediately, but because it is a blood product, there are current concerns about its long-term safety. Hepatitis A vaccine is also available in

---

Medical Kit Check List

Although you'll find well-stocked pharmacies all through Russia and China, consider taking a basic medical kit, including:

Antibiotics – useful if you're travelling well off the beaten track, but they must be prescribed; carry the prescription with you.

Antidiarrhoea drugs, eg, Imodium (Loperamide) or Lomotil – these gut-paralysing drugs suppress the symptoms of diarrhoea and are only for emergency use!

Antihistamine (eg, Benadryl) – useful as a decongestant for colds and allergies, to ease the itch from insect bites or stings, and to help prevent motion sickness. Antihistamines may cause drowsiness and may interact with alcohol, so care should be taken when using them; take one you know and have used before if possible.

Antinausea drugs such as prochlorperazine (eg, Stemetil) or metaclopramide (eg, Maxalon) – for nausea and vomiting.

Antiseptic such as povidone-iodine (eg, Betadine) – for cuts and grazes.

Anti-itch cream such as calamine lotion or aluminium sulphate spray (eg, Stingose) – to ease irritation from bites or stings.

Bandages and **Band-Aids**

Cold & flu tablets and some **throat lozenges** Pseudoephedrine hydrochloride (eg, Sudafed) may be useful if flying with a cold to avoid inner ear damage.

Insect repellent, sunscreen, chap stick and, if you're hiking, **water-purification tablets**

Multivitamins – especially for long trips when dietary vitamin intake may be inadequate.

Painkillers – aspirin or paracetamol (acetaminophen in the USA) – for pain or fever.

Rehydration mixture – for treatment of severe diarrhoea; particularly important when travelling with children.

Scissors, tweezers and a **thermometer** (note that mercury thermometers are prohibited by airlines).

a combined form, Twinrix, with hepatitis B vaccine. Three injections over a six-month period are required, the first two providing substantial protection against hepatitis A.

Hepatitis B Travellers who should consider vaccination against hepatitis B include those on a long trip, as well as those visiting countries where there are high levels of hepatitis B infection, where blood transfusions may not be adequately screened or where sexual contact or needle sharing is a possibility. Vaccination involves three injections, with a booster at 12 months. More rapid courses are available if necessary.

Japanese B Encephalitis Consider vaccination against this disease if spending a month or longer in a high-risk area (particularly the Russian Far East) or making repeated trips to a risk area. The course involves three injections over 30 days.

Meningoccal Meningitis A single injection gives good protection against the major epidemic forms of the disease for three years and should be considered by anyone heading off the beaten Trans-Siberian path.

Polio Everyone should keep up to date with this vaccination, which is normally given in childhood. A booster every 10 years maintains immunity.

Rabies Another vaccination to be considered by longer-term travellers in this region, especially if they are planning on cycling, handling animals, caving or going to remote areas, and for children (who may not report a bite). Pretravel vaccination involves three injections over 21 to 28 days. After a scratch or bite by an animal, two booster jabs are required; those not vaccinated require more.

Tuberculosis The risk of TB to travellers is usually very low unless they are living with or closely associated with local people. Vaccination against TB (BCG) is recommended for children and young adults living in these areas for three months or more.

Typhoid Vaccination against typhoid may be required if you are travelling for more than a couple of weeks in most parts of Central and Eastern Europe or Asia. It is now available either as an injection or as capsules to be taken orally.

Malaria Medication Although malaria is not something you'll have to be concerned about in Russia or Mongolia, in parts of China it is a real risk. Antimalarial drugs do not prevent you from being infected but kill the malaria parasites during a stage in their development and significantly reduce the risk of becoming very ill or dying. Expert advice on medication should be sought, as

Everyday Health

Normal body temperature is around 37°C (98.6°F); more than 2°C (4°F) higher indicates a high fever. The normal adult pulse rate is 60 to 100 beats per minute (children 80 to 100, babies 100 to 140). As a general rule the pulse increases about 20 beats per minute for each 1°C (2°F) rise in fever.

Respiration (breathing) rate is also an indicator of illness. Count the number of breaths per minute: between 12 and 20 is normal for adults and older children (up to 30 for younger children, 40 for babies). People with a high fever or serious respiratory illness breathe more quickly than normal. More than 40 shallow breaths a minute may be an indicator of pneumonia.

there are many factors to consider, including the area to be visited, the risk of exposure to malaria-carrying mosquitoes, the side effects of medication and your medical history.

Other Preparations Make sure you're healthy before you start travelling. If you are going on a long trip make sure your teeth are OK. If you wear glasses take a spare pair and your prescription.

If you require a particular medication take an adequate supply, as it may not be available locally. Take part of the packaging showing the generic name rather than the brand, which will make getting replacements easier. It's a good idea to have a legible prescription or letter from your doctor to show that you legally use the medication.

Make sure that you have adequate health insurance to cover you in case of emergencies. See Travel Insurance under Visas & Documents earlier in this chapter.

Basic Rules
Food & Drink Being cautious about what you eat and drink is the best protection against diseases of poor sanitation such as diarrhoea, giardiasis and hepatitis A.

In some Russian cities tap water is safe to drink; in others – notably St Petersburg – it definitely isn't. To play safe, don't drink it; that includes avoiding ice in your drinks and brushing your teeth with it. Decent hotels and restaurants should have safe bottled mineral water. Mineral water from shops and kiosks may not be pure. Imported bottled water is available in some shops in larger towns. An electric water heating element is a useful thing to carry for boiling your own water.

Locals insist that tap water in Beijing and Ulaan Baatar is safe to drink. Bottled water is readily available in all major cities and towns, however, so there is really no reason to take a risk. If you travel in the countryside, be sure to boil water before drinking.

Cheap vodka bought from shops or kiosks can make you ill. Look for name brands in unopened bottles.

In tourist hotels and good restaurants along the route, food can be considered safe. But choose food from street vendors and cafeterias (stolovaya) in Russia with care. Go for hot, fresh-looking dishes. Don't eat anything you don't like the look, taste or smell of. Avoid salads. Be suspicious of fish and shellfish and avoid undercooked meat. Peel fruit yourself or wash it in water you trust. Ice cream is OK, except possibly the soft extruded kind. In remote areas milk may be unpasteurised (with a risk of tuberculosis), although yogurt and sour milk (kefir) are usually hygienic.

Medical Problems & Treatment

Self-diagnosis and treatment can be risky, so you should always seek medical help. An embassy, consulate or five-star hotel can usually recommend a local doctor or clinic. Although we give drug dosages in this section, they are for emergency use only. Correct diagnosis is vital. In this section we have used the generic names for medications – check with a pharmacist for brands available locally.

Note that antibiotics should ideally be administered only under medical supervision. Take only the recommended dose at the prescribed intervals and use the whole course, even if the illness seems to be cured earlier. Stop immediately if there are any serious reactions and don't use the antibiotic at all if you are unsure that you have the correct one. Some people are allergic to commonly prescribed antibiotics such as penicillin; carry this information (eg, on a bracelet) when travelling.

Environmental Hazards

Hypothermia Hypothermia occurs when the body loses heat faster than it can produce it and the core temperature of the body falls.

It is surprisingly easy to progress from very cold to dangerously cold due to a combination of wind, wet clothing, fatigue and hunger, even if the air temperature is above freezing. It is best to dress in layers; silk, wool and some of the new artificial fibres are all good insulating materials. A hat is important, as a lot of heat is lost through the head. A strong, waterproof outer layer is essential. Carry basic supplies, including food containing simple sugars to generate heat quickly and fluid to drink.

Symptoms of hypothermia are exhaustion, numb skin (particularly toes and fingers), shivering, slurred speech, irrational or violent behaviour, lethargy, stumbling, dizzy spells, muscle cramps and violent bursts of energy. Irrationality may take the form of sufferers claiming they are warm and trying to take off their clothes.

To treat mild hypothermia, first get the person out of the wind and/or rain, remove

Water Purification

Hikers drinking from streams might be at risk of waterborne diseases (eg, gastroenteritis or, rarely, typhoid), especially if they take water downstream of unsewered villages.

The simplest way of purifying water is to boil it thoroughly for 10 minutes. However, at high altitude water boils at a lower temperature, so germs are less likely to be killed.

Simple filtering doesn't remove all dangerous organisms, so if you can't boil water it should be treated chemically. Chlorine tablets (Puritabs, Steritabs or other brand names) will kill many but not all nasties, including giardia and amoebic cysts. Iodine is very effective in purifying water and is available in tablet form (such as Potable Aqua); remember to follow the directions carefully as too much iodine can be harmful.

If you can't find tablets, use tincture of iodine (2%). Four drops of tincture of iodine per litre of clear water is the recommended dosage; the treated water should be left to stand for 20 to 30 minutes before drinking. Iodine crystals (very dangerous things to have around as they are highly toxic and give off toxic gas when exposed to air) can also be used to purify water but this is a more complicated process, as you have to first prepare a saturated iodine solution.

their clothing if it's wet and replace it with dry, warm clothing. Give them hot liquids – not alcohol – and some high-kilojoule, easily digestible food. Do not rub victims: instead, allow them to warm themselves slowly. This should be enough to treat the early stages of hypothermia. The early recognition and treatment of mild hypothermia is the only way to prevent severe hypothermia, which is a critical condition.

Motion Sickness Eating lightly before and during a trip will reduce the chances of motion sickness. If you are prone to motion sickness try to find a place that minimises movement – near the wing on aircraft, close to midships on boats, near the centre on buses. Fresh air usually helps; reading and cigarette smoke don't. Commercial motion-sickness preparations, which can cause drowsiness, have to be taken before the trip commences. Ginger (available in capsule form) and peppermint (including mint-flavoured sweets) are natural preventatives.

Sunburn You can get sunburnt surprisingly quickly, even through cloud. Use a sunscreen, a hat, and a barrier cream for your nose and lips. Calamine lotion or a commercial after-sun preparation are good for mild sunburn. Protect your eyes with good quality sunglasses, particularly if you will be near water, sand or snow.

Infectious Diseases
Diarrhoea Simple things like a change of water, food or climate can all cause a mild bout of diarrhoea, but a few rushed toilet trips with no other symptoms is not indicative of a major problem.

Dehydration is the main danger with any diarrhoea, particularly in the elderly or children as dehydration can occur quite quickly. Under all circumstances *fluid replacement* (at least equal to the volume being lost) is the most important thing to remember. Weak black tea with a little sugar, soda water, or soft drinks allowed to go flat and diluted 50% with clean water are all good in this situation.

With severe diarrhoea a rehydrating solution is preferable to replace the minerals and salts lost. Commercially available oral rehydration salts (ORS) are very useful; add them to boiled or bottled water. In an emergency you can make up a solution of six

teaspoons of sugar and a half teaspoon of salt to a litre of boiled or bottled water. You need to drink at least the same volume of fluid that you are losing in bowel movements and vomiting.

Urine is the best guide to the adequacy of replacement – if you have small amounts of concentrated urine, you need to drink more. Keep drinking small amounts often. Stick to a bland diet as you recover.

Gut-paralysing drugs such as loperamide or diphenoxylate can be used to bring relief from the symptoms, although they do not actually cure the problem. Only use these drugs if you do not have access to toilets, eg, if you *must* travel. Note also that these drugs are not recommended for children under 12 years.

In certain situations antibiotics may be required: diarrhoea with blood or mucus (dysentery), any diarrhoea with fever, profuse watery diarrhoea, persistent diarrhoea not improving after 48 hours and severe diarrhoea. These suggest a more serious cause of diarrhoea and in these situations gut-paralysing drugs should be avoided.

Two other causes of persistent diarrhoea experienced by travellers are giardiasis and amoebic dysentery.

Giardiasis is caused by a common parasite, *Giardia lamblia*. Symptoms include stomach cramps, nausea, a bloated stomach, watery, foul-smelling diarrhoea and frequent gas. Giardiasis can appear several weeks after you have been exposed to the parasite. The symptoms may disappear for a few days and then return; this can go on for several weeks.

Amoebic dysentery is caused by the protozoan *Entamoeba histolytica*, and is characterised by a gradual onset of low-grade diarrhoea, often with blood and mucus. Cramping abdominal pain and vomiting are less likely than in other types of diarrhoea, and fever may not be present. It will persist until treated and can recur and cause other health problems.

You should seek medical advice if you think you have giardiasis or amoebic dysentery, but if this is not possible, tinidazole or metronidazole are the recommended drugs. Treatment is a 2g single dose of tinidazole or 250mg of metronidazole three times daily for five to 10 days.

Hepatitis Hepatitis is a general term for inflammation of the liver. There are several different viruses that cause hepatitis, and they differ in the way that they are transmitted. The symptoms are similar in all forms of the illness, and include fever, chills, headache, fatigue, feelings of weakness and aches and pains, followed by loss of appetite, nausea, vomiting, abdominal pain, dark urine, light-coloured faeces, jaundiced (yellow) skin and yellowing of the whites of the eyes. People who have had hepatitis should avoid alcohol for some time after the illness, as the liver needs time to recover.

Hepatitis A is transmitted by contaminated food and drinking water. You should seek medical advice, but there is not much you can do except rest, drink lots of fluids, eat lightly and avoid fatty foods. Hepatitis E is transmitted in the same way as hepatitis A; it can be particularly serious in pregnant women.

There are almost 300 million chronic carriers of **hepatitis B** in the world. It is spread through contact with infected blood, blood products or body fluids, for example through sexual contact, unsterilised needles and blood transfusions, or contact with blood via small breaks in the skin. You can become infected by being shaved, tattooed or body pierced with contaminated equipment. The symptoms of hepatitis B may be more severe than type A and the disease can lead to long-term problems such as chronic liver damage, liver cancer or a long-term carrier state. Hepatitis C and D are spread in the same way as hepatitis B and can also lead to long-term complications.

There are vaccines against hepatitis A and B, but there are currently no vaccines against the other types of hepatitis. Following the basic rules about food and water (hepatitis A and E) and avoiding any risk situations (hepatitis B, C and D) are important preventative measures.

HIV & AIDS Infection with the human immunodeficiency virus (HIV) may lead to acquired immune deficiency syndrome (AIDS), which is a fatal disease. Any exposure to blood, blood products or body fluids may put the individual at risk. The disease is often transmitted through sexual contact or dirty needles – vaccinations, acupuncture, tattooing and body piercing can be potentially as dangerous as intravenous drug use. HIV/AIDS can also be spread via infected blood transfusions; Russia's record of blood screening is not perfect.

If you do need an injection, ask to see the syringe unwrapped in front of you, or take a needle and syringe pack with you.

Fear of HIV infection should certainly never preclude treatment for serious medical conditions.

Sexually Transmitted Diseases HIV/AIDS and hepatitis B can be transmitted through sexual contact – see the relevant sections earlier for more details. Other STDs include gonorrhoea, herpes and syphilis; sores, blisters or rashes around the genitals and discharges or pain when urinating are common symptoms. In some STDs, such as wart virus or chlamydia, symptoms may be less marked or not observed at all, especially in women. Chlamydia infection can cause infertility in men and women before any of the symptoms have been noticed. Syphilis symptoms eventually disappear completely but the disease persists and can cause severe problems in later years. While abstinence from sexual contact is the only 100% effective prevention, the use of condoms is also effective. The treatment of gonorrhoea and syphilis is with antibiotics. The different sexually transmitted diseases each require specific antibiotics.

Cholera The current injectable vaccine against cholera is poorly protective and has many side effects, so it is not recommended for travellers. Cholera is the worst of the watery diarrhoeas and medical help should be sought. Outbreaks of cholera are generally widely reported, so you can avoid such problem areas. *Fluid replacement is the most vital treatment* – risk of dehydration is severe as you may lose up to 20L a day. If there is a delay in getting to hospital, then begin taking tetracycline. The adult dose is 250mg four times a day. It is not recommended for children under nine years nor for pregnant women. Tetracycline may help shorten the illness, but adequate fluids are required to save lives.

Diphtheria There have been extensive epidemics of diphtheria in Russia over the past few years. The disease is potentially fatal and is generally transmitted by the inhalation of infected cough or sneeze droplets. There is a higher risk of catching the disease in urban areas. Symptoms include coughing, shortness of breath and swelling around the throat. Medical help must be sought. Vaccination against the disease is available.

Typhoid Typhoid fever is a dangerous gut infection caused by contaminated water and food. Medical help must be sought.

In its early stages sufferers may feel they have a bad cold or flu on the way, as early symptoms are a headache, body aches and a fever that rises a little each day until it is around 40°C (104°F) or more. The victim's pulse is often slow relative to the degree of fever present – unlike a normal fever where the pulse increases. There may also be symptoms of vomiting, abdominal pain, diarrhoea or constipation.

In the second week the high fever and slow pulse continue and a few pink spots may appear on the body; trembling, delirium, weakness, weight loss and dehydration may occur. Complications such as pneumonia, perforated bowel or meningitis may also occur.

Tuberculosis TB is a bacterial infection usually transmitted from person to person by coughing but which may also be transmitted through the consumption of unpasteurised milk. Milk that has been boiled is normally safe to drink, and the souring of milk to make yogurt or cheese also kills the bacilli.

Travellers are usually not at great risk as close household contact with the infected person is usually required before the disease is passed on. You may need to have a TB test before you travel as this can help diagnose the disease later if you become ill.

Insect-Borne Diseases

Ticks You should always check all over your body if you have been walking through a potentially tick-infested area as ticks can cause skin infections and other more serious diseases. If a tick is found attached to your body, press down around the tick's head with tweezers, grab the head and gently pull upwards. Avoid pulling the rear of the body as this may squeeze the tick's gut contents through the attached mouth parts into the skin, increasing the risk of infection and disease. Smearing chemicals on the tick will not make it let go and is not recommended.

You might want to consider a vaccination against tick-borne encephalitis if you plan to do extensive hiking between May and September.

Lyme Disease This is a tick-transmitted infection that may be acquired in temperate forested areas of the region. It does not occur in the tropics. The illness usually begins with a spreading rash at the site of the tick bite and is accompanied by fever, headache, extreme fatigue, aching joints and muscles and mild neck stiffness. If untreated, these symptoms usually resolve over several weeks but over subsequent weeks or months disorders of the nervous system, heart and joints may develop. There is no vaccination against Lyme disease. Treatment works best early in the illness and medical help should be sought.

Cuts, Bites & Stings

Cuts & Scratches Wash well and treat any cut with an antiseptic such as povidone-iodine. Where possible avoid bandages and Band-Aids, which can keep wounds wet.

Bedbugs & Lice Bedbugs live in various places, but particularly in dirty mattresses and bedding, evidenced by spots of blood on bedclothes or on the wall. Bedbugs leave itchy bites in neat rows. Calamine lotion or a sting-relief spray may help.

All lice cause itching and discomfort. They make themselves at home in your hair (head lice), clothing (body lice) or in pubic hair (crabs). You catch lice through direct contact with infected people or by sharing combs, clothing and the like. Powder or shampoo treatment will kill the lice and infected clothing should then be washed in very hot, soapy water and left in the sun to dry.

Bites & Stings Bee and wasp stings are usually painful rather than dangerous. However, in those people who are allergic to them severe breathing difficulties may occur and require urgent medical care. Applying Calamine lotion or a sting relief spray will give relief and ice packs will reduce the pain and swelling.

Rabies This fatal viral infection is found in rural areas. Many animals can be infected (such as dogs, cats and bats) and it is their saliva that is infectious. Any bite, scratch or even lick from an animal should be cleaned immediately and thoroughly. Scrub with soap and running water, and then apply alcohol or iodine solution. Medical help should be sought promptly to receive a course of injections to prevent the onset of symptoms and further complications.

Women's Health

Gynaecological Problems Antibiotic use, synthetic underwear, sweating and contraceptive pills can all lead to fungal vaginal infections, especially when travelling in hot climates. Fungal infections are characterised by a rash, itch and discharge and they can be treated with a vinegar or lemon-juice douche, or with yogurt. Nystatin, miconazole or clotrimazole pessaries or vaginal cream are the usual treatments. Maintaining good personal hygiene and wearing loose-fitting clothes and cotton underwear may help prevent these infections.

Sexually transmitted diseases are a major cause of vaginal problems. Symptoms include a smelly discharge, painful intercourse and sometimes a burning sensation when urinating. Medical attention should be sought and male sexual partners must also be treated. For more details see the section on Sexually Transmitted Diseases earlier.

Pregnancy Most miscarriages occur during the first three months of pregnancy. Miscarriage is not uncommon and can occasionally lead to severe bleeding. The last three months should also be spent within reasonable distance of good medical care. A baby born as early as 24 weeks stands a chance of survival, but only in a good modern hospital.

Pregnant women should avoid all unnecessary medication, although vaccinations and malarial prophylactics should still be taken where needed. Additional care should be taken to prevent illness and particular attention should be paid to diet and nutrition. Alcohol and nicotine, for example, should be avoided.

WOMEN TRAVELLERS

Bring sanitary towels or tampons only if there is a brand you absolutely must use. Otherwise you can find locally produced Western brands like Tampax everywhere. Western and Russian-made soap and other toiletries are widely available but you might want to bring your own soap as hotels only supply meagre quantities.

Attitudes Towards Women

You're unlikely to experience sexual harassment on the streets in most parts of Russia though sexual stereotyping remains strong. In remoter areas, the idea that women are somehow less capable than men may persist, and in some Muslim areas women are treated as second-class people. In rural areas of the country, revealing clothing will probably attract unwanted attention (whereas on hot days in Moscow women wear as little as possible).

Russian women relish the chance to talk alone with a foreign woman, and the first thing they'll tell you is how hopeless their menfolk are. When journeying by train, women might consider buying a platskartny (open carriage) rather than a kupeyny (compartmentalised carriage) ticket and risk getting stuck in a closed compartment with three shady characters. If you do decide to travel kupeyny and don't like your cabin mates, tell the conductor who more than likely will find you a new place.

China and Mongolia are probably among the safest places in the world for foreign women to travel alone. Women are generally treated respectfully, especially in China, where principles of decorum are ingrained deeply in the Chinese culture.

Safety Precautions

You need to be wary; a woman alone should certainly avoid private taxis at night. Never get in any taxi with more than one person – the driver – already in it. In Russia, any young or youngish woman alone in or near flashy bars frequented by foreigners risks being mistaken for a prostitute.

GAY & LESBIAN TRAVELLERS

While girls walking hand in hand and drunken men being affectionate are common sights throughout Russia, open displays of same-sex love are not condoned. In general, the idea of homosexual acts is well tolerated by the younger generation, though overt gay behaviour is frowned upon.

There is an active gay and lesbian scene in Moscow and St Petersburg with the *Moscow Times* and the *St Petersburg Times* both containing listings of gay clubs and bars and publicising gay events. Away from the two major cities, however, the gay scene is much less open. One of the most up-to-date Web sites is W www.gay.ru/english/, with good links and other information.

Chinese law is ambiguous on the issue of homosexuality, but authorities generally take a dim view of gays and lesbians. The scene in Beijing is definitely quiet. For up-to-date information on the latest gay and lesbian hot spots in Beijing and elsewhere in China, take a look at the Web site W www.utopia-asia.com/tipschin.htm.

In Mongolia, there is little, if any, gay and lesbian culture. In 2000, the gay and lesbian rights group Tavilan (Destiny) was formed to promote understanding and to network with overseas groups. This group may be contacted at PO Box 405, Ulaan Baatar 210644.

DISABLED TRAVELLERS
Russia, China and Mongolia can be difficult places for disabled travellers. Most buildings, buses and trains are not wheelchair accessible. In China and Russia, crossing busy streets often requires using underground walkways with many steps. Uneven pavements in the cities and rough roads in the countryside make for uncomfortable and potentially dangerous travel.

Before setting off, get in touch with your national support organisation (preferably with the travel officer, if there is one). In the UK contact Radar (☎ 020-7250 3222, W www.radar.org.uk), 250 City Rd, London EC1V 8AF, or the Holiday Care Service (☎ 01293-774 535). In the USA, contact Mobility International USA (☎ 1-541-343 1284, W www.miusa.org), PO Box 10767, Eugene, Oregon, 974400. In Australia, try Nican (☎ 02-6285 3713, W www.nican.com.au), PO Box 407, Curtin, ACT 2605.

SENIOR TRAVELLERS
Respect for the elderly is far more ingrained in Russia than in some countries. Organisations in your home country, like the American Association of Retired Persons (W www.aarp.org), which you can join even if you're not retired or a senior, can assist with age-specific information before you leave.

China is a reservoir of the influenza virus. The elderly are particularly prone, and pneumonia can be a fatal complication. Older travellers should be sure that their influenza vaccinations are up to date. Apart from this, China poses no particular problems for seniors. There is also no reason why senior travellers would not enjoy Mongolia, although extreme temperatures and lack of medical care may be a problem.

TRAVEL WITH CHILDREN
Travelling in Russia with children can be a ball as long as you come well prepared with the right attitudes, equipment and patience. In Moscow there are the old stand-bys of the zoo, Gorky Park and the circus, but elsewhere, diversions are more problematic. On trains, children are likely to find playmates of their own age, but as many distractions such as toys and books as you can manage would be wise. Consider using the trip as an opportunity to teach children a little about the region's history and geography.

One thing to inquire about in the summer months are the children's railway parks, run by the Ministry of Railways and dotted all across Russia. They have actual working trains which are accurate small-scale replicas of the bigger ones. Children take part in all of the activities from ticket sales to engineers; it's all in Russian, but it could also be interesting to watch and you could arrange for a guide to assist you with translations. A Web site (again all in Russian) gives details of the parks: W railways.id.ru.

The Chinese, like the Russians, are open and affectionate towards children, and you may enjoy a particularly warm reception if you are travelling with your kids. Beijing is a city notable for its historical and architectural masterpieces, which may bore the kids to pieces. That is, only until they spot the toboggans at the Great Wall at Mutianyu, the dinosaur park at the Old Summer Palace and the flying saucer boats at Beihai Park. Other favourite spots for children include Ritan Park and the Beijing Zoo. Popular children's spots in Harbin include the Children's Park and the Siberian Tiger Park.

Ulaan Baatar does not cater so much to visiting children, although the dinosaur exhibit at the Natural History Museum in Ulaan Baatar will certainly capture their imaginations.

Lonely Planet's *Travel with Children* by Cathy Lanigan contains useful advice on how to cope with kids on the road and what to bring to make things go more smoothly.

Travels with Barnaby, the Trans-Sibearian Bear

As any six-year-old in the UK can tell you, Barnaby is a small bear who gets up to all kinds of adventures around the world – all in the name of primary education. As luck would have it we caught up with Barnaby and his minder Dean Arthur, a geography teacher who is based at the British School of Bahrain, just before he was about to set off on the Trans-Mongolian (or should that be Trans-Sibearian?) train. This is what happened to him:

'The 1st-class cabin was very nice coming complete with shared shower, an important element for all travelling bears. Apart from Dean, I was sharing with a large Mongolian woman who spoke little English and no bear. It transpired she was a doctor and wife of a Mongolian diplomat. The rest of our carriage was rather empty, with only three other travellers – two Germans and another English guy – all humans. They more than made up for the lack of numbers with beer and vodka parties each night, using the feeble excuse that it helped them sleep.

As a bear who hibernates his way through the winter I was happy to keep watch. So, I took a good bear's-eye view of the scenery. From Moscow to Irkutsk, there was some lovely pine and conifer forest but otherwise it was a little boring – far too similar to regular bear country. Our carriage filled up at Irkutsk with French and Swiss travellers, who must have felt right at home near glittering Lake Baikal and all that Alpine scenery – just as I did.

The three hours spent at the Russian border saw another drinking spree from the humans, while I dealt with customs. Mongolian border formalities were made far easier for me, compared to the others on the train, by the diplomatic passport our Mongolian companion had. Wish I had smuggled more than a Russian Soviet poster (of bears, of course).

By this time – day six of the journey – I was feeling a little like my poor cousins who live in cages, despite the 1st-class comforts. Awaking next morning, though, was the highlight of the trip. The rolling plains and hills of Mongolia were unbearlievable – no evidence of glaciation here. I am a geography bear after all!'

Barnaby the Bear, Moscow to Ulaan Baatar, July 2001

DANGERS & ANNOYANCES

Russia, China and Mongolia are generally safe countries and crime against foreigners is rare. Pickpocketing is probably the biggest threat for the traveller, especially in crowded places such as public transport, markets and tourist attractions. The risk is greatly reduced if you keep valuables in money belts or under a layer of clothes. The hotels are generally quite safe, but leaving valuables lying around your room would be tempting providence. Always take precautions at youth hostels and guesthouses, where other travellers may be trying to subsidise their journeys.

You needn't be too concerned about the so-called 'Mafia' – Russia's organised crime problem is far more complex, and far less of a threat to visitors, than one might guess from reading an issue of *Newsweek*. In general, Moscow and St Petersburg's streets are about as safe, or as dangerous, as those of New York or London and, with the possible exception of Irkutsk (where some muggings have been reported), you're highly unlikely to suffer any problems in Siberia or the Russian Far East.

The key here is to be neither paranoid nor insouciant. Use common sense and be aware that it's pretty obvious you're a Westerner. Anything you can do to try to fit in is a good idea, so scrap the day-pack and carry your goods in a plastic bag.

On the whole the trains are reasonably safe (you're certainly less likely to be involved in a fatal accident on a train than on one of Russia's dodgy airlines), but it pays to take simple precautions with your luggage – see the boxed text 'Playing it Safe'. If you've got the compartment to yourself, ask the provodnitsa to lock it when you leave for the restaurant car or get out at the station platforms.

Annoyances

Things are getting better, but in Russia be prepared for the tone-deaf hotel staff, monosyllabic shop 'assistants' with strange paralyses that make them unable to turn to face customers, and so on.

One thing you can't do anything about is the tangle of opening hours whereby every shop, museum and cafe seems to be having its lunch or afternoon break, or day off, or is *remont* (closed for repairs), or is simply closed full stop, just when you want to visit.

Queuing is basically nonexistent in China and Mongolia and there are very specific rules for it in Russia (see the boxed text 'The Rules of Queuing' in the Krasnoyarsk to Irkutsk & Lake Baikal chapter). In most cases, neither being polite nor getting angry will help. If you have the head for it, sharpen your elbows, learn a few scowling phrases in the appropriate languages, and plough headfirst through the throng. Good luck.

Spitting in China is only slightly less popular than badminton. Although it is technically illegal in Beijing, everyone does it everywhere, loudly and flamboyantly.

LEGAL MATTERS

Do your best to avoid contact with the myriad types of police. Some are known to bolster their puny incomes by robbing foreigners either outright or through various sham 'fines'. There is zero tolerance of any alcohol consumption by drivers and if you're caught with illegal drugs of any kind you'll be in big trouble. The age of consent for both sexes is 14.

If you are arrested, the Russian authorities are obliged to inform your embassy or consulate immediately and allow you to contact it without delay – but don't expect it to happen (see the boxed text 'Arrested in Siberia' in the Krasnoyarsk to Irkutsk & Lake Baikal chapter). Be polite and respectful towards officials and things are likely to go far more smoothly. *'Pa-ZHAHL-stuh, ya kha-TYEL bi pahz-vah-NEET v pah-SOLST-vih ma-YEY STRAHN-ih'* means 'I'd like to call my embassy'.

BUSINESS HOURS

In Russia government offices open from 9am or 10am to 5pm or 6pm weekdays. Banks usually open from 9am to noon Monday to Friday; those in major cities often also open from 1pm to 6pm. Currency-exchange booths open long hours, and on Saturday and sometimes Sunday too. Museum hours change often, as do their weekly days off. Most stop selling tickets 30 minutes or an hour before closing.

Playing it Safe

Security can be a very real concern on the Trans-Siberian trains, but they are quite safe with a few simple precautions.

The main rule is to NEVER leave important or precious belongings in the carriage. If you're getting off at a platform stop or going to the restaurant car, take valuable items with you or ask someone trustworthy to guard them. On our train one (thankfully honest) couple had brought along a normal British gas-meter key, which also happened to open train compartment doors. Losing passports and visas is a nightmare to be avoided at all cost. The easy solution is to keep these documents with you at all times.

Always lock the door at night. People will likely try to steal belongings even when you're in the cabin and asleep. Wear body belts or neck purses in bed. It's important to tell someone in your carriage if you're going to the toilet and leaving the door unlocked. A loud shout will usually scare thieves off – there's usually no violence involved but a strange face and attempted grab at your bag can give you a nasty shock.

The door-locks on some trains are dodgy. Test them well when you first board; you may need to improvise some security measures. We used a strong pair of knickers to tie the door lock, but strong cord would also work.

As well as the thieves, people sometimes come looking for spare (and better) carriages during the night. Be wary, but don't be too paranoid. Most visitors are either drunk Russians who can't find their way back from the toilet or confused next-door neighbours. We unfortunately 'karate kicked' the nice Russian family man from next door who stumbled into our carriage during the night!

Daniel & Sioned Williams, St Petersburg to Beijing, July–August 2001

Most Russian shops are open Monday to Saturday, although increasingly you will find seven-day and even some 24-hour operations. Food shops tend to open from 8am to 8pm except for a break *(pereryv)* between 1pm and 2pm or 2pm and 3pm; some close later, some open Sunday until 5pm. It's rare not to be able to find kiosks selling food and drink around the clock. Restaurants typically open from noon to midnight

Mongolian Insurance Scam

We have received reports from travellers of a scam operating on the Trans-Mongolian route. Do your best to ignore anyone who approaches you on the train insisting that you need to pay US$10 for mandatory health insurance to visit Mongolia. There is no such requirement for this – tell them you have your own health insurance.

except for a break between afternoon and evening meals.

Government offices and businesses in China and Mongolia operate on a five-day work week, generally from 9am to 5pm, often closing for lunch between noon and 2pm. Shops and museums are usually open on weekends, and may be closed instead for one or two days mid-week. Some branches of the Bank of China may be open on the weekend.

In Mongolia, however, the banks usually open only from 10am to 3pm weekdays. Many museums and tourist attractions have shorter hours and more days off in winter.

PUBLIC HOLIDAYS

The following are major public holidays in the three countries along the Trans-Siberian, Trans-Mongolian and Trans-Manchurian.

New Year's Day (Russia, China & Mongolia) 1 January

Russian Orthodox Christmas Day (Russia) 7 January

Spring Festival (Chinese New Year or Tsagaan Sar in Mongolia) end of January or beginning of February

Defenders of the Motherland Day (Russia) 23 February

International Women's Day (Russia & China) 8 March

International Labour Day/Spring Festival (Russia & China) 1 & 2 May

Youth Day (China) 4 May

Victory (1945) Day (Russia) 9 May

Children's Day (China & Mongolia) 1 June

Independence Day (Russia) 12 June

Anniversary of the Founding of the CCP (China) 1 July

National Day Celebrations (Mongolia, Naadam festival) 11–13 July

Anniversary of the Founding of the PLA (China) 1 August

National Day (China, celebrating the founding of the PRC in 1949) 1 October

Day of Reconciliation and Accord (the re-branded former Revolution Day) (Russia) 7 November

Constitution Day (Russia) 12 December

Easter Monday is also widely celebrated in Russia. Much of Russia shuts down for the first half of May and its wealth of holidays.

SPECIAL EVENTS
Russia

Some of the more important events and festivals are:

January

Russian Orthodox Christmas (Rozhdestvo) 7 January – celebrations begin with midnight church services.

February to April

Goodbye Russian Winter (Maslennitsa) Late February and/or early March – folk shows and games to celebrate the approach of the end of winter.

Tibetan Buddhist New Year (Tsagaalgan) Held in February or March, lasting 16 days and celebrating the lunar new year, hence advances by about 10 days a year. Mainly celebrated at family level in Buryatia and Tuva (where it's known as *Shagaa*).

Easter (Paskha) The main festival of the Orthodox Church year, held in March/April. Easter Day begins with celebratory midnight services, after which people eat special dome-shaped cakes called *kulichy* and curd cakes called *paskha*, and may exchange painted wooden Easter eggs. The devout deny themselves meat, milk, alcohol and sex in the 40-day, pre-Easter fasting period of Lent.

May

Graduates Day Held on or near the 24th – a day when those finishing school parade about their home towns in traditional student garb.

June

St Petersburg White Nights All of June – there's general merrymaking and staying out late, plus a dance festival.

July

Maitreya Buddha Festival Held at Ivolginsk *datsan* (monastery) near Ulan Ude.

Buryatia Folk Festival Celebrated at the ethnographic museum in Ulan Ude.

November

Great October Socialist Revolution Anniversary 7 November – now the holiday has been taken over by the noncommunists (see Public

Holidays earlier), this is a big day for marches by the Communist Party.

December
Sylvestr & New Year 31 December & 1 January – the main winter and gift-giving festival. Gifts are put under the traditional fir tree *(yolka)*. See out the old year with vodka and welcome the new one with champagne while listening to the Kremlin chimes on TV.

Russian Winter Festival Tourist *troyka* (vehicle drawn by three horses) rides and folklore performances at Irkutsk.

China
Spring festival, which is otherwise known as Chinese New Year, is the biggest festival of the year, starting on the first day of the first month according to the traditional lunar calendar. It is a great time to visit Beijing, where fairs take place at parks and temples around the city. The fairs feature food, arts and crafts, and dragon dancers.

Fifteen days after the New Year is the Lantern Festival, another colourful time to visit Beijing. In Harbin, the Ice Lantern Festival has evolved into a peak tourist season (for details, see the section on Harbin in the Tarskaya to Beijing chapter).

Mongolia
The Naadam festival, held on the anniversary of the founding of the Mongolian People's Republic, is the most celebrated event in Mongolia (see the boxed text 'The Naadam Festival' in the Zaudinsky to Beijing chapter).

Tsagaan Sar (White Month) is another wonderful festival, celebrating the start of the lunar new year in the midst of winter. The fattest sheep is killed for a feast on the first day. The days are filled with traditional songs and greetings, and gallons and gallons of airag.

ACTIVITIES
For details of operators offering adventure activities along the Trans-Siberian route see the Travel Agencies & Organised Tours section of the Getting There & Away chapter and the destination chapters.

Banya
A combination of dry sauna, steam bath, massage and plunges into ice-cold water, the banya is a weekly event that is a regular part of Russian life. All Russian cities will have banya, and they're generally worth visiting. For more details see the boxed text 'Bathtime at the Sandunovskiye' in the Moscow chapter.

Beaches
There are some good beaches at the Vladivostok end of the Trans-Siberian, especially if you head out to the more remote areas of Primorsky Kray. Also in St Petersburg, the locals are partial to a spot of sunbaking beside the Peter & Paul Fortress. Perhaps more surprising are the opportunities to strip off and lounge on the sand within Russia. Moscow, Kazan and Khabarovsk all have riverside beach areas where the locals flock on steamy days. On the artificial Ob Sea at Novosibirsk (see the Yekaterinburg to Krasnoyarsk chapter) there's even a nudist beach.

Cycling
Poor roads and manic drivers are two of the main hazards to cyclists in Russia. Otherwise you will find rural Russians quite fascinated and friendly towards long-distance riders. Just make certain you have a bike designed for the harshest of conditions and that you carry plenty of spare parts. Some local agencies run cycle tours, including Team Gorky Adventure Travel in Nizhny Novgorod who offer a program peddling around the Golden Ring towns (for contact details see the Getting There & Away chapter).

Cycling is a practical means of transport, as well as an entertaining way to explore Beijing. The neighbourhoods and *hutong* (narrow alleyways) seem to have been built with bicycles in mind, as they are the only vehicles that can fit down some of them. The courtyard complex of Qing Prince Zeng Gelin and the surrounding hutong are wonderful places to toodle around on a bike. The journey to the Summer Palace can also be an enjoyable ride.

In Ulaan Baatar, cycling is more enjoyable (and safer) outside the city, with one of the best rides along the Tuul Gol, south of the centre.

Fishing
Siberia, particularly the Russian Far East, is an angler's paradise with rivers swollen with grayling and various species of salmon. Unfortunately, organised fishing trips can be heart-stoppingly expensive. While it

is possible to go it alone and just head off with rod and tackle, most regions have severe restrictions on fishing. Travel agencies in Khabarovsk and Vladivostok can arrange fishing trips in the Russian Far East.

Horse & Camel Riding

A visit to Mongolia is not complete without a ride on a horse and/or camel. Ger camps at Terelj National Park rent horses and can direct riders to trails with some spectacular scenery. Most travel agencies also organise more extensive treks. Camel riding is more common in the Gobi Desert, where camels can be rented by the hour or just for a photo opportunity.

Mountain Climbing

Along the Trans-Siberian route possibilities for climbing exist in the Altay (south of Novosibirsk on the Kazakhstan and Mongolian borders), the neighbouring but less-elevated Kuznetsky Alatau, the Sayan Mountains (on the Mongolian border) and in the Baikalsky Range on the western shore of Lake Baikal. Frith Maier's book *Trekking in Russia & Central Asia* contains information on worthwhile climbs and the difficulties they present.

An experienced English-speaking guide who can arrange mountain climbing tours throughout Russia is Sergei Ginzburg; contact him through Megatest (☎ 095-126 9119, fax 126 1136, ⓔ admin@megatest.msk.ru, ⓦ www.megatest.ru).

River Trips & Rafting

River trips are offered across Russia from May to October, with cruises along the Volga being particularly popular. It's possible to sail between St Petersburg and Kazan, with stops at Moscow and Nizhny Novgorod en route. Other river trips include excursions along the Irtysh between Omsk and Tobolsk, along the Yenisey from Krasnoyarsk and on the Amur from Khabarovsk. And, of course, there are also the sailings down the Angara River from Irkutsk to Lake Baikal.

For those looking for a bit more adventure on the water, rafting trips can be organised out of Nizhny Novgorod (with Team Gorky), Yekaterinburg (with the Ekaterinburg C&V Bureau & Guide Centre), Novosibirsk as a base for the Altay, and Vladivostok.

Trekking

The best place for trekking along the Trans-Siberian route is around Lake Baikal, with the most adventurous options being at the northern end of the lake. Many of the towns along the Baikal-Amur Mainline (BAM) are good bases for heading out into the wilds and farther afield. The Altay Mountains, accessed from Novosibirsk, are great places to explore. The Stolby Nature Reserve in Krasnoyarsk is a striking landscape in which you can easily organise a day's hike. The hills and islands around Vladivostok also provide a full range of trekking options.

Both China and Mongolia offer excellent opportunities for hiking within day trips of the capitals. The most popular (and deservedly so) locales for hikes near Beijing are along the Great Wall, with a wide variety in terms of levels of challenge and degree of remoteness. Hiking destinations near Ulaan Baatar include Manzshir Khiid, Tsetseegun Uul and Terelj National Park.

Winter Sports

With all that snow could you really pass up the chance to indulge in some winter sports while crossing Siberia? Possibilities include cross-country skiing, skating, troyka rides – even dog sledding in Yekaterinburg!

COURSES
Russia

There are plenty of opportunities for language study in Russia. The English-language publications in Moscow and St Petersburg (for details see Newspapers & Magazines earlier in the chapter) regularly carry listings of and advertisements for Russian-language schools and tutors. The cost of formal course work varies widely, but one-on-one tutoring can be a great bargain given the low local wage levels.

Several of the Russian travel agencies (for example, Patriarshy Dom in Moscow and Baikalcomplex in Irkutsk) can arrange Russian-language tutors and combine them with homestay programs.

Another option for learning Russian is through one of the many international universities in Moscow and St Petersburg. These are usually affiliated with a school in either Britain or the USA. To find out about what programs are available, inquire at any college or university, which will have reams of information on international study programs worldwide.

China

Language Prices and quality of language courses in Beijing vary widely. At the low end of the range, four hours of instruction per day, five days a week, might cost around US$500 per month.

Beijing Language and Culture University (☎ 8230 3088, fax 8230 3902, **W** www .blcu.edu.cn) 15 Xueyuan Lu, Haidian
Beijing Normal University (☎ 6220 7986, fax 6220 0567, **e** isp@bnu.edu.cn) 19 Xinjiekouwai Dajie
Beijing University (☎ 6275 1230, fax 6275 1233, **e** cqlb@pku.edu.cn) 5 Yiheyuan Lu, Haidian
Taiwan Language Institute (☎ 6466 3311 ext 3509, **e** tli@bj.col.com.cn) 40 Liangmaqiao Lu

Cooking Try Chang's Club (☎ 6416 0377, **e** cchang@unet.net.cn), at the southern end of Bar Street (near the Butterfly Bar), which offers cooking instruction in English and allows clients to choose their dishes.

Mongolia

The most cost-effective way to learn some Mongolian is by hooking up with a private tutor or a student learning English. Ask around at the National University of Mongolia and the Institute of Foreign Languages in Ulaan Baatar. Other options language courses in the city include:

Bridge Mongolian Language Center (☎ 367 149, **e** bridgeinst@magicnet.mn) Sunrise Center room 205, Jalhanz Hutagt Damdinbazer St
Santis (☎ 318 313, fax 326 373, **e** santis@ magicnet.mn) Unen Newspaper Bldg 5th floor, east of Tuvshin Hotel

If you are interested in Buddhism, The Federation for the Preservation of Mahayana Tradition (☎ 9911 9765, **e** fpmt-mongolia@ magicnet.mn) is involved in reviving Buddhist culture in Mongolia. The centre gives free lectures and courses on various aspects of Buddhist tradition and meditation. Lectures are in English and they are held in the two-storey building next door to the Zanabazar Museum.

WORK

Opportunities for paid work in Russia are scarce, except perhaps in large cities where native speakers of English and sometimes German or Japanese are in demand. Private English-language schools are thin on the ground, but you probably won't find it too difficult arranging a private tutorship or setting up your own private class with the help of an advertisement in a local newspaper or by word of mouth. Also check the classified sections of the print and online versions of the *Moscow Times* and *St Petersburg Times*. The Peace Corps has teachers around Russia and similar agencies may offer voluntary work.

'We all must be happy in our work', said Chairman Mao. Foreigners seeking happiness in Beijing will likely wind up teaching English or other languages. You won't get rich (average pay is Y2000 per month for 12 hours a week), but there are often fringe benefits such as low-cost housing. Contact the universities directly to get more information about teaching. Another option is freelance writing for Beijing's expat magazines. The going rate is about Y1 per word. Foreign companies usually recruit from overseas to fill their plum positions, so these are harder to come by. A useful Web site to check is **W** www.zhaopin.com.

Finding work in Mongolia is much more difficult, due to stringent hiring regulations and minimal demand. Even organisations recruiting volunteers prefer to be contacted through their head offices overseas. Informal, short-term work teaching English may be possible through private universities such as the International School (☎ 452 959) or the Mongolian Knowledge University (☎ 327 165, fax 358 354).

ACCOMMODATION

For train accommodation options see the Train Bookings section earlier in this chapter.

Russia

You may find it useful to book a few nights in advance for Moscow, St Petersburg and Irkutsk, particularly during the busy summer travel period. Reservations can be problematic – sending a fax is preferable to email.

Russian hotels run the gamut from dirtcheap flophouses to megabuck, five-star palaces. Standards are on the rise; don't be surprised to come across places charging

$50 a night or more that are shockers. Although less common now in Moscow and St Petersburg, elsewhere you'll still find that, as a foreigner, you'll have to pay more for a room than a Russian.

Single prices often refer to single occupancy of a double room. Beds are almost always single. A *lyux* room is a kind of suite, often with a sitting room in addition to the bedroom and bathroom. Note that in summer some hotels can be without hot water for a month or more when the neighbourhood system is shut down for maintenance (the better hotels manage to avoid this).

For cheaper accommodation, Moscow and St Petersburg each has one or more youth or backpacker hostels, most able to offer visa support. Homestays (see the boxed text) can be a great way to experience Russian life – see also the individual city listings for more details. Camping in the wild is generally permitted: check with locals if you're in doubt.

Komnaty otdykha (resting rooms) are found at all major stations along the Trans-Siberian route and are very cheap – which is precisely why they are often booked up. Rooms are usually shared and there are often no bathrooms. At the bigger stations, such as Novosibirsk, the komnaty otdykha are excellent and the luxe rooms are well worth the extra expense. At many other stations the rooms are very basic.

At virtually all hotels you have to show your passport and visa when you check in – staff may keep it for a few hours to register your presence with the local OVIR. Often each floor has a floor lady *(dezhurnaya)* to keep an eye on it and to supply guests with snacks, bottled drinks or boiled water. They might even do your laundry. Hotels with significant numbers of foreign guests also attract prostitutes.

Check-out time is usually noon, but it's unlikely that anyone will mind if you stay an extra hour or two. It's usually no problem storing your luggage.

China

Camping is not really feasible in China, especially within sight of a town or village. Wilderness camping is more appealing, but most areas require special permits, which are difficult to obtain. The good news, however, is that other cheap accommodation options

Homestays

A lot of the Russian tourist companies and overseas agencies offer homestays as a cheap alternative to hotels. The standard price is about $30 a night, usually including breakfast. See the Travel Agencies & Organised Tours section of the Getting There & Away chapter for details of some agencies.

One reliable Russian organisation is the St Petersburg-based Host Families Association (see Places to Stay in the St Petersburg chapter for details). It can arrange homestays in many other cities along the Trans-Siberian route including Moscow, Yaroslavl, Vladimir, Nizhny Novgorod, Yekaterinburg, Tyumen, Omsk, Novosibirsk, Tomsk, Krasnoyarsk, Irkutsk, Listvyanka, Khabarovsk and Vladivostok. It also offers visa support.

In Australia, Eastern Europe Travel Bureau and Gateway Travel in Sydney, and Passport Travel in Melbourne can book rooms in Russia. In the UK, try Interchange (☎ 020-8681 3612, fax 8760 0031, ⓦ www.interchange .uk) which offers homestays in Moscow (for £43 a night) and St Petersburg (£34 a night). In the USA, Russian Home Travel (toll-free ☎ 1-800-861 9335, ⓦ russiahome@aol.com) offers visa support and represents hosts in Moscow and St Petersburg.

are available. University dormitories sometimes rent rooms to tourists, and several youth hostels have opened in Beijing in more recent years. A dorm bed in the centre of town goes for about US$7.

The price and quality of hotels in China vary considerably, especially in Beijing. A typical hotel room is a 'twin' – two single beds in one room. A 'single room' or a Western 'double' (one large bed for two people) is a foreign concept and rare in China. In Beijing, twins start around US$25.

Mongolia

With 1.5 million sq km of unfenced and unowned land, spectacular scenery and freshwater lakes and rivers, Mongolia is perhaps the most perfect camping destination in the world. Excellent camping sites are everywhere, even near Ulaan Baatar in places such as Terelj. If you are travelling in the countryside, camping is an even better option, considering the lack of hotels and the expense of ger camps. Be sure to carry enough supplies and water for the duration of your stay, since they may be hard to come by, depending on where you are.

A tourist ger camp is a 'camping ground' with traditional gers, a separate building for toilets and showers, and a restaurant/bar. The gers are furnished with two or three beds. Toilets are usually clean. Prices are US$30 to US$40 per person per night, which includes three hearty meals. Prices are negotiable, and they may drop considerably if you bring your own food. Most ger camps in Terelj are open from June to September. In the Gobi, they are open from May to October.

Ulaan Baatar has a handful of guest-houses, which target foreign backpackers. Most are in apartment blocks and have dorm beds for US$3 to US$5. Many guesthouses also offer cheap meals, laundry service, Internet connection and travel services. Some of the guesthouses can also arrange for more long-term guests (one week or more) to rent a private apartment. At US$10 to US$20 per day, an apartment is much better value than the hotels in Ulaan Baatar.

Hotels in Ulaan Baatar are decent but overpriced. You will be hard-pressed to find a double for less than US$40. Comfortable and clean, these rooms usually have hot water and satellite TV, and maybe even English-speaking staff members. In the countryside, hotels are usually decrepit, empty and very cheap. Service is pretty poor wherever you go, except for a few top-end hotels in Ulaan Baatar. It is all part of the post-communist experience.

FOOD
On The Trains

At times a Trans-Siberian trip can seem like an endless picnic with all manner of foods being picked over and shared among fellow passengers. The dining car is favoured more for its makeshift role as a social centre than for any gastronomic qualities. It becomes the place to meet, hang out, drink beer and play cards (see the boxed text 'Restaurant Car Entrepreneurs').

The dining cars are changed at each border, so en route to Beijing you get Russian, Chinese and possibly Mongolian versions. Occasionally, between the Russian border and Ulaan Baatar there is no dining car. For what we think of the different dining cars of each country see the boxed text 'A Culinary Study of the Trans-Mongolian'.

You pay in roubles in the Russian car, RMB in the Chinese and dollars in the Mongolian, and a meal in either will rarely cost above $5. Dining cars are open from approximately 9am to 9pm local time, although this is by no means certain and with the time difference it can be a constant guessing game when to turn up.

In the dining car there's often a table of pot noodles, chocolate, alcohol, juice and the like being peddled by the staff. They sometimes make the rounds of the carriages, too, with a trolley of snacks and drinks. The provodnitsas also offer their own drinks and nibbles. Prices are cheap but overinflated compared to what you'd pay at the kiosks or to the babushkas at the station halts.

Shopping for supplies at the stations is part of the fun of a Trans-Siberian trip. The choice of items – all incredibly cheap – is often excellent, with fresh milk, ice cream, grilled chicken, boiled potatoes, home cooking such as *pelmeni* (dumplings) or *pirozhki* (savoury pies), buckets of forest berries and smoked fish all on offer. It's a good idea to have plenty of small change on hand, but you rarely have to worry about being overcharged.

Most of the way between Moscow and Vladivostok it's possible to eat perfectly well on supplies bought solely from the babushkas; however in Mongolia, as along the BAM route, there seems to be less on offer.

Russia

The country is a long way off developing a fully-fledged dining-out culture, but this said there are now modern restaurants serving decent and reasonably priced food all across Russia. Visitors to Moscow and St Petersburg have the best choice (at a price). The pickings in smaller Siberian towns are slim but there'll always be a market *(rynok)*, selling all manner of fresh produce and dried goods, and in the big cities there are well-stocked supermarkets and food stores.

Meals in some of the better new restaurants can be fine renditions of Russian classics made with fresh and tasty ingredients. In contrast, food in run-of-the-mill, old-style Russian restaurants tends to be bland, rich and heavy on meat, potatoes and overboiled or

Restaurant Car Entrepreneurs

The main thing I remember was the restaurant car – if you could call it that. Despite a long and impressive menu, there was nothing to eat except cucumber, nothing to drink except Russian champagne. We were the only people naive enough to try eating in the restaurant; everyone else came simply to drink and gamble at cards.

We got to know the main waiter reasonably well. He was a little guy and one day we asked him how he coped with these huge, drunk and belligerent Russians, all decommissioned soldiers travelling back from the east. By way of reply he pulled a small canister of CS gas out of his pocket. And we know he used it.

He was constantly on the make. While we were waiting for our sliced cucumber he would open up the bench seats and bring out boxes with little *Rossiya* tie pins, ties crudely embroidered with 'Perestroika', souvenir train timetables etc – all $1. Then as the journey progressed we were offered a samovar from the kitchen and even a *Rossiya* plaque that had been unscrewed from the side of the train. It was really lovely, with the crest and everything, and only $40, but far too unwieldy to carry – and tricky to explain away at customs.

The waiter and his team were real entrepreneurs. These experts in arbitrage bought sought-after foodstuffs and other commodities from one part of the country and sold them off at premium prices farther down the line. We happened to be in the restaurant car as the *Rossiya* approached Moscow. The waiters were counting stacks of money piled high on the tables.

The other thing I remember is how incredibly generous the other passengers – all Russians – were with their food. Everyone came well prepared, toting bags of supplies to last the journey, and were constantly plying us with thick slabs of bread to eat with boiled eggs, preserved fish, home-cured sausages and other local delicacies. It made a welcome change from cucumber and champagne.

Jan Dodd, Vladivostok to Moscow, 1992

pickled vegetables. Such canteen fodder is what you'll get at a stolovaya, one of the cafeteria-style places usually found near stations, and in office blocks and government institutions, where a meal rarely busts the $1 mark. A *bufet* is a snack bar, usually in a hotel, selling cheap cold meats, boiled eggs, salads, bread, pastries etc.

Get into the Russian way of starting with a few hors d'oeuvres *(zakuski)*, which are often the most interesting items on the menu and usually a good choice for a vegetarian. Soups, such as *borshch*, made with beetroot, *lapsha* (chicken noodle), and *solyanka* (a thick broth with meat, fish and a host of vegetables) can be a meal in themselves, served with piles of bread and a thick dollop of sour cream. Main dishes often come with a salad garnish.

Western fast-food chains have hit Moscow, St Petersburg and other cities, where they're incredibly popular. During summer, outdoor pizza and *shashlyk* (kebab) stalls pop up everywhere. Other standard snacks are pirozhki (pies) and *bliny* (pancakes served with a range of fillings). Useful for nibbling on long journeys is *kolbasa*, a salami-like sausage, which is made in a wide variety of styles and can go down pretty well with bread, tomato and raw onion.

China

In northern Chinese cuisine, the *fàn*, or grain, in the meal is usually wheat or millet, rather than rice. Its most common incarnations are as *jia* (steamed dumplings) or *chunjuan* (spring rolls). The most famous northern dish, Peking duck (or Beijing duck as it is called today), is also served with typical ingredients: wheat pancakes, spring onions and fermented bean paste. The range of *cài* (vegetable or other accompanying dishes) is limited in the north. The cuisine relies heavily on freshwater fish, chicken and most of all, cabbage.

The influence of the Mongols is evident in northern Chinese cuisine. Mongolian hotpot and Mongolian barbecue are adaptations from Mongol field kitchens. Animals that were hunted on horseback could be cooked in primitive barbecues made from soldiers' iron shields on top of hot coals. Alternatively, a soldier could use his helmet as a pot, filling it with water, meat and condiments. Mutton is now the main ingredient in Mongolian hotpot.

The most common method of cooking in Beijing is 'explode-frying', or deep-frying in peanut oil. Although northern Chinese cuisine has a reputation for being bland and unsophisticated, it has the advantage of being filling and therefore well suited to the cold climate.

In Beijing, of course, diners are not limited to northern cuisine. Every region of China and most regions of the world are represented on Beijing's restaurant scene. The options range from the street stalls at Dong'anmen Night Market to chic (and pricey) fusion restaurants where East meets West. Eating out in this cosmopolitan city is an adventure which should be seized with both chopsticks!

Mongolia

Mongolia, on the other hand, may leave your stomach growling. At least Ulaan Baatar has well-stocked restaurants that serve some international dishes. If you leave the capital, however, be prepared for gastronomical purgatory.

Dairy products – known as 'white foods' – are the staple for herdsmen in the summer. Camel's milk, thick cream, dried milk curds and fermented cheese are just a few of the delicacies you may sample (most of which taste like bitter, plain yogurt). During winter, the vast majority of Mongolians survive only on boiled mutton and flour. Likewise, in cheap restaurants throughout the country, mutton is the special of the day every day: mutton with rice, mutton in goulash etc. A *guanz* is a canteen that often offers nothing but mutton and noodles. In the countryside, the guanz is often housed in a ger and may be a traveller's only eating option.

Fortunately, many places in Ulaan Baatar – as well as ger camps that cater to foreigners – have expanded their menus. A few restaurants serve Mongolian hotpot and Mongolian barbecue, but these are really Chinese adaptations of ancient Mongolian cooking techniques. You are more likely to sustain yourself on *buuz* (steamed dumplings) and *khuushuur* (fried pancakes with mutton).

Self-catering is a necessity for travellers spending any length of time in Mongolia, especially in the countryside. Vegetarians especially will need to bring all of their own supplies from Ulaan Baatar.

A Culinary Study of the Trans-Mongolian

Rumour has it that the food is delish on the Chinese trains. Whoever said that must have been travelling east, and thus visiting the Chinese dining car after having their fill of its Russian and Mongolian counterparts. After a veritable food fiesta in Beijing, however, Chinese train food was quite underwhelming, to say the least. But it did fill my stomach for about US$4 (payable in yuan). And it was the last time I ate any vegetables besides cabbage.

I skipped the Mongolian dining car, but reports from fellow passengers sounded like this: 'We ordered *khuushuur*, which is supposed to be like a crepe filled with meat, but it was really filled only with rice and onion'. Or, 'I got a cheese omelette, but it was really just beaten egg whites'. Again, meals cost about $4 (payable in US dollars or Mongolian tögrög), and 'tolerable' was the description that rang most true. Following what seems to be national policy, the restaurant car actually had only a few of the items that were offered on the menu. (Note that the Mongolian train only has a dining car between Dzamyn-Üüd and Ulaan Baatar. Be sure to bring some snacks in case you get hungry between Ulaan Baatar and the Russian border.)

Once in Russia, the dining car was much less crowded than in China and Mongolia. Most likely, passengers were filling up on home-made pirozhki and dried *omul*, which were being sold by the babushkas on the platforms. Others had raided their stocks of instant noodles and canned fruit, which they could and would eat for days straight, and with pleasure.

The highlight of Russian cuisine is its soups, and I did enjoy a delectable *solyanka* somewhere between Ulan Ude and Irkutsk. For the most part, however, the Russian restaurant car was not going to win any international awards either. (I understand that the situation gets worse towards the journey's end, when the trains have been known to run out of provisions!)

After extensive research in three countries, I came to the conclusion that the quality of the train cuisine transcends national boundaries (for better or for worse).

Mara Vorhees, Beijing to Irkutsk, July 2001

DRINKS
Russia

Vodka can be bought everywhere. Be very suspicious of cheap stuff from kiosks, though: some of it can be bad and make you ill. Only buy screw-top bottles and always check to see that the seal is not broken. Two reliable 'plain' vodkas are Stolichnaya, which is in fact slightly sweetened with sugar, and Moskovskaya, which has a touch of sodium bicarbonate. Supermarket and liquor-store prices range from around $1 for half a litre of Stolichnaya or Moskovskaya to $20 for the most exotic brands.

These days, beer is overtaking vodka in popularity and for good reason – the quality is excellent and it's cheap at around $0.30 a half-litre bottle. The market leader is Baltika, making a range of brews from the No 0 nonalcoholic beverage to the lethally strong No 9. No 3, the most common, is a very quaffable lager.

Champagne *(shampanskoe)* comes very dry *(bryut)*, dry *(sukhoe)*, semidry *(polusukhoe)*, semisweet *(polusladkoe)* and sweet *(sladkoe)*. Anything above dry is sweet enough to turn your mouth inside out. Most other wine comes from outside the CIS (Eastern European brands are the cheapest), though you can find Georgian, Moldovan and Crimean wine.

Brandy is called *konyak*, though local varieties certainly aren't Cognac. The best stuff is Armenian, and anything classified five star is usually fine. *Kvas* is fermented rye bread water, often dispensed on the street from big, wheeled tanks. It's mildly alcoholic, tastes not unlike ginger beer, and is cool and refreshing in summer.

Tap water is suspect in some cities and should definitely be avoided in St Petersburg. Many people stick to mineral water, which is ubiquitous and cheap.

Russians are world-class tea drinkers: the traditional brewing method is to make an extremely strong pot, pour small shots of it into glasses and fill the glasses with hot water from the samovar. Putting jam, instead of sugar, in tea is quite common.

Coffee comes in small cups and is supposed to be thick, but quality – and sometimes supplies – is erratic. Almost any cafe, restaurant or bufet, and some bakery shops, will offer tea or coffee or both. Other drinks, apart from the ubiquitous canned soft drinks, include *sok* (juice) and *kefir* (yogurt-like sour milk).

China

Legend has it that tea was first cultivated in China about 4000 years ago in the modern-day province of Sichuan. Today, green tea is the most popular beverage throughout the country. Other local beverages include sugary soft drinks as well as lychee-flavoured carbonated drinks. A surprising treat is fresh, sweet yogurt, available from street stalls and shops everywhere. It is typically sold in small milk bottles and consumed through a straw.

If tea is China's most popular beverage, beer must be a very close second. The best Chinese brew is Tsingtao, produced in the formerly German town of Qingdao (the Chinese inherited the brewery). A notable Beijing brand is Yanjing. China is also a wine-producing country, although many Chinese 'wines' are actually spirits. Many of these are used primarily for cooking or medicinal purposes. The Chinese reds and

Drinking the Russian Way

The nearest thing to a pub is a *traktir* (tavern), but most drinking goes on in restaurants and cafes. If you find yourself sharing a table with locals, it's odds-on they'll press you to drink with them. Even people from distant tables, spotting foreigners, may be seized with hospitable urges.

If it's vodka that's being drunk, they'll want a man to down the shot – neat of course – in one; women are usually excused. This can be fun to start with, but vodka has a knack of creeping up on you from behind and the consequences can be appalling. A slice of heavily buttered bread before each shot, or a beer the morning after, are reckoned to be good vodka antidotes.

Refusing a drink can be very difficult. The Russians may continue to insist until they win you over. If you can't manage to stand quite firm, take it in small gulps with copious thanks, while saying how you'd love to indulge but have to be up early in the morning etc. And if you're really not in the mood, the only tested and true method of warding off all offers is to say *'Ya alkogolik'* (*alkogolichka* for women) – 'I'm an alcoholic'.

whites tend to unanimously get the thumbs down from Westerners.

Imported beverages such as soda, beer and coffee are available at many shops and restaurants. Coca-Cola, introduced to China by American troops in 1927, is now produced in Beijing. And yes, Starbucks coffee has opened its doors in Beijing.

Mongolia

Mongolians commence every meal with a cup of tea to aid digestion. In the countryside, many people drink *süütei tsai*, a salty tea, which is a taste that is hard to acquire.

The most famous Mongolian alcoholic drink is airag, fermented mare's milk. Herders make it at home with an alcohol content of about 3%. If further distilled, it becomes the more dangerous *shimiin arkhi* with 12% alcohol content. Mongolians have inherited a penchant for vodka from their Russian patrons. Mongolia is home to over 200 distilleries. Mongolians used to export vodka to Russia, but now consume much of it themselves. Two pubs in Ulaan Baatar brew their own light and dark beers. Imported beer is also available.

ENTERTAINMENT

While it's 'make your own fun' on the journey, there's no shortage of entertainment in Moscow and St Petersburg and, to a lesser extent, the larger cities along the Trans-Sib route, such as Yekaterinburg. The relevant chapters list the options as well as sources of local information about what's on.

Classical, jazz and rock music, ballet, opera and drama all thrive in Russia, the cultural flagships being St Petersburg's Kirov Ballet & Opera, Moscow's Bolshoi Ballet & Opera, and orchestras including the State Symphony Orchestra, the Russian National Symphony Orchestra and the St Petersburg Philharmonic. Many major cities have their own ballet and opera companies and orchestras. For the Bolshoi Ballet expect to pay around $50 a ticket; for the regional theatres the cost is much less.

Much culture and entertainment lies dormant between about June and September as companies go on tour or holiday.

Bars and clubs abound in Moscow and St Petersburg, and it's rare for a Trans-Siberian city these days not to have at least one megaclub combining a high-energy disco with a strip show, restaurant, bowling alley and whatever else the local entrepreneurs feel like chucking in. These can be fun (if you can hack the music), but at around $7 entrance plus pricey drinks they're far from a cheap night out.

Away from Moscow and St Petersburg, it can be hard to find regular bars. This said, in larger Russian cities, the 'authentic Irish pub' is popping up as fast as the factories in the old sod can pop them out. During the summer months, the ubiquitous simple street cafes can be fine places to while away the warm nights.

In China, Beijing has a vibrant and varied nightlife. Bars, discos and music performances abound, especially in the Sanlitun area. Karaoke is particularly popular among the wealthy Chinese. For tourists, traditional performances such as acrobatics and Chinese opera are excellent sources of entertainment in Beijing. See that chapter for details.

Entertainment in the Western mould in Mongolia is pretty well limited to the capital. Ulaan Baatar has a handful of discos and pubs, some of which levy a hefty cover charge in order to keep out the poorer 'unwelcome' Mongolians. A thriving opera and drama program is one worthwhile legacy of Soviet domination; plays and operas are shown regularly (more often in winter) at the theatre in Ulaan Baatar.

Traditional Mongolian music and dance is a favourite pastime for locals and a fascinating display for tourists. See the section on Ulaan Baatar in the Zaudinsky to Beijing chapter for details.

SHOPPING
Russia

The classic Russian souvenir is the *matryoshka*, the set of wooden dolls within dolls. Although often kitsch, they're a true folk art, and there are all manner of intricate painted designs. A small, mass-produced set should cost just a couple of dollars, but the best examples may set you back $100. For this price you can also take along a family photo to Izmaylovsky Park in Moscow and come back the following week to collect your very own personalised matryoshka set.

Other items to look out for include:

- *Palekh* – enamelled wooden boxes, each with an intricate scene painted in its lid

- *Khokhloma* ware – the gold, red and black wooden bowls, mugs and spoons from near Nizhny Novgorod
- *Gzhel* – blue-and-white ornamental china
- *Platok Pavlovo Posad* – the floral-designed 'Babushka scarf'
- *Yantar* – amber from the Baltic coast, though beware of fake stuff in some St Petersburg and Moscow outlets

Russian records and cassettes – rock, jazz, classical – are a bargain at about $1 or $2. For the same price you can get all manner of pirated CDs, video cassettes and software – just don't expect any of them to be of decent quality. Other ideas include paintings from the street; posters, both old Socialist exhortation and modern social commentary, from bookshops or specialist poster *(plakat)* shops; and little Lenin busts at street stands and in tourist markets.

China

Although tourists are unlikely to find true antiques at bargain prices, China is still a great place to buy handmade arts and crafts and furniture. Even if the seller claims it is old, it is more likely a reproduction, but that does not mean that it is not a good buy. Most Chinese markets are chock full of exquisite traditional furniture, iron teapots, bronze figures and Tibetan carpets, most of which are sold at prices considerably lower than in the West. Shoppers can get fantastic bargains on jewellery, especially pearls. Silk is high quality and low priced compared to material you can buy in the West. China also offers an impressive selection of fake brand-name clothing and pirated CDs and DVDs for very cheap prices.

Mongolia

Mongolian crafts are made almost exclusively for tourist consumption, and they are expensive. Some potentially good buys are traditional Mongolian clothing and boots, landscape paintings and Mongolian games such as *khorol* (checkers) and *shagai* (dice). Cashmere sweaters are an important export item, but they are usually over-priced, especially for the limited selection. Traditional musical instruments can be a beautiful and unique memento of a trip.

See the destination sections in the route chapters for details on where to shop.

Getting There & Away

While most travellers will start this route in either Moscow or Beijing, it's quite possible to fly into or out of other major gateways along the way, such as St Petersburg or Vladivostok. There are also many options for overland approaches from Europe or Asia – mainly by rail but also by road – as well as arriving in or departing from the Far East by sea.

This chapter covers getting to points on the route by air, land and sea, and outlines onward travel from the region. Since you're planning a train trip, we've left out the usual Getting Around chapter on travel within the region. This said, many Trans-Siberian travellers will want to make use of internal flights and trains within Russia and China and so we've included some information on these services here, too.

AIR

There are daily services to Moscow and Beijing from most major European capitals and New York, as well as frequent services from Hong Kong and other Asian centres. There are no direct services between Russia and Australasia; you will need to get to an Asian, European or US gateway and proceed from there.

There are also international flights to St Petersburg, Vladivostok and Ulaan Baatar as well as Khabarovsk, Nizhny Novgorod, Perm, Yekaterinburg, Novosibirsk, Krasnoyarsk and Irkutsk. More often than not, though, your best connection to anywhere in Russia along the Trans-Siberian route will be through Moscow, which handles the bulk of domestic flights. However, this will inevitably require a change of airports, which can be potentially costly, inconvenient and time consuming.

Airports & Airlines

The two major international airports on the route are Moscow's Sheremetevo-2 (which handles most international flights, although a few services now use Domodedovo airport) and Beijing. It's possible that you could also fly into or out of St Petersburg's Pulkovo-2, Vladivostok, Ulaan Baatar or a few other Siberian cities with international connections.

Since most travellers will be using either Moscow or Beijing as an entry or departure point for this trip, we have included fare details for these cities. For information on other flights see the destination chapters.

Major airlines flying into Moscow or Beijing include Aeroflot, Air China, Air France, Alitalia, American Airlines, Austrian Airlines, British Airways, CSA Czech Airlines, Delta Airlines, Dragonair, El-Al Israel Airlines, Finnair, Japan Airlines, KLM, Korean Air, LOT Polish Airlines, Lufthansa, Mongolian Airlines (MIAT), Qantas, Singapore Airlines, Swissair and Turkish Airlines.

Buying Tickets

The plane ticket will probably be the single most expensive item in your budget, and buying it can be an intimidating business. There is likely to be a multitude of airlines and travel agencies hoping to separate you from your money and you're going to want to get the best deal possible. With a bit of research – ringing around travel agencies, checking Internet sites, perusing the travel ads in newspapers – you can often get yourself a good travel deal. Start early as some of the cheapest tickets need to be bought well in advance and popular flights can sell out.

Full-time students and people under 26 years of age (under 30 in some countries) have access to better deals than other travellers. To qualify for these discounts, you have to show a document proving your date of birth or a valid International Student Identity Card (ISIC) when buying your ticket and boarding the plane.

Generally, there is nothing to be gained by buying a ticket direct from the airline. Discounted tickets are released to selected travel agencies and specialist discount agencies, and these are usually the cheapest deals going.

One exception to this rule is the expanding number of 'no-frills' carriers, which mostly sell only direct to travellers. Unlike the 'full-service' airlines, no-frills carriers often make one-way tickets available at around half the return fare, meaning that it is easy to put together an open-jaw ticket when you fly to one place but leave from another.

The other exception is booking on the Internet. Many airlines, both full-service and no-frills, offer some excellent fares to Web surfers. They may sell seats by auction or simply cut prices to reflect the reduced cost of electronic selling.

Use the fares quoted in this book as a guide only. They are approximate and based on the rates advertised by travel agencies at the time of going to press. Quoted air fares do not necessarily constitute a recommendation for the carrier.

You may find the cheapest flights are advertised by obscure agencies. Most such firms are honest and solvent, but there are some rogue fly-by-night outfits around. Paying by credit card generally offers you protection, as most card issuers provide refunds if you can prove you didn't get what you paid for. Similar protection can be obtained by buying a ticket from a bonded agent, such as one covered by the Air Travel Organiser's Licence (ATOL) scheme in the UK. Agencies who accept only cash should hand over the tickets straight away and not tell you to 'come back tomorrow'. After you have made a booking or paid your deposit, call the airline and confirm that the booking was made. It's generally not advisable to send money (even cheques) through the post unless the agency is very well established – some travellers have reported being ripped off by fly-by-night mail-order ticket agencies.

If you purchase a ticket and later want to make changes to your route or get a refund, you need to contact the original travel agency. Airlines issue refunds only to the purchaser of a ticket – usually the travel agency who bought the ticket on your behalf. Many travellers change their routes halfway through their trips, so think very carefully before you buy a ticket that's not easily refunded.

You may decide to pay more than the rock-bottom fare by opting for the safety and reliability of a better-known agency. Firms such as STA, who have offices worldwide, Council Travel in the USA or Travel CUTS in Canada are not going to disappear overnight, leaving you clutching a receipt for a nonexistent ticket, but they do offer good prices to most destinations.

Open-Jaw Tickets These are return tickets where you fly out to one destination but return from another, which saves you having to backtrack to your arrival point. It's unlikely that you'll find a return ticket into Moscow and out of Beijing or Vladivostok (or vice versa) with the same airline, but travel agencies will certainly be able to put together two one-way tickets with different airlines. This gives you peace of mind and something to show immigration officials, but sacrifices flexibility. It means you have to be at the other end on a certain date, or go through the hassle of changing your flight en route. It will not be any cheaper to do it this way as one-way tickets to major destinations can be purchased reasonably cheaply and at short notice in Moscow, St Petersburg, Beijing and elsewhere. Generally, you'll be better off buying a one-way ticket into your destination and another one-way ticket out when you finish the trip.

Buying Tickets Online There are many Web sites specifically aimed at selling flights, where you can look up fares and timetables by selecting your departure point and destination, then book a ticket online using your credit card. Your ticket will (hopefully) be mailed out to you, or it may be an 'electronic ticket' that you claim at the airport before checking in for your flight.

Sometimes these fares are cheap, often they're no cheaper than those sold at a standard travel agency, and occasionally they're way too expensive – but it's certainly a convenient way of researching flights from the comfort of your own home or office. Many large travel agencies also have Web sites, but not all allow you to look up fares and schedules.

Web sites worth checking out include:

W **www.cheapestflights.co.uk** This site really does post cheap flights (out of the UK only) but you have to get in early to get the bargains.

W **www.dialaflight.com** This site offers worldwide flights out of Europe and the UK.

W **www.expedia.msn.com** A good site for checking worldwide flight prices.

W **www.flifo.com** The official site of OneTravel .com for travellers on a budget.

W **www.flychina.com** Has good deals on flights to China from the USA and Canada.

W **www.lastminute.com** This site deals mainly in European flights but does have worldwide flights, mostly package returns. There's also an Australian version.

W **www.statravel.com** STA Travel's US Web site. You can also check the local sites for the UK (W www.statravel.co.uk) and Australia (W www .statravel.com.au).

W **www.travel.com.au** A good site for Australians to find cheap flights, although some prices may turn out to be too good to be true.

W **www.travelonline.co.nz** A good site for New Zealanders to find worldwide fares from their part of the world.

Departure Taxes

Russian departure taxes are usually included in the price of the ticket (there's a $25 tax payable in roubles for all flights from Khabarovsk, though).

Departing from Beijing airport, you must pay a Y90 international departure tax or a Y50 domestic departure tax. Both fees are payable in renminbi at a special counter near the airport entrance. You will need the receipt to check into your flight.

Travellers with Special Needs

If they're warned early enough, airlines can often make special arrangements for travellers, such as wheelchair assistance at airports or vegetarian meals on the flight. Children under two years travel for 10% of the standard fare (or free on some airlines) as long as they don't occupy a seat. They don't get a baggage allowance. 'Skycots', baby food and nappies should be provided by the airline if requested in advance. Children aged between two and 12 can usually occupy a seat for around two-thirds of the full fare, and do get a baggage allowance.

The disability-friendly Web site W www .everybody.co.uk has an airline directory that provides information on the facilities offered by various airlines.

Flights from Outside the Region

The USA Discount travel agencies in the USA are known as consolidators (although you won't see a sign hanging on the door saying Consolidator), and they can be found through the *Yellow Pages* or travel sections of major daily newspapers such as The *New York Times*, the *Los Angeles Times*, and the *San Francisco Examiner*. Good deals can generally be found at travel agencies in San Francisco, Los Angeles, New York and other big cities.

Council Travel (toll-free ☎ 800-226 8624, W www.counciltravel.com), which is the largest student travel organisation, has about 60 offices throughout the USA, including its headquarters at 6 Hamilton Place, 4th Floor, Boston, MA 02108. Another good option is STA Travel (☎ 800-781 4040, W www .statravel.com), also with an wide network of offices.

Ticket Planet (W www.ticketplanet.com) is a leading consolidator in the USA.

Economy class air fares from New York to Moscow can go as low as one-way/return $450/550 with Aeroflot, while you can get Beijing one way/return for US$500/750. From Los Angeles you're looking at one-way/return fares to Moscow of $550/960, to Beijing of $400/900.

Canada Discount agencies in Canada are also known as consolidators. They advertise their specials in major newspapers such as the *Toronto Star* and the *Vancouver Sun*. The national travel agency specialising in student fares is Travel CUTS (☎ 866-246 9762, W www.travelcuts.com).

In general, fares from Canada to Moscow and Beijing cost 10% more than those from the USA. For a one-way/return flight from Vancouver to Moscow the cost is US$720/ 1150; if you are travelling from Montreal it's US$770/940.

The main carriers between Canada and China are Air Canada, United and Air China. From Vancouver, one-way/return fares are US$550/900 year-round. Fares from Montreal are US$750/1400 in the low season, rising to US$850/2000 in the high season.

Australia Cheap flights from Australia to Europe generally pass through South-East Asian capitals, and involve stopovers at Kuala Lumpur, Bangkok or Singapore. If a long stopover between connections is necessary, transit accommodation is sometimes included in the price of the ticket. If the fare requires you to pay for transit accommodation yourself, it may be worth considering a more expensive ticket.

Quite a few travel offices specialise in discount air tickets. Some travel agencies, particularly smaller ones, advertise cheap air fares in the travel sections of weekend newspapers, such as *The Age* in Melbourne and *The Sydney Morning Herald*.

Two well-known agencies for cheap fares with offices throughout Australia are:

STA Travel (☎ 03-9349 2411, W www.statravel .com.au). Call ☎ 131 776 Australia-wide for the location of your nearest branch.
Flight Centre (☎ 131 600 Australia-wide, W www.flightcentre.com.au)

The most direct flight you're likely to get would be something like Sydney to Bangkok and from there Bangkok to Moscow; a Qantas/Aeroflot one-way/return deal starts at A$1100/1450.

To Vladivostok, the most straightforward route would be from Sydney to Seoul, South Korea, from where there are direct flights to the Trans-Siberian's eastern terminus. Alternatively you could fly to Japan; from here there are regular services to Vladivostok from Osaka, Niigata and Toyama.

The cost of a one-way/return flight from Australia to Japan starts at A$1200/1400. For onward flights from Japan to Russia and China see the Japan section later in this chapter.

To Beijing the one-way/return fares from Sydney with carrier Air China start at about A$1100/1649.

New Zealand The *New Zealand Herald* has a travel section in which the travel agencies advertise fares. Flight Centre (☎ 09-309 6171) has a large central office in Auckland at National Bank Towers (at the corner of Queen and Darby Sts) and many branches throughout the rest of the country.

The main office of STA Travel (☎ 09-309 0458, W www.statravel.com.au) is at 10 High St, Auckland, and there are other offices in Auckland as well as branches in Hamilton, Palmerston North, Wellington, Christchurch and Dunedin.

Fares from New Zealand to Russia and China are similar to those for flights that originate in Australia.

The UK Newspapers and magazines such as *Time Out* and *TNT Magazine* in London regularly advertise very low fares to places such as Moscow and Beijing. A good place to start shopping for fares is with the major student-or backpacker-oriented travel agencies such as STA and Trailfinders. Through these reliable agencies you can get an idea of what's available and how much you're going to pay – although a bit of ringing around to the smaller agencies afterwards will often turn up cheaper fares.

Addresses of some reputable agencies in London are:

Bridge the World (☎ 0870-444 7474 or 020-7813 3350, W www.b-t-w.co.uk) 4 Regent Place, London W1R 5FB
Flightbookers (☎ 0870-010 7000, W www .ebookers.co.uk) 34-42 Woburn Place, London WC1H 0TA
STA Travel (☎ 0870-1600 599, W www .statravel.co.uk) 40 Bernard Street, London WC1N 1LJ
Trailfinders (☎ 020-7938 3939, W www .trailfinders.co.uk) 194 Kensington High St, London W8 7RG

Shop around and you might be able to find a low-season one-way/return fare to Moscow for £150/200. Flights to St Petersburg are usually a bit more expensive at about £200/250 one way/return. Aeroflot generally offers the cheapest deals and it also has fares through to Ulaan Baatar should you wish to start or finish your Trans-Siberian journey in Mongolia.

Return fares from London to Beijing start at £500 with Air China, Air France and British Airways.

Continental Europe Although London is the travel discount capital of Europe, there are several other European cities in which you will find a range of good deals. Generally, there is not much variation in air fares from the main European cities. All the major airlines are usually offering some sort of deal and travel agencies generally have a number of deals on offer, so shop around.

One French travel agency that specialises in youth and student fares is OTU Voyages (☎ 01 40 29 12 12, W www.otu.fr) at 39 ave Georges Bernanos, 75005 Paris. Another general travel agency offering good services and deals is Nouvelles Frontières (☎ 01 45 68 70 00, W www.nouvelles-frontieres.fr), 87 blvd de Grenelle, 75015 Paris. Both of these agencies have a number of branches around the country.

STA Travel (☎ 01805-456 422, W www .statravel.de) in Germany also offers some good fares.

South-East Asia Although most Asian countries are now offering fairly competitive air-fare deals, Bangkok and Singapore are still the best places to shop around for discount tickets.

Khao San Rd in Bangkok is the budget travellers headquarters. Bangkok has many excellent travel agencies but there are also some suspect ones; ask the advice of other travellers before handing over your hard-earned cash. STA Travel (☎ 02-236 0262), 33/70 Surawong Rd, is a good and reliable place to start.

Aeroflot has direct flights to Moscow from Bangkok.

In Singapore, STA Travel (☎ 737 7188) 33A Cuppage Rd, Cuppage Terrace, offers competitive discount fares for Asian destinations and beyond. Singapore, like Bangkok, has hundreds of travel agencies, so you can compare prices on flights.

Another useful Asian connection with the Trans-Siberian route is from South Korea. There are flights from Seoul to Beijing, Vladivostok, Krasnoyarsk and Khabarovsk. Pusan is also connected with Vladivostok on a twice-weekly service.

Some sample prices for one-way/return flights from South-East Asia are: Bangkok to Beijing US$397/531; Singapore to Beijing US$377/745; Seoul to Beijing US$333/433.

Hong Kong & Macau Apparently reunification doesn't apply in the airline industry, as flights between Hong Kong and Macau and the rest of the country are considered international. This classification means that travellers have to go through Immigration and Customs, and that they must pay inter-

national rates and departure tax. However, on the positive side, it also means that the international standards of safety and service are maintained.

Only three carriers fly the Beijing-Hong Kong route at present: Air China, China Eastern and Dragonair. The former two are PRC airlines. Dragonair, a CAAC-Cathay Pacific joint venture, offers better service and lower prices. One-way/return tickets between Beijing and Hong Kong start at Y2200/4324.

Japan There are branches of STA Travel (☎ 03-5485 8380, fax 5485 8373, W www .statravel.co.jp) on the 1st Floor, Star Plaza Aoyama Building, 1-10-3 Shibuya, Shibuya-Ku, Tokyo, and in Osaka (☎ 06-6262 7066) 6th Floor, Honmachi Meidai Building, 2-5-5 Azuchi-Machi, Chuo-ku. Other reliable discount agencies include No 1 Travel (☎ 03-3200 8871, W www.no1-travel.com) and A'cross Travel (☎ 03-3373 9040, W www .across-travel.com).

One-way/return flights from Tokyo to Moscow are generally around ¥130,000/ 221,000, although at certain times of the year 60-day excursion fares on Aeroflot can go as low as ¥60,000 return.

Vladivostok Avia flies twice a week to Niigata and Toyama (one-way ¥38,000). It also flies to Osaka but only between May and September. There are also regular flights between Niigata and Khabarovsk using Dalavia (¥40,000).

Air China and Japan Airlines have several flights per week from Tokyo and Osaka to Beijing. One-way fares from Tokyo start at ¥23,000.

Flights within the Region

Russia Every Siberian city or large town has an airport with direct flights to Moscow. Usually these flights go at least daily. There are also regular flights between most major cities along the Trans-Siberian route. So, if you're tired of the train by the time you reach Irkutsk you could always hop on a plane to Vladivostok to finish the journey. There are also flights between Moscow, Beijing and Ulaan Baatar.

The chaotic situation created by decentralisation of the former Soviet state airline Aeroflot into scores of here-one-day-gone-the-next airlines has calmed somewhat.

Foreigners now also pay the same price as Russians for tickets and there are generally many places around the cities where you can buy them (often there's a booth selling tickets in train stations or at the central train ticketing offices). Tickets can also be purchased at the airport right up until the actual departure of the plane and sometimes even when you've previously been told the plane is full.

This said, the idea of schedules being stuck to remains in the realms of fantasy. Delays and cancellations are common. More worrying, the regulation of airlines and their safety records have not improved, making flying in Russia still very much a lottery. Reliable information on the relative safety records of the various airlines is impossible to get. In some cases, though, because of time restraints or lack of rail or road connections, if you want to get to a particular place in Russia, there will be no option but to fly.

Aeroflot has direct flights connecting Beijing and Moscow one way/return from US$310/620. MIAT and Aeroflot connect Moscow and Ulaan Baatar, with the cheapest fare being around US$310/660 one way/return. There are also flights from Irkutsk to Ulaan Baatar in Mongolia, and Shenyang in China, and from both Vladivostok and Khabarovsk to Harbin in China.

China The sole Chinese domestic air carrier is the Civil Aviation Administration of China (CAAC), which operates some 630 air routes around the country via regional subsidiaries. CAAC publishes comprehensive domestic and international timetables, in both English and Chinese, which come out in April and November each year. They are available at the CAAC office in the World Trade Center in Beijing.

Legally, domestic air tickets are fixed by the government at a standard price. Foreigners and Chinese now pay the same rate for domestic air travel. Some smaller travel agencies (illegally) offer discounted fares (up to 20% off the standard fare), which may be advertised in local Chinese-language newspapers.

Mongolia Although Mongolians rely heavily on air transport to get around their vast country, less than half of their 81 airports can be used year-round and just eight of these are paved.

MIAT is the major domestic airline. Its flights are often delayed or cancelled and it has a poor safety record and reputation for losing passengers' luggage.

If you do choose to fly within Mongolia, as a foreigner you must pay several times more for your ticket than a local. You must also pay with US dollars and get a 'dollar-denominated ticket'; otherwise you won't be allowed on the plane.

LAND

Russia has borders with 11 other countries and China with 14, so if you're planning on travelling overland to join or leave the Trans-Siberian route there are plenty of options. Our own Trans-Siberian travels began in London with a Eurostar service to Paris then onward across Eastern Europe to St Petersburg. For those who absolutely love trains, the longest possible trip entirely by rail is from Vila Real de Santo Antonio in Portugal to Ho Chi Minh City (Saigon) in Vietnam – a journey of 17,852km via the Trans-Mongolian route.

More often than not it will be by train that you cross into or leave this region. There are also several useful bus services; we list some here.

No Russian or Chinese visas that are useful for Trans-Siberian travellers are issued at the borders. You should also check well in advance whether you'll need a visa for any of the countries you'll pass through en route to Russia or China. For more details on visas and customs regulations see those sections in the Facts for the Visitor chapter.

Border Crossings

For details of the border crossings between Russia and Mongolia and Russia and China see the boxed texts in the Zaudinsky to Beijing and Tarskaya to Beijing chapters respectively. Other likely places you may cross overland into Russia are Belarus, Estonia, Finland, Kazakhstan and Latvia.

Routes into China are even more varied than into Russia: below we list details for Kazakhstan, Kyrgyzstan, Laos, Myanmar (Burma), Nepal, North Korea, Pakistan and Vietnam. For details of the Mongolia-China crossing see the boxed text in the Zaudinsky to Beijing chapter.

The UK & Europe

Travelling overland from the UK or Europe will be no cheaper than flying (in most cases it will cost considerably more) and, from London, takes a minimum of two days and nights. It is, however, a great way of easing yourself into the rhythm of a Trans-Siberian journey. If you have time, there are plenty of interesting places to stop along the way, not least in Eastern Europe from where the direct train connections to Russia are best.

Train There are no through-trains from the UK to Russia. The most straightforward route is on the Eurostar (**W** www.eurostar .com) to Brussels from where you can transfer to a train to Cologne and the service that goes straight through to Moscow via Warsaw and Minsk in Belarus. The cost will be around £280.

Crossing the Poland-Belarus border at Brest takes several hours while the wheel bogies are changed for the Russian track. All foreigners visiting Belarus need a visa, including those transiting by train – it's best to sort this out before arriving in Belarus otherwise you're likely to be fined.

To avoid this hassle, consider taking the train to St Petersburg from Vilnius in Lithuania that runs several times a week via Latvia. There are daily connections between Vilnius and Warsaw.

From Moscow there are also regular international services to Belgrade, Berlin, Bratislava, Budapest, Prague, Sofia, Vienna, Venice and Warsaw, and from St Petersburg to Berlin and Budapest.

For full details of European rail timetables try **W** mercurio.iet.unipi.it/misc/timetabl .html, which provides a central link to all of Europe's national railways. Most (but unfortunately not the Russian Railways site) have an English version.

Bus From May to October there's a weekly direct bus service to Moscow from London's Victoria Station, Leicester and Manchester via Berlin and Minsk. The journey, which takes just under 48 hours, costs £110/160 one way/return from London, and £130/180 from Leicester and Manchester. Contact Eastern European Travel Ltd (**☎** 01706-868 765, **e** eetravel@breathe.co.uk) for details of departures.

From Berlin, Cologne, Hamburg, Munich and Stuttgart it's also possible to take a coach to Riga in Latvia or Tallinn in Estonia, where there are direct bus connections to Moscow. For full details about these services, contact Eurolines (**W** www.eurolines.com).

Finland & the Baltic Countries

There are two daily daytime trains between St Petersburg and Helsinki: the *Repin* is the Russian-run service and the *Sibelius* is the Finnish-run service. Both train journeys take around six hours and cost sitting/*kupe* class $51/86. There are also daily buses to/from Helsinki ($52, seven hours) with Finnord (**☎** 812-314 89 51) and also Sovavto (**☎** 812-123 51 25).

Moscow is also connected with Helsinki by a daily night train ($125 2nd class/kupe, 14 hours).

From Estonia there's a daily train between Tallinn and St Petersburg (kupe $40, 11 hours). The daily express bus is faster (eight hours) and cheaper.

From Latvia trains run daily between Riga and Moscow ($57, 17 hours) and St Petersburg ($50, 12 hours). There is a daily bus to St Petersburg (14 hours) and a weekly option to Moscow (18 hours).

For details of the St Petersburg bus links with Riga and Tallinn contact Eurolines (**☎** 812-168 27 40), ulitsa Shkapina 10, 50m west of Baltisky Vokzal, or you can check its Web site.

Central Asia

To and from Kazakhstan trains run every two days between Moscow and Almaty ($102, 4¼ days). There's also a Novosibirsk-Almaty service, and some of the services between Yekaterinburg and Omsk also cut through Kazakhstan, stopping at the city of Petropavlovsk.

Between Kazakhstan and China, there are two trains a week between Ürümqi and Almaty. There are also buses from Almaty, which use the year-round road crossing to Ürümqi via the border post at Khorgos and Zharkent.

Approaching China from neighbouring Kyrgyzstan, from at least June to September it's possible to cross the dramatic 3752m Torugart Pass on a rough road from Bishkek to Kashgar. Even the most painstaking arrangements, however, can be thwarted by

The Finland Crossing

Almost missing your first train is not the best way to start a railway adventure from Finland to southern China, especially when your entire luggage and a distraught partner are on board. Sprinting down the Helsinki platform in an adrenalin rush, I banged on the last doorway of the carriage, which was opened by a startled attendant, and grabbing the handrails hauled myself aboard. And I didn't even spill my (capped) cups of coffee.

Near the Finnish-Russian border our compartment received a visit from a travelling bank. Basically it was a trolley with money but we were able to change various currencies into roubles and reclaim tax on goodies bought in Helsinki.

The border is still there in much the same fashion as it would have been during the Cold War – watchtowers, a swathe of emptiness cut through the forest, impregnable fences and guards with dogs. Crossing it had changed. Our Russian customs official was not the hard man with steely-grey eyes in a crisp militaristic uniform that I expected – just a man in shoddy overalls shambling down the carriage corridor.

The politely offered customs form asked if I was importing dutiable items but gave no description of what they might be. Without looking at our extensive luggage the customs official told me to write no, sign the form and return it. Later, a similar form offered at the Mongolian border asked the same question – I neither filled it in nor signed the form and no-one cared or noticed. Similarly, the immigration procedures at both ends of Russia were a breeze.

**Patrick Horton,
Moscow to Beijing, July 2001**

logistical gridlock on the China side or by unpredictable border closures (eg, for holidays or by snow). Ensure you have a valid Kyrgyzstan visa.

Pakistan & Nepal

The China-India border is closed, but from Pakistan the exciting trip on the Karakoram Hwy, over the 4800m Khunjerab Pass and what is said to be the world's highest public international highway, is an excellent way to get to or from Chinese Central Asia. There are regular bus and 4WD services when the pass is open – normally between May and early November. If you're considering this option see Lonely Planet's *Karakoram Highway* guide for more information.

To and from Nepal the 920km road connecting Lhasa with Kathmandu is known as the Friendship Hwy. It's a spectacular trip over high passes and across the Tibetan plateau. By far the most popular option for the trip is renting a 4WD through a hotel or travel agency and then sorting out a private itinerary with the driver. A 4WD from Lhasa to the Nepalese border will cost approximately Y2400 for the three-day journey. The going rate for a 4WD is Y2.50 to Y3.50 per kilometre.

Visas for Nepal can be obtained in Lhasa, or even at the Nepalese border. When travelling from Nepal to Lhasa, foreigners must arrange transport through tour agencies in Kathmandu. If you already have a Chinese visa, you could try turning up at the border and organising a permit in Zhangmu. This is a gamble, however, as the rules and regulations change hourly – it's far better to join an economy tour to Lhasa in Kathmandu. The occasional traveller slips through (even a couple on bicycles). At Zhangmu you can hunt around for buses, minibuses, 4WDs or trucks heading towards Lhasa.

South-East Asia

Laos From the Mengla district in China's southern Yunnan province it is legal to enter Laos via Boten in Luang Nam Tha province if you possess a valid Lao visa. From Boten there are morning and afternoon buses onward to the provincial capitals of Luang Nam Tha and Udomxai, three and four hours away, respectively.

The majority of travellers from Kunming go via Jinghong to Mengla and thence to the border at Mohan. As the bus journey from Jinghong will take the better part of the day, you will probably have to stay overnight at Mengla. Lao visas can be obtained in Beijing; alternatively, the Lao consulate in Kunming, Yunnan, issues both seven-day transit and 15-day tourist visas for Laos.

The Lao border town of Boten is accessible by four buses per day from Luang Nam Tha. Chinese visas should be obtained in advance as they are not available at the border. Again, an overnight stay is likely to be required, and facilities are better in Mengla on the Chinese side.

Myanmar (Burma) Originally built to supply the forces of Chiang Kaishek in his struggle against the Japanese, the famous Burma Road runs from Kunming, in China's Yunnan province, to the city of Lashio. Nowadays the road is open to those travellers carrying permits for the region north of Lashio, but you can only legally cross the border in one direction – from the Chinese side (Ruili) into Myanmar via Mu-se in the northern Shan state. This appears to be possible only if you book a visa-and-transport package from Chinese travel agencies in Kunming. Once across the border at Mu-se, you can continue on to Lashio and farther south to Mandalay and Yangon.

A second route, a little farther north-west from Lwaigyai to Bhamo, is also open in the same direction. You cannot legally leave Myanmar by either route.

North Korea There are twice-weekly trains between Beijing and Pyongyang, but visas are difficult to arrange to North Korea and at the time of research it was totally impossible for US and South Korean citizens. Those interested in travelling to North Korea from Beijing should get in touch with Koryo Tours (**e** tours@koryogroup.com, **w** www .koryogroup.com) who can get you there (and back).

Vietnam In the finest bureaucratic tradition, travellers require a special visa for entering Vietnam overland from China. A one-month tourist visa costs Y470 and takes three days to issue. Travellers who have tried to use a standard visa to enter Vietnam overland from China have fared poorly, and it no longer seems possible to bribe your way in.

Exiting from Vietnam to China is much simpler. The Chinese don't require anything more than a standard tourist visa, and Chinese visas do not indicate entry or exit points. However, your Vietnamese visa must have the correct exit point marked on it, a change that can easily be made in Hanoi. Ironically, it seems to be possible to bribe your way out.

The Vietnam-China border crossing is open 7am to 4pm, Vietnam time, or 8am to 5pm, China time. Set your watch when you cross the border – the time in China is one hour later than in Vietnam. Neither country observes daylight-saving time. There are currently two border checkpoints, detailed below, where foreigners are permitted to cross between Vietnam and China.

Friendship Pass The busiest border crossing is at the Vietnamese town of Dong Dang, 164km north-east of Hanoi. The closest Chinese town to the Vietnamese border is Pingxiang in Guangxi province, but it's about 10km north of the actual border gate. The crossing point (Friendship Pass) is known as Huu Nghi Quan in Vietnamese or Youyi Guan in Chinese.

The nearest city to Dong Dang is Lang Son, 18km to the south. Buses and minibuses on the Hanoi-Lang Son route are frequent. The cheapest way to cover the 18km between Dong Dang and Lang Son is to hire a motorbike for $1.50. There are also minibuses cruising the streets looking for passengers. Just make sure they take you to Huu Nghi Quan – this is the only point where foreigners can cross – and not to the other nearby checkpoint.

There is a customs checkpoint between Lang Son and Dong Dang. Sometimes there are long delays here while officials gleefully rip apart the luggage of Vietnamese and Chinese travellers. For this reason, a motorbike might prove faster than a van since you won't have to wait for your fellow passengers to be searched. Note that this is only a problem when you're heading south towards Lang Son, not the other way.

On the Chinese side, it's a 20-minute drive from the border to Pingxiang by bus or share taxi – the cost for the latter is $3. Pingxiang is connected by train to Nanning, capital of China's Guangxi province. Trains to Nanning depart from Pingxiang at 8am and 1.30pm. More frequent are the buses (once every 30 minutes), which take four hours to make the journey and cost $4.

There is a walk of 600m between the Vietnamese and Chinese border posts.

A word of caution – because train tickets to China are expensive in Hanoi, travellers have bought a ticket to Dong Dang, walked across the border and then bought a domestic train ticket on the Chinese side. This is not the best way because it's several kilometres from Dong Dang to Friendship Pass, and you'll have to hire someone to take you by motorbike. If you're going by train, it's better to buy a ticket from Hanoi just to Pingxiang, and then in Pingxiang get the ticket to Nanning or beyond.

Trains on the Hanoi-Dong Dang route run according to the following schedule:

train No	depart Dong Dang	arrive Hanoi
HD4	8.30am	8.00pm
HD2	5.40pm	1.50am

train No	depart Hanoi	arrive Dong Dang
HD3	5.00am	1.30pm
HD1	10.00pm	5.10am

There is also a twice-weekly international train running between Beijing and Hanoi, which stops at the Friendship Pass. You can board or exit the train at numerous stations in China. The entire Beijing-Hanoi run is 2951km and takes approximately 55 hours, including a three-hour delay (if you're lucky) at the border checkpoint.

Schedules are subject to change, but at the time of research, train No 5 departed from Beijing at 10.51am on Monday and Friday, arriving in Hanoi at 11.30am on Wednesday and Sunday, respectively. Going the other way, train No 6 departed from Hanoi at 2pm on Wednesday and Saturday, arriving in Beijing at 5.18pm on Thursday and Sunday, respectively.

There's also a railway linking Hanoi with Kunming. The border town on the Vietnamese side is Lao Cai, 294km from Hanoi. On the Chinese side the border town is called Hekou, 486km from Kunming. At the time of research the international services along this route had been suspended, however there are domestic trains that run daily on both sides of the border.

Trains within China

China has some 52,000km of domestic train lines, and this is in fact the most comfortable and reliable way to travel around the country. The network covers every province except Tibet.

All express trains go through Beijing station or Beijing West station. Both of these stations have special International Passenger Booking Offices, which saves travellers queuing with the masses. Even better, tickets are sold for a small surcharge at hotels and travel agents around the city. The Great Wall Sheraton Hotel (☎ 6590 5210) has a train-ticket counter at its back entrance, which is open 8am to noon and 1pm to 5pm. Any long-distance trains, especially express trains, should be booked well in advance, especially during busy summer months.

Your degree of comfort on the train depends on your class of travel. The 'hard-seat' actually – technically – has padded seats. But this class is still hard on one's sanity, as it is generally dirty, noisy and smoky. You may or may not have a seat reservation. Some shorter journeys have 'soft-seat' carriages, where overcrowding and smoking are not permitted. The 'hard-sleeper' carriage consists of doorless compartments with half a dozen bunks in three tiers. 'Soft-sleeper' is relative luxury: four comfortable bunks in a closed compartment. Once you are on the train, the conductor may be able to upgrade your ticket if space is available in other carriages. The cost of the upgraded ticket is prorated to the distance travelled in the higher class.

Food and beverages are for sale on the trains and at stations. Toilets – especially in hard-seat carriages – can be on the nose. Be sure to bring toilet paper.

International Although Hong Kong is officially part of mainland China, the Beijing to Hong Kong train is an international route and subject to immigration and customs controls. This train is relatively fast, making the 2470km journey in 29 hours. It's also the most luxurious train in China; a one-way hard/soft-sleeper goes for Y776/1027. The train presently runs every second day.

An international train runs twice a week between Beijing and Hanoi. The total trip – 2951km – takes 55 hours, including a three-hour delay at the border.

SEA
Russia

Biznes Intur Servis (☎ 4232-49 74 03, e bis@ints.vtc.ru, w www.bisintour.com), 3rd floor, Moskoi Vokzal, 1 Okeansky prospekt, Vladivostok, and the United Orient Shipping & Agency Co (☎ 03-3249 4412, fax 3249 4430), 6th floor, Kashikichi Ningyocho Bldg, 3-10-1 Nigyocho Nihonbashi, Chuo-ku, Tokyo 103, handle bookings for the ferries between Vladivostok and the

Japanese port of Fushiki from March to October. Regular services operate between May and October. Only once or twice a season there are also sailings to Niigata in Japan and Pusan in South Korea.

The voyage takes 42 hours and 3rd-class passage (lower deck, four berths per cabin) is $260, 2nd class (as for 3rd but on the main deck) is $270, while 1st (twin-bed cabins) is $450. All meals are included in the price. The ship is rarely full so chances are you'll have a cabin to yourself anyway. The food's not bad, but the crossing can be rough so be prepared to eat little and suffer seasickness.

You might also be able to catch a ship from Japan's northernmost main island of Hokkaido to Korsakov, the southernmost port on the Russian island of Sakhalin. From here you can fly to Vladivostok or Khabarovsk or take another ferry to the mainland.

From Fuyuan, a small port on the Amur River in north-eastern China, a hydrofoil sails every other day to Khabarovsk – see that section of the Irkutsk to Vladivostok chapter for details.

Opportunities to reach European Russia by sea have dried up. There is no scheduled passenger service on the Baltic Sea and nothing at all on the Black or Caspian Seas.

China

Beijing's nearest seaport is Tianjin Municipality's port district of Tanggu. Ships travel between Tianjin and Kobe, Japan, once a week and the fare for passengers is between $200 and $300. You can buy tickets at the Tianjin office (☎ 022-2311-2842), 89 Munan Dao, Heping District, or at the Kobe port (☎ 078-321 5791).

Every fourth day, the Jincheon Ferry goes from Tianjin to the port (☎ 032-888 7911) at Incheon, South Korea.

TRAVEL AGENCIES & ORGANISED TOURS

If you have time, and a certain degree of determination, organising your own Trans-Siberian trip is easily done. But, for many, opting for the assistance of an agency in drawing up an itinerary, booking train tickets and accommodation, not to mention helping with the visa paperwork, will be preferable. You might also want to arrange activities such as trekking or rafting, for which the services of an expert agency is almost always required. Others will want to go the whole hog and have everything taken care of on a fully organised tour.

The following agencies provide a range of travel services and tours to Russia, China and Mongolia. Numerous more locally based agencies can provide tours once you are there (for details see the destinations in the route chapters), and many of those listed below work in conjunction with overseas agencies.

Russia

Baikalcomplex (☎/fax 3952-38 92 05, e youry@ travel.baikal.ru, w www.baikalcomplex.irk.ru) PO Box 3598, Irkutsk 664074. One of the most experienced Russian agencies, offering reasonably priced tours and homestays along both the Trans-Sib and BAM railways, as well as a wide range of adventure activities including jeep rides, hikes, mountain biking and rafting around Lake Baikal.

Dalgeo Tours (☎ 4212-74 77 84, fax 32 67 02, e dalgeo@dgt.khv.ru, w www.dalgeotours .khv.ru) 34A ul Dzerzhinskogo, Khabarovsk. As well as homestays and tours around the city of Khabarovsk, this agency offers various trips in the Russian Far East to Sakhalin Island, Yakutia and Kamchatka, and cruises along the Amur River.

Ekaterinburg C&V Bureau & Guide Centre (☎ 3432-68 16 04, fax 55 60 19, e ecvisitor@ mail.ur.ru) 2nd floor, Urals Mineralogical Museum, ul Krasnoarmeyskaya 1, Yekaterinburg. Run by the enthusiastic Konstantin Brylyakov, this agency can arrange a wide variety of tours in the Urals, including rafting during summer. Also offers a wide range of city-based activities and can book accommodation including homestays.

G&R International (☎ 095-378 00 01, fax 378 28 66, e hostelasia@mtu-net.ru, w www.hostels .ru) Hostel Asia, Zelenodolskaya ul 2/3, Moscow. It can arrange visas, train tickets and various tours.

Intour-Khabarovsk (☎ 4212-38 73 17, fax 33 87 74, e int115@intour.khv.ru) Hotel Intourist, Amursky bul 2, Khabarovsk. Friendly agency with lots of experience dealing with foreigners, usually large groups with planned itineraries. It offers an impressive range of tours in the area and longer Trans-Siberian packages.

Lucky Tour (☎ 4232-22 33 33, fax 26 78 00, w www.luckytour.com) ul Sukhanova 20, Vladivostok. It can book Trans-Siberian tickets out of Vladivostok as well as the ferry to Japan. Also offers a wide range of tours in the area, including trekking, rafting and wildlife-watching trips.

The Trans-Siberian Route by Road

There is nothing remotely approaching a continuous Trans-Siberian highway, but a few intrepid souls have been known to rise to the challenge of driving, even cycling, across the country. Most famously, *Corriere della Sera* journalist Luigi Barzini documented the road trip he made from Beijing to Paris in 1907, led by Prince Scipione Borghese. The journey took them two months, during which time they frequently resorted to driving along the train line rather than the mud tracks that constituted Siberian roads.

Today, the main road, such as it can be called, still peters out in the swamps east of Chita and doesn't re-emerge as a driveable surface for another couple of hundred kilometres. There is a track that follows the BAM line but this is even more of an unlikely route to follow given the scarcity of people in these parts. It would only be possible in summer, anyway.

Bearing in mind the numbing monotony of the landscape, the frequently dire quality of the roads, lack of adequate signposting, keen-eyed highway police on the lookout for a bribe, and the difficulty of obtaining petrol, not to mention spare parts, there are few advantages for a motorist in Siberia. Besides, the majority of settlements cling tenaciously to the lifeline of the railway and there are not many off-the-beaten-track places that can easily be reached by road.

There are a few exceptions. The Altay Mountains, Khakassia, Tuva and the Russian Far East around Khabarovsk and Vladivostok have reasonable road systems and interesting scenery with a fair number of scattered towns and villages to provide accommodation. Also for short jaunts away from the Trans-Siberian line (say from Novosibirsk to Tomsk), driving is usually far faster and more convenient than going by train.

Given the number of Russians who act as taxi drivers (practically anyone with a car), there's no need to bring your own vehicle to Russia, or to drive yourself once there. But should you feel so inspired, outlined below are the crucial points to keep in mind.

The Basics

To drive a car or motorcycle in Russia you'll need to be 18 years old and have an International Driving Permit with a Russian translation of your licence, or a certified Russian translation of your full licence (you can certify translations at a Russian embassy or consulate).

You will also need your vehicle's registration papers, proof of insurance (be sure it covers you in Russia) and a customs declaration promising that you will take your vehicle with you when you leave. To get the exact details on all this it's best to contact your automobile association (eg, the AA or RAC in the UK) at least three months before your trip.

Road Rules

Russians drive on the right-hand side of the road and traffic coming from the right has the right of way. Speed limits are generally 60km/h in towns and between 80km/h and 110km/h on highways. There may be a 90km/h zone, enforced by speed traps, as you leave a city. Children under 12 may not travel in the front seat, and safety-belt use is mandatory. Motorcycle riders (and passengers) must wear crash helmets.

Marlis Travel (☎ 095-453 43 68, fax 456 66 06, W travel.world.co.uk/marlis. Moscow branch of UK-based tour agents *The Russia Experience*. It receives good recommendations from locals for booking train tickets and making other travel arrangements.

Paradise Travel Agency (☎ 3912-65 26 52, fax 65 26 49, e paradise@paradise-travel.ru, W www.siberiaparadise.com) ul Lenina 24, Krasnoyarsk. A reliable agency that can book Trans-Siberian tickets and Yenisey River cruises, as well as arrange homestays and other accommodation. Also offers a range of tours,

including nine-day fully guided small group tours to Tuva and Khakassia (around $1700).

Sibalp (☎ 3832-49 59 22, fax 54 13 74, e sibalp@online.nsk.su) Office 515, ul Karla Marxa 2, Novosibirsk. This is one of the most experienced agencies offering trekking and rafting trips around the Altay region. Can also arrange tours and accommodation in and around Novosibirsk.

Sokol Tours (☎/fax 095-424 7988, W www.sokoltours.com) 4th floor, Semyonovskaya pl 7A, Moscow 105318, and (☎/fax 617-269 2659, toll free in USA & Canada ☎ 1-800-55-RUSSIA), PO Box 382385, Cambridge, MA 02238-2385,

The Trans-Siberian Route by Road

Technically the maximum legal blood-alcohol content is 0.04%, but in practice it is illegal to drive after consuming *any* alcohol at all. This is a rule that is strictly enforced. The normal way of establishing alcohol in the blood is by a blood test, but apparently you can be deemed under the influence even without any test.

Traffic lights that flicker green are about to change to yellow, then red.

The GAI

The State Automobile Inspectorate, GAI (*gah-yee*, short for Gosudarstvennaya Avtomobilnaya Inspektsia), skulks about on the roadsides, waiting for speeding, headlightless or other miscreant vehicles. Officers of the GAI are authorised to stop you (they do this by pointing their striped, sometimes lighted, stick at you and waving you towards the side of the road), issue on-the-spot fines (in roubles only – you should get a receipt) and, worst of all, shoot at your car if you refuse to pull over.

The GAI also hosts the occasional speed trap – the Moscow-Brest, Moscow-Oryol and Vyborg-St Petersburg roads have reputations for this. In cities, the GAI is everywhere, stopping cars for no discernible reason and collecting 'fines' on the spot. There are permanent GAI checkpoints at the boundary of many Russian cities and towns. For serious infractions, the GAI can confiscate your licence, which you'll have to retrieve from the main station. GAI guys have been known to shake down foreigners. Don't give them any hard currency. Get receipts for any fine you pay and if you think you've been ripped off, head for the nearest GAI office and complain. Get the shield number of the arresting officer.

On the Road

Russian main roads are a really mixed bag – sometimes they are smooth, straight dual carriageways, sometimes rough, narrow, winding and choked with the diesel fumes of the slow, heavy vehicles that make up a high proportion of Russian traffic. Driving much more than 300km in the course of a day is pretty tiring.

Russian drivers use indicators far less than they should, and like to overtake everything on the road – on the inside. Priority rules at roundabouts seem to vary from area to area: all you can do is follow local practice. Russian drivers rarely switch on anything more than sidelights – and often not even those – until it's pitch black at night. Some say this is to avoid dazzling others, as for some reason dipping headlights is not a common practice.

Fuel

Joint-venture and other Western-style petrol stations are becoming common. Petrol comes in four main grades – 76, 93, 95 and 98 octane. Prices are cheap by European standards: $0.25 a litre for 76 octane and $0.35 a litre for 98 octane. Unleaded petrol is becoming available in major cities – BP or Castrol stations usually always have it. Diesel (*dizel*) is available. Stations aren't often more than 100km apart, but don't rely on it.

USA. Canadian-Russian joint-venture company offering a wide range of Siberian tours including train trips and rafting in the Altay.

Team Gorky Adventure Travel (☎ 8312-65 19 99, fax 63 24 44, **e** adv@teamgorky.ru, **w** www .teamgorky.ru) ul 40 Let Oktyabrya 1A, Nizhny Novgorod 603062. Agency specialising in adventure travel offering rafting, trekking, biking and fishing tours around Nizhny Novgorod, in the Altay, and also in Siberia. A three-day biking tour of the Golden Ring is $220, a weekend rafting trip on the Lukh River near Nizhny Novgorod $55.

Vizit Co (☎/fax 4232-26 91 72, **e** vizit@online .vladivostok.ru, **w** www.tour-vizit.vladivostok .ru) ul Svetlanskaya 147, Vladivostok. Arranges trips along the BAM line to the north as well as Trans-Siberian itineraries and other adventure tours in the Russian Far East.

Wild Russia (☎/fax 812-27 36 5 14, **e** yegor@ wildrussia.spb.ru, **w** www.wildrussia.spb.ru) ul Mokhovaya 28/10, St Petersburg, 191028. Adventure travel specialist whose numerous wide-ranging trips include horse riding, trekking and white-water rafting in Kamchatka and the Altay Mountains.

China

To purchase train tickets out of Beijing, contact:

Beijing Tourism Group (BTG; ☎ 8610-6515 8562, fax 6515 8603) Beijing Tourist Building, 28 Jianguomenwai Dajie (between the New Otani and Gloria Plaza Hotels), Beijing. Formerly known as the China International Travel Service (CITS)

Juulchin (☎ 8610-6512 6688 ext 4015, fax 6525 4339, Ⓔ julnpek@public.bta.net.cn) Beijing International Hotel, 9 Jianguo Mennei Ave, Beijing

Monkey Business (☎ 8610-6591 6519, fax 6591 6517, Ⓦ www.monkeyshrine.com) 12 Dong Da Qiao Xie (above the Hidden Tree on Sanlitun), Beijing. This experienced company offers tours in both directions on the Trans-Manchurian and the Trans-Mongolian, with stops in Ulaan Baatar, Irkutsk and/or Yekaterinburg. Although some clients have complained of inflated prices, it continues to be a popular option.

Moonsky Star Ltd (☎ 852-2723 1376, fax 2723 6653) Chung King Mansion, E-4-6, Nathan Road 36-44, Kowloon, Hong Kong. The Hong Kong partner of Monkey Business caters to clients who wish to start in Hong Kong.

Mongolia

Several travel agencies can assist with the purchase of train tickets out of Ulaan Baatar:

Juulchin (☎ 9761-328 428, fax 320 246, Ⓦ www .mol.mn/juulchin) Bayangol Hotel, 5B Chingisiin Örgön Chölöö

UB Tour (☎ 9761-324 740, fax 324 730, Ⓔ ubour@mongol.net) Ulaan Baatar Hotel, 4th floor, 14 Sükhbaatar Square

The USA

Boojum Expeditions (☎ 800-287 0125 or 406-587 0125, fax 585 3474, Ⓦ www.boojum.com) 14543 Kelly Canyon, Bozeman MT 59715. Experienced operator of Mongolian adventure tours, including horse riding, biking and rafting.

Far East Development (☎ 206-282 0824, fax 281 4417, Ⓦ www.traveleastrussia.com) 131 W Emerson #6, Seattle, WA 98119. An eco-adventure tour company specialising in far eastern Russia.

Mir Corporation (☎ 206-624 7289, fax 624 7360, Ⓦ www.mircorp.com) 85 South Washington Street, Suite 210, Seattle, WA 98104. Among lots of other trips in Russia, this agency offers upmarket private train tours in Pullman-style carriages from $4495 for a 15-day Moscow to Vladivostok itinerary.

Nomad Travel Planners (☎ 888-345 0313, fax 907-243 0333, Ⓦ www.nomad-travel.com)

3430 East 142nd Ave, Anchorage, Alaska 99516. It can organise fishing, rafting, sledding and other excursions in the Russian Far East.

Russiatours (☎ 800-633 1008, fax 251 6685, Ⓦ www.russiatours.com) 13312 N 56th St, Suite 102, Tampa, FL 33617. This agency specialises in luxurious group tours to Moscow and St Petersburg.

White Nights (☎/fax 916-979 9381, Ⓦ www.con course.net/bus/wnights) 610 La Sierra Drive, Sacramento, CA 95864. White Nights is perhaps the only US-based agency that will assist with purchasing tickets or obtaining visas without requiring clients to book an entire tour. It also has offices in the Netherlands, Germany and Switzerland.

Canada

The Adventure Centre (☎ 416-922 7584, fax 922 8136, Ⓦ www.theadventurecentre.com) 25 Bellair St, Toronto, Ontario M5R 3L3. Canada's top adventure tour agency offers Sundowners' Trans-Siberian packages (see Australia following). Also has branches in Vancouver, Edmonton and Calgary.

Australia

Eastern Europe Travel Bureau (☎ 02-9262 1144, fax 9262 4479, Ⓔ eetb@optusnet .com.au) Level 5, 75 King St, Sydney, NSW 2000. Can arrange Trans-Siberian tickets, homestays, visas and put together individual itineraries throughout Russia.

Gateway Travel (☎ 02-9745 3333, fax 9745 3237, Ⓦ www.russian-gateway.com.au) 48 The Boulevarde, Strathfield, NSW 2135, Australia. Experienced Russia specialist company with its own range of Trans-Siberian tours as well as a host of accommodation packages for the major cities. It arranges visas and individual tickets, too.

Passport Travel (☎ 03-9867 3888, fax 9867 1055, Ⓔ passport@werple.net.au, Ⓦ www .travelcentre.com.au) Suite 11A, 401 St Kilda Rd, Melbourne, VIC 3004. As well as Trans-Siberian packages, this agency can arrange your visa invitations, independent itineraries, language courses, and more.

Sundowners (☎ 03-9672 5300, fax 9672 5311, Ⓦ www.sundowners-travel.com) Suite 15, 600 Lonsdale St, Melbourne, VIC 3000. One of the premier Trans-Siberian tour operators offering both small group tours, ranging from eight to 25 days at various levels of comfort, and unescorted trips. Its budget eight-day Trans-Mongolia package, including two nights in Moscow, costs from A$1200; it can also book individual tickets and homestays.

The UK

The China Travel Service (☎ 020-7836 9911, fax 7836 3121, Ⓦ www.ctshorizons.com) 7 Upper

St Martins Lane, London WC2H 9DL. It's worth checking with this agency for interesting add-on tours within China as well as for its Moscow-to-Beijing packages and other travel services.

Exodus Discovery Holidays (☎ 020-8675 5550, fax 8673 0779, ⓦ www.exodus.co.uk) 9 Weir Rd, London SW12 0LT. This overland adventure-tour specialist has itineraries in Mongolia that could be usefully added on to a Trans-Mongolian trip.

GW Travel Ltd (☎ 0161-928 9410, fax 941 6101, ⓦ www.gwtravel.co.uk) 6 Old Market Place, Altringham, Cheshire WA14 4NP. If you're looking to travel the Trans-Siberian route in luxury this is the group to hook up with. Tours on private Pullman-style carriages with restaurants, showers and lectures start from US$4495. It occasionally runs steam-train tours, including one scheduled for the Trans-Siberian centenary celebrations in 2003.

The Imaginative Traveller (☎ 020-8742 3049, fax 8742 3045, ⓦ www.imaginative-traveller .com) 14 Barley Mow Passage, Chiswick, London W4 4PH. UK agent for Sundowners' Trans-Siberian tours (see Australia).

Intourist Travel (☎ 020-7538 8600, fax 7538 5967, ⓦ www.intourist.com/UK/index.shtml) Intourist House, 219 Marsh Wall, London E14 9PD. It offers 2nd-class Moscow-Vladivostok tickets for £405, and Trans-Manchurian and Trans-Mongolian packages from £566 to £731.

Regent Holidays (☎ 0117-921 1711, fax 925 4866, ⓦ www.regent-holidays.co.uk) 15 John St, Bristol BS1 2HR. Often-recommended agent with lots of experience in arranging tours and individual trips in this part of the world.

The Russia Experience (☎ 020-8566 8846, fax 8566 8843, ⓦ www.trans-siberian.co.uk) Research House, Fraser Rd, Perivale, Middlesex UB6 7AQ. Agency with years of experience in Russia, who can help with transport, tours and bookings, or put together an all-inclusive adventure. It also runs the Beetroot Bus (ⓦ www .beetroot.org), a backpacker-style tour between St Petersburg and Moscow, and adventurous programs in the Altay and Tuva.

Russian Gateway (☎ 07951-694 620, fax 07050 803 161, ⓦ www.russiangateway.co.uk) This is a Web-based agency offering ticketing services for the Trans-Siberian on all available trains between Russia, China and Mongolia. Also provides hotel and excursion add-ons in all three countries and full visa support.

Steppes East (☎ 01285-65 1010, fax 88 5888, ⓦ www.steppeseast.co.uk) The Travel House, 51 Castle St, Cirencester, Glos GL7 1QD. This agency specialises in catering to more offbeat requirements and has plenty of experience in the region.

Voyages Jules Verne (☎ 020-7616, fax 7723 8629, ⓦ www.vjv.co.uk) 21 Dorset Square, London NW1 6QG. Its upmarket 'Central Kingdom Express' tour uses private Pullman-style carriages to cover the 15-night journey between Moscow and Beijing. Prices start at around £2795.

Germany

Experienced agents include:

Lernidee Reisen (☎ 030-786 0000, fax 786 5596, ⓦ www.lernidee-reisen.de) Dudenstrasse 78, 10965 Berlin

Travel Service Asia (☎ 7351-37 3210, fax 37 3211, ⓔ TSA-Reisen@t-online.de, ⓦ www .travel-service-asia.de) Schmelzweg 10, 88400 Biberach/Riss

Japan

A couple of agencies in Tokyo who specialise in Trans-Siberian tours and who can also arrange ferry tickets across from Japan to Vladivostok are:

MO Tourist CIS Russian Centre (☎ 03-5296 5783, fax 5296 5759, ⓔ sales@motcis.co.jp, ⓦ www.motcis.com) 2F Kandatsukasa-cho Bldg, 2-2-12 Kandatsukasa-cho, Chiyoda-ku, Tokyo 101 0048

Euras Tours (☎ 03-5562 3381, fax 5562 3580, ⓔ euras-tyo@ma.neweb.ne.jp) 1-26-8 Higashi-Azabu, Minato-ku, Tokyo 106 1044

St Petersburg
Санкт Петербург

☎ 812 • pop 4.6 million

If it wasn't for the summer mosquitoes, it would be almost impossible to believe that a mere three centuries ago St Petersburg was little more than a giant swamp. Such is the visual power of this handsome city with a history and European savoir-faire that few other places in Russia possess. For this alone you should consider starting (or finishing) your Trans-Siberian journey here.

St Petersburg – always the Russian trendsetter since Peter the Great created it as his 'window on the West' – is the home of the country's first railway (the line out to Tsarkoe Selo) and still has an excellent railway museum. Art lovers will not want to miss out on the world-class museums, the most famous being, of course, the Hermitage.

Those in search of fun will not be disappointed since Piter, as it's affectionately known to residents, has a lively club and music scene and prides itself on the quality of its performing arts. Whether you choose to sink a beer at one of the myriad outdoor bars that sprout on the streets every summer, or lick an ice cream while the winter snow highlights the pastel-painted buildings to best effect, St Petersburg is a city that demands to be savoured.

HISTORY

Having trounced the occupying Swedes, Peter the Great founded the Peter & Paul Fortress on the marshy estuary of the Neva River in 1703. This was the start of what would become St Petersburg, a city built to grand design by mainly European architects. By Peter's death in 1725, 40,000 people lived here and 90% of Russia's foreign trade passed through the city.

In the early 19th century St Petersburg had firmly established itself as cultural centre of the empire, a role it still jealously guards today. But at the same time as writers, artists and musicians such as Pushkin, Turgenev and, later, Tchaikovsky and Dostoevsky, lived in and were inspired by the city, political and social problems were on the rise.

Industrialisation brought a flood of poor workers, and associated urban squalor, to St

Highlights

- Cruise the canals and admire the city's elegant, crumbling architecture.
- Lose yourself amid the artistic riches of the Hermitage or the Russian Museum.
- Watch the bridges rise along the Neva River during the summer white nights.
- Enjoy the opera or ballet at the beautiful Mariinsky Theatre.
- Wander through the splendid country estates of Petrodvorets and Tsarkoe Selo.

Petersburg. Revolution against the monarchy was first attempted in the short-lived coup of 14 December 1825. The leaders (who included members of the aristocracy and who became known as the Decembrists) were banished to the outer edges of the empire, becoming some of the earliest European Trans-Siberian travellers. See the boxed text 'The Decembrist Movement' in the Krasnoyarsk to Irkutsk & Lake Baikal chapter.

The next revolution was in 1905, sparked by the 'Bloody Sunday' of 9 January when more than a hundred people were killed and hundreds more were injured after troops fired on a crowd petitioning the tsar outside the Winter Palace. The tsar's government limped on, until Vladimir Lenin and his Bolshevik followers took advantage of Russia's disastrous involvement in WWI to instigate the third successful revolution in 1917. Again, St Petersburg (renamed a more Russian-sounding Petrograd in 1914) was at the forefront of the action.

To break with the tsarist past, the seat of government was moved back to Moscow, and St Petersburg was renamed Leningrad after the first communist leader's death in 1924. The city – by virtue of its location, three million-plus population and industry – remained one of Russia's most important, thus putting it on the frontline once more during WWII. For 872 days Leningrad was besieged by the Germans, causing one million to perish in horrendous conditions.

After the war, Leningrad was almost entirely reconstructed. As the Soviet Union came tumbling down, the city was poised to again become the modern European face of Russia, and took the opportunity to rename itself St Petersburg in 1991. The city is now looking forward to – and furiously renovating for – its 300th birthday celebrations in 2003.

ORIENTATION

St Petersburg sprawls across and around the delta of the Neva River, at the end of the easternmost arm of the Baltic Sea, known as the Gulf of Finland.

If you arrive, as most visitors do, by the train from Moscow, your entry point will be Moscow Station (Moskovsky Vokzal) at the eastern end of Nevsky prospekt, St Petersburg's main thoroughfare, which heads west for 3km through the heart of the city towards the south bank of the Neva and the Winter Palace. Trains from Berlin, Budapest and Kyiv arrive at Vitebsk Station (Vitebsky Vokzal), 2km south-west of Moscow Station, as do those from Warsaw and the Baltic countries. Warsaw Station (Varsharvsky Vokzal), another kilometre in the same direction, is under reconstruction. Trains from Helsinki end up at Finland Station (Finlyandsky Vokzal) on the northern side of the Neva in the eastern area known as the Vyborg Side.

The other two main areas north of the Neva are Vasilevsky Island, on the westernmost side of the city – at its eastern end is the Strelka (Tongue of Land) where many of the city's fine early buildings still stand; and the Petrograd Side, a cluster of delta islands whose southern end is marked by the Peter & Paul Fortress.

INFORMATION
Tourist Offices

The official tourist office is at Nevsky prospekt 41 (☎ 311-28 43, e info@ctic.spb.ru, w www.tourism.spb.ru). The staff can help with individual queries, but they don't book accommodation and there's nothing in the way of official literature, although they sell Lonely Planet guidebooks. A city walking tour from here is $25.

More helpful is the HI St Petersburg Hostel (☎ 329 80 18), 3-ya Sovietskaya ulitsa 28,

where you'll also find the budget travel agency Sindbad Travel (see Travel Agencies).

Consulates

See the Facts for the Visitor chapter.

Money

There are plenty of places to change money, particularly around Moscow Station and along Nevsky prospekt. Ligovsky (☎ 325 10 93), Ligovsky pereulok 2, is reliable. ATM machines are inside every metro station, department stores, main post offices and along major streets. American Express (☎ 329 60 60) has a full-service office at the Grand Hotel Europe, Mikhailovskaya ulitsa 1/7.

Post & Telephone

The central post office (glavpochtamt) is at ulitsa Pochtamtskaya 9. A smaller, more user-friendly branch is at Stremyannaya ulitsa 14. For courier service, try Express Mail Service inside the central post office or the pricey Westpost (☎ 275 07 84) at Nevsky prospekt 86, which reliably mails letters and parcels via Finland.

The Central Telephone Office is at ulitsa Bolshaya Morskaya 3/5 where you can prepay the operator to connect you; there's a smaller office at Nevsky prospekt 88. You can also call direct from any of the green, card-operated phone booths all over the city. Cards can be purchased from metro stations and telephone offices. Rouble coin-operated phones are found inside every metro station.

Private telephone companies offering direct country service from St Petersburg include MCI (☎ 8 10 800 497 7222), Sprint (☎ 095 155 61 33) and AT&T (☎ 325 50 42).

Email & Internet Access

Internet cafes are becoming ubiquitous – the standard rate charged is around $2 per hour. At the central telephone office each terminal has its own booth; you must pay in advance.

Active Centre Internet (☎ 311 6338), Kazanskaya ulitsa 5, is on the northern side of the Griboedov Canal. Head towards the Church of the Resurrection of Christ from Nevsky prospekt. It has fast terminals, is open long hours and serves drinks.

Travel Agencies

Sindbad Travel (☎ 327 83 84, fax 329 8019, w www.sindbad.ru) at the HI St Petersburg

CENTRAL ST PETERSBURG

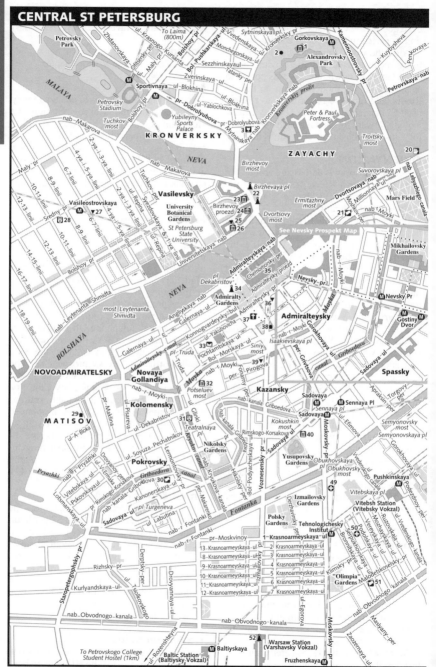

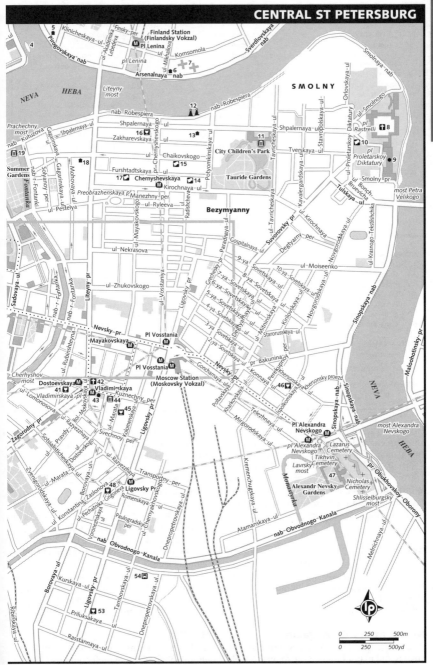

CENTRAL ST PETERSBURG

CENTRAL ST PETERSBURG

PLACES TO STAY
5 Hotel St Petersburg
Гостиница Санкт-
Петербург
6 Holiday Hostel
13 Marshal Hotel
18 Hotel Neva
Гостиница Нева
29 Matisov Domik
Матисов Домик
38 Hotel Astoria; Angleterre
Hotel
Гостиница Астория

PLACES TO EAT
25 Restoran
Ресторан
27 Karma Sutra
Камасутра
36 Tandoor
39 Café Idiot

CONSULATES
10 UK Consulate
14 German Consulate
15 Finnish Consulate
17 US Consulate
21 French Consulate
30 Chinese Consulate
51 Canadian Consulate

BARS & CLUBS
3 Faculty
Факультет
16 JFC Jazz Club
41 Mollies Irish Bar
45 Time Out

46 Moloko
Молоко
48 Griboedov
Грибоедовъ Клуб
53 Metro Club

MUSEUMS
11 Tauride Palace
Таврический Дворец
19 Summer Palace
Летний Дворец
23 Central Naval Museum
(Old Stock Exchange)
Центральный Военно-
Морской Музей
24 Museum of Zoology
Зоологический Музей
26 Museum of Anthropology &
Ethnography
Музей Антропологии и
Этнографии (
Кунтскамера)
32 Yusupov Palace
Юсуповский Дворец
40 Railway Museum
Железная Дорога Музей
44 Dostoevsky Museum
Музей ФМ Достоевского

OTHER
1 Planetarium
Планетарий
2 Amusement Park
Аттракционы
4 Cruiser Aurora
Крейсер Аврора
7 Kresty Prison

8 Smolny Cathedral
Смольный Собор
9 Smolny Institute
12 Sphinx Monuments
Сфинксы
20 Summer Garden Landing
22 Rostral Columns
Ростральные Колонны
28 Teatr Satiry
Театр Сатиры
31 Mariinsky Theatre
Мариинский Театр Оперы
и Балета
33 Central Post Office
Главпочтамт
34 The Bronze Horseman
Медный Всадник
35 Admirality
Адмиралтейство
37 St Isaac's Cathedral
Исаакиевский Собор
42 Our Lady of Vladimir Church
Церковь Владимирской
Уожей Матери
43 Kuznechny Market
Кузнечный Рынок
47 Alexandr Nevsky Monastery
Лавра Александра Невского
49 Poliklinika No 2 (Medical
Centre)
Поликлиника И2
50 American Medical Center
52 Lenin Statue
Памятник ВИ Ленину
54 Avtovokzal No 2 (Bus
Station)
Автовокзал и2

Hostel, 3-ya Sovietskaya ulitsa 28, is a reliable student and discount air-ticket office. It can also arrange train tickets and visas.

Ost-West Contaktservice (☎ 812-327 34 16, ℮ sales@ostwest.com, Ⓦ www.ostwest .com), ulitsa Mayakovskogo 7, deals professionally with most travel needs, including arranging visa support and homestays in the city.

Bookshops
Anglia (☎ 279 82 84), at naberezhnaya Fontanka 40, has the city's best selection of English-language books, including a full range of Lonely Planet guides. ISIC cardholders get a 5% discount.

Newspapers & Magazines
Pick up the free daily *St Petersburg Times* at hostels and major hotels; its also on the Web (Ⓦ www.times.spb.ru). The monthly *Pulse*, a colour freesheet focusing on entertainment and features, is also worth a look.

Medical & Emergency Services
Treatment of Western standard is available at the expensive American Medical Center (AMC; ☎ 326 17 30) at Serpukhovskaya ulitsa 10, which offers 24-hour emergency care. Poliklinika No 2 (☎ 316 62 72), at Moskovsky prospekt 22, is also recommended – and much cheaper.

Apteka Petrofarm is a 24-hour pharmacy at the corner of Nevsky prospekt and Bolshaya Konyushennaya ulitsa. Apteka, at Liteyny prospekt 56 is open 8am to 10pm daily.

Health
Under no circumstances should you drink unboiled tap water, which contains *Giardia*

lamblia, a nasty parasite that causes nausea and diarrhoea. Recommended treatments are Metronidazole (Flagyl) and Tinidazole (Fasigyn).

THINGS TO SEE & DO

In a few days you'll only be able to scratch the surface of what St Petersburg has to offer, particularly if you include a day trip to one of the country palaces. The following are the major sights; for more detailed information see Lonely Planet's *St Petersburg* city guide.

Summer Garden

As a great place to chill out, the lovely Summer Garden *(Letny sad; ☎ 314 03 74; adult/ student $0.20/0.13; open 9am-10pm daily May-Oct, 10am-6pm Oct–mid-Apr)* are perfection. Laid out for Peter the Great with fountains, statues and pavilions, the leafy park also contains the modest **Summer Palace** *(Muzey Letny Dvorets Petra I; ☎ 314 04 56; adult/student $1.80/0.60; open 11am-7pm Wed-Mon early May-early Nov)*, St Petersburg's first royal residence, built between 1704 and 1714.

Smolny Cathedral

The best thing about the Rastrelli-designed Smolny Cathedral *(Smolenksy sobor; ☎ 278 55 96, pl Rastrelli; admission $3.30; open 11am-5pm Fri-Wed)*, 3km east of the Summer Garden, is the sweeping view from the top of one of its 63m-tall belfries.

Yusupov Palace

Just over a kilometre south-west of Nevsky along the Moyka River is the delightful Yusupov Palace *(☎ 314 98 83, nab reki Moyki 94; adult/student $5/2.50; open 11am-4pm daily)*. Although notorious as the scene of Rasputin's grisly murder in 1916, there's a particularly attractive set of rooms, that include a jewel box of a theatre where performances are occasionally still held. If you want to see the cellar where the Machiavellian mystic supped his last meal (re-created in a kitsch waxwork tableaux) a separate $3/2 ticket and advance booking is required.

Railway Museum

Every schoolboy's model-train dream is realised at the Railway Museum *(Zheleznaya Doroga muzey; ☎ 168 80 05, 50 ul Sadovaya; admission free; open 11am-5pm Sun-Thur,* *closed last Thur of month)*. This is a surprisingly fascinating and large collection of scale locomotives and model railway bridges often made by the engineers who built the real ones. Apparently it is also the oldest such collection in the world since the museum was established in 1809, 28 years before Russia had its first working train! Trans-Sib travellers will be particularly interested in the models of the ship that once carried passengers and trains across Lake Baikal, the sumptuous 1903 wagon complete with piano salon and bathtub, and Krasnoyarsk's Yenisey Bridge. It's a good idea to bring along someone to translate if you don't speak Russian.

Vasilevsky Island

Stand on the Strelka (Tongue of Land), beside the Rostral Columns and admire one of the best views in the city. Immediately behind is the **Central Naval Museum** *(Tsentralny Voenno-Morskoy muzey; ☎ 218 25 02,* **W** *www.museum.navy.ru, Birzhevaya pl 4; adult/student $2.25/1.10; open 10.30am-5.30pm Wed-Sun)*, housed in the old Stock Exchange, and a must for naval enthusiasts.

Among the area's other sights worth visiting is the nearby **Museum of Zoology** *(Zoologichesky muzey; ☎ 218 01 12, Univer sitetskaya nab 1/3; adult/student $0.75/0.35, free on Thur; open 11am-6pm Sat-Thur)* with incredibly lifelike stuffed animals from all over the world, including a complete 44,000-year-old woolly mammoth thawed out of the Siberian ice in 1902.

Jarred mutant foetuses and the like, from Peter the Great's personal collection of 'curiosities', are the star attractions at the **Museum of Anthropology & Ethnography** *(Kunstkammer; ☎ 218 14 12,* **W** *www.kunst kamera.ru, Universitetskaya nab 3; admission $1.50; open 11am-6pm Fri-Wed; last entry 4.45pm)*, housed one block west in the blue and white building with the steeple. The entrance is around the corner on Tamozhyonny pereulok.

Peter & Paul Fortress & Around

Founded in 1703, the Peter & Paul Fortress *(Petropavlovskaya krepost; ☎ 238 45 40; Metro: Gorkovskaya; free entry to the grounds, adult/student $3/1.50 to all buildings; open 10am-6pm Thur-Mon, 10am-4pm Tues)* is the oldest building in St Petersburg. Its main use up to 1917 was as a political

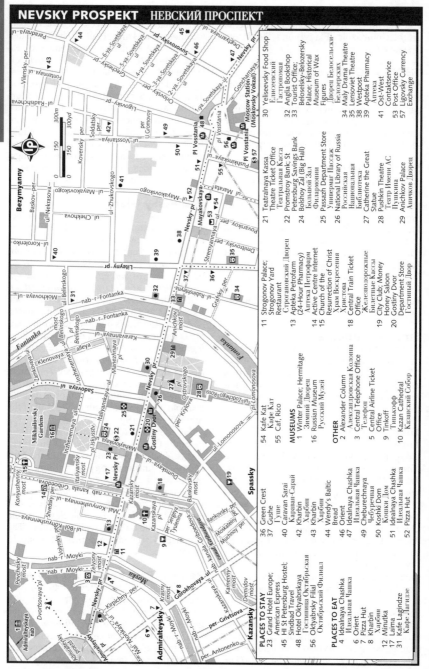

NEVSKY PROSPEKT   НЕВСКИЙ ПРОСПЕКТ

PLACES TO STAY
23 Grand Hotel Europe;
   American Express
45 HI St Petersburg Hostel;
   Sindbad Travel
48 Hotel Oktyabrskaya
   Гостиница Октябрьская
56 Oktyabrsky Filial
   Октябрьский Филиал

PLACES TO EAT
4 Idealnaya Chashka
   Идеальная Чашка
6 Orient
7 Pizza Hut
8 Kharbin
   Харбин
12 Minuta
17 Laima
31 Kafe Lagindze
   Кафе Лагидзе
36 Green Crest
37 Gushe
   Гуше
40 Caravan Sarai
   Караван-Сарай
42 Kharbin
   Харбин
43 Kharbin
   Харбин
44 Wendy's Baltic
   Bread
46 Orient
47 Idealnaya Chashka
   Идеальная Чашка
49 Cheburechnaya
   Чебуречная
50 Koshki Dom
   Кошки Дом
51 Idealnaya Chashka
   Идеальная Чашка
52 Pizza Hut
54 Kafe Kat
   Кафе Кат
55 Caf, Rico

MUSEUMS
1 Winter Palace; Hermitage
   Зимний Дворец
16 Russian Museum
   Русский Музей

OTHER
2 Alexander Column
   Александровская Колонна
3 Central Telephone Office
   Телефон
5 Central Airline Ticket
   Office
9 Tinkoff
   Тинькофф
10 Kazan Cathedral
   Казанский Собор
11 Strogonov Palace;
   Strogonov Yard
   Restaurant
   Строгановский Дворец
13 Apteka Petrofarm
   (24-Hour Pharmacy)
   Аптека Петрофарм
14 Active Centre Internet
15 Church of the
   Resurrection of Christ
   Храм Воскресения
   Христова
18 Central Train Ticket
   Office
   Железнодорожные
   билетные Кассы
19 City Club; Money
   Honey Saloon
20 Gostiny Dvor
   Department Store
   Гостиный Двор
21 Teatralnaya Kassa
   Theatre Ticket Office
   Театральная Касса
22 Promstroy Bank; St
   Petersburg Savings Bank
24 Bolshoy Zal (Big Hall)
   Большой Зал
   Филармонии
25 Passazh Department Store
   Универмаг Пассаж
26 National Library of Russia
   Российская
   Национальная
   Библиотека
27 Catherine the Great
   Statue
28 Pushkin Theatre
   Театр Имени АС
   Пушкина
29 Anichkov Palace
   Аничков Дворец
30 Yeliseevsky Food Shop
   Елисеевский
   Гастрономия
32 Anglia Bookshop
33 Tourist Office;
   Beloselsky-Belozersky
   Palace; Historical
   Museum of Wax
   Figures
   Дворец Белосельских-
   Белозерских
34 Maly Drama Theatre
35 Lensoviet Theatre
38 Westpost
39 Apteka Pharmacy
   Аптека
41 Ost-West
   Contaktservice
53 Post Office
57 Ligovsky Currency
   Exchange

prison; famous residents include Peter's own son Alexey, Dostoevsky, Gorky and Trotsky. At noon every day a cannon is fired from the **Naryshkin Bastion**. Most spectacular of all is the **Cathedral of SS Peter & Paul**, with its landmark needle-thin spire, magnificent baroque interior and Romanov family crypt.

Around 500m east of the fortress is the cruiser **Aurora** *(Avrora;* ☎ *230 84 40, Petrovskaya nab; admission free; open 10.30am-4pm Tues-Thur & Sat-Sun)*, which fired the (blank) shot that signalled the start of the October 1917 Revolution.

PLACES TO STAY
Apartments & Homestays

Ost-West Contaktservice (see Travel Agencies earlier in this chapter) can arrange apartments and central homestays from $25 per person including breakfast.

The Host Families Association (HOFA; ☎/fax 275 19 92, **e** alexei@hofak.hop.stu .neva.ru, **W** webcenter.ru/~hofa) is a long-established St Petersburg University-based agency that can place travellers with English-speaking families around town or arrange apartments. Its cheapest program offers B&B for $25/40 singles/doubles for a minimum of two nights. It also issues visa invitations and has accommodation in many other cities along the Trans-Sib route.

Apartment City (**W** www.apartment.spb .ru) has accommodation from $30 a day; the Web site gives you virtual tours of places that are available.

Hostels

HI St Petersburg Hostel (☎ *329 80 18, fax 329 80 19,* **e** *ryh@ryh.ru, 3-ya Sovetskaya ul)* Metro: Ploshchad Vosstania. Bed in 3- to 6-bed dorm adult/student or HI member $19/17, one double $48; all including breakfast. Prices about 20% cheaper Nov-Mar. St Petersburg's longest-running hostel is nothing fancy but a smooth operator all the same. You'll be able to clue into what's going on and arrange all onward travel details with its excellent inhouse agency Sindbad Travel (see Travel Agencies earlier).

Holiday Hostel (☎*/fax 542 73 64, 327 10 70,* **e** *info@hostel.spb.ru, ul Mikhailova 1)* Bed in 3- to 6-bed dorm $12, doubles $15; all including breakfast. Just south of Finland Station and next door to the Kresty Prison, this hostel is basic and quiet.

Petrovskogo College Student Hostel (☎ *252 75 63, fax 252 65 12, ul Baltiskaya 26)* Metro: Narvsakya. Doubles/triples $4/6. While not close to the centre, this friendly hostel has excellent deals. From the metro, walk left (south) down prospekt Stachek to ulitsa Baltiskaya, where you turn left and continue another 500m.

Hotels – Budget

Hotel Oktyabrskaya (☎ *277 63 30, fax 315 75 01, Ligovsky prosp 10)* Singles/doubles/triples from $37/53/54. In an ultra-convenient location opposite Moscow Station, this rambling Soviet-style place offers a wide range of rooms, some quite modern (but avoid the cheapest ones overlooking the noisy square if you want to sleep). Note that prostitutes actively work the corridors at night.

Oktyabrsky Filial (☎ *277 72 81, fax 315 75 01, Ligovsky prosp 43/45)* Singles/doubles with breakfast from $26.50/34. All the rooms have been upgraded at this sister establishment to the Hotel Oktyabrskaya, and it's run in a similar style.

Hotel Neva (☎ *278 05 35, fax 273 25 93, ul Chaykovskogo 17)* Singles/doubles from $28/46. This one-time bordello was obviously once more sumptuous. Still, travellers seldom have a bad report about it and the staff seem willing to sort out visa registration hassles that other places won't.

Hotels – Mid-Range & Top End

Hotel St Petersburg (☎ *542 94 11, fax 248 80 02,* **W** *www.hotel-spb.ru, Pirogovskaya nab 5/2)* Doubles from $77. This big three-star hotel has many rooms with great views over the Neva. Not a bad deal but it's a 15-minute walk to ploshchad Lenina, which is the nearest metro station.

Matisov Domik (☎ *318 70 51, fax 318 74 19,* **W** *www.businessweb.ru/'matisov, nab reki Pryazhki 3/1)* Singles/doubles with breakfast $60/100. A fine family-run option, Matisov Domik is a 10-minute walk west of Mariinsky Theatre. The rooms are super-clean, all with phone, TV and soft drinks. Tram 22 stops nearby.

Marshal Hotel (☎ *279 99 55, fax 279 75 00,* **e** *marshal.hotel@tpark.spb.ru, Shpalernaya ul 41)* Doubles with breakfast from $80. This is a new small hotel, on the way to the Smolny Cathedral, with reasonably large rooms.

Walking Tour: Nevsky Prospekt & Around

To get a feel for St Petersburg's grand architecture you need wander little farther than Nevsky prospekt, Russia's most famous thoroughfare. The inner 2.5km to Moscow Station is where locals come to shop and play but the street actually runs 4km from the Admiralty on the south bank of the Neva to the Alexandr Nevsky Monastery, from which it takes its name. To stroll the full length with various detours will take at least a couple of hours, but reckon on a full day if you linger at the sights.

Starting at Dvortsovy, most take a moment to admire the sweep on the Neva and the view across the water to the Strelka end of Vasilevsky Island, studded by the brick-red **Rostral Columns**, and the spire of the SS Peter & Paul Cathedral on the Petrograd Side.

Immediately to the west of Nevsky is the **Admiralty** *(Admiralteysky)*, topped with a gilded spire. This was the headquarters of the Russian navy from 1711 to 1917 and is now a naval college. In the neighbouring **ploshchad Dekabristov** (Decembrists' Square), named after the Decembrists' Uprising of 1825, is the most famous statue of Peter the Great, the **Bronze Horseman**.

Behind the statue rises the vast golden dome of **St Isaac's Cathedral** *(Isaakievsky sobor;* ☎ *315 97 32, Isaakievskaya pl; adult/student $8/4; open as a museum 11am-6pm Thur-Tues)*, built between 1818 and 1858. Don't miss the panoramic city views from the **colonnade** *(adult/student $2.75/$1.40; same opening hours)* around the drum of the dome. Note that photography is not permitted inside.

Your attention is likely to be grabbed by what's immediately to the east of Nevsky: **Dvortsovaya ploshchad** (Palace Square), bordered by the wedding-cake-like **Winter Palace** *(Zimny Dvorets)*, commissioned from Rastrelli in 1754 by Empress Elizabeth. The palace's 1057 rooms are now home to the **Hermitage** *(*☎ *110 90 79,* Ⓦ *www.hermitage.ru; admission $10, free for ISIC card-holders; open 10.30am-6pm Tues-Sat, 10.30am-5pm Sun)*, one of the world's great art museums. The ticket hall is inside the main entrance on the river side of the palace.

The 47.5m **Alexander Column** in the middle of the square commemorates the 1812 victory over Napoleon as does the giant **arch** topped with a victory chariot at the square's southern end leading on to ulitsa Bolshaya Morskaya. The arch is currently under wraps following damage caused by fireworks during January 2000 New Year's Eve celebrations.

Head down Nevsky, crossing the Moyka River, to No 17 – another Rastrelli extravaganza – the **Stroganov Palace** (1752–54). This green building, once the home of the prominent Strogonoff family whose chef created a rather well-known beef dish, now has a popular tourist cafe in its courtyard (see Places to Eat).

One block east are the great colonnaded arms of the awesome **Kazan Cathedral**. In summer many outdoor cafe-bars are open here, making it an ideal spot to take in the passing parade. A short detour behind the cathedral along Griboedov Canal is **Bankovsky Most**, the much-photographed bridge suspended by cables emerging from the mouths of golden griffins.

Return to Nevsky along the canal and continue to follow the waterway towards the striking **Church of the Resurrection of Christ** *(Khram Voskresenia Khristova;* ☎ *315 16 36, Konyushennaya pl; adult/student $7.50/3; open 11am-6pm Thur-Tues)*. Modelled on St Basil's in Moscow, it's also known as the Church of Spilled Blood since it was here that Alexander II was assassinated in 1881. The elaborate exterior is more impressive than the interior.

East of the church are the tranquil **Mikhailovsky Gardens** on to which backs the former Mikhailovsky Palace, now the excellent **Russian Museum** *(Gosudarstvenny Russky muzey;* ☎ *311 14 65,* Ⓦ *www.rusmuseum.ru; ul Inzhenernaya 4; adult/student $8/4, open 10am-5pm Wed-Mon)*. Here you'll find one of the country's two finest collections of Russian art (the other is in Moscow's Tretyakov Gallery). The main entrance is off **ploshchad Iskusstv** (Arts Square) on the opposite side of the building. A statue of Pushkin, erected in 1957, stands in the middle of this attractive tree-lined square.

From here it's just a short hop past the Grand Hotel Europe to Nevsky and the popular department stores **Gostiny Dvor** and **Passazh**, which stand opposite each other and provide an excellent

ST PETERSBURG

Russian-style shopping experience. Another shop worth a look is the sumptuous grocery **Yeliseevsky** *(Nevsky prosp 56)*. Built in Style Moderne from 1901 to 1903, it has sculptures and statues on the outside, and a gorgeous mirrored ceiling and stained-glass windows on the inside.

Nineteenth-century representation of St Isaac's Cathedral

Opposite Yeliseevsky is **ploshchad Ostrovskogo**, sometimes referred to as the Catherine Gardens because of the large statue of Catherine the Great (1873) that stands amid the chess, backgammon and occasionally even mah jong players who crowd the benches here. At the empress' heels are renowned statesmen of the 19th century, including her lovers Orlov, Suvorov and Potyomkim .

The western side of ploshchad Ostrovskogo is taken up by the lavish **National Library of Russia**, St Petersburg's biggest with some 31 million items, nearly a sixth of which are in foreign languages. Rossi's **Pushkin Theatre** (formerly the Alexandrinsky) at the southern end of the square is one of Russia's most important.

On the western side of the Fontanka Canal is the **Anichkov Palace** (1741–50), which now houses after-school clubs for children. Nevsky continues over the canal via the Anichkov Most, with dramatic statues of rearing horses at its four corners. A photogenic baroque backdrop is provided by the (currently rather faded) red 1840s **Beloselsky-Belozersky Palace**. It's now home to the city's tourist office and a missable **Historical Museum of Wax Figures** *(☎ 312 36 44, Nevsky prosp 41; adult/student $4/2; open noon-6pm daily)*. Concerts are also occasionally held here.

Along the 750m from Fontanka to Moscow Station, Nevsky is mainly shops, restaurants and cinemas; a more interesting diversion is to head south along Liteyny prospekt towards Vladimirskaya/Dostoevskaya metro station. Clustered around here you'll find the attractive **Our Lady of Vladimir Church**, the bustling **Kuznechny market** and the interesting **Dostoevsky Museum** *(☎ 164 69 50, Ⓦ www.md.spb.ru, Kuznechny per 5/2; adult/student $2/1; open 11am-5.30pm Tues-Sun)*, in the house where the writer died in 1881.

Dividing Nevsky and Stary (old) Nevsky prospekts is **ploshchad Vosstania** (Uprising Square), on one side of which is Moscow Station. The Cyrillic sign on top of the Hotel Oktyabrskaya across from the station translates as 'Hero City Leningrad' in recognition of St Petersburg's heroism and losses during WWII.

The lower-key Stary Nevsky juts off the square at a 45-degree angle and heads a kilometre southeast towards the operational **Alexandr Nevsky Monastery** *(☎ 274 36 05, pl Alexandr Nevsky)*, founded in 1713 by Peter the Great. You can wander freely around most of the grounds, but you'll need a ticket from the kiosk on your right by the main gates to enter its two most important graveyards, the Tikhvin and Lazarus cemeteries *(admission $1; open 11am-6pm Fri-Wed Mar-Sept, 11am-3.30pm Oct-Feb)*. **Tikhvin Cemetery** *(Tikhvinskoe Kladbishche)*, on the right as you enter the monastery, contains the most famous graves, including those of Tchaikovsky, Rimsky-Korsakov and Dostoevsky.

Hotel Astoria (☎ 210 57 57, fax 313 51 33, W www.rfhotels.com, ul Bolshaya Morskaya 39) Singles/doubles from $300/350. There are bags of old-world charm at this top hotel in front of St Isaac's Cathedral. Adjacent and cheaper, **Angleterre Hotel** (☎ 313 56 66, fax 313 51 25, e reservations@angleterrehotel .spb.ru) is managed by the same company and has a fitness centre, pool and sauna.

The **Grand Hotel Europe** (☎ 329 60 00, fax 329 60 01, W www.grand-hotel-europe.com, Mikhailovskaya ul 1/7) is top of the range. Rooms start at $295/335.

PLACES TO EAT
Restaurants & Cafes
Restoran (☎ 327 89 79, Tamozhenny per 2) Mains from $9. The stark interior is ultra-stylish, but the food is very good and not overpriced. The salad bufet is a bargain, but don't fill up if you're having a main course, too, because they're huge.

Café Idiot (☎ 315 16 75, nab reki Moyki 82) Most dishes under $5. This firm fixture on the tourist trail is still well worth visiting. It has a relaxed atmosphere that will encourage you to linger. All the food is vegetarian, and there's a nonsmoking room.

Kharbin (☎ 279 99 90, ul Nekrasova 58) Mains $4. We ate at this branch of this mini Chinese restaurant chain (the others are at ulitsa Zhukovskogo 34/2 and naberezhnaya reki Moyki 48) and found the food very acceptable and reasonably priced.

Caravan Sarai (☎ 272 7129, Cnr Liteyny prosp & ul Nekrasova) Mains $5. Some good Uzbek cuisine is served here in an atmospheric setting with a side order of belly dancing.

Kafe Kat (☎ 311 33 77, Stremyannaya 22) Mains $3. Fake vines hang from the ceiling of this cosy Georgian restaurant. A selection of appetisers plus the cheese bread will fill you up. Other good, more workaday Georgian cafes are **Cheburechnaya** (☎ 277 53 85, ul Vosstania 13) and **Kafe Lagindze** (ul Belinskogo 1).

Karma Sutra (☎ 323 38 81, ul 6-ya Liniya 25). The food here is not quite Indian, but tasty all the same (not to mention the rather racy decor!). It's on a newly pedestrianised street that looks set to become a hot social spot. For more authentic Indian dishes (but at higher prices) try **Tandoor** (☎ 312 38 86, Voznesensky prosp 2).

The Stroganoff Yard (☎ 315 2315, Nevsky prosp 17) Mains from $5. Use the telephones on each table to chat with fellow diners, while grazing on the good-value $5 lunch bufet ($8 at night), which includes some tasty traditional Russian dishes.

Vegetarians will find contentment at the simple cafes **Green Crest** (☎ 113 13 80, Vladimirsky prosp 7) and **Gushe** (☎ 113 24 05, Vladimirsky prosp 5), both of which serve a pretty similar menu of fresh salads, soups and cutlets for less than $3 a head.

Coffee lovers can get their fix at **Idealnaya Chashka** (Nevsky prosp 15, 112 & 130), the local equivalent of Starbucks, or at the similar **Café Rico** (☎ 325 64 40, Pushkinskaya ul 1).

Fast Food
Laima (☎ 232 44 28, kanala Griboedova 14 & ☎ 315 55 45, Bolshoy prosp 88, Petrograd Side) Dishes under $3. Open 24 hrs. The huge menu at the undisputed champion of the Russian fast-food concept includes about 20 salads, soups, stuffed peppers, chicken and fish fillets, kebabs, freshly squeezed juices and milkshakes. Ask for the English menu.

Orient (☎ 277 57 15, Suvorovsky prosp 1/8 & ☎ 314 64 43, Bolshoya Morskaya 25) Dishes under $3. This is an excellent option for quick, cheap, quality meals. Comparable is **Koshki Dom** (ul Vosstania 2 & Liteyny prosp 23).

If only Western-style fast food will do, there's **Pizza Hut** (nab reki Moyki 71/76 & Nevsky prosp 96), plenty of McDonald's, and **Minutka** (Nevsky prosp 20), the Russian version of Subway.

Self-Catering
For fresh produce head to the city's liveliest food market **Kuznechny** (Kuznechny per 3) next to Vladirmiskaya metro. There's a well-stocked supermarket in the basement of the **Passazh** shopping centre (Nevsky prosp 48).

For your breakfast supplies and bakery items try **Wendy's Baltic Bread** (Grechesky prosp 25).

ENTERTAINMENT
Ballet, Opera, Theatre & Classical Music
September to early summer is the main performing season. During June, the **White Nights Dance Festival**, includes numerous

events ranging from folk to ballet. Most theatres and concert halls are closed Monday.

The beautiful ***Mariinsky Theatre*** *(☎ 114 52 64,* W *www.kirovballet.com, Teatralnaya pl 1)*, home to the Kirov Ballet and Opera, is worth attending whatever is on, just for the opportunity to enjoy its glittering decor.

Maly Drama Theatre *(☎ 113 20 49, ul Rubinshteyna 18)* This internationally recognised theatrical company often stages experimental and frequently unforgettable pieces. Also worth checking out are performances at the ***Lensoviet Theatre*** *(☎ 113 21 91, Vladimirsky prosp 12)* and the clever, off-beat plays at ***Teatr Satiry*** *(☎ 314 70 60, Sredny prosp 48, Vasilevsky Island)*.

Bolshoy Zal *(☎ 110 42 57, ul Mikhailovskaya 2)* Also known as the Shostakovich Academic Philharmonic Big Hall, this grand hall hosts concerts by St Petersburg's renowned Philharmonic Symphony Orchestra.

Bars & Clubs

Most bars and clubs are open daily until the early hours of the morning.

Mollies Irish Bar *(☎ 319 97 68, ul Rubinshteyna 36)* The bar that first brought Guinness to the city on the Neva is still going strong. Its pub food is also decent.

Tinkoff *(☎ 314 8485, ul Kazanskaya 7)* Drinkable ales are produced at this microbrewery with a hip beer hall and sushi bar.

Buying Tickets

The city's top venues, including the Mariinsky, Mussorgsky, Hermitage and Maly theatres, charge far higher prices for tickets for foreigners than Russians. You'll pay even more for a ticket purchased through a hotel concierge or travel agency, so if you have the time go along to the theatre box offices first.

If you can prove that you are working or studying in Russia, you'll pay the Russian price. You'll usually be able to buy Russian tickets from scalpers outside the venue, but check carefully to make sure you're not sold a fake. Be warned though: if you have a Russian ticket and are caught inside the theatre, you'll be made to pay the difference.

The best booking office at which to buy tickets for classical and rock concerts, plays and ballet is the Teatralnaya kassa (☎ 314 93 85) at Nevsky prospekt 42.

Time Out *(☎ 113 24 42, ul Marata 36)* Your average sports bar, with pool table and satellite TV, Time Out also has a foreign book exchange, good pizza from $3 and a happy hour from 5pm to 8pm.

For the following clubs expect cover charges of at least $3 at the weekends.

City Club/Money Honey *(☎ 310 05 49, Apraksin dvor 14)* Upstairs (City Club) there's a dance floor and pool tables and space to mingle, downstairs there's the Money Honey Saloon, which has great live rockabilly and country bands. It's lively but sometimes gets rowdy. Enter via the courtyard off ulitsa Sadovaya.

JFC Jazz Club *(☎ 272 98 50, ul Shpalernaya 33)* This cosy, New York-style space offers some of the city's best jazz and blues – book on weekends.

Metro Club *(☎ 166 02 04, Ligovsky prosp 174)* For a boogie, the cavernous Metro is hugely popular, has three dance halls, theme nights and is a lot of fun.

Moloko *(☎ 274 94 67, Perekupnoy per 12)* Open 7pm-midnight Thur-Sun. A dimly lit cellar provides a performance space for good live bands. It's also one of the few places to work up an atmosphere earlier in the evening.

Faculty *(☎ 233 06 72, Dobrolyubova prosp 6)* There's a trendy student-union vibe going here, with some odd performances thrown in with the danceable music.

Griboedov *(☎ 164 43 55, ul Voronezhkaya 2A)* An artfully converted bomb shelter has become the city's hottest club, with a no-pop-music policy. Weekends tend to get stiflingly crowded here – the best nights are Wednesday and Thursday.

GETTING THERE & AWAY
Train

Of St Petersburg's four major long-distance train stations the one most Trans-Sib travellers will use is Moscow Station (Moskovsky Vokzal), at ploshchad Vosstania. From here there are about 10 trains daily to and from Moscow; the majority are sleeper services leaving late at night and taking around eight hours. The premium trains are the No 1 (Red Arrow) departing at 11.55pm and No 5 (Nikolaevski Express) departing at 11.35pm. Four-berth *(kupe)*/two-berth (SV) tickets on these trains cost $30/60. Both have smart liveries and pricey all-night dining cars. The SV ticket includes a packed breakfast.

ST PETERSBURG

Tickets on train Nos 27 and 29, leaving at 10.30pm and 9.55pm respectively, cost $20/40, while the fastest train – the ER200 – leaves early in the morning (around 7am), takes five hours and costs $30/60.

Trains to Helsinki depart from Finland Station (Finlyandsky Vokzal), ploshchad Lenina, Vyborg Side. Those to Berlin, Budapest, Kyiv, Minsk, Prague, Riga, Tallinn, Vilnius and Warsaw depart from Vitebsk Station (Vitebsky Vokzal), Zagorodny prospekt 52. For details of all these international services see the Getting There & Away chapter.

Tickets In high season (June to September) you'll find both the general ticket halls at Moscow Station and the Central Train Ticket Office, naberezhnaya kanala Griboedova 24, awash with daunting crowds. Don't waste your time in these queues since plenty of other purchasing options are available.

At Moscow Station, the Intourist ticket counters (Nos 40 to 43), near the statue of Peter the Great and on the right-hand side of the main hall as you enter from the street, are the places to head. At the Central Train

---

Historic Railway Stations

As the birthplace of Russia's railway system it's not surprising that St Petersburg has some grand stations. The most elegant is Vitebsk, also the oldest, originally built in 1837 for the line to Tsarskoe Selo. The current building dates from 1904 and is partly graced with gorgeous Style Moderne (Russian Art Nouveau) interior decoration which is best appreciated in the cafe upstairs on the right of the building.

While at Moscow Station look up at the expansive ceiling mural in the main entrance hall. There's a striking giant bust of Peter the Great in the hall leading to the platforms. In the same hall you'll also find a small wall display on the history of Russia's railways.

Rebuilt after WWII, Finland Station is famous as the place where Lenin arrived from exile and gave his legendary speech atop an armoured car in the square in April 1917. When the progress of the revolution began to look iffy, it was from here that Lenin hightailed it off to Finland, only to return again in October to seize power. Lenin's statue, pointing across the Neva towards the old KGB headquarters, stands outside the station.

Ticket Office, try the counters upstairs where trainee ticket issuers practise their craft. Better still, head to the Central Airline Ticket Office at Nevsky prospekt 7/9, which has a quiet desk issuing train tickets, or to Sindbad Travel (see Travel Agencies). If you have luck at none of these places, your final – and most expensive – option is the concierge at any of the luxury hotels.

Air

There are direct air links with most major European capitals – see the Getting There & Away chapter for details.

Between other cities along the Trans-Sib route there are daily flights to Moscow (one way/return $59/118), and services four times weekly to Yekaterinburg ($116/174), three times weekly to Novosibirsk ($133/247) and Irkutsk ($157/264); and weekly to Khabarovsk ($246/415) and Vladivostok ($264/448). Tickets can be purchased at the Central Airline Ticket Office, Nevsky prospekt 7, and at travel agencies such as Sindbad Travel.

Bus

St Petersburg's bus station, Avtovokzal No 2 (☎ 166 57 77) – there is no No 1 – is 1km from Ligovsky Prospekt metro at naberezhnaya Obvodnogo kanala. It serves Moscow, Novgorod and other smaller destinations.

For international bus services see the Getting There & Away chapter.

GETTING AROUND

Metro tokens (zhetony) cost $0.12, and a variety of magnetic-strip cards for multiple entry are also available from booths in the stations, which open around 5.30am and close just after midnight daily. Tickets for buses, trolleybuses and tramways are bought inside from controllers. To order a taxi, call ☎ 265 13 33 or ☎ 312 00 22.

Around St Petersburg

PETRODVORETS
ПЕТРОДВОРЕЦ
☎ 812

Russia's 'Versailles' is Petrodvorets (☎ 427 95 27; admission to grounds adult/student $4/1.75; open 9am-9pm year-round), the grandiose estate built by Peter the Great 29km west of St Petersburg. It was badly damaged by the Germans in WWII (many say it was further trashed by the Soviets after the war) and is largely a reconstruction, but still mightily impressive – even when swarming with tourists, as it frequently is.

The centrepiece is the **Grand Cascade & Water Avenue**, a symphony of over 64 fountains and 37 bronze statues. Between the cascade and the **Upper Garden** is the **Grand Palace** *(adult/student $8/4; open 10am-6pm Tues-Sun)*. Amid all the eye-boggling interiors, many find the finest room is the simplest – Peter's study, apparently the only one to survive the Germans. The estate features several other buildings of interest – all with their own admission charges and separate opening hours – which can easily take up half a day to tour fully.

Getting There & Away

The easiest way to Petrodvorets is to take the double-deck bus Nos 849 or 851 from the Baltic Station ($1, 40 minutes), which leave regularly and will drop you at the main entrance on Sankt Peterburgsky prospekt.

Cutting off the Tsar's Finger

In October 2001, the busy, 150-year-old rail link between Moscow and St Petersburg was closed for 24 hours so that workers could finally cut off the protruding finger of Tsar Nicholas I. Not his actual finger, but a long bend in the track attributed to the royal digit.

Legend has it that, when Tsar Nicholas commanded the route to be built in 1850, he accidentally drew around his own finger on the ruler as he traced out a straight line along the 650km between the tsarist northern capital and Moscow. Engineers, too afraid to point out the error, duly incorporated the kink into the plans, which became a 17km bend near the town of Novgorod.

The truth is somewhat more prosaic. The curve was actually built to circumvent a steep gradient that Russian steam locomotives of the time were not powerful enough to climb. Today's trains, however, have been forced to slow down in order to negotiate the Tsar's Finger. Straightening the line will cut an hour off the journey, reducing the trip to just under four hours.

From May to September, the *Meteor* hydrofoil ($10, 30 minutes) leaves from opposite St Petersburg's Hermitage every 20 to 30 minutes from 9.30am to at least 7pm.

TSARKOE SELO & PAVLOVSK
ЦАРКОЕ СЕЛО И ПАВЛОВСК
☎ 812

Be prepared for crowds again at Tsarkoe Selo (previously called Pushkin), the estate created by Empresses Elizabeth and Catherine the Great between 1744 and 1796, 25km south of St Petersburg. The big draw here is the Rastrelli-designed baroque **Catherine Palace** *(☎ 466 66 69; adult/student $8.50/4; open 11am-5pm Wed-Mon)*, built between 1752 and 1756, but practically destroyed in WWII. The exterior and 20-odd rooms have since been expertly restored; the Great Hall's gilt and mirrors are particularly dazzling.

Just wandering around **Catherine Park** *(adult/student $2/1; open 9am-5.30pm daily)* surrounding the palace is a pleasure. In the outer section of the park is the **Great Pond**, fringed by an intriguing array of structures including a Chinese Pavilion, purposely Ruined Tower and Pyramid where Catherine the Great buried her dogs.

To escape the masses head 4km farther south to Pavlovsk *(admission to grounds $0.80; open 9am-6pm daily)*, the park and palace designed by Charles Cameron between 1781 and 1786, and one of the most exquisite in Russia. Pavlovsk's **Great Palace** *(☎ 470 21 55; adult/student $6/3; open 11am-5pm Sat-Thur)* was a royal residence until 1917, burnt down in WWII and fully restored by 1970. The sprawling park itself is a delight to explore.

Getting There & Away

At Vitebsk Station head to platform 1 for the suburban train to Detskoe Selo Station (zone 3 ticket) for Tsarkoe Selo, and to Pavlovsk Station (zone 4) for Pavlovsk (a 30-minute trip to either). Note that while there are several trains prior to 9am, there are far fewer later in the day.

From Detskoe Selo Station, a five-minute ride on bus No 370, 371, 378, or 381 takes you to within two minutes' walk of Catherine Palace. From Pavlovsk Station, you can either cross the road and walk through the park to the palace, or take bus No 370, 383, 383A or 493 (under 10 minutes).

Moscow
Москва

What a difference a decade has made to Moscow. The stern-faced, awe-inspiring former capital of the communist world has evolved into a dutiful disciple of capitalism, with glitzy shops, modern colourful ads and a booming restaurant and cafe scene. These days it's but a short stroll from the technicolour domes of St Basil's to the largest Internet cafe in Eastern Europe, while at night you can lounge in clubs so hip that by the time we report on them, they're likely to be passé.

Many visitors will still find Moscow's vast scale forbidding, its extremes of wealth and poverty upsetting, its nouveau riche trappings ridiculous. Take comfort from the fact that service standards are on the rise, prices – post the 1998 crash – are more realistic and getting around is a cinch, thanks to the magnificent Metro – a tourist attraction in its own right.

Most importantly, Moscow is the benchmark against which the rest of Russia (with the possible exception of St Petersburg) measures itself. The city reeks of history and power, nowhere more so than in the Kremlin and precincts of Red Square. Those in search of Russia's rich cultural heritage will be delighted by museums, such as the Tretyakov Gallery, or institutions such as the Bolshoi. Give yourself at least three days here – who knows, like countless previous visitors you may find yourself less than inclined to leave.

HISTORY

The founding of the city is traditionally ascribed to Yury Dolgoruky, prince of Suzdal, who is recorded as giving a feast here in 1147. In 1238 Moscow lay in ruins following the Tatar invasion but by 1326 it had revived to become the seat of the Russian Orthodox Church, overtaking Golden Ring towns such as Vladimir and Suzdal (see the Moscow to Yekaterinburg chapter) in importance.

It was during the prosperous reigns of Ivan III (the Great) and Ivan IV (the Terrible) in the 15th and 16th centuries that many of Moscow's most distinctive build-

Highlights

- Take a relaxing cruise down the Moscow River.
- Toast the sunset over the city in the bar atop the Academy of Sciences.
- Wander the leafy grounds of Kolomenskoye, the tsar's suburban retreat.
- Pay your respects to Lenin in Red Square.
- Sweat off your Trans-Siberian grime at the Sandunovskiye Baths.

ings – including the walls of the Kremlin and St Basil's Cathedral – were constructed. The 17th century was chaotic in comparison; Moscow was subjected to one of its periodic sackings in 1612 by invading Poles.

In 1712 the capital was shifted to St Petersburg by Peter I. Despite this, Moscow's importance as an economic centre endured and the city was significant enough for Napoleon to advance on it a century later. Three-quarters of Moscow was destroyed by the time the French forces were in retreat, but the city – ever one to rise from the ashes – was quickly rebuilt and industrialised. By 1914 its population head reached 1.4 million.

In 1918 Lenin reinstated Moscow as the capital. His successor Stalin devised a comprehensive urban plan that resulted in broad roads and the monumental Gothic skyscrapers that still make Moscow so distinctive today. In comparison, the often wacky projects of the current mayor Yury Luzhkov and his chief artist Zurab Tsereteli – such as the outlandish statue of Peter the Great (who actually detested the city) on the Moscow River – seem almost insignificant.

Scene of dramatic confrontations during the fall of the Soviet Union in 1991, Moscow's White House again became a battleground for President Boris Yeltsin in September 1993 in his struggle against a hostile parliament. Violence again erupted at the end of the decade in a series of bomb blasts linked to the conflict in Chechnya. Security on the streets and at public buildings has been raised ever since, but on the whole these days there's little to fear wandering about the city.

ORIENTATION

Picture Moscow as four road rings that spread out from the centre. Radial roads spear out across the rings, and the Moscow River meanders across everything from north-west to south-east. The Kremlin is at Moscow's heart in every way, and sits at the northern tip of the river's biggest loop.

About 2.8km north-east of the Kremlin is Yaroslavl Station (Yaroslavsky Vokzal), the most important of Moscow's nine train stations for Trans-Siberian travellers. This is where all the major eastward services depart and arrive. Next door is Leningrad Station (Leningradsky Vokzal), for services to and from St Petersburg, while across the road is Kazan Station (Kazansky Vokzal) the terminus for some trains from the Urals including the main service from Yekaterinburg.

If you're arriving in Moscow on trains from Western and Eastern Europe your likely entry points will be Belorussia Station (Belorusskaya Vokzal), 2.8km north-west of the Kremlin, or Kiev Station (Kievsky Vokzal), 2.4km to the west.

The main shopping street heading north-west from the Kremlin is Tverskaya ulitsa, while directly west are Novy Arbat ulitsa and the pedestrianised Arbat ulitsa, other important commercial avenues.

INFORMATION
Tourist Offices

There's no official tourist office. Information is best sought from travel agencies or at hotel front desks.

Maps

You can find plenty of maps in Cyrillic at kiosks in and around metro stations. The top hotels will have free maps in English.

Atlas (☎ 928 61 09), at Kuznetsky Most ulitsa 9, stocks a good range of Russian-produced maps for around the country plus a few English-language ones.

For the most comprehensive map of the Russian railway system go to Transportnaya Kniga bookshop (☎ 262 25 13) at ulitsa Spasskaya 21, next to Krasnye Vorota metro station, which also stocks timetable books for Moscow's major stations.

Visas & Documents

For visa extensions, the main OVIR office, known in Moscow as UVIR (Upravleniye viz i registratsii; ☎ 200 84 97; Metro: Kurskaya) is at ulitsa Pokrovka 42. It's open 10am to 1pm and 3pm to 6pm Monday, Tuesday and Thursday and 10am to 1pm and 3pm to 5pm Friday.

If you need someone to register your visa, G&R Hostel (see Places to Stay) will do it for $7. Or try Andrews Consulting (☎ 258 51 98, Ⓦ www.andrews-consulting.ru), on the 5th floor at Novaya ploshchad 10, near Kitay-Gorod metro.

For details of embassies see that section of the Facts for the Visitor chapter.

Money

Cash can be changed at the many small exchange offices around the city. You'll also be able to get cash from the equally ubiquitous ATM machines.

Travellers cheques are best cashed at an established bank, such as Alfa Bank (☎ 202 35 35), at ulitsa Arbat 4/1. American Express (☎ 933 66 36, fax 933 66 35) has an office at ulitsa Usacheva 33.

Post & Telephone

A convenient, central post office is in the Central Telegraph (Tsentralny Telegraf) at Tverskaya ulitsa 7, from where you also can call, fax and email 24 hours a day. Moscow's main post office (glavpochtamt) is at Myasnitskaya ulitsa 26, on the corner of Chistoprudny bulvar. Courier services include DHL Worldwide Express (☎ 956 10 00) and Fedex (☎ 234 34 00).

Most of the pay phones you will find in Moscow are the blue-and-white booths, which are operated by cards widely available in shops and kiosks. Private telephone companies offering direct country service include MCI (☎ 8 10 800 497 7222), AT&T (☎ 8 10 800 110 1011 or 325 5042) and Sprint (☎ 235 6133 or 144 6133).

Email & Internet Access

Time Online (☎ 363 00 60), on the lower level of Okhotny Ryad shopping mall near Red Square, claims to be the largest Internet

MOSCOW

MOSCOW

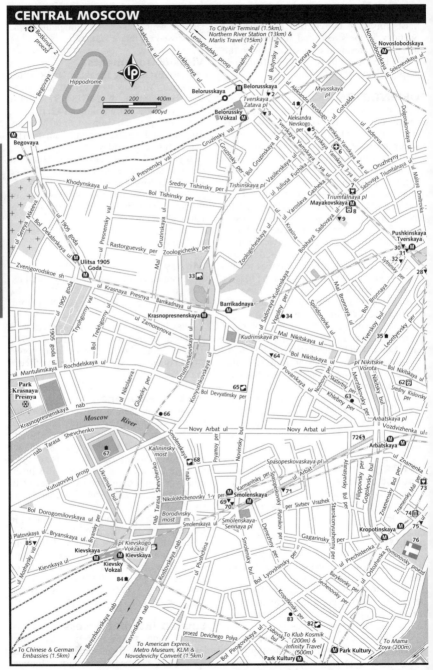

CENTRAL MOSCOW

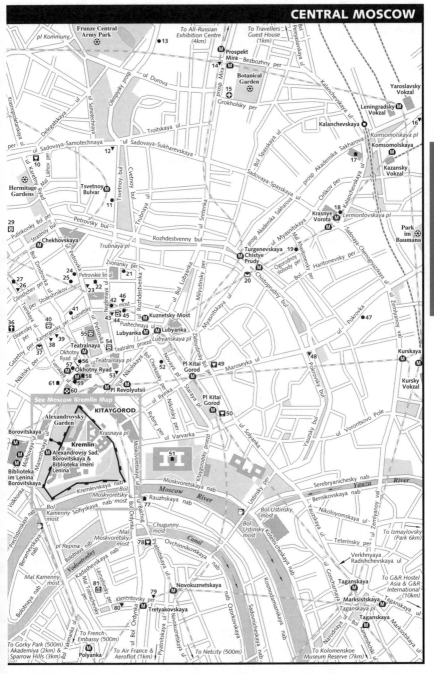

CENTRAL MOSCOW

MOSCOW

CENTRAL MOSCOW

cafe in the whole of Eastern Europe. No drinks are served, but its 200-plus zippy terminals are open for use 24 hours and rates go as low as $1/hour from 1am to 11am.

Drinks and competitive rates are also available at the equally central Internet Club (☎ 924 21 40), Kuznetsky Most ulitsa 12. It is open from 10am to midnight daily. Netcity (☎ 969 21 25), Paveletskaya ploshchad 2, has fast terminals and more of a cafe feel with sofas, drinks and snacks.

Digital Resources

The official Moscow government Web site is W www.moscow-guide.ru. Live views of the Kremlin can see seen on the Internet at W www.kremlinkam.com.

Travel Agencies

G&R International (☎ 378 00 01, fax 378 28 66, e hostelasia@mtu-net.ru, W www.hostels.ru) is a reputable agency that also runs the G&R Hostel Asia (see Places to Stay later in this chapter). It can arrange visas, train tickets and various tours.

Marlis Travel (☎ 453 43 68, fax 456 66 06, e wshtg@online.ru, W www.travel.world.co.uk/marlis) is the Moscow operation of UK-based tour agents The Russia Experience. It is recommended by locals for booking train tickets and making other travel arrangements.

Galileo Rus (☎ 929 87 01, fax 928 15 97, e galileo@galileo.ru), 15/13 ulitsa Petrovka, is also experienced at booking trains and other forms of transport.

Intourist (☎ 797 30 74, fax 927 11 61), ulitsa Stoleshnikov 11, offers the full range of tourist services.

Infinity Travel (☎ 234 65 55, fax 234 65 56, W infinity.ru) and the student- and youth-fare agency Star Travel (☎ 797 95 55) are both affiliated with Traveller's Guest House (see Places to Stay) and offer domestic and (discount) international air tickets. They can also buy train tickets with a $15 commission.

Bookshops

Anglia (☎ 203 58 02), at pereulok Khlebny 2/3, has Moscow's best selection of English-language books and is open 10am to 7pm Monday to Saturday and 10am to 5pm Sunday. The closest metro station is Arbatskaya.

Angliyskaya Kniga na Kuznestkom (☎ 928 20 21), Kuznetsky Most 18/7, near Kuznetsky Most metro station, is also worth checking out. It's open 10am to 2pm and 3pm to 7pm Monday to Friday and 10am to 2pm and 3pm to 6pm Saturday.

Newspapers & Magazines

You can pick up the *Moscow Times* (W www.themoscowtimes.ru) at many hotels, restaurants, cafes and shops around the city from Monday to Saturday. It's an excellent, free English-language newspaper. Also worth looking out for is the irreverent *The Exile* (W www.exile.ru), a free weekly focusing on entertainment listings.

Medical & Emergency Services

The American Medical Center (☎ 933 77 00, fax 933 77 01) at Grokholsky pereulok 1, offers 24-hour emergency service, consultations (from $175), a full range of specialists, including paediatricians and dentists, and an English-speaking pharmacy (open 8am-8pm Mon-Fri, 9am-5pm Sat & Sun). Get off at Prospekt Mira metro station.

The European Medical Center (☎ 956 79 99), 2-y Yamskoy Tverskoy pereulok 10, is similar in terms of both service and cost.

Botkin Hospital (☎ 945 00 45), 2-y Botkinsky proezd 5, is the main Moscow hospital for foreigners.

Apart from the American Medical Center, you'll also find several pharmacies along Tverskaya ulitsa.

To report a crime, call Petrovka 38, the state police, on ☎ 200 8924 for an English-speaking officer. The English-Language Crisis Line (☎ 244 3449) is a 24-hour hotline. Call, say 'crisis line', leave your number and a counsellor will call back.

Dangers & Annoyances

There's a strong chance that you'll be stopped in central Moscow (particularly in and around Red Square) by *militsia* asking for your passport. If you've not been registered by UVIR, your hotel or visa invitation agency you could have a lot of your time wasted, or at worst be made to pay a fine. This is often something of a scam, but stay calm, be polite, and try to check the person's identity before handing over your passport.

THINGS TO SEE & DO

The first place you're likely to head is Red Square and the adjacent Kremlin (see the

MOSCOW

The Kremlin

The apex of Russian political power and once the centre of the Orthodox Church, the Kremlin is not only the kernel of Moscow but also the whole country. It's from here that tsars, communist dictators and democratic presidents have done and continue to do their best – and worst – for Russia.

Occupying a roughly triangular plot of land covering little Borovitsky Hill on the north bank of the Moscow River, the Kremlin is enclosed by high walls 2.25km long with Red Square outside the east wall. The best views of the complex are from Sofiyskaya naberezhnaya across the river and the upper floors of the Rossiya hotel.

History

Kreml, in Russian, means fortress and every medieval town had one, including Moscow where the first wooden walls surrounding the settlement were built in the 1150s. In the 1320s, the Kremlin became the headquarters of the Russian Church, which shifted from Vladimir.

The 'White Stone Kremlin' – which had limestone walls – was built in the 1360s with almost the same boundaries as today. This lasted until the 1475–1516 reconstruction commissioned by Ivan the Great, when master builders from Pskov and Italy came to supervise the building of new walls and towers (most of which still stand), the three great cathedrals and more.

The Romanov dynasty added various palaces and although Peter the Great shifted the capital to St Petersburg, the tsars still showed up here for coronations and other celebrations. Repairs were needed after Napoleon blew parts of the Kremlin up before his retreat from Moscow in 1812; the citadel wouldn't be breached again until the Bolsheviks stormed the place in November 1917.

Until 1955 the Kremlin was closed to the public, most of whom would have feared death entering the terrifying lair of Stalin. It was Stalin who, in 1935, had the imperial double-headed eagles removed from the wall's five tallest towers and replaced with the distinctive red glass stars still there today.

Visiting Details

Before entering the **Kremlin** (☎ 921 47 20, Ⓦ *www.kremlin.museum.ru; adult/student $7/4, after 4pm $3.50/2; open 10am-6pm Fri-Wed*) deposit any bags you have at the left-luggage office (open 9am-6.30pm, $0.30 per bag), beneath the Kutafya Tower, just north of the main ticket office. Don't wear shorts or you won't be let in either.

The main ticket office, in the Aleksandrovsky Garden just off Manezhnaya ploshchad (metro: Aleksandrovsky Sad, Borovitskaya or Biblioteka imeni Lenina), closes at 4.30pm. The ticket covers entry to all buildings except the Armoury and Diamond Fund Exhibition (see below); it's a good idea to buy tickets for these two here as well to avoid having to queue up again once you're inside the Kremlin. A photography permit is $3. There's also an entrance at the southern Borovistkiye Gate, mainly used by those heading straight to the Armoury.

Inside the Kremlin police will keep you from straying into areas that are out of bounds. Numerous freelance guides tout their services near the Kutafya Tower; prices (anything from $10 to $20 per hour) and quality varies widely. **Patriarshy Dom** (see the Organised Tours section later in this chapter) offers regular tours of the main sights and occasionally runs tours of the off-limits Great Kremlin Palace. The following buildings are listed in order of the walking tour shown on the Kremlin map, starting at the Kutafya Tower.

Government Buildings

The **Kutafya Tower,** which forms the main visitors entrance today, stands away from the Kremlin's west wall, at the end of a ramp over the Alexandrovsky Garden leading up to the **Trinity Gate Tower**. On the way to the central Sobornaya ploshchad you'll pass the following buildings, which are closed to visitors. On the right is the 17th-century **Poteshny Palace**, where Stalin lived, and the bombastic marble, glass and concrete **State Kremlin Palace,** formerly the Palace of Congresses, built in 1960–61 for Communist Party congresses and now used by both the Bolshoi and Kremlin Ballet companies. On the left is the **Arsenal**, home to the Kremlin guard and ringed by 800 captured Napoleonic cannons, and the yellow, triangular former **Senate** building, now the ultimate seat of power in the modern Kremlin, the offices of the president of Russia. Next to the Senate is the 1930s **Supreme Soviet** building.

Patriarch's Palace
The first buildings open to visitors are the Patriarch's Palace *(Patriarshy Dvorets)* and attached five-domed **Cathedral of the Twelve Apostles** *(Sobor Dvenadtsati Apostolov)*, built in the 17th century. The palace now contains the **Museum of 17th-century Russian Applied Art & Life,** displaying church regalia, furniture and household items.

Assumption Cathedral
On the northern side of Sobornaya ploshchad, with five golden helmet domes and four semicircular gables facing the square, is the Assumption Cathedral *(Uspensky sobor)* built between 1475 and 1479. As the focal church of pre-revolutionary Russia, it's the burial place of most of the heads of the Russian Orthodox Church from the 1320s to 1700. The tombs are against the north, west and south walls.

The **iconostasis** dates from 1652 but its lowest level contains some older icons, including the *Virgin of Vladimir* (Vladimirskaya Bogomater), an early 15th-century Rublev school copy of Russia's most revered image, the *Vladimir Icon of the Mother of God* (Ikona Vladimirskoy Bogomateri). The 12th-century original, now in the Tretyakov Gallery, stood in the Assumption Cathedral from the 1480s to 1930.

Ivan the Great Bell Tower
With its two golden domes rising above the eastern side of Sobornaya ploshchad, the 16th-century Ivan the Great Bell Tower *(Kolokolnya Ivana Velikogo)* is the Kremlin's tallest structure, visible 30km away. Exhibitions from the Kremlin collections are shown on the ground level and require an extra $5 ticket. Beside the bell tower stands the world's biggest bell, the **Tsar-kolokol**, a 202-tonne monster that never rang. It was cast in the 1730s for Empress Anna Iovanovna.

Other Buildings
Back on Sobornaya ploshchad, the 1508 **Archangel Cathedral** *(Arkhangelsky sobor)* at the square's south-eastern corner was for centuries the coronation, wedding and burial church of tsars. The tombs of all of Moscow's rulers from the 1320s to the 1690s – bar one (Boris Godunov, buried at Sergiev Posad) – are here.

Dating from 1489, the **Annunciation Cathedral** *(Blagoveshchensky sobor)*, at the south-western corner of Sobornaya ploshchad, contains the celebrated icons of the master painter, Theophanes the Greek. They have a timeless beauty that appeals even to those usually left cold by icons.

Archangel Michael (the third icon from the left on the largest of the six tiers of the iconostasis), is ascribed to Andrey Rublev, who may also have painted the adjacent *St Peter*. Rublev is also reckoned to be the artist of the first, second, sixth, seventh and probably the third and fifth icons of the row above.

Both the **Hall of Facets** and the **Terem Palace** are closed to the public.

The Armoury
The 700-room **Great Kremlin Palace** is the official residence of the Russian president and is home to the Armoury *(Oruzheynaya palata; adult/student $18.30/4.60; visit on tours only at 10am, noon, 2.30pm & 4.30pm Fri-Wed)*, a numbingly opulent collection of treasures accumulated over centuries by the Russian State and Church. Also in the Great Kremlin Palace is the equally dazzling State Diamond Fund *(Almazniy Fond; admission $18.30; 10am-5pm Fri-Wed)*, which boasts the world's largest sapphire and the whopping 190-carat Orlov Diamond.

Of the Armoury's nine rooms, Room 6 is one of the most fascinating, with thrones and royal regalia. There's the joint coronation throne of boy tsars Peter (the Great) and his half-brother Ivan V (with a secret compartment from which Regent Sofia would prompt them), the 800-diamond throne of Peter's father, Tsar Aleksey Mikhailovich, and the coronation dresses of 18th-century empresses.

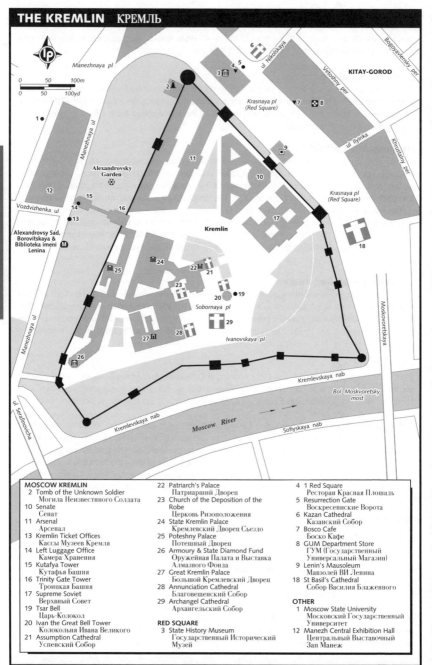

THE KREMLIN КРЕМЛЬ

MOSCOW KREMLIN

2 Tomb of the Unknown Soldier
  Могила Неизвестного Солдата
10 Senate
  Сенат
11 Arsenal
  Арсенал
13 Kremlin Ticket Offices
  Кассы Музеев Кремля
14 Left Luggage Office
  Камера Хранения
15 Kutafya Tower
  Кутафья Башня
16 Trinity Gate Tower
  Троицкая Башня
17 Supreme Soviet
  Верхный Совет
19 Tsar Bell
  Царь-Колокол
20 Ivan the Great Bell Tower
  Колокольня Ивана Великого
21 Assumption Cathedral
  Успенский Собор

22 Patriarch's Palace
  Патриарший Дворец
23 Church of the Deposition of the
  Robe
  Церковь Ризоположения
24 State Kremlin Palace
  Кремлевский Дворец Сьездо
25 Poteshny Palace
  Потешный Дворец
26 Armoury & State Diamond Fund
  Оружейная Палата и Выставка
  Алмазного Фонда
27 Great Kremlin Palace
  Большой Кремлевский Дворец
28 Annunciation Cathedral
  Благовещенский Собор
29 Archangel Cathedral
  Архангельский Собор

RED SQUARE

3 State History Museum
  Государственный Исторический
  Музей

4 1 Red Square
  Ресторан Красная Площадь
5 Resurrection Gate
  Воскресенские Ворота
6 Kazan Cathedral
  Казанский Собор
7 Bosco Cafe
  Боско Кафе
8 GUM Department Store
  ГУМ (Государственный
  Универсальный Магазин)
9 Lenin's Mausoleum
  Мавзолей ВИ Ленина
18 St Basil's Cathedral
  Собор Василия Блаженного

OTHER

1 Moscow State University
  Московский Государственный
  Университет
12 Manezh Central Exhibition Hall
  Центральный Выставочный
  Зап Манеж

boxed text 'The Kremlin'), a full tour of which will take up a day. There's enough in the heart of Moscow to occupy you for several more days, but we only list the major sights here; for more detailed information see Lonely Planet's *Moscow* city guide.

Red Square & Around

Most visitors approach Red Square *(Krasnaya ploshchad*, from the old Russian word for 'beautiful'), through the northern **Resurrection Gate** *(Voskresenskiye vorota)*, which perfectly frames the building that, more than any other, says 'Russia': **St Basil's Cathedral** *(Sobor Vasiliya Blazhennogo; ☎ 298 33 04, Krasnaya pl 2; admission $3; open 11am-5pm Wed-Mon).*

Rising from the slope at the square's southern end, St Basil's crazy confusion of colours and shapes was created between 1555 and 1561, replacing an existing church, to celebrate Ivan the Terrible's taking of the Tatar stronghold of Kazan. Its design is the culmination of a wholly Russian style that had been developed for building wooden churches. Legend has it that Ivan had the

LPP

St Basil's Cathedral, Red Square, Moscow

two architects responsible blinded so that they could never build anything comparable.

Lenin's Mausoleum *(Mavzoley VI Lenina; admission free; open 10am-1pm Tues-Thur, Sat & Sun)*, standing at the foot of the Kremlin wall, is another of Red Square's must-sees, especially since (if some people get their way) the former leader is eventually buried beside his mum in St Petersburg. After trouping past the embalmed, oddly waxy figure, emerge from his red and black stone tomb and inspect where Stalin, Brezhnev and many of communism's other heavy hitters are buried along the Kremlin wall.

A counterpoint to all this is the handsome **GUM** State Department Store (Gosudarstvenny Universalny Magazin), lining the north-eastern side of Red Square. Built in the 19th century to house over 1000 shops, it's still a bright, bustling place.

Tiny **Kazan Cathedral** *(Kazansky sobor; Nikolskaya ul 3; admission free; open 8am-7pm, evening service 8pm Mon)* is opposite the northern end of GUM. It's a replica of the original founded in 1636 and demolished on Stalin's orders in 1936, allegedly because it impeded the flow of parades through Red Square.

The red-brick building opposite the cathedral is opposite the **State History Museum** *(Gosudarstvenny Istorichesky muzey; ☎ 292 37 31; admission $5; open 11am-7pm Wed-Mon).* Although it has an enormous collection covering the whole Russian empire from the Stone Age, only a few galleries have so far been opened up to the public.

A good place to relax after all that sightseeing is the pleasant **Alexandrovsky Garden** *(admission free)* along the Kremlin's western wall. At the garden's northern end is the **Tomb of the Unknown Soldier**, containing the remains of a soldier who died in December 1941 at Km 41 of Leningradskoe shosse – the nearest the Nazis came to Moscow. The changing of the guard here happens every hour from 10am to 7pm in summer, and to 3pm during winter. Opposite the gardens is Manezhnaya ploshchad and the vast underground **Okhotny Ryad Shopping Mall**, a popular meeting spot for young Muscovites.

Pushkin Fine Arts Museum & Around

The Pushkin Fine Arts Museum *(☎ 203 95 78, ul Volkhonka 12; Metro: Kropotkinskaya;*

adult/student $5.50/2; open 10am-6pm Tues-Sun), 400m south-west of the Kremlin, is famous for its collection of impressionist and post-impressionist paintings, but it also has a broad selection of European works from the Renaissance onwards.

Near the museum is the gigantic **Cathedral of Christ the Saviour** *(Khram Khrista Spasitelya; ☎ 201 28 47, ul Volkhonka 15; admission to church free, guided tours $20 for up to 15 people; open 10am-6pm daily)*, rebuilt at an estimated cost of $360 million by Mayor Luzhkov on the site of the original, which was destroyed by Stalin. It replaces what was the world's largest swimming pool.

Tretyakov Gallery

The not-to-be missed Tretyakov Gallery *(Tretyakoskaya gallereya; ☎ 951 13 62, Lavrushinsky per 10; Metro: Tretyakovskaya; adult/student $7/$1.30; open 10am-7.30pm Tues-Sun)*, 1km south of the Kremlin, contains the world's best collection of Russian icons and an outstanding collection of other pre-revolutionary Russian art.

Novodevichy Convent

One of Moscow's most beautiful buildings is Novodevichy Convent *(Novodevichy monastyr; ☎ 246 85 26, Novodevichy proezd 1; Metro: Sportivnaya; adult/student $1/0.50; open 8am-6pm daily)*, a cluster of sparkling domes behind handsome turreted walls near the Moscow River. Founded in 1524 to celebrate the re-taking of Smolensk from Lithuania, the convent is notorious as the place where Peter the Great imprisoned his half-sister Sofia for her part in the Streltsy rebellion.

Enter the convent under the red-and-white Moscow baroque **Transfiguration Gate-Church**, built in the north wall between 1687 and 1689. The oldest and dominant building in the grounds is the white **Smolensk Cathedral** *(adult/student $2.20/1.10)*, which was built in 1524–25. Sofia's tomb lies among others in the south nave.

The **bell tower** against the convent's east wall, completed in 1690 with a gold dome topping six red-brick tiers with white detail, is generally regarded as Moscow's finest. The adjacent **cemetery** *(admission $0.70; open 9am-6pm daily)* contains the tombs of a host of Russian notables, including Chekhov, Gogol, Mayakovsky, Prokofiev

and Stanislavsky, and is a fascinating place to wander around.

Gorky Park & Around

Part ornamental park, part funfair Gorky Park *(admission $1.50; open 10am-10pm summer, 10am-9pm winter daily)*, stretching almost 3km along the Moscow River upstream of Krymsky Most, is a good place to escape the hubbub of the city. In winter the park turns into a gigantic **skating rink** *(admission $0.80)* – you can rent low-quality skates for $1. The skating is better at the privately run **Frozen Beach** *(admission $3.20)* near the Buran space shuttle in the park or at the Hermitage Gardens (see Bars & Clubs later). The park's main entrance is on ulitsa Krymsky Val, 500m from either Park Kultury or Oktyabryskaya metro.

Opposite the main entrance is **Iskussty Park,** which has become home to many old communist statues removed from around the city. Here you'll also find a big modern block housing both the **Central House of Artists** *(Tsentralny Dom Khudozhnika; admission $0.50; open 11am-8pm Tues-Sun)*, showcasing contemporary art and furniture, and the **New Tretyakov Gallery** *(Novaya Tretyakovskaya galereya, ☎ 238 13 78; admission $7; open 10am-7.30pm Tues-Sun)*, with a fascinating collection of 20th-century Russian art.

Kolomenskoye Museum-Reserve

An ancient royal country seat and Unesco World Heritage Site, set amid 4 sq km of parkland on a bluff above a bend in the Moscow River, is Kolomenskoye Museum-Reserve *(☎ 115 23 09; Metro: Kolomenskaya; grounds free; open 10am-9pm daily; ticket to all museums $4; open 10am-5pm daily)*. This is the best excursion in the outer suburbs. Lots of **festivals** are held here and it's well worth checking to see if anything is happening during your visit.

Entering through the **Saviour Gate**, you'll pass the **Kazan Church** before reaching the reserve's most impressive collection of buildings – the white, tent-roofed 17th-century **Front Gate & Clock Tower,** parts of which house an interesting museum, and the rocket-like **Ascension Church**, built between 1530 and 1532 for Grand Prince Vasily III, father of Ivan the Terrible. Among the other buildings scattered amid the trees is a simple

wooden cabin in which Peter the Great lived while supervising ship and fort building in Archangelsk in the 1700s.

All-Russia Exhibition Centre

No other place in Moscow sums up the rise and fall of communist Russia quite as well as the All-Russia Exhibition Centre or VDNKh. The initials stand for Vystavka Dostizheny Narodnogo Khozyaystva SSSR (USSR Economic Achievements Exhibition). Although it was created in the 1950s and '60s to impress one and all with the success of the Soviet economic system, it's now a big fun fair and shopping centre for cheap imported goods.

VDNKh, 2km long and 1km wide, is composed of wide pedestrian avenues and grandiose pavilions that once glorified every aspect of socialist life from education to agriculture. Scattered about are the most kitsch of socialist-realist statues – don't miss the colossal *Worker and Collective Farm Girl*, designed for the 1937 Paris Expo by Vera Mukhina.

The main entrance, 200m off prospekt Mira, is approached from VDNKh metro,

beside which is a soaring 100m titanium obelisk – a monument to Soviet space flight. In its base is the **Museum of Cosmonautics** *(Muzey Kosomonavtiki; ☎ 283 79 14, prosp Mira 111; admission $1; open 10am-7pm Tues-Sun, closed last Fri of month)*, housing a series of displays from the glory days of the Soviet space program.

ACTIVITIES
River Trips

For an alternative view of the capital, take a boat ride along the Moscow River. Stopping at six points along the way, the main route runs between landings at Kiev Station and Novospassky Most, near the Novospassky Monastery, 1km west of Proletarskaya metro. The boats run every 20 to 30 minutes, noon to 8pm daily from late April to early October. One-way tickets are $2 on weekdays, $4 on weekends, regardless of whether you go one stop or the full trip (90 minutes).

Banya

There can be few more pleasurable experiences than a good clean up at a traditional Russian *banya* – especially after a long

---

Bathtime at the Sandunovskiye

From the moment I climbed the gilded and elaborately tiled staircase of the *banya* known to regulars as the Sanduny, I knew I wouldn't be regretting a couple of hours of hard sweat in the heart of Moscow.

The changing room, with its vaulted mahogany ceiling and turquoise and gold, fleur de lis patterned walls, felt like a baroque gentlemen's club. I left my clothes at a space on one of the high-backed leather banquettes, deposited my valuables with an attendant, donned my cotton sheet like a Roman senator and strode towards the baths.

Outside the steam room *(parilka)* lay bundles of dried birch leaves *(veniki)* that Russians enthusiastically beat themselves with while in the sauna. Such flagellation is said to open up the pores, helping the body rid itself of toxins; it was enough for me to concentrate on sweating and wondering whether, like my bathing companions, I should be wearing a funny felt hat to protect my hair.

The sweat is followed by the quick freeze – a lightening dip in one of the wooden barrel baths filled to the brim with cold water. The sensation is amazing, but better still was the following swim in the main pool, amid a room designed like a Grecian shrine with columns, statues and mosaic floors.

The optional extra of a massage ($20) was well worth the indulgence, the full body soap and rub not as rough as a Turkish pummelling. I also recommend stringing the whole affair out by nipping back to the changing room, as the regulars do, for restorative cups of tea and snacks that you can order from the attendants.

Simon Richmond

Trans-Siberian journey without a proper bath. As far as opulence goes, there's no better banya to choose than the elegant **Sandunovskiye Baths** (☎ *925 46 31; ul Neglinnaya 14; general baths $16.60, luxe baths $20, hire of towel & sandals $1.60; open 8am-10pm Wed-Mon, last entry 8pm*). There are separate entrances to the baths for men and women off Zvonarsky pereulok. See the boxed text 'Bathtime at the Sandunovskiye' for more details.

ORGANISED TOURS

Patriarshy Dom Tours (☎/fax *795 09 27,* W *www.expat.ru, Vspolny per 6*) operates a varied and interesting program of English-language tours in and around Moscow. Walking tours start at $10 and you'll pay little more for other tours apart from entrance fees. It can also organise private guides and language classes (from $13 per hour) as well as arranging visa support.

PLACES TO STAY – BUDGET

Most travel agencies and tour companies offering Trans-Siberian packages (see the Facts for the Visitor chapter) can arrange *homestays* in Moscow, as can HOFA (see Places to Stay in the St Petersburg chapter).

Guesthouses

G&R Hostel Asia (☎ *378 00 01, fax 378 28 66,* e *hostelasia@mtu-net.ru, Hotel Asia, Zelenodolskaya ul 2/3*) Dorm beds/singles/doubles with breakfast $16/20/25. Twenty minutes from the centre by metro, this hostel on the top floors of an old hotel is one of the best budget options. The management is clued up and there's a travel agency that can book Trans-Siberian tickets. Leave Ryazansky Prospekt metro from the end of the train and look for the tallest building around – that's the hostel.

Art Hostel (*hostel* ☎ *251 28 37, central reservations* ☎ *812-275 15 13, fax 275 45 81,* W *www.arthostel.net, Tverskaya 3-ya ul 58/5*) Dorm beds/singles/doubles with breakfast $15/20/30. Only open 1 January to 1 March and 12 June to 6 September (when prices are about $5 higher per person), Art Hostel has a prime location, two minutes' walk from Belorusskaya metro, in a student hostel run by kindly *babushkas*. Rooms are well furnished and facilities include a modern kitchen with microwave and washing machine. The entrance is the third door on the left on Aleksandra Nevskogo pereulok. Note: there's a 1am curfew.

Travellers Guest House (☎ *971 40 59, fax 280 76 86,* e *tgh@glasnet.ru,* W *tghmoscow .hypermart.net, Bolshaya Pereyaslavskaya ul 50, 10th floor*) Dorm beds/singles/doubles with breakfast $15/30/40, 5% discount for ISIC cards, 10% for IYHF cards. Not the backpackers hotspot that it once was, this lacklustre place is a 10-minute walk north of Prospekt Mira metro. Rooms and shared toilets are basic but clean and there's almost always space. It remains a reliable source of information and the affiliated Infinity Travel and budget STAR travel agencies can help you arrange all onward tickets. They also offer a $99 special for a 25-day tourist visa, airport pick-up and two days' dorm accommodation, which is a good deal if you want to arrange your own train tickets.

Hotels

Hotel Leningradskaya (☎ *975 18 15, fax 975 18 02, Kalanchevskaya ul 21/40*) Singles/doubles from $26/53. Arriving at this looming Stalinist skyscraper in the dead of night is likely to strike fear into your heart, but in daylight this showpiece Soviet hotel retains much of its grand 1950s style and is worth considering as a base for a couple of nights.

Hotel Tsentralnaya (☎ *229 89 57, fax 292 12 21, Tverskaya ul 10*) Singles/doubles with shared bathrooms $38/58. The only things going for this crumby place are its central location and cheap prices.

Hotel Rossiya (☎ *232 44 34, 232 43 01, Varvarka ulitsa 6*) Singles/doubles from $40/45. Another fall-back from the Soviet school of hotel management, this confusingly huge building seems perpetually on the up-grade. Rooms with Kremlin views are double the price.

PLACES TO STAY – MID-RANGE

East West Hotel (☎ *290 04 04, fax 291 46 06,* W *www.col.ru/east-west, Tverskoy bul 14/4*) Singles/doubles with breakfast from $100/130. It's kitsch, but the East West is a rather charming small hotel on one of central Moscow's most pleasant streets. Features include a quiet and secure courtyard and a sauna for warming up in winter.

Hotel Budapest (☎ *921 10 60, fax 921 52 90,* e *reservations@hotel-budapest.ru,*

Petrovskie Linii 2/18) Singles/doubles with breakfast from $95/137. Prices are 20% lower at the weekend at this elegant central hotel, with friendly management and larger than average rooms.

Hotel Moskva (☎ 292 60 70, fax 928 59 38, e root@hotel-moskva.aha.ru, Okhotny Ryad 2) Singles/doubles from $49/80. The atmosphere is sombre here but the rooms are reasonably comfortable (you'll pay more for the upgraded ones). West-facing rooms have views of the Kremlin.

Hotel Ukraina (☎ 243 30 30, fax 956 20 78, Kutuzovsky prosp 2/1) Singles/doubles from $79/89. Facing the White House across the Moscow River, this giant hotel popular with tour groups, echoes Stalinist pomp in its hallways and old-fashioned, stately rooms, many with terrific views.

PLACES TO STAY – TOP END
Le Royal Meridien National (☎ 258 70 00, fax 258 71 00, W www.national.ru, Mokhovaya ul 15/1) Singles/doubles from $324/420. Better known as the National, this early-20th-century beauty faces the Kremlin and boasts gorgeous rooms.

Radisson-Slavyanskaya Hotel (☎ 941 80 20, fax 240 32 17, W www.radissonmoscow .ru, Berezhkovskaya nab 2) Doubles from $224. Bright and modern, this hotel is almost a village in itself with a large business centre, a shopping mall and a cinema playing English-language movies.

Hotel Baltschug Kempinski (☎ 230 65 00, fax 230 65 02, W www.kempinski-moscow .com, ul Balchug 1) Doubles from $500. Dating from 1898, this is one of Moscow's most elegant hotels with top-class service and buffet breakfasts and brunches that are well worth the splurge.

PLACES TO EAT
Restaurants
Yolki-Palki (☎ 928 55 25, ul Neglinnaya 8/10) Dishes under $5. One of several outlets for this excellent country-cottage-style Russian chain, specialising in simple, traditional dishes. The beer is cheap and there's a brilliant salad bar. We also liked the Mongolian barbecue branch on Tverskaya ulitsa at Pushkinskaya ploshchad.

Moo Moo (☎ 241 13 64, Arbat ul 45/24 & ☎ 245 78 20, Komsomolskaya prosp 26) Dishes around $5. Dig that spotted cow

decor and the easy serve-yourself approach to standard Russian favourites such as *borshch*, *pelmeni* and some violently coloured desserts.

Mekhana Bansko (☎ 241 31 32, Smolenskaya pl 9/1) Mains around $10. This Bulgarian restaurant occupies an atmospheric basement space close by the exit of the metro. Its traditional *shopska* salad made with baked peppers is recommended along with *shkembe chorba*, veal boiled in milk.

Yakitoria (☎ 250 53 85, 1-ya Tverskaya-Yamskaya 1/29) Mains $6-15. Moscow is in the grip of a sushi craze and this chain is one of the best places to try it and other Japanese dishes such as yakitori (here called *shashlyk*) and tempura. We found the food delicious at this original branch.

Tibet Kitchen (☎ 923 24 22, Kamergersky per 5/6) Mains $10. The cosy interior of this basement place, on one of the Kuznetsky Most's trendiest streets, will whisk you to Lhasa – ask the management to tone down the spice to more authentic Tibetan levels if you wish.

Jagannat (☎ 928 35 80, Kuznetsky Most 11) Mains $6. This funky contemporary vegetarian cafe, restaurant and store does great food. It also offers a traditional Chinese tea ceremony with a wide range of varieties.

A couple more reliable and inexpensive options are *Starlight Diner (☎ 290 96 38, ul Bolshaya Sadovaya 16)*, set in an authentic 1950s American diner and great for blow-out breakfasts; *Soleil Express (☎ 725 64 74, ul Sadovaya Samotechnaya 24/27)*, a convivial bistro serving a good range of dishes; and the Georgian restaurant *Mama Zoya (☎ 242 85 50, Frunzenskaya nab 16)*, which now has this branch on a boat, where fleet-footed dancers and musicians accompany the delicious shashlyk and cheese bread.

When money is no object try *CDL (☎ 291 15 15, ul Povarskaya 50)*, offering grand decor and expensive modern Russian cuisine, in one part of the historic House of Writers. Also here is the less costly but atmospheric *Zapisky Okhotnika (Hunter's Sketches)*. The name refers both to the historic graffiti-clad walls, the dining room and its extraordinary stuffed menagerie (the present owners are hunters).

1 Red Square (☎ 925 36 00, Krasnaya pl 1) Mains around $20. Another luxury choice is this intimate restaurant inside the History

MOSCOW

Museum, high on style and service. There's an extensive menu, including classic Russian dishes from the tsar's era, and a good business lunch for $18.

Cafes

Moscow's booming cafe scene is beginning to make long-standing imports like Deli-France look decidedly old hat.

Coffee Bean *(Pokrovka ul 18 & Tverskaya ul 10)* Both branches are classic coffee bars with high ceilings, no smoking, good drinks, cakes and simple sandwiches.

Orange *(pl Revolyutsii)* Central and unmissably orange, this place is good for anything from a coffee to a light meal and offers delightfully dippy service to match the funky decor.

Zen Coffee *(☎ 234 17 84, Lesnaya ul 1/2 & ☎ 292 51 14, Kamergersky per 6)* The first of these modern, pleasant cafes is opposite Belorusskaya Vokzal, the second is on the popular pedestrian boulevard leading from Tverskaya to Kuznetsky Most.

A couple of luxury options are parisienne-style ***Aldebaran*** *(☎ 953 63 06, Bolshoy Tolmachovsky per 6)*, handy to the Tretyakov Gallery, and the swish Italian ***Bosco Cafe*** *(☎ 929 31 82, GUM, Krasnaya pl 3)*, where you sip your cappuccino and have a ringside seat on Red Square.

Fast Food

Fighting for prime retail space with the inevitable ***McDonald's*** is ***Russkoe Bistro***, an equally omnipresent local chain endorsed (and, coincidentally, co-owned) by Mayor Luzhkov. It serves cheap, traditional goodies such as *pirozhki* (pies) and *bliny*.

Patio Pizza *(☎ 201 56 26, ul Volkhonka 13A)* Pizzas from $8. Although it's all over town, this branch across from the Pushkin Museum is considered the best. The pizzas come hot from wood ovens. The salad bar is huge. Often next to a Patio Pizza you'll also find a ***Rostiks***, run by the same company, and serving up deep-fried chicken, chips and the like.

There's a handy, but pricey food court in the basement of the Okhotny Ryad shopping mall.

Self-Catering

Ramstore *(Komsomolskaya pl 6)* Open 24 hours daily. Conveniently opposite Yaroslavl Station, this branch of the giant supermarket chain is *the* one-stop place to stock up on provisions for your Trans-Sib trip.

Stockmans *(Smolensky Passage, Karmanitsky prosp)* Open 10am-10pm daily. In the basement of this department store, beside Smolenskaya metro, is one of the city's top foreign-goods supermarkets.

Yeliseevsky *(Tverskaya ul 14)* Open 8am-9pm Mon-Sat, 10am-6pm Sun. Come to gawp at the luxurious pre-revolutionary decor of the surroundings and the old Soviet style of selling goods.

Dorogomilovsky Market *(Mozhaysky Val 10)* Open 7am-7pm daily. One of the best spots for fresh food, this market overflows along Kievskaya ulitsa to Kiev Station.

ENTERTAINMENT

Check the Thursday or Friday edition of the *Moscow Times* or *The Exile* for the latest places to go and what's on where. Note that from late June to early September there are no performances by the regular companies at places such as the Bolshoi.

Classical Music, Opera & Ballet

For top-notch classical music, look up what's playing at the ***Tchaikovsky Concert Hall*** *(☎ 299 03 78, Triumfalnaya pl 4/31)*, Moscow's largest concert venue and home of the famous State Symphony Orchestra. You can also try the ***Moscow Tchaikovsky Conservatoire*** *(☎ 229 94 03, Bolshaya Nikitskaya ul 13)*.

Bolshoi *(☎ 292 99 86, W www.bolshoi.ru, Teatralnaya pl 1)* An evening here remains one of Moscow's best nights out. The atmosphere in the glittering, six-tier auditorium is electric. To buy tickets (expect to pay around $85), you either have to buy in advance from one of a few specific outlets or hang around outside the theatre before the performance and get one from a tout (for more tips see the boxed text 'Buying Tickets' in the St Petersburg chapter).

Leading dancers also appear with the Moscow Classical Ballet Theatre. This company and the Bolshoi both perform at the ***State Kremlin Palace*** *(☎ 929 79 01, ul Vozdvizhenka 1)*.

Theatre & Circus

Your enjoyment of theatre in Moscow will obviously depend on how much Russian you understand. You may be able to catch a rare English-language performance at the **Chekhov Moscow Art Theatre** (☎ 229 87 60, Kamergersky per 3), also known as MKhAT, the birthplace of method acting.

Otherwise, a good bet is **Lenkom Theatre** (☎ 299 07 08, ul Malaya Dmitrovka 6), which specialises in flashy, musical productions that are more generally understandable to a non-native audience.

Maly Theatre (☎ 923 26 21, Teatralnaya pl 1/6) is a lovely venue, founded in 1824, where you can catch performances of the classics and some newer plays.

The most atmospheric of Moscow's two circuses is the central **Old Circus** (☎ 200 68 89, Tsvetnoy bul 13), where performances start at 7pm, or 6.30pm on weekends.

Bars & Clubs

Come summer, **outdoor beer tents** and **shashlyk stands** pop up all over the city.

One of the most pleasant places to head is the Hermitage Gardens (Pushkinskaya/ Tverskaya metro). You can dress and look as you like while drinking at the places here, unlike at some of Moscow's trendier clubs where 'face control' rules are arbitrarily imposed by thuggish bouncers.

Kitaysky Lyotchik Dzhao-Da (☎ 924 56 11, Lubyansky proezd 25) In a basement close to Kitay-Gorod metro station, this is one of the best and most relaxed club/ restaurants of the moment. It often has live music for which there's an entrance charge of around $4.

Propaganda (☎ 924 57 32, Bolshoy Zlatoustinsky per 7) Thursday is the night to get down to this hip hang-out where the DJs spin a cool mix for the beautiful people to dance.

Trety Put (☎ 951 87 34, ul Pyatnitskaya 4) The antithesis of Moscow trendy, this cheap and delightfully grungy club can be a fun place to hang out. Expect anything from a punk band to heated philosophical discussions.

Akademiya (☎ 938 57 75, Academy of Sciences, Leninsky prosp 32A) On the 22nd floor, with a magnificent view of the city, is this retro bar/club popularly known as 'The Brains', after the surreal metallic structure that tops the building.

As for expat bars you can't go far wrong at **American Bar and Grill** (☎ 251 0151, ul 1-ya Tverskaya-Yamskaya 2/1) or **Rosie**

O'Grady's (☎ 203 9087, ul Znamenka 9/12), both of which are pretty self-explanatory.

BB King (☎ 299 82 06, ul Sadovaya Samotechnaya 4/2) is a good place to hear jazz and blues. If there's live music, expect to pay a $3 cover charge.

Klub Kosmik (☎ 246 36 66, ul Lva Tolstogo 18) This is the place to head if you fancy a spot of high-tech bowling (it has several psychedelic fluorescent lanes) or pool. Drinks are good value and it's around $20 per hour per lane.

SHOPPING

For souvenirs the ideal place to head is the **Vernisazh market** (Izmaylovsky Park; admission $0.20; open 10am-6pm daily), best on weekends when stalls are most plentiful. Also worth a look are the weekend street **stalls** on ulitsa Krymsky Val, opposite Gorky Park's entrance and at the Sparrow Hills (Vorobyovy Gory) beside the University of Moscow, overlooking the river bend toward Luzhniki Stadium. There are daily stalls along the Arbat.

If you are looking for anything else you should be able to find it in the shops along Novy Arbat, Tverskaya ulitsa and streets around Kuznetsky Most, this area being home to Moscow's most stylish boutiques.

GETTING THERE & AWAY
Train

For Trans-Siberian travellers the most important of Moscow's nine stations is Yaroslavl (Komsomolskaya metro) where the major trains to Siberian cities, Vladivostok, Ulaan Baatar and Beijing all depart from and arrive. See the Facts for the Visitor chapter for details of specific services. You can change money in the main waiting hall. There's a left-luggage office (kamera khraneniya) beneath this and alongside platform 1.

St Petersburg trains depart from and arrive at Leningrad Station next to Yaroslavl Station. Across the road is Kazan Station, the terminus for trains from Central Asia and some western parts of Siberia. Go to Kursk Station (Kurskaya metro) for the express train to Vladimir.

Trains for London, Berlin and Warsaw leave from Belarus Station (Belorusskaya metro), those to Latvia from Riga Station (Rizhskaya metro) and those to Budapest,

MOSCOW

Prague or Kyiv (Kiev in Russian) from Kiev Station (Kievskaya metro). See the Getting There & Away chapter for more details.

Tickets If you encounter long queues at the long-distance ticket *kassa* at Yaroslavl Station, try the Central Railway Agency offices either to the east or west of the main building. Better still, head to the service centre at the entrance to the main waiting hall where, for a $3 charge, there's a numbered ticket queuing arrangement and you can wait in air-conditioned comfort – important in the height of summer.

Of the several Central Railway Agency offices around the city a good one is at Maly Kharitonyevsky pereulok 6 (☎ 262 25 66). It's open from 8am to 1pm and 2pm to 7pm daily and the nearest metro is Chistye Prudy. You can book tickets here for stations outside Moscow; useful if you're planning to stop off at various places along the Trans-Siberian route.

Alternatively, many travel agencies (see earlier in this chapter) can buy or issue tickets. This is much simpler and well worth the charge of between $5 and $10 to avoid any hassles at the station or Central Railway Agency offices where, generally, only Russian will be spoken.

Air

Moscow has five airports, each of which serves specific destinations.

The airports that are most likely to be used by Trans-Siberian travellers are: Sheremetevo-2 (☎ 578 91 01), 30km north-west of the city centre, for flights to/from outside the former Soviet Union; Sheremetevo-1 (☎ 575 57 91), across the runways from Sheremetevo-2 airport, for flights to/from St Petersburg, the Baltic countries, Belarus and northern European Russia; and Domodedovo (☎ 933 66 66), around 40km south of the city centre, for flights to/from eastern Russia, including the cities along the Volga and Siberia, as well as some of the international flights.

If you're not stopping in Moscow, it's likely that you'll find yourself flying into one and out of another airport on any connecting flight, so check details carefully before departure and double check about transfers between terminals, for which you are usually left to your own devices.

You can buy domestic airline tickets at most travel agencies and Aeroflot offices all over town, including the user-friendly one at ulitsa Korovy Val 7 (☎ 158 80 19). Transaero airlines also has a number of ticket offices, including one in the corner of the Hotel Moskva (☎ 241 76 76, Okhotny ryad 2).

International airline offices in Moscow include:

Air France (☎ 937 38 39) ul Korovy Val 7
British Airways (☎ 956 46 76) ul 1-ya Tverskaya Yamskaya 34
Delta (☎ 937 90 90) Gogolevsky bul 11
Finnair (☎ 933 00 56) Kropotkinsky per 7
KLM (☎ 258 36 00) ul Usacheva 33/2
Lufthansa (☎ 737 64 00) Renaissance Moscow Hotel, Olimpiysky prosp 18
SAS (☎ 925 47 47) ul Kuznetsky Most 3

Domestic one-way fares and frequency of flights to destinations along the Trans-Sib route covered in this book include:

destination	cost	frequency
St Petersburg	$59	daily
Nizhny Novgorod	$61	six times weekly
Perm	$106	twice weekly
Kazan	$77	daily
Yekaterinburg	$119	daily
Tyumen	$104	daily
Omsk	$143	daily
Novosibirsk	$136	daily
Tomsk	$144	daily
Krasnoyarsk	$193	daily
Irkutsk	$104	daily
Ulan Ude	$187	daily
Chita	$207	four times weekly
Khabarovsk	$203	five times weekly
Vladivostok	$293	daily

Bus

Buses are not very comfortable and tend to be slower than trains. To book a seat (it's advisable to do so in advance) you have to travel out to the long-distance bus terminal, the Shchyolkovsky Avtovokzal, right beside Shchyolkovskaya metro station (east of the city). Queues can be bad here.

Boat

The Moscow river terminus for departures to St Petersburg, Yaroslavl, Nizhny Novgorod, Kazan and other cities along the Volga River is the Northern River Station

(☎ 459 74 76) at Leningradskoe shosse 51, around 15 minutes' walk west of Rechnoy Vokzal metro. Ships operated by the Capital Shipping Company (☎ 277 39 02) run several times a week from early June to mid-October.

GETTING AROUND
To/From the Airports

The City Air Terminal at Leningradsky prospekt 37 has bus services to/from all the airports. However, the terminal itself is about 1km from Dinamo metro and services from the terminal are infrequent and confusing.

To reach Sheremetevo-1 or Sheremetevo-2 airports, there are buses to and from Rechnoy Vokzal metro ($0.30). It's best to pre-arrange a taxi transfer with a travel agency or tour company (for around $30) if you want to avoid being stung by the airport taxi mafia eagerly awaiting your arrival.

The easiest way to Domodedovo airport is from Paveletsky Vokzal – see the airport's Web site (W www.eastline.ru/domodedovo /index_e.asp) for details.

Metro

The metro is the easiest, quickest and cheapest way of getting around Moscow. A ticket (prisnoy bilet) – sold at booths in the metro stations – for one trip costs $0.20. However, you're better off buying a stored-value ticket for two, five, 10, 20 or 60 trips – with each ride becoming cheaper the more trips you buy. Maps of the system, with stations' names in Roman and Cyrillic letters, are in each carriage.

Bus, Trolleybus & Tram

Buses, trolleybuses and trams run almost everywhere the metro doesn't. You need to validate your ticket on board. *Bilety*, which cost about $0.20 each, can be bought from drivers and street kiosks that display them.

Taxi

Practically any car is a taxi in Moscow – to hail one just stand on the street and stick your arm out. Don't hesitate to wave on a car whose occupant(s) you don't like the look of. Always agree on a price before you get in. For a short ride $2 is plenty; to cross the city shouldn't be more than $5. To book a taxi in advance, call the Central Taxi Reservation Office (☎ 927 00 00) 24 hours daily.

Touring the Metro

Used by up to nine million people daily, the Moscow Metro, with over 120 stations, around 250km of track (and still growing) and trains running every 1 or 2 minutes at peak times, is one of the city's marvels. The first stations date from 1935 and were dug so deep to also act as bomb shelters. Many are now rightly considered art and design classics.

Patriarshy Dom (see Organised Tours earlier in this chapter) often run Metro tours, but it's easy enough to go sightseeing on your own; outside rush hours and Sunday mornings are best. Stations to look out for include:

Kievskaya – on the circle line, with its vivid mosaics of Ukrainian history and delightful images of a happy and well-fed proletariat.
Komsomolskaya – on the circle line, the one with the chandeliers and gold-encrusted mosaics. On the Sokolnicheskaya (red) line are panels depicting heroic metro workers.
Mayakovskaya – grand prize winner at the 1938 World's Fair in New York, has a central hall that's all stainless steel and marble with 36 oval ceiling mosaics on the theme of sport and aviation.
Novokuznetskaya – with military bas-reliefs and industrial ceiling mosaics. The elegant marble benches came from the original Church of Christ the Saviour.
Ploshchad Revolyutsii – life-sized bronze statues in the main hall and beside the escalators illustrate the idealised roles of common men and women.

If you want to know more about the system, check out the small **Metro Museum** (☎ 222 73 09, Khamovnicheski val 35; call ahead for tours 9am-4pm Thur only) at the Luzhniki Sports Complex end of Sportivnaya Station – look for the *Militsia* office on the right as you exit the station and climb up the stairs.

Around Moscow

The ancient towns of the Golden Ring, north-east of the city, are where most visitors head on day trips out of Moscow. Their churches, monasteries, kremlins (fortifications) and museums make an incredibly picturesque portfolio of early Russian architecture and craftwork. They were the centre of culture and politics before Moscow became the capital. For more about the Golden Ring and its rich history see the 'Architecture of the Golden Ring' boxed text in the Moscow to Yekaterinburg chapter.

Until June 2001, all of the Trans-Siberian trains passed through Sergiev Posad, Rostov-Veliky and Yaroslavl, which are each covered in this chapter. Now trains head towards the Urals via Vladimir – if your time is limited we recommend you take this route and stop off at Suzdal, the most beautiful Golden Ring destination.

That said, express trains make all the Golden Ring towns accessible on long day or overnight trips from Moscow. However, be selective about which towns you visit – impressive as the numerous religious and historic buildings in these towns are, see too many and you run the risk of becoming 'churched out'.

SERGIEV POSAD
СЕРГИЕВ ПОСАД
☎ 254 • pop 100,000

Home to the evocatively medieval Trinity Monastery of St Sergius, Sergiev Posad (still sometimes called by its Soviet name of Zagorsk), is the obvious half-day trip from Moscow. The monastery, surrounded by stout white walls and towers, was founded around 1340 and is one of Russia's most important religious and historical landmarks.

Since it's only 70km north-east of the capital, there's not much reason to stop overnight here (although there is one good accommodation option). However you could combine a visit to Sergiev Posad and Rostov-Veliky (see later in this section), staying at the latter's Kremlin.

The Sergiev Posad train and bus stations are opposite each other, roughly 250m east of prospekt Krasnoy Armii, the main central street that runs north-south past the easy-to-spot monastery.

There are exchange bureaus and banks near the station and on Krasnoy Armii.

Trinity Monastery of St Sergius

To get the most out of a visit to the Trinity Monastery of St Sergius *(Troitse-Sergieva Lavra; ☎ 4 53 56, prosp Krasnoy Armii; admission to grounds free; open 9am-6pm daily)* it's best to take a tour (available 9am

SERGIEV POSAD
СЕРГИЕВ ПОСАД

PLACES TO STAY & EAT
1 McDonald's
2 Sever
   Север
4 Trapeza na Makovtse
   Трапеза на Маковце
16 Russky Dvorik Cafe/Restaurant
   Русский Дворик
17 Russky Dvorik Hotel
   Гостиница Русский Дворик

OTHER
3 ATM
5 Tsar's Chambers
   Царские Палаты
6 Kalichya Tower
   Каличья Башня
7 Bell Tower
   Колокольня
8 Grave of Boris Gudonov
9 Assumption Cathedral
   Успенский Собор
10 Gate Church of St John the Baptist/Main Gate
   Церковь Иоанна Предтечи
11 Chapel-at-the-Well
   Надкладезная Часовня
12 Church of the Descent of the Holy Spirit
   Духовская Церковь
13 Old Russian Applied Art Section
   Отдел Древнерусского Прикладного
   Искусства (Ризница)
14 Trinity Cathedral
   Троицкий Собор
15 Refectory Church of St Sergius
   Трапезная Церковь Св Сергия
18 Exchange Bureau
19 Bus Station

to 4.40pm daily), which needs to be booked in advance. For photography within the complex requires a $3 permit bought at the gate.

The monastery's most important building is the **Trinity Cathedral** *(Troitsky sobor)*, built in the 1420s over the grave of St Sergius. A memorial service to him goes on all day, every day. The icon-festooned interior, lit by oil lamps, is largely the work of the great medieval painter Andrey Rublyov.

In the centre of the compound is the **Assumption Cathedral** *(Uspensky sobor)*, with its star-spangled blue domes. Outside the west door is the grave of Boris Godunov, the only tsar not buried in the Moscow Kremlin or St Petersburg's SS Peter & Paul Cathedral. Nearby is the baroque **Chapel-at-the-Well** *(Nadkladeznaya Chasovnya)*, built over a holy spring, and the five-tier, wedding cake-like **bell tower**.

The **Old Russian Applied Art Section** *(Otdel Drevnerusskogo Prikladnogo Iskusstva; admission $5; open 10am-5.30pm Tues-Sun)*, in the vestry behind the Trinity Cathedral, houses the monastery's extraordinarily rich **treasury**, bulging with 600 years of donations by the rich and powerful – tapestries, jewel-encrusted vestments, solid gold chalices and more.

For a great view of the whole attractive ensemble head up into the monastery walls and the **Kalichya Tower** *(admission $0.70)*.

Places to Stay & Eat
Russky Dvorik *(☎ 7 53 92, fax 7 53 91, ul Mitkina 14/2)* Singles/doubles with breakfast $45/60. This delightful small hotel, a short walk east of the monastery, is decorated in rustic style but is quite modern. It also has a separate ***cafe/restaurant*** *(☎ 4 51 14, Krasnoy Armii 134)*, that gets overrun with tour groups for lunch but is quite pleasant at other times (try the delicious pancakes).

The touristy restaurant ***Trapeza na Makovtse*** *(☎ 4 11 01, Krasnoy Armii 131)* tends to be rather pricey for what you get. ***Sever*** *(☎ 4 12 20, prosp Krasnoy Armii 141)* is cheaper but the food is as hit and miss as the Soviet-style service. There's also a ***McDonald's*** farther up prospekt Krasnoy Armii.

Getting There & Away
From Moscow's Yaroslavl Station, suburban trains to Sergiev Posad leave every hour or so, taking roughly 90 minutes and costing

just under $1 (Zone 8 if you use one of the ticket machines).

The fastest option is the daily Express train to Yaroslavl departing at 8.32am (1st/2nd class $3/2, 55 minutes) and returning at 7.16pm; tickets for this service need to be bought from the ticket counters.

It is often more convenient to take one of the frequent buses ($1, 70 minutes) from outside Yaroslavl Station, near the statue of Lenin, or from the All-Russia Exhibition Centre (VDNkh), which is on the metro.

To continue to Rostov-Veliky by train you may have to change at Alexandrov. Alternatively try to catch one of the through buses from Moscow to Yaroslavl, many of which stop en route in Rostov.

ROSTOV-VELIKY
РОСТОВ-ВЕЛИКИЙ
☎ 08536 • pop 40,000
After Suzdal, Rostov-Veliky (also known as Rostov-Yaroslavsky) is the prettiest of the Golden Ring towns – a tranquil, rustic place with a magnificent kremlin and beautiful monasteries magically sited by shimmering Lake Nero. Around 220km north-east of Moscow, it is one of Russia's oldest towns, first chronicled in 862.

The train and bus stations are together in the drab, modern part of Rostov. From here it's a direct 1.5km walk south to the kremlin, around which the old town consists mostly of *izbas* (traditional wooden cottages), trees and grassy spaces.

The main post and telephone office is at ulitsa Severnaya 44 is around 1km east of the kremlin. There's no bank but you may be able to change money at the Lion Gift Shop near the old trading arcades next to the kremlin.

Things to See & Do
The unashamedly photogenic **Kremlin** *(☎ 3 12 44; admission to grounds $0.05, around $0.20 for each of the museums or $1.60 for all; open 10am-5pm)*, dominated by the **Cathedral of the Assumption** *(Uspenksy sobor)* just outside its north wall, is Rostov's main attraction. Although established in the 12th century, nearly all the buildings here date from the 1670s and 1680s.

The west gate (the main entrance) and north gate are straddled by the **Gate Church of the Resurrection** *(Tserkov Voskreseniya)* and the **Gate Church of St John the Divine** *(Tserkov Ioanna Bogoslova)*, respectively. Both are richly decorated with 17th-century frescoes. Like several other buildings within the complex these are only open from 1 May to 30 September.

The metropolitan's private chapel, the **Church of the Saviour-over-the-Galleries** *(Tserkov Spasa-na-Senyakh)*, has the most beautiful interior. There are museums filled with icons, paintings and painted enamelware *(finift)*, in the metropolitan's house as well as the **White Chamber** *(Belaya palata)* and **Red Chamber** *(Krasnaya palata)*.

Although you can take bus No 1 or 2 for 1.5km west of the kremlin to the restored **Monastery of St Jacob** (the fairy-tale apparition you'll see as you approach Rostov by road or rail), it's a very pleasant walk there alongside Lake Nero. Heading east of the kremlin, bus No 1 will also bring you to the dilapidated **Monastery of St Avraam**, with a cathedral dating from 1553.

For a great view of the kremlin from the lake, hire a boat (around $2) from near the delightful cafe/craft gallery gallery **Khors.**

Places to Stay & Eat

Dom na Pogrebakh *(☎ 3 12 44, fax 3 15 02)* Rooms $6-11. Right inside the kremlin, this is among the most atmospheric places to stay in Russia. The clean, wood-panelled rooms vary in size and view. All share clean toilets and showers.

Khors *(☎/fax 3 24 83, ul Podozerka 30)* Rooms $6 & $12. A short walk towards the

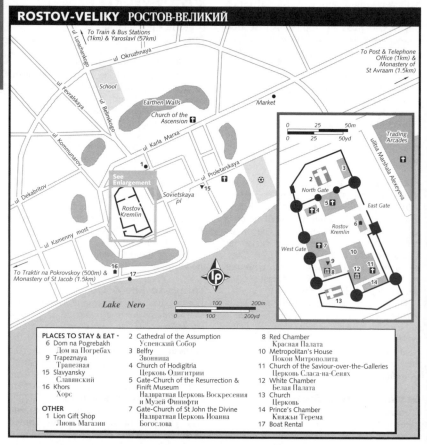

ROSTOV-VELIKY РОСТОВ-ВЕЛИКИЙ

PLACES TO STAY & EAT	2	Cathedral of the Assumption	8	Red Chamber
6 Dom na Pogrebakh		Успенский Собор		Красная Палата
Дом на Погребах	3	Belfry	10	Metropolitan's House
9 Trapeznaya		Звонница		Покои Митрополита
Трапезная	4	Church of Hodigitria	11	Church of the Saviour-over-the-Galleries
15 Slavyansky		Церковь Одигитрии		Церковь Спаса-на-Сенях
Славянский	5	Gate-Church of the Resurrection &	12	White Chamber
16 Khors		Finift Museum		Белая Палата
Хорс		Надвратная Церковь Воскресения	13	Church
		и Музей Финифти		Церковь
OTHER	7	Gate-Church of St John the Divine	14	Prince's Chamber
1 Lion Gift Shop		Надвратная Церковь Иоанна		Княжьи Терема
Лионь Магазин		Богослова	17	Boat Rental

lake as you exit the monastery will bring you to this small gallery and B&B in a two-storey wooden house. If the door is locked, knock at the house to the left. There are two very tiny but clean rooms with shower and kitchen.

You'd be hard pushed to spend over $3 at any of Rostov's restaurants. Inside the kremlin is the unfussy *Trapeznay* restaurant, open 9am to 8pm. *Slavyansky* (☎ 3 22 28, *Sovetskaya pl 8*), 100m east of the kremlin, is a new ritzier place that is locally recommended. *Traktir na Pokrovskoy* (☎ 3 55 74, *ul Pokrovskaya*), around 750m west of the kremlin, is also worth a look.

Getting There & Away

The fastest train from Moscow is the Express service leaving Yaroslavl Station at 8.32am (1st/2nd class $3.50/2.25, three hours). Otherwise try for a ticket on one of the long-distance trains stopping at Rostov en route to Yaroslavl or beyond, or go by suburban train, changing trains halfway at Alexandrov, which takes about five hours.

If you're travelling to/from Yaroslavl, it's much more convenient to take one of the frequently departing buses ($1, 70 minutes).

YAROSLAVL
ЯРОСЛАВЛЬ
☎ 0852 • pop 680,000

The most metropolitan of the Golden Ring towns, Yaroslavl, 250km north-east of Moscow, is a relaxed and generally attractive place. Its wealth of churches, Monastery of the Transfiguration of the Saviour and position along the Volga are the main draws and they all merit an overnight stay.

In 1010, the Kyivan prince Yaroslav the Wise took an interest in a trading post where the Kotorosl River enters the Volga. According to legend, the locals responded by setting a sacred bear on him. Yaroslav killed the bear with his axe and founded a town on the spot, putting both the bear and his weapon on its coat of arms.

Yaroslavl was the centre of an independent principality by the time the Tatars came. Developed during the 16th and 17th centuries as the Volga's first port, it became Russia's second-biggest city of the time, growing fat on trade with the Middle East and Europe. Rich merchants competed to build churches bigger than Moscow's, with bright decorations and frescoes on contemporary themes.

Orientation & Information

Yaroslavl Glavny Station is 3km west of the town centre, between the Volga and the Pervomayskaya ulitsa inner ring road. Most of the major sights are easy walking distance of here, although a few major churches lie south of the Kotorosl River, which forms the southern edge of the city centre.

For information try Intourist (☎ 30 50 58, fax 30 54 13) at the Hotel Yubileynaya. It can provide English-, French- and German-speaking guides.

You can change money at the Sebrbank at ulitsa Kirova 16, open 10am to 5pm daily (closed Sunday). The main post and telephone office is at ulitsa Komsomolskaya 22 on Bogoyavlenskaya ploshchad (opposite the Transfiguration Monastery). It's open 8am to 8pm daily (until 6pm Sunday).

Internet access is available at the post offices at ulitsa Svobody 79 and ulitsa Bolshaya Oktyabrskaya 124 for $1 per hour.

Things to See & Do

The **Monastery of the Transfiguration of the Saviour** *(Spaso-Preobrazhensky monastyr; Bogoyavlenskaya pl; admission to grounds free, museums $0.70 each; grounds open 8am-7.30pm, museums 10am-5pm daily)*, surrounded by white wall and towers, was founded in the 12th century.

Entry is through the **Holy Gate** *(Svyatye vorota)* on the river side. There are several small museums to visit within the grounds, but the most exciting thing to do is climb the **bell tower** *(zvonnitsa; admission $0.70)* for a panorama of the city and a close-up view of the spiked golden bulbs atop the monastery buildings.

West of the monastery, off Bogoyavlenskaya ploshchad, is the red-brick 17th-century **Church of the Epiphany** *(Tserkov Bogoyavlenia)*, covered with bright exterior ceramic tiles, a Yaroslavl speciality. It's now in the process of being restored as a working church. The central **statue** in the square is of Yaroslav the Wise.

Down Pervomayskaya ulitsa, past the 19th-century **Trading Arcades**, is **Znamenskaya Watchtower**, built in 1658 on what was then the edge of the city.

Of the numerous other churches in the old town, the **Church of Elijah the Prophet** *(Tserkov Ilyi Proroka; Sovietskaya pl; admission $0.30; open 10am-5pm daily*

May–Sept) contains some of the Golden Ring's brightest frescoes.

South of the Kotorosl River is the unique, 15-domed **Church of St John the Baptist** *(Tserkov Ioanna Predtechi; 2-ya Zakotorosl-naya nab; admission $0.30; open 10am-5pm Wed-Sun)*, displaying intricate brick and tilework. Take tram No 2 west along Bolshaya Oktyabrskaya ulitsa to prospekt Tolbukhina. Walk across the bridge; the church is on the right, near the river.

The parks and avenues along the Volga and Kotorosl embankments make a pleasant stroll. Beside the Volga you'll find **Yaroslavl Art Museum** *(Yaroslavsky Khudozhestvenny muzey; ☎ 30 34 95, Volzhskaya nab 23; admission $1.25; open 10am-5.30pm Tues-Sun)*, in the elegant old Governor's Mansion

and displaying a fine collection of 18th- to 20th-century Russian art. The museum's extensive collection of **old Russian art** starting from the 13th century is housed farther along the street in the 17th-century **former Metropolitan's Chambers** *(Mitropolichyi palaty; ☎ 72 92 87; admission $1; open 10am-5.30pm Sat-Thur)*.

In the summer, consider taking a short **boat trip** along the Volga to the pretty village of **Tolga**, 35 minutes from Yaroslavl ($0.50). Boats depart irregularly from just beyond the River Station. You can also get there on bus No 21 from Krasnaya ploshchad ($0.10).

Places to Stay & Eat

HOFA (see Places to Stay in the St Petersburg chapter) can arrange *homestays* in Yaroslavl.

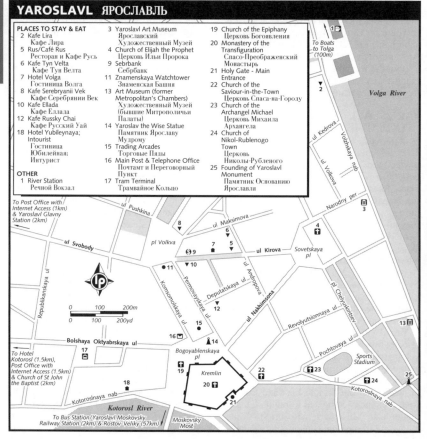

YAROSLAVL ЯРОСЛАВЛЬ

PLACES TO STAY & EAT
2 Kafe Lira
   Кафе Лира
5 Rus/Café Rus
   Ресторан и Кафе Русь
6 Kafe Tyn Velta
   Кафе Тын Велта
7 Hotel Volga
   Гостиница Волга
8 Kafe Serebryanii Vek
   Кафе Серебряний Век
10 Kafe Ellada
   Кафе Еллада
12 Kafe Russky Uai
   Кафе Русский Уай
18 Hotel Yubileynaya;
   Intourist
   Гостиница
   Юбилейная;
   Интурист

OTHER
1 River Station
   Речной Вокзал

3 Yaroslavl Art Museum
   Ярославский
   Художественный Музей
4 Church of Elijah the Prophet
   Церковь Ильи Пророка
9 Sebrbank
   Сбербанк
11 Znamenskaya Watchtower
   Знаменская Башня
13 Art Museum (former
   Metropolitan's Chambers)
   Художественный Музей
   (бывшие Митрополичьи
   Палаты)
14 Yaroslav the Wise Statue
   Памятник Ярославу
   Мудрому
15 Trading Arcades
   Торговые Ряды
16 Main Post & Telephone Office
   Почтамт и Переговорный
   Пункт
17 Tram Terminal
   Трамвайное Кольцо

19 Church of the Epiphany
   Церковь Богоявления
20 Monastery of the
   Transfiguration
   Спасо-Преображенский
   Монастырь
21 Holy Gate - Main
   Entrance
22 Church of the
   Saviour-in-the-Town
   Церковь Спаса-на-Городу
23 Church of the
   Archangel Michael
   Церковь Михаила
   Архангела
24 Church of
   Nikol-Rublenogo
   Town
   Церковь
   Николы-Рубленого
25 Founding of Yaroslavl
   Monument
   Памятник Основанию
   Ярославля

Volga River

To Boats
to Tolga
(100m)

ul Kedrova

Volzhskaya nab

ul Volkova

To Post Office with
Internet Access (1km)
& Yaroslavl Glavny
Station (2km)

ul Pushkina

ul Maksimova

ul Svobody

pl Volkva

ul Kirova

Sovetskaya
pl

Narodny per

Republikanskaya ul

Komsomolskaya ul

Pervomayskaya ul

Deputatskaya ul

Andropova

ul Nakhimsona

pl Chelyuskintsev

Revolyutsionnaya ul

Pochtovaya ul

Sports
Stadium

0   100   200m
0   100   200yd

Bolshaya Oktyabrskaya ul

Bogoyablenskaya
pl

To Hotel
Kotorosl (1.5km),
Post Office with
Internet Access (1.5km)
& Church of St John
the Baptist (2km)

Kremlin

Kotorosl River

Kotoroslnaya nab

Kotoroslnaya nab

To Bus Station/Yaroslavl Moskovsky
Railway Station (2km) & Rostov-Veliky (57km)

Moskovsky
Most

Church of the Epiphany

Hotel Kotorosl (☎ 21 24 15, fax 21 64 68, *e* *kotorosl@yaroslavl.ru, ul Bolshaya Okt-yabrskaya 87)* Singles/doubles $16/26. This is the best-value accommodation in Yaroslavl, within walking distance of the train station and offering modern rooms and quite decent facilities.

Hotel Volga (☎/fax 22 91 31, ul Kirova 10) Singles/doubles from $16.50/26. A great location in the centre of the town is this hotel's best feature. The cheapest rooms have shared bathrooms and are a bit dingy; better to pay a bit more for the renovated ones with their own bathrooms.

Hotel Yubileynaya (☎ 30 92 59, fax 30 29 52, Kotoroslnaya nab 11A) Singles/doubles $29/48. Yaroslavl's top hotel would win no architectural prizes but it does overlook the Kotorosl River and has comfortable rooms. There's a restaurant, bar and business centre with Internet connections.

You'll find several good places to eat along pedestrianised ulitsa Kirova, which in summer fills up with outdoor tables and beer stalls.

Rus/Café Rus (☎ 72 94 08, ul Kirova 10) The cheap traditional cafe downstairs is the pay first, then eat variety, while upstairs it's all Art Nouveau elegance and fine dining

for around $10 per head. The trendier *Kafe Ellada (ul Kirova 11)* is also worthwhile checking out.

Kafe Serebryanii Vek (☎ 32 83 80, ul Trefoleva 1) offers good food in modern surroundings and also has a fancier restaurant upstairs. *Kafe Lira (☎ 72 79 38, Volzhskaya nab 43)* is a popular and pleasant option near the Volga serving a wide range of Russian dishes for $3.

For breakfast or a snack you can't go far wrong at *Kafe Russky Chai (ul Deputatskaya 9)* which serves cheap, tasty pastries and bliny along with the no-frills tea and coffee. For a nightcap our choice is the cost and stylish *Kafe Tyn Velta (☎ 72 92 94, ul Andropova 25).*

Getting There & Away

The main station is Yaroslavl Glavny, about 3km west of the centre of town at the end of ulitsa Svobody. If your train coming into Yaroslavl happens to stop at the lesser Yaroslavl Moskovsky station, 2km south of the Kotorosl River on Moskovsky prospekt, there's no harm getting off there, since transport to the centre is not a problem to organise.

Around eight trains a day run between Yaroslavl Glavny and Moscow's Yaroslavl Station, the fastest Express service making the journey in under four hours (1st/2nd class $4/2.50), the rest taking five hours. Several services depart in the dead of night. There's also a daily service to/from St Petersburg and Nizhny Novgorod.

For Rostov-Veliky (two hours), take one of the infrequent suburban trains to Rostov itself, Beklemishevo or Alexandrov, or catch the more regular buses from outside Yaroslavl Moskovsky station. There are also at least five buses daily from here to Moscow ($4.50, six hours).

Boat During the summer, from early June to early October, the long-distance Volga passenger boats stop every couple of days in Yaroslavl on their way between Moscow ($20, 1½ days) and cities like Nizhny Novgorod and Kazan.

The ships are not very often full and tickets are normally available at short notice. Timetables are displayed at the river station (☎ 27 23 38), which also has an information window.

MOSCOW

MOSCOW

Getting Around

From Yaroslavl Glavny Station to reach the town centre, either take tram No 3 along Bolshaya Oktyabrskaya ulitsa to the tram terminus, a short walk west of Bogoyavlenskaya ploshchad, or trolleybus No 1 along ulitsa Svobody to ploshchad Volkova.

If you want to get etween the bus station and Yaroslavl Moskovsky train station, trolleybus No 5 or 9 from the far side of the main road outside the station will get you to Bogoyavlenskaya ploshchad. All city buses, trams and trolleybuses cost $0.05 per ride.

Title page: Ea series steam locomotive with plaque at Vladivostok station (Simon Richmond).

Top: The P36 series steam locomotive, the most powerful to run on the Trans-Siberian, Severobaikalsk.

Middle: An old Su series steam locomotive forever out of service near Ulan Ude.

Bottom: Another member of the P36 series waits for one last passenger at Taiga.

TRACKS ACROSS SIBERIA: HISTORY OF THE RAILROAD

In the second half of the 19th century, the more advanced industrial states engaged in a world-wide contest for strategic advantage, economic fortune and imperial expansion. The competition took the form of continental conquest. Across Africa, Asia and the Americas, expeditions set off to explore hidden interiors, exploit material riches and tame 'uncivilised' natives. As industrial empires arose, railways became a means to and a symbol of great power and status. The number of miles of laid track and the production of more powerful locomotives became indicators of industrial might, while the exquisite designs of railway stations and great halls became expressions of imperial pomp.

Russia's ambitions turned eastward towards the immense Siberian hinterland and distant Pacific coastline. Russia sought to consolidate existing holdings and to extend her influence in the region. At stake was Russia's claim over the still undeveloped and even undiscovered natural wealth of inner Eurasia. But these ambitions were checked by the Russian state's limited reach across these far-flung eastern territories. Until this time, the distance between St Petersburg and the Pacific was measured in an arduous overland trek or a hazardous sea voyage. The solution was found in the construction of the world's longest railroad, the Great Siberian Railway.

Age of Industrial Empire

Russia was a latecomer to the industrial revolution. Russian society had long been dominated by a bloated autocratic state with close ties to an obsolete, land-owning aristocracy. With industrial entrepreneurs in short supply, the state was compelled to take the initiative in economic innovation, often by granting special concessions to foreign developers.

By the mid-19th century, Russia was slipping from the ranks of Europe's great powers. In 1857, Tsar Alexander II issued a Railway Decree, by which the state determined to reinvigorate the economy's pre-industrial infrastructure with modern railway routes. Between 1860 and 1890, Russia constructed more kilometres of track than any other country except the United States. Railroads connected the central industrial region to the raw materials of the Urals and the agricultural products of the Black Earth region. Moscow became the hub of Russia's rail system, the terminus of nine different lines. This spurt of construction, however, was mostly confined to European Russia. Fear of British encroachment from the Indian subcontinent prompted a Trans-Caspian line, which penetrated deep into Central Asia in the 1880s. Siberia, however, continued to remain a distant and undeveloped land.

In the 1840s, a geological expedition had discovered that the Chinese had left the Amur River region unsettled and unfortified. Shortly thereafter, the tsar appointed the ambitious and able Nikolai Muravyov as the governor general to Eastern Siberia. Unlike his predecessors, Muravyov was not content merely to reap the graft harvest that came with the office. He believed it was Russia's destiny

Russia's Earliest Rails

Russia's first public railway, operating with British-built locomotives, was a 24km line connecting the tsar's palace in St Petersburg to his summer residence in Tsarkoe Selo. It served no particular economic interest. A short industrial line supporting the Urals mining industry was constructed in the 1830s. The Urals line employed the first Russian-manufactured steam locomotives, modelled after an early design by George Stephenson, Britain's locomotive pioneer. In the 1840s, Tsar Nicholas I took ruler and pencil and drew a straight line on a map between St Petersburg and Moscow. The resulting rail connection, known as the Nicholas Railroad, and later as the Red Arrow, bypassed the towns en route.

to develop the Siberian Far East. With the tsar's approval, he collected some Cossacks and cruised the Amur, establishing towns for Russia and provoking fights with China. Preoccupied with foreign encroachment along the eastern seaboard, China was in no mood for hassles over Siberian forests. Thus, without bloodshed, Muravyov was able to redraw the border with China along the Amur River in the north and the Ussuri River in the east in exchange for some cash and a promise of mutual security. At the tsar's request, Muravyov henceforth attached the sobriquet 'Amursky' to his name.

Muravyov-Amursky continued to pursue his vision of Siberian colonisation. He became a leading advocate of a railway that would connect European Russia to the Far East. He attracted a long line of suitors from Russia, England and the United States, offering their own proposals for a railroad to the Pacific. But these petitions went unheeded in St Petersburg, where neither political support nor financial backing was forthcoming. In the last quarter of the 19th century, however, domestic and international events prompted a change in attitude in St Petersburg.

First, Russia's estate economy came under stress in the 1880s. Population growth and bad weather caused widespread famine and led to peasant unrest in the countryside. As a solution to the overcrowded villages and bread shortages, the government considered a policy of migration to the uncultivated lands of western and southern Siberia. The land-owning nobility were persuaded of the policy's merits as reports of pummelled foremen and torched manor houses became more frequent.

Second, in the late 19th century, a regional intelligentsia began to write resentfully about Siberia's colonial status and admiringly about the American west. Regional elites tried to define a distinct Siberian cultural identity, which was rooted in the region's multi-ethnic frontier society. Their words fuelled fears that Siberia might go the same way as the Americas and seek political independence. In response, a consensus formed in Russia's ruling circles that Siberia's radicals and renegades needed to be reined in.

Third, the decline of the Chinese empire provided the opportunity for the great powers to whet their avaricious appetites in the Far East. Russia's vulnerability in the Pacific was made clear as early as the

1850s, when British and French war ships launched assaults on the coastal town of Petropavlovsk during the Crimean War. The opening of the Suez Canal and the completion of the Canadian-Pacific Railway provided the British with easy access to the region. As a result, the 'Great Game', in which Russia and Great Britain vied for strategic leverage along the mountain passes of Central Asia, now spread to the coast of the Far East.

Finally, the most important event was a leadership change. In 1881, Tsar Alexander II was assassinated and succeeded by his son. Alexander II had earned a reputation as the 'Tsar Reformer', instituting sweeping internal changes meant to modernise and liberalise Russian society. Among his most notable reforms were abolishing serfdom and introducing local representative assemblies. By contrast, Alexander III was a political reactionary. He embraced the old regime's ideological pillars: autocracy, orthodoxy, empire. He aspired to rule through a strong centralised state. Much more so than his father, Alexander III embodied the nationalist spirit that infused the Age of Industrial Empire. He was anxious to join the competition for new territorial possessions and he swore to defend Russia's existing claims.

In 1886, Alexander III responded to a petition for support from the governor general of Irkutsk: 'How many reports from Siberian governors have I not read already, and I have to admit with shame and grief that until now the government has done nothing to satisfy the requirements of this rich but neglected region. It is time, high time'. In March 1891, the Tsar officially proclaimed the undertaking of a Trans-Siberian railway, from the Urals to the Pacific, and dispatched his son and heir apparent, Nicholas, to lay the first stone at Vladivostok.

From the Archive

Your Imperial Highness!

Having given the order to build a continuous line of railway across Siberia, which is to unite the rich Siberian provinces with the railway system of the Interior, I entrust to you to declare My will, upon your entering the Russian dominions after your inspection of the foreign countries of the East. At the same time, I desire you to lay the first stone at Vladivostok for the construction of the Ussuri line, forming part of the Siberian Railway, which is to be carried out at the cost of the State and under direction of the Government. Your participation in the achievement of this work will be a testimony to My ardent desire to facilitate the communications between Siberia and the other countries of the Empire, and to manifest My extreme anxiety to secure the peaceful prosperity of this Country.

I remain your sincerely loving
Alexander

Letter from Tsar Alexander III to the Grand Duke Tsarevitch, from the *Guide to the Great Siberian Railway*, 1900

A State within a State

The task of building the Trans-Siberian Railway fell to one of Imperial Russia's most industrious and talented statesmen, Sergei Witte. His rise to the highest levels of state service, given his modest pedigree, was testimony to his skills and shrewdness.

The son of a colonial bureaucrat in the Caucasus and a graduate in mathematics, young Sergei Witte took a job selling train tickets in Odesa for the Southwest Railway Company just as Russia's railway boom got under way. He quickly mastered the logistics and finances of rail transport and was promoted to stationmaster, and then company director. Witte's rare ability to turn a profit from the line and his efficient dispatch of troops during the first Balkans War earned him a post in the central railway administration in St Petersburg. His upward ascent continued with appointments as Minister of Transport and Minister of Finance, probably the most powerful portfolio in the government.

Elite society considered Witte an outsider; his forceful personality and sudden appearance inside the tsar's court was much resented. But in Alexander III he had a most admiring patron. Moreover, Witte genuinely shared the tsar's vision of a Trans-Siberian Railway, describing it as 'one of the largest and most important undertakings of the 19th century, not only for the Motherland, but for all the world'.

Witte was entrusted by the tsar with overseeing the pedestrian details underlying his imperial vision. The Trans-Siberian Railway was no ordinary project and, thus, was not left to the ordinary process. The Siberian Railway Committee, a special panel with enhanced powers, was created to override the inevitable bureaucratic obstacles. At Witte's urging, the tsar named his son Nicholas to head the Committee. In so doing, Witte was able to exert influence on and curry favour with the 23-year-old tsarevitch.

As work progressed, the Committee's scope expanded. It assumed responsibility for peasant resettlement to Siberia, diplomatic relations in the Far East and security forces along the route. In a jealous pique, the minister of foreign affairs remarked that Witte had built his own 'state within a state'.

For decades, proposals for a transcontinental railway had been quashed by frugal finance ministers. But that situation changed once the post was occupied by Witte, a devout Keynesian (even before Keynes!). After months of wooing the Rothschilds, they suddenly pulled out to protest Russian anti-Semitic legislation. Alexander, meanwhile, was swayed by the argument of economic nationalists, who warned against foreign participation in a project of such great strategic value. Witte was forced to raise money from a lean domestic economy.

Witte implemented a host of financial policies and manoeuvring to raise the necessary funds, including issuing bonds, raising taxes and taking out foreign loans. Finally, he set off a wave of inflation by printing extra roubles to cover the soaring construction costs. 'Better to lose money than prestige', he explained to the concurring tsar.

The Trans-Siberian also provided Witte with the opportunity to play diplomat, when he proposed to build a 560km shortcut across Manchuria, rather than follow the northern bend in the Amur to

Vladivostok. Already besieged with foreigners, the Chinese emperor rejected this indignity.

A determined Witte changed tactics. He bought the influence of senior Chinese statesmen, offered a generous loan to the close to bankrupt Chinese government and repackaged his proposal to look like a Chinese-Russian joint venture. The result was an 80-year lease agreement over a corridor of territory for the railway. The Manchurian diversion led to the formation of the East Chinese Railway Company and the Russo-Chinese Bank, which were both in fact fronts for the Russian Ministry of Finance.

In 1898, Witte negotiated further territorial concessions, allowing Russia to build a Southern Manchurian line to a warm-water outlet at Port Arthur (Dalian), on the southern tip of the Liaodong Peninsula. The minister of finance, in effect, became the tsar's chief envoy to the Far East.

Witte was truly a character of historic magnitude. He saw himself as Russia's Cecil Rhodes, an empire builder, and the Trans-Siberian Railway gave him the opportunity to realise this ambition.

Working on the Railroad

Construction on the railway got under way almost immediately after the tsar's decree was issued in 1891. Perhaps the biggest question concerning the route had already been decided: the railway would forge a path across southern Siberia. Beginning at Chelyabinsk, in the southern Urals, the line would run parallel to the old post road as far as Irkutsk. Then it would blaze an iron trail eastward through the untamed Baikal, Amur and Ussuri regions to Vladivostok, the eastern terminus on the Pacific.

This route was selected out of consideration for the south's warmer weather conditions and more arable lands, which would hopefully encourage new agricultural settlements. The chosen route caused the industrialists and merchants to seethe, since it bypassed many larger mining colonies and river towns in the north. The line was later altered to accommodate these influential economic lobbies by including Perm, Yekaterinburg and Tyumen.

Right: Built in 1902 and styled on an old Russian fort, Yaroslavl Station in Moscow marks the start of the Trans-Siberian Railway.

JOHN S KING

Building the world's longest railroad across a formidable landscape posed ongoing challenges of engineering, supply and labour. The railroad cut through thick forests, crossed countless rivers, scaled rocky mountains and traversed soggy quagmires. Work brigades were poorly outfitted. The heavy work was carried out using shovels and picks, while horses and humans did the hauling.

The builders had to keep the workers supplied with huge quantities of stone, timber and iron as well as with necessary food and fodder. Maintaining supply lines in Siberia's unsettled hinterland required the utmost resourcefulness.

No ready labour supply existed for this immense project. Workers were recruited, or conscripted, from all over the empire as well as from abroad. They toiled from dawn to dusk in sweltering heat and freezing cold. They endured bouts with deadly disease, forest bandits and even hungry tigers.

The construction work was divided into seven territorial segments, starting simultaneously from the eastern and western terminus points.

Western Siberian 1892–96

From Chelyabinsk in the west, it ran through Omsk and on to the Ob River, the site of present-day Novosibirsk. The western Siberian section was 1440km long and the easiest to build. For the engineers, the main

SIMON RICHMOND

Left: Yenisey railway bridge, almost a kilometre in length, spans the Yenisey River.

challenge was to span the many rivers that fed the Ob Basin. The crossings for the Irtysh and Ob Rivers both required the building of bridges that were almost 1km long. The region did not suffer from a shortage of materials or labour. The free peasants of western Siberia willingly enlisted in the work brigades, although many disappeared during harvest season.

Central Siberian 1893–98

The central Siberian section covered a distance of 1920km from the Ob through Krasnoyarsk and on to Irkutsk, west of Lake Baikal. The work of the engineers became more complicated on this leg, because of the mountainous terrain and the steep river valleys. The Yenisey River required a steel bridge nearly a kilometre in length. The earth – frozen until July and then swampy after the thaw – was less than ideal for digging. Water from the drained bogs collected in stagnant pools, which bred swarms of bloodthirsty mosquitoes around work sites.

Supply and labour now became chronic problems. Unlike the plains, the line ran through forests with few settlements to tap for workers or provisions. The builders advertised throughout the empire, offering higher wages and bonuses to entice fresh forces. The shortage of skilled labour required for the stonework was especially acute.

Ussuri 1891–97

Meanwhile, construction was under way in the east on the Ussuri section of the railway. Beginning in Vladivostok, the line ran northward through the Ussuri River Valley to Khabarovsk, a distance of about 800km. The forest terrain was more difficult for the engineers. Moreover, after the first tracks had been laid, it was discovered that the Amur rose as much as 10m during the spring, which meant redrawing the route and starting again. The builders faced severe labour shortages in this remote corner of the Far East. Despite initial misgivings, the construction brigades recruited over 8000 workers from the local Korean population and migrant Chinese labourers, over one-half of the total work force for this section. They received lower wages than the Russian workers because, the foremen said, their work was inferior (though it might have been that they did not run tabs in the company canteen).

The builders of the Ussuri line introduced convict labour to the railroad, when 600 prisoners destined for incarceration on Sakhalin Island were instead ordered to start digging. Some prisoners escaped from their inexperienced handlers and went on a local crime spree. The project as a whole eventually employed nearly 15,000 convicts and exiles, with far better results. Many brigade foremen praised their contribution. Convicts, in turn, could work time off their sentences and the living conditions were a small improvement over the tsar's prisons.

Circumbaikal 1901–04

Heading east from Irkutsk, the builders encountered their most formidable obstacle, Lake Baikal – 640km long, 100km wide and nearly a mile deep. No previous experience prepared the engineers for the frigid lake's steep rocky cliffs, which dominated the shoreline.

JOHN S KING

While the engineers sorted out the logistics, a ferry line – modelled after a similar crossing on the Great Lakes in northern Michigan – was implemented as a short-term solution. Two heavy British-built ice-breakers were pressed into service, one shuttling passengers and the other hauling the train itself. In the meantime, construction commenced on a railroad, skirting the southern edge of the lake. The project was overseen by VA Savrimovich, a highly regarded engineer and surveyor.

The Circumbaikal was a world-class engineering marvel. The line was literally carved out of rock and held up by extensive and elaborate masonry work. The Circumbaikal consumed four times as much stone as the entire Transbaikal section. Workers chiselled 33 tunnels into the lake's craggy capes and erected over 100 bridges and viaducts above its rivulets and falls. Some tunnels required more than two years of painstaking digging. For additional information on the Circumbaikal railway line, see that section in the Krasnoyarsk to Irkutsk & Lake Baikal chapter.

TransBaikal 1895–1900

The TransBaikal section ran from the eastern shore of Lake Baikal past Ulan Ude and Chita, then on to Sretensk on the Shilka River. For the engineers, this section of 1072km of dense forest was nearly as daunting as the Circumbaikal, and would prove more frustrating. The railroad had to scale the Yablonovy Mountains, rising 5630m above sea level. The rivers were not so wide, but they ran in torrents and cut steep valley walls. The tracks were laid on narrow beds along high mountain ledges. Dynamite was used to dig deeper into the permafrost to erect sturdier supports. Harsh weather including summer droughts and heavy rains exacerbated the difficulties. The great flood of 1897 washed away over 300km of laid track and 15 completed bridges.

Amur 1907–16

The 2080km-long Amur section presented similar engineering, supply and labour challenges. It required some of the longest and

Left: The icebreaker *Angara*, once used to ferry Trans-Siberian passengers across Lake Baikal before the railway line was built around it in 1905, now rests near Irkutsk.

most complicated bridges, including a span of almost 2km across the Amur. The builders relied heavily on convict labour, supplemented by army units and Chinese migrants. Building materials, including iron rails, had to be imported from British and North American suppliers.

The Amur was the last section of the Trans-Siberian to be built, going into operation only in 1916. The railway's first travellers transferred into boats at Sretensk for a long river voyage down the Amur to Khabarovsk, where they could reboard the train. Later travellers bypassed the Amur, when the railway was diverted through northern China.

East Chinese 1897–1901

In 1894, Russia secured the agreement from the desperately weak Chinese empire that allowed for a Manchurian section of the Trans-Siberian Railway. From Chita, the 1440km-long East Chinese Railway turned south-east, crossing the Argun River and rolling through Harbin on its way to Vladivostok. It sliced over 600km off the journey. Chinese officials had insisted on a narrow gauge to fit their existing rail system, but after a one-sided negotiation the Russian wide gauge was chosen. The terrain of flat steppe lands, wide mountain passes and fertile river valleys elated the exhausted builders.

The problems that arose during construction of the East Chinese line were political rather than practical. In 1899, having suffered repeated indignation and intimidation, Chinese nationalism mobilised into a rancorous antiforeigner movement, the self-proclaimed 'Fists of Higher Justice'. Better known as the Boxer Rebellion, the movement quickly spread to Manchuria and the Russian-controlled railway. Stations and depots were set ablaze, 480km of track were torn up and besieged railroad workers took flight. The line was only able to return to service after the Russian military intervened.

For state leaders, time was of the essence, so the work brigades pressed on, driving a modern wedge into an ancient wilderness. Despite the many obstacles, construction proceeded apace. In August 1898, the first train rolled into the station at Irkutsk, two years ahead of schedule. In the same year, the line between Vladivostok and

Right: Obelisk commemorating the 10th anniversary of the building of the Trans-Siberian Railway, Irkutsk.

SIMON RICHMOND

Khabarovsk went into operation. In 1900, service began on the Trans-baikal section. At this point, a train journey across Siberia was possible, although supplemented in stages by water transport. The completion of the Amur line in 1916 represented the possibility of travelling exclusively by rail from St Petersburg in the west to the Pacific entirely within Russian territory.

Riding the Rails

The Trans-Siberian Railway was introduced to the world at the Paris Exhibition in 1900. Visitors to the Russian pavilion were treated to visual images of Siberia's pristine rugged landscape and exotic native cultures. They were also impressed by the luxuriously decorated mock-up wagon displays. The 1st-class sleepers offered comfortable and commodious compartments. The dining car enticed visitors with caviar, sturgeon and other Russian delicacies. The exhibit featured a handsome smoking car, a music salon with piano, a well-stocked library, a fully equipped gymnasium and a marble and brass bath. The exhibit also boasted that the Trans-Siberian would shave off 10 days from the present travel time of five weeks from London to Shanghai. Here was elegance and efficiency, provided in inimitable Russian style.

The personal accounts of early travellers suggest that the actual journey did not live up to its advance billing. Although 1st-class accommodation was comfortable enough, most of the other promised indulgences were underwhelming, to say the least. East of Baikal the train routinely ran out of food and had to stop once a day at small stations en route. 'Today we did not eat until 3pm, and then it was vile', wrote one cranky American traveller in 1902. 'There was one wretched little eating room filled with Russians. You may stand around and starve for all they care.'

In addition, the Trans-Siberian did not succeed in providing a more expeditious route to the Far East. The hastiness that went into construction was exposed in operation. Travellers experienced frequent delays, sometimes lasting days. The Trans-Siberian had the highest accident rate of any other line in the empire. Ties splintered, bridges buckled, and rails warped. The locomotives chugged along at no more than 25km/h because of the risk of derailment at higher speed. One Beijing-bound passenger scribbled in resignation: 'A traveller in these far eastern lands gradually loses his impatience and finally ceases to care whether his train goes fast or slowly, or does not go at all. Certainly we have been two hours at this station for no apparent reason.' (This sentiment may ring true even for travellers today.)

A principal goal of the railway was to facilitate the resettlement of European Russia's rural inhabitants, in the hopes of easing social tensions and offering economic opportunities. In the 1800s, the tsar had officially lifted restrictions on internal migration and opened up Siberia for colonisation. Between 1860 and 1890, less than 500,000 people moved to Siberia. But once the train came on line, the population's eastward drift turned into a raging torrent.

Between 1891 and 1914, over five million new immigrants settled in Siberia. Station halls were packed with hundreds of waiting peasants sleeping on the floor. Third-class fares were kept low so that ordinary subjects could ride the rails. One could travel for more than 3200km on the Trans-Siberian for less than 20 roubles. These wagons dispensed with any pretension of style or comfort. A 1st-class rider observed: 'The 3rd-class passengers are packed like sardines. Their cars hold nothing save wooden bunks, two tiers thereof, and each has four and some- times six. One's health would certainly be jeopardised by a passage through them. I notice that our car is constantly guarded. I am not sur- prised, and do not object in the least.'

War and Revolution

Alexander III saw the Trans-Siberian Railway as the means by which the Russian empire would act as a great power in the Far East. Under his less able successor, Nicholas II, the construction of the railway instead provoked confrontations that exposed the manifold weak- nesses of imperial Russia. The railway and railroad workers played prominent supporting roles in the tumultuous political events that subsequently toppled the tsarist autocracy and brought radical social- ism to power in the early 20th century.

The Russo-Japanese War

The East Chinese Railway involved Russia in the multilateral dismem- berment of the Chinese empire. In the subsequent grab for territorial and commercial concessions in Manchuria, Russia came into direct conflict with imperial Japan. Witte was always inclined towards diplo- macy in Russia's Far Eastern policy, but Nicholas fell under the sway of more adventurous advisors. 'What Russia really needs', the Minister of Interior opined, 'is a small victorious war'.

The Tsar's aggressive stance in the Far East provoked Japan to attack Port Arthur in February 1904. The overconfident Nicholas was dazed by the rapid string of defeats in the field. Japanese forces quickly seized the advantage over Russia's outnumbered troops, while the reinforce- ments remained stalled at Lake Baikal. The single-track, light-rail Trans- Siberian was simply overwhelmed by the demands of war. The tsar dispatched his prized Baltic fleet. In May 1905, the war concluded when – upon reaching the Tsushima Straits – the fleet was annihilated in just one afternoon. Nicholas summoned Witte to salvage Russia's dignity in the peace negotiations. Under the Treaty of Portsmouth, Russia agreed to vacate southern Manchuria, but managed to hold on to the East Chinese Railway.

The 1905 Revolution

Russia's woeful performance in war unleashed a wave of protest at home. The reactionary impulses of the regime were fully displayed in January 1905 when peaceful demonstrators, led by an Orthodox priest, were shot down in front of the Winter Palace. The 'Bloody Sunday' massacre did not quell the unrest, but instead incited more people to take to the streets. Among the most radical participants in the 1905 Revolution were the railroad workers.

Like most Russian workers, railroad employees laboured under harsh conditions, received scant wages and suffered tyrannical bosses. Unlike other sectors, however, the railroad workers could paralyse the economy by going on strike. The government maintained a special railway police force, 8000 strong, which spent its time intimidating labour organisers.

Railroad workers were quick to join the protest movement, as 27 different lines experienced strikes in the first two months of 1905. In April, they coordinated their efforts by forming an All-Russia Union of Railroad Workers. At first, they demanded economic concessions, such as higher wages and shorter hours, but soon their demands became more political, such as the rights to organise and strike.

The government attempted to impose martial law over the railway system. The railway union responded by calling for a total shut-down of service. The strike started in Moscow, spread to every major railway line and sparked a nationwide general strike. The movement only subsided after the tsar issued the October Manifesto, which promised to reform the autocracy into a constitutional monarchy.

The Bolshevik Revolution

Radical railroad workers also played a crucial role in the Bolshevik Revolution of 1917. Exhausted by its involvement in WWI, the tsarist regime lost its will to rule and fell to street demonstrators in February 1917. Nicholas' abdication created a power vacuum in the capital. The liberal provisional government hesitated to make decisions or end the war, which swung public sentiment towards the more radical political parties.

In an attempt to restore order, General Kornilov ordered his troops at the front to march on St Petersburg, with the intention of declaring martial law. Radicals and liberals alike took cover. But Kornilov's men never made it. Railroad workers went on strike, refusing to transport them, and the putsch petered out. Within weeks, Lenin and the Bolsheviks staged a palace coup, deposed the provisional government and declared themselves rulers of Russia.

SIMON RICHMOND

Left: Colourful Lenin mural at Krasnoyarsk station.

The Russian Civil War

The Bolsheviks' claim on power was soon challenged. In the spring of 1918, as the war in Europe continued without Russia, a legion of Czech prisoners of war attempted to return home to rejoin the fighting. Unable to cross the front line in the west, they headed east. Along the way, they provoked a confrontation with the Bolsheviks. When the White Army, hostile to the Bolsheviks, came to the immediate support of the Czechs, Russian civil war was under way.

The Czech legion seized control of the western half of the Trans-Siberian Railway; in the meantime, the Japanese, who had landed in Vladivostok, took control of the railway east of Baikal. A separatist Siberian Republic was formed in Omsk, that is, until the tsarist naval officer Admiral Kolchak overthrew the Omsk government and proclaimed himself supreme ruler of Siberia. Another former tsarist general reigned over the East Chinese Railway in Manchuria. Cossacks menaced the Transbaikal and Amur regions. Siberia had returned to the era of warlords.

It took the Bolsheviks more than three years to secure complete control over the Trans-Siberian and to establish Soviet power across Siberia. Kolchak was arrested, tried and shot for his less-than-sterling performance as supreme ruler.

The Development of Siberia

The construction of the Trans-Siberian Railway was intended to foster industrial development in Siberia. As such, an engineering and technical school was founded in the city of Tomsk, to become Siberia's first university. Scores of factories, mills and mines sprung up along the route to feed the railroad's huge appetite for iron, bricks and lumber. However, Siberia's fledgling industries could not keep pace with the growing demand.

The project served as an economic stimulus for other regions. The mining and metal works in the Urals became the chief supplier of iron and steel. The sprawling manufacturing works around St Petersburg and Moscow were contracted to supply the rolling stock. By 1905, over 1500 locomotives and 30,000 wagons had rolled out of Russian factories. At the same time, the railway system as a whole employed over 750,000 workers involved with engines and rolling stock, traffic management, track maintenance and administration. Higher wages, as much as 50% above the norm, attracted railway employees to the Trans-Siberian line.

After coming to power, Russia's new Soviet rulers were committed to rapid industrial development. To meet this goal, they needed to gain wider access to Siberia's plentiful raw materials. Thus, they invested heavily in upgrading the Trans-Siberian Railway. A second track was built alongside the original single line. The light rails were replaced with heavier, more durable rails. Wooden bridges and supports were replaced with iron and steel. Working conditions on the railway did not improve much under the new socialist regime, but railway workers were now extolled for being in the vanguard of the industrial proletariat.

In the 1930s, the Soviet regime launched a state-managed campaign of industrialisation, in which large-scale projects in Siberia figured

SIMON RICHMOND

prominently. The Kuznets Basin became a prodigious supplier of coal, coke, iron and steel.

At the same time, the paranoid and vengeful Soviet dictator, Josef Stalin, was engaged in a 'class war' against his own citizens and comrades. The victims of Stalin's terror who were not shot were sent to forced labour camps. Siberia's industrial revolution was built on the backs of millions of imaginary 'enemies of the people'.

In WWII, Nazi Germany's blitzkrieg invasion was an unintended impetus for Siberia, when the industrial stock of European Russia was hastily evacuated to safer interior locations. During the German occupation, the Trans-Siberian Railway served as a lifeline for Soviet survival. It furnished the front with the reinforcements and equipment that eventually wore down the formidable Nazis.

In the 1950s, Siberian development was energised by the discovery of oil and gas. While these deposits were in the north, they promoted development in the cities along the railway, such as the oil refinery in Omsk and the chemical plant in Irkutsk.

Soviet development policies changed the face of Siberia. As industry moved east, so did the population. In 1911, Siberia recorded about nine million inhabitants; by 1959, the number had increased to nearly 23 million. In the postwar period, Stalin's reform-minded successor, Nikita Khrushchev, denounced his former boss and liberated millions of labour-camp inmates.

Meanwhile, incentive-laden offers lured new workers to the region. The population of Siberia became highly skilled and urban based. A uniquely planned, elite academic community was created near Novosibirsk. Military industry flourished in secret cities, sheltering well-tended scientists and technicians. By 1970, thirteen Siberian cities had populations of 250,000 or more, eight of which were located along the railway.

During this time, Siberia's indigenous populations were increasingly assimilated into the lifestyle and culture of Soviet Russian society. In 1900, native peoples accounted for more than 15% of Siberia's total population but, by 1970, the number had fallen to less than 4%.

An ugly side of Siberian development was – and continues to be – widespread ecological degradation. Obsessed with fulfilling production

Left: Built in 1940, the grand Novosibirsk Station, is the largest on the Trans-Siberian Railway and a popular halfway stop for passengers.

SIMON RICHMOND

plans, Siberian managers showed little regard for the harmful practices of their factories. As a result, the major industrial areas in the Kuznets Basin, Irkutsk and Krasnoyarsk, have since been declared environmental catastrophes, with irreparably damaged soil and water. Lake Baikal served as a receptacle for raw waste, discharged from paper mills and towns along its shore. In the 1970s, a scheme was concocted to divert the waters from the Ob River into a 1000km canal, which would replenish the exhausted Aral Sea Basin in Central Asia. The river-diversion project aroused the indignation of Siberians, who organised a protest movement in response. The project was finally cancelled in 1986.

Branching Out

The Soviet regime intended to further develop overland access to the Eurasian continent so that travellers could reach ever more remote corners of the Far East. The construction and operation of branch lines throughout the Far East were entangled in the politics of the region for most of the 20th century.

The Trans-Manchurian

The Trans-Manchurian line connects Beijing to the Trans-Siberian at Chita, via the Russian-built East Chinese and South Manchurian Railways. The South Manchurian, however, fell to Japan as a spoil of war in 1905. At this time, the American railroad baron, EH Harriman, made several generous bids to buy these routes from their respective operators. He saw a rare opportunity to realise his ambition of building a railroad line that circumnavigated the globe. Harriman's offers, however, were rebuffed.

In 1922, China persuaded Soviet Russia – which was weakened by war and revolution – to renegotiate the status of the East Chinese Railway between Vladivostok and Port Arthur (Dalian). The Soviet government renounced its special economic privileges in Manchuria and agreed to joint custody of the railway. As Manchuria was the scene of an ongoing power struggle, the Russians had to continuously defend their (partial) claim to the railway line. During the 1920s, the Russian

Right: The stark, grey stone facade of Zima Station.

managers were arrested by a Manchurian warlord and again by Chiang Kaishek, both of whom seized control of the railroad. In each case the aggressors were forced to relinquish their prizes and prisoners. In 1932, the Japanese took control of Manchuria, renaming it Manchukuo and installing the last Manchu emperor, Puyi, as a puppet ruler. Under pressure, Russia sold her interest in the East Chinese Railway to the new rulers in 1935.

This was not the end of the line, however. According to the secret protocols negotiated at Yalta, Churchill and Roosevelt conceded back to Stalin the East Chinese and South Manchurian rail lines, as part of the price of Soviet entry into the Pacific War. Russia's return to Manchuria was brief; the lines were given back to China in 1952 as a goodwill gesture to its new communist regime.

Ironically, geopolitics proved stronger than ideology. In the 1960s, relations between China and Russia worsened, and the border was closed. Since the 1980s, however, Russian-Chinese relations have warmed considerably, which has allowed the Trans-Siberian to be reconnected to the Trans-Manchurian.

The Trans-Mongolian

The 2080km Trans-Mongolian line was built along the route travelled by the ancient tea caravans, from Beijing through Mongolia to Ulan Ude. The line was built piecemeal, a direct result of fluctuations in the Russian-Chinese relationship.

During the late 19th century, Mongolia was formally part of the Chinese Manchu empire. After centuries of neglect, China's officials became more interested in the region at this time, much to the irritation of the Mongols. Plans were made to construct a railroad from Beijing to Örgöö (Ulaan Baatar). Instead, the Chinese empire collapsed in 1911.

Mongolia was eager to be rid of its Chinese overlord but was too weak to fend for itself. Russia conveniently emerged as a protective patron of Mongolian independence. The Soviet Union consolidated its influence in 'independent' Mongolia with the signing of agreements on economic and military cooperation. In 1936, a short rail route was announced, linking Mongolia to Soviet Buryatia, whose peoples shared close ethnic ties. This line between Ulan Ude and Naushki was completed in 1940. In 1949, it was extended to the capital, Ulaan Baatar.

In the early 1950s, relations between the Soviet Union and communist China relaxed a bit, allowing the Chinese to finally begin work on the long-planned railroad connecting Beijing to Ulaan Baatar. Although train service began on this line in 1956, the Sino-Soviet split in the 1960s closed the border. Like the Trans-Manchurian, the Trans-Mongolian line was reopened in the 1980s.

The Turkestan-Siberian

The Turkestan-Siberian (Turk-Sib) connects the Trans-Siberian to Central Asia. From Novosibirsk, the 1680km line heads south over the Altay Mountains and across the Kazakh steppe to Almaty. The line was first planned in the last years of the tsarist empire, when the initial segment of track was laid between Barnaul and Semipalatinsk. It was not completed, however, until the Soviet period, after Stalin made the Turk-Sib one of the more prominent construction projects of the first five-year plan.

The route was opened in 1931. The railway was built to facilitate the exchange of Central Asian cotton for western Siberian grain. This trade would keep the looms busy in the textile factories of the north, while the import of cheap food would free up more land for cotton cultivation in the south. The construction of the Turk-Sib was also meant to stimulate industrial development in the region, hence its nickname, 'the Forge of the Kazakh Proletariat'. The project was featured in a classic example of socialist-realist cinema by Soviet film director Viktor Turin in 1929.

In 1996, newly independent Kazakhstan took over its section of the line for a state-managed railway firm. From the southern terminus at Lugovaya, the line extends to Chimknet in western Kazakhstan and to Bishkek in Kyrgyzstan.

The Baikal-Amur Mainline

The 4300km Baikal-Amur Mainline (Baikalo-Amurskaya Magistral, or BAM) begins west of Irkutsk and passes north of Lake Baikal on its way east to the Pacific coast. Work was begun on this second Trans-Siberian line in the 1930s. It was abandoned in WWII and stripped so its tracks could be used to lay a relief line to the besieged city of Stalingrad. In 1974, the project was resumed with much fanfare. Hailed as the 'Hero Project of the Century', the call went out to the youth of all the Soviet Union to rally to the challenge of constructing the BAM. The response is evident from the names of towns along the line: Estbam, Latbam and Litbam, so called for the young workers from the Baltic states who built them.

The BAM was badly mismanaged. Instead of a construction chief, 16 different industrial ministries organised their own separate work teams with minimal coordination. By 1980, 50% of the managers had been replaced for 'unsatisfactory work'. The project employed 100,000 workers, including 20,000 communist youth league 'volunteers'. Lacking housing and electricity, few workers re-enlisted and others simply deserted.

The BAM epitomised the best and worst of Soviet industrialisation. It blazed a trail through inhospitable climate and terrain, providing access to the region's mineral-rich basins. The BAM towns expanded with the new railway, which was being forced through virgin wilderness. Overcoming Siberia's swamps and mountains, its seemingly infinite number of rivers and, in particular, its vast swathe of permafrost pushed the cost of the project to a staggering US$25 billion (the original Trans-Siberian is estimated to have cost the equivalent of $500 million).

Officially opened in 1991, the line still isn't finished. Although it is possible to travel the whole length of the BAM, from Tayshet to Sovetskaya Gavan on the Pacific coast, one section is bypassed by a temporary line that is particularly susceptible to landslides. The final Severomuysk tunnel is anticipated to be completed within the next few years. In any case, there is very little traffic on the line and many of its settlements have become ghost towns.

The Trans-Korean

A new branch line is tentatively planned for the future. The Trans-Korean line, from Seoul in the south to Wonson in the north, would re-create the old Kyongwan Railway, from the early 20th century. The line would connect with the Trans-Siberian at Vladivostok, establishing an overland rail route between the Korean Peninsula and Central Asia and Europe.

A small but significant step forward was taken in September 2000, when North and South Korean leaders agreed to restore a short train service across the world's most heavily fortified border. To promote the project, North Korean leader Kim Jong Il made a much publicised junket on the Trans-Siberian in the summer of 2001. In Moscow, Kim met with Russian President Putin, and they announced that the Trans-Korean was 'entering the stage of active development'.

Siberia in Transition

After decades of overbearing central control, the fall of the communist regime in 1991 ignited a spontaneous diffusion of power across Russia's regions. This process was accelerated by Russian President Boris Yeltsin, who, in looking for allies in his feud with Mikhail Gorbachev, urged regional leaders to 'take as much sovereignty as you can swallow'.

Kim's Big Trip

The most notorious Trans-Siberian traveller during the northern summer of 2001 was undoubtedly Kim Jong Il, the leader of the Democratic People's Republic of Korea (otherwise known as North Korea). Travelling in his own 21-carriage armoured train, fully equipped with a global positioning system and Internet connections and an entourage of 150 bodyguards and officials, Comrade Kim was retracing his father's 1984 journey from Pyongyang to Moscow.

The beloved leader's paranoia about security caused a monumental disruption all along the Trans-Siberian route, with trains being stopped and stations closed as Kim passed through. So while President Putin was welcoming the world's last Stalinist dictator with open arms, his fellow Russians were fuming over train delays and cancellations. Muscovites in particular were incensed that their weekend *dacha* trips were thrown into chaos when Yaroslavl Station was closed down on a Friday evening.

Apart from an in-principle only agreement to extend the Trans-Siberian Railway route through to North Korea and onwards to South Korea, the visit revealed a few tantalising personal details about the famously secretive Kim. In St Petersburg, the governor Vladimir Yakovlev let slip that Kim had been to Russia before with his father in 1959. Kim also took a particular shine to Baltika beer, overstaying his visit to Russia's top beer factory by an hour and leaving with several cases of the product for the trip home. No doubt to wash down his favourite food – roasted 'heavenly cow' – otherwise known as donkey.

Celebrating the Trans-Sib Centenary

While crossing Russia you won't fail to notice the posters, plaques and stickers at stations and on trains celebrating the centenary, in 2000, of the Trans-Siberian Railway. But given that there are several dates that could qualify for the 100th anniversary of the route's operation, what exactly is the significance of 1900?

We asked Valeria Burkova, custodian of the Museum of History of the Far Eastern Railway, and received this frank reply: 'It's nothing to do with history, only politics. It was a government decision that we should celebrate the centenary in 2000. The real anniversary should be in either August 2003 *when the first regular passenger services started* or 2004 *after the completion of the Circumbaikal line.*'

Then again some historians would go for 1916 when the Amur bridge at Khabarovsk was opened, thereby completing the route still used by trains today. So will these dates be commemorated too? 'Of course,' says Valeria, 'The Russian people love celebrations.'

Poster at Ilanskaya Station commemorating the arrival of the railway.

In Siberia, these dramatic events rekindled the separatist spirit. Siberian Accord, a confederation of regional political actors, was founded in Novosibirsk in 1991. Resentful of Moscow's grabbing hand, they were determined to wrest control of Siberia's natural resources away from central-government ministries. President Yeltsin, a former regional governor himself, defused the conflict through a negotiated compromise, by which Siberia's regions were granted greater political autonomy and a larger share of the region's wealth. His successor, Vladimir Putin, however, has pursued an policy of gradual recentralisation.

In some ways, post-communist Siberia has come to resemble the 'Wild Wild East' of olden days. The privatisation of state property has given rise to a new breed of economic adventurer. Those who have succeeded in gaining control over Siberia's prized natural resources have reaped great fortunes.

As in the old days, this new economic elite has close connections to political power, using influential patrons to secure lucrative concessions and special privileges. Siberia's regional governors openly defy the Kremlin's edicts and pillage the local economy for private gain. The retail trade and service sector is dominated by gangsters and racketeers who engage in periodic turf wars for control over supply and distribution networks.

Meanwhile, the bankrupt state can no longer provide for the region's industrial, military and academic communities. Wages and pensions go unpaid, heat and electricity are turned off. Outlying towns and villages have been abandoned for lack of food. As a result, people are now leaving Siberia in droves.

The Trans-Siberian Railway has been centre stage in the regional transition of postcommunist Russia. Most dramatically, embittered Siberian coal miners laid across the tracks and held up train services for days during 1998, forcing the government to pay back wages owed. On a more positive note, the major cities along the railway, which were closed even to Soviet citizens, have been opened and integrated into the new post-Soviet Siberia. In foreign affairs, the improvement in Russian-Chinese relations has re-opened the border in the Far East. The old Trans-Siberian link to Manchuria has been re-established and now supports a thriving business in cross-border petty trade and smuggling.

Some things, however, never change. For reasons of national security and public service, the Trans-Siberian Railway remains a state-managed monopoly, for better or worse. It continues to be one of the busiest railway lines in the world. Most importantly, the Trans-Siberian endures as the vital lifeline for the people of Siberia.

READING BETWEEN THE LINES:
LITERATURE OF THE TRANS-SIBERIAN

Norbert Schürer

Siberia

When you ride the Trans-Siberian Railway, chances are there will be moments when it is too dark to look out the window, when the landscape becomes too monotonous, or when conversation with your fellow travellers is simply no longer stimulating. One way to spend these times is to take the opportunity to learn about the history, culture and literature of the peoples of the vast territories to your north and south – from books.

Siberia Today

Of course, many people have taken a trip on the Trans-Siberian Railway before you, and some of them have written down their experiences. The best of these travelogues is Colin Thubron's *In Siberia*, where in addition to travelling along the route of the Trans-Siberian Railway, Thubron takes detours to places such as the Entsy village of Potalovo near the Arctic Ocean and Magadan on the Sea of Okhotsk. To some extent, his journey is rather depressing, showing a population let down by communism, but unable to develop an alternative, and nature on the verge of an ecological catastrophe. But at the same time, Thubron meets extraordinary and inspiring individuals such as a group of elderly ladies at a restored monastery or a shaman in Tuva's capital Kyzyl, the centre of Asia. Also appropriate reading for a Trans-Siberian journey are Thubron's earlier works *Among the Russians* and *Behind the Wall*.

In *Siberian Dawn: A Journey Across the New Russia*, Jeffrey Tayler paints an even bleaker picture of Siberia. The Russian-speaking author decided to fly east to Magadan and make his way back to Poland by bus and train, through some pretty hair-raising situations. But even worse, all he can find among the people he encounters is alcoholism, organised crime and despair. In spite of this gloom, Tayler's account is readable because he concentrates less on the big picture and more on evocative details and personal experiences.

One of the first Westerners to travel extensively in Siberia after the collapse of the Soviet Union was Friedrich Kempe, who tells the story of his trip down the Ob River in *Siberian Odyssey: A Voyage Into the Russian Soul*. Kempe presents excellent vignettes of his visits to Kemerovo, where US labour activist Big Bill Haywood tried to found a worker's utopia in 1921, to Yurga, where Stalin exiled many of the so-called Volga Germans in 1941, and to Baidaratsky Bay, where Nentsy herders run a reindeer farm the size of the Netherlands.

One of the classics of travel along the Trans-Siberian Railway is Paul Theroux's *The Great Railway Bazaar: By Train Through Asia*, in which the last chapter is devoted to the Trans-Siberian. Ten years later, he returned to Asia in *Riding the Iron Rooster: By Train Through China*, travelling on the Trans-Mongolian as well as Trans-Manchurian routes. Theroux himself praises another classic account, Eric Newby's 1978 *The Big Red Train Ride*. During the reign of Brezhnev, Newby and his wife Wanda spent eight days on the railway with a government guide and a photographer. Even earlier, Peter Fleming spent time on the

133

Trans-Siberian Railway in 1933 as a correspondent for the *London Times*, an experience he recounts in *One's Company*. Fleming's anecdote of a crash on the railway remains particularly vivid.

Histories of Siberia

In addition to these travelogues, descriptions of Siberia from a historical or cultural perspective are available. James Forsyth's *A History of the Peoples of Siberia: Russia's North Asian Colony 1581–1990* is the most comprehensive book on Siberian history, though because it is an academic book you might not find it an easy read. Forsyth places particular emphasis on the 20th century, where he investigates the impact of Soviet Stalinism, Siberia in the 1980s and the bearing these developments have on individual Siberian tribes. Similarly, Victor Mote's *Siberia: Worlds Apart* does cover the area's prehistory briefly, but soon moves into the 20th century. Mote's short book is vivid because of its pictures, graph and maps, and because the author is not afraid to include personal anecdotes.

The most visually stunning volume on contemporary Siberia – though large enough to take up significant room in your luggage – is *The Peoples of the Great North* by ethnographers Valentina Gorbacheva and Marina Federova. This book has interesting essays on nature, indigenous life and shamanism in Siberia (also discussed in *Riding Windhorses* by Sarangerel and in *Entering the Circle* by Olga Khartidi). It offers the best available list of indigenous peoples with numbers, locations, lifestyle, religion and language – but unfortunately no map to place them. The volume's real strength is its gorgeous and well-reproduced pictures, which come in three categories: contemporary scenes of nature and culture; cut-outs of native artefacts such as clothes, carvings and religious objects; and photographs of indigenous life from the early 20th century.

In *Siberian Survival: The Nenets and Their Story*, authors Andrei Golovnev and Gail Osherenko concentrate on the particular tribe. They conclude that the Nenets, like many other indigenous people, have been successful in resisting Russian and later Soviet attempts to 'modernise' them because of a special combination of nomadic lifestyle, economic autonomy and a minimalist and antimaterial ethic – all of which are constantly under threat.

Along the Route

While these books look at Siberia as a whole or at individual tribes, others consider particular aspects, locations or events. Most obviously pertinent is Steven Marks' *Road to Power: The Trans-Siberian Railroad and the Colonization of Asian Russia*, the definitive account of the building of the railway. Marks summarises the historical context around 1890, when plans were first made to develop such a route, covers the bureaucratic debates surrounding the building of the railway and narrates the actual construction. He argues that political concerns over the competition with China and Korea in the Far East played as much of a role in the success of the Trans-Siberian Railway as the economic interest in developing Siberia.

Early in your trip from the west, you will pass through Yekaterinburg, formerly known as Sverdlovsk. In April and May of 1979 at least 66 people died here from a mysterious illness. It soon emerged that the cause of death was anthrax, the deadly biological weapon that has recently become notorious again. In *Anthrax: The Investigation of a Deadly Outbreak*, Jeanne Guillemin painstakingly reconstructs the catastrophe, down to pinpointing the location of the victims at the time of the accident and showing how the anthrax was spread through the air from its origin at the nearby military installation Compound 19.

A more pleasant, and intentional, experiment was the community of Akademgorodok outside Novosibirsk. Here, academics founded a utopian city in the late 1950s with the goal of being able to do research unfettered by politics and bureaucracy. However, as Paul Josephson argues in *New Atlantis Revisited: Akademgorodok, the Siberian City of Science*, the city lost its privileged status when political support failed and the USSR encountered economic difficulties as early as the late 1960s.

With *Lost in the Taiga*, Russian journalist Vasily Peskov presents the amazing story of a family of 'Old Believers' – Orthodox Christians who disagreed with the modernisations instituted by Patriarch Nikon in 1653 and sided with Archpriest Avvakum instead – who had refused to follow civilisation for many generations. Because of the increasing encroachment from Soviet authorities, the Lykov family moved to an inaccessible valley in the Altay Mountains south of Krasnoyarsk in 1945 and did not have any contact with other human beings until 1982, when they were accidentally discovered by geologists doing research in the area. At that time, the Lykovs still spoke a 17th-century Russian dialect, wore birch-bark shoes and had not heard of space travel or even cars. Today, Agafia, the last remaining family member, lives in a 140,000-hectare 'reserve' intended to keep tourists as well as scientists out. Peskov's book is absolutely fascinating in its human portraits of strong individuals who make conscious choices to reject certain aspects of modernity.

Past Irkutsk, you will reach Ulan Ude, the surprising home of supermodel Irina Pantaeva. In *Siberian Dream*, Pantaeva, who is a member of the Buryat people, spends most of her time trying to get away from her home; still her bizarre story – from designing her own clothes in a small Siberian fashion factory, getting training in Vladivostok and moving to Moscow, Paris and New York, where she acted in Woody Allen's *Celebrity* – is inspiring.

Siberian Village presents a description of the tiny village of Djarkhan in the Sakha Republic west of Yakutsk. Author Bella Bychkova Jordan's mother was herself a native of the village, while Bella's husband and co-author Terry Jordan-Bychkov is only the sixth foreigner ever to visit Djarkhan. The book offers a geographical description of the area as well as a cultural history divided into pre-Soviet, Soviet and post-Soviet times. It is particularly touching because of the author's personal involvement. Probably the most surprising fact to emerge from *Siberian Village* is how little impact the successive waves of Russians, Christianity and communism had on life there.

Towards the end of the eastward trip on the Trans-Siberian Railway, you will pass through Birobidzhan, which Thubron describes as 'a conventional Siberian settlement'. However, the town has a questionable past as the centre of Stalin's answer to the 'Jewish question'. As Robert

Weinberg describes in *Stalin's Forgotten Zion*, the Russian ruler tried to establish a (voluntary) homeland here for the Jews of his country as an alternative to Palestine. While officially Birobidzhan is still Jewish, these days Jews make up only a small minority of the citizens – the rest have emigrated after all.

Early-20th-Century Siberia

While the Trans-Siberian Railway with its completion in 1916 is relatively new, travellers have been following routes similar to yours, from Moscow to Vladivostok, for a long time. In 1890, for instance, Russian playwright Anton Chekhov decided to investigate the situation on Sakhalin Island in the Sea of Okhotsk, which Russia had acquired from Japan in 1875 and turned into an immediately notorious penal colony. He recounted his arduous journey through Yekaterinburg, Irkutsk and Omsk, which took 2½ months by sled and carriage, in dispatches to the journal *New Times* and later collected in *From Siberia*. On his return Chekhov produced the treatise *Sakhalin Island*, an in-depth but dispassionate description of the trip and the conditions on Sakhalin. These two works, as well as some of the letters Chekhov wrote on his way, are collected in *A Journey to Sakhalin*.

Among the works Chekhov himself read in preparation for his journey to Sakhalin Island was a series of articles published beginning in 1888 by the American journalist George Kennan. Sponsored by *The Century*, Kennan produced 25 articles beautifully illustrated with black-and-white drawings (available today at Cornell University's 'Making of America' Web site at ⓦ cdl.library.cornell.edu/moa) in which he indicted the exile system and attacked the ruling tsarist government. These essays, which were later collected in *Siberia and the Exile System* and shaped US public opinion about Russia at least until WWI, were of course immediately banned in Russia, but continued to circulate in underground translations.

Also around the start of the 20th century, several scientific expeditions surveyed the country north of Vladivostok. In 1917 Viktor Arseniev, a geographer on three of those expeditions, wrote a book inspired by his native guide *Dersu the Trapper*, a member of the Nanai (Gold) tribe. *Dersu*, a mixture of fact and fantasy, is a kind of combination of Lewis and Clark with the Leatherstocking tales and chronicles the surprisingly tender crosscultural friendship between the Russian and the Nanai. The fascinating narrative is driven not by a plot but by the rambling movements of the surveying company across the countryside, observing flora and fauna through the ravages of nature, and by Dersu's intimate knowledge of the land, which he imparts in pidgin Russian/English. The book was turned into a movie, *Dersu Uzala*, in 1976, by Akira Kurosawa.

Siberian Folklore

The population of Siberia generally falls into two categories: indigenous people such as Dersu, and western Russians, who come as exiles looking for economic opportunities or to distance themselves from the rest of the world. The latter group can further be divided into those who give up and those who turn their banishment into a source of strength and inspiration (such as the Lykovs). Both exiles

Right: Iurii Rytkheu, dramatises his Chukchi people's confrontation with modernity.

and indigenous people have turned their experiences into fiction that you can include in your reading material for your trip on the Trans-Siberian Railway.

The oldest form of native literature, folk tales, are collected by James Riordan in *The Sun Maiden and the Crescent Moon*. Riordan distinguishes between tales of creation, tales of spirits and everyday life and animal tales in his informative introduction, but does not make this distinction in the body of the text. The 40-odd fascinating tales come from peoples as far west as the Saami on the Kola Peninsula and as far east as the Chuckchi in north-eastern Siberia.

Kira van Deusen has begun the challenging task of collecting the tales of the Tuva and other Siberian people on the border to Mongolia and Manchuria and so far has produced three slim but significant volumes through her publishing company, Ugadan Books. *Fox Mischief* is a short cycle of stories involving Solika the Fox and *Shyaan am!*, which literally means 'This now!', and is an invitation to tell stories, includes eight tales from the Tuvan people. But most impressively, van Deusen has translated and retold the Tuvan epic *Woman of Steel*, the almost-feminist story of Kang-Kys, the woman of steel, who has to fight evil-doer Shoi-Togus to regain her birthright as a warrior and ruler. The book is illustrated with drawings by Tuvan artist Alexei Sedipkov. If you are interested in the Tuvans, whom Thubron calls 'a sturdy people with high, burnished cheeks – trim women and crop-haired men', you should try to watch the Oscar-nominated documentary *Genghis Blues* on the uniquely Tuvan vocal technique of throat-singing.

Indigenous Literature

In addition to this folklore, authors from various indigenous peoples of Siberia have begun to write 'literature' in the Western sense in recent decades. Unfortunately, very little of this work – which is usually composed in the authors' native languages or in Russian – is available in English. Chukchi Iurii Rytkheu (1930–) has been writing since 1950, but apart from the short-story collection *Stories from Chukotka* none of his work has been translated into English (though most of his novels are available in German). Nivkhi Chuner Taksami has contributed to art history catalogues that also only exist in German. The Khanty Yeremei Aipin is the author of the novella *I Listen To the Earth* and is also prominent as a political activist. His article 'Not By Oil Alone' (*International Work Group for Indigenous Affairs Newsletter*, 1989) is an impassioned plea to allow his people to preserve their culture. The short story 'About That For Which There Is No Name' by Nenets author Anna Nerkagi (1952–), in the mostly nonfiction anthology *Anxious North*, is an allegorical vision of the decline and corrupted state of the native people, framed by a plea from the narrator not to let the vision come true.

MW

Among the many other indigenous writers are the Yukagir Semyon Kurilov, who wrote the novel *Khanido and Khaleka*, the Chuckchi poetess Antonina Kymytval, the Nivkhi novelist Vladimir Sangi (*Kevongy's Wedding*), the Yukagir Teki Odulok, the Mansi poet Yuvan Shestalov and the Nanai historian and author of a Nanai-Russian dictionary, Sulungu Onenko. Unfortunately, in order to read any of these, you will have to learn Russian at the very least.

Russian Literature on Siberia

Fortunately, there are also plenty of Russian writers who have made Siberia the topic of their work and many of these have been translated into English. The most famous of them is certainly Boris Pasternak (1890–1960), Nobel Prize winner in 1958, who set large parts of his masterpiece *Doktor Zhivago* in the Far East. Pasternak's hero finds refuge in the Ural Mountains but is sent to Siberia as a physician in the civil wars following the October 1917 Revolution. *Zhivago* is not so much an indictment of the Soviet system as a panorama of life in Russia in the first 35 years of the 20th century.

One hundred years earlier, Fyodor Dostoevsky (1821–81) received a sentence of four years in a Siberian labour camp. He fictionalised his experiences in the novel *The House of the Dead*, supposedly the autobiography of a Russian farmer sent to Siberia. In this book, Dostoevsky emphasises the individual's need for freedom and shows how the penal system degrades and dehumanises prisoners as well as guards. Thubron thinks Siberia allowed this author to experience 'a half-mystical reconciliation with the peasant Russian people'.

About the same time, Vladimir Korolenko (1853–1921) was exiled to the Amga region for refusing to sign an oath of allegiance to Tsar Alexander III. Korolenko went on to defend indigenous people such as the Udmurt (some of whom were on trial for ritual murder) in journalism and to write 'Siberian' stories collected in *Makar's Dream*. Korolenko also wrote a novel based on his visit to the US, *In a Strange Land*, in which the Russian protagonist searches for his sister's husband, who has run away to America.

Two centuries earlier, the Orthodox archpriest Avvakum (1620–82) – the same one whom the Lykovs still follow – was one of the first victims of the Siberian exile system. As a young man, Avvakum resisted the changes Patriarch Nikon was instituting such as crossing oneself with three rather than two fingers, was imprisoned several times and ultimately exiled to Siberia. During his final spell in jail, Avvakum wrote his *Life*, the first Russian spiritual autobiography and arguably the first work in the genre of prison writing. Avvakum describes the natives of Siberia – he travelled at least as far east as Lake Baikal – as heathens and barbarians, but

TC

also occasionally as kind and helpful. His Russian compatriots were hardly any nicer, though, executing him in 1682.

Writing in Exile

Of course, the most brutal system of Siberian penal colonies was not instituted until Stalin's time, when many authors found themselves in exile for supposed anticommunist behaviour or writings. As a young man, Dimitry Stonov (1892–1962) became friends with Vladimir Korolenko, and perhaps inspired by this connection, dared to resist the Soviet system. To continue his literary work in a labour camp near Krasnoyarsk, Stonov removed tobacco from cigarettes and then scribbled stories on the cigarette paper in a tiny script. These stories, which contrast the betrayal and loneliness of the prison camps with the transcendence of the human spirit, are available as *In the Past Night: The Siberian Stories*.

Similarly, Varlam Shalamov (1907–82) was exiled to Siberia, where he spent 16 years as a prisoner and then as a 'free' worker. He survived probably only because he became a paramedic, recording his experiences in a series of over 150 short stories, *Kolyma Tales*. In contrast to Stonov, Shalamov finds absolutely no redeeming features in prison life, but dwells on the atrocities and the savagery. Nevertheless, he does not seem to condemn any of his characters, but presents them with an eerie, detached moral neutrality reminiscent of Chekhov.

Because of the Nobel Prize in Literature he received in 1970, Alexander Solzhenitsyn (1918–) is the most prominent of the authors who spent time in exile in Siberia. His novel *One Day in the Life of Ivan Denisovich* draws on Solzhenitsyn's own experiences to describe the hardships and struggles in a typical day in the life of a prisoner innocently jailed in a Siberian camp. Other works with thinly veiled autobiographical backgrounds are the novels *The First Circle* and *Cancer Ward* and the nonfiction, seven-part *The Gulag Archipelago*, which led to his exile from the Soviet Union entirely.

Siberian Authors

As much as you can criticise the Soviet Union for its treatment of Siberia and use as a penal colony, it did bring education to many people who in previous generations would have remained illiterate. For this reason, Siberia itself has produced numerous and innovative writers in the last 50 years – writers whose background is Russian rather than native, ie, who are the descendants of individuals who moved to Siberia voluntarily or in exile in earlier times.

Sergei Zalygin (1913–2000), for instance, was born in the Ufa Province in the Ural Mountains, lived in Barnaul in the Altay Mountain region and studied in Omsk. In his most ambitious novel, *The Commission*, Zalygin interweaves realism with legend and philosophical speculation in the story of an honest peasant in the village of Lebyazhka destroyed by his environment during the Civil War. However, Zalygin's greatest influence perhaps came through his editorship of the literary magazine *Novy Mir*, which he used to challenge the Soviet authorities.

Left: The prison-camp experiences of Fyodor Dostoevsky had a profound impact on his beliefs and writings.

Viktor Astafiev (1924–) was born in Krasnoyarsk and published his first collection of short stories in 1953. His novella *Queen Fish* deals with the ecological destruction perpetrated not only by individual poachers, but by industrial pollution – one of the first 'green' books in Russian literature. The first volume of a trilogy about a group of Siberian soldiers during WWII, *The Cursed and the Dead*, was published in Russia in 1992. Unfortunately, today Astafiev is associated more with his nationalist and anti-Semitic political stance than with his writing.

Vasilii Shukshin (1929–74), from Srostki in the Altay region, is sometimes counted as part of the Village Prose movement, a group of writers who attempted to portray rural Russia with respect and almost nostalgia. His novel *Snowball Berry Red* combines this approach with a comedic portrayal to tell the story of a criminal who half-heartedly tries to start a new life after his release from prison. The novel was ground-breaking for its depiction of Russian criminality and the underworld and hugely influential through a 1974 film version which starred Shukshin himself. *Stories from a Siberian Village* collects short stories – which many critics consider Shukshin's strongest form – from throughout Shukshin's career for an English audience.

Yevgeny Yevtushenko (1933–) hails from the Irkutsk region. Poet, prose writer and actor, Yevtushenko is most famous for his narrative poem *Winter Station*, which tells the story of a poet's return to his birthplace, Zima Station, from Moscow. The poem has narrative as well as philosophical parts that address subjects such as growth, youth and truth, and is mostly composed in iambic pentameter. Yevtushenko has also written 'Babi Yar', one of the few literary treatments of a Russian massacre of Jews in Kyiv in 1941, which provided the text for a Shostakovich symphony and the novel *Wild Berries*, also set at Zima Station.

Aleksander Vampilov (1937–72) from Kutulik attended Irkutsk University and died an untimely death in a boating accident on Lake Baikal. In his plays, Vampilov attacked the new Soviet bureaucrats for their egoistical and materialistic stance. His most famous drama *Duck-Hunting* is structured around flashbacks of the main character Zilov, who begins and ends the play with preparations for the hunt. In between, he examines the relationships with and between his friends, which are characterised by mutual insults, ruthless provocation and insincere opportunism.

Valentin Rasputin (1937–) is the most prominent contemporary Siberian author. He was also politically active as a member of Gorbachev's presidential council, but his impact has been marred by his association with ultranationalist causes. Rasputin's novel *Farewell to Matyora* is the final and best work of the Village Prose movement. It follows three generations of Russian peasants in Matyora in the weeks before the destruction of their village by flooding because of a new hydroelectric dam. The novel deals with the death of the village, of Russia and of nature, and it questions the psychological impact of modernisation, ending with a wonderfully ambiguous scene in the fog among the rising waters. Almost as important is Rasputin's earlier novel *Live and Remember*, which tells the story of a couple at the end of WWII; a deserter who has to live across the river outside the village where his wife is trying to survive. In addition to his fictional work – which more recently has taken an antimodernist bent, attacking contemporary Russian youth for their embrace of Western values in works such as *Siberia on Fire* – Rasputin is also the author of the only work on Siberia by a Siberian native, *Siberia, Siberia*. In agreement with most outsiders, Rasputin worries about the ecological future of his homeland, making the destruction of Lake Baikal the centrepiece of his book.

Mongolia

South of the Trans-Siberian Railway, where the Trans-Mongolian Railway branches off, lies the mysterious, mystical and mythical country Mongolia, home of spiritual shamans, of restless nomads and of Chinggis Khaan. Long almost impossible to reach for political reasons, the country is slowly moving towards democracy and opening up to the West. It also offers you a body of literature quite distinct from books about Siberia.

Travel Writing

The most recent traveller to write about her time in Mongolia is Canadian Jill Lawless, who describes her stay in *Wild East: Travels in the New*

Right: Chinggis Khaan has inspired travellers through the ages to follow in his footsteps and record their adventures in Mongolia.

Mongolia. Lawless acutely – and frequently in hilarious detail – observes the efforts of the country to make it on its own, and the struggles of resilient individuals in that process. One anecdote, for instance, offers the description of a marmot barbecue where 'the carcass is stuffed with hot rocks, inserted through the anus, and a blowtorch is used to burn off the fur'. The cover of Lawless's book, showing a satellite dish next to a traditional *ger* (nomad's tent), is a perfect expression of past and future meeting in Mongolia today.

Stanley Stewart, author of *In the Empire of Genghis Khan*, retraced the journey of medieval traveller William of Rubruck, 1600km on horseback in a 8000km trip from Istanbul to Mongolia. Stewart argues that the lives of Mongolian nomads have changed little since Rubruck's time and that Soviet culture has made few inroads. He believes that the combination of physical movement and cultural stasis explains the persistence of customs in Mongolia.

British adventurer Benedict Allen's beautifully illustrated *Edge of Blue Heaven: A Journey Through Mongolia* is the companion volume to Allen's BBC TV series on the country. In the company of reindeer, camels and horses, Allen spent five months in Mongolia, sliding from calamity into catastrophe. Coming from Siberia, he travels along the western border of the country and the Gobi Desert, ending up at the Trans-Mongolian Railway near the Chinese border.

Don Croner concentrates on the northern part of the country in *Travels in Northern Mongolia*. The three sections of the book narrate the search for the source of the Yenisey-Angara-Selenga River system, which drains into Lake Baikal; the visit to sites associated with Zanabazar (1635–1723), the first Bogd Gegen – a reincarnated Buddhist spiritual leader similar to the Dalai Lama – of Mongolia; and a trip to the 'Three Rivers Region' that, according to *The Secret History of the Mongols* (see the History, Culture and Folklore section later), is the people's birthplace.

Nick Middleton's *The Last Disco in Outer Mongolia* compares Mongolia before and after 'opening' in a wonderful mix of laugh-out-loud comic scenes and historical background.

John DeFrancis' *In the Footsteps of Genghis Khan* describes a journey that took place in the mid-1930s, when, as an interpreter, DeFrancis accompanied a military historian researching the Mongolian conquest of China. Moving by camel, raft and train, they were on the road (or river or railway) over five months, encountered temperatures up to 60°C (140°F), met Chinese communists on the Long March and travelled along the Silk Road. About the same time as DeFrancis, Henning Haslund was travelling in Mongolia. He recounts his classic adventures in *Men and Gods in Mongolia* and *In Secret Mongolia*.

Medieval Travellers

Even earlier, travellers throughout the middle ages had also come to Mongolia for trade, religion or adventure. Most famously, of course, you probably know about Marco Polo taking up his family's tradition of trade with the East and spending four years at the court of the Mongolian ruler Kublai Khan in his summer residence Shang-tu (Coleridge's Xanadu) and his winter home Ta-tu (today's Beijing) between 1271 and 1295. However, it remains unclear to what extent his book, known in Italian as *Il milione* (literally, *The Million,* and metaphorically perhaps *Tall Tales*) and in English simply as *Travels of Marco Polo*, is a truthful account or the inventions of a self-aggrandising traveller.

Earlier, the French Franciscan friar William of Rubruck had visited the Great Khan in Karakorum – the ancient capital on the Orhon River in northern Mongolia – on an informal mission from Louis IX of France from 1253 to 1255. However, his *Journey of William of Rubruck to the Eastern Parts of the World* was overshadowed by Marco Polo's work.

Similarly, another Franciscan monk, Giovanni Da Pian Del Carpini, had been sent to the Mongol empire on an official mission from the Pope in 1245. Travelling over 4800km on horseback in about 100 days, Del Carpini witnessed the official election and enthronement of the new khan Güyük. Unfortunately, his report *Historia Mongalorum Quos Nos Tartaros Appellamus* (History of the Mongols Whom We Call Tartars) was not available in full until 1839.

In the other direction, the Chinese priest Rabban Sauma seems to have been the first Asian to visit Western Europe on a pilgrimage supported by Kublai Khan around 1275. While his own writings are hard to come by in English, there is a book by Morris Rassabi, *Voyager from Xanadu*, that summarises and contextualises his amazing story.

History, Culture and Folklore

The Mongolians have their own account of their origins in *The Secret History of the Mongols*, a text originally written in the 14th century that combines a biography of Chinggis Khaan with the story of the formation of the Mongol Empire. Paul Kahn's translation also includes an introduction, maps, genealogical charts and 'The Death of Chingis Khan', a passage from a 17th-century elegy. In *The Mongols*, David Morgan presents a historical study of the 12th to 14th centuries, when the Mongol 'hordes' conquered the entire world – from China to Europe – in a matter of generations and disappeared with equal speed. Morgan relies on sources such as *The Secret History of the Mongols* as well as the accounts of Rubruck and Del Carpini to give the most comprehensive story of the Mongols in this period.

Martha Avery spent time in Mongolia in the early 1990s and collected a series of fascinating interviews in *Women of Mongolia*. She discerns the themes of continuity, change and resilience in almost all interviews, but this commonality obscures the amazing variety of her subjects – from Inkhe, a beautiful young lady holding her baby giving the recipe for marmot roast (take out the stomach immediately, or the animal will bloat, but wait till it puffs up on the fire, which shows it is ready), to Tumen, a palaeoanthropological scientist who is just beginning to use DNA analysis to investigate the origins of the ancient nomadic population. Avery's fantastic volume includes black-and-white pictures of the subjects as well as images of their activities.

Finally, examples of the ancient oral tradition of the Mongolian people are collected by Hillary Roe Metternich in the gorgeous *Mongolian Folktales*. The first tale appropriately recounts 'How Storytelling Began Among the Mongol People'. The stories themselves are well worth reading, but the spectacular original papercut illustrations by Mongolian artist Norovsambuugiin Baatartsog make the book an absolute must. For

'The Four Friendly Animals,' for instance, Baatartsog shows the elephant (with a butterfly sitting on his trunk) on a different level from the monkey, hare and dove (who are gesticulating as if talking), all framed by the trunk and leaves of a fruit-bearing tree, the grass meadow and a decorative design; all are beautifully cut from a single piece of paper. Metternich classifies the stories into five groups – 'those about animals, those about magic and especially the magical horse, those about domestic affairs, satirical tales and, lastly, tales about relations between man and nature or about the origins of nature' – which should cover all aspects of your trip along the Trans-Siberian Railway.

TRANS-SIBERIAN

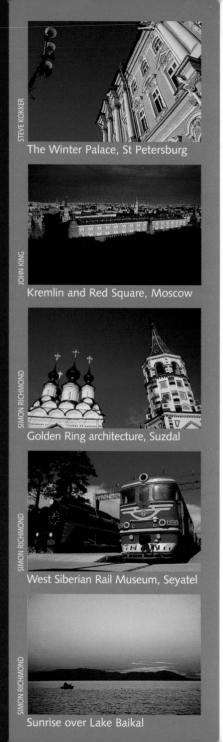

The Winter Palace, St Petersburg

STEVE KOKKER

Kremlin and Red Square, Moscow

JOHN KING

Golden Ring architecture, Suzdal

SIMON RICHMOND

West Siberian Rail Museum, Seyatel

SIMON RICHMOND

Sunrise over Lake Baikal

SIMON RICHMOND

TRANS-SIBERIAN
Did you know?

- The world's largest country, Russia covers 17.1 million sq km. Mainly flat, the country rises slightly in the Urals, which mark the border between European Russia and Siberia. On a Trans-Sib journey possibly the most impressive geographical feature you'll pass in European Russia is the 3690km Volga River, Europe's longest waterway.

- There are over one million lakes in Siberia, the largest of which is Lake Baikal, the world's deepest, holding nearly one-fifth of the planet's fresh water.

- January night temperatures on the Trans-Siberian route average -20°C to -25°C, with cold snaps to -35°C – spring comes in late April or May. July and August temperatures average 15°C or 20°C and can reach 30°C.

- Siberia and the Russian Far East include some of the northern hemisphere's most polluted rivers, swathes of dead taiga and air around some industrial towns that is so defiled that you'll never need tinted windscreens. Russia's navy dumped nuclear waste in the Sea of Japan and the Arctic Ocean. Multinational logging concerns, in partnership with Russia, are queuing up to clear-fell the Siberian forests and Lake Baikal was once a dump for waste products from pulp and paper companies.

- Most of Russia's 145 million people are ethnic Russian. There are scores of small ethnic groups – many in Siberia – with their own languages, traditions and religions. The Buryats, mostly living near Ulan Ude, is the largest indigenous group. Other minorities include Tatars, Yakuts, Tuvans, Evenki and Nentsy.

Moscow to Yekaterinburg

The Route

Moscow to Vyatka (Kirov)

Since June 2001, all Trans-Siberian trains have taken a new eastern route out of Yaroslavl Station, through Moscow's grey suburbs and sylvan satellite communities of *dacha*, towards **Vladimir** (191 km), where there's a 20-minute stop. As you approach Vladimir look out for the golden spires and domes of the Assumption Cathedral (see the boxed text 'Architecture of the Golden Ring'), high on the embankment to the north.

Cast your gaze northward as you pull out from Vladimir for a glimpse of the 12th-century monastery complex at **Bogolyubovo** (200km), then do a quick turn to the south-facing window to see the beautiful Church of the Intercession on the Nerl, sitting in splendid isolation at the confluence of the Nerl and Klyazma Rivers.

There is a stop (12 minutes) at **Nizhny Novgorod** (441km), Russia's third most populous city, where the station is still called by the city's Soviet-era name Gorky. Services to Kazan run south from Nizhny Novgorod, via **Arzamas II** (562km).

The *Rossiya* and other services to Siberia, China and Mongolia all head north-east from Nizhny, crossing the mighty Volga River about a kilometre outside the station. You'll then chug along past the farmland and taiga of Gorkovskaya oblast towards **Kotelnich** (869km), the junction with the old Trans-Siberian route westwards towards Yaroslavl. Here the time is Moscow time plus one hour.

Moscow time + 0100

Just outside Kotelnich the train crosses the Vyatka River, a meandering 1367km waterway that gives its name to Vyatka (956km) which is also called Kirov, its old Soviet title, on train timetables. There's a 15-minute stop here, but little reason to get out and explore other than to stretch your legs or to search the kiosks for supplies.

Vyatka (Kirov) to Perm

Yar (1126km) is the first town you'll pass through in the Udmurt Republic, home to the Udmurts, one of Russia's four major groups of Finno-Ugric people. Around here

Highlights

- Wander through the fairy-tale Russian landscape of Suzdal.
- Explore Nizhny Novgorod's kremlin and its charming museum of wooden architecture.
- Cruise down the Volga to the serene Makariev Monastery.
- Discover Islamic Tatar culture in the ancient capital of Kazan.
- Enjoy the gentle scenery of the Urals on the approach to Perm.

the countryside becomes picturesque with plenty of pretty painted log cabins to be spotted. At **Balyezino** (1192km) there's a change of locomotive during the 19-minute halt.

At **1221km** the route crosses the Cheptsa River. About 40km after **Cheptsa** (1223km), the junction for the line to Perm from Kazan, you'll cross into Perm oblast and the foothills of the **Ural Mountains**, which stretch 2000km from Kazakhstan to the Arctic Kara Sea. The mineral-rich, densely wooded Urals rarely break 500m above sea level in this area, so it's difficult to actually *tell* you're in a mountain range. Still with increasing glimpses above the pine and birch forests across verdant rolling landscapes, this is one of the more attractive sections of the Trans-Siberian route.

Around **Vereshchagino** (1314km), a station named after the great late 19th-century painter VV Vereshchagin, turn forward your watch as local time becomes Moscow time plus two hours.

Moscow time + 0200

Crossing the broad Kama River (1432km) you'll see the industrial city of Perm (1434km) where trains make a 15-minute stop. There's a green and red steam locomotive on the northern side of the train as you pull into the station.

From **Kungur** (1535km) the railway follows the Sylva River. The crucial thing to keep an eye out for beyond here is the **Europe-Asia Border Obelisk** (1777km), a

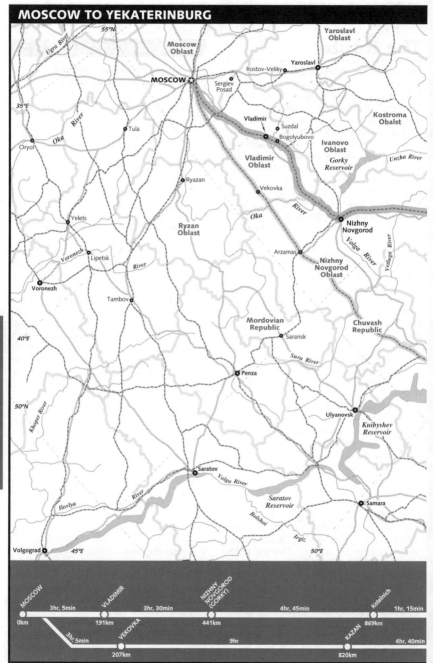

MOSCOW TO YEKATERINBURG

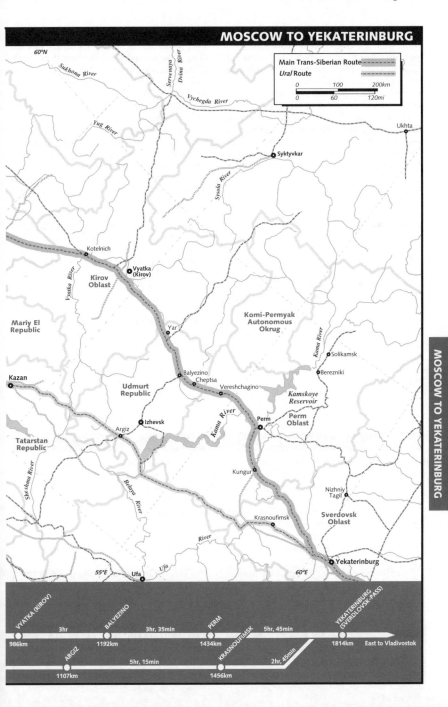

MOSCOW TO YEKATERINBURG

Main Trans-Siberian Route
Ural Route

| 0 | 100 | 200km |
| 0 | 60 | 120mi |

60°N

Sukhona River

Servernaya Dvina River

Vychegda River

Yug River

Ukhta

Syktyvkar

Sysola River

Kotelnich

Vyatka
(Kirov)

Kirov
Oblast

Komi-Permyak
Autonomous
Okrug

Vyatka River

Mariy El
Republic

Yar

Kama River

Solikamsk

Berezniki

Kazan

Udmurt
Republic

Balyezino
Cheptsa

Vereshchagino

*Kamskoye
Reservoir*

Argiz

Izhevsk

Kama River

Perm

Perm
Oblast

Tatarstan
Republic

Shc-ihma River

Belaya River

Kungur

Nizhniy
Tagil

River

Krasnoufimsk

Sverdovsk
Oblast

Ufa

Ufa

55°E

60°E

Yekaterinburg

MOSCOW TO YEKATERINBURG

VYATKA (KIROV)

3hr

986km

BALYEZINO

3hr, 35min

1192km

ARGIZ

1107km

PERM

1434km

KRASNOUFIMSK

5hr, 45min

1456km

5hr, 15min

2hr, 45min

YEKATERINBURG
(SVERDLOVSK-PASS)

1814km

East to Vladivostok

large white monument on the southern side of the train. In *The Big Red Train Ride* Eric Newby wasn't impressed: 'We were in Asia, at last – but ... there was nothing to see except a lot of deciduous trees in leaf, which had been planted as windbreaks and which effectively blocked any views.'

The views south of the train approaching **Yekaterinburg** (1814km), still called Sverdlovsk on timetables, are certainly pleasant as you pass several lakes along the Usovaya River. The first major station in Asian Russia – but still 260km short of the official beginning of Siberia – Yekaterinburg is where trains make a 15- to 30-minute stop.

VLADIMIR
ВЛАДИМИР
☎ 09222 • pop 360,000
🕐 Moscow time

Little evidence remains of Vladimir's medieval heyday when it was Russia's capital, 178km north-east of Moscow. However, what does remain (see the boxed text 'Architecture of the Golden Ring' later in this chapter) is worth pausing briefly to see en route to or from the more charming town of Suzdal, 35km north and the better place to stay.

Vladimir's main street is ulitsa Bolshaya Moskovskaya. This is where you'll find the cathedrals of the Assumption and St Dmitry. Both are 15 minutes' walk west of the train and bus stations, which are next to each other

at the foot of the steep embankment about 1km south-east of the 12th-century Golden Gate at the town centre. To reach the Church of the Intercession on the Nerl, around 11km east of the town of Bogolyubovo, it's best to catch a taxi. You should not have to pay any more than \$5 for the return trip, including waiting time.

There's an ATM in the lobby of the Hotel Vladimir and an Internet cafe at ulitsa Bolshaya Moskovskaya 51. It's open 8.30am to 9pm Monday to Friday.

If you decide to stop over the best option is *Hotel Vladimir (☎ 32 30 42, fax 32 72 01, 🅴 tour@gtk.elcom.ru, ul Bolshaya Moskovskaya 74)* Singles/doubles \$14.30/18.60. English is spoken here and room standards are higher than at Vladimir's other rather shoddy hotels. The town's best restaurant (at least where all tour groups seem to be taken) is *Zoloyte Vorota (☎ 32 31 16, ul Bolshaya Moskovskaya 15)* where a meal will set you back around \$8.

Getting There & Away
All Trans-Siberian trains stop at Vladimir, but the quickest way of getting here from Moscow is on one of the two daily Express services from Moscow's Kursk station (1st/2nd/3rd class \$4.50/3,80/2, two hours 40 minutes). No 146 departs at 7.51am, No 116 at 6.04pm; from Vladimir No 115 heads to Moscow at 7.25am and No 145 at 5pm.

Moscow to Yekaterinburg on the *Ural*

Apart from the main Trans-Siberian route from Moscow to Yekaterinburg outlined in this chapter, there is also the more southerly line traversed by the No 16 *Ural* service. This flagship train is worth considering if you plan to travel directly between these two cities.

One of the *Ural*'s most memorable stops is at **Vekovka** (207km), home to a glassware factory. Along the platform the food and drink hawkers are vastly outnumbered by factory workers flogging off sets of cut-glass tumblers, giant brandy glasses, vases, hideous chandeliers and the like.

At the Tatarstan capital of **Kazan** (820km) there's a 16-minute halt at 8.54pm; take the opportunity to inspect the handsomely restored station building. For more information see the Kazan section later in this chapter.

Continuing east there's a useful breakfast stop of 10 minutes at Argiz-1 (1107km), where you may spot old steam locomotives still in use for shunting. At 1150km the *Ural* crosses the Kama River around which there are good views.

We can personally vouch for the quality of raspberries and other forest fruits sold on the platform at the small country station of **Krasnoufimsk** (1456km). When you stop here the local time will be two hours ahead of Moscow. From there on to **Yekaterinburg** (1814km), you'll pass through similar rolling Ural Mountains scenery as on the route from Perm, and as you near the terminus there will be lake views to the south.

It shouldn't be any problem catching a local *elektrichka* train eastward to Nizhny Novgorod ($2.60, four to five hours, two daily). However, if you want a place on one of the faster and more comfortable *skoryy poezd* (fast trains) sort it out in Moscow (see Getting There & Away in the Moscow chapter) rather than in Vladimir, where the queues at the station's ticket offices can be bad and ticket availability is limited.

There are plenty of buses to/from Moscow (from $2.30) and Suzdal ($0.30) and seven services daily to Nizhny Novgorod ($4.50).

SUZDAL
СУЗДАЛЬ
☎ 09231 • pop 12,000
◷ Moscow time

You have to pinch yourself in Suzdal, 35km north of Vladimir, to be reminded that you have not slipped back in time to medieval Russia. Such is the enchanting quality of this architecturally protected town with its profusion of old monasteries, convents and churches and intricately decorated *izbas* dotted in green fields around the meandering Kamenka River.

Yury Dolgoruky made Suzdal the capital of Rostov-Suzdal principality in the first half of the 12th century and it developed into a wealthy monastic centre a century later. To best experience the town's unique atmosphere an overnight stay is recommended.

Suzdal's attractions are spread out, but it's easy enough to get around on foot. The main street ulitsa Lenina is a 2km walk west of the bus station along ulitsa Vasilevskaya; at the junction you'll face Torgovaya ploshcad and the early-19th-century Trading Arcades. Some 200m to the north along ulitsa Lenina is the post and telephone office on Krasnaya ploshchad. A further 400m along the street is the Saviour Monastery of St Euthymius.

There's no Internet access in Suzdal and you'll be better off changing money in Vladimir or Moscow before you arrive.

Things to See & Do
Start at **Saviour Monastery of St Euthymius** *(Spaso-Yevfimievsky monastyr; ul Lenina; admission $4; open 10am-6pm Tues-Sun, closed last Thur of month)*, founded in the 14th century. The highlight of the complex is the seven-domed, 12th- and 13th-century **Cathedral of the Transfiguration of the**

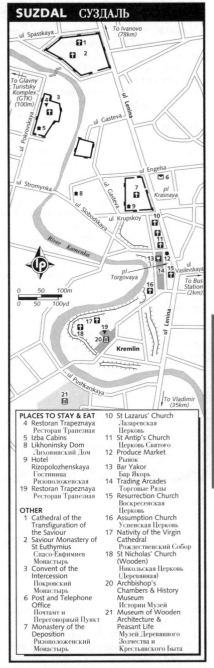

SUZDAL   СУЗДАЛЬ

PLACES TO STAY & EAT
4   Restoran Trapeznaya
   Ресторан Трапезная
5   Izba Cabins
8   Likhoninsky Dom
   Лихонинский Дом
9   Hotel
   Rizopolozhenskaya
   Гостиница
   Ризоположенская
19 Restoran Trapeznaya
   Ресторан Трапезная

OTHER
1   Cathedral of the
   Transfiguration of
   the Saviour
2   Saviour Monastery of
   St Euthymius
   Спасо-Евфимиев
   Монастырь
3   Convent of the
   Intercession
   Покровский
   Монастырь
6   Post and Telephone
   Office
   Почтамт и
   Переговорный Пункт
7   Monastery of the
   Deposition
   Ризоположенский
   Монастырь

10 St Lazarus' Church
   Лазаревская
   Церковь
11 St Antip's Church
   Церковь Святого
12 Produce Market
   Рынок
13 Bar Yakor
   Бар Якорь
14 Trading Arcades
   Торговые Ряды
15 Resurrection Church
   Воскресенская
   Церковь
16 Assumption Church
   Успенская Церковь
17 Nativity of the Virgin
   Cathedral
   Рождественский Собор
18 St Nicholas' Church
   (Wooden)
   Никольская Церковь
   (Деревянная)
20 Archbishop's
   Chambers & History
   Museum
   Истории Музей
21 Museum of Wooden
   Architecture &
   Peasant Life
   Музей Деревянного
   Зодчества и
   Крестьянского Быта

To Ivanovo (78km)
To Glavny Turistsky Komplex (GTK) (100m)
ul Spasskaya
ul Lenina
ul Gasteva
ul Engelsa
ul Stromynka
ul Slobodskaya
ul Krupskoy
ul Pokrovskaya
River Kamenka
pl Krasnaya
ul Vasilevskaya
pl Torgovaya
To Bus Station (2km)
ul Lenina
Kremlin
ul Pushkarskaya
To Vladimir (35km)
0 50 100m
0 50 100yd

MOSCOW TO YEKATERINBURG

Architecture of the Golden Ring

The Golden Ring (Zolotoe Koltso) is the modern name for a loop of very old towns north-east of Moscow that preceded the present capital as the political and cultural heart of Russia. Best known is little Suzdal, officially protected against industrial development and littered with so many protected buildings that it's almost one big museum. The other towns are more lived-in but are equally rich in churches, monasteries or kremlins. Made from stone, these buildings have outlived most wooden structures, although a good collection of these can be seen in Suzdal's Museum of Wooden Architecture & Peasant Life.

History

The Golden Ring's main towns began as outposts of the Kyivan (Kievan) Rus state. At the start of the 12th century, Prince Vladimir Monomakh of Kyiv (Kiev in Russian) founded a fort at Vladimir and gave the Rostov-Suzdal principality in which it lay to his son Yury Dolgoruky.

After Yury died in 1157, his son and successor Andrey Bogolyubsky spurned the chance of establishing himself in Kyiv and moved to the more secure northern base of Vladimir, which became the effective capital of Russia in 1169. During this era other Golden Ring settlements, including Suzdal, Yaroslavl and Rostov-Veliky (see the Moscow chapter) flourished and sprouted cathedrals, monasteries and massive city walls.

In 1237, the Tatars invaded Russia, sacking and burning as they went. Having made their point, they were then mostly content to rule and collect taxes through local princes, which they did for the next 250 years. In the meantime the importance of Moscow increased to the point that the headquarters of the Russian Orthodox Church was transferred there from Vladimir in the 1320s. By the end of the 15th century the entire region around Vladimir and Suzdal was part of Muscovy, the Moscow state.

Architecture & Art

The majority of the Golden Ring's surviving architectural monuments date from spurts of building and rebuilding after the collapse of Tatar power. Most in the 16th century (particularly the fort-monasteries of Suzdal) were bankrolled by the Moscow princes, and from the 17th century by the Church (as happened in Rostov) and a new class of rich merchants (as in Yaroslavl).

However, the buildings that gave the region a key place in the story of Russian architecture were constructed before the Tatars came. Most important are three 12th-century buildings in and near Vladimir: the cathedrals of the Assumption and St Dmitry, and the Church of the Intercession on the Nerl. These buildings are the vital link between the architecture of 11th-century Kyiv and that of 15th-century Moscow – early northern interpretations, in majestic, finely carved white stone, of Kyiv's Byzantine brick churches.

The Vladimir-Suzdal region was also a chief inheritor of Kyiv's Byzantine artistic traditions, though only a few fragments of 12th- and 13th-century frescoes survive in the Vladimir and Suzdal cathedrals.

Saviour. Inside you can admire vivid frescoes while a choir of monks gives a short and heavenly a cappella performance each morning around 10.30am. CDs and tapes are, naturally, available to buy. This is followed outside by a delightful, 10-minute bell-ringing concert from the tall bell tower, built to mark the birth of Ivan the Terrible.

It's a pleasant walk around St Euthymius' fortress walls and across the wooden bridge over the Kamenka River towards the attractive Intercession Convent (Pokrovsky sobor; ul Pokrovskaya), founded in 1364 and still home to a small community of nuns. There's accommodation and a good restaurant here (see Places to Stay & Eat).

Back near the pillared Trading Arcades, are St Lazarus' Church and St Antip's Church. Stretching south is the 1.4km earth rampart of Suzdal's Kremlin, founded in the 11th century. In the Kremlin area is the Nativity of the Virgin Cathedral (Rozhdestvensky sobor), its dirty blue domes spangled with gold stars, its frescoed interior under restoration. Also here you'll find the attractive wooden St Nicholas' Church and the Suzdal History Exhibition (☎ 2 04 44; admission $1; open 10am-5pm Wed-Mon, closed last Fri of

Architecture of the Golden Ring

While still primarily Byzantine, these works show a bold use of colour and a range of emotions that heralds later Russian artistic developments.

Assumption Cathedral

Begun in 1158, the Assumption Cathedral *(Uspensky sobor; admission $0.70; open 1.30pm-5pm daily)* is a white-stone version of Kyiv's brick Byzantine churches. Its simple but majestic form is adorned with fine carving, innovative for the time. Extended on all sides after a fire in the 1180s, and at the same time gaining four outer domes, the cathedral has changed little since.

Inside the working church a few restored 12th-century murals of peacocks and prophets holding scrolls can be dimly made out about halfway up the inner wall of the outer north aisle; this was originally an outside wall. The real treasures are the *Last Judgment* frescoes by Andrey Rublyov and Daniil Chyorny, painted in 1408 in the central nave and inner south aisle, under the choir gallery towards the western end.

Adjoining the cathedral on the northern side (beside the path up from ulitsa Bolshaya Moskovskaya) are an 1810 **bell tower** and the 1862 **St George's Chapel**.

Cathedral of St Dmitry

A moment's stroll east of the Assumption Cathedral is the smaller Cathedral of St Dmitry *(Dmitrievsky sobor)*, built between 1193 and 1197, where the art of Vladimir-Suzdal stone carving reached its pinnacle. The church is permanently closed, but its exterior walls, covered in an amazing profusion of images, are the attraction here.

The top centre of the north, south and west walls all show King David bewitching the birds and beasts with music. The Kyivan prince Vsevolod III, who had this church built as part of his palace, appears at the top left of the north wall, with a baby son on his knee and other sons kneeling on each side. Above the right-hand window of the south wall, Alexander the Great ascends into heaven, a symbol of princely might; on the west wall appear the labours of Hercules.

Church of the Intercession on the Nerl

The village of **Bogolyubovo**, 10km east of Vladimir, boasts the picturesque monastery-palace complex of Prince Andrey Bogolyubsky, as well as the Church of the Intercession on the Nerl *(Tserkov Pokrova na Nerli)*, one of Russia's loveliest churches. Its beauty lies in its simple but perfect proportions, a brilliantly chosen waterside site and sparing use of delicate carving.

Taxis will drive down to the church across the fields from Bogolyubovo, but it's also a pleasant walk here from the monastery-palace complex. Take ulitsa Frunze downhill towards the railway bridge, follow the path under the bridge and to the left along the side of a small wood. The church appears across the meadows, about 1.25km away.

month), reached from the tent-roofed 1635 bell tower on the eastern side of the yard.

South of the Kremlin, the **Museum of Wooden Architecture & Peasant Life** *(Muzey Derevyannogo Zodchestva i Krestyanskogo Byta; admission $1; open 9.30am-3.30pm Wed-Mon, closed last Fri of month)* is a short walk across the river. As well as log houses, windmills, a barn and lots of tools and handicrafts, its highlights are the 1756 **Transfiguration Church** *(Preobrazhenskaya tserkov)* and the simpler 1776 **Resurrection Church** *(Voskresenskaya tserkov)*. Building interiors are open only from May to October.

Places to Stay & Eat

It's important to book accommodation ahead in Suzdal, particularly at weekends and during holiday periods.

Likhoninsky Dom *(☎ 2 19 01, fax 32 70 10, ul Slobodskaya 34)* Singles/doubles with breakfast $14/21. This small guesthouse, with only four rooms in a traditional izba, is the nicest place to stay in town, but you'll need to book well ahead.

Hotel Rizopolozhenskaya *(☎ 2 05 53, ul Lenina)* Singles/doubles from $4.50/8. In the grounds of the decrepit Monastery of the Deposition opposite the post office, many of the cheaper rooms at this hotel are pretty crumby; ask to check out the more costly *lux* ones for $16.

If you're on a tour, it's likely you'll end up at the charmless but reasonably comfortable ***Glavny Turistsky Komplex*** *(GTK;* ☎ *2 09 08, fax 2 07 66,* 🄴 *gtk@tcsuz.vladimir.ru)* Singles/doubles with breakfast $14/19.50.

Contact GTK if you want to book one of the *izba cabins* within the grounds of the Intercession Convent, which are $44 for two people. The convent also has the good ***Restoran Trapeznaya*** *(open 9am-10.30am, noon-5pm & 6pm-10pm daily)* where a meal of traditional dishes costs around $10.

There's another ***Restoran Trapeznaya*** *(*☎ *2 17 62, open 11am-11pm daily)*, in the Archbishop's Chambers in the kremlin, which does decent Russian fare for $7 a meal. For a spot of self-catering check out the daily ***produce market*** beside the Trading Arcades and for a lovely view with your beer or ice cream grab an outdoor table at ***Bar Yakor*** *(Anchor; ul Lenina 63)* on the western side of the Arcades.

Getting There & Away
There are buses roughly every hour from Vladimir to Suzdal ($0.30, one hour). A taxi between the two takes half the time and costs around $10. From Moscow there's also a direct bus at 5pm daily ($2.60, 4½ hours).

NIZHNY NOVGOROD
НИЖНИЙ НОВГОРОД
☎ 8312 • pop 2 million
🕘 Moscow time

On the banks of the mighty Volga, Nizhny Novgorod, Russia's third largest city, is markedly less cosmopolitan than Moscow and St Petersburg, but has a low-key charm that makes it a pleasant place to spend a few days. A stroll along the high embankment above the river is a must, as is a promenade on the central shopping street Pokrovskaya. There's a handful of interesting museums and the chance to take a short cruise along the Volga to an ancient monastery.

History
Founded in 1221, Nizhny Novgorod has been an important trading centre for a long time. Barges used to dock on the river and exchange goods. Later this floating market was formalised as a huge trade fair, the Yarmarka, a tradition that continues to this day. During the 19th century it was said 'St Petersburg is Russia's head, Moscow its heart, and Nizhny Novgorod its wallet'.

In Soviet times the city was named Gorky after the writer Maxim Gorky (born here in 1868); this name is still sometimes used on train timetables. The presence of many industries connected with the military (eg, submarine construction) meant that Nizhny Novgorod was closed to foreigners for many decades. This is one reason the late physicist, dissident and Nobel laureate Andrey Sakharov was exiled here in the 1980s.

Building on the city's long history of international trade, the reform-minded local government is again actively encouraging joint ventures with Western firms. The district is also known for traditional crafts, including *matryoshka* dolls and Khokhloma ware – wooden spoons, cups and dishes painted gold, red and black and par;ially covered by designs of flowers – named after a town about 100km north of Nizhny.

Orientation & Information
Nizhny Novgorod lies on the southern bank of the Volga River and is also split by the Oka River. The western bank includes the train station and Hotel Tsentralnaya on ploshchad Lenina. The high eastern bank has the kremlin on ploshchad Minina, from which the main streets span out, including the pedestrianised Bolshaya Pokrovskaya ulitsa with many shops and restaurants.

Good maps in Russian showing local transport routes are widely available for $1; try Dom Knigi (House of Books) in the same building as Hotel Tsentralnaya. Open 10am to 7pm weekdays, 10am to 6pm Saturday and 11am to 4pm Sunday, it also has a small selection of English-language books.

Alfabank (☎ 30 09 55), ulitsa Semashko 9, is open 8am to 8pm weekdays. Besides the usual exchange services, it handles Western Union transfers, Visa and MasterCard cash advances and has an ATM linked to foreign networks.

The post office is at the ploshchad Gorkogo end of Bolshaya Pokrovskaya ulitsa and is open 24 hours. Internet Sitek (☎ 77 58 44), is on the 8th floor of the Hotel Tsentralnaya, ulitsa Sovetskaya 12

At the time of research, Alye Parusa (☎/fax 77 58 24, 🄴 parus@nnov.sitek.net)

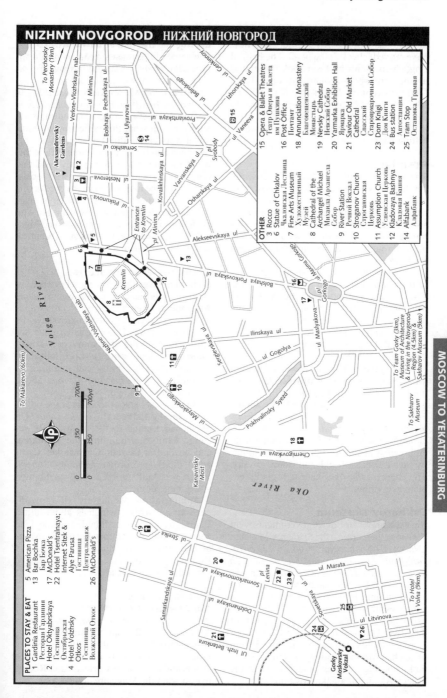

NIZHNY NOVGOROD НИЖНИЙ НОВГОРОД

PLACES TO STAY & EAT
1 Gardinia Restaurant
  Ресторан Гардиния
2 Hotel Oktyabrskaya
  Гостиница
  Октябрьская
4 Hotel Volzhsky Otkos
  Гостиница
  Волжский Откос
5 American Pizza
13 Bar Bochka
  Бар Бочка
17 McDonald's
22 Hotel Tsentralnaya;
  Internet Sitek &
  Alye Parusa
  Гостиница
  Центральнаяж
26 McDonald's

OTHER
3 Rocco
6 Statue of Chkalov
  Чкаловская Лестница
7 Fine Arts Museum
  Художественный
  Музей
8 Cathedral of the
  Archangel Michael
  Михаила Архангела
  Собор
9 River Station
  Речной Вокзал
10 Stroganov Church
  Строгановская
  Церковь
11 Assumption Church
  Успенская Церковь
12 Kladovaya Bashnya
  Кладовая башня
14 Alfabank
  Альфабанк

15 Opera & Ballet Theatres
  Театр Оперы и балета
  им Пушкина
16 Post Office
  Почтамт
18 Annunciation Monastery
  Благовещенский
  Монастырь
19 Nevsky Cathedral
  Невский Собор
20 Yarmarka Exhibition Hall
  Ярмарка
21 Saviour Old Market
  Cathedral
  Спасский
  Старинармарочный Собор
23 Dom Knigi
  Дом Книги
24 Bus Station
  Автостанция
25 Tram Stop
  Остановка Трамвая

MOSCOW TO YEKATERINBURG

was on the 8th floor of the Hotel Tsentral-naya, ulitsa Sovetskaya 12, but may now have moved; check at the hotel. The helpful English-speaking staff can book flights and arrange transport around the city. Team Gorky Adventure Travel (☎ 65 19 99, fax 63 24 44, adv@teamgorky.ru), at ulitsa 40 Let Oktiabria 1A, organises outdoor travel in the region and farther afield, including rafting trips.

Kremlin

The main entrances to Nizhny's Kremlin, perched above the Volga, are off ploshchad Minina. The present walls, with 11 towers, date from the 16th century – either walk around the base for free, or climb up into the **ramparts** *(admission $0.20; open 10am-7pm daily)* through the cafe-bar in the Kladovaya Bashnya gate.

Inside the Kremlin one of the best views of the city and the Volga is from behind the 17th-century **Cathedral of the Archangel Michael** *(Mikhailo-Arkhangelsky sobor; open 9am-2pm Mon-Sun)*, built in 1631 and a functioning church. Here you'll also find an eternal flame and a striking monument to the heroes of WWII.

Most of the buildings within the Kremlin are used as government offices, but at the north-eastern end of the grounds the former governor's house is now home to the worthy **Fine Arts Museum** *(Khudo-zhestvenny muzey; ☎ 39 13 73; admission $1.30, open 10am-5pm Wed-Mon)*. Exhibits range from 14th-century icons to 20th-century paintings by such artists as Rerikh and Borovikovsky. The cheery *babushkas* here will gladly explain everything.

Sakharov Museum

Revealing how far Soviet governments went to silence their critics, the Sakharov Museum *(Muzey AD Sakharova; ☎ 66 86 23, prosp Gagarina 214, admission $0.50; English tour $1; open 10am-5pm Sat-Thur)* makes for sobering but fascinating viewing. In the actual ground-level flat Sakharov shared with his wife Yelena Bonner while they were exiled here, the museum contains artefacts of their lives before and after their exile.

To get there catch bus No 3, 5 or 43 from ploshchad Minina heading towards Shcher-binki housing complex and get off at the Muzey Akademika Sakharova bus stop.

Museum of Architecture & Living in the Novgorod Region

The name of this museum *(Muzei Architekt-yur i Bita Narodov Nizhegorodskogo Povol-zhya; ☎ 65 15 98, ul Gorbatovskaya 39, Shchyolokovsky Khutor; adult/student $1.70/0.50; open Tue, Wed, Fri-Sun 10am-4.15pm & Thur 10am-2.15pm)* is a mouthful, but it well sums up what this collection of traditional wooden buildings is about.

Only a handful of the 14 structures in this woodland site (featuring a weedy pond that is a popular spot for swimming with locals) are open on the tour. When we showed up the tour was conducted expertly by eight-year-old Zhenya, deputising for his babushka who made sure no facts were missed. The highlight is the **Pokrovskaya tserkov**, a beautiful wooden church dating from 1731.

Churches & Monasteries

Nizhny has many churches; most have been or are being renovated. The 17th-century stone **Assumption Church** *(Uspenskaya tserkov)* is on a hill at the end of ulitsa Pokrovskaya. Its design was normally for wooden churches only. The baroque **Stroganov or Nativity Church** *(Stroganovskaya tserkov)*, built at the turn of the 18th century and retaining its magnificent stone carvings, is just above ulitsa Mayahkovskogo.

On the west bank of the Oka is the prominent **Nevsky Cathedral** *(Nevsky sobor)*. On ploshchad Lenina is the handsomely restored exhibition building, the **Yarmarka**, and beyond is **Saviour Old Market Cathedral** *(Spassky Staroyarmarochny sobor)*, which was built in 1822 with an impressively large dome.

Annunciation Monastery *(Blagovesh-chensky monastyr)*, which is above ulitsa Chernigovskaya, was founded in the 13th century. The 17th-century **Pechorsky Monastery** *(Pechorsky monastyr)*, off ulitsa Rodinova overlooks the Volga. Both can be viewed from the outside only.

Places to Stay

Hotel Volzhsky Otkos (☎ 39 19 71, fax 19 48 94, Verkhne-Volzhskaya nab 2A) Singles with shared bathroom $5, singles/doubles with bathroom from $10. A delightful Soviet relic with friendly staff, decent unrenovated rooms and a reasonably priced cafe. Rooms overlooking the Volga are around $20.

Hotel Tsentralnaya (☎ 77 55 00, fax 77 55 66, **W** www.hotel-central.ru, ul Sovetskaya 12) Singles/doubles $23/29. It's close to the station and has helpful staff, but otherwise the old-style rooms are overpriced (as is the cafe) and the ones with river views suffer from traffic noise.

Hotel Oktyabrskaya (☎ 32 06 70, fax 32 05 50, **e** oktbr@kis.ru, Verkhne-Volzhskaya nab 9A) Singles/doubles with breakfast $50/100. There are cheaper, unrenovated rooms at this acceptable modern business hotel, but they're likely to be booked up (or just not offered to you).

Hotel Volna (☎ 96 19 00, fax 96 14 14, **W** volna.nnov.ru, ul Lenina 98) Singles/doubles with breakfast from $120/180. Nizhny's only four-star hotel is professionally run and offers all the facilities you could wish for at this price. The location, 4.5km south of the station (but near the end of the metro), is not in its favour.

Places to Eat

Bolshaya Pokrovskaya ulitsa has many restaurants and cafes – the entire city seems to turn up here for a stroll on a summer evening. The other popular spot – great for sunset views and a cold beer or ice cream from one of the many stalls – is the terrace above the Aleksandrovsky Gardens facing the Volga, particularly around the statue of Chkalov, the trans-polar aviator.

American Pizza (☎ 39 18 44, Verkhne-Volzhskaya nab 2A) Meals $5. This modern place offers authentic, tasty pizza, salads and beers with a view of the Volga.

Gardinia (☎ 19 41 01, Verkhne-Volzhskaya nab) Meals $8. Basically this cafeteria has most of the Russian-style dishes on display so ordering is as easy as pointing. The food is OK, the river views better.

Bar Bochka (☎ 33 55 61, 14 ul Bolshaya Pokrovskaya) Mains around $7. Excellent Georgian cuisine is served at this restaurant hidden by two sets of doors behind a convivial bar where there's often live music.

There are also a couple of branches of *McDonald's* – one opposite the station, the other on ploshchad Gorkogo.

Entertainment

Rocco (☎ 36 03 53, ul Minina 10B) Admission $4. Open 10pm-5am daily. Nizhny's top nightclub pounds to a high-energy disco beat and offers nightly cabaret and laser shows, a casino and small bowling alley.

Productions at the city's *opera* and *ballet theatres* on ulitsa Belinskogo are also recommended.

Getting There & Away

Train Gorky-Moskovsky Vokzal is on the western bank of the Oka River at ploshchad Revolyutsii. Trains from Moscow (seven hours) cost $16 for a *kupe* ticket on the *firmennye* Trans-Siberian services, less on the other services. Heading on to Perm (12½ hours) costs $25 to $30 for kupe or $30 to $35 to Yekaterinburg (18½ hours). Train No 41 is the direct service to Kazan (nine hours) and costs $10.

Buying tickets at the stations is generally not a problem, although in the peak summer period you may find getting exactly the train you want tricky.

Air There are two daily flights to Moscow (Domodedovo) for around $50, and a daily flight to Yekaterinburg for $90. Lufthansa (☎ 75 90 85) flies three times a week to/from Frankfurt.

Bus The bus station is across from the train station. There are five daily buses to/from Moscow (Shchyolkovsky bus station) that cost $13 (nine hours).

Boat The river station (☎ 30 36 66) is on Nizhne-Volzhskaya below the kremlin. Apart from short trips along the Volga (see Around Nizhny Novgorod), this is where you can find out about the summer cruises linking the city with Kazan, Moscow and St Petersburg.

Getting Around

Tickets for the trams, trolleybuses and buses cost around $0.10 and can be bought on board. Tram No 1 is convenient, starting from the train station, crossing the Kanavinsky Bridge and climbing the hill to the Kremlin. From the train station, cross the street and walk past the kiosks to reach the stop.

There are plans to extend the metro (one trip $0.10) across the river but it's unlikely to happen in the life of this book. Currently you might use it only to get to the Hotel Volna.

If you can bargain like a local, a taxi from the train station to the Kremlin costs $1 or $5 to the airport.

AROUND NIZHNY NOVGOROD
Makarevo
Макарево

A trip to the sleepy village of Makarevo, around 60km east along the Volga from Nizhny Novgorod, is highly recommended. The main attraction is the **Makariev Monastery** (☎ *249-2 69 67; admission $3; open 9am-5pm*), the fortified stone walls and church domes of which look magnificent on the approach from the river.

The monastery was founded in 1435 and it thrived along with the surrounding village because of regular trade fairs, precursors for Nizhny's famous Yarmarka. When the fairs moved permanently to Nizhny in the 19th century, Makarevo's importance and that of its monastery dwindled. Devastating floods also forced the villagers to relocate. Like many others, the monastery was closed in the Soviet period and used as an orphanage and hospital. In 1991, a few nuns returned to help restore the churches, four of which are now operating. Only 20 nuns live here now; ask for Fortinia who speaks English and may be able to give you a tour.

The village of 180 people is made up of rustic wooden cottages and there's a small **museum** (free) in the old schoolhouse that's worth a look. Most locals come here, though, for a quiet day out sunbathing on the beach by the river. Bring a picnic since there are only a couple of shops with limited supplies.

Boats to Makarevo depart daily from near the Rechnoy Vokzal in Nizhny Novgorod where advance tickets can be bought; for tickets on the day, go to the kiosk on the waterfront under the main building or pay on the boat. Times change, but generally there's a boat at 9am returning at 5pm. The trip takes three to four hours and costs $1.70. By taxi it's only 1½ hours from Nizhny Novgorod to Makarevo but is $35.

VYATKA
ВЯТКА

☎ 8332 • pop 490,000
🕐 Moscow time + 0100

Still often called Kirov, the name given to it in 1934 in honour of the assassinated communist leader, Vyatka is not a priority stop – something you'll find out pretty quickly if you arrive here without an onward ticket. Queues at the station for tickets are horrendous, mainly because the train is practically

the only means in and out of this regional administrative centre – and most people seem to want out.

Founded in 1181, the city lies on the west bank of the Vyatka River, with the station around 3km from Teatralnaya ploshchad, more or less the centre of this otherwise sprawling place. You can change money in and around the old Hotel Tsentralnaya, ulitsa Lenina 80, which is now a shopping and office centre. The main post office is at ulitsa Drelevskogo 43. There's an Internet cafe (☎ 62 49 84, ⓦ www.inetcafe.vyatka .ru) on the 4th floor at ulitsa Svoboda 67.

Things to See & Do

If you have time to kill, the most interesting place to head is the **Fine Arts Museum** (*Khudozhestvenny muzey;* ☎ *62 79 41, ul Karla Marxa 70; admission $1.75; open 10am-6pm Wed-Sun*), dedicated to the local impressionist painters and brothers BM and AM Vasnetsov. Their works hang alongside a good collection of paintings from the 18th century on, impressive and beautiful icons and some photography exhibits.

If your Russian is up to it, the quirky **Museum of Aviation & Space** (*Muzey KE Tsiolkovskogo, Aviatsy i Kosmonavtiki; ul Engelsa 16; admission $0.50; open 10am-6pm Wed-Sun*), dedicated to the Russian inventor of the rocket, is worth a quick look.

Places to Stay & Eat

Hotel Vyatka (☎/*fax 64 64 10, prosp Oktyabrski 145*) Singles/doubles from $10/12.50. The cheap rooms are perfectly acceptable at this friendly, spick and span hotel. There's a lively disco at weekends and an inexpensive cafe on the 5th floor.

Shinok (☎ *38 34 33, ul Moskovskaya 10*) Mains around $3. Service is slow, but the food excellent at this stylish Ukrainian restaurant in a brick-lined cellar.

American Saloon (☎ *62 24 82, ul Karla Marxa*) Mains around $3. This modern place is open round the clock and serves an all-American menu, plus a few Russian dishes. There's a bowling alley here too ($8 per hour, open 6pm till late Thursday to Sunday).

Getting There & Away

All Trans-Siberian services pass through Vyatka, but you should sort out your onward ticket in Moscow, since securing one here can be a long and frustrating experience. The best service is No 32/31, the *Vyatka*, leaving Moscow at 8.25am and Vyatka at 8.35pm ($15 kupe, 13 hours).

Trolley bus Nos 3 and 5 run between the station and the city centre; tickets cost $0.20.

PERM
ПЕРМЬ

☎ 3422 • pop 1 million
⊙ Moscow time + 0200

Largely industrial and dominated by ugly concrete blocks, Perm itself is another missable stop on the Trans-Siberian route. You will, however, need to disembark here if you wish to explore the ice caves at nearby Kungur or visit the ethnographic architecture museum at Khokhlovka.

By the time Catherine the Great decreed Perm as a provincial capital in 1780, it was well on its way to being the major trading gateway to Siberia and Asia from Europe. It was however another of Soviet Russia's closed cities, when it was renamed Molotov, after the foreign minister who also gave his name to the explosive cocktail.

The city has a renowned ballet school and literary associations. Boris Pasternak lived and wrote *Doktor Zhivago* here. More telling, Chekov used Perm as inspiration for the city his *Three Sisters* were so desperately longing to leave.

Information & Orientation

Perm sprawls along the south bank of the Kama River, with Perm II station about 2.5km west of the city centre around the intersection of ulitsa Lenina and Komsomolsky prospekt.

Sebrbank, ulitsa Lenina 31, cashes travellers cheques and gives credit-card advances. Its exchange office is open 10am to 8pm with a break from 2pm to 3pm. The black-market dealers who hang around the post office next door (which also has an exchange office offering a lousy rate) offer better deals for cash.

The central post office is at ulitsa Lenina 29. The main telephone office, at ulitsa Lenina 66, has an Internet service charging $1.80 per hour.

JSC Permtourist (☎ 34 35 60, fax 12 48 43, ⒠ travel@permtourist.ru), at ulitsa Lenina 58, can arrange all manner of tours and travel services.

Things to See

Perm does have a rather good **art gallery** (*Permskaya Gosudarstvennaya galereya;* ☎ 12 33 95, Komsomolsky prosp 4; admission $0.50; open 11am-5.30pm Tues-Sun), easily identified by the spire and cupola of its building, a former cathedral. The gallery was opened in 1922 and houses one of the largest icon collections in the country.

Next door, the **Ethnographic Museum** (*Permsky Oblastnoy Kraevedchesky muzey;* ☎ 12 25 69; Komsomolsky prosp 6; admission $0.50; open 10am-6pm Sat-Thur) has numerous stuffed local animals.

Sergei Diagilev Museum (*Dom SM Dyagileva;* ☎ 12 06 10, ul Sibirskaya 33; admission free; open 9am-6pm Mon-Fri) is a lovingly curated small exhibition on the world-famous ballet and opera impresario (1872–1929) whose family came from the Perm region. On show are posters and a few costumes from his productions.

Places to Stay & Eat

Hotel Prikamye (☎/fax 34 86 62, Komsomolsky prosp 27) Singles/doubles $15.50/20. Undergoing renovation when we visited (so standards and prices are likely to rise) the rooms here, all with their own bathroom and TV, are good value and the staff friendly.

Hotel Ural (☎ 34 44 17, fax 90 62 20, ⒠ ural-hotel@permtourist.ru, ul Lenina 58) Singles/doubles from $6.50/10. It's a monolith, but is the best place to stay. Better rooms with facilities such as a telephone and TV go for around $20. There's a cafe with an English menu on the 7th floor and the appropriately named **Grot Bar** in the basement.

Kafe Staraya Perm (☎ 12 68 68, ul Sibirskaya 8) Mains around $4. Seductively dark and plush, this restaurant does nicely presented Russian dishes.

Sunshine Blues (☎ 12 72 55, Komsomolsky prosp 16) Convivial blues bar with good food and an outdoor terrace in summer. Breakfast is from 9am to noon, after which a good-value, three-course lunch costs $3. You'll spend around $6 for dinner.

Rock'n Roll Pizza (☎ 19 52 66, ul Kirsanova 12A) is a fun round-the-clock operation serving decent pizza with imaginative toppings from $1 a slice. After, try the ice cream at **Baskin Robbins** (Komsomolsky prosp 7).

For self-catering supplies try the daily open-air **market** behind Hotel Ural, or the

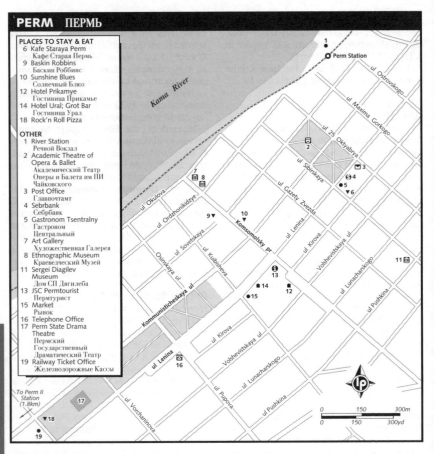

PERM ПЕРМЬ

PLACES TO STAY & EAT
6 Kafe Staraya Perm
   Кафе Старая Пермь
9 Baskin Robbins
   Баскин Роббинс
10 Sunshine Blues
   Солнечный Блюз
12 Hotel Prikamye
   Гостиница Прикамье
14 Hotel Ural; Grot Bar
   Гостиница Урал
18 Rock'n Roll Pizza

OTHER
1 River Station
   Речной Вокзал
2 Academic Theatre of
   Opera & Ballet
   Академический Театр
   Оперы и Балета им ПИ
   Чайковского
3 Post Office
   Главпочтамт
4 Sebrbank
   Сбербанк
5 Gastronom Tsentralny
   Гастроном
   Центральный
7 Art Gallery
   Художественная Галерея
8 Ethnographic Museum
   Краеведческий Музей
11 Sergei Diagilev
   Museum
   Дом СП Дягилеба
13 JSC Permtourist
   Пермтурист
15 Market
   Рынок
16 Telephone Office
17 Perm State Drama
   Theatre
   Пермский
   Государственный
   Драматический Театр
19 Railway Ticket Office
   Железнодорожные Кассы

To Perm II
Station
(1.8km)

Kama River

Perm Station

ul Ostrovskogo

ul Maxima Gorkogo

ul 25 Oktyabrya

ul Sibirskaya

ul Gazety Zvezda

ul Okulova

ul Ordzhonikidze

ul Lenina

ul Kirova

ul Sovetskaya

Komsomolsky pr

Volshevitskaya ul

ul Lunacharskogo

ul Pushkina

Osinskaya ul

Kuibisheva

Kommunisticheskaya ul

ul Kirova

Volshevitskaya ul

ul Lunacharskogo

ul Lenina

ul Vorchaninova

ul Pupova

ul Pushkina

0   150   300m
0   150   300yd

---

well-stocked **Gastronom Tsentralny** *(ul Sibirskaya 6)*, open 8am to 9pm Monday to Saturday and 9am to 6pm Sunday.

Entertainment
The outdoor stalls that set up in the summer on the terrace overlooking the Kama River just outside the art gallery are good places for beer and shashlyk.

The **Academic Theatre of Opera & Ballet** *(Akademichesky Teatr Opery i Baleta;* ☎ *12 30 87, Kommunisticheskaya ul 25)* in Reshetnikova Garden is one of Russia's top schools and stages good productions.

Getting There & Away
Train Perm II, the city's major train station, is on the Trans-Siberian route from Moscow

($39 kupe, 20 hours). Yekaterinburg ($4, six hours) is the next major city east, while back west is Vyatka ($8, seven hours) and Kazan ($10, 15¼ hours); cheaper *platskartny* tickets to all these destinations are available.

Perm II is a major rail junction and buying a ticket here can be a trial if you opt to queue with everyone else. The easiest alternative option is to use the *zal povishennoi komfortnosty*, the first-class lounge next to the ticket offices. For around $2.50 commission the attendants here will get your ticket for you.

In Perm itself, there is a ticket office *(zheleznodorozhnye kassi)* at ulitsa Kirsanova 19, officially open from 6am to 6pm daily, although it was still open when we turned up at 7.30pm. The lines here are more manageable and you'll pay a booking fee of just under $1.

The crumbling Perm Station, 1km east of the centre, is used by suburban trains only, but there's an old steam locomotive outside it.

Air There are two daily Aeroflot flights to/from Moscow ($148). Lufthansa (☎ 28 44 42) flies to/from Frankfurt twice a week. There's an airline ticket office in the lobby of Hotel Ural, open 9am to 8pm daily.

Boat The river station (☎ 19 93 04), is at the eastern end of ulitsa Ordzhonikidze, is opposite Perm station. Boats down the Kama River to the Volga depart about once a week during summer. On summer weekends local tour boats depart every hour and cost $1.

Getting Around

Bus Nos 110, 119 and 120 serve the airport from the centre ($0.25, 35 minutes). A taxi costs about $8. Take any bus or trolleybus, or tram No 7, for $0.10, to get from the Perm II station to Hotels Ural and Prikamye. A taxi costs around $2.50.

AROUND PERM
Khokhlovka
Хохловка

Set in rolling countryside at Khokhlovka, 45km north of Perm, is an **Architecture-Ethnography Museum** *(Arkhitekturno-Etnografichesky muzey Khokhlovka;* ☎ *979 71 82; admission $0.60; open 10am-6pm Mon-Sun, late May-Oct)* with eight wooden buildings. Two churches date back to the turn of the 18th century, while the other structures are from the 19th or early 20th century. During the first weekend of May, a folk and culture festival celebrates the coming of spring. Several buses a day serve Khokhlovka from Perm. JSC Permtourist runs tours here (see Information & Orientation in the Perm section).

Kungur
Кунгур

About 100km south-east of Perm, and on the Trans-Siberian route (but not a scheduled stop), is the atmospheric old Urals town of Kungur. Lying in a gigantic natural bowl where three rivers meet, Kungur was founded in 1648 by runaway serfs. In the 19th century the town's already prosperous merchants established trade relations with Asia and became the largest tea dealers in the country.

Although it's now a backwater, Kungur still has many notable if somewhat dilapidated buildings including the **All Saints Church** *(Vsekh Svyatikh tserkov)*, a 17th-century **governor's house** and 19th-century shopping arcade **Gostiny dvor**.

There's also a **Regional Local Studies Museum** *(Krayevedchesky muzey; ul Gogolya 36; admission $0.40; open 11am-5pm)*.

The main attraction, however, is **Kungur ice cave** *(Ledyanaya peshchera; admission $3; open 10am-5pm daily)*, 5km out of town, which is famous for unique ice formations with frozen waterfalls and underground lakes. JSC Permtourist (see Perm Information & Orientation) can arrange tours here, as well as accommodation in the adjacent **Stalagmit Hotel** *(☎ 271-3 97 23)*, which has singles/doubles from $5/10.

Getting There & Away The train and bus stations in Kungur are on ulitsa Bachurina. There are eight trains a day from Perm II station ($0.80, two hours 20 minutes). A day trip from Perm is possible if you start early (there's a train at 5.40am and then a big gap till 1.50pm), with the last train back to Perm II at 7.27pm – but check these times first at the station.

KAZAN
КАЗАНЬ

☎ 8432 ● pop 1.1 million
🕓 Moscow time + 0200

Famous for its historic Kremlin, Kazan has an intriguing atmosphere redolent of Central Asia, particularly around its several mosques and in its teeming central market where you'll find everything from pineapples to pigs heads. Its riverside beaches are fine places to relax and it's fun to join the people strolling along the lively pedestrianised shopping street Baumana ulitsa.

As the capital of Tatarstan, this is also the place to find out more about the Tatars, Turkic people who ruled parts of Russia for over 300 years. Nationalism is strong here – you'll frequently see the green, white and red striped Tatar flag, and all the streets are bilingually signposted.

History

Kazan, one of Russia's oldest Tatar cities, dates back to around 1005. Capital of part of the Golden Horde in the 15th and 16th centuries, it was famously ravaged in 1552 by Ivan the Terrible, who forced the Muslim khan to become Christian. St Basil's Cathedral in Moscow was built to celebrate Kazan's capture.

The city later flourished as a gateway to Siberia. Leo Tolstoy was educated here, as was Lenin, who was thrown out of Kazan University for being too bolshie.

During Soviet times, Kazan became the capital of the Tatar Autonomous Republic. In autumn 1990, this oil-rich region (now renamed Tatarstan) declared its autonomy from the rest of Russia, launching several years of political warfare with Moscow. Full independence remains unlikely given that 43% of the 3.7 million people within the republic are Russian.

Orientation & Information

Most places of interest lie within easy walking distance of the station on the east bank of the Volga. The main drag, Baumana ulitsa is around 500m east of the station. There are nice beaches on the north bank of the Kazanka River which flows into the Volga.

There's a foreign exchange booth in the long-distance booking office at the train station. Ak Bars Bank (☎ 49 35 56), at ulitsa Dekabristov 1, will cash travellers cheques and is open 9am to 7pm Monday to Friday and 9am to 5pm Saturday. It's five minutes from the station by tram No 14 or 21; get off at the first stop after crossing the causeway.

The main post and telephone office is at ulitsa Kremlyovskaya 8 and a convenient telephone office, with Internet facilities, is

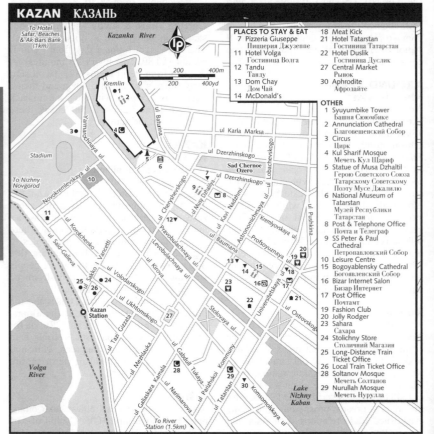

KAZAN КАЗАНЬ

To Hotel Safar, Beaches & Ak Bars Bank (1km)

Kazanka River

Kremlin

Stadium

To Nizhny Novgorod

Volga River

Kazan Station

To River Station (1.5km)

Lake Nizhny Kaban

PLACES TO STAY & EAT
7 Pizzeria Giuseppe
   Пиццерия Джузеппе
11 Hotel Volga
   Гостиница Волга
12 Tandu
   Танду
13 Dom Chay
   Дом Чай
14 McDonald's
18 Meat Kick
21 Hotel Tatarstan
   Гостиница Татарстан
22 Hotel Duslik
   Гостиница Дуслик
27 Central Market
   Рынок
30 Aphrodite
   Афродайте

OTHER
1 Syuyumbike Tower
   Башня Сююмбике
2 Annunciation Cathedral
   Благовещенский Собор
3 Circus
   Цирк
4 Kul Sharif Mosque
   Мечеть Кул Шариф
5 Statue of Musa Dzhaltil
   Герою Советского Союза
   Татарскому Советскому
   Поэту Мусе Джалилю
6 National Museum of
   Tatarstan
   Музей Республики
   Татарстан
8 Post & Telephone Office
   Почта и Телеграф
9 SS Peter & Paul
   Cathedral
   Петропавловский Собор
10 Leisure Centre
14 Bogoyablensky Cathedral
   Богоявленский Собор
16 Bizar Internet Salon
   Бизар Интернет
17 Post Office
   Почтамт
19 Fashion Club
20 Jolly Rodger
23 Sahara
   Сахара
24 Stolichny Store
   Столичний Магазин
25 Long-Distance Train
   Ticket Office
26 Local Train Ticket Office
28 Soltanov Mosque
   Мечеть Солтанов
29 Nurullah Mosque
   Мечеть Нурулла

Moscow's 1812 Victory Arch in a winter mist.

Orator Lenin, outside Finland Station, Moscow.

St Isaac's Cathedral at dusk, St Petersburg.

Church of the Resurrection of Christ, St Petersburg.

GUM state department store, Moscow.

Cathedral of Christ the Saviour, Moscow.

JOHN KING

JONATHAN SMITH

SIMON RICHMOND

GEORGI SHABLOVSKY

SIMON RICHMOND

SIMON RICHMOND

SIMON RICHMOND

Multiple Matryoshka dolls.

SCOTT DARSNEY

Bolts of fabric on sale at Ulaan Baatar's Khar Zakh market.

MARLENE GOLDMAN

Everything a Mongolian horseman could need, Khar Zakh market.

SIMON RICHMOND

Fresh Irkutsk produce.

SIMON RICHMOND

Decorative enamelled boxes.

SIMON RICHMOND

Dried *omul* from Lake Baikal, to supplement your journey..

on the corner of ulitsa Pushkina and ulitsa Profsoyuznaya. Bizar Internet Salon, in room 313 of the old Sovet Hotel, at ulitsa Universitetskaya 7, is open 9am to 10pm daily. It charges $1.25 per hour.

Kremlin

Declared a Unesco World Heritage Site in November 2000, Kazan's striking Kremlin (main entrance at the northern end of ulitsa Kremlyovskaya), is best admired from a distance. It has been rebuilt a number of times over the last five centuries. At the time of research no buildings were open to visitors, although it's a pleasant stroll through the grounds and around bits of the white limestone walls dating from the 16th and 17th centuries.

Undergoing renovation when we visited, the 1562 **Annunciation Cathedral** *(Blagoveshchensky sobor)* was designed by the same architect responsible for St Basil's Cathedral in Moscow. Nearby the slightly leaning 17th-century, 59m **Syuyumbike Tower** *(Bashnya Syuyumbike)* is named after a long-suffering princess married to three successive khans.

Legend claims the reason for the siege of Kazan by Ivan IV was Syuyumbike's refusal to marry the tsar. To save her city, she agreed to marry him only if a tower higher than any other mosque in Kazan could be built in a week. As soon as the tower was completed, though, Syuyumbike killed herself by jumping from its upper terrace.

Today the tower has a rival landmark. Under construction since the mid-1990s and nearing completion is the enormous **Kul Sharif Mosque** *(Mechet Kul Sharif)*, with a turquoise blue dome and four minarets.

Museums, Cathedrals & Mosques

Outside the Kremlin's main entrance is an imposing **statue** of Tatar poet Musa Dzhaltil, who was taken prisoner in Germany during WWII. Opposite is the **National Museum of Tatarstan** *(Muzey Respubliki Tatarstan; ☎ 92 89 84, ul Kremlevskaya 2; adult/student $1.25/0.20; open 10am-5pm Tues-Sun)* in an ornate building dating from 1770. Following fire damage the museum is very slowly being restored; at present all that is open is a ground-floor exhibition of Tatar treasures, which are worth a look.

> ## The Tatars
>
> Around one-third of Russia's 2.8 million Tatars form nearly half the population of the Tatarstan republic. The rest of this mostly Muslim people are scattered around the federation with large groups in Eastern Siberia, particularly around ancient Tatar cities such as Tobolsk. They are descended from the Mongol-Tatar armies of Chinggis Khaan.

Among Kazan's several Russian Orthodox churches, the most attractive is the **SS Peter & Paul Cathedral** *(Petropavlovsky Sobor; ul Musy Dzhalila 21; admission free; open noon-3pm Mon, 1pm-3pm Tues-Sun)*. Built between 1723 and 1726, this baroque cathedral, with its heavily decorated facade and soaring iconostasis, commemorates Tsar Peter I's visit to the city in 1722.

On Baumana ulitsa is the striking 90m red-brick tower and the separate golden-domed **Bogoyablensky Cathedral** *(Bogoeblinsky sobor)*. There is also a statue of opera singer Fydor Chalyapin who apparently loved performing in Kazan. Maybe it's in his honour that buskers and karaoke singers gather along this street on summer nights.

There are several 19th-century mosques in the city centre, too. Close by the central market is the **Soltanov Mosque** *(Sultanovskaya mechet; ul Gabdull Tukaya 14)* dating from 1867 and nearby the **Nurullah Mosque** *(Nurulla mechet; ul Kirova 74)*, which has been rebuilt several times since it first went up in 1849.

Places to Stay

Kazan's hotels are an ugly bunch, at least from the outside.

Hotel Volga *(☎ 31 64 58, fax 92 14 69, ul Said-Galeeva 1A)* Singles/doubles $9/15. Best of the cheapies, this clean hotel is closest to the station (so suffers from traffic and train noise), but the rooms are acceptable enough for a night or so.

Hotel Tatarstan *(☎ 38 83 79, fax 38 85 68, ul Pushkina 4)* Singles/doubles from $14/17. This hideous concrete-slab hotel has a good location and some slightly more expensive upgraded rooms. The renovated doubles are cheaper than the renovated singles because they're on a lower floor. Take Tram No 2 from the station.

Hotel Duslik (☎ 92 33 20, fax 92 35 92, ul Pravo-Bulachnaya 49) Singles/doubles from \$15/28. Much the same as the Hotel Tatarstan with a mix of cheaper old rooms and more expensive but bland renovated rooms.

Hotel Safar (☎ 43 97 43, fax 43 98 43, [e] reception@safar.tbit.ru, ul Krasnoselskaya 1) Singles/doubles with breakfast \$34/52. North of the river, this comfortable modern business hotel has reasonable facilities, but little style. Some rooms have impressive views of the Kremlin.

Places to Eat

Dom Chay (ul Baumana 64) Meals about \$1. Serving local dishes such as *mantee* (dumplings) and *lapsha* (a noodle soup), this good self-service cafe is on two floors with the waitress-service room open noon to 8pm.

Aphrodite (☎ 93 45 49, ul Tatarstan 3/2) Mains around \$1.75. Between 11am and 4pm this pleasant restaurant offers self-service Greek (well sort of) and Russian dishes. In the evening there's waitress service from a full menu in English.

Tandu (☎ 92 31 22, ul Baumana 38/17) Mains around \$3. Treat yourself to real Chinese food and decor at this attractive place on a historic strip opposite the old Hotel Kazan.

Meat Kick (☎ 92 93 32, ul Profsoyuznaya 9) Mains around \$8. Your average Western-style steak house, this place is modern and roomy, with a good English menu and a salad bar for a little under \$3.

Pizzeria Giuseppe (☎ 32 09 38, ul Kremlyovskaya 15) Pizza \$1. Best stick with the pizzas, pastries and ice creams here – we found the young staff were clueless on how to operate the expresso machine and we ended up with bitter coffee.

Need we say **McDonald's** (ul Baumana 70A) is one of the most popular pitstops?

The colourful, sprawling **central market** (ul Mezhlauka) is worth browsing even if you don't want to go shopping for supplies for your train journey or for a picnic lunch. The **Stolichny** store opposite the station is handy for last-minute purchases for the train trip.

Entertainment

Once you've taken your constitutional down Baumana ulitsa, Kazan presents a variety of evening entertainment. That UFO-looking building on Yarmarochnaya ulitsa is actually the **circus**; look for posters to see if there's a show on here. Nearby, the giant glass pyramid (still under construction when we visited) promises to be a state-of-the-art **leisure centre** with cinemas and bowling alley. **Jolly Rodger** (☎ 36 63 43, ul Pushkina 15) has an excellent jazz band playing nightly; it serves food too, although we weren't brave enough to order the 'chicken chest in woodoo style'. There's dancing at the **Fashion Club** (ul Profsoyuznaya 25).

The brightly decorated pub/cafe/club (take your pick) **Sahara** (☎ 60 57 51, ul Pravo-Bulachnaya 47) does have an African theme, though you'd hardly know it from the food – basically shashlyk on plastic plates.

Getting There & Away

Train Frequent trains link Kazan to Moscow's Kazan Station (\$24 kupe, 15 hours). Several also serve Yekaterinburg (\$35, 16 to 17 hours). Train No 212 goes to Perm daily at 10.35pm (\$10.50, 15½ hrs).

The beautifully restored original train station, an attraction in itself, is only a waiting room. Just north, the tatty 1960s building handles suburban tickets. Farther north, long-distance tickets are sold in a new building that's sleek inside and out. If the ground-floor ticket counters are busy, try the 2nd floor.

Air Tickets for flights to Moscow (Domodedovo; 1½ hours, twice daily) and St Petersburg (3¾ hours, three times weekly) can be purchased in the long-distance ticket office at the train station or at the Avia Kassa (☎ 37 97 65), Levo-Bulachnaya ulitsa 42. Lufthansa has twice-weekly flights to/from Frankfurt.

Bus There are buses three times a week to Moscow (18 hours, \$8.50) that go via Nizhny Novgorod (seven hours, \$5.50) The long-distance bus station (☎ 93 04 00) is where ulitsa Tatarstan meets ulitsa Portovaya and is served by tram No 7 from the train station.

Boat The river station for cruises along the Volga is at the end of Tatarstan ulitsa.

Getting Around

Bus, tram or trolleybus tickets cost \$0.05; pay once you're on board. The airport bus leaves roughly hourly from 4am to 10.30pm. The stop is in front of the Stolichny store across from the train station. Tram No 7 links the train and river stations.

Yekaterinburg to Krasnoyarsk

The Route

Yekaterinburg to Omsk

All major east-bound trains halt at **Yekaterinburg** for 15 to 30 minutes. There are several places to get food in and just outside the station building, which was being upgraded when we visited. For more on Yekaterinburg see that section later in this chapter.

Siberia officially begins at **2102km**, the border between Sverdlovskaya and Tyumenskaya oblasts. Not long after, the train makes a 15-minute stop in **Tyumen** (2138km), oil capital and the oldest city in Siberia. In a letter to Lonely Planet one reader accurately summed up this station as 'a gaudy modernist concrete slab with an oversized clock'.

From Tyumen our route detours 274km north-east off the official Trans-Siberian line to the old Siberian capital of **Tobolsk**. It's an interesting trip through deciduous forest and near the 212km marker from Tyumen marshland there's a spectacular view of Tobolsk's kremlin in the distance.

Back on the main Trans-Siberian route east, the next major stop is **Ishim** (2428km) – for 15 minutes – another long-established trade town on the west bank of the Ishim River. At **2497km**, local time becomes Moscow time plus three hours. Around here the land is swampy, providing good opportunities for bird-spotters.

Moscow time + 0300

There's another 15-minute halt at Nazyvaevskaya (2562km); you'll now be into day three of your journey from Moscow. After crossing the six-span bridge over the Irtysh River, the train pauses for 25 minutes in Omsk (2716km), where Dostoevsky was exiled in 1849.

Omsk to Krasnoyarsk

After Omsk you'll notice a sharp increase in the number of passing freight trains. This is the busiest section of railway in the world for freight, most of it coal from the Kuzbas Basin east of Novosibirsk heading for the smelting works of the Urals.

At **Barabinsk** (3035km), which was once a place of exile for Polish Jews, there's a 17-minute stop. You're now in the midst of

Highlights

- Walk through a visual textbook of modern Russian history in Yekaterinburg.

- Explore Tobolsk's elegant kremlin and quietly crumbling old town.

- Discover the charming Siberian wooden architecture of Tomsk.

- Indulge in Novosibirsk's big-city restaurants and nightlife.

- Inspect the antique locos and carriages at the West Siberian Rail Museum.

the Barabinsk Steppe, a boggy expanse of grassland and lakes that was once the homeland of the Kirghiz people.

Around **3330km** get ready for the seven-span, 870m-long Ob River bridge, which crosses one of the world's longest rivers, flowing over 4000km from its source in the Altay Mountains to the Arctic Ocean. Just before the bridge, a small community of wooden cottages, to the north of the train, stand in contrast to the modern city – Siberia's largest – on the other side.

During the 20-minute stop at **Novosibirsk** (3343km), take a moment to inspect the grand interior of the station building – a real Temple of the Trans-Siberian – or seek out the replica of the first steam engine used at the station, which is mounted on the platform. Novosibirsk is also the junction for the Turk-Sib route through to Almaty in Kazakhstan, where you can transfer to the *Genghis Khan Express* to Ürümqi in China (for full details read Lonely Planet's *Central Asia*).

Moscow time + 0400

At 3479km, the frontier between the Novosibirskaya and Kemerovskaya oblasts, Trans-Siberian time shifts ahead again to make it Moscow time plus four hours. The 25-minute halt at Taiga (3565km), provides plenty of time to contemplate a switch to the branch line to Tomsk, 79km north. British readers of a certain age will know the name of this old Siberian city, founded

YEKATERINBURG TO KRASNOYARSK

in 1604, through the kids TV program The Wombles – its attractive traditional architecture certainly makes it worth a detour.

Mariinsk (3713km), a 20-minute stop, was the focus of a Siberian gold rush in the 19th century, when 50 tons of the metal were dug up in the region. Keep an eye out for the engine repair yard to the south of the train as you approach the station. Leaving town the route crosses the Kiya River.

The border between western and eastern Siberia is at **3820km**, the start of Krasnoyarsky Kray. A *kray* is a large territory and this one covers 2.5 million sq km, a region of great mineral and forest wealth stretching all the way to the Arctic coast.

After **Bogotol** (3846km), where there's an eight-minute stop, the route descends to

cross the Chulim River just after **Achinsk-1** (3914km), where there's another brief pause. 'You'll be bored from the Urals to the Yenisey,' wrote Chekhov about his crossing of Siberia along the old post road. Though he'd have surely changed his mind along this stretch of the railway; the landscape is gloriously cinematic, the train twisting through forests and over hills.

A small white obelisk at **3932km**, south of the train line and difficult to spot, marks the halfway point between Moscow and Beijing (via Ulaan Baatar). Around **4079km** wooden cabins are picturesquely sited north of the train. A 1989 brick locomotive shed marks the approach to **Krasnoyarsk** (4098km), capital of the kray beside the Yenisey River, where all major services stop for 20 minutes.

YEKATERINBURG TO KRASNOYARSK

Main Trans-Siberian Route
Alternative Routes

0	100	200km
0	60	120mi

Khanty-Mansi
Autonomous
Okrug

Nizhnevartovsk

Vasyugan River

Tym

Krasnoyarsky
Kray

Tomsk
Oblast

Ket

Uluyul River

Lesosibirsk

Tara River

Barabinsk

Tomsk

Taiga

Mariinsk

Bogotol

Achinsk

Kemerovo
Oblast

Novosibirsk
Oblast

Kemerovo

Krasnoyarsk

Ob Sea

Novosibirsk

Divnogorsk

BARABINSK		NOVOSIBIRSK		TAIGA		MARIINSK	Bogotol	Achinsk-1		KRASNOYARSK
	3hr, 30min		3hr, 35min		2hr	1hr, 50min	1hr		3hr	
3035km		3343km		3565km		3713km	3846km	3914km		4098km

East to Vladivostok

YEKATERINBURG
ЕКАТЕРИНБУРГ

☎ 3432 • pop 1.37 million
🕐 Moscow time + 0200

With a notoriously bloody and secret history – something to which high-profile Mafia killings in the 1990s added a contemporary edge – Yekaterinburg, birthplace of Boris Yeltsin and focus of the Ural's industrial and mineral wealth, is an intriguing place on paper. In reality, it's even better – a pleasant city to stroll through, with stacks of museums (26 of them!), a fascinating variety of architecture, and an above-average range of accommodation, restaurants and entertainment possibilities.

Sometimes written as Ekaterinburg (and still called Sverdlovsk, its Soviet name, on railway timetables), the city is a good base for trips farther afield into the Ural Mountains for adventure activities such as river rafting (don't expect rapids though) in the summertime, and dog sledding and cross-country skiing in winter. If you have time, a visit to the architectural museum at Nizhnyaya Sinyachikha, 150km north-east of Yekaterinburg, is also recommended.

History

Founded as a factory-fort in 1723 as part of Peter the Great's push to exploit the Ural region's mineral riches, the city was named after two Yekaterinas – Peter's wife (later Empress Catherine I), and Russia's patron saint of mining. After discovering his wife's infidelity a year later, Peter had her lover's

Boris Yelstin, former Russian president and Yekaterinburg son, believes in alternative after-care techniques for open-heart surgery.

head cut off and placed in a jar of surgical spirits in her bedroom.

By the 19th century Yekaterinburg, already wealthy through the machinery that it supplied to the Ural mines, also became a gold-rush town. Gold is still being discovered here – a find in the 1980s during excavations for the city's metro helped to pay for the metro line itself.

Yekaterinburg is most famous, though, as the place where Tsar Nicholas II, his wife and children were murdered by the Bolsheviks in July 1918. Six years later, the town was renamed Sverdlovsk, after Yakov Sverdlov, a leading Bolshevik who is said to have arranged the murders.

WWII turned the city into a major industrial centre as hundreds of factories were transferred here from vulnerable areas west of the Urals. It was closed to foreigners until 1990 because of its many defence plants. Remnants of this era still litter the city with fighter planes proudly displayed in school yards and missiles arranged outside the city's Military History Museum.

It was one such missile that in 1960 brought down the US pilot Gary Powers and his U2 spy plane in this area. Powers, who bailed out successfully, was exchanged for a Soviet spy in 1962. In 1979, 64 people died of anthrax after a leak from Sverdlovsk-19, a biological weapons plant in the city.

In 1991, Yekaterinburg reclaimed its original name. After economic depression and

Mafia lawlessness in the early 1990s, business is now on the up, the local economy growing by some 20% in 2000. Factories designed for military production are now tailoring their talents to civilian uses. One that used to make tanks and air-defence systems now specialises in CD ROMs in partnership with the Dutch firm Phillips.

Orientation

The train station is 2km north of the city centre, which is roughly bordered by prospekt Lenina in the north, ulitsa Malysheva in the south, ploshchad 1905 Goda in the west and ulitsa Lunacharskogo in the east. Ulitsa Sverdlova runs south from the station, changing its name to ulitsa Karla Libknekhta closer to the centre. Prospekt Lenina crosses the dammed Iset River three blocks west of ulitsa Karla Libknekhta.

Although changes to some street names have long been on the cards, the old names are likely to be used by locals for the foreseeable future. Just in case changes are made, they include:

old name	new name
ul Sverdlova	Arsenevsky prosp
nab Rabochey-Molodyozhi	nab Gimnazicheskaya
prosp Lenina	Glavny prosp
ul Malysheva	Pokrovsky prosp
ul Kuybysheva	Sibirsky prosp
ul Lunacharskogo	Vasnetsovskaya ul
ul Karla Libknekhta	Voznesensky prosp
ul Rozy Lyuxemburg	Zlatoustovskaya ul

Maps Karta (☎ 75 62 90), at ulitsa Pervomayskaya 74, offers the best range of maps for both the Yekaterinburg area and the rest of the country. It's open 9am to 1pm and 2pm to 6pm Monday to Friday. The Knigi bookshop near the train station opposite the end of ulitsa Sverdlova, also stocks maps of the city and surrounding areas.

Information

Tourist Offices For information head to Ekaterinburg C&V Bureau & Guide Centre (☎ 68 16 04, fax 55 60 19, ⓔ ecvisitor@ mail.ur.ru) on the 2nd floor of the Urals Mineralogical Museum. It's at ulitsa Krasnoarmeyskaya 1, on the corner of the Bolshoy Ural Hotel behind the Opera Theatre.

The Kazakhstan Connection

From 1892 to 1895 the West Siberian Railway was constructed between Chelyabinsk, 252km south of Yekaterinburg, and the small settlement of Novo Nikolayevsk (which later became Novosibirsk). There are still trains between Yekaterinburg and Omsk along this route, which passes through the city of Petropavlovsk, now in northern Kazakhstan. If you take this service, it's a good idea to have a transit visa for Kazakhstan since your passport may be checked.

Money There are many exchange bureaus around town, including ones at the railway station in Hall No 1 and at the post office. The Uralvneshtorgbank, ulitsa Generalskaya 7, cashes American Express travellers cheques. It's open 9am to 1pm and 2pm to 8pm weekdays, and until 6pm on weekends.

Post & Communications The main post office, prospekt Lenina 39, offers Internet connections and international telephone services in room 148 (turn right as you enter the building). The Pochtovaya Lavka on the western corner of the building is a good place to buy stamps and postcards. It's open 10am to 7pm Monday to Friday.

Internet access is available at the fast-food cafe Pingvin, prospekt Lenina 40/8, open 10am to 10pm daily. The entrance is on ulitsa Karla Libknekhta.

Bookshops Knigi Druzhba, at ulitsa Voevodina 4, is open 10am to 2pm and 3pm to 7pm Monday to Friday, and 10am to 5pm on Saturday and Sunday. It stocks a small selection of English-language classics.

Visa Registration The OVIR (Department of Visas & Registration) is at ulitsa Krylova 2 in a red-brick building (take tram No 2, 13 or 18 to the ulitsa Krylova stop). It's open 10am to 5pm on Monday, from 9am to 5pm on Wednesday and 9am to 4pm on Friday (closed noon to 2pm).

Travel Agencies Ekaterinburg C&V Bureau & Guide Centre (see Information earlier) is run by the enthusiastic Konstantin Brylyakov who can arrange inexpensive hotel and homestay accommodation and a wide range of English-language tours of the city and surrounding area, including one-day rafting trips in the Urals from $35 to $75 per person (depending on numbers). City walking tours lasting three hours start at $20 per person, including entry to one museum.

Sputnik (☎ 59 83 00, fax 71 34 83, e sputnik@dialup.mplik.ru), ulitsa Pushkina 5, is a long-standing agency that handles bookings for the major hotels and it can arrange all kinds of air tickets. Its tours include three-hour sightseeing tours of the city in English for $65 and geology and other tours out to the Europe-Asia border that last up to four hours at a maximum cost of $110 per person.

Dangers & Annoyances Make sure you boil the tap water before drinking it.

Museums

Among Yekaterinburg's many museums our favourite – and one of the most original we've found in Russia – is the **Museum of Youth** (*Muzey Molodyozhi;* ☎ *51 77 93, ul Karla Libknekhta 32; admission $0.50; open 10am-6pm Mon-Fri*). The highly imaginative and often surreal displays, relating to 20th-century history, were created by local art students.

Almost as interesting is the neighbouring **Museum of Photography** (*Muzey Fotografii;* ☎ *71 38 14, ul Karla Libknekhta 36; admission $0.30; open 11am-5.30pm Wed-Mon*), where you can see some evocative photographs of old Yekaterinburg as well as modern exhibitions.

The star exhibit of the **Museum of Fine Arts** (*Muzey Izobrazitelnykh Iskusstvs;* ☎ *51 06 26, ul Voevodina 5; admission $1; open 11am-7pm Wed-Sun*), at the southern end of Istorichesky skver, is the elaborate Kasli Iron Pavilion that won prizes in the 1900 Paris Expo. There are other good examples of local crafts and arts here.

Across the river, the **Museum of City Architecture & Urals Industrial Technology** (*Muzey Istorii Arkhitektury Goroda i Promyshlennoy Tekhniki Urala;* ☎ *71 40 45, ul Gorkogo 4 & 5; admission $0.30; open 11am-6pm Mon & Wed-Sat*) is housed in an old (though not the original) mining-equipment factory and mint buildings. Inside you'll find antique machinery and an exhibition on the growth of the city.

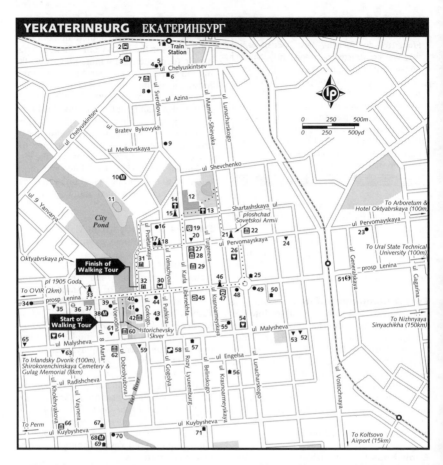

YEKATERINBURG ЕКАТЕРИНБУРГ

Train Station

ul Chelyuskintsev

ul Sverdlova

ul Azina

ul Mamina-Sibiryaka

ul Lunacharskogo

ul Chelyuskintsev

ul Bratev Bykovykh

ul Melkovskaya

ul Shevchenko

ul 9 Yanvarya

City Pond

Shartashskaya ul

ploshchad Sovetskoi Armii

ul Proletarskaya

ul Tolmachova

ul Pervomayskaya

ul Turgeneva

Oktyabrskaya pl

Finish of Walking Tour

pl 1905 Goda

To OVIR (2km)

prosp Lenina

ul Karla Libknekhta

Start of Walking Tour

ul Voevodina

ul Sakko

ul Pushkina

Istorichevsky Skver

ul Malysheva

ul 8 Marta

ul Dobrolyubova

ul Khokhryakova

ul Vaynera

ul Rozy Lyuksemburg

ul Gogolya

ul Belinskogo

ul Krasnoarmeyskaya

IsetRiver

To Irlandsky Dvorik (100m), Shirokorenchinskaya Cemetery & Gulag Memorial (8km)

ul Radishcheva

To Perm

ul Kuybysheva

ul Kuybysheva

ul Engelsa

ul Krasnoarmeyskaya

ul Lunacharskogo

ul Generalskaya

ul Gagarina

prosp Lenina

ul Krasnoarmeyskaya

ul Vostochnaya

To Arboretum & Hotel Oktyabrskaya (100m)

ul Pervomayskaya

To Ural State Technical University (100m)

To Nizhnyaya Sinyachikha (150km)

To Koltsovo Airport (15km)

0   250   500m
0   250   500yd

The **Military History Museum** *(Voenno-istorichesky muzey; ☎ 55 17 42, ul Pervo-mayskaya 27; admission $0.30; open 9am-4pm Tues-Sat)* is a must-see for military buffs, but unfortunately it's not always open. To check, call ahead or ask at the Ekaterinburg C&V Bureau & Guide Centre (see Information earlier). A few scraps of metal in case 13 upstairs are all that's left on display of Gary Power's shot-down American spy plane.

The **Regional Local Studies Museum** *(Oblastnoy kraevedchesky muzey; ☎ 76 47 58, ul Malysheva 46; admission $1; open 11am-6pm Mon & Wed-Sat, closed first Mon of month)* has some interesting exhibits dedicated to the Old Believers in the Ural region, and old Yekaterinburg.

Serious geologists should visit the **Ural Geology Museum** *(Uralsky Geologichesky muzey; 29 49 38, ul Kuybysheva 39; admission $1; open 11am-5.30pm Mon-Wed & Fri, 2pm-6pm Thur)*, which has over 500 carefully catalogued Ural-region minerals and a collection of meteorites. Less specialised is the **Urals Mineralogical Museum** *(Muzey Kamiya; ☎ 55 60 19, ul Krasnoarmeyskaya 1A; admission $1; open 10am-6pm Tues-Sat)*, which has an impressive, but not very imaginatively displayed, collection of rare minerals and semiprecious stones from the surrounding area.

Finally, for railway enthusiasts, there's a small **museum** *(☎ 58 53 22, ul Chelyuskin-tsev 102; admission free; noon-6pm Tues-Sat)* in the **House of Culture of Railway**

YEKATERINBURG ЕКАТЕРИНБУРГ

PLACES TO STAY

1	Komnaty Otdykha
	Комнаты Отдыха
6	Hotel Sverdlovsk
	Гостиница Свердловск
25	Hotel Iset
	Гостиница Исет
50	The Academy of Geology Hotel
56	Premier Hotel
57	Hotel Tsentralnaya
	Гостиница Центральная
67	Hotel Magistr
	Гостиница Магистр
69	Hotel of the Urals Academy of State Service
71	Atrium Palace Hotel & City Bar
	Атриум Палас Отель

PLACES TO EAT

5	Stolovaya
	Столовая
20	Sem Sorok
	Семь Сорок
24	Stolovaya Kompaniya Proviant
	Столовая Компания Провиант
35	Mak Pik
	Мак Пик
52	Master
	Мастер
53	Elephant Kafe
	Элефант Кафе
59	Kamenny Most
	Каменний Мост
61	Akvarium
	Аквариум
63	La Gradara
	Ла Градара
65	Nigora
	Нигора

METRO STATIONS

3	Uralskaya
	Уралская
10	Dinamo
	Динамо
38	Ploshchad 1905 Goda
	Площадь 1905 Года
68	Geologicheskaya
	Геологическая

OTHER

| 2 | Bus Station; Train Ticket Office |
| | Автостанция |

4	Knigi Bookshop
	Магазин Книги
7	House of Culture of Railway Employees
	Дворец Культуры
	Железнодорожников
8	Kirovsky Supermarket
	Кировский
9	Central City Railways Office
	Центральные Городские
	Железнодорожные Кассы
11	Dinamo Stadium
	Стадион Динамо
12	Rastorguev-Kharitonov Mansion
	Усадьба Расторгуева-
	Харитонова
13	Ascension Church
	Вознесенская Церковь
14	Church of Blood
15	Romanov Death Site
	Место Убийста Романовых
16	Bandstand
17	Siberian Trakt Post House
	Объединенный Музей
	Писателей Урала Дом-Музей
	ФМ Решетникова
18	Pushkin Statue
19	Philharmonic
	Филармония
20	Afghanistan War Monument
22	Military History Museum
	Военно-Исторический Музей
23	Karta Map Shop
	Карта Магазин
26	Malakhit
	Малахит
27	Museum of Photography
	Музей Фотографии
28	Museum of Youth
	Музей Молодёжи
29	Yekaterinburg History Museum
	Музей Истории
	Екатеринбурга
30	Post Office
	Почтамт
31	Governor's Residence
	Резиденция Губернатора
32	Nikolai Sevastianof Mansion
	Дом Николай Севастианоф
33	Lenin's Statue
34	Souvenir Market
36	Toilet
	Туалет

37	City Hall
	Городской Совет
39	Knigi Druzhba
	Книги Дружба
40	Water Tower
	Водонапорная Башня
41	Nature Department
	Отдел Природы
42	Museum of City Architecture & Urals Industrial Technology
	Музей Истории Архит-
	ектуры Города и
	Промышленной Техники
	Урала
43	Sputnik; Lufthansa
	Спутник; Луфтганса
44	Regional Government Building
45	Pingvin Internet Café
	Пингвин
46	Sverdlov Statue
	Памятник ЯМ Свердлову
47	Opera & Ballet Theatre
	Театр Оперы и Балета
48	Gastronom Tsentralny
	Гастроном Центральный
49	Transaero
	Трансаэро
51	Uralvneshtorgbank
	Уралвнешторгбанк
54	Gans
	Ганс
55	Ekaterinburg C&V Bureau & Guide Centre; Urals Mineralogical Museum
	Екатеринбургский Центр
	Гидов; Музей Камня
58	UK & US General Consulates
	Генеральное Консульство
	Великобритании и
	Генеральное Консульство
	США
60	Fine Arts Museum
	Музей Изобразительных
	Искусств
62	Regional Local Studies Museum
	Историко-Краеведческий
	Музей
64	The Old Dublin Irish Pub
66	Ural Geology Museum
	Уралский Геологический
	Музей
70	Circus
	Цирк

Employees, on the corner opposite the Hotel Sverdlovsk. Outside, as well as a small mounted steam locomotive, you'll find a replica of the first Russian steam locomotive invented by father and son EA & ME Cherepanov in 1834.

University & Arboretum

Ural State Technical University (*Uralsky Gosudarstvenny Tekhnichesky Universitet*), an imposing 1930s Soviet classical edifice at the eastern end of prospekt Lenina 3km from the centre, is the biggest Russian university

Yekaterinburg Walking Tour

'My fondest memory of Yekaterinburg was the amazing profusion of statues. I found it to be a city that rewards the aimless wanderer. In the park behind the city pond we saw some old *babushkas* wandering around repainting all the benches. No wet paint signs or anything. We saw many people with paint across the back of their trousers and dresses, and Mum was one of them!'
Brett Hyland, St Petersburg to Irkutsk, July 2001

We hope that you don't get caught by the bench painters (as Brett's mum did) but we can certainly recommend Yekaterinburg as a place for a relaxed walking tour – an ideal way to take in the scope of the city's tumultuous history.

Start at **Istorichesky skver** *(Historical Square)* where prospekt Lenina crosses a small dam forming the Gorodskoy prud (City Pond) on its northern side, with the Iset River funnelled through a narrow channel on the southern side. This was where Yekaterinburg began back in 1723. Water from the dam (reconstructed twice since that date) powered an iron forge below it. A mint and a stone-cutting works soon followed.

Istorichesky skver is surrounded by a clutch of statues, old buildings turned into museums (see Museums later) and on its western side **Geological Alley** (Geologicheskaya alleya), a small park dotted with large, labelled rocks from the Ural region. Here you'll also find a time capsule to be opened in 2023 (when it will be interesting to see what the communists 50 years earlier wanted preserved of their era).

About 100m west along prospekt Lenina is another square, **ploshchad 1905 Goda** – the looming **statue of Lenin** here occupies the spot where once stood one of Yekaterinburg's main cathedrals, destroyed in the Soviet period. Farther west prospekt Lenina is split by a strip of tree-shaded park where souvenir sellers gather daily.

Returning to the bridge you'll pass the striking red-sculpted Order of Lenin given to the city for honourable service during WWII. Ahead on prospekt Lenina are several buildings that show how much architecture changed in Yekaterinburg over a century. On the corner by the bridge the eclectic 19th-century **Nikolai Sevastianof mansion** (now a trade union headquarters), the exotic creation of a rich merchant who wanted his house to outshine that of the governor's, which stands next door.

In total contrast are the clean lines of the **central post office** and the **regional government building** opposite, both prime examples of 1930s constructivism. Heading farther east along Lenina you'll pass the attractive **Opera & Ballet Theatre**. The strip of park in front has a **statue of Yakov Sverdlov**, the Communist Party official who ordered the massacre of the tsar and his family, and who died himself a year later in 1919.

At the roundabout head north up ulitsa Lunacharskogo for 700m to reach **ploshchad Sovetskoi Armii**, dominated by one of the most powerful statues you're likely to see in Russia. The giant soldier with downcast head is primarily a **monument** commemorating lives lost in the Afghanistan War (1979–89) but plaques around the statue also remember those lost in other Soviet conflicts of the Cold War years.

east of the Ural Mountains. It's still known as UPI – the initials of its old name, Uralsky Politekhnichesky Institut (Ural Polytechnical Institute), when it was renowned as a stepping stone to high political office – for Boris Yeltsin, among many others.

There's a nice, quiet open-air **arboretum** *(Dendrologichesky Park-Vystavka)* a block north of the university, on the corner of ulitsa Pervomayskaya and ulitsa Mira. You can reach the university by tram No 4, 13, 15 or 18 or bus No 28 east along prospekt

Lenina. Get off the tram when it turns right down ulitsa Gagarina, a block before the university.

Places to Stay – Budget
You'll have to be lucky to score a place at the station's *komnaty otdykha* (Level 4, west wing, main train station). Doubles/triples with shared bathroom $5, doubles with bathroom $13. The rooms are clean and will do for a night but the station is so busy that they fill up quickly.

Yekaterinburg Walking Tour

Continue north from the square along ulitsa Mamina-Sibiryaka to the entrance of a pretty park that climbs up the hill, known locally as the Yekaterinburg Acropolis. At the top is the ostentatious classical-fronted mansion of a rich 19th-century gold family called **Rastorguev-Kharitonov** (now used for after-school clubs), and the restored **Ascension Church** (Voznesenskaya tserkov; ul Karla Tsetkin 11), used as a nature museum during the Soviet era.

Immediately ahead of the church, across ulitsa Karla Libknekhta, is the **Romanov Death Site**. It was here that Tsar Nicholas II, his wife and five children were murdered on the night of 16 July 1918 in the cellar of a house known as Dom Ipateva, after its owner, Nikolay Ipatev. It was demolished by local governor Boris Yeltsin in 1977 (on Politburo orders, he says). Today, the site is marked by an iron cross dating from 1991, and another of marble from 1998 when the Romanovs' remains were sent to St Petersburg for burial in the family vault. Beside the crosses stands the pretty little wooden **Chapel of the Revered Martyr Grand Princess Yelisaveta Fyodorovna** (Chasovnya vo Imya Prepodobnomuchenitsy Velikoi Knyagini Yelisavety Fyodorovny; open 9am-5.30pm daily).

Grand Princess Yelisaveta, great-aunt of the royal family, was a pious nun who, soon after her relatives' murders, reportedly met an even worse end. When she survived being thrown down a mine, poisonous gas was pumped in and the shaft filled with earth. You can visit this spot, where a monastery has recently been built, on a trip to Nizhnyaya Sinyachikha (see Around Yekaterinburg later in this chapter). Inside the chapel are modern paintings of Yelisaveta and the Romanovs.

The chapel is already overshadowed by the neighbouring Byzantine-style **Church of the Blood** (Tserkov na Krovi), construction of which was well under way when we visited. This will honour the Romanovs, now elevated to the status of saints.

Head south from here along ulitsa Karla Libknekhta, turn west at the ulitsa Pervomayskaya, then north along the second street you come to, ulitsa Proletarskaya (also called Ofitserskaya), where several of the wooden buildings are small museums dedicated to local writers. At No 6 is an old **Siberian Trakt post house** marked by a pole showing the distances – in the ancient Russian measurement of versts – to Moscow and St Petersburg.

Near here is the inevitable **statue of Pushkin**, although in a non-traditional pose; it's supposed to be the poet waking in the middle of the night gripped by inspiration but, surrounded by snow, the poor man just looks like he's freezing. There's also a small **bandstand** at the end of the street where free concerts are held on weekends in June and July. From here it's not very far to the city pond and back to Istorichesky skver.

Tsar Nicholas II and Tsarina Alexandra

The Ekaterinburg C&V Bureau & Guide Centre (see Information earlier) arranges homestays and can get you into the following two hotels otherwise not available to walk-in guests.

The Academy of Geology Hotel (Bldg 6, prosp Lenina 54) Singles/doubles with breakfast $26/30. This is the best budget option with smart, spacious rooms in a quiet complex tucked away off the main road.

Hotel of the Urals Academy of State Service (ul 8 Marta 70) Dorm beds/singles $14/30. Used by visiting civil servants the rooms here are old-fashioned but decent enough. There's a cheap *bufet* on the ground floor, open 10.30am to 3pm. Tram No 15 going west from anywhere along prospekt Lenina will take you there (ask for the Dekabristov stop).

Hotel Tsentralnaya (☎ 55 11 09, fax 55 69 79, ul Malysheva 74) Singles/doubles from $14/24. This is another hotel where you'll need to book ahead for the cheaper rooms. The upgraded doubles are fine but cost $58.

Hotel Sverdlovsk (☎ 53 65 74, fax 53 62 48, ul Chelyuskintsev 106) Singles/doubles from $14/20. The cheap rooms are dilapidated, the upgraded ones overpriced, the corridors so long they seem to fade into infinity. In its favour is its great location opposite the station.

Places to Stay – Mid-Range & Top End

Hotel Iset (☎ 55 69 43, fax 56 24 69, e hotel _resr@etel.ru, prosp Lenina 69) Singles/ doubles from $52/69. In a building shaped like a hammer and sickle, this hotel has bright and comfortable rooms, all with their own bathrooms. The staff are friendly.

Hotel Oktyabrskaya (☎ 74 15 95, fax 74 50 16, e man@gw.ural.ru, ul Sofyi Kovalevskaya 17) Singles/doubles 1st night from $42/61, following nights $32/47. This former Communist Party hang-out is in a leafy neighbourhood 3km east of the centre, off ulitsa Pervomayskaya. It's a comfortable choice with professional staff and service.

Hotel Magister (☎ 22 42 06, fax 22 56 74, e magister@mail.utnet.ru, ul 8 Marta 50) Singles/doubles with breakfast $88/100. Stylishly furnished rooms at this small hotel are popular with businesspeople (so you will need to reserve a couple of weeks in advance). Tram No 15 running west along prospekt Lenina goes past the door. Get off just before the circus.

Premier Hotel (☎ 56 38 97, fax 56 38 80, ul Krasnoarmeyskaya 23) Singles/doubles $83/117. This is a new place with big, stylishly decorated rooms.

Atrium Palace Hotel (☎ 59 60 00, fax 59 60 01, e info@aph-ural.ru, ul Kuybysheva 44) Singles/doubles with breakfast $198/ 251. The Atrium Palace is the top option, with a good restaurant, popular bar and a nightclub. Use of the gym with sauna and pool is included in the price.

Places to Eat

Restaurants The menu is short but sweet at *Nigora* (☎ 76 39 41, ul Malysheva 19). This small basement place specialises in Uzbek cuisine, such as *plov* (a meaty pilaf) and the noodle stew *lagman* for about $2.

Akvarium (☎ 59 82 19, ul Voevodina 6) Mains around $6. Watch fish swim in tanks dotted around this cosy restaurant, where – surprise, surprise – there is mainly fish on the menu!

Sem Sorok (☎ 55 70 17, ul Pervomayskaya 9) Excellent Jewish food, including *gefilte fish* and *cholent* (a meat stew) is served at this classy restaurant.

Kamenny Most (☎ 56 19 55, ul Malysheva 56A) Mains from $6. A pleasant and friendly restaurant offering good Russian dishes in stylish surroundings, Kamenny Most overlooks the Iset River.

Elephant Kafe (☎ 24 01 95, ul Malysheva 108) Mains $10. The quirky design features of this upmarket restaurant ape those of a cafe from a popular WWII spy drama on Russian TV. The food's recommended.

For reasonably priced Italian food, but expensive wine, try *La Gradara* (☎ 59 83 66, ul Malysheva 36).

Fast Food, Snacks & Self-Catering For a taste of old-Soviet-style dining try the *Stolovaya Kompaniya Proviant* (2nd floor ul Pervomayskaya 56), where the food resembles school dinners but won't set you back more than $3. Similarly basic, but convenient is the *Stolovaya* (ul Chelyuskintsev 25) around the corner from the station, where you can also get a beer.

Mak Pik (☎ 51 83 98, prosp Lenina 24/8) Meals $3. This funkily decorated burger bar, that also does pizza, *pelmeni* and, of all things, sushi, is a major hang-out. Similar, although sticking to pizzas and salads, is *Master* (ul Malysheva 114), where a small pizza will only set you back $1.50.

Kirovsky (ul Sverdlova 27) is a Western-style supermarket near the train station. *Gastronom Tsentralny* (prosp Lenina 48) has a reasonable range, and there are usually people selling fresh fruit and veges outside.

Entertainment

Classical Music, Opera & Ballet Tickets for the *Opera & Ballet Theatre* (☎ 55 80 57, prosp Lenina 45A) start as low as $1. Those for the *Philharmonic* (☎ 51 73 77, ul Karla Libknekhta 38) are more expensive (from $5) but both institutions are said to put on good shows.

Bars & Clubs At the authentic *The Old Dublin Irish Pub* (☎ 10 91 73, ul Khokhryakova 23) we were sad to be missing out on the forthcoming 'great potato party', but found the desserts, as well as the Guinness, seductive. *Irlandsky Dvorik* (☎ 763 318, ul

Malysheva 11) is also a pleasant place with good food and drink.

Gans *(ul Malysheva 61)* is a German beer bar, with some very quaffable but pricey ales and food.

City Bar *(Atrium Palace Hotel, ul Kuybysheva 44)* is a good place to meet Westerners, especially during its Friday evening happy hour, when cheap fish and chips are served for around $4.

Yekaterinburg's top club is **Malakhit** *(☎ 56 40 48, ul Lunacharskogo 128)*. It's a typically flash place with plenty of options if you don't want to dance. There's a restaurant, strip bar, bowling alley, even a bucking bronco! It's open 9pm to 6am Wednesday to Sunday. Admission on Friday and Saturday is $8 for men and $5 for women. On Wednesday it's $2.50 and $3 on Thursday.

Getting There & Away

Train Yekaterinburg is a major rail junction and apart from the main services between Moscow and Vladivostok or Beijing, there are numerous other daily trains to different cities. Eastbound, some go via Tyumen ($10, 4¼ hours) to Omsk ($40, 12 hours); others via Kurgan and Petropavlovsk (in Kazakhstan) to Omsk. Westbound, some Moscow trains go via Kazan ($35, 15 hours) rather than Perm (see the Kazan section in the Moscow to Yekaterinburg chapter). There are also direct services to/from Tobolsk (12½ hours).

To travel to and from Moscow (Kazan Station), a good choice is the daily flagship *Ural* (No 15/16), which starts and finishes in Yekaterinburg and travels via Kazan ($46, 27½ hours).

Tickets In summer buying a last-minute ticket from Yekaterinburg to Moscow is rarely a problem, however, securing one eastward to Irkutsk and beyond can be tricky. If you're on a tight schedule, it's advisable to make an advance booking through a travel agency, such as Ekaterinburg C&V Bureau & Guide Centre (see the Information section earlier for contact details).

Long-distance tickets are sold on level three in the west wing of the main train station, although you'd be better off trying the service centre on the ground floor first, where you'll pay a $1 commission. Also handy (and generally quieter) is the ticket office in the bus station immediately west of the train station – here the commission will be $2.50.

The Central City Railways Office, ulitsa Sverdlova 25, was closed when we visited, but may re-open in the future.

Air The main airport is Koltsovo (☎ 24 99 24), 15km south-east of the city centre. Daily flights go to/from Moscow ($130, 2½ hours) and Irkutsk ($120, four hours) and there are services several times a week to/from St Petersburg ($120, 2½ hours), Novosibirsk ($80, two hours) and Vladivostok ($240, 11 hours). Lufthansa flies to/from Frankfurt three times weekly ($520, six hours).

The Lufthansa office (☎ 59 83 00) operates from the Sputnik office (see Travel Agencies earlier). Transaero (☎ 65 91 65, fax 77 73 97) is at prospekt Lenina 50 and can handle bookings for all airlines.

Getting Around

Bus No 1 links the train station and Koltsovo airport every 10 to 20 minutes from 5.30am to 11pm. The trip takes around 45 minutes. A taxi to/from the airport costs about $8, but will cost double at night.

Many trolleybuses (pay on board, $0.20) run up and down ulitsa Sverdlova/ulitsa Karla Libknekhta between the train station and prospekt Lenina. Tram Nos 4, 13, 15 and 18 and bus No 28 cover long stretches of prospekt Lenina, with tram Nos 4 and 15 also serving the bus station.

The metro ($0.20) currently runs from the Uralmash machine-tool factory in the north to the train station and into the centre near ploshchad 1905 Goda. A new station, Geologicheskaya, near the circus and Hotel Magistr, should open soon.

AROUND YEKATERINBURG
Shirokorenchinskaya Cemetery & Gulag Memorial
Широкоренчинская

A trip to Shirokorenchinskaya Cemetery, 8km west of the city along the Moskovsky Trakt road, reveals some of Yekaterinburg's more recent history. At the entrance you'll see monumental graves to casualties of gang warfare in the 1990s. One has a life-size engraving of a 35-year-old gangster, with his hand dangling Mercedes keys, a symbol of his wealth.

On the opposite side of the road is a vast memorial, opened in 1992, dedicated to victims of the Gulag (see the boxed text) and the massacres during Stalin's rule. Some 25,000 people were killed in Yekaterinburg and many of their bodies were later discovered to have been secretly buried here.

You can catch a taxi from the city to the cemetery for about $10 return. Alternatively, Ekaterinburg C&V Bureau & Guide Centre (see Information earlier) runs short tours here from $15 to $35 per person depending on numbers.

If you missed the obelisk beside the railway line en route from Perm or if you just wish to have one foot in Europe and one in Asia, then head 32km from here to another Europe-Asia marker. Erected in 1837 at a 413m highpoint in the local Ural Mountains, the marker is in a forest clearing and

is a popular spot for wedding parties to visit on their post-nuptial video and photo jaunts.

Nizhnyaya Sinyachikha & Around
Нижняя Синячиха

The pretty village of Nizhnyaya Sinyachikha, around 150km north-east of Yekaterinburg and 12km north of the town of Alapaevsk, is home to an open-air **architecture museum** *(Muzey Uralskoi Narodnoi Zhevolisi; ☎ 246-7 51 18; admission $0.60; open 10am-4pm Thur-Sun)*. Here are 15 traditional Siberian log buildings, with displays of period furniture, tools and domestic articles. The stone cathedral houses a collection of Ural region folk art, which is one of the best of its kind, and this alone makes it worth the trip.

About 2km west of Nizhnyaya Sinyachikha is a new monastery dedicated to Grand Princess Yelisaveta (see the boxed text 'Yekaterinburg Walking Tour' earlier), on the spot where she died. Back in Alapaevsk there's also a **museum** *(admission $1; open 10am-4pm Tues-Sat)* dedicated to Tchaikovsky in a house where the composer lived as a child.

There are local trains to Alapaevsk from Yekaterinburg, but they're infrequent. It's much better to take a bus from Yekaterinburg or arrange a day trip with Ekaterinburg C&V Bureau & Guide Centre (prices range from $40 to $80 per person depending on the numbers).

TYUMEN
ТЮМЕНЬ
☎ 3452 • pop 600,000
🕓 Moscow time + 0200

Situated on the Tura River, Tyumen is the Dallas of Siberia. The oblast of which it is the capital stretches all the way to the Arctic and is rich in gas and oil. The wealth generated by these resources has made Tyumen noticeably more prosperous and provided it with the mirror-glass tower blocks that seem to be characteristic of oil cities the world over.

It's not all modern; the first Russian fort in Siberia was founded here in 1586 and there are some attractive parts to the city, including a picturesque monastery. But on the whole, you'd be better advised moving sharply on to the much more rewarding old Siberian city of Tobolsk.

The Gulag

The exile system was abolished at the start of the 20th century, but Stalin brought it back with a vengeance, expanding it into a full-blown, home-grown slave trade. It was during his rule that Siberia became synonymous with death. He established a vast bureaucracy of resettlement programs, labour colonies, concentration camps and special psychiatric hospitals, commonly known as the Gulag (Glavnoe Upravlenie Lagerey, or Main Administration for Camps).

The Gulag's inmates – some of whose only 'offence' was to be Jewish, a modern artist or high-profile Buryat, or simply to have shaken the hand of such a person – cut trees, dug canals, laid railway tracks and worked in factories in remote areas, especially Siberia and the Russian Far East. A huge slice of the north-east was set aside exclusively for labour camps, and whole cities such as Komsomolsk-on-Amur and Magadan were developed as Gulag centres.

An estimated 20 million people died in the Gulag. Nadezhda Mandelstam, whose husband Osip Mandelstam, a highly regarded poet, was exiled to Siberia in 1934, wrote that a wife considered herself a widow from the moment of her husband's arrest. She was almost right – Osip lasted four years before dying at the Vtoraya Rechka transit camp in Vladivostok.

Orientation & Information

The train station is 1.5km south of the main street ulitsa Respubliki, which runs across town from the Trinity Monastery, overlooking the Tura River, to the bus station in the south-east of town. Ulitsa Ordzhonikidze runs through the city centre, between ulitsa Respubliki and the parallel street, ulitsa Lenina.

There are exchange bureaus and ATMs in the Quality Hotel and Hotel Vostok, as well as at many banks and exchange offices in ulitsa Respubliki.

The post office is at ulitsa Respubliki 56, the long-distance telephone office nearby at No 51. The latter is open 24 hours and also has a cheap Internet salon (around $0.70 an hour) with fast computers.

Things to See

Opposite the Quality Hotel, the **Fine Arts Museum** *(Muzey Izobrazitelnykh Iskusstv; ☎ 46 91 15, ul Ordzhonikidze 47; admission $0.35; open 10am-6pm Tues-Sun)* is Tyumen's most interesting attraction. Its eclectic collection ranges from a gallery of ornate window frames saved from the city's old wooden houses to tiny, intricately carved bone figures. There are also special exhibitions for which you'll pay extra.

Russian Orthodox church fans should get along to the **Museum Church of St Peter and Paul** *(Tserkov Petra i Pavll; ☎ 46 24 12, ul Kommunisticheskaya 10; admission $0.50; open 10am-5pm Wed-Sun)*, part of an attractive old stone-walled monastery in a fine position above the Tura. The displays, including icons, household objects and local religious practices, are nothing special. Behind the church and within the monastery walls, the black-domed **Cathedral of Trinity Monastery** *(Sobor Troitskogo Mykhskogo monastyr)* is being renovated – you may be able to peek inside.

Also closed for repairs (when we showed up) were the nearby **Town Hall Museum** *(☎ 46 80 71, ul Respubliki 2)*, which contains stuffed animals, mammoth fossils and the like, and the **Marsharov Mansion Museum** *(Dom muzey Masharova; ☎ 46 13 10, ul Lenina 24)*, the house of a rich 19th-century factory owner. The **House Museum of 19th- & 20th-Century History** *(Muzey Istorii Doma; ☎ 46 49 63, ul Respubliki 18; admission $0.25; open 10am-1pm & 2pm-5pm Wed-Sun)* was open and has some marginally interesting displays on the original merchant owner of the house, Ikonnikov, who hosted the future tsar there in 1837, and Blukhera, a Bolshevik general who took up residence during the revolution and was later executed by Stalin.

A block to the north is the baroque, sky blue-and-white, multidomed **Cathedral of the Holy Cross** *(Znamenskii sobor; ul Semakova 13)*, an operating church built in 1786. This area of town is full of attractive **old wooden houses** and is worth a stroll.

Places to Stay & Eat

Other than their price and location, there is very little to recommend the *resting rooms (komnaty otdykha Tyumen)*. Dorm beds/ singles $2.30/5.50. The entrance is from in front of the station.

Hotel Tura (☎/fax 22 99 69, ul Melnikaite 103A) Singles/doubles with breakfast $21/35. Once you get over the very swirly carpets, this small hotel has decent, well-priced rooms and a restaurant.

Hotel Vostok (☎/fax 22 61 24, ul Respubliki 159) Singles/doubles with breakfast both $28. Sure, it's a huge Soviet Intourist-mould hotel, but the unrenovated rooms, all with bathrooms, TV & fridge, are OK. The staff can also be quite friendly when they try. There's a good *supermarket* in the same building, but avoid the restaurant in the evenings if you are not into karaoke-style crooning.

Hotel Prometei (☎/fax 25 14 23, ul Sovetskaya 61) Singles/doubles $30/40. It offers a similar deal to the Vostok, but this hotel is more central.

Quality Hotel (Kvoliti Otel Tyumen; ☎ 49 40 40, fax 49 40 50, e *quality@sbtx.tmn.ru, ul Ordzhonikidze 46)* Singles/doubles with breakfast $78/93. Tyumen's best hotel, this is worth splashing out on. Facilities include a good sauna and gym ($6.70 for use of both, open 11am to 3am daily), the formal *Four Seasons (Vremetna Goda)* restaurant, and more casual but equally salubrious *Cafe Vienna*. Both the restaurants are good value and serve tasty food.

Maksim (☎ 46 60 83, ul Semakova 19) Mains $3-4. Open 11am-late daily. Maksim is an intimate, relatively stylish place, where the well-prepared Russian dishes live up to their photos on the menu.

YEKATERINBURG TO KRASNOYARSK

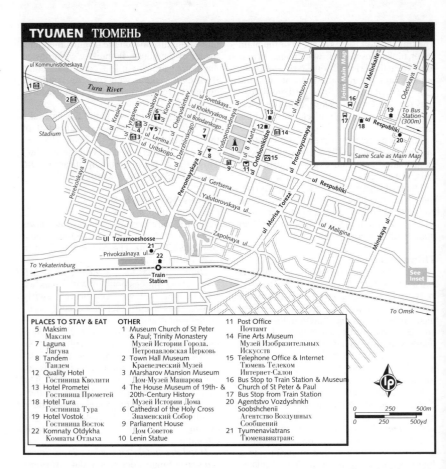

TYUMEN ТЮМЕНЬ

PLACES TO STAY & EAT
5 Maksim
   Максим
7 Laguna
   Лагуна
8 Tandem
   Тандем
12 Quality Hotel
   Гостиница Кволити
13 Hotel Prometei
   Гостиница Прометей
18 Hotel Tura
   Гостиница Тура
19 Hotel Vostok
   Гостиница Восток
22 Komnaty Otdykha
   Комнаты Отдыха

OTHER
1 Museum Church of St Peter
   & Paul; Trinity Monastery
   Музей Истории Города.
   Петропавловская Церковь
2 Town Hall Museum
   Краеведческий Музей
3 Marsharov Mansion Museum
   Дом-Музей Машарова
4 The House Museum of 19th- &
   20th-Century History
   Музей Истории Дома
6 Cathedral of the Holy Cross
   Знаменский Собор
9 Parliament House
   Дом Советов
10 Lenin Statue

11 Post Office
   Почтамт
14 Fine Arts Museum
   Музей Изобразительных
   Искусств
15 Telephone Office & Internet
   Тюмень Телеком
   Интернет-Салон
16 Bus Stop to Train Station & Museum
   Church of St Peter & Paul
17 Bus Stop from Train Station
20 Agentstvo Vozdyshnkh
   Soobshchenii
   Агентство Воздушных
   Сообщений
21 Tyumenaviatrans
   Тюменавиатранс

250   500m
250   500yd

Laguna (☎ *46 24 70, ul Respubliki 33*) Mains $5. Open noon-midnight daily. Part of the World Trade Center, this slick restaurant offers an upmarket range of dishes including a 'caviar sandwich' for $5.

For a slice of piping-hot pizza and a beer try *Tandem* (*ul Respubliki 48*), which is very popular with locals.

Getting There & Away
There are regular links to all Trans-Siberian destinations, including Moscow ($50 to $60, 35 hours), Yekaterinburg ($5, 4½ hours), Omsk ($6.50, 7½ hours) and Novosibirsk ($35 to $40, 18 hours). At least three trains run daily to/from Tobolsk ($6, five hours).

Agentstvo Vozdyshnkh Soobshchenii, ulitsa Respubliki 156, opposite the Hotel Vostok, sells train as well as air tickets. It's a good alternative if the ticket hall at the station is too busy.

Tyumenaviatrans (☎/fax 25 05 32), which is opposite the train station, handles airline reservations. There are services to/from Moscow daily ($100, two hours) and several times weekly to St Petersburg ($133, 2½ hours), as well as to other destinations in the region.

From the bus station on ulitsa Permyakova at the junction with ulitsa Respubliki there are many daily services to Tobolsk.

Getting Around
Any bus ($0.20) from the train station will take you along ulitsa Pervomayskaya to ulitsa Respubliki or ulitsa Lenina. To return

Attendant on the *Okean* train.

Your friendly *provodnitsa* on the No 9/10 Irkutsk-Moscow line.

A relatively luxurious restaurant car on the Trans-Mongolian route.

Stocking up, Krasnoyarsk.

Who needs a washroom?

Enjoying a bowl of *airag* (fermented mare's milk), Mongolia.

Vladivostok's ornate station.

The first stone building at Irkutsk Station was built before 1900.

There are few people to greet the train as it pulls into Sainshand station in Mongolia.

Must see where we are going!

A big red loco awaits a signal to push ahead at Krasnoyarsk.

to the station take bus No 13 on ulitsa Respubliki. Bus No 30 runs the length of ulitsa Respubliki to the monastery.

TOBOLSK
ТОБОЛЬСК
☎ 34511 • pop 118,000
🕐 Moscow time + 0200

Although it's well off the main Trans-Sib route, the old Siberian capital of Tobolsk, 247km north-east of Tyumen at the confluence of the Irtysh and Tobol Rivers, is worth visiting. Its star attractions are a handsome kremlin and an old town on the point of collapse but packed with old wooden houses and churches. Also noteworthy are the late-19th-century mosque and cultural centre of the city's Tatars, who make up some 30% of Tobolsk's population.

History
In 1582, Yermak Timofeevich and his band of Cossack mercenaries sacked the nearby Tatar stronghold of Sibir, later establishing a fort at Tobolsk's strategic location on the Irtysh. This soon became the political, military and religious centre of Russian Siberia, a position it continued to hold until the early 19th century.

Tobolsk was the seat of Siberia's first bishopric from 1620 (set up, incidentally, with the express purpose of stamping out incest, wife-renting and wife-stealing by sexually frustrated Cossacks). From 1708 to 1839 the governor resided here, exercising administrative power throughout Siberia and the Far East.

Tobolsk's importance waned from the 1760s, when the new Great Siberian Trakt road east took a more southerly route, but it remained a significant centre of learning and culture until the early 20th century. This was reinforced by the arrival of educated Decembrists and their families in the 1830s (see the boxed 'The Decembrist Movement' in the Krasnoyarsk to Irkutsk & Lake Baikal chapter).

In 1850, Dostoevsky did time at Tobolsk's jail, en route to his eventual exile in Omsk, while Tsar Nicholas II and the royal family spent several months here in 1917 before being taken to Yekaterinburg. Today the local economy relies on a giant petrochemical plant producing propane, butane and the like, much of it bound for Germany.

Orientation & Information
The railway station is 10km north-east of the modern city centre, an area of ugly Soviet-era concrete blocks that on first sight is not encouraging. The kremlin and the old town, which begins at the foot of the hill and extends south across the valley of the Irtysh River, is 3km south of the city centre.

Turisticheskoe Agenstvo Slavyanskaya (Slavyanskaya Tourist Agency; ☎ 9 91 14, fax 5 58 76, 🇪 sputnik@tob.ru), on the 2nd floor of the Hotel Slavyanskaya (see Places to Stay & Eat later), has knowledgeable staff who, with advance notice, can arrange tours of the city and environs with an English-speaking guide.

You can change cash at the reception of the hotel and there's a Sebrbank on prospekt Mendeleeva, about 500m west of the Hotel Slavyanskaya. The post and telephone office is 900m south along Komsomolsky prospekt. Internet access is available at the Hotel Slavyanskaya.

Kremlin & Around
The elegant 18th-century kremlin, the first in Siberia to be made of stone, is a part of the **Tobolsk State Historian-Architectural Museum Reserve** (☎ 6 41 47, 🇪 museum@ttknet.ru, Krasnaya pl 5), which has ambitious plans for the complex. To find out the latest, contact the museum's Viacheslav Novitsky (☎ 5 41 60) who speaks good English and will happily show you around.

At the time of research part of the notorious 19th-century **prison** (closed since the late 1980s), where Dostoevsky spent time, was under repair to allow anyone who so wishes to stay overnight in one of its dank, cramped cells. The **Gostiny Dvor** (trading arcades), dating from 1703 and currently occupied by the city's archives, will be remade into shops and possibly a hotel. A small **Fine Art Museum**, in the old House of Pioneers just outside the kremlin opposite the Hotel Sibir, should now also be open.

Inside the kremlin *(grounds open 8am-8pm)* the blue-domed **St Sofia Cathedral** *(Sofiysky sobor)*, built in 1686, is the oldest church, while the **Intercession Cathedral** *(Pokrovsky sobor)* is from the 1740s. The **bell tower** was built for the Uglich bell (see the boxed text 'The First Siberian Exile'). The Arkhereisky Dom now houses the **Museum of the Spiritual Cultures of Western Siberia**

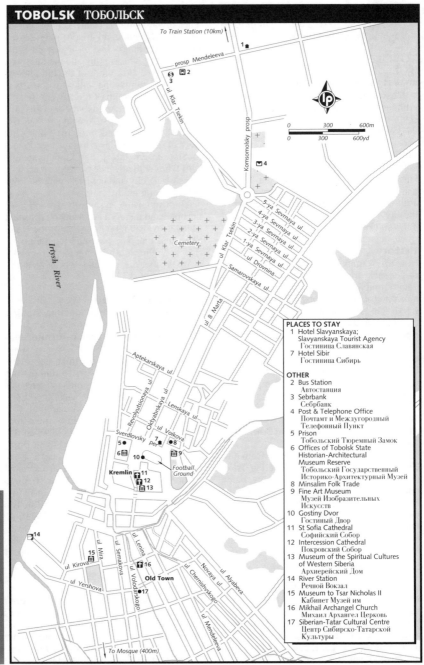

TOBOLSK ТОБОЛЬСК

To Train Station (10km)

prosp Mendeleeva

ul Klar Tsekin

Komsomolsky prosp

Irtysh River

Cemetery

5-ya Sevrnaya ul
4-ya Sevrnaya ul
3-ya Sevrnaya ul
2-ya Sevrnaya ul
1-ya Sevrnaya ul
ul Dromina

Samarovskaya ul

ul 8. Marta

Aptekarskaya ul

Revolutsionaya ul

Oktyabrskaya ul

Lenskaya ul

ul Voikova

Sverdlovsky per

Kremlin

Football Ground

ul Mira

ul Semakova

ul Kirova

ul Yershova

ul Lenina

Old Town

Novaya ul

ul Chernishevskogo

ul Alyabeva

ul Volodarskogo

Mendeleeva

To Mosque (400m)

0   300   600m
0   300   600yd

PLACES TO STAY
1 Hotel Slavyanskaya;
  Slavyanskaya Tourist Agency
  Гостиница Славянская
7 Hotel Sibir
  Гостиница Сибирь

OTHER
2 Bus Station
  Автостанция
3 Sebrbank
  Себрбанк
4 Post & Telephone Office
  Почтамт и Междугородный
  Телефонный Пункт
5 Prison
  Тобольский Тюремный Замок
6 Offices of Tobolsk State
  Historian-Architectural
  Museum Reserve
  Тобольский Государственный
  Историко-Архитектурный Музей
8 Minsalim Folk Trade
9 Fine Art Museum
  Музей Изобразительных
  Искусств
10 Gostiny Dvor
  Гостиный Двор
11 St Sofia Cathedral
  Софийский Собор
12 Intercession Cathedral
  Покровский Собор
13 Museum of the Spiritual Cultures
  of Western Siberia
  Архиерейский Дом
14 River Station
  Речной Вокзал
15 Museum to Tsar Nicholas II
  Кабинет Музей им
16 Mikhail Archangel Church
  Михаил Архангел Церковь
17 Siberian-Tatar Cultural Centre
  Центр Сибирско-Татарской
  Культуры

The First Siberian Exile

In the late 16th century, a 300kg bell from Uglich became the first exile to Siberia when it was dragged to Tobolsk by the town's banished citizens. The bell had fired Tsar Boris Gudonov's wrath when it was used to call an insurrection on the murder of the imperial heir Tsarevich Dimitri in 1581. Gudonov ordered the bell to be publicly flogged and its tongue to be ripped out before it was banished to Tobolsk. A small tower was built for the bell in the kremlin where eventually it would again find its voice. The original bell has long since been returned to Uglich but a replica can be seen in the kremlin's museum.

(admission $1; open 10am-5pm Mon-Fri), which has a mixture of exhibits ranging from a mammoth skeleton to good ethnographic displays and a section on the last tsar.

Next door to the Fine Art Museum is **Minsalim Folk Trade** *(☎ 6 26 50, ul Oktjabrskaja 2)*, an interesting craft and art shop. Here you'll find good examples of different crafts from the region plus Minsalim himself, an irrepressible Tatar who carves miniature models from bone and who will happily allow you to try the same tasks in his workshop.

The Old Town
Head through the gate at the southern end of the kremlin and walk down the wooden stairs to the foot of the cliff and the river to start exploring the old town. Here you will find many dilapidated wooden homes, some ruined churches and a sprinkling of baroque and neoclassical stone administrative buildings, including one housing a tiny **museum** *(Kabinet-muzey Imperatora Nikolaya II; ul Kirova)*. This is dedicated to the last tsar who stayed here with his family briefly before making their final, fatal journey to Yekaterinburg.

Beautiful **Mikhail Archangel Church** *(ul Lenina 24)* has been restored, and its swirling wrought-iron fence and gates and equally colourful interior are worth seeing. This is where Natalia Fonvezena prayed when she was not cultivating pineapples in her hothouse. Pushkin apparently modelled Tatianna Larina in his epic *Eugene Onegin* on Natalia, the wife of an exiled Decembrist.

The **Siberian-Tatar Cultural Centre** *(Tsentr Sibirsko-Tatarskoi Kultur; ☎ 6 27 13, ul Yershova 30; admission $0.05, open 9am-noon & 1pm-5pm Mon-Fri)* is on the 2nd floor of a modern building. Here the chatty curator will show you around three rooms displaying Tatar cultural items.

A 10-minute stroll west towards the river will bring you to the handsome red-brick **mosque** *(ulitsa Pushkina 27)*, built at the turn of the 19th century and replacing an earlier wooden structure.

Places to Stay & Eat
At the train station is the **komnaty otdykha** *(☎ 9 55 22)* Dorm beds/doubles without bathroom $2.20/3. Rooms are fine but they are inconveniently far from town. Look for the sign by the colourful mosaic in the station waiting hall.

Hotel Sibir *(☎ 6 23 90, ul Oktyabryskaya 1)* Singles/doubles with toilet $5.40/7.60, doubles with bathroom $24. The cheap rooms at this old-fashioned hotel, opposite the kremlin, will do for a night. The most expensive doubles are decorated in a quaint kitsch style. Food at the **restaurant** is good and cheap (around $3 a meal); we enjoyed the borshch and pelmeni here.

Hotel Slavyanskaya *(☎/fax 9 91 20, Mikrorayon 9)* Singles/doubles with breakfast from $23/48. This hotel offers some unexpected comfort and value (despite foreigners being charged more than locals). Rooms are very modern. There is a sauna and swimming pool in the basement as well as a bar and two decent **restaurants** where main dishes cost around $10.

Getting There & Away
At least three trains run every day between Tobolsk and Tyumen ($6, five hours), including the Omsk-Surgut service. There's at least one direct link daily with Yekaterinburg. A few buses also make the trip daily from Tyumen (4 hours).

Catch bus No 4 from the station to the city centre – it stops at Hotel Slavyanskaya and continues on to the kremlin.

From around June to September boats ply the Irtysh and Ob Rivers and it's possible to take a short cruise from Omsk to Tobolsk or vice versa. It takes about three days and costs $40. Boats dock at the River Station (Rechnoy Vokzal) in Tobolsk's old town.

OMSK
ОМСК
☎ 3812 • pop 1.3 million
🕐 Moscow time + 0300

Don't let first impressions of Omsk, 568km east of Tyumen, put you off. Crossing the Irtysh River you'll see a line of giant cranes like skeletal giraffes and the usual rows of drab apartment blocks. But head towards the city centre, where the Om River joins the Irtysh, and the scene couldn't be more different.

This older part of Omsk has lots of parks and a surprising collection of quirky public sculptures. A stretch of stately 19th-century buildings along ulitsa Lenina, the main shopping drag, have been given a spruce white-wash, and is topped off by the ornate Drama Theatre at the northern end of the street.

As with Tyumen there's no compelling reason to break your journey here. However, if you're a Dostoevsky fan or you just want a rest from the train, Omsk is a fine place to idle a day away.

History

Omsk started out in 1716 as a Cossack outpost, then in 1824 replaced Tobolsk as the seat of the governor general of Siberia.

It became a major dumping ground for exiles, the best known of whom was Fyodor Dostoevsky. In *Buried Alive in Siberia*, he wrote about his wretched years in prison here (1849–53), during which he nearly died from a flogging. During the Civil War, Admiral Kolchak made Omsk the seat of his anti-Bolshevik government – until it was overrun in 1919.

A famous modern-day exile Alexander Solzhenitsyn paused in Omsk on his way to a labour camp in Kazakhstan. Today the jails have gone and Omsk has become another city doing quite nicely on the proceeds of Russia's oil money and booming economy.

Orientation & Information

The train station is 4km south of ploshchad Lenina (dominated by the hideous Soviet-era musical theatre, with a roof like a giant ski jump) and the city centre. Prospekt Marxa forms Omsk's main artery along with ulitsa Lenina, which runs over the Leningradsky Most to the Drama Theatre north of the Ob River, then kinks to the east and becomes ulitsa Gertsena.

The main post office is at ulitsa Gertsena 1 and is open 8am to 7pm Monday to Thursday and Saturday, 9am to 7pm Friday, and 10am to 5pm Sunday.

A good Internet cafe is Perekrestok, at ploshchad Leningrad 3, where ulitsa Lenina meets ulitsa Maslennikova. It's open 24 hours daily, charges $1.40 per hour and you can get drinks here. Kokos, ulitsa Lenina 3, opposite the Drama Theatre, is another Internet cafe (without drinks), open 9am to 6.40pm Monday to Thursday, till 5.40pm on Friday and 5pm on Saturday.

Things to See & Do

In the park on the north bank of the Ob River and west of ulitsa Lenina is the **Literature Museum** *(Literaturny muzey;* ☎ *24 29 65, ul Dostoevskogo 1; admission $0.70; open 10am-6pm Tues-Sun)*, which includes a section on Fyodor Dostoevsky. It's all in Russian and monochromatic, but does have its moments – Dostoevsky's death mask provides a macabre touch. So does the creepy miniature tableaux in a cramped cellar – here, in a crevice in the wall, you can see tiny renderings of Dostoevsky's books, plus a beetle in chains!

More conventional is the **Omsk State History Museum** *(Omskiy Gosudarstvenniy Istoriko-Kraevadcheskiy muzey;* ☎ *31 47 47, ul Lenina 23A; admission $0.35; open 10am-7pm Tues-Sun)*, which offers a traditional resume of local history from prehistoric finds in the area to modern-day links with Omsk's sister city of Milwaukee, Wisconsin. The ethnographic sections on Kazak, Tatar and Russian peasant life are particularly good, and there's a nice old map, in a smart metal frame, of the original Trans-Sib line running from Chelyabinsk to Vladivostok.

A block south of the museum along ulitsa Lenina is stately 19th-century **St Nicholas Cathedral**, a working church, used as a cinema during Soviet times.

Omsk has several pretty, traditional Siberian wooden buildings – one of the easiest to find is directly opposite the musical theatre on ploshchad Lenina. Dating from 1911, this building now houses the **Liberov Centre** *(Liberov Tsentr;* ☎ *30 16 45; ul Dumskaya 3; admission $0.18; open 10am-5pm Tues-Sun)*, where you'll find works by the renowned artist Alexei Liberov along with changing displays of other local artists.

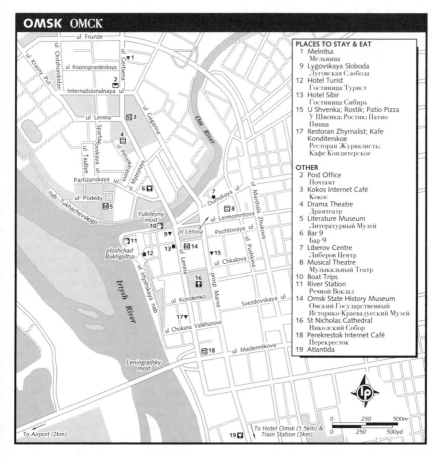

OMSK OMCK

PLACES TO STAY & EAT
1 Melnitsa
    Мельница
9 Lygovskaya Sloboda
    Луговская Слобода
12 Hotel Turist
    Гостиница Турист
13 Hotel Sibir
    Гостиница Сибирь
15 U Shvenka; Rostik; Patio Pizza
    У Швенка; Ростик; Патио
    Пицца
17 Restoran Zhyrnalist; Kafe
    Konditerskoe
    Ресторан Журналисть;
    Кафе Кондитерское

OTHER
2 Post Office
    Почтамт
3 Kokos Internet Café
    Кокос
4 Drama Theatre
    Драмтеатр
5 Literature Museum
    Литературный Музей
6 Bar 9
    Бар 9
7 Liberov Centre
    Либеров Центр
8 Musical Theatre
    Музыкальный Театр
10 Boat Trips
11 River Station
    Речной Вокзал
14 Omsk State History Museum
    Омский Государственный
    Историко-Краеведческий Музей
16 St Nicholas Cathedral
    Никольский Собор
18 Perekrestok Internet Café
    Перекресток
19 Atlantida

To Airport (2km)

To Hotel Omsk (1.5km) &
Train Station (3km)

0   250   500m
0   250   500yd

If you fancy a short **river trip** along the Irtysh, boats depart roughly on the hour from 9am to 9pm daily in the summer months from just west of Yubileyny Most. The one-hour round trip, which heads north along the Irtysh River, costs $0.80. The scenery is nothing special but, since the point is to relax, eat and drink, this doesn't really matter. A racier four-hour trip departs at midnight, has a strip show and costs $1.40.

Places to Stay
On the left as you exit the station are the *komnaty otdykha*. Singles/doubles without bathroom $3/4. Rooms are quite acceptable and cheap, although you'll likely have to make do with a cold shower.

Hotel Omsk (☎ 31 07 21, fax 31 52 22, *ul Irtyshskaya nab 30*) Singles/doubles from $8/16. This one is not particularly convenient to the city centre, and the old rooms are beginning to look shabby, but there are good views of the river and you could pay double for a renovated room.

Hotel Turist (☎/fax 31 64 14, *ul Broz Tito 2*) Singles/doubles $20/26.50. Housed in an unlovely tower block but with some brightly decorated rooms and good river views, this a reasonable choice. The staff are friendly too.

Hotel Sibir (☎ 31 25 71, *ul Lenina 22*) Singles/doubles without bathroom $10/17, with bathroom $20/41. Though the corridors are gloomy, the Sibir has a fine location and spacious, if old-fashioned, rooms.

Places to Eat & Drink

The bakery and cafe *Lygovskaya Sloboda* (☎ *31 15 40, ul Lenina 20)* is deservedly popular. Its spotless kitchens are on view from the street windows and in the cafe (open 10am to 10pm daily) the food is excellent. We found the hearty borshch was brimming with beef chunks and served with garlic rolls, a meal in itself.

Restoran Zhyrnalist (☎ *31 47 79, ul Lenina 34)* Mains around $4. Open noon-1am daily. This imaginatively designed place is in an old brick building. The menu is on newsprint in the style of old advertisements (making it more difficult to decipher than usual) but the standard of the Russian cuisine makes it worth the effort. A pianist tinkles away in the evening. Next door in an equally attractive wooden house is *Kafe Konditer-skoe* doing a nice line in gooey cakes.

Melnitsa (☎ *25 23 88, ul Gertsena 12A)* Mains $3-4. Open 10am-2am daily. Come here for a modern restaurant/bar with a beer garden and usual menu of Russian dishes, including good salads and very nice bliny. Its windmill logo harks back to the wooden structures that used to stand outside the city in the 19th and early 20th centuries.

The Czech beer bar and restaurant *U Shvenka*, chicken fast-food outlet *Rostik* and the pizzeria *Patio Pizza* form a cluster of reliable chain restaurants in a big complex at prospekt Marxa 5 opposite the children's theatre.

A trendy central watering hole is *Bar 9* (☎ *23 24 74, ul Lenina 14)*. Omsk's obligatory megaclub *Atlantida* (☎ *53 03 30, prosp Marxa 18/2)* costs $7 to enter on weekends ($3.50 other nights). If the disco, floor show and glitzy restaurant upstairs leave you cold there are a small bowling alley and billiard tables (both extra fees).

Getting There & Away

Omsk is on the main Trans-Siberian line. Westbound trains go to Moscow (42 hours), Yekaterinburg (12 hours) and Tyumen ($6.50, 7½ hours). Heading west to Novosibirsk, the best train to catch is No 88, the *Irtysh* ($27, 9½ hours).

There's a service centre at the station (9am to 9pm daily) for tickets, where you'll pay a $1 commission. In the city centre, train tickets as well as air tickets can be bought at the River Station *(Rechnoy Vokzal)* open 8am to 7pm daily. This is where you should also come to inquire about the two-night river cruises to Tobolsk that run between June and September.

Omsk's airport is on the west bank of the Irtysh and linked to the city centre by several buses. Among other places there are flights several times a day to/from Moscow ($138, three hours), and three times a week to St Petersburg ($110, four hours) and Irkutsk ($93, two hours).

Many trolley buses and buses ($0.20) run from the station along prospekt Marxa to ploshchad Lenina.

NOVOSIBIRSK
НОВОСИБИРСК

☎ 3832 • pop 1.9 million
🕓 Moscow time + 0300

Despite its daunting scale, Novosibirsk, straddling the Ob River, is a very relaxed, friendly and surprisingly stylish city. Pride of place goes to the silver-domed Opera & Ballet Theatre, Russia's biggest and the home of a respected ballet company and school. Less highbrow entertainment is plentiful since Novosibirsk also offers a sybaritic range (for Siberia) of fine restaurants and rockin' bars.

Rail enthusiasts will want to stop here to tour the city's superb open-air train museum and check out the biggest train station in Siberia. There's the full range of winter sports come winter, or water sports on the artificial beach beside a dammed section of the Ob River in summer. Novosibirsk is also the main access point for the alpine Altay region (see the boxed text 'Adventures in the Altay' later), a magnet for hikers, mountaineers and rafters.

History

This is a city that wouldn't exist if not for the Trans-Siberian Railway. It was founded in 1893 and until 1925 was known as Novonikolaevsk, after the last tsar. Suffering badly during the Civil War and its immediate aftermath, when some 60,000 citizens died of typhus, Novosibirsk quickly recovered. It's phenomenal growth into Siberia's biggest metropolis began in the 1920s when it was purpose-built as an industrial and transport centre, between the coal fields to the east and the mineral deposits of the Urals to the west.

In the 1930s the construction of the Turkestan-Siberian (Turk-Sib) railway south from Novosibirsk to Almaty in Kazakhstan made the city a crucial transport link between Russia and Central Asia. In 1958 Novosibirsk was chosen as the location for an experimental city of scientists – Akademgorodok (see Around Novosibirsk).

Orientation & Information

Vokzalnaya magistral runs 1.5km from the train station, along the east bank of the Ob River, to the city centre around ploshchad Lenina. Krasny prospekt runs north-south through ploshchad Lenina and is the main axis of the city.

Dom Knigi, 51 Krasny prospekt, has a good selection of maps, including ones for parts of the Altay Mountains if you're heading for the hills. It's open 10am to 8pm daily.

You can change money at the post office, in the Service Centre at the train station and in the lobbies of the Hotel Sibir and Hotel Novosibirsk. You can get cash advances on your Visa card at the Sibirsky Bank, ulitsa Lenina 4.

The main post office and long-distance telephone office are a few doors apart on ulitsa Lenina. The post office has fax, telegram, an EMS express-post service and an email service. It's open 8am to 7pm weekdays and until 6pm weekends.

Internet Klub, downstairs at ulitsa Trudovaya 1 (take the lane running west behind the cylindrical, tiled kiosk on Krasny prospekt, just north of ploshchad Lenina), is the best place to access the Web. The rates are $1 an hour and it's open round the clock.

OVIR (☎ 29 04 85) is on the corner of ulitsa Oktyabrskaya and ulitsa Kamenskaya, behind the large Globus Theatre (enter from ulitsa Oktyabrskaya). It registers foreigners between 3pm and 5pm on Monday and between 10am and noon on Thursday.

For city tours and trips to the Altay, contact Sibalp (☎ 49 59 22, fax 54 13 74, e sibalp@online.nsk.su) at ulitsa Karla Marxa 2 (office 515), on the left bank of the Ob close to metro Ploshchad Marxa. The director, Sergey Kurgin, will meet clients at their hotel. The helpful Intourist service bureau (☎ 23 02 03) in the Hotel Sibir lobby can book train and air tickets and arrange tours.

Things to See & Do

Novosibirsk's top attraction is the grand **Opera & Ballet Theatre** *(☎ 18 07 59, pl Lenina; tickets from $1.50)*. There are no performances from July through to the end of September. The sculptural ensemble out front features Lenin, the *de rigueur* peasant, soldier and worker piece, and a couple representing the socialist future, who look like they're directing traffic.

Across the square in Novosibirsk's oldest stone building is the **Local Studies Museum** *(Kraevedchesky muzey; ☎ 18 17 73, Krasny prosp 23; admission $3; open 10am-6pm Tues-Sun)*, with excellent displays on Altay culture and the city's history, including a section on the building of the railway. A second branch of the **museum** *(☎ 21 70 31, Vokzalnaya magistral 11; admission $3; open 10am-6pm Tues-Sun)* focuses on natural history and is not so interesting. Its entrance is actually a few yards up prospekt Dimitrova behind the fire-gutted TsUM building.

The **Art Gallery** *(Kartinnaya galereya; ☎ 22 20 42, Krasny prosp 5; admission $1; open 10am-6pm Wed-Mon)* includes numerous works by the Russian painter Nikolay Rerikh (which the artist himself donated), plus changing exhibitions. Rerikh, who now enjoys international cult status, was obsessed for a while by the beauty and mystical qualities of the Altay Mountains south of Novosibirsk.

The pretty little **Chapel of St Nicholas** *(Chasovnya Svyatitelya Nikolaya)*, in the middle of Krasny prospekt south of ploshchad Lenina, is reckoned to be at the geographical centre of Russia. Originally built in 1915 to celebrate (two years late) 300 years of the Romanov dynasty, it was knocked down in the 1930s but rebuilt in 1993 for Novosibirsk's centenary.

About 700m farther down Krasny prospekt is **Alexander Nevsky Cathedral** *(Sobor Alexandra Nevskogo)*. This brick building was closed for reconstruction when we visited but, near the circus, you can go inside to admire the beautiful blue-and-gold domed **Cathedral of the Ascension** *(Voznesenskaya sobor; ul Sovietskaya 91)* dating from the early 1900s.

Tsentralny Park, north of the Opera & Ballet Theatre, has horse-drawn carts, a children's railway, cafes and outdoor music on summer weekends. There's also a sobering

NOVOSIBIRSK НОВОСИБИРСК

PLACES TO STAY
- 4 Gostinitsa Vokzala Novosibirsk-Glavny
  Гостиница Вокзала Новосибирск-Главный
- 5 Hotel Novosibirsk
  Гостиница Новосибирск
- 14 Hotel Sibir; Intourist
  Гостиница Сибирь; Интурист
- 21 Hotel Oktyabrskaya
  Гостиница Октябрьская
- 25 Hotel Tsentralnaya
  Гостиница Центральная

PLACES TO EAT
- 9 Balkan Grill
  Балкан-Грилъ
- 16 New York Pizza & New York Times
  Нью-Йоркпицца
- 18 Zolotoye Kolos
  Золотой Колос
- 20 Planet Sushi; Patio Pizza & Rostik's
  Планта Суши; Патио Пицца и Ростик
- 24 Tsentralny Komplex; Arkada; Traveler's Coffee; Grill Master
  Центральный Комплекс; Аркада; Грилъ-Мастер
- 31 Mexico Kafe
  Мехсико Кафе
- 33 Shanghai Café
  Шанхай Кафе

OTHER
- 1 Circus
  Цирк
- 2 Cathedral of the Ascension
  Восксенский Собор
- 3 Central Market
  Центральный Рынок
- 6 TsUM
  ЦУМ
- 7 Local Studies Museum (natural history section)
  Краеведческий Музей
- 8 Banya
  Фёдоровския Бани
- 10 Tsentralny Park
  Центральный Парк

- 11 Old Irish
- 12 Dom Knigi
  Дом Книги
- 13 Internet Klub
  Интернет Клуб
- 15 Pub 501
- 17 St Patrick's & Cerp i Molot
  Серп и Молот
- 19 Sibirsky Bank
  Сибирский Банк
- 22 Siberian Airlines
- 23 Opera & Ballet Theatre
  Театр Оперы и Балета
- 26 Post Office
  Почтамт
- 27 Telephone Office & Internet
  Международный Телефонный Пункт
- 28 Locomotive Monument
- 29 Local Studies Museum
  Краеведческий Музей
- 30 Chapel of St Nicholas
  Часовня Святителя Николая
- 32 OVIR
- 34 Art Gallery
  Картинная Галерея
- 35 Alexander Nevsky Cathedral
  Собор Александра Невского
- 36 Bus Station
  Автостанция

War Memorial on the west bank of the river; take the metro to Ploshchad Marxa and head north for a block along ulitsa Rimskogo Korsakovo.

Cold? Try a traditional Russian **banya** (☎ 17 19 99, ul Sovietskaya 36; admission $0.60 for 1hr, massage $5; open 24 hrs Tues-Sun). It's women only on Wednesday, Friday and Sunday, men only on other days.

Places to Stay

The best option, though so popular you're likely to find it difficult scoring a room, is the **Gostinitsa Vokzala Novosibirsk-Glavny** (☎ 29 23 76, Novosibirsk Vokzal). Singles/doubles from $8.50/13.50. The reception for these superior resting rooms is on the 2nd floor at the northern end of the station building. The lux rooms ($36.70) are worth the extra expense if that's all that's available.

Hotel Tsentralnaya (☎/fax 22 76 60, ul Lenina 3) Singles/doubles $26.70/33.50. Rooms here are a fine choice, boasting a central location and good value, even if they are somewhat old fashioned.

Hotel Novosibirsk (☎ 20 11 20, fax 21 65 17, Vokzalnaya magistral 1) Singles/doubles with breakfast from $34.70/90.70. There are cheaper rooms at this huge Soviet-era monstrosity, but as a foreigner, you are not likely to be offered them. It's conveniently located opposite the train station (with great views) and is reasonably comfortable. There's a small supermarket in the lobby and breakfast is served in the bar.

Hotel Oktyabrskaya (☎ *22 62 87, fax 23 27 22, ul Yadrintsevskaya 14*) Singles/doubles $26.70/30. Leaf-patterned wallpaper and wooden floors give this decent hotel's rooms a retro feel.

Hotel Sibir (☎ *23 02 03, fax 23 87 66,* e *centre@gk-sibir.sibnet.ru, ul Lenina 21*) Singles/doubles with breakfast $44/74. A smart Intourist operation, the Hotel Sibir features pleasant rooms and a reliable *restaurant*.

Places to Eat

Novosibirsk has Siberia's best range of restaurants, with several of the bars serving good food, too.

Traveler's Coffee (*2nd floor, Arkada, pl Lenina*) is a trendy Starbucks-style place with a prime view of the Opera & Ballet Theatre. It does good cappuccinos, sandwiches and cakes. There's also a branch of the bright local chain *New York Pizza* (*ul Lenina 12*). *Grill Master* (*ul Lenina 1*) is another very popular fast-food operation serving a wide range of items.

Planet Sushi (☎ *22 18 46, Krasny prosp 29*) Meals $10. This is the better of the city's two Japanese restaurants, where a deluxe sushi dinner costs around $20. In the same building and run by the same company is the reliable *Patio Pizza* and the fried-chicken outlet *Rostik's*.

There are also a few Chinese restaurants in the city centre, including the swank *Shanghai Cafe* (☎ *23 46 87, Krasny prosp 13*). However, the best place for enjoying this style of cuisine is on the west bank of the Ob at *Fei Lun* (☎ *46 15 40, Blukhera 32/1*), just a couple of minutes' walk from Studentsyeskaya metro. Here the food is simple, tasty and shouldn't cost more than $10 a head.

Balkan Grill (☎ *17 22 85, ul Frunze 3*) Meals $10. Serving gut-busting grills, with attentive service, this is one of the town's best restaurants and packed to prove it. Prices are 20% cheaper from noon to 4pm, Sunday to Wednesday.

Mexico Kafe (☎ *10 34 20, Oktyabrskaya magistral 49*) Mains from $5. There are tacos, burritos, chilli and the whole enchilada on offer at this reasonably authentic Mexican restaurant/bar where you can sip Coronas and listen to live music 8pm to 11pm, Tuesday to Sunday.

Adventures in the Altay

One of the best reasons for hopping off the train at Novosibirsk is to head south to the Altay Mountains – one of the most beautiful and pristine parts of Siberia. These mountains, declared a Unesco World Heritage Site in 1998, rise in the Altay Republic (Respublika Altay), which begins 450km south-east of Novosibirsk, and stretch south into Kazakhstan, China and Mongolia. Siberia's highest peak, 4506m Mt Belukha, stands on the Kazakhstan border.

To reach the Altay Republic from Novosibirsk (there are both train and bus services), you must cross the separate Altay Territory (Altaysky kray), which usually involves making transport connections in one of its two main towns, Barnaul or Biysk. The capital of the Altay Republic is Gorno-Altaysk, 467km from Novosibirsk; it's useful only for transport connections to the mountains and you should have it listed on your visa to avoid any problems.

The 71,000-strong Altay ethnic group forms about 28% of the population of this mountainous republic. They are a Turkic-speaking people, and from the 15th to 18th centuries were ruled by the fearsome Oyrats of western Mongolia who scared the Kazakhs into joining Russia in the 18th century.

Few foreigners get to this remote corner of Siberia but those who do – to trek, climb, raft the Altay's wild rivers or explore its archaeological sites – won't forget its haunting beauty. The Katun River, flowing down the centre of the republic from Gebler glacier on Mt Belukha, and the Chulyshman in the east, flowing into Lake Teletskoe, provide some of Russia's most challenging white-water rafting.

A few tour companies offer packages (see the Activities section in the Facts for the Visitor chapter), but it's possible to travel here on your own and to find good adventure guides in Novosibirsk, Barnaul or even locally. June to August are the best months to visit, though it can rain at any time. For more details see Lonely Planet's *Russia, Ukraine & Belarus*.

The traditional Russian bakery *Zolotoye Kolos* (*ul Lenina 2*) stocks an excellent range of breads, pastries and cakes and has a stand up bar that's perfect for breakfast or quick snack.

There is a reasonable *supermarket* inside the *Tsentralny Komplex*, near ploshchad Lenina, and the large, bustling *central market (ul Gogolya)* has an excellent range of fresh produce.

Bars

Old Irish (Krasny prosp 37) Mains from $5, business lunch $3. Here, in Siberia, is your standard Irish-theme bar, serving great steaks and other food. There's Guinness and Kilkenny (a pint is $9) on tap and a menu in English. It's a great place to meet the city's expats and there's live music from 9pm Thursday to Saturday nights.

St Patrick's (☎ 22 44 77, ul Lenina 8) is a similar operation, distinguished by the eccentric *Cerp i Molot (Hammer & Sickle)* karaoke bar hidden away in the basement. Head through the door at the back of the pub to discover a world where the iconography of the Soviet years is gently mocked. A pair of earplugs is recommended once the singing gets going though.

Pub 501 (☎ 18 09 39, ul Lenina 20) Mains from $5, business lunch $3. Tired of Irish bars? Try this cowboy-theme one, which offers up a similarly slick and pricey range of alcoholic beverages and food.

New York Times (☎ 22 78 09, ul Lenina 12) is directly beneath New York Pizza and is a great place to hear live rock, blues and jazz, as well as kick up your heels with a spot of dancing.

Shopping

Hotel Sibir has a souvenir stall and the Krasny prospekt branch of the *Local Studies Museum* sells some folk art. The main department store *TsUM*, on Vokzalnaya magistral was gutted by a fire at New Year 2001; it may reopen. The city's fanciest mall is *Arkada* on ploshchad Lenina.

The huge *Barakholka* flea market is on at weekends in the east of the city. Hang on to your wallet! Buses run from the train station.

Getting There & Away

Train All the major Trans-Siberian and China-bound trains stop in Novosibirsk, but you might find it easier to get a ticket on one of the trains that start or finish here. No 25/26 the *Sibiryak* connects Novosibirsk with Moscow ($75 to $80, 51 hours) and also Yekaterinburg ($40 to $45, 20 hours). Head-

ing eastward, No 8 goes alternate days to Krasnoyarsk ($25, 12¼ hours) and onward to Irkutsk and Vladivostok.

Services to places off the main Trans-Siberian line include trains at least daily to Barnaul (six to 10 hours) for the Altay Mountains, and every second day to Severobaikalsk (43 hours) and beyond on the Baikal-Amur Mainline (BAM) line (see the BAM Line section in the Krasnoyarsk to Irkutsk & Lake Baikal chapter). On the Turk-Sib line south, there's a daily service to/from Almaty (32 to 37 hours) in Kazakhstan.

For tickets and information the best place to head is the excellent service centre (8am to 7.30pm daily) on the ground floor at the northern end of the station; English is spoken and a $1 commission is charged here. Intourist in the Hotel Sibir can also get you tickets ($2 commission).

Air Novosibirsk has two airports. The one you're most likely to use is Tolmachyovo, 30km west of the centre off the Omsk road.

From Tolmachyovo, there are three flights daily to/from Moscow ($115, four hours), most days to St Petersburg ($140, five hours), Irkutsk ($100, 2¼ hours) and Vladivostok ($233, 7½ hours).

From the city airport, which is 10km from the centre, flights go to/from Krasnoyarsk twice weekly ($46, two hours).

Regular international flights by Siberian Airlines (☎ 22 33 22), Krasny prospekt 38, include services to Tel Aviv ($425), Hanover ($285) and Frankfurt ($365).

Bus The bus station is at Krasny prospekt 4, 1.5km south of ploshchad Lenina. There are 14 buses daily to Barnaul (three hours) and seven to Tomsk ($4, four hours), but it will be quicker taking one of the shared *marshrutnye* taxis to Tomsk (three hours) for $10.

Getting Around

An express bus runs to Tolmachyovo (about 50 minutes) from the street in front of Hotel Novosibirsk roughly half-hourly from 5.30am to 7pm, but marshrutnye taxis are inexpensive, faster and operate most of the night. Trolleybus No 5 runs between the city airport and the Oktyabrskaya metro. Trolleybus No 2 connects the train station and city airport. A taxi to the city airport should be no more than $5, to Tolmachyovo $10.

Buses and trolleybuses ($0.20) travelling around the city centre don't seem to follow any handy routes but there's a useful metro system. There is just one line, running beneath Krasny prospekt much of its length, with a one-stop branch to Ploshchad Garina-Mikhaylovskogo, at the train station. The interchange station is Sibirskaya/Krasny Prospekt. Ploshchad Lenina is one stop south of Sibirskaya/Krasny Prospekt.

Boat From the river station by the Hotel Ob (metro Rechnoy Vokzal) there are some occasional excursions on the Ob River from April/May to September/October. Information can be obtained at the inquiry desk.

AROUND NOVOSIBIRSK
West Siberian Rail Museum
Западо Сибская Жепезная Дорога Мчзей

Beside Seyatel station, around 2km north of Akademgorodok (see below), is the West Siberian Rail Museum *(Zapado Sibirskaya Zheleznaya Doroga muzey,* ☎ *29 20 33; admission free; open 11am-5pm Sat-Thur)*, a star attraction for any train enthusiast. Here you'll find 69 brightly painted and lovingly maintained locomotives and carriages, that date from 1891 to the present day. There are engines fitted with giant snow ploughs for clearing the tracks in winter, and even one carriage rumoured to have been used by the last tsar.

Akademgorodok & the Ob Sea
Академгоподок и Обское Море

Nestled in the taiga around 30km south of Novosibirsk is Akademgorodok, the academic township founded in the 1950s as a Siberian branch of the Soviet Academy of Sciences. Those who lived in this once-elite community, with 23 highly prestigious institutes, enjoyed perks unavailable to their fellow Soviet citizens. However, since the collapse of the system that created it, central government funding has largely dried up, leaving the residents little better off than everyone else.

Many academics have now left for overseas and better salaries. Still, research here continues and the town itself, all but hidden by the trees, is a pleasant place to wander around. In the winter there are cross country ski trails. It's also close to the Ob Sea

---

The Trans-Siberian Station Manager

Viktor Kholodov is the man in charge of Novosibirsk Station, the largest and grandest in Siberia, coping with 10,000 passengers daily on 59 different services. This smart-suited, walkie-talkie clutching executive looks more like Richard Branson than a stock Soviet railwayman of old. He spared us five minutes in his busy routine to answers some questions.

LP: How long have you worked at the station?
Kholodov: For 18 years. I began as a duty manager looking after the arrival and departure of all trains. I'm now in charge of the 617 people who work here and all the station's operations.
LP: What do you like about your job?
Kholodov: Everything. But mainly working with both passengers and the staff.
LP: How is the Russian railway system doing?
Kholodov: It's getting better. Now the first purpose of our work is to make the trip more comfortable and to improve service.

Simon Richmond

(Obskoe More), the lake created by the damming of the Ob River, along which there are artificial beaches (including a nudist beach). The most developed beach is called Bambook and has restaurants, bars and various water sports.

There are some museums in the institutes. One of the most interesting is the **Geology Institute** *(☎ 33 28 37, ul Koptyuga; admission $0.60; open 9am-4pm Mon-Fri)* where you can see examples of all the mineral wealth of Siberia, including diamonds from Mirny and the incredibly rare purple charoite from Yakutia.

Suburban trains ($1, one hour) run fairly frequently from Novosibirsk Glavny Station or the River Station (Rechnoy Vokzal) to Obskoe More station. Akademgorodok's main street ulitsa Ilicha is where you'll find the shops and the good ***Hotel Zolotaya Dolina*** *(☎ 35 66 09, fax 35 42 40, ul Ilicha 10)*, with comfortable singles/doubles from $13.50/20. It's around 10 minutes' walk east of the station along Morskoi prospekt. A taxi from Novosibirsk shouldn't cost more than $5 one way.

TOMSK
ТОМСК
☎ 3822 • pop 473,000
🕐 Moscow time + 0400

You can't help feeling as you walk the tree-lined streets of Tomsk, 270km north-east of Novosibirsk and 80km off the Trans-Sib route, that its isolation has been a blessing. This largely undiscovered gem of a place is home to some of the best examples of traditional wooden architecture in Siberia.

Founded in 1604, Tomsk was an important administrative and commercial town on the Great Siberian Trakt at its Tom River crossing. When it was bypassed by the railway, Tomsk's commercial importance declined as Novosibirsk's rose. (One story says it was a ghastly miscalculation by Tomsk's city fathers, who felt that trains would just bring noise, dirt and disruption.)

In Soviet times Tomsk became even further cut off because of Tomsk-7, 16km to the north, part of Siberia's 'nuclear archipelago' of secret weapons research and production centres. Tomsk-7 is still firmly off limits, and radioactive leaks and dubious waste disposal methods haven't exactly encouraged tourism in the area anyway. Tomsk itself, though, upriver of Tomsk-7, is said to be safe.

The Tomsk oblast's oil wealth keeps the local economy afloat and the respected university – the first in Siberia – gives the city the faint atmosphere of a Siberian Oxford.

Orientation & Information
The train station and bus station, next door to each other, are about 2.5km south-east of Tomsk's main commercial street, prospekt Lenina. The university is at the street's southern end and the city administration at the northern end.

The post office is at prospekt Lenina 95, where you'll also find an airline ticket office.

Internet access is available at Inferno (☎ 23 03 26), ulitsa Gagarina 35. It's open 9am to 11pm daily and one hour costs less than $0.50. Next door the Graft nightclub hosts an English club at 6pm each Sunday.

Things to See
Tomsk is the kind of place that rewards casual wanderers, with many fine wooden houses lining the main inner city streets. To find some of the best examples start off on

TOMSK ТОМСК

PLACES TO STAY & EAT
2 Siberian Bistro
  Сибирский Бистро
3 Hotel Oktyabrskaya
  Гостиница Октябрьская
8 Golden Dragon
  Золотой Дракон
9 Hotel Sibir
  Гостиница Сибирь
16 Praga
  Прага
18 Trattoria
  Траттория
19 Kakadu
  Какаду
20 Hotel Tomsk
  Гостиница Томск

OTHER
1 Ascension Church
  Воскесенская Церковь
4 City Administration
  Областная
  Администрация

5 Peter & Paul Cathedral
  Петропавловский
  Собор
6 Hospital
  Больница
7 Post Office
  Почтамт
10 Inferno Internet Café
  Инферно
11 Graft Nightclub
  Графт
12 Dragon House
  Дом Дракона
13 Peacock House
  Дом Павлина
14 University
  Томский
  Государственный
  Университет
15 Russian-German House
  Российско-Немецкий
  Дом
17 Bus Station
  Автостанция

ulitsa Kirova, the broad leafy boulevard that runs east off prospekt Lenina, and head north up ulitsa Krasnoarmeiskaya.

The elaborate **Russian-German House** *(Rossiisko-Nemetskii dom,* ☎ *52 17 25, ul Krasnoarmeiskaya 71; admission free; open 9am-6pm daily)*, built in 1906, is one of the best preserved wooden buildings. It's now a cultural centre for the oblast's 50,000 ethnic Germans, many exiled here during Stalin's era. You'll also find the *Baden Baden* cafe here.

A block farther north and set back from the main road, at ulitsa Krasnoarmeiskaya 67A, is **Peacock House**, so called because its gables are decorated with silhouettes of the bird. Over a century old, this remarkable building would have had a preservation order slapped on it in many Western countries; here it's a communal residence kept in dubious repair. Equally striking is the **Dragon House** at No 68, which now serves as a clinic.

After passing the **hospital** on ulitsa Krasnoarmeiskaya, turn up the hill along ulitsa Altayskaya to reach **Peter & Paul Cathedral** *(Petropavlovskaya sobor)*, a 200-year-old brick structure with five silver domes and colourful murals in its interior.

There's another attractive church with a green dome and bell tower to be found 2km farther north along Krasnoarmeiskaya. Turn west along ulitsa Pushkina at the crossing, pass the small pond Ozero Beloye, and continue on towards the tall yellow **Ascension Church** *(Voznesenskaya tserkov)*, with five black spires. From around here there's a good view across the city down towards the river. Head in this direction and you'll eventually hit prospekt Lenina along which there are several handsome 19th-century stone buildings.

Follow prospekt Lenina south for 3km and you'll pass the leafy grounds of the **university** and eventually end up at an impressive **WWII memorial**.

Places to Stay & Eat

The station has decent *komnaty otdykha* that cost from about $3.50 without a bathroom. To find them go upstairs just before the ticket hall.

For a bit more comfort try *Hotel Tomsk (*☎ *52 41 15, prosp Kirova 65)* Doubles $18.50. It's immediately opposite the bus and train stations.

Hotel Sibir (☎*/fax 22 64 52, prosp Lenina 91)* Standard singles/doubles from $6/11.50, lux singles/doubles $18/24. The cheapest rooms at this old-fashioned hotel are fine but overlook the noisy main street; better to stump up for the lux rooms. There's a good gift shop in the lobby selling birch-bark crafts from the Altay.

Hotel Oktyabrskaya (☎ *51 21 51, ul Karla Marxa 12)* Singles/doubles from $16.50/47. The rooms are not renovated, but smart enough at this hotel beside the Tom River.

Mlechni Put is an ornately decorated restaurant in Tomsk railway station that's worth a look and is reasonably priced for salads, pelmeni and main dishes.

Close by the station are *Trattoria (per Nakhimova 2)*, a spick and span modern pizzeria serving pizza slices from $0.60, and *Kakadu (ul Yelizarovkh)*, a popular restaurant and disco that has absolutely nothing to do with Australia.

Praga (ul Kirova 27) does good salads and excellent shashlyk for around $5. There's a shady outdoor area in summer.

There are also plenty of dining options along prospekt Lenina, which include the *Siberian Bistro (prosp Lenina 127)* and the *Golden Dragon (prosp Lenina 56)*, a Chinese restaurant.

Getting There & Away

Local *elektrichka* trains run to Tomsk from Taiga ($1.80, two hours), which is on the main Trans-Siberian line. It's a pleasant journey through wooded countryside dotted with villages, but there are only a couple of trains a day. There are direct trains from Novosibirsk, but they go in the middle of the night, take five hours and are expensive. A better option would be to take one of the frequent buses or shared taxis that run between the two cities in under three hours for between $3 and $10.

There are flights to Tomsk from Moscow and other major Russian cities.

Krasnoyarsk to Irkutsk & Lake Baikal

The Route

Krasnoyarsk to Tayshet

During the 20-minute stop at **Krasnoyarsk** (4098km) you will have enough time to admire the large, colourful mural of Lenin & co at the north-eastern end of the station. This is where you'll need to change trains if you're heading south to the remote republics of Khakassia and Tuva, both cradles of Siberian civilisation. It's also a more comfortable station to change trains for the BAM line to the north of Lake Baikal and beyond – see 'The BAM Line' section later.

Heading east out of the station, trains cross a 1km-long bridge over the **Yenisey River** (4102km). In the language of the local Evenki people, Yenisey means 'wide water', and each summer passenger boats travel the river from Krasnoyarsk almost to the Arctic Kara Sea (see the boxed text 'Voyage to the Arctic Circle' later in this chapter). The original bridge, built in 1898 and winner of a gold medal at the Paris Expo two years later, was replaced by a new construction in 1999.

The *Rossiya* makes short stops at both **Zaozernaya** (4264km), from where a line runs north to the off-limits space centre of Krasnoyarsk-45 and **Kansk-Yeniseysky** (Kansk; 4344km), a town that was once a major transit point for travellers into Siberia. From there the train crosses the Kan River.

Ilanskaya (Ilansky; 4377km) has a small **museum** *(open 10am-5pm Mon-Fri)* in the 100-year-old, red-brick locomotive depot at the western end of the station, and an old locomotive and water tower behind the wooden station building. You'll have 20 minutes, but we really recommend that you *don't* take photographs – see the boxed text 'Arrested in Siberia' later in this chapter.

There's a brief pause at **Reshoti** (4452km) and then shortly after, at **4474km**, the train passes into Irkutsk oblast and local time becomes Moscow time plus five hours.

Moscow time + 0500

Tayshet (4515km), where the Rossiya has a five-minute stop, is the Trans-Siberian's westernmost junction with the BAM line.

Highlights

- Relax in a *banya* in a Siberian village on the shores of Lake Baikal.
- Ride the thrilling Circumbaikal railroad along the lakeshore's cliffs and through its tunnels.
- Head well off the beaten track on the BAM to the beautiful northern end of Lake Baikal.
- Cruise up the Yenisey to the hydro-electric dam at Divnogorsk.
- Hike through the weird rock formations of Krasnoyarsk's Stolby Nature Reserve.

The city, established in 1897 when the railway arrived, became infamous as a transit point for Gulag prisoners, many of whom were pressed into building the line from here to Bratsk, where one of Siberia's biggest hydro-electric stations was built in the 1950s.

The BAM Line

To detour through some of the remotest parts of Siberia, consider riding the Baikalo-Amurskaya Magistral (Baikal-Amur Mainline or BAM), the second Trans-Siberian railway. The BAM extends to Komsomolsk-on-Amur and Sovetskaya Gavan. This part of the route, starting in Tayshet and snaking east over 2500km to Bamovskaya, takes around three days to travel without breaks.

The first major stop is at **Bratsk** (main station: Anzyebi, 292km from Tayshet), a sprawling city of 280,000 on the edge of the Bratsk Sea, an artificial lake created in 1955 by the building of the Bratsk Hydroelectric Station. The train line actually crosses the top of this gigantic 1km-long dam on the Angara River, and there are spectacular views on both sides.

The *taiga* closes in on the line as you travel the next 600km towards the jagged mountains hemming in the northern end of Lake Baikal. Get off at **Severobaikalsk** (1064km) to explore this beautiful spot. The modernist

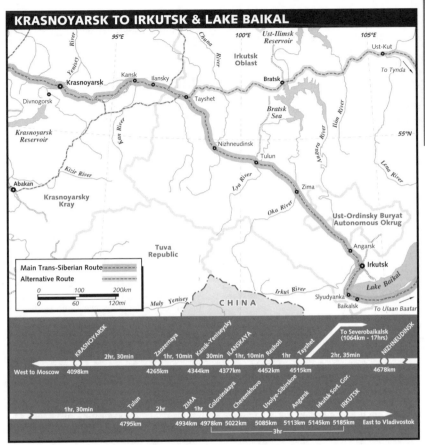

station here is one of the most striking along the line and outside there's a statue commemorating the workers who built the BAM. For more details on Severobaikalsk see the Northern Baikal section later in this chapter.

From Severobaikalsk to the fishing village of **Nizhneangarsk**, 28km north, the line runs along beside Lake Baikal before stopping at **Nizhneangarsk 2** (1104km) station near to the airport. From here for the next 1300km, if you haven't already, you will really begin to appreciate the massive engineering achievement of the BAM. Many consider this the most interesting section of the line as it climbs over densely forested, mountainous terrain along switchbacks and through several tunnels. The longest one of 17km at Severomuisk (1400km) is still to be finished.

Tynda (2364km) is *the* BAM town, home of the BAM construction company's headquarters and of the best BAM **museum** *(city library, ul Profsoyuznaya 3)*. It is from here the Amuro-Yakutskaya Magistral (Amur-Yakutsk Mainline or AYaM) heads north towards Yakutsk, although there's still over 450km of line to be constructed before it eventually reaches the capital of the Sakha Republic. Passenger services only run as far as Aldan.

To rejoin the main Trans-Siberian route from here you'll need to head south 180km along the little BAM, the line linking Tynda with **Bamovskaya** (7273km from Moscow). Alternatively you can stay on the BAM from Tayshet to Komsomol-on-Amur and Sovetskaya Gavan.

KRASNOYARSK TO LAKE BAIKAL

Peoples of Central Siberia

The 210,000 Tuvans are, like the Buryats, a Tibetan Buddhist Mongol people, however they are Turkic-speaking. Nearly all of them live in the Tuva Republic (capital: Kyzyl), in the upper Yenisey basin on the Mongolian border, where they make up 64% of the population. Traditionally, they have been hunters or herders of cattle, horses, sheep and yak.

Tuva was part of the Chinese Empire in the 18th and 19th centuries; a nominally independent communist Tannu Tuva Republic existed from 1921 to 1944. Mongolia also has a sizable Tuvan population.

Partly shamanist and partly Christian, the Khakass number about 80,000 but make up only about 11% of the population of the Khakassia Republic (capital: Abakan). These Turkic people, formerly nomad herders, are the local remnants of the 'Yenisey Kyrgyz' empire that stretched from Kazakhstan to Lake Baikal from the 6th to the 13th century.

Tayshet to Irkutsk

By the time you leave Tayshet you'll be well into the fourth day of your journey from Moscow – midway point for those heading for the Pacific. Battle the overwhelming urge to go stir-crazy by contemplating the scenery that for the next 100km or so runs along the foothills of the **Sayan Mountains**. Here the endless birch and pine forests of the taiga begin, and a real sense of wilderness sets in.

There are good photo opportunities as the line rises above the taiga at around **4560km** and sweeps around bends for another 100km.

At **Nizhneudinsk** (4678km) there's a stop for 15 minutes, after which the landscape becomes flatter and the forests thin out – mainly because this is a prime area for logging. At **Tulun** (4795km), where a road heads 225km north to Bratsk, there's a pause of two minutes.

The next opportunity to stretch the legs comes at **Zima** (4934 km), meaning 'winter' and once a place of exile. After 20 minutes, the train heads south-east, shadowing the Angara River, through several inconsequential stops where it pauses for no longer than a couple of minutes.

Three kilometres outside of the station, the train crosses the River Irkut, from which **Irkutsk** (5185km) takes its name. At one time known as the 'Paris of Siberia', Irkutsk is the one Siberian city where most people plan to stop, so they can visit Lake Baikal, 65km farther south-east.

KRASNOYARSK
КРАСНОЯРСК
☎ 3912 • pop 871,000
🕓 Moscow time + 0400

On the banks of the magnificent Yenisey River, Krasnoyarsk is a pleasant place to pause en route to Irkutsk (or Novosibirsk if you're heading west). It has one of the best-designed museums in Siberia, there are good walks in the Stolby Nature Reserve and there's the chance to cruise part of the river – as far north as the Arctic Circle should you wish.

This is also the jumping-off point for adventures farther afield in the remote central Siberian republics of Khakassia, where you'll find statues and burial mounds dating back millennia, and Tuva, where taiga gives way to steppe and an ancient nomadic culture. For more details see Lonely Planet's *Russia, Ukraine & Belarus*.

Krasnoyarsk grew from a 17th-century Cossack fort to its present size thanks to the discovery of gold in the 19th century; there are still several handsome buildings from this period and the 20th century along prospekt Mira. The arrival of the Trans-Siberian Railway further boosted the city's fortunes, as did the shifting of factories to here during WWII and the building of the nearby hydroelectric dam on the Yenisey at Divnogorsk in the 1950s.

Krasnoyarsk was off limits to foreigners during Soviet times, but these days you're likely to bump into American families with local babies since the city has become a major centre for international adoption.

Orientation & Information

The train station is on the western side of the city, along ulitsa Karla Marxa, one of the two main east-west streets (the other is prospekt Mira). It's 3km from Hotel Krasnoyarsk, the best orientation point. The Yenisey splits the city into the north and south banks, with most of interest to visitors, other than the Stolby Nature Reserve, on the north bank.

Up-to-date city maps are in short supply; try the bookshop Knizhny Mir, at prospekt Mira 86, or the Hotel Krasnoyarsk, which had the best one we could find – and it also doubled as a 1998 wall calendar.

Inkombank, prospekt Mira 108, gives cash advances on Visa, American Express and EuroCard. It is open 9.30am to 1pm and 2pm to 6pm Monday to Friday. There's an ATM machine in the Hotel Krasnoyarsk.

The main post office is at ulitsa Lenina 49, and the long-distance telephone office at prospekt Mira 102. Internet cafe Port (☎ 27 72 18), ulitsa Surikova 2, is open 24 hours and serves drinks.

For registering your passport (Pasportno-vizovaya sluzhba) go to the office at prospekt Mira 16. It's open 10am to 1pm and 2pm to 5pm Monday to Friday, 9am to noon on Saturday.

Paradise Travel Agency (☎ 65 26 52, fax 65 26 49, ⓔ paradise@paradise-travel.ru, ⓦ siberiaparadise.com), ulitsa Lenina 24, is a reliable agency that can book all tickets, arrange homestays and organise a range of tours, including 9-day, fully guided small group tours to Tuva and Khakassia (around $1700). Alf Tour (☎ 27 16 26) in the Hotel Krasnoyarsk can also book air tickets and arrange city tours.

Museums & Churches

Housed in an incongruous Egyptian-style temple building (the building's architect was obsessed with Egypt), the totally renovated **Krasnoyarsk Regional Museum** (*Kraevedchesky muzey;* ☎ 27 69 70, *ul Dubrovinskogo 84; admission $0.60; open 11am-7pm Tues-Sun*) has an excellent range of displays on local history and culture. Exhibits include a full-scale replica of a boat used by the Cossack explorers of the area, and a fine ethnographic section, in the basement, on indigenous peoples.

The leading 19th-century Russian historical painter Vasily Surikov (1848–1916) was born and lived in Krasnoyarsk and his home is now the **Surikov Museum-Estate** (*Muzey-usadba V I Surikova;* ☎ 23 15 07, *ul Lenina 98; admission $0.60; open 10am-6pm Tues-Sat*). Pass through the wooden gate and you enter another world of Siberian tranquillity. Apart from the preserved house with many of Surikov's paintings and sketches, there's a garden that demands to be lingered in.

There is more of Surikov's work on show at **Surikov Art Museum** (*Khudozhestvenny muzey imeni V I Surikova;* ☎ 65 28 81, *ul*

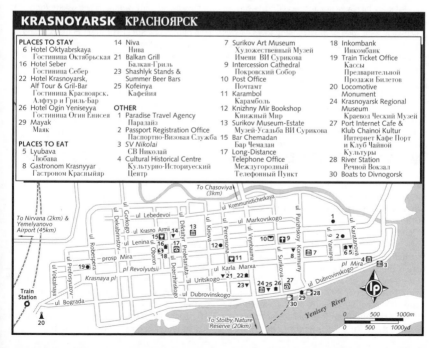

KRASNOYARSK КРАСНОЯРСК

PLACES TO STAY		
6 Hotel Oktyabrskaya Гостиница Октябрьская	14 Niva Нива	7 Surikov Art Museum Художественный Музей Имени ВИ Сурикова
16 Hotel Seber Гостиница Себер	21 Balkan Grill Балкан-Гриль	9 Intercession Cathedral Покровский Собор
22 Hotel Krasnoyarsk, Alf Tour & Gril-Bar Гостиница Красноярск, Алфтур и Гриль-Бар	23 Shashlyk Stands & Summer Beer Bars	10 Post Office Почтамт
	25 Kofeinya Кафейня	11 Karambol Карамболь
26 Hotel Ogin Yeniseyya Гостиница Огин Енисея	**OTHER**	12 Knizhny Mir Bookshop Книжный Мир
29 Mayak Маяк	1 Paradise Travel Agency Парадайз	13 Surikov Museum-Estate Музей-Усадьба ВИ Сурикова
	2 Passport Registration Office Паспортно-Визовая Служба	15 Bar Chemadan Бар Чемадан
PLACES TO EAT	3 SV Nikolai СВ Николай	17 Long-Distance Telephone Office Междугородный Телефонный Пункт
5 Lyubava Любава	4 Cultural Historical Centre Культурно-Исторический Центр	
8 Gastronom Krasnyyar Гастроном Красныйяр		

18 Inkombank Инкомбанк		
19 Train Ticket Office Кассы Предварительной Продажи Билетов		
20 Locomotive Monument		
24 Krasnoyarsk Regional Museum Краевод Ческий Музей		
27 Port Internet Cafe & Klub Chainoi Kultur Интернет Кафе Порт и Клуб Чайной Культуры		
28 River Station Речной Вокзал		
30 Boats to Divnogorsk		

To Chasoviya (3km)
To Nirvana (2km) & Yemelyanovo Airport (45km)
ul Kommunisticheskaya
ul Lebedevoi
Gorkogo
ul Dekabristov
ul Krasno Armii
ul Markovskogo
ul Kirova
Peterosna
ul Vyerbauma
Parizhskoy Kommuny
Surikova
Karatanova
ul Lenina
Oborony
Diktaty
Proletariata
Dezerzhinskogo
pl Revolyutsii
prosp Mira
ul Karla Marxa
Krasnaya pl
ul Uritskogo
ul Dubrovinskogo
pl Mira
Train Station
ul Bograda
ul Dubrovinskogo
Yenisey River
To Stolby Nature Reserve (20km)
To Volzinaya
Prof soyuzov
Robespera
0   500   1000m
0   500   1000yd

Arrested in Siberia

It was at Ilansky (station: Ilanskaya), 4377km from Moscow, that I began to experience both the worst and best day of my Trans-Siberian travels. I had arrived there at 10.15am en route to Irkutsk. There was a 15-minute stop, just enough time, I thought, to check out the museum in the locomotive depot next to the station.

The gate to the depot, a rather handsome red-brick complex, with neat flower gardens, was open. When I asked in the office about the museum all I got was a shrug from one of the employees. On leaving I made the fatal mistake of raising my camera to snap a water tower and a poster commemorating the depot's centenary.

Moments later two men approached and grabbed me. I thought I was being robbed and started to yell. A third man joined in and I was briskly dragged towards a corner of the compound into what transpired was the security office. The men were convinced they had caught a *spion* (spy).

With the seconds ticking down to my train departure, I was frantic with worry and begged the guards (there were two of them – acting out a Russian bad-cop and badder-cop routine) to at least let me return to get my luggage. The badder cop said if I didn't shut up he'd handcuff me to the chair. I shut up. For a minute. Then I started wailing again.

Whipping out the business card of a contact at the British embassy provoked a series of phone calls – but none to Moscow. All I had on me – apart from the incriminating camera – was my passport, my notebook and less than 1000 roubles. The rest of my belongings, including my computer, research notes and practically all my cash, were by now continuing their merry way into the midst of Siberia.

Next thing I found myself being hustled out the office and running with bad cop to the police building closer to the tracks. Perhaps sense had prevailed after all? No such luck. This was where the cast of characters involved began to grow, but later I realised how fortunate I had been in that they all had a good sense of humour and patience with a crazy foreigner who had now missed his train and was separated from all his luggage.

After a while Svetlana, the local OVIR agent, showed up, brandishing *protokols* and asking for my documents. At least she smiled. She was accompanied by several plain-clothes police. It turned out Ilansky is some kind of drug-running town – I was shown photos of smugglers caught in the past and told the reason I couldn't go to the post office to call Moscow was that I'd be mugged on the way.

The phone in the police station didn't allow long-distance calls either so I couldn't call the embassy from there, or even the guide who was expecting me in Irkutsk. I had little choice but to sign the protokols – basically admissions of my guilt. At least then they agreed to put me on the next train.

Except the next train was the *firmennye* No 8 from Novosibirsk and the train directors – one bleached-blond dominatrix in a grey uniform, the other like Brezhnev's mother in her nightie – absolutely refused to let me on. Something about rule No 5 of the railway department, or some other such nonsense, but they wouldn't budge, despite many entreaties from the police. As the train pulled away we all agreed they were 'very bad women'.

Parizhskoy Kommuna 20; admission $0.60; open 11am-6pm Tues-Sun), along with other Russian art ranging from the 18th to 20th centuries.

There are sometimes exhibitions in the ugly concrete **Cultural Historical Centre** on ploshchad Mira. Permanently docked below here is the **SV** *Nikolai (admission $0.20; open 10am-6pm Tues-Sun),* a boat on which Lenin lived briefly in 1897 during his Siberian exile. It's now a museum with a variety of displays ranging from Russian sea voyages to a collection of 20th-century household objects. If it all gets too much there's a *bar* here, too, open 2pm to midnight.

The 10-rouble note showcases Krasnoyarsk's most famous church, the **Chasoviya** (chapel), a small stone building now in the place of the 17th-century wooden original. It's clearly visible on a hill overlooking the city from the north; a walk up here takes about 30 minutes, with the view as a reward. The newly restored, red-brick **Intercession Cathedral** *(Pokrovsky sobor)* on the corner of prospekt Mira and ulitsa Surikova is Krasnoyarsk's most attractive church.

Arrested in Siberia

In the meantime, the motherly Ola from the baggage office had been chasing down my luggage and had been told it would be offloaded at Nizhneudinsk – another five hours east – where I could pick it up and sort out a replacement ticket to Irkutsk. That was assuming there would be any luggage to pick up.

The next train through was the much less fancy Penze to Vladivostok service, practically all *platskartny* carriages. The train director Slava was much more accommodating and soon I found myself sharing with some 50-odd other passengers in their dorm on rails. The irony was that until now I had purposefully avoided taking platskartny trains.

'The Lord always has a purpose,' said Leonid, the Molodovian Seventh Day Adventist priest travelling home with his family to Sakhalin Island, and a perfect English speaker who befriended me on the train. And in this case the purpose was to show me how much fun (at least for a day) travelling platskartny can be. If you really want to meet Russians, experience their great hospitality and make friends, this is the way to do it.

We arrived in Nizhneudinsk at 8pm where Leonid and I dashed to the *militsia* to see if they had my bags. They knew who I was, but told me my luggage had gone on to Irkutsk. There was a new ticket waiting for me, for which I paid Sasha 350 roubles, leaving me a couple of hundred in my wallet. If my bags had gone forever, as Marina, the jolly blonde *provodnitsa* of my carriage was certain, this was all I had left. I finally broke and felt the tears welling up, but Leonid told me to have courage and invited me to eat with his family.

At 4.30am we arrived at Irkutsk, where my guide had been waiting for me since 11pm. He didn't have my bags and knew nothing about my day, so we set off again for the militsia. On the way, however, we were intercepted by a statuesque blonde (and her rather squatter mate) who screamed at me 'Anglichan?' (English?) and then delivered a tirade about what a night she'd had on my account.

Turned out Sveta, the blonde, and Ina, her mate, were provodnitsas from Minsk (my original train had originated in Minsk). Their colleagues had entrusted them with my bags and ever since they had been waiting for me to turn up. So we all trekked out to the station sidings where Sveta and Ina's train was lodged for the night.

When we eventually reached the carriage, Sveta said 'Now big trouble'. We had to wake the train director, Sergey, who understandably was rather grumpy and informed us that the militsia had carted my bags back to the station! So off we all went again.

Finally I found myself at 5.30am in the militsia office carefully going through all my luggage against a check list detailing every item down to 'seven pairs of dirty underwear', and every last coin and note secreted in the many (I thought) secret compartments of my rucksack. 'This is the Russian way', said my guide, and for once I could only applaud it. Such scrupulous honesty by so many people was incredible, especially when I considered that the money I had received back in full was more than all the onlookers in the room (and there were plenty of them) would have earned together in a year.

Simon Richmond

Stolby Nature Reserve

The highlight of a visit to Krasnoyarsk is hiking through the woods and past the strange volcanic-rock pillars (called *stolby* in Russian) in the Stolby Nature Reserve (Zapovednik stolby). The reserve is on the south-western edge of the city, around 25km from the centre. A map at the entrance to the 17,000-hectare reserve gives a basic idea of the trails.

Take bus 50 or 50A that passes Hotel Krasnoyarsk across the Zheleznodozhny bridge and stay on for around 20km as it heads west towards Turbaza. From here walk along the river uphill for a couple of kilometres to reach the reserve entrance.

Divnogorsk

The 45-minute cruise up the Yenisey River to Divnogorsk, 30km west of Krasnoyarsk, is highly recommended. The scenery is spectacular and the 1km-long hydroelectric dam, built between 1956 and 1972, an impressive piece of engineering.

Taxis wait at Divnogorsk to ferry visitors to the foot of the dam about 5km away – a return trip is around $3, or $6 if you want to go to the top and look down into the reservoir on the other side. This will also give you a chance to see up close the remarkable moving basin that allows ships to cross the dam. An English-speaking guide, Konstatin Ziranov, may be around to give a short lecture with original photographs – well worth the $1 charge.

High-speed boats sail from quay 4 at Krasnoyarsk's river station (rechnoy vokzal) roughly every two hours from 10am to 6pm from May to the end of September. The cost is $1 and you can pay on board.

Places to Stay

Only a handful of hotels will readily accept foreigners. If your Russian skills are good you could chance the cheapies – **Hotel Seber** (☎ 22 41 14, ul Lenina 21) or **Hotel Ogin Yeniseyya** (☎ 27 52 69, ul Dubrovinskogo 82) where rooms start at around $3 a single.

Also in the might-not-let-you-stay category is the hotel-ship **Mayak** (☎ 29 04 81, Rechnoy Vokzal, ul Dubrovinskogo), an atmospheric place, based on a good-looking old cruise ship and with small single/double cabins without bathrooms from $3/4.

Hotel Krasnoyarsk (☎ 27 37 54, fax 27 02 36, e hotelkrs@ktk.ru, ul Uritskogo 94) Singles/doubles with breakfast from $18.50/ 23.50. This big hotel offers the best all-round value. The upper-floor rooms at the front have great views over the river and are spacious and comfortable. The buffet breakfast is good too.

Hotel Oktyabrskaya (☎ 27 19 16, ☎ 27 05 81, e october@krsk.ru, prosp Mira 15) Standard singles/doubles $40/45, renovated singles & doubles from $50. Professionally run and with quite smart rooms, renovated or not, the Oktyabrskaya has a restaurant and decent bufet as well. To get here from the station take trolleybus No 7.

Places to Eat & Drink

Balkan Grill (☎ 23 45 49, ul Perensona 9). Mains $10. Make sure you're hungry – this highly professional place serves huge portions of delicious food.

Kofeinya (☎ 23 26 96, ul Dubrovinskogo 82) Mains $5.50. Open 8am-midnight daily. Another excellent choice – try the soup in a bread roll or any of a range of traditional dishes. The outdoor tables are the best choice on summer evenings.

Lyubava (ul Mira 7A) Mains from $2. Open noon to midnight daily. You'll find some dubious attempts here at nouvelle Russian cuisine of the fruit-with-meat variety, but otherwise there's respectable grub.

On the corner of the Hotel Krasnoyarsk is the **Gril-Bar** serving a decent range of snacks and good for coffee and drinks in the evening on the terrace.

In summer you'll find **Klub Chainoi Kultur** (Cnr ul Surikova & ul Dubrovinskogo), a new-agey outdoor cafe specialising in the Chinese tea ceremony, outside the Internet cafe Port; in winter it decamps to the Cultural Historical Centre on ploshchad Mira.

In summer check out the **shashlyk stands** and **outdoor cafes** overlooking the water alongside the river station and the beer bars in the square with the fountains outside Hotel Krasnoyarsk, which takes on the feel of an Italian piazza at night when it's packed with crowds.

For self-catering **Gastronom Krasnyyar** (prosp Mira 50A), open 24 hours daily, has a good range of foodstuffs. Outside of the grocery store **Niva** (ul Lenina 112) there are fresh food sellers and inside a cheap cafe and bakery.

Bar Chemadan (☎ 23 02 59, ul Oboron 2B) is a stylish basement bar and **Karambol** (ul Perensona 20) a popular central night club. You could also try **Nirvana** (ul Kirenskogo 86), a big dance club about 3km west of the train station. Entry is around $3, and its open 9pm to 6am Friday and Saturday.

Getting There & Away

Train All major Trans-Siberian and China-bound trains stop at Krasnoyarsk. If you are coming/going straight from/to Moscow, the three-times-weekly Yenisey (train No 55/56) is a good service ($105, 60 hours). To Novosibirsk ($25, 12½ hours) there are at least nine daily services with the No 83 starting in Krasnoyarsk.

Eastbound, there are about six trains a day to/from Irkutsk ($24, 18 hours). There are daily trains on alternate days along the BAM line – one to Severobaikalsk ($19), the other continuing to Tynda ($37) and Neryungri. To/from Abakan, the capital of Khakassia, train No 23/24 ($20, 12 hours) is the best service.

Voyage to the Arctic Circle

In August 2001, as part of his Trans-Siberian travels, Stephen Hammond, hopped off the train in Krasnoyarsk at 7am and an hour later found himself on the passenger boat B Chkalov steaming up the Yenisey River towards the Arctic Circle. Here are his impressions of the nine-day, round trip voyage.

'It was an elegant boat from 1953, with wood panelling and naval brass fittings, that my cleaner, the ever-smiling Tatiana, kept shiny. I was in a top-deck 1st-class cabin, which had a washbasin; baths were shared and on the middle deck. There was a couch-bed that was really big enough for one, so I wondered how two people might share this space.

For practically all the voyage I didn't eat in the restaurant because I couldn't read the cursive Cyrillic script on the menu and didn't have sufficient Russian to order food on my own – instead I made do with snacks from the bufet. I was the only foreigner on the boat and only about a third of the way into the trip did I find another English-speaker – the ship's doctor. He helped me to order in the restaurant, so I tried the borshch and it was good.

The voyage, in effect, was a supplies mission, with the top deck full of small cars and the two lower decks jammed packed with merchandise obscuring many windows and blocking the walkways. Once all this had been off-loaded in Dudinka (the most northerly stop on the voyage) the ship became more liveable and I could explore and take photos.

The ship doesn't pay any attention to the official schedule. It stops wherever anyone wants it to stop, and for as long as it needs to – usually in the middle of the river where speed boats come up to load and unload cargo and people. As a result you can't really get off and walk around, the exceptions being in Igarka (just within the Arctic Circle) where the ship did in fact stop, as scheduled, for two hours, and Dudinka, where we berthed overnight for 15 hours.

Igarka was dingy and dirty and had obviously seen better days, but Dudinka was interesting – a hustling, bustling place where it was quite inspiring to see the stevedores unloading the cargo by hand. The town's main landmark is its restored Orthodox church – I could see its golden cupolas from the boat. There's also apparently a museum about the local Dolgan and Nenets people, but, sadly, I couldn't find it.

On leaving Dudinka, I had my greatest adventure of the trip, which was nearly missing the boat! I returned to the port in good time for the scheduled departure, but the boat had vanished. Thinking I saw it downriver I set off in that direction, only to find I was wrong. By the time I made it back to where I'd started, the Chkalov had reappeared, but had just set sail. Feeling dejected, I showed my ticket to a bystander who called over a boatman who very kindly took me across to the ship.

The highlight of the voyage was the marvellous scenery along the Yenisey. You're in tundra territory just like the National Geographic map says. In Dudinka there was also the 'white nights' with the sun hanging like a blood-red ball low in the sky. I just spent my time gazing out the window at it all.'

If there are queues at the station, try the ticket office (Kassi Predvaritelnoi Prodazhi Biletov) at ulitsa Robespera 29, open 8am to 8pm Monday to Friday, 9am to 6pm Saturday and 9am to 3pm Sunday (with a lunch break from 1pm to 2pm daily). You can also book flights here.

Air Yemelyanovo airport is 45km northwest of the city. There are three flights daily to/from Moscow ($170, 4½ hours); four times weekly to St Petersburg ($150, six hours); three times weekly to Khabarovsk ($124, four hours), twice weekly to Irkutsk ($59, 2½ hours) and Yekaterinburg ($120, three hours); and weekly to Novosibirsk ($42, two hours). On Krasair there are also weekly international services to Seoul ($295 one way), Frankfurt ($365 one way) and Hanover ($520 one way).

Boat Passenger boats ply the Yenisey from the end of May to mid-September between Krasnoyarsk and the arctic Kara Sea. The main service is to the port of Dudinka, 1989km north and well within the Arctic Circle. It takes nearly four days (and nearly six days coming back, against the current). You can fly out of Dudinka.

Sailings to Dudinka, with 18 stops (or sometimes 13 stops on a faster service), are around twice weekly. There's a ticket office in Krasnoyarsk's river station, open 8am to 7pm: the boats are not usually full, but you may not get the class you want if it's very close to departure time. Paradise Travel Agency (see Orientation & Information) can also book tickets.

First-class, one-way fares to Dudinka are around $100; for this you get a place in a two-person cabin with a washbasin. For details of the trip see the boxed text 'Voyage to the Arctic Circle'.

There are many more upmarket 11-day cruises operating on the same route on the Swiss-managed *Anton Chekhov*. The cost is from $1050 per person rising to $1540 in 1st-class, two-berth cabins with toilet and shower – again Paradise can make the bookings.

Getting Around

Bus No 135 runs between Yemelyanovo airport and the bus station behind the Hotel Krasnoyarsk. The ride is about 50 minutes. A taxi costs about $15.

Several buses and trolleybus No 7 ($0.20, pay on board) run from the train station via the city centre towards Hotel Oktyabrskaya. Some follow ulitsa Karla Marxa, others prospekt Mira. From the centre to the train station, you can pick up bus No 11 and trolleybus Nos 7 and 14 on ulitsa Lenina between ulitsa Surikova and ulitsa Perensona.

IRKUTSK
ИРКУЦК

☎ 3952 • pop 591,000
🕐 Moscow time + 0500

Still retaining vestiges of its eclectic history, Irkutsk is one of the most intriguing cities on the Trans-Siberian trail. Most people stop here en route to Lake Baikal, since Irkutsk is the best place to arrange activities around this natural wonder.

The town itself – with the cultural heritage of its aristocratic exiles, whole quarters of traditional Siberian wooden buildings and the Asiatic influences of nearby Mongolia and China – is also worth a day or two of your time.

History

Irkutsk was founded in 1651 as a Cossack garrison to establish authority over the indigenous Buryats. In the 1700s, it was the springboard for expeditions to the far north and east. Under trader Grigory Shelekhov, expeditions even went across the Bering Strait into Alaska (referred to at that time as the 'American district of Irkutsk').

Irkutsk became Eastern Siberia's trading and administrative centre. From here, Siberian furs and ivory were sent to Mongolia, Tibet and China in exchange for silk and tea. A major junction on the exile road, its most illustrious 19th-century residents were the Decembrists and Polish rebels. The exiles formed a rough-hewn aristocracy who emphasised education, arts and political awareness (see the boxed text later in this chapter).

When gold was discovered in the Lena basin in the 1880s, the city boomed. The newly rich built brick mansions and grand public buildings, many of which are still standing. The shops filled with luxuries and imported goods, and Irkutsk became known as 'the Paris of Siberia'.

A city of well-to-do merchants and highbrow socialites, Irkutsk did not welcome the news of the Great October Socialist Revolution. The city finally succumbed to the Red tide in 1920, with the capture and execution of Admiral Kolchak, the head of the White army. Soviet-era planning saw Irkutsk develop as an industrial and scientific centre, which it remains today.

Orientation & Information

The bustling train station is on the west bank of the Angara River, directly across from the city centre. The city's axes are ulitsa Lenina, which runs parallel to the Angara, and ulitsa Karla Marxa. The administrative centre is ploshchad Kirova at the northern end of Lenina.

The most useful banking facility is Alfa-Bank, at bulvar Gagarina 38, which cashes travellers cheques and has an ATM. The exchange bureau at Hotel Intourist, bulvar Gagarina 44, is open 24 hours to change US dollars or give cash advances.

The main post office on ulitsa Stepana Razina is open every day and offers Internet service. The main telephone and telegraph office is on ulitsa Sverdlova, opposite the circus. Faxes can be sent from either office.

The Internet cafe at ulitsa Marata 38 is in the basement; enter through the unmarked door on Marata. Web-Ugol has two locations, both with surprisingly speedy connections.

IRKUTSK ИРКУЦК

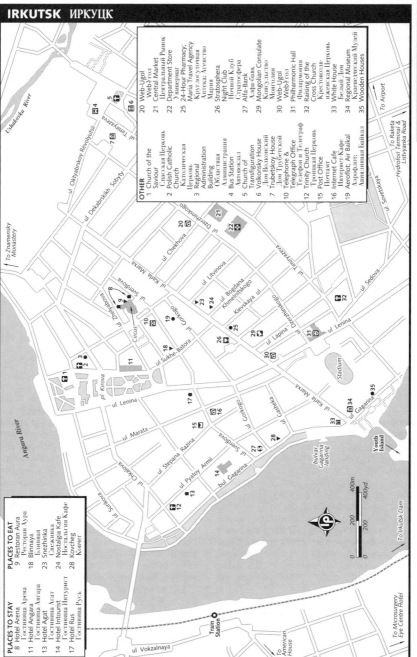

PLACES TO STAY
8 Hotel Arena
   Гостиница Арена
11 Hotel Angara
   Гостиница Ангара
13 Hotel Agat
   Гостиница Агат
14 Hotel Intourist
   Гостиница Интурист
17 Hotel Rus
   Гостиница Русь

PLACES TO EAT
9 Restoran Aura
   Ресторан Аура
18 Blinnaya
   Блинная
23 Snezhinka
   Снежинка
24 Nostalgia Kafe
   Ностальгия Кафе
28 Kovcheg
   Ковчег

OTHER
1 Church of the
   Saviour
   Спасская Церковь
2 Polish Catholic
   Church
   Католическая
   Церковь
3 Regional
   Administration
   Building
   Областная
   Администрация
4 Bus Station
   Автовокзал
5 Church of
   Transfiguration
6 Volkonsky House
   Дом Волконский
7 Trubetskoy House
   Дом Трубецкой
10 Telephone &
   Telegraph Office
   Телефон и Телеграф
12 Trinity Church
   Троицкая Церковь
15 Post Office
   Почтамт
16 Internet Cafe
   Интернет-Кафе
19 Aeroflot; Air Baikal
   Аэрофлот;
   Авиалиния байкал
20 Web-Ugol
   Web-Угол
21 Central Market
   Центральный Рынок
22 Department Store
   Универмаг
25 24-Hour Pharmacy;
   Maria Travel Agency
   Круглосуточная
   Аптека; Агенство
   Мария
26 Stratosphera
   Night Club
   Ночной Клуб
   Стратосфера
27 Alfa-Bank
   Альфабанк
29 Mongolian Consulate
   Консульство
   Монголии
30 Web-Ugol
   Web-Угол
31 Philharmonic Hall
   Филармония
32 Raising of the
   Cross Church
   Крестовоздви-
   женская Церковь
33 White House
   Белый Дом
34 Regional Museum
   Краеведческий Музей
35 Wooden Houses

The first (☎ 56 48 45), at ulitsa Lenina 13), is open every day from 10am to 10pm. The second (☎ 205 928), near the central market at ulitsa Chekhova 19, is only open until 7pm (5pm on Sunday).

A useful Web site for the history of the city and region, plus tourist information, is ⓦ www.irkutsk.org.

Travel Agencies Local tour operators are useful not only for organising excursions, but also for booking hotels and train tickets, both of which can be tricky.

Baikalcomplex (☎/fax 38 92 05, ⓦ www.baikal complex.irk.ru) One of the veterans in the business, owner Yury Nemirovsky specialises in organising homestays on Lake Baikal. The one-day excursion on the Circumbaikal Railway is brilliant.

Green Express (☎ 38 01 11, ⓔ info@greenex press.ru, ul Chelnokova 46) In addition to the charming hotel in Listvyanka (see the Listvyanka section), Green Express runs adventure tours, including mountain biking and horse riding.

Irkutsk-Baikal Intourist (☎ 29 01 61, Hotel Intourist, bul Gagarina 44) Although the ticketing service is helpful, don't bother with the overpriced tours.

Maria (☎ 24 02 39, fax 25 80 10, ⓦ www.baikal -maria.irk.ru, ul Kievskaya 2) Enter from ul Karla Marxa). Maria can organise stays at tourist bases in Bukhta Peschanaya and Olkhon Island.

Decembrist Houses

After completing their terms of labour near Chita, many Decembrists settled in Irkutsk with their wives and families, who had earlier followed them into exile. Two of the homes – those of Prince Sergey Trubetskoy and Count Sergey Volkonsky – are now rather touching museums, complete with furnishings and pictures of family and friends.

The smaller building is **Trubetskoy house** *(Muzei Trubetskoi; ☎ 27 75 32, ul Dzerzhinskogo 64; admission $2.50; open 10am-6pm Wed-Mon).* In addition to the living quarters, in the cellar it displays maps and paintings of exile life.

If you follow the dusty road that runs past the church, you will find **Volkonsky house** *(Muzei Volkonski; ☎ 27 34 38, per Volkonskogo 10; admission $3.50; open 10am-6pm Tues-Sun).* It is a large, unmarked bluish-grey building, which you enter through the courtyard. The upper floor houses exhibits about the lives of the women who followed their husbands into exile.

Neither museum has English explanations; before coming, you may want to read *The Princess of Siberia*, Christine Sutherland's account of the life of Maria Volkonskaya.

Irkutsk Regional Museum & Around

In the 1870s this Victorian building was the museum of the Siberian Geographical Society, a club of explorers and researchers. It is now the Regional Museum *(Kraevedchesky muzey; ☎ 33 34 49, ul Karla Marxa 2; adult/student $2.50/1.50; open 10am-4pm Tues-Sun).* The best exhibitions focus on indigenous tribes and their nomadic culture.

The **obelisk** across the road was erected on the 10th anniversary of the arrival of the Trans-Siberian Railway. The faces are those of Yermak (the 'conqueror of Siberia'), Count Muravyov-Amursky (the governor general regained the Amur River from the Chinese) and Speransky, another governor.

Churches

Another local museum is housed in the **Church of the Saviour** *(Spasskaya tserkov; ul Sukhe-Batora; admission $2; open 10am-6pm Wed-Sun).* Exhibits include a collection of stuffed animals and early Evenki, Buryat and Yakuty clothing. The interesting exhibit upstairs focuses on local religious history.

The heart of old Irkutsk was the magnificent Annunciation Cathedral, at the northern end of ploshchad Kirova. After suffering extensive damage in the Civil War, the cathedral was demolished to make way for the hulking Party headquarters, now the regional administration building. The cathedral is still visible in photos exhibited in the belfry of the Church of the Saviour.

Nearby on ulitsa Sukhe-Batora is Siberia's only Gothic building, a Catholic **Polish church** *(Polskaya Kostyol)*, built by exiles in 1881. In the 1930s it became a concert hall and still hosts organ recitals during summer.

Znamensky Monastery *(Znamenskaya tserkov)*, built in 1763, was restored by exiled nuns after WWII and reopened. The remains of St Innokent, a Siberian missionary, are a supposed source of miracles for believers. In the cemetery are the graves of the merchant-explorer Grigory Shelekhov,

The Decembrist Movement

After participating in the Napoleonic campaigns in 1812, a group of educated, aristocratic army officers began a movement advocating for reforms in the tsarist regime. They championed constitutional monarchy and abolition of serfdom, but they had little popular support outside their intellectual circles. One of these groups, the Northern Society, was based in St Petersburg.

When Alexander I died in 1825, his successor was not immediately apparent, and a minor dynastic crisis ensued. The Northern Society took advantage of this confusion to persuade a group of conspiring officers to stage a mutiny against the chosen successor. On 26 December, the day designated to swear allegiance to the new Emperor Nicholas I, the plotters occupied Senate Square in St Petersburg. The rebels thus earned their name in Russian history, the 'Decembrists'.

The rebels were poorly organised and misguided. Loyal tsarist troops outnumbered them, but Nicholas I was loathe to mark the start of his reign with a domestic massacre. After a stand-off, which lasted most of one day, troops fired several canister shots into the square. They killed about 60 people and dispersed the rebels. After the uprising, five leaders of the Decembrist movement were executed, and the rest of the 121 participants were sentenced to hard labour, prison and exile in Siberia.

There, the Decembrists became romantic heroes of a sort, especially when a group of their wives and fiancees abandoned their lives of comfort, and sometimes even their families, to follow their men into exile. The first was the faithful Yekaterina Trubetskaya. The story goes that she travelled 6000km by coach to Nerchinsk, and then immediately descended into the silver mines to find her husband.

A prominent group of Decembrists settled in Irkutsk in 1844. The role that these aristocratic exiles played in the city's cultural and intellectual development is unrivalled. They opened schools, formed scientific societies and edited newspapers. Maria Volkonskaya, popularly known as the 'Princess of Siberia', founded a local hospital and opened a concert theatre, in addition to hosting musical and cultural soirees in her home.

The Decembrists were granted amnesty when Nicholas I died in 1855. Many of them, including Maria Volkonskaya, returned to St Petersburg. Yekaterina Trubetskaya had died three years earlier, and she and her three children are buried at Znamensky Monastery.

Princess Trubetskaya and three of her children. The monastery is 1.5km north-east of ploschad Kirova, accessible via trolleybus No 3 from the southern end of the square.

Built in 1758, the baroque **Raising of the Cross Church** (*Krestovozdvizhenskaya tserkov*) on ulitsa Sedova is one of the few churches that remained open to worshippers during the Soviet era. It dominates the skyline of Irkutsk seen from the Trans-Siberian.

Other Historic Structures

Charming **wooden cabins** are prevalent in Irkutsk's older neighbourhoods, especially between ulitsa Karla Marxa and ulitsa Timiryazeva. The lacy, wood-carved decoration on some of these buildings is exquisite. Two structures, side by side on bulvar Gagarina, illustrate the stylistic differences between early Siberian and later Russian architecture. At No 14, the women's quarters upstairs face the courtyard and there are few front windows. The house at No 16 has 'wooden lace' decoration and many high windows facing the street.

Opposite the Irkutsk Museum on ulitsa Karla Marxa is the **White House** (*Bely dom*), built in 1804 as the residence of the governors general of Eastern Siberia. It's now a university science library.

Moored near the Raketa hydrofoil terminal is the icebreaker ferry *Angara*, one of two old boats that originally ferried Trans-Siberian passengers and trains across the lake. There were plans to turn this ship into a museum, but you can still go on board and look around.

Places to Stay

Tourist agencies, such as Baikalcomplex, arrange *homestays* in Irkutsk and villages around Lake Baikal. The price is usually $20 to $25 per person with meals. Without the help of a tourist agency, finding accommodation in Irkutsk can be tricky. Most hotels will not make a reservation over the phone, although they might do so if you confirm by fax.

Budget There are a few options in Irkutsk for the budget traveller.

SIMON RICHMOND

Traditional, carved wooden window treatments.

American House (☎ 43 26 89, ul Ostrovskogo 19) B&B $20. Open Apr-Oct. This friendly guesthouse is in a private home, 20 minutes' walk from the train station. Climb the stairs across from the train station, and follow the dirt road between the apartment blocks and up a steep hill. A brick church is on your left; Ulitsa Ostrovskogo is on your right. Alternatively, a taxi from the train station should be less than $2.

Hotel Arena (☎ 34 46 42, ul Zhelyabova 8A) Doubles from $18. Also known as the Circus Performers' Hotel, the Arena appears to be run by clowns. You cannot complain about the location or the price, however. The hotel has two entrances. On the northern side of the circus, newer rooms have a television and telephone. On the southern side, rooms are more basic, but cheaper.

Hotel Agat (☎ 29 73 25, ul 5-ii Pyatoy Armii 12, entrance no 2) Singles/doubles with shared bathroom $12/24. On the first floor of an apartment block next to Trinity Church, this place has clean, basic rooms.

Mid-Range & Top End If you're looking for something with a bit more comfort, try one of the following places.

Hotel Rus (☎ 25 64 00, fax 24 07 33, ul Sverdlova 19) Singles/doubles with breakfast $22/42. This small, comfortable hotel is the best value in the city, but it is often booked out.

Hotel Angara (☎ 25 51 05, fax 25 51 03, W www.angarahotel.ru, ul Sukhe-Batora 7) Singles/doubles with breakfast $40/50. An unbeatable location and efficient service make up for the lack of charm.

Microsurgery Eye Centre Hotel (☎ 56 41 37, fax 42 20 35, ul Lermontova 337) Trolleybus No 1, 7 or 10 or minivan No 3. Singles/doubles $40/50. It's a 10-minute bus ride across to the west bank of the Angara, but this place is clean (clinically so) and modern. The staff is friendly and guests can use the cafe and sauna.

Hotel Intourist (☎ 29 01 68, fax 29 03 14, bul Gagarina 44) Singles/doubles with breakfast $117/133. It's no beauty, but the hotel does have a fine setting on the Angara River. It offers plain, clean rooms and a multitude of services.

Places to Eat

The larger hotels all have restaurants, the best of which is *Restaurant Rus* in the hotel of the same name. The Russian food is reasonably priced and guests are not subjected to live entertainment.

Snezhinka (☎ 34 48 62, ul Litvinova 2) Lunch/dinner $3/7. This bright bar/restaurant advertises a 'business lunch' ($2.50), 'musical program' (no cover), and 'romantic dinner' (priceless).

Restoran Aura (☎ 33 61 39, ul Zhelyabova) Dinner $5-10. Open noon-1am daily. This tiny restaurant in the Circus building features Siberian dishes and live cabaret every night. Enter to the left of the main entrance.

Kovcheg (☎ 33 07 63, bul Gagarina 38) Mains $10. The modern art adds a nice touch to this professionally run place.

Nostalgia Kafe (☎ 34 34 05, ul Bogdana Khmelnitskogo 1) Dinner $10-15. Open noon to midnight daily. With fish tanks, colourful linen and gold-trimmed plates, this elegant cafe is frequented by the *novie russkie* (new Russians). Dishes such as beef à la Siberia or *bliny* (crepes) with caviar are delish.

Blinnaya (Cnr ul Sverdlova and ul Sukhe-Batora) is a quick place for bliny between 10am and 6pm.

A great place to get food is the lively **central market** on ulitsa Chekhova. Fresh produce, meats and cheeses are a treat for the eyes as well as the palate: fish from the barrel, berries by the bucket, bread hot from the oven. This is also the best place to stock up for train journeys.

Entertainment

Circus (☎ 33 61 39, ul Zhelyabova) Just east of ploshchad Kirova, the circus is seasonal but in the summer break the auditorium is used by other travelling shows. Check the foyer posters for details.

Philharmonic Hall (☎ 24 50 76, ul Dzerzhinskogo 2) Despite its dilapidated appearance, this 1890 hall, opposite the stadium on ulitsa Lenina, still has regular events. Check at the ticket office for details.

Stratosphera Night Club (ul Karla Marxa 15) Cover charge $2.50. This is the hot spot in town. It's a two-storey disco and bowling alley extravaganza; coffee is a whopping $3.50.

Getting There & Away

Train The daily express train, the No 9/10 *Baikal* connects Moscow and Irkutsk ($123, 88 hours). The *Rossiya* stops in Irkutsk on its way between Moscow and Vladivostok ($108, 74 hours). There are several trains per day to Ulan Ude ($10, eight hours), and additional trains to Novosibirsk ($60, 30 hours) and Khabarovsk ($92, 62 hours).

If you are heading to Beijing ($100 to $110 depending on the service), the Trans-Manchurian passes through Irkutsk on Wednesday and the Trans-Mongolian on Saturday. There are two trains per week that originate in Moscow and go to Ulaan Baatar, passing through Irkutsk on Friday and Saturday. The *Angara*, No 264, goes daily between Irkutsk and Ulaan Baatar ($55, 35 hours).

Tickets You are able to get your tickets at the international ticket window, or *mezhdunarodnaya kassa (☎ 28 28 20)*, even if you are buying a domestic ticket. Alternatively, Irkutsk-Baikal Intourist (in the Intourist Hotel) and Baikalcomplex can book tickets for a small fee.

Air International flights go to Beijing ($390 one way, twice weekly) and Shenyang ($168 one way, twice weekly) in China. Domestic flights include Moscow, St Petersburg ($180), Novosibirsk, Bratsk ($60), Khabarovsk ($130) and Krasnoyarsk ($82). Aeroflot (☎ 27 69 17) is at ulitsa Gorkogo 29, and Air Baikal is next door.

Ferry Between June and September there are hydrofoil services from Irkutsk to Bratsk on the BAM line on Wednesday, Thursday and Saturday ($50, 12 hours) and to Severobaikalsk on Wednesday only ($65, 12 hours).

Getting Around

From the train station, bus Nos 7, 16 and 20 cross the river and go to ploshchad Kirova. To reach the Raketa hydrofoil terminal, take southbound bus No 16 from the train station, or trolley bus No 5 from the north-western corner of ploshchad Kirova. The Raketa is the fourth stop after the *Angara* steamship (25 minutes). A taxi from the Raketa terminal or from the airport to ploshchad Kirova should cost no more than $2.

AROUND LAKE BAIKAL

Lake Baikal, the 'Pearl of Siberia', is a crystal clear body of the bluest water, surrounded on all sides by rocky, tree-covered cliffs, and dotted with tiny settlements of colourful wooden cottages.

The lake itself is a living museum of flora and fauna, 80% of which is found nowhere else on the planet (see the 'Nature Guide' special section). Shaped like a banana, Lake Baikal is 636km from north to south, but only 60km wide. It is the world's deepest lake: 1637m near the western shore. As such, it contains nearly one-fifth of the world's fresh water – more than North America's five Great Lakes combined. Swimmers brave enough to face Baikal's icy waters (never warmer than about 15°C) risk vertigo, as it is possible to see down as far as 40m.

Lake Baikal was formed by a collision of two tectonic plates which left a rift 9km deep. Over the course of 25 million years, 7km of sediment has collected at the bottom. So, although the lake is less than 2km deep now, it is gradually getting deeper as the plates separate, and will eventually become the earth's fifth ocean, splitting the Asian continent.

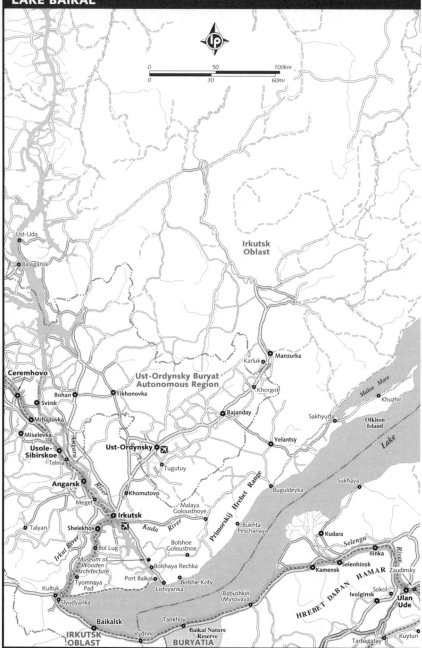

LAKE BAIKAL

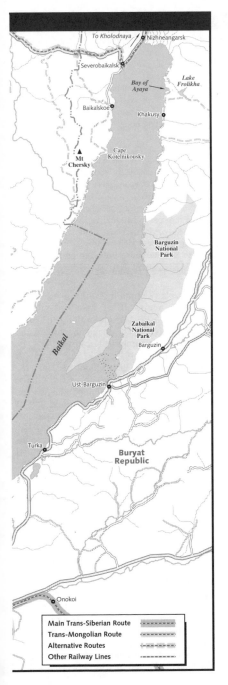

Museum of Wooden Architecture
Музей Деревянного Зодчества

On the road from Irkutsk to Listvyanka, is the Museum of Wooden Architecture *(Muzey derevyannogo zodchestva)*. The old wooden Siberian buildings include three renovated farmsteads, two chapels and a 17th-century village watchtower. If you stop, go back 100m along the road to see the 'wishing trees' – shrubs tied with bits of cloth by picnickers and newlyweds for good luck. Supposedly a shamanist hangover, it's also reminiscent of the prayer flags of Tibetan Buddhism, the religion of most Buryats.

Port Baikal
Порт Байкал

It was from Port Baikal that the *Angara* and *Baikal* steamships used to ferry the whole Siberian express train and its passengers across the lake to pick up the tracks again at Mysovaya. Nowadays, there is not much to see in Port Baikal unless you are riding or walking the Circumbaikal Railway.

Listvyanka
Листвянка

☎ 3952 • pop 2500
🕐 Moscow time + 0500

Within striking distance of Irkutsk, the tourist-wise village of Listvyanka offers a charming village atmosphere and striking views of the lake. It is centred on ferry landings and ship-repair workshops. Unfortunately, a highway follows the lakeshore for the length of the village, so it limits the opportunities for hiking and swimming.

Things to See & Do Many of the villagers live in the picturesque area called Krestovka, nestled on the valley floor just south of the boat landings. **St Nicholas Church** *(Svyato-Nikolskaya tserkov)* has services twice a day. The windows and naturally lit interior are unusual for a Russian Orthodox church.

South of Krestovka, 3km along the lakeside promenade, is the Baikal Limnological Institute, housing the cramped **Baikal Ecological Museum** *(☎ 112 155, ul Akademicheskaya 1; admission $1; open 10am-5pm daily)*. This disappointing museum has examples of some of the rare species of marine life to which Baikal is home, as well as plenty of maps, diagrams and models. Down the road, the institute has opened a new

The Rules of Queuing

Russia conjures up images of endless queues for non-existent or worthless products. It's true that the queues are endless, but the product – a train ticket – can be highly valuable, hence the queue, I guess. The original way (still common outside the big cities) to secure a ticket to anywhere in Russia is to spend a few hours in the queue at the station.

Russians are astonishingly good at standing in queues. You can save someone's place (or have your place saved) for hours, even days if necessary. Once your place is reserved (as simple as asking the person just ahead or writing your name on the list) you can go and do something else entirely, and come back just before your turn. And even if they have been waiting hours themselves, no one will mind if you muscle in to the front because your train is leaving soon.

The queues have some stupid rules too. The stupidest (and fortunately almost extinct in this egalitarian age) are the special queues for foreigners. Imagine my dismay when, after waiting half an hour to get a train ticket in Irkutsk, the clerk tells me that I have to wait in the special queue for foreigners. I explain to her that my train is leaving in five minutes and the foreigners desk is closed for another 45 minutes; in effect, I will miss my train. She shrugs. I swear.

In the end the train I finally got a ticket on was six hours late (the train the clerk could not sell me a ticket for left dead on time). So her refusal to serve me cost me 10 hours of my life. And it would have only taken two minutes of hers. For which she is paid. The beautiful irony is that the special queues for foreigners were designed to speed things up.

Hayden Glass, Vladivostok to St Petersburg, July-September 2001

Aquarium *(admission $1; open 10am-5pm daily)*. 'Aquarium' is perhaps an exaggeration, but visitors do get an up-close meeting with 'Leika', a friendly freshwater seal.

On the hill behind the Limnological Institute, a 2.5km path climbs to an **observation point**, with excellent views of the lake and mountains, Port Baikal and the Angara River.

Places to Stay Baikalcomplex and other travel agencies can organise *homestays* in Listvyanka for about US$20 per person. Most are in the apartment blocks behind the Limnological Institute. If you wish to experience the quaint atmosphere of the village, you can choose from a number of *B&Bs* on ulitsa Chapaeva, just south of the port. Prices range from US$5 to US$10 per person, including breakfast. Keep in mind that the 'quaint' village atmosphere features outhouses for toilets and Russian *banya* instead of showers.

National Park Hotel (☎ 112 520, ul Gorkogo 39) Beds $7. On the main road along the lakeshore, this place is mainly an information centre about the Pribaikalsky National Park, but there are also nine beds, as well as kitchen and bath facilities.

Green Express Hotel (☎ 11 25 99, ⓔ info@greenexpress.ru, ul Gornaya 16) Doubles with breakfast $50. This small, charming hotel has an excellent Russian

banya with a swimming pool, and a summer cafe with views of the lake and village. From the port, walk south along the main road. The hotel sits up on the hill in the south-western corner of Krestovka.

Hotel Baikal (☎ 29 03 91, fax 25 03 14) Singles/doubles/deluxe $40/44/63. This 118-bed Intourist hotel is south of the village behind the Limnological Institute. Rooms are posh by Siberian standards, and half of them have unbeatable views of the lake.

Places to Eat You will also discover innumerable places to buy smoked fish and shashlyk close to the port and along the lakeshore. The Russian/Siberian food at *Hotel Baikal* is supposed to be excellent.

Proshlii Vek (☎ 11 25 54, ul Gorkogo 5) Dinner $5-8. Open noon to midnight. Along the main road overlooking the lake, this restaurant is a nice alternative, serving fresh fish and *ukho* (traditional fish soup) in a pleasant but not overly touristy atmosphere.

Getting There & Away Between 5.30am and 6pm each day there are four buses between Irkutsk bus station and Listvyanka village, though it is also possible to catch a minibus. The bus also stops near the Limnological Institute.

From mid-May to late September, a hydrofoil makes the return trip between Irkutsk,

Listvyanka and Bolshie Koty once a day on Tuesday and Wednesday, twice on Friday and Saturday, and three times on Sunday. The price is $1 for each leg. This schedule seems to change every summer, so double check with a travel agent or at the Raketa terminal in Irkutsk.

Western Shore of Lake Baikal
Западная Берега Озера Байкала

In theory, ferries and hydrofoils go to a number of the landings along the western shore. Maintenance problems, financial constraints and weather patterns all play a deciding role in what services are running. The only guaranteed source of accurate, up-to-date information is the Raketa terminal in Irkutsk.

Bolshie Koty The name of this town translates not as 'big cats' but as 'big boots', referring to the footwear worn by the gold miners who worked here in the 19th century. Now this tiny, picturesque village 15km north of Listvyanka is home to 300 people (100 in winter) and a small, biological research station.

Hiking trails follow the lakeshore heading both north and south out of the village. Hikers will be rewarded with spectacular views: rocky cliffs overlooking the lake; green valleys overflowing with wildflowers; and isolated beaches where you can take a (quick) dip in the icy water. Green Express (in Irkutsk or Listvyanka) organises horse riding here for $50 per day.

Baikalcomplex can arrange a homestay here, or you can probably just show up and find accommodation in a guesthouse or private dacha. At the time of writing, hydrofoils from Irkutsk made the return trip (via Listvyanka) on Tuesday, Wednesday, Friday, Saturday and Sunday, but this schedule is subject to change.

Bukhta Peschanaya The appropriately named Sandy Bay, 80km from Listvyanka village, is a popular spot for Russian vacationers because of its sandy beaches and dramatic capes. Once a week, the hydrofoil from Irkutsk makes the 3½-hour trip. There is accommodation available in tourist bases here, but you should probably make arrangements in advance through Baikalcomplex or Green Express.

Olkhon The large island off Baikal's western shore (70km long) is one of the most mysteriously beautiful places on the lake. The western shore of the island is steppe bounded by dramatic orange cliffs. In the interior of the island are half a dozen lakes and the 1300m-high Zhima Peak. The only settlement of any size is the fishing village of Khuzhir. The northern end of Olkhon, once the domain of religious shamans, is reportedly a good place to see Baikal seals.

During summer, buses leave Irkutsk bus station for Olkhon once a week, taking eight torturous hours over pot-holed roads to reach Sakhyurta, the nearest mainland village to the southern tip of the island (there's a ferry crossing point a few kilometres up the road). Both Maria and Green Express organise trips to Olkhon from Irkutsk.

Eastern Shore of Lake Baikal
Восточная Берега Озера Байкала

The eastern shore of Lake Baikal is some of Buryatia's wildest and least explored territory, not only untrodden by backpackers but also relatively uncolonised by Buryats and Russians. Farther north there's not the slightest trace of civilisation for hundreds of kilometres, until the single-minded swathe of the BAM ploughs through the taiga beyond the northern end of the lake.

The tracts of land that have remained free of habitation or development now fall within the boundaries of **Barguzin National Reserve** (*Barguzinsky zapovednik*). Created in 1917, this is Russia's oldest national reserve. With more than 263,000 hectares of protected flora and fauna, the park has long provided valuable virgin research territory for small armies of scientists, hermitted away in the coastal settlement of Davsha. Linked only by boat to Ust-Barguzin 120km to the south, Davsha can also act as a reception centre for visitors.

Immediately south of the Barguzin Reserve is **Zabaikal National Park** (*Zabaikalsky Natsionalny Park*), a more accessible, but still controlled, stretch of forested Baikal coastline. Within the boundaries of the national park are the Ushkani Islands, four small mountain peaks out in the lake that are the favourite basking place of Baikal's seals.

The place to start exploring the eastern shore is **Ust-Barguzin**, where you can hire transportation into Zabaikal or get additional information about Barguzin at the national park headquarters. There is a daily bus to Ust-Barguzin from Ulan Ude.

NORTHERN BAIKAL

Compared to the much-visited south of Lake Baikal, the northern end is practically virgin territory. This is the best area to enjoy the serenity of the lakeside scenery and ideal for camping or indulging in other wilderness pursuits such as trekking, rafting, mountaineering or, in winter, skiing.

Train enthusiasts and admirers of grand engineering schemes will also be drawn by the dual achievements of the BAM railway and the huge hydroelectric station at Bratsk (see The BAM Line in The Route section earlier in this chapter). Whatever one may think of the environmental impact of these projects (which has been significant), here one can really grasp the scale of Soviet industrial fantasies and marvel at what the Russians can do when they're inspired.

The best base for the area is Severobaikalsk, linked with Irkutsk by train, plane and a weekly hydrofoil. Despite this range of transport options, it's important to keep in mind that the weather around the north of the lake is highly changeable, particularly affecting flight schedules. Therefore you should give yourself plenty of time not only to explore the area but also to get there and back – four days is the safe minimum.

Severobaikalsk
Севепобайкальск

☎ 30139 • pop 35,000
🕐 Moscow time + 0500

Severobaikalsk rose out of virgin taiga almost overnight in the early 1970s. The first dwellings were temporary – railroad carriages and shacks built from scavenged railway construction materials. Soon a small, permanent, concrete-block town followed, built by workers from Leningrad.

Despite the fact that the best views of Baikal are from the railway yard and the coal-fired electricity plant, Severobaikalsk is not unattractive . In minutes by car you're out of the concrete and in the wilderness beside cool, clear rivers that run gurgling from rounded olive-green mountains.

The town is an excellent base from which to explore the northern end of the lake and

has some very good accommodation. Several transport links with Irkutsk also makes Severobaikalsk easily accessible from the main Trans-Siberian rail route.

Orientation & Information The main street, Leningradsky prospekt, runs north from the train station 600m to Tsentralny ploshchad (Central Square) – and that's about the extent of the town. Running east to west in front of the station is the snappily named prospekt 60 let SSSR (60 Years of the USSR Ave). Turning right at the eastern end of this street will bring you to the port on Lake Baikal, 1.5km south of the station.

On the eastern side of Tsentralny ploshchad is the Torgovy tsentr, a miniature department store, and just to the south is the post office. The telephone and telegraph office is just east of the southern end of Tsentralny ploshchad. The local bank – the only place in town to change money – is next door. It's closed on weekends.

Never designed with tourism in mind, Severobaikalsk is not the sort of place you can just show up and hope things will fall into place. The most useful person to contact is long-time guide and ex-BAM worker *Rashit Yahin* (☎/fax 2 15 60, 🄴 baikal@ iname.com, 🅆 www.gobaikal.com, ul Oktyabrya 16-2). Despite a stroke in the mid-90s, Rashit remains an active and determined presence on the north Baikal tourist scene and can help arrange trips as well as homestays from $21 per person per night.

Things to See There's not much to see in Severobaikalsk itself. The mid-1950s **steam engine**, parked some 50m west of the station along prospekt 60 let SSSR, makes for a good photo. You could also tick off the **Palace of Culture**, on the northern side of Tsentralny ploshchad, which sometimes has exhibitions of local art and also hosts musical performances.

Around 1km east of the square is the **BAM museum & gallery** (☎ 2 76 44, ul Mira 2; admission $1.50; open 10am-5pm Tues-Sun), with small displays on the building of the BAM and a few Buryat artefacts. The gallery, in a separate building around the corner on ulitsa Druzhba, has a limited collection of work by local artists. They're not

[Continued on page 221]

Nature Guide

GRAHAM BELL

RAY TIPPER

ABWP

DAVID TIPLING

Title page: Wander along the beach with the local wildlife, Bay of Ayaya, northern Lake Baikal (Simon Richmond)

Title page inset: Juvenile Peregrine Falcon *(Falco peregrinus)* (Chris Mellor)

Top left: The Baikal Teal *(Anas formosa)* on the Lena River in northern Siberia

Top right: Little Ringed Plover *(Charadrius dubius)*

Middle: Grey Heron *(Ardea cinerea)* alert in the water

Bottom: European Brown Bear *(Ursos arctos)*

NATURE GUIDE
Graham Bell

No railway journey in the world engenders such fascination, mystery, romance and excitement as the Trans-Siberian Railway – the enormous length of the track, the vast landscapes and even the very name 'Siberian' stir the imagination and evoke strong emotion.

Part of this attraction for any traveller with even the slightest interest in natural history is the wildness of the largely uninhabited terrain along the route and the abundance of wildlife it holds – a major part of the heritage and ecosystem of this part of Siberia. Much of the region's wildlife is naturally shy, hidden from view or too distant to be observed well, but the traveller will nevertheless see many interesting things from the train compartment, sometimes very close to the track. Moreover, there will be frequent opportunities to get off and explore the countryside at leisure and in more detail.

The extent and variety of habitat – mountains, steppes (plains), rivers, lakes, marshes, scrub, *taiga* (dense, often impenetrable forest) – provide a huge range of species, so many in fact that we can only sketch an outline of this rich fauna and flora here, selecting only those that are typical and significant as samples of what the area has to offer.

Vegetation
It is impossible to divide the vegetation bordering the railway into clearly demarcated zones as it is constantly changing and mixing. However, taiga is the habitat through which much of the railway passes. In some places it is dominated by conifers, particularly Siberian pine *(Pinus sibirica)*, in others mixed conifer and deciduous and in yet others all deciduous. Silver firs, spruce, larch and birch often mingle with maple and aspen, while by the innumerable lakes, ponds and rivers willows and poplars dominate – in late summer their white fluffy seed floating everywhere like snow.

Coniferous trees change little in appearance seasonally, except when the snows of winter blanket them, but the broad-leaved deciduous trees undergo dramatic transformations. Bare in winter, decked with green in spring and summer, they blaze with russet and gold in autumn.

A particularly beautiful species of birch *(Betula dahurica)* with an unusual dark bark grows near Lake Baikal, while at the far eastern end of the journey, in Ussuriland, the traveller will see the impressively tall white-barked elms *(Ulmus propingua)* and Manchurian firs *(Abies holophylla)* – the latter with pink, purple or orange-buff bark – as well as the more familiar cork, walnut and acacia trees. The almost subtropical climate here is quite different from the harsher conditions farther west in Siberia, allowing a lush profusion of exotic flowers.

The leaf litter at the base of trees swarms with all forms of invertebrate life, which not only transforms the dead vegetation into fertile humus, but also provides food for animals and birds.

Here on the forest floor mosses, lichens, ferns and fungi thrive, including the colourful but deadly fly agaric *(Amanita muscaria)*. The dense leaf canopy above inhibits the growth of flowering plants and shrubs below, but in more open areas and clearings it is a different picture; in such places flamboyant rhododendrons, azaleas, ryabina, spiraea, asters, daisies, gentians and vetches all combine to delight the eye in summer.

Top: Juvenile Peregrine Falcon *(Falco peregrinus)*. (Chris Mellor)

Though still extensive, much of the forest has been cleared for agricultural purposes or to sell to the Japanese timber trade, so large tracts of cultivated fields and eroded scrubland where trees once stood are a common sight. There are also extensive but natural open treeless landscapes known as steppes. Of the many kinds of grass that grow wild here the most attractive are the aptly named feather grasses, which rise and ripple in the wind like the surface of the sea.

Animals

The wild animals living in the area bordering the railway are amazingly varied, recalling what Western Europe was like before civilisation took its toll. What follows is a selection of the most characteristic species (if not always the most easily observable).

DEER FAMILY
Moose (Elk) *Alces alces*
These impressive creatures, the largest of the deer family, are common, particularly in the wetter and more open parts of the forest. Submerged in water up to their chests, they will raise their heads from rooting up vegetation from the bottom of shallow lakes to stare at the passing train, water dripping from their muzzles and dewlaps. Standing in water also cools them in summer and affords some respite from the swarms of blood-sucking insects (best to keep the train compartment windows closed in these areas!).

Easily identified by a huge head, downward-pointing snout, humped shoulders and sloping back, the males also sport large palmate antlers up to 2m wide. These males can stand over 2m high at the shoulders and weigh over 800kg. As with reindeer in the Arctic, moose have been domesticated in places for their meat and milk, but those that the sharp-eyed Trans-Siberian Railway traveller will spot are most likely to be wild.

Red Deer (Maral) *Cervus elaphus*
Unlike the musk deer, the Siberian race of red deer, otherwise known as the maral, is a highly sociable if timid animal. The stags aged three years and over and the hinds with their young live in separate groups for most of the year. The stag is a sturdy animal with a powerful chest, hefty neck and long, slender legs. He carries impressive antlers, shed annually in early spring but immediately starting to grow again. In the late summer he sheds the velvety skin that covers the new antlers.

Autumn is the rutting season and now the stag puts on a great show of strength, claiming a harem of hinds he defends aggressively and noisily; in September his roaring can be heard from the depths of the forest – quite an intimidating sound. However, the stag is not quite as macho as he pretends to be, for he will flee at the least sign of danger, leaving his harem of hinds to defend themselves – which they are quite capable of doing, always being better organised. At no time do the two sexes form anything like a permanent bond.

Musk Deer *Moschus moschiferus*

Another creature of the forest is the well-known but rare musk deer, standing not more than 60cm at the shoulders. Unlike other deer, the males do not grow antlers; instead, both sexes have tusks (actually extended upper canines) protruding about 6cm in males, less in females. These are not just decoration – they are used with deadly effect in the rutting season in December/January.

Highly active at all times of year, these diminutive deer can reach up twice their height into the branches of trees when winter snow covers the ground; they can even climb when necessary.

Unfortunately, they have long been prized by man for their musk – a pungent secretion produced in their abdominal glands – widely used in the manufacture of expensive perfumes and fetching exorbitant prices in the world of commerce (worth more than its weight in gold). The musk deer's solitary nature and mainly nocturnal habits in these remote areas have not prevented it being relentlessly hunted.

Roe Deer *Capreolus capreolus*

This elegant and abundant deer is much smaller than the red, with much shorter, more vertical antlers. It is also more likely to be seen out in the open – at the edge of the forest and in the fields where it browses on all kinds of vegetation including crops. But it is equally suited to life among trees and thickets, where its small size and antlers enable it to move quickly through dense undergrowth or conceal itself. Moreover, having hind legs longer than its fore legs, it is particularly nimble and adept at jumping over fallen trees and other obstacles at high speed. They are sometimes even seen bounding along the train line.

CANINE FAMILY
Wolf *Canis lupus*

All the previously mentioned deer, and many other creatures, are potential prey of wolves. In Western Europe these much feared and hated predators have been persecuted so much that they now only survive in a few remote areas. Siberia, however, is so vast that wolves are still a significant and important part of the ecosystem. They are always wary of man and so no one is more likely to hear the unmistakable distant howling than meet them face to face. (The howl, incidentally, is a contact call to assemble or keep the pack together.)

Left: Red deer or Maral *(Cervus elaphus).*

Right: The dwindling yet predatory wolf *(Canis lupus).*

The wolf resembles a large Alsatian dog, but is typically greyer with a broader head, smaller ears and pale yellow eyes. It regularly hunts in packs and takes a huge variety of prey, from tiny voles to the mighty elk.

Despite its bad reputation, the wolf deserves to be regarded as more than a savage killer. In wolf society there is a strong sense of responsibility, obedience, cooperation and sharing. The species also performs a useful function in keeping populations of other animals under control and should only be destroyed when its activities are in direct conflict with man's raising of his domestic animals. We can only hope that the wolf's intelligence, flexible hunting techniques and catholic choice of habitat will enable it to fare better here than it has managed to do elsewhere in the world.

Fox *Vulpes vulpes*

A member of the same family (Canidae) as the wolf, the fox is much more familiar and easily observed. It is also readily identified by its sharp snout, long ears, russet-brown fur and pale-tipped long bushy tail – about one-third of the length of the whole animal (about a metre). With luck, you will be able to glimpse a fox anywhere alongside the track – in the forest, on the open steppes or even around human habitation. This carnivore has a wide range of habitat in which it hunts its favourite prey: small rodents, though it will eat anything from birds and insects to carrion and human domestic rubbish. Apart from being a useful scavenger, an efficient predator of rats and mice, and an aesthetically attractive animal in its own right, the fox has a little-known characteristic to commend it: faithfulness to the same mate for life.

MUSTELID FAMILY
Otter *Lutra lutra*

It is not generally realised that otters belong to the same family as stoats and weasels (which also occur widely in the Trans-Siberian region); somehow, their aquatic habits make them more appealing.

The otter is certainly well-adapted for its lifestyle. Its thick brown fur – thicker in winter and kept well lubricated by cutaneous glands – sleek, supple body with a long tail used as a rudder, flat head and webbed feet enable it to move with great dexterity through the water in search of the fish on which it mainly feeds. To enable it to sense its prey, it has a ring of stiff bristles round its muzzle. It can stay submerged for up to seven minutes at depths of up to 9m.

Otters are mainly crepuscular or nocturnal hunters, so early morning or dusk are the best times to have a chance of seeing them. You are at least as likely to spot them on land, bounding along quickly, with head and shoulders held low and hindquarters held high in the manner of all mustelids. They always eat their fish (or other prey) on land too. Moreover, they are well adapted to the bitterly cold conditions of the Siberian winter and have no need to hibernate or migrate. Hence they are active and visible year-round.

Left: The common otter (*Lutra lutra*) survives over a wide range in the Trans-Sib region.

Wolverine *Gulo gulo*

We call someone a glutton if they are greedy and always hungry. Why? Well, glutton is the old name for the wolverine, an animal with an insatiable appetite and completely omnivorous, literally consuming anything from minute plants, berries and insects to carrion and the largest species of deer – elk and maral – which it stalks and ambushes with endless patience. Immensely strong, it has the habit of ripping the head off its prey. Decapitated heads of animals as large as reindeer, complete with antlers, have been found high up in conifer trees; seemingly it regards its victim's head as a special delicacy and likes to enjoy it well above ground, out of the way of other inquisitive or jealous competitors!

The largest of the mustelids, the wolverine somewhat resembles a long brown badger in shape, but its fur is brown, with lighter patches on its head and flanks. Like all fur-bearing animals it has suffered at the hands of trappers and their cruel gin-traps. However, this species has got its own back to some extent, as it is well known (and unpopular) for robbing their traps!

Sable *Martes zibellina*

Most of the fauna found in the area along the railway is also found elsewhere in the world – though usually in smaller numbers owing to the impact of greater human population pressures and demands. The sable, however, is almost exclusively a Siberian animal. It is virtually confined to the vast stretches of forest that traverse this huge country, mostly to the east of the Yenisey River and notably in the forests around Lake Baikal, where the Barguzin Reserve was established in 1916.

Of all the mustelid family, the sable has the most luxurious dark brown fur – long, thick and soft – a fact that brought it to the brink of extinction as a result of relentless trapping. At the time of the October 1917 Revolution there was only a handful left, but the Barguzin Reserve and other measures have managed to reverse the tide. Now there are perhaps several thousand in the wild, counting those inside and outside the reserve. Though still obtained by trapping and shooting wild animals, most sable furs now come from farmed animals.

Unlike stoats (ermine) which turn white in winter, sable retain their dark-coloured coats – usually brown, but sometimes black – throughout the year.

RODENT FAMILY
Muskrat *Ondatra zibethica*

A number of rodents have adapted to an aquatic life, including the dark, silvery brown muskrat. It is shaped like a large rat, with a tail almost as long as its body and flattened vertically in contrast with the beaver. An excellent swimmer, it is most often seen gliding effortlessly along the surface of the water with only its head showing. However, it is equally at home using its partially webbed hind feet to propel it along the

Above: The wily and not so fussy wolverine *(Gulo gulo)*.

bottom of rivers, streams and lakes in search of plants and invertebrates (especially swan mussels – its favourite).

The name of the species comes from the highly developed scent glands, which emit a pungent musky odour during the breeding season. Where these animals occur they can be very abundant, since the females have a short gestation period (four weeks) and produce between five and 10 young in a litter three times a year.

Beaver *Castor fiber*
The best-known aquatic rodent is the beaver, owing to its habit of building dams to raise the water levels of rivers and streams, and also constructing a lodge of sticks in the middle.

The beaver is the largest rodent in the northern hemisphere, growing up to 1.3m in length and weighing up to 40kg. Perfectly designed for an amphibious lifestyle, it has dense brown fur, eyes and nose situated high on its head, and webbed feet. Uniquely among rodents, it has a long, scaly and horizontally flattened tail, used as a rudder for steering and also for slapping loudly on the water surface to warn other members of the colony of danger. Exclusively vegetarian, its favourite food is the bark and branches of waterside trees, particularly willows, poplars and aspens. It stores branches and other vegetation for the winter in underwater chambers inside its lodge, where the young are also born. These lodges are wonderful feats of engineering, with an elaborate system of interconnected chambers and tunnels for different purposes, with ventilation shafts incorporated.

Though beavers are not frequently seen by the casual observer (nowadays they are rarer because of being hunted for fur), their conspicuous dams and lodges are clear evidence of their presence along the stretches of river where they occur. Conspicuous, too, are the gnawed ends of the stumps and trunks of trees felled by the incredibly sharp and powerful teeth in the dam-building process: worth looking out for.

This section on rodents should not end without brief mention of squirrels, chipmunks, rats, voles and mice, which though largely inconspicuous, overlooked and comparatively uninteresting to the average traveller, nevertheless form an integral part of the ecosystem. On a massive scale, they replenish the soil through their regular burrowing and eating routines and provide an indispensable food source for creatures higher up the food chain.

BEAR FAMILY
Brown Bear Ursus arctos
No sight in nature is more appealing than a mother brown bear with her cubs, and we are all familiar with stories and fairy tales about bears from our childhood. And we all know they love honey – even the Russian word for brown bear – medved – reflects this. Unfortunately these gentle giants are not usually held in such esteem by Russian hunters, who kill them even in winter, when specially trained dogs are used to scent out the lairs in which they hibernate.

Despite this, and the high mortality of the cubs dependent on their mothers for two or three years, brown bears still occur widely, if sparsely, in Siberia, with several distinguishable races. The huge size, humped shoulders and long snout make it impossible to confuse with any other animal on the continent. It is easily the heaviest animal of the area, males weighing up to 350kg and females up to 250kg.

Both sexes are great wanderers, covering enormous distances in search of food, and there is always a chance of seeing one in a forest clearing or ambling lazily along the shores of a lake.

CAT FAMILY
Lynx *Felis lynx*

Another carnivore typical of the forest, particularly in the more northern areas, is the very distinctive lynx. Rarely seen, but easily identified by the tufted ears and short black-ringed tail, this medium-sized member of the cat family is solitary and nocturnal. It hunts animals up to the size of hares, badgers, foxes and young deer, as well as catching smaller prey such as mice, voles and insects. Cats are popularly supposed to dislike water, but the lynx regularly pounces on ducks, fish and other aquatic creatures, and is in fact a strong swimmer.

Mating occurs in spring and the young are born in summer; the latter are dependent on their mother for the first year of their lives and will die if she is killed – which is always a possibility when trappers are at work. The lynx's much-prized coat of fur is reddish or greyish in background colour, more or less covered with indistinct dark spots.

Siberian Tiger *Panthera tigris altaica*

We end this account of the animals with one that is now so rare and seen by so few people that it is almost mythical. The Siberian tiger (also known as the Amur or Manchurian tiger) used to occur throughout the country's vast forests, but its valuable fur and propensity for hunting domestic animals when the opportunity arose, has led to its demise over virtually all of its former territory. Though nobody really knows, probably fewer than 300 remain in remote, isolated pockets in the Far East, where last-ditch efforts are being made to save it from extinction.

Though the chances of even glimpsing one are virtually nil, Trans-Siberian travellers should at least close their eyes and visualise this magnificent lord of the carnivores stalking through the world's largest forests; this has to be the ultimate Siberian wildlife sighting – the tiger in the taiga!

Birds

Bird species are more numerous than other animal species and are also seen more often. Indeed, the traveller will undoubtedly see more birds – species and individuals – than any other wild creatures on the journey. Of course, many birds are shy and secretive, have restricted habitat preferences or are absent in winter. What follows is a representative selection of those that might be encountered or are typical of the area.

Right: Prized for its fur, the lynx *(Felis lynx)* is seldom spotted.

NATURE GUIDE

WATERBIRDS
Greylag Goose *Anser anser*
This is the largest of the 'grey' geese and familiar as the ancestor of the domestic farmyard goose. Though not as common in Siberia as in parts of Western Europe, it is nevertheless likely to be encountered on marshes and lakes. Look for its heavy body and neck, big bill and, in flight, conspicuously pale forewing.

Bean Goose *Anser fabalis*
In contrast to the greylag, the bean goose is now rare in Western Europe but still widespread in Siberia as a nesting species. Smaller and darker than greylag, it has orange legs and a black and orange bill.

Mallard *Anas platyrhynchos*
This widespread species is common on marshes and lakes everywhere and is the origin of the domestic duck. The sexes of the wild birds are, as in most ducks, very different in appearance though approximately the same size. The females are basically mottled brown; the drakes have the characteristic bottle green head. Both have a white-bordered purple patch (speculum) on the wing.

Baikal Teal *Anas formosa*
This super bird has to be mentioned as one of the main desiderata for birders visiting Siberia. The drake is very colourful, with a distinctive half moon mark near the nape and black and yellow stripes below the eye. Despite its name its only known breeding grounds are in north-eastern Siberia, and it migrates south and south-east for the winter.

Falcated Teal *Anas falcata*
As with the Baikal teal, this is a scarce and little-known duck with a very limited breeding distribution. It nests on lakes and ponds in the taiga in southern Siberia. It has a beautiful mane of feathers hanging from its nape and another drooping from its closed wing. It winters in South-East Asia.

Coot *Fulica atra*
Coots prefer the more open areas of lakes, so are easily visible. They are readily identified by their all black rounded bodies, small heads and white beak and forehead. They dive regularly to bring up the water weeds on which they feed.

Common Gull *Larus canus*
As its name suggests, this gull is widespread throughout the region, particularly on the larger lakes and rivers. It is identified by green legs and beak, and by its weak mewing cry – its alternative name is mew gull.

Black-Headed Gull *Larus ridibundus*

Another abundant gull species, the black-headed is distinguishable from others by the red beak and legs and, in flight, by the white wedge along the edges of the wings in both sexes and at all seasons.

Little Gull *Larus minutus*

This, the world's smallest gull at only 26cm long, is a particularly graceful and dainty bird, usually seen gliding and dipping over lakes picking mosquitoes off the surface. It is only present in summer, when the very dark underwing contrasts markedly with the pale upper side – a unique combination.

Common Tern *Sterna hirundo*

Terns are sea and freshwater birds, related to gulls but more slender with black caps, long thin beaks and forked tails. The present species has a red beak and red legs, and may be seen hovering over lakes and wide rivers before plunging in to catch fish.

Common Crane *Grus grus*

Not common, despite its name, this species is nevertheless widespread over the area, nesting in open or wooded swamps. Its huge size, long legs, black and white striped neck and bushy appearance at the rear end mark it out from all other birds. In autumn, large flocks set off on migration with loud bugling calls, returning the following spring to breed. Its elaborate dancing rituals when courting and mating are well known.

WATERSIDE BIRDS
Grey Heron *Ardea cinerea*

This species of heron is the only one likely to be seen near the train line. Tall and grey, with a long shaggy crest, it will be seen wading cautiously through shallow water or standing hunched on the shores of lakes and rivers. In flight the neck is retracted in an S curve, as in all members of the heron and egret families.

Lapwing *Vanellus vanellus*

This is a widespread, attractive wading bird, easily identified by its wispy crest and, in flight, very rounded wings. In spring it is noticeable as it tumbles about the sky in its wild mating display, uttering the call which gives it its other name 'pewit'. It can be observed on dry fields and areas of short grass, as well as in wetter localities.

Left: Coots *(Fulica atra)* patrol the lake for food.

Right: A common tern *(Sterna hirundo)* on the alert.

Little Ringed Plover *Charadrius dubius*

A member of the same wader family as the lapwing, this species is much smaller, sandy brown above, white below with a black collar. Its preferred habitat is the stony shores of lakes and rivers, where it lays its well-camouflaged eggs on the bare ground.

Yellow Wagtail *Motacilla flava*

This dainty bird is a summer visitor to marshes, water meadows and lake edges throughout the whole area. The male is mainly yellow-ish, the female more buffish. Both sexes have the long tail characteristic of the wagtail family. They have a great time in the Siberian summer, chasing the hordes of insects that throng around all the aquatic habitats.

RAPTORS (BIRDS OF PREY)
White-Tailed Eagle *Haliaeetus albicilla*

No sight is more impressive than that of this magnificent bird soaring over a lake or rapidly gliding down to snatch an unsuspecting fish from near the surface. Its huge size, very broad wings and short wedge-shaped tail identify it. Young birds are mainly dark, but adults are a paler brown, with a huge yellow beak and pure white tail.

Golden Eagle *Aquila chrysaetos*

Another magnificent bird, the golden eagle, is slightly smaller than the white-tailed, with a longer tail and, in the adult, a golden brown head and hind neck. It hunts over open forest and steppes. Immature birds show patches of white beneath the wings and at the base of the tail.

Common Buzzard *Buteo buteo*

This is one of the most numerous and often-seen raptors. It soars end-lessly over all kinds of habitat, but is never very far away from trees. The general shape is not dissimilar to an eagle, but a buzzard is considerably smaller, with a less protruding head. It feeds mainly on rodents and carrion.

Black Kite *Milvus migrans*

With more angled and longer wings than a buzzard, the Black Kite is another soaring raptor. Its most distinctive feature is its long, shallowly forked tail. It's actually omnivorous, but its main food is carrion.

Peregrine *Falco peregrinus*

For sheer speed the peregrine's stoop is unsurpassed. It rises above its intended victim – a flying duck or pigeon perhaps – and with lightning speed (over 150km/h) it strikes a deadly blow with its outstretched talons. Like all falcons, the peregrine has rather pointed wings in comparison with those of eagles, buzzards and hawks. The heavy black moustachial stripe is a diagnostic feature.

Goshawk *Accipiter gentilis*

This is the largest of the hawks. It hunts quite differently from eagles, buzzards, kites and falcons. Surprise is the key to its hunting success; it glides low to the ground, swerving in and out of the trees, hoping to catch a thrush or pigeon unawares and seize it after a quick dash. It is capable of catching prey up to the size of a goose – hence its name.

Left: Black Kite *(Milvus migrans).*

Sparrowhawk *Accipiter nisus*

This may be regarded as a smaller and commoner version of the goshawk. It hunts in the same way, but takes smaller prey like finches, buntings and, of course, sparrows.

CROW FAMILY
Raven *Corvus corax*

The raven is the largest and most intelligent of the crow family. They are distinguished by their long wedge-shaped tails: crows are also all black, but their tails are shorter and only slightly rounded at the tip. The deep croak of the raven is a typical sound of almost all kinds of habitat.

Siberian Jay *Cractes infaustus*

Reminiscent and close relative of the better-known European jay, the Siberian jay is smaller and greyish brown all over with rusty patches on the rump, wings and tail. Along with the raven, it is one of the few birds that stay to survive the harsh Siberian winter. Like its European counterpart, it hides food in caches in preparation for the hard times ahead.

On arrival in Vladivostok at the end of the journey from Moscow, the traveller will have reached the Sea of Japan – and a whole lot more birds and other wildlife. But that's another story!

The Ecology of Lake Baikal

The highlight of the journey has to be Lake Baikal, the Blue Eye of Siberia. This is the world's deepest and oldest freshwater lake – nearly 650km long, up to 50km wide and, astonishingly, up to 6000m deep. Its volume of water nearly equals that of all North America's Great Lakes put together; it holds, in fact, a fifth of all the liquid fresh water in the world. It has been in existence for some 26 million years, with accumulated sediment up to 5km thick at the bottom of the world's deepest continental trough. Revered as sacred by the local Buryat people for its majesty, beauty and mystery, its unique wildlife is priceless.

Although now polluted by the industrial combines at Baikalsh and on the Selenga River – Baikal's main tributary on the eastern shore – it still contains an astonishing richness.

Thanks to warm water entering from vents in the bottom of the lake, and the filtering action of countless millions of minute crustaceans called epishura, the water is exceptionally clear and pure – although unfortunately less so now than formerly. Uniquely for a deep lake, life exists right down to the bottom – not just in the top layer. Over 1000 species of plants and animals live in it (nearly all endemic), including over 200 of shrimp and 80 of flatworm; one of the latter is the world's largest and eats fish!

Several of the lake's species of sponge are found nowhere else, including one which has been traditionally used to polish silverware!

Right: A true survivor of the harsh winters, the Siberian Jay *(Cractes infaustus)* plans ahead for the lean times.

The many kinds of fish include the endemic omul, Baikal's main commercial fish. A remarkable species, the omul is reputed to emit a shrill cry when caught. It spawns in the Selenga River, but its main food source is the endemic Baikal alga, melosira, which has declined drastically because of pollution.

Another remarkable fish is the golomyanka – a pink, translucent oilfish with large pectoral fins. Endemic to Baikal, it too has suffered from pollution. It is unusual among fish in having no scales and being viviparous – giving birth to live young, about 2000 at a time. It is the lake's commonest fish. By day it lives in the deep, dark depths, rising at night to near the surface.

Golomyanka is the preferred food of the most famous denizen of the lake – the Baikal seal, or nerpa *(Phoca siberica)*. This is the world's only freshwater seal, with no relatives nearer than the ringed seal of the Arctic. Nerpas are attractive, gentle creatures with unusually large eyes set in round flat faces, enabling them to hunt down to at least 1500m below the surface – even at night. Despite their size (less than 1.5m – the world's smallest seal) they have particularly strong claws for forcing their way through winter ice and keeping their breathing holes open. Pups are born in late winter. At the top of the food chain, Baikal seals have been greatly affected by pollution and are still harvested by local people. However, their population still hovers around the 50,000 mark.

There is plenty of other wildlife around the lake. The huge delta, 40km wide, formed by the sediment brought down to the lake by the Selenga River, is a great attraction to wildfowl and wading birds. In summer such beautiful and rare species as Asiatic dowitcher and white-winged black tern nest there, while in autumn vast numbers of waterfowl from the north use the mudflats and marshes to rest and feed on their migration south – a sort of international bird airport – while many overwinter there too.

Vast numbers of caddis flies and other insects hatch and swarm on the lake in summer, providing a rich and vital food source for all kinds of wildlife, from fish to birds. Despite their lack of visual impact for the Trans-Siberian traveller, these tiny insects, along with the microscopic plant and animal organisms, form the base of the pyramid of wildlife that graces this unique area.

The whole of Lake Baikal and its wildlife is a famous and urgent cause célèbre for conservation in Russia, giving hope that this priceless jewel will be preserved, albeit degraded from its former pristine state, for future local communities to inhabit, scientists to study, and everyone to admire and enjoy.

REFERENCES

Trans-Siberian Handbook by Bryn Thomas
A Field Guide to the Birds of Russia by VE Flint et al
Collins Guide Birds of Russia by Algirdas Knystautas
Realms of the Russian Bear by John Sparks
Baikal's Hidden Depths by John Massey Stewart

[Continued from page 208]

always open and even locals will tell you they're not worth visiting.

Places to Stay The one pleasant surprise of Severobaikalsk is its good range of accommodation possibilities.

For those on a budget, the station's clean *komnaty otdykha* will do fine for less than $3 a bed; there's no shower though.

Hotel Podlemore (☎ 2 31 79, prosp 60 let SSSR 26A) Singles/doubles $6.50/13. Right next to the station (and thus a bit noisy) is this brand-new hotel with friendly staff and more than acceptable rooms with good bathrooms and hot water.

Beside the hydrofoil landing, are seven attractive and cosy wooden *cottages* for $10 a night. For bookings for these and the up-market *Baikal Servis* chalets on the eastern edge of the town, about a 20-minute walk from the train station, contact Yevgeniya Kuznetsova (☎/fax 2 39 12, Russian only).

The four railway-owned *BAM guest cottages*, and the adjacent and rather incongruous brick building known to locals as *Hotel Santa Barbara*, are close to the lake in a woodland setting. All are well furnished and at $30 a night a bargain. The cottages are 25 minutes' walk from the train station, over the footbridge, then right along the road parallel to the tracks; take the first surfaced road on the left, then the first right, bearing left at the fork. Follow this road for 1km until Sibirskaya 12, a two-storey yellow house on your left, which is where the cottage warden lives. At night the whole of this lonely route is unlit so bring a torch. Contact Rashit Yahin (see Orientation & Information earlier) about the cottages and *homestays*.

Places to Eat There are half a dozen *food shops* plus an open-air *market* in the square.

Tikonov i Synovya (☎ 2 16 25, 2nd floor, Leningradsky prosp) Meals $4. Open 10am-1pm & 8pm-1am daily. Overlooking the main square and to the left of the central library is this smartish restaurant with a decent range of Russian dishes on the menu, including *omul* from the lake.

Kafe Ayana (☎ 2 12 24, Leningradsky prosp) Meals $3. Open 9am-6pm & 7pm-1am daily. From the short menu, we found the speciality of *pozy*, the big Buryat-style

dumplings, disappointingly unspicey but quite edible. We left as the customers started to dance, but if you feel in the mood to boogie there's also the *Piter* disco at the back of the Torgovy tsentr. Entrance is $1 before midnight and slightly more after.

Getting There & Away There's no ideal way of travelling back and forth from Severobaikalsk, but a combination of the following options can make for an interesting journey and the cost differences are negligible.

Train The cheapest, but longest ($15, 30 hours) way to or from Irkutsk is by *plats-kartny* carriage – *kupe* tickets cost around $35. Train Nos 71/72 link Severobaikalsk and Irkutsk, running on odd-numbered days. On other days you may be able to change to an Irkutsk- or Severobaikalsk-bound service at Anzyebi station in Bratsk.

From Severobaikalsk heading west are the No 75 going on odd-numbered days to Moscow and No 197 on even-numbered days to Krasnoyarsk. From June to September there's also No 97 to Kislovodsk in the Caucasus, which passes through twice a week, and No 131 to Moscow on even-numbered days. Eastbound, train No 76 leaves for Tynda ($21, 25½ hours) on odd-numbered days, while No 98 does the same route on Wednesday and Sunday.

Air The airport is at Nizhneangarsk, 28km north-east of Severobaikalsk. There are around six flights a week to Ulan Ude ($40, 1½ hours) and flights twice a week to Irkutsk ($35, one hour). The danger with flying is that there can be long delays and even cancellations due to bad weather. However, the views over the lake as you come in to land are spectacular.

Boat From June to the end of August a hydrofoil service runs the length of Lake Baikal between Severobaikalsk and Irkutsk. There's only one service a week in both directions – from Irkutsk to Severobaikalsk on Wednesday, the return trip on Saturday. One-way tickets are $35.

Getting Around You'll have to flag down cars; most drivers will stop. A ride to Nizhneangarsk is about $2, to Baikalskoe around $10 return.

The Circumbaikal Railway Круглобайкальская Железная Дорога

When the first trains began traversing Siberia in 1901, they still faced a major obstacle in getting around (or across, as the case may be) Lake Baikal. Engineers had decided that construction of a railroad line around the lake would be impossibly expensive, due to the lakeside cliffs and rocky terrain.

Instead, the Russian government commissioned a British firm to construct a ferry that could smash through the ice and transport the train carriages and passengers across the lake. In April 1900, the steamer *Baikal* commenced making its daily journey (twice daily in summer) between Port Baikal on the western shore and Mysovaya on the eastern shore. Later that year, a second ship, the *Angara*, was also put into operation. Today, the *Baikal* is somewhere at the bottom of Baikal, but the *Angara* is moored in Irkutsk near the Raketa hydrofoil terminal.

Ferrying entire trains (and trainloads) across the lake did not prove to be too efficient, especially due to impassable thick ice in winter and stormy seas in summer. This hindrance became a national security threat in 1904 when the Russians had no way to transport troops and supplies to the front during the Russo-Japanese War. Tracks were actually laid across the ice in an attempt to expedite the military movement. Tragically, the ice cracked under the very first train to attempt this crossing, and it sank into Baikal's icy waters.

Despite earlier hesitation, the decision was made in 1901 to begin construction of a railway line that would skirt the southern edge of the lake, connecting Port Baikal and Mysovaya. The cliffs around the lake required a tunnel or bridge almost every kilometre, making this the most challenging section of the Trans-Siberian to build. Tsar Alexander III brought in Armenian and Italian masons to design the elaborate portals and arched bridges. The pride of Mother Russia at the time, this section of the railroad earned the nickname 'the Tsar's Jewelled Buckle'.

In the 1950s, the Angara River was dammed, submerging the railway line between Irkutsk and Port Baikal. At the same time, a short-cut line was built between Irkutsk and Slyudyanka, bypassing this flooded section. This is the route that is still used today.

The remaining 94km of the Circumbaikal Railway has become a somewhat neglected branch line. Three or four times a week the train chugs to and fro with supplies for the isolated villages along the way. The ride on this line, however, is thrilling. The train goes through 39 tunnels and over more than 200 bridges, most of which have been constructed from the natural rock formations of lakeside cliffs. Every bend reveals new, spectacular views of craggy cliffs, flower-filled valleys and sun-sparkling surf.

Hiking the Circumbaikal

The easiest way to get a glimpse of the Circumbaikal is to take the ferry from Listvyanka to Port Baikal, where you can hike along the railway line at your leisure. Six boats go daily in each direction. One option would be to leave in the morning (make sure it is a day that the train runs) and to hike to one of the villages along the route, then catch the train back to Port Baikal in the afternoon. Alternatively, if you are prepared to camp, you can hike the whole distance from Port Baikal to Slyudyanka.

Frith Maier describes this route in detail in her book *Trekking in Russia & Central Asia*. Here are a few practical details from Edward Gowan, a traveller from Moscow to Ulaan Baatar (and back again) in July-August 2001.

• The path is very poor for the vast majority of the walk and requires walking on the sleepers of the track.
• The tunnels are wide and safe to walk through. Designed for a double track railway, they leave plenty of space for a group of walkers if one of the infrequent trains passes.

Around Severobaikalsk

Boats represent the main means of getting around Baikal's northern end. Contact *Viktor Kuznetsov* (☎ 30130-5 10 05, fax 5 10 30, e *frolicha@mail.ru*) in Nizhneangarsk, whose boat can be chartered for $100 a day.

A glorious day trip (although you'll need to start around 6am) is to sail from Nizhneangarsk to the Bay of Ayaya, then on to Khakusy for a hot-spring dip and lunch and finally to the pretty fishing village of Baikalskoe.

The Circumbaikal Railway Круглобайкалская Железная Дорога

• Places to camp are abundant at either end of the track. The number drops off rapidly, however, if you are more than a day's walk from either Port Baikal or Kultuk. In this section, take any good spots you see, even if you are not quite ready to break for the day.

• Don't expect to buy ANY provisions locally. We came across exactly one shop, which was selling a lot of fruit juice and not much of anything else.

• As two 19-year-old men, we completed the walk in four days. It would take longer for the unfit, but the seven days suggested by Frith Maier is perhaps excessive.

• Lake Baikal is incredibly cold. Drip-drying is recommended only on hot, sunny days.

• The Russian trekkers are a good laugh, but be prepared for many tales about Chechnya and many more shots of vodka.

Riding from Slyudyanka

At the time of research, the train travelled from Slyudyanka to Port Baikal on Wednesday, Friday, Saturday and Sunday, leaving at 2pm and arriving at 7pm. The return trip was at night. (This schedule seems to change every year, so be sure to check the timetable at Irkutsk station.) In theory, you can take a local train from Irkutsk to Slyudyanka in the morning, ride the Circumbaikal to Port Baikal in the afternoon, and catch the last ferry to Listvyanka at 8pm.

Riding from 'Kilometre 149'

If you wish to combine your ride with a hike through the forested hillsides or a stroll through some of the Circumbaikal's picturesque tunnels, a better option is to take a local train *(prigorodny poezd)* from Irkutsk to Tyomnaya Pad, or Dark Valley.

About 30km before Slyudyanka, the stop at Tyomnaya Pad is little more than a kilometre marker along the side of the tracks. It is also the starting point for a one-hour walk down to the lakeshore, where you can pick up the Circumbaikal. When you get off the train in Tyomnaya Pad, follow the railroad tracks towards the tunnel and look for the path that goes off to the left. The path leads downhill to a small village, known only as 'Kilometre 149'. Walk through the village to see the shiny blue lake sparkling in the distance and the old train tracks overgrown with wildflowers. In theory, the Circumbaikal passes the 149km at 3pm. Be ready (because the next train may not come for several days) but not too ready (because it is usually late).

Places to Stay

Several of the remote villages along the Circumbaikal line have well-equipped *lakeside resorts* and *tourist camps*. They are popular with Russian tourists in the summer, so you will need to make reservations. Any of the tourist agencies in Irkutsk can make these arrangements.

Getting There & Away

Be aware that the Circumbaikal rarely runs on time. Chances are the train will not actually arrive in Port Baikal until after 8pm, but the ferry tends to wait for the train before it makes its final departure to Listvyanka. Otherwise, there is no accommodation in Port Baikal, so you may have to get one of the local fishermen to give you a lift across the river.

Some of the agencies also organise day trips on the Circumbaikal from Irkutsk or Listvyanka. For about $100, Baikalcomplex offers a wonderful package, which includes a picnic lunch on the lakeshore, a knowledgeable guide, and a thrilling ride through the tunnels on the front of the locomotive.

Nizhneangarsk Нижнеангарск Nizhneangarsk is a small fishing village with approximately 10,000 people, 28km northeast of Severobaikalsk. It is home to the regional airstrip and a fish-processing plant. The town itself is attractive – made up of mainly wooden buildings – and in the high school there is a small **museum** that traces the history of the fishing settlement back to the 17th century.

The hydrofoil for Irkutsk begins its journey in Nizhneangarsk.

Bay of Ayaya & Khakusy Губа Аяя и Хакусы

A three-hour boat ride across the lake from Nizhneangarsk is the shaman-haunted Bay of Ayaya (which in the local Evenki language means 'very, very beautiful'). It's possible that you'll encounter reindeer ambling along the beach here, re-introduced to the area by the Evenki, and camping fishermen.

Inland about 7km from Ayaya is a pretty mountain lake, **Frolikha**. It's a good hike and you could camp here and then hike 15km south downhill to Khakusy where there's a holiday camp and good hot springs ($0.20 for entry to the nature sanctuary of which Khakusy is a part; $1 for the hot springs). Alternatively, continue by boat from Ayaya to Khakusy which takes around 1½ hours.

Baikalskoe Байкальское

On a lakeside bluff at the foot of a steep, emerald-green hill, the tiny fishing village of Baikalskoe is absurdly picturesque – a community of little gingerbread cottages with bright-blue shutters and small, neat, green and flowery gardens. The first cottages were built here over a century ago but life in the village has changed so little since then that they are indistinguishable from the more recently built houses.

It takes less than half an hour to explore the village, which includes a rebuilt church and the fishermen's collective hall, but the surrounding area is good for **walking**. Take the path north that leads up past a small hillside cemetery and continues along the top of some steep cliffs for a sweeping vista of the village and lake. Heading south out the village will bring you to an ancient wooden bridge across a river.

By car it is a good one-hour drive from Severobaikalsk to Baikalskoe along (for these parts) a sealed road of a reasonable standard. By boat the trip is around four hours directly from Nizhneangarsk.

Cape Kotelnikovsky Мыс Котельник-овский

This remote, uninhabited spot on the western shore of Lake Baikal, 65km south of Severobaikalsk, is known locally for its hot springs. About 10km inland from the springs are the peaks of the Baikalsky Range – the scenery around the highest peak, Mt Chersky (2588m), 40km by foot directly inland from Kotelnikovsky, is said

---

The Evenki

Probably the most ancient of the Siberian tribes, the 30,000-strong Evenki, or Tungus, spread widely from the middle Yenisey River to the eastern seaboard and south to Lake Baikal, the Amur River and Manchuria. Their language is related to Chinese, though they're culturally closer to Mongolians. They form 14% of the population of the huge Evenk Autonomous District (Okrug), north of Krasnoyarsk.

Related tribes are the Evens, hunter-fishers who number 17,000 scattered around the north-east, and the 12,000 Nanai, in the lower Amur River basin.

---

to be some of the most spectacular in Siberia, with waterfalls and glacial lakes.

It's possible to make a day trip to Kotel-nikovsky by chartering a skippered boat from Baikalskoe. The trip along the lake takes about three hours each way. For the day's hire of a boat with room aboard for four passengers you should expect to pay around $150.

Kholodnaya Холодная

The Evenki are one of the original indigenous peoples of the North Baikal region. Their village of Kholodnaya, 20km north-east of Nizhnean-garsk, which was originally an encampment of birch-bark yurts, is still quite attractive and offers an insight into traditional life in deepest Siberia.

About 10km from Kholodnaya are the re-mains of a **Gulag camp** (see the boxed text 'The Gulag' in the Yekaterinburg to Krasnoy-arsk chapter) where, in the late 1930s, prison-ers mined mica. The camp was closed shortly before WWII but several buildings survive, along with fallen towers, barbed-wire fences and three abandoned mine shafts.

The camp is in the Akikan Valley and the strenuous trek to reach it takes three to four hours. From Kholodnaya train station on the Kichera road, cross the river and con-tinue up the hill until the 42km marker. A little beyond, off to the left, is an overgrown dirt track which eventually, after about an hour, becomes a path beside a stream and winds up the valley to the camp. The best time for hiking here is July and August to avoid dangerous ticks (see Health section of the Facts for the Visitor chapter).

Irkutsk to Vladivostok

The Route

Irkutsk to Ulan Ude

As the train leaves Irkutsk, it cuts away from the Angara River and takes a more direct route straight to the southern tip of Lake Baikal. North of the line, at **5228km**, a cheery Lenin waves from the hillside.

Now, whatever is happening in the train stops dead, and everyone runs to the windows. The mind-numbing Siberia-scapes suddenly give way to the dramatic shores and icy blue waters of the world's deepest lake. For 200km, the line runs along the southern shore of **Lake Baikal** (5300km to 5500km) and through a series of tunnels blasted into the cliffs along the water's edge.

The train passes through **Kultuk**, the junction with the Circumbaikal line (see the boxed text in the Krasnoyarsk to Irkutsk & Lake Baikal chapter), before it stops in **Slyudyanka** (5312km). In the old days, passengers at Slyudyanka station would run down to the lakeshore and dip their hands in Baikal's supposedly healing waters. Today, however, the stop is shorter and the *provodnitsa* will strongly advise against (read 'forbid') leaving the platform.

From here, the railroad follows the southern shore of the lake, rolling past the Khamar Daban Mountains south of the line. Around 5390km, the train crosses the river that marks the border of Buryatia, one of Russia's semiautonomous ethnic republics. Although closely related to the Mongols, the Buryats have given up their nomadic herding lifestyle. Many cultural similarities remain, however, including the prevalence of Tibetan Buddhism in this region.

The town of **Tankhoy** (5426km) lies in the centre of the Baikal Nature Reserve. Farther along the shore, **Mysovaya** (5477km) is the port where the *Baikal* and *Angara* used to start (or finish) their journeys across the lake, ferrying train carriages and their passengers, before the railway was completed. The obelisk at the railway station marks the spot where revolutionary Ivan Babushkin was shot by tsarist forces in 1906.

If you are travelling west, keep a look out for the lake from around **5507km**, when the train suddenly pulls out from between the

Highlights

- Sail around Vladivostok's picturesque harbour and visit its early-20th-century forts.

- Cross the Amur River bridge at Khabarovsk, the longest on the Trans-Siberian route.

- Witness the revival of Buddhism in Russia at Ivolginsky Datsan.

- Ponder the relics of Buryatia's indigenous cultures at Ulan Ude's Ethnographic Museum.

- Savour the excitement of reaching the Pacific after a week's travel across a third of the globe.

forested hillsides and reveals a glorious view of Baikal's clear blue waters and the cliffs on the other side.

Just before the town of **Selenga** (5562km), the train line hooks up with the Selenga River, which it will follow all the way into Mongolia if you are on the Trans-Mongolian. Between here and Ulan Ude, the river valley provides ample photo opportunities, such as at 5630km, when the train crosses the river.

The train stops for about 15 minutes in **Ulan Ude** (5640km), capital of Buryatia. At the north-western end of the platform you can admire the old steam locomotive that sits in front of the depot. If you have time, climb up the footbridge at the northern end of the station and snap some photos of this busy railway station.

Ulan Ude to Chita

The Trans-Mongolian junction is at **Zaudinsky** (5655km), just east of Ulan Ude. If you are taking the Trans-Mongolian, turn to the Zaudinsky to Beijing chapter.

Around 5750km, the train crosses the border into the Chita Oblast, where the *taiga* gives way to rolling meadows, hills and deciduous woodland. Between the cities are quaint log-cabin settlements – see the boxed text 'Gingerbread Villages'. (During the summer of 1998, this entire area was flooded, in some places up to the tracks, and

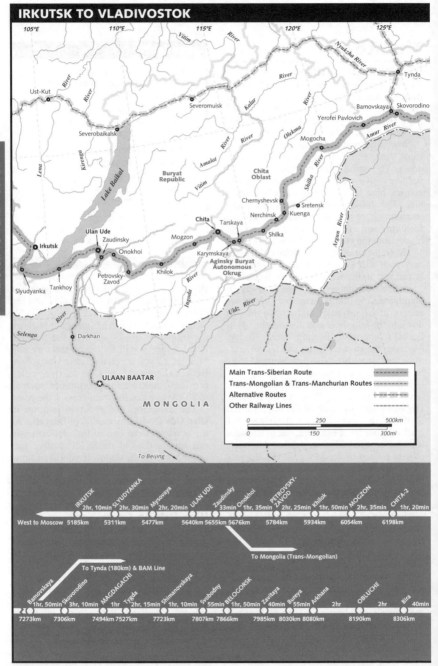

IRKUTSK TO VLADIVOSTOK

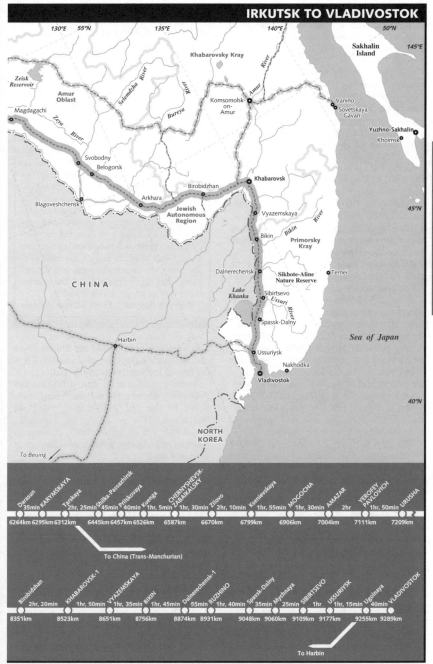

IRKUTSK TO VLADIVOSTOK

130°E 55°N 135°E 140°E 50°N 145°E

Sakhalin Island

Zeisk Reservoir

Amur Oblast

Magdagachi

Komsomolsk-on-Amur

Vanino
Sovetskaya Gavan

Yuzhno-Sakhalin
Kholmsk

Svobodny
Belogorsk

Khabarovsk

Blagoveshchensk
Arkhara
Birobidzhan

Jewish Autonomous Region

Vyazemskaya
45°N

Bikin

Primorsky Kray

CHINA
Dalnerechensk

Sikhote-Aline Nature Reserve
Ternei

Lake Khanka
Sibirtsevo
Spassk-Dalny

Harbin

Ussuriysk
Nakhodka

Sea of Japan

Vladivostok
40°N

NORTH KOREA

To Beijing

IRKUTSK TO VLADIVOSTOK

Darasun	KARYMSKAYA	Tarskaya	Shilka-Passazhirsk	Priiskovaya	Kuenga	CHERNYSHEVSK-ZABAIKALSKY	Zilovo	Ksenievskaya	MOGOCHA	AMAZAR	YEROFEY PAVLOVICH	URUSHA
35min		2hr, 25min	45min	40min	1hr, 5min	1hr, 30min	2hr, 10min	1hr, 55min	1hr, 30min	2hr	1hr, 50min	
6264km	6295km	6312km	6445km	6457km	6526km	6587km	6670km	6799km	6906km	7004km	7111km	7209km

To China (Trans-Manchurian)

Birobidzhan	KHABAROVSK-1	VYAZEMSKAYA	BIKIN	Dalnerechensk-1	RUZHINO	Spassk-Dalny	Mychkaya	SIBIRTSEVO	USSURIYSK	Ugolnaya	VLADIVOSTOK
2hr, 20min	1hr, 50min	1hr, 35min	1hr, 45min	55min	1hr, 40min	35min	25min	1hr	1hr, 15min	40min	
8351km	8523km	8651km	8756km	8874km	8931km	9048km	9060km	9109km	9177km	9255km	9289km

To Harbin

only the roofs of some cottages and the tops of haystacks were visible.) At **5771km**, local time becomes Moscow time plus six hours.

Moscow time + 0600

The train stops for about 12 minutes at Petrovsky-Zavod (5784km), the station for the town of Petrovsk-Zabaikalsky. The station name (and the old name of the town) means 'Peter's Factory', so called for the huge ironworks you can still see from the train. Some of the Decembrists (see the boxed text in the Krasnoyarsk to Irkutsk & Lake Baikal chapter) were jailed here from 1830 to 1939, an event commemorated in a large, photogenic mural at the station.

From here, the train turns to the northeast to follow the river valley of the Khilok, a tributary of the Selenga. The **Yablonovy Mountains** (between 5800km and 6300km) are blue shadows in the distance. At the small town of **Bada** (5884km), look for the MiG fighter monument and the cluster of old aircraft on the runway to the north.

Around **5925km**, the train slows as it leaves the valley and moves into the mountains, affording inspiring views of the winding river and fields filled with wildflowers. It may pause briefly in **Khilok** (5932km), where there is a machine shop for repairing train engines. An old locomotive stands at the eastern end of the platform. There is another 15-minute stop at **Mogzon** (6053km), which is a good place to get some homemade *bliny* (crepes) or *vareniki* (dumplings) from the babushkas on the platform.

The train halts for 20 minutes at **Chita-2** (6198km), the main station of Chita, capital of Chitinskaya Oblast.

Chita to Mogocha

For the next 250km east, the Trans-Siberian route follows the Ingoda River, which is south of the train. There are good views of the river around **Darasun** (6264km) where the train pauses briefly.

In **Karymskaya** (6293km), the station for the industrial town of Karymskoe, there's a 20-minute stop, shortly before **Tarskaya** (6312km), the Trans-Manchurian junction – if you're travelling this route turn to the Tarskaya to Beijing chapter.

The main Trans-Siberian route continues north-east on through **Shilka-Passazhirsk** (6445km), where there's a five-minute halt.

Gingerbread Villages

If anyone throughout all of vast Russia ever equalled Siberians in the art of wooden ornamentation, it could only have been the peasants from their ancestral homeland...from which the first settlers of Siberia brought their craft. They brought it with them, developed it to a point of astonishing perfection and endless, whimsical imagination, overlaid with new expanses and new life, and cultivated it here, there and everywhere – in town and country, among rich and poor, among plowmen, workmen and hunters. Only someone totally poverty-stricken in pocketbook or spirit, after putting up a dwelling, did not ornament it, cover it with design, paint it or work magic on it...Created to delight people, they continue to bring us joy to this day despite their advanced age. Even the most insignificant house with the plainest decoration, a good deal of which has already been lost, still preserves its attractiveness and dignity along with the noble soul of the master craftsman, which remains in it forever.

Valentin Rasputin, From *Siberia, Siberia*

The village here is beside the Shilka River and was once a popular health resort. Look for an old locomotive near the station.

There's another brief stop at **Priiskovaya** (6484km), where a 10km branch line heads north to the old gold-mining town of Nerchinsk. This is where the Treaty of Nerchinsk was signed in 1689, carving up Russian and Chinese spheres of influence in the Far East.

Around **6510km** keep an eye out for a picturesque church and a few other buildings on the flood plain across the Shilka River, south of the train.

At **Kuenga** (6526km) the Trans-Sib route turns sharply north, while a 52km branch line heads to Sretensk, the eastern terminus of the Transbaikal Railway. Until the Amur Railway was completed in 1916 Trans-Sib passengers used to disembark from the train here and climb aboard steamers to Khabarovsk. For more about the Transbaikal and Amur Railways see the 'Tracks Across Siberia' history special section.

Chernyshevsk-Zabaikalsky (6587km) is named after the 19th-century exile Nikolai Chernyshevsky whose silver-painted statue is on the platform. There's an 18-minute stop here giving you plenty of time to stock up from the various food and drink sellers.

Around **6660km** there are sweeping views to the north of the train across the Siberian plains. The next long stop (15 minutes) is at **Mogocha** (6906km), an ugly place scorched by summer sun and frozen solid during the long winter.

Mogocha to Khabarovsk

For about 700km, starting at around **7000km**, the line runs only about 50km north of the Amur River, the border with China. At one time, strategic sensitivity meant that carriages containing foreigners had their window blinds fastened down during this stretch – there's still not a whole lot to see with the blinds up!

At **Amazar** (7004km) there's a graveyard of steam locomotives – you'll have 15 minutes here to explore. The terrain now gets so rugged that roads stop and don't resume again until across the border at **7075km** between Chitinskaya and Amur Oblasts. This is also where Siberia officially ends and the Russian Far East begins.

Yerofey Pavlovich (7111km) was named in honour of the Siberian explorer Yerofey Pavlovich Khabarov (the remainder of his name went to the big city farther down the line). There's a 20-minute halt here and one of 16 minutes at **Urusha** (7209km).

You'll be well into day six of your journey from Moscow by **Skovorodino** (7306km), on the Bolshoi Never River, where there's a five-minute pause. This is where you'll need to hop out and change trains to go north along the BAM; the junction is back at **Bamovskaya** (7273km) – for more details about the BAM line see The Route section of the Krasnoyarsk to Irkutsk & Lake Baikal chapter. If you're on the *Rossiya* or any other major east-bound service you'll have to get off at Skovorodino and catch a local train back the 33km to Bamovskaya.

At **Magdagachi** (7494km) there's an 18-minute stop, and then a series of short stops before arriving in **Belogorsk** (7866km). This is the place to change trains if you wish to head south-west to the border town of Blagoveshchensk, the administrative capital of Amur Oblast.

At **8184km**, the border between Amur Oblast and the Jewish Autonomous Region (Yevreyskaya Avtonomnaya Oblast), local time becomes Moscow time plus seven hours. **Birobidzhan** (8351km), is the capital of the Jewish Autonomous Region – note the station name in Hebrew letters during the five-minute stop here.

Moscow time + 0700

The Jewish Autonomous Region is also part of Khabarovsky Kray, the 788,600-sq-km territory, rich in timber, minerals and oil, that stretches 2500km north along the Sea of Okhotsk.

Approaching **Khabarovsk** (8523km) from the west, the train crosses a 2.6km bridge over the 2824km-long Amur, the longest span on the whole line and the last stretch of the Trans-Siberian to be completed in 1916. The railway now runs across a new bridge, with a road along the top, completed in the 1990s. There's also a 7km tunnel under the Amur, secretly completed during WWII, and the longest such tunnel on the Trans-Sib route; it's now used only by freight trains.

From Khabarovsk you can take a train to connect with the BAM at Komsomolsk, or go direct to Port Vanino for a boat to Sakhalin Island. A statue of Khabarov stands in the square outside the station, which is undergoing a long reconstruction to mirror the fancy design of the old *duma* (parliament) in the city on ulitsa Muravyova-Amurskogo. The *Rossiya* stops here for a luxurious 33 minutes.

Khabarovsk to Vladivostok

This is day seven, and your last 13 hours on the train usually pass in the night. One reason for the cover of darkness is that the line comes within 10km of the sensitive Chinese border in places. From Khabarovsk south to Vladivostok the route shadows the Ussuri River, the border with China. At **8597km** you'll cross the Khor River.

At **Vyazemskaya** (8651km) there's a 16-minute stop; there'll be plenty of people selling food, including fresh salmon caviar. From here the forests are dominated by deciduous trees, such as maple and elm, which briefly blaze in a riot of autumn colours during September.

You'll probably be settling down to sleep by the time the train reaches **Bikin** (8756km) where there's a 24-minute halt; the line crosses the Bikin River here and follows it south to the border between Khabarovsky and Primorsky Krays. The southern forests of Primorsky Kray are the world's most northerly monsoon forests and home to black and brown bears, the rare Siberian tiger and the virtually extinct Amur leopard. The territory covers 165,900 sq km, has the Sikhote-Alin Mountains and runs 2000km from north to south.

There's a 15-minute pause in the dead of night at **Ruzhino** (8931km). Some 40km west of **Sibirtsevo** (9109km) – a 20-minute stop – is Lake Khanka, one of the ecological wonders of Primorsky Kray. This shallow lake covers 4000 sq km and is famous for its 2m-wide lotus flowers.

At **Ussuriysk** (9177km), you have 10 minutes in which to contemplate changing to the branch line north to Harbin in China; check your dates first, though, since the train goes only twice a week. Ussuriysk, formerly named Nikolskoe in honour of the tsarevitch's 1891 visit, was once of greater size and importance than nearby Vladivostok. There's also a line from here south to Pyongyang in North Korea, which may open again for passengers in the future (see the 'Tracks Across Siberia' special section).

By dawn – and after a week of travel from Moscow – you'll have your first glimpse of the Pacific to the south of the train at around **9245km**. You'll now be travelling along the hilly peninsula that forms the eastern side of Amursky Gulf. Near **Sanatornaya** (9269km) are some of Vladivostok's forlorn beaches and an enclave of hotels.

The city rises in a series of concrete tower blocks on the hillsides; you'll pass older buildings nearer the terminus – **Vladivostok** (9289km). Before leaving take a moment to admire the old locomotive on the platform beside the monument commemorating the completion of the great railroad you've just travelled along.

ULAN UDE
УДАН УДЭ
☎ 3012 • pop 380,000
⏲ Moscow time + 0500

Despite an archetypal Stalinist centre dominated by Vladimir Illych Lenin's surreal head, Ulan Ude is quite remarkable for its un-Russian ambience. The ethnographic museum features local indigenous cultures and the nearby Ivolginsk Datsan (monastery) is the centre of Buddhism in Russia.

The town was founded in the 17th century as a Cossack garrison on the Selenga River and chartered as Verkhne-Udinsk in 1775. A trading post on the tea-caravan route between Irkutsk and China, the town grew to 10,000 in the early 1900s. By 1930 this number had risen tenfold with the onset of Soviet industrialisation.

The indigenous Buryat people of the region put up stiff resistance to Sovietisation, as they had earlier to Russian colonisation, and grimly clung to their language, their cultural identity and the Tibetan-Buddhist faith they had adopted from their cousins in Mongolia. In 1934, as part of the Soviet recognition of national minorities, the city got its present name, which is Buryat for 'Red Uda' (the Uda River is a local tributary).

Because of Soviet installations on the Mongolian border, the city was closed until 1987 and could only be visited with special permission. Heavy industry was the backbone of the region with a large locomotive works, a metal-processing plant and an aircraft factory. Much of this industry has since shut down, leaving the workers to find other jobs, mainly in cross-border trade.

Orientation & Information
The city's axis is the tree-lined ulitsa Lenina; the central square, ploshchad Sovietov, is at its northern end and shopping areas are around the old trading arcades in the south. The train station is north of the square. From there, cross the footbridge over the tracks and walk south along ulitsa Borsoeva for 150m. Take any of the small side roads on the right and cut through the outdoor market area. Bear slightly left, towards the red-brick Hotel Geser, and the central square is two blocks east of the hotel.

There are exchange bureaus at Hotel Geser (open 9am to 6pm) and Hotel Buryatia (open 9am to 6pm). Hotel Buryatia also has an ATM, which operates on Western networks.

The main post office is on ulitsa Sukhe-Batora, at the north-western corner of ploshchad Sovietov. The telephone, telegraph and fax office, on ulitsa Borsoeva near the railway footbridge, is open 8am to 10pm. You may use the Internet at the main post office or at the Hotel Geser business centre, which is open 9am to 5pm, Monday to Friday.

Buryat-Intour (☎ 21 69 54, fax 21 92 67) has an office in Hotel Geser. The friendly,

English-speaking staff operates tours to Ivolginsk Datsan and to the eastern shore of Lake Baikal.

Merchants' Quarter

The town's historical main artery, ulitsa Lenina, is lined with elegant, faded architecture from the mid-19th century. In 1907 a rich merchant built the brown **mansion** with statues near ulitsa Kalandarashvili. The classically styled building along ulitsa Kuybysheva, which is now a clinic, was once a **Merchants' Yard** (1825). The central department store is now built into the middle of the crumbling old **trading arcades**.

On the corner of ulitsa Kirova and ulitsa Kommunisticheskaya is a large, pink house, which was the **home of Colonel Morrow**, an American mercenary who helped the Whites in the Civil War. Some blatant profiteering (stealing gold from the Barguzin Valley) caused a local surge of support for the Reds and he was run out of town.

South of ulitsa Kuybysheva is the oldest quarter characterised by its decorative log houses. Broken-down **Hodigitria Cathedral** *(Odigitrievsky sobor)* was once the pride of Verkhne-Udinsk.

Museums

Ethnographic Museum One of Russia's best exhibitions of indigenous and early Russian life is 6km north of Ulan Ude at the open-air Ethnographic Museum *(Etnografichesky muzey; Bus No 8; admission $2; open 10am-5pm daily June-Aug)*. Exhibits begin with reconstructions of prehistoric burial mounds and stone totems, and trace the region's vernacular history through to the wooden buildings of the early 20th century. A map in Russian is available.

Through the woods to the right is a complex of Evenki teepees, including a shaman's hut with totems in the yard. The small zoo houses some traditional herding animals, as well as some bears and lynx in miserably small cages. Continuing along the path, the Buryat complex includes a collection of *ger* (yurts), as well as cabins that were adopted by the eastern Buryats when they settled down in the 19th century. Nearby, a small Buddhist temple has an exhibit on temple architecture. The last collection of buildings at the front of the park is a re-creation of an Old Believers' settlement.

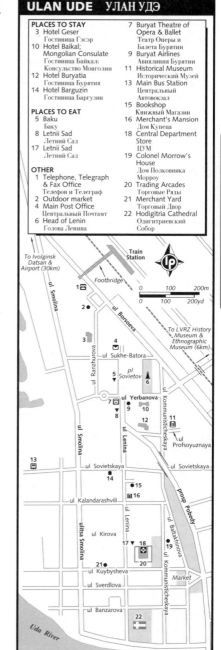

ULAN UDE УЛАН УДЭ

PLACES TO STAY
3 Hotel Geser
  Гостиница Гэсэр
10 Hotel Baikal;
  Mongolian Consulate
  Гостиница Байкал:
  Консульство Монголии
12 Hotel Buryatia
  Гостиница Бурятия
14 Hotel Barguzin
  Гостиница Баргузин

PLACES TO EAT
5 Baku
  Баку
8 Letnii Sad
  Летний Сад
17 Letnii Sad
  Летний Сад

OTHER
1 Telephone, Telegraph
  & Fax Office
  Телефон и Телеграф
2 Outdoor market
4 Main Post Office
  Центральный Почтамт
6 Head of Lenin
  Голова Ленина

7 Buryat Theatre of
  Opera & Ballet
  Театр Оперы и
  Балета Бурятии
9 Buryat Airlines
  Авиалиния Бурятии
11 Historical Museum
  Исторический Музей
13 Main Bus Station
  Центральный
  Автовокзал
15 Bookshop
  Книжный Магазин
16 Merchant's Mansion
  Дом Купеца
18 Central Department
  Store
  ЦУМ
19 Colonel Morrow's
  House
  Дом Полковника
  Морроу
20 Trading Arcades
  Торговые Ряды
21 Merchant Yard
  Торговый Двор
22 Hodigitria Cathedral
  Одигитриевский
  Собор

The Buryats

This Mongol people is the largest indigenous group in Russia, numbering 420,000. Just over half of them live in the Buryatia Republic south and east of Lake Baikal, which was Chinggis Khaan's home territory. Others are in rural autonomous districts (okrugi) west of Irkutsk and near Chita, as well as in Mongolia and northern Xinjiang in China.

Many Buryats converted to Tibetan Buddhism in the 18th century, though many Western Buryats later turned to Orthodox Christianity.

To get to the Ethnographic Museum from ploshchad Sovietov, take bus No 8 then walk the remaining 1km. Alternatively you can catch a taxi for $3.

Historical Museum Those exhibits that were used during Soviet times as an anti-religious museum now make up the Ulan Ude's Historical Museum *(Istorichesky muzey; ul Profsoyuznaya 29; admission $2; open 10am-5pm Tues-Sun)*. You can view the collected remains of pre-revolutionary Buddhism in Russia, salvaged from Buryatia's monasteries and temples on the eve of their destruction.

LVRZ History Museum Ulan Ude is home to the Locomotive Wagon Repair Factory *(Lokomotivo Vagono Remontinii Zavod; LVRZ)*, which has been building and repairing engines since 1932. Although the factory no longer allows tourists to visit its facilities, you can visit the LVRZ History Museum *(☎ 34 43 40, ul Komsomolskaya 23; Bus No 37; admission free; open 9am-5pm Mon-Fri)*. This small museum on ploshchad Slava traces the history of the factory, including its construction, its operation during WWII and its most famous employees (including the current president of Buryatia). Although there are not too many exhibits on the trains themselves, there are photos of the factory and models of engines that were built and repaired there.

Places to Stay

Hotel Barguzin (☎ 21 57 46, ul Sovietskaya 28) Singles/doubles $6/10. The Barguzin is the cheapest – and bleakest – hotel in town.

It does not have hot water in summer, but it does have a giant stuffed bear in the lobby!

Hotel Buryatia (☎ 21 18 35, fax 21 17 60, e hotel@burnet.ru, ul Kommunisticheskaya 47A) Singles/doubles/deluxe $10/15/23. Although readers have complained of abrupt Brezhnevesque service, the Buryatia has reasonably comfortable rooms and a host of other services available.

Hotel Baikal (☎ 21 37 18, ul Yerbinova 12, pl Sovietov) Singles/doubles/deluxe $10/12/24. This hotel features acceptable rooms with views of the giant Lenin head.

Hotel Geser (☎ 21 61 51, fax 21 40 88, ul Ranzhurova 11) Singles/doubles with breakfast $15/25. This old Party hang-out is the most comfortable place in town. It is a modern, well-maintained hotel. One annoyance – a feature of many upmarket Russian hotels – is the hourly phone calls from the local escort service.

Places to Eat

Ulan Ude is nearly devoid of eating establishments. Your best bets for a decent meal are the hotel restaurants. For a more informal experience (to put it mildly), visit one of the *letnii sad* (summer gardens) along ulitsa Lenina.

Restaurant Buryatia (Hotel Buryatia) Dinner $5. Open 11am-3am. This restaurant is popular as the town's number-one party spot. If you prefer to eat, the food is reasonable enough and includes some local specialities.

Hotel Geser Cafe/restaurant meals $3/7. If you stay at the hotel, you will probably get enough of the 24-hour cafe at breakfast. Even though prices are higher, the larger restaurant, open noon to 11pm, has tasty Siberian food and a pleasant atmosphere.

Baku (☎ 21 08 85, pl Sovietov) Dinner $4. Specialising in Azeri food, Baku is the best restaurant in town (which does not say too much, as it seems to be the only restaurant in town!).

Getting There & Away

Train The *Rossiya*, which travels between Moscow and Vladivostok every second day (in both directions), stops in Ulan Ude. There are also additional trains to Chita, Novosibirsk and Khabarovsk.

If you are heading to Beijing, the Trans-Manchurian passes through Ulan Ude on

Baikalskoe's lake jetty.

Alone on vast Lake Baikal.

Enjoying the company of a local boatman on Lake Baikal.

Traditional painted cottage at the picturesque village of Baikalskoe.

WWII memorial, Nizhneangarsk.

BRADLEY MAYHEW

The modern Mongolian man.

DIANA MAYFIELD

An earlier Chinese fashion.

JONATHAN SMITH

Tradition in St Petersburg.

ROBYN ROSENFELDT

One for now and one for later.

JONATHAN SMITH

Ice cream eaters in St Petersburg's sunshine.

JOHN KING

Pins to exchange?

DIANA MAYFIELD

Beijing Opera preparations.

GRAHAM TAYLOR

Distilling mare's milk for *airag*.

Wednesday and the Trans-Mongolian passes through on Saturday. There are two trains per week which originate in Moscow and go to Ulaan Baatar, passing through Ulan Ude on Friday and Saturday. If you want to go to Ulaan Baatar, however, you are better off catching the *Angara*, which runs daily between Irkutsk and UB and stops in Ulan Ude along the way.

Tickets Buy your tickets at the international ticket window *(mezhdunarodnaya kassa)*, even if you are buying a domestic ticket. Alternatively, the Buryatia-Intour office may be able to help you get tickets.

Air There are direct flights daily to/from Irkutsk, Moscow and Vladivostok. There are also flights to Chita, Omsk and St Petersburg once or twice a week. The regional Aeroflot subsidiary, Buryat Airlines, has an office at the corner of ploshchad Sovietov and ulitsa Lenina.

Bus Daily buses go to Ust-Barguzin, on the eastern shore of Lake Baikal, and to Kyakhta, on the Russian-Mongolian border.

CHITA
ЧИТА
☎ 30222 • pop 315,000
🕓 Moscow time + 0600

Chita was founded in 1653 as a Cossack stockade at the confluence of the Ingoda River and its tributary the Chita. In 1827 it became the home of a group of exiled Decembrists (see the boxed text in the Krasnoyarsk to Irkutsk & Lake Baikal chapter). After building their own prison, the exiles went on to dig irrigation systems and to cultivate the land. Under the influence of the group, Chita developed into a busy commercial and agricultural centre. In addition to the insightful Decembrists Museum, the present-day city still has a commemorative ulitsa Dekabristov. Unfortunately, ulitsa Damskaya (Ladies' Street), named in honour of the Decembrists' wives, seems to have disappeared.

Since the Trans-Siberian Railway was completed, light engineering has grown to form the backbone of the regional economy of Chita. When the East Chinese Railway opened in 1901 (see the Tarskaya to Beijing chapter), Chita became the guardian of this route into Manchuria and home to a large military presence. For this reason the city was closed to all foreign visitors until the late 1980s.

Orientation & Information
Central Chita is laid out on a grid pattern with the train line running along its southern edge. Immediately north of the train station is the sports stadium and, two blocks beyond, the awesome expanse of ploshchad Lenina. Bisecting the square, running east-west, is the wide, boulevard-like ulitsa Lenina, the city's main thoroughfare. Many of the Places to Stay are on ulitsa Profsoyuznaya, a north-south street that starts one block east of the train station.

The main post office is in the wooden building on the south-western corner of ploshchad Lenina. Two blocks north, the Internet cafe Magellan, on ulitsa Chaikovskogo 24, is open 9am to 8pm Monday to Friday and 9am to 5pm on Saturday.

Things to See
The city is probably not worth the hassle of a special visit, but you may have to stop here if you are trying to catch the train into China. In this case, you could be entertained for a day or two. The impressive building at the top of ulitsa Profsoyuznaya is the **Officers' Club**, where you may be able to sneak a peek at the military men battling it out on the chess boards. Next door is the **Military Museum** *(ul Lenina 86; admission $0.20; open 10am-5pm Wed-Sun)*. The most interesting exhibit is about the recent exhumation of a nearby mass grave, which contained local victims of Stalin's purges. If you missed the museums in Irkutsk, you may want to visit the **Decembrists Museum** *(☎ 34 803, Archangel Michael Church, ul Dekabristov 3B; admission $1; Open 10am-6pm Tues-Sun)*.

Places to Stay & Eat
Accommodation and food options in Chita are sparse, to say the least. Heading away from the train station there are some options.

Hotel Dauria (☎ 623 65, ul Amurskaya 80) Doubles $20. Upstairs from a popular Chinese restaurant and nightclub, rooms are a bit dismal, although they do have a television and telephone. Enter from ulitsa Profsoyuznaya.

IRKUTSK TO VLADIVOSTOK

Ivolginsk Datsan Иволгинский Дацан

This monastery at the foot of the Khamar-Daban Mountains is reason enough to visit Ulan Ude. Ivolginsk is perhaps not as elaborate as Gandan Khiid in Ulaan Baatar. It is worthwhile, however, to see the incarnation of Buddhism in Russia – perhaps the strongest evidence of the close relationship between Mongolia and Buryatia.

Buddhism in Russia

Many Buryats converted to Buddhism in the 18th century, when Mongolian and Tibetan lamas first founded monasteries in the regions east of Lake Baikal. In 1764, the high priest of the then-oldest monastery in the region, Tasongolski Datsan, became Band Hambo Lama, head of all Buddhist clergy.

Buddhists were, of course, persecuted during the Soviet period, perhaps even more than followers of other religions. During the height of Stalinist repression in the 1930s, temples throughout the country were shut down and thousands of lamas were sent to labour camps. After WWII the Soviet stance on religion softened somewhat; exactly two monasteries were allowed to reopen. Ivolginsk Datsan was rebuilt and reopened in 1946. Since then, it has been the centre of Buddhism in Russia.

Today it is the residence of about 30 lamas, mostly trained in Mongolia. The majority of the monks are of Buryat descent, but the monastery houses a handful of young Russians following a five-year course of study in Tibetan Buddhism. They belong to the Gelugpa, or Yellow Hat, sect. This 'School of Virtue' is a branch in the Mahayana tradition.

The practice of Buddhism in Russia differs slightly from the more traditional practices in Mongolia and Tibet. Many Russian lamas marry, for example, and wives and families might reside at the datsan.

In recent years, an interest in female monasticism has grown. A Buddhist Women's Centre in Kalmykia is supposedly constructing a Buddhist convent, where nuns from Mongolia will train female followers. Another apparent trend in Buryatia is a revival of interest in meditative hermit practices.

Visiting Ivolginsk

The main temple, near the front gate, was built in 1972. Inside, it is a riot of colour: multicoloured flags, golden dragons, shiny Buddhas. Most of the Buddha images and *tangkas* (paintings) were saved from other temples in Russia. The four 'guardians' at the rear are recent paintings by Buryat artists. Another smaller temple is in the front corner of the compound.

To the left is a round shrine to Maitreya, or Maidar, the future Buddha. Maitreya is the object of adoration during a two-day holiday in midsummer. The first day is spent in prayer. On the second

---

Hotel Obkomovskaya (☎ 652 70, ul Profsoyuznaya 18) Although this oblast administration hotel received good reviews from readers, it was closed for renovation at the time of our research. The cafe downstairs remains open and is a pleasant place to eat.

Hotel Zabaikale (☎ 355 51, ul Leningradskaya 36) Singles/doubles without bath $7/9, with bath $14/19. This rival for the cheapest place is on the 2nd floor of the shopping centre that is at the corner of ulitsa Lenina (facing the square).

Hotel Turist (☎ 652 70, ul Babushkinskaya 42) Trolleybus no 1 or 5 from the train station. Singles/doubles $9/14. In the north-eastern corner of the centre, the Hotel Turist has surly service and average rooms. It has two restaurants, so if you make your way out here, you nearly double your eating options.

Getting There & Away

Chita is 6199km from Moscow and 3090km from Vladivostok. The *Rossiya* stops here every day, travelling in either direction. Other trains go as far as Novosibirsk, heading west, and Khabarovsk, heading east.

If you are going to China, try to get a ticket for the once-weekly *Vostok*, which passes through on Tuesday on its way to Beijing. Otherwise, you will have to catch the overnight train, which goes every day to the border town of Zabaikalsk ($12 *kupe*). For more information on this route, see the 'Border Crossings' boxed text in the Tarskaya to Beijing chapter.

The Service Centre in the railway station is very helpful with obtaining train tickets. Look for the signs and enter from the eastern side of the building.

day, the monks process around the datsan, carrying a gilded statue of Maitreya on a chariot adorned with silk ribbons. Much fanfare accompanies this parade, including drumming and conch blowing, reading of Scripture and spectators throwing money. This procession symbolises the Maitreya radiating grace throughout the universe.

In the rear of the complex, the white building is a library containing the pride of the monastery: a rare edition of the 108-volume Ganjur, or Buddhist scripture. All of the volumes are artfully handwritten in Tibetan with a special ink made from precious metals. The library also contains a complete collection of the 225-volume Danjur, or commentaries, in Sanskrit. The Danjur comments on all aspects of Buddhist practice, including theology, philosophy, logic, medicine, art, architecture and rituals. Other items in the library include hundreds of Tibetan and Mongolian texts, each wrapped in silk.

The oldest building at the datsan, built in 1946, is the green temple in the rear of the complex. The sacred reliquary, or *stupa*, contains the remains of a former head of the monastery. The tree nearby is supposedly grown from a cutting of the original Bodhi Tree from Delhi. The lamas' houses are at the back. The one with the stone lions is for the head lama, who is also head of all Buddhists in Russia.

The prayer wheels around the perimeter are turned clockwise to 'activate' them. In fact, everything is done clockwise so as to keep one's right side to venerated objects.

Visitors are welcome in the temples and may observe the ceremonies, which tend to start around 9am and go on for two or three hours. The temple is closed in the evening. Ceremonies include chanting and drumming, and perhaps worshipping by pilgrims who are visiting the monastery. When you enter the temple, you must not step in front of the monks. Instead, go clockwise around the back. You can approach the altar to make a small cash offering, then bow before the altar.

Getting There & Away

Ivolginsk is 30km west of Ulan Ude. From the bus station, bus No 104 to Kalyonaya goes directly to the monastery three times a day. Alternatively, bus No 130 departs more frequently for the village of Ivolga. From there follow the road out of the village and you'll see the datsan glinting off in the distance to your right. It's a 4km to 5km walk, and considerably longer if you attempt a short cut across the marshy plain. The easiest way to see the monastery is to catch a taxi from the bus station. Negotiate the price in advance, but for about $15 your driver will wait at the datsan and drive you back.

BIROBIDZHAN
БИРОБИДЖАН
☎ 42162 • pop 90,000
🕐 Moscow time + 0700

The pleasantly leafy city of Birobidzhan, 180km west of Khabarovsk, is not an essential stop, but has an interesting history. The big Hebrew letters spelling out the station's name are one of the rare present-day indications of Birobidzhan's status as capital of the Jewish Autonomous Region (Yevreyskaya Avtonomnaya Oblast).

This 36,000-sq-km swampy, mosquito-infested territory on the Bira and Bidzhan Rivers, tributaries of the Amur, was opened to settlement in 1927, when the Soviet authorities conceived the idea of a homeland for Jews in the sensitive border region of the Far East. Some 43,000 Jews, mainly from

Belarus and Ukraine but also from the USA, Argentina and even Palestine, made the trek. The harshness of the land and climate (temperatures can drop as to low as -40°C here), meant only a third stayed.

Despite being proclaimed the Jewish Autonomous Region in 1934, the anti-Semitism and persecutions of the later Soviet years killed off the project. All Jewish institutions in the region, including the schools and synagogue, were shut down and the use of Hebrew was banned. Since 1991, and the establishment of diplomatic ties between Russia and Israel, there has been a further outpouring of Jews.

Today, although probably less than 10,000 Jews account for only 7% of the region's population, there is a tiny, but noticeable revival of Jewish culture in the town. Apart from the synagogue there's a cultural centre, newspaper in Yiddish (the polyglot language of Eastern European Jews), and Hebrew and Yiddish are also taught in schools.

Orientation & Information

The city's main streets run east-west, parallel to and squeezed between the train line and the Bira River to the south. From the station, the streets are ulitsa Kalinina, ulitsa Lenina, ulitsa Sholom-Aleykhema (the main axis), ulitsa Pionerskaya and prospekt 60 let SSSR with its twin squares, ploshchad Lenina and ploshchad Sovietov.

The main post and telephone office is at prospekt 60 let SSSR 14, where you can also access the Internet.

Things to See

The closest you'll get to a Siberian tiger is likely to be the stuffed one at the **Regional Museum** (*Kraevedchesky muzey;* ☎ 6 83 21, *ul Lenina 25; admission $2; open 9am-1pm & 2pm-6pm Tues-Fri*), that also has a room devoted to the Jewish history of the region.

A better place to go if you want to find out about the town's Jews is **Freid** (☎ 4 15 31, *ul Sholom-Aleykhem 14A*), a Jewish community centre with its main entrance at ulitsa Lenina 19, easily spotted because of the giant menorah outside. Freid means 'happiness' in Yiddish. A new synagogue is being built next to here, but for the time being there's the tiny pale-blue painted **prayer hall** (*ul Mayakovskogo 11*) – follow ulitsa Sholom-Aleykhema east into ulitsa Komsomolskaya, on into ulitsa Sovietskaya, and Mayakovskogo is left at the end.

Places to Stay & Eat

The *komnaty otdykha* on the top floor of the station has single rooms without bathrooms for $4, four-bed dorms for $2.50.

Hotel Vostok (☎ 6 53 30, *ul Sholom-Aleykhema 1*) Singles/doubles $16/32. The Vostok is Birobidzhan's only hotel and has acceptable accommodation. Skip the cafe, where the staff basically can't be bothered, in favour of the restaurant that sometimes serves Jewish-style cuisine for tour groups.

Next door to the hotel is the town's lively *market* where you'll find plenty of food for a picnic.

Otherwise, try *Restaurant Birobidzhan* (☎ 6 84 19, *ul Golkogo 10*), on the corner

of ulitsa Lenina, where a reasonable meal of Russian dishes costs around $2.

Getting There & Away

You might find it difficult getting a ticket on the *Rossiya* or any other long-distance trains that pause in Birobidzhan – it's easier to take the twice-daily *elektrichka* service to/from Khabarovsk ($1.50, three hours).

Buses from the bus station next to Birobidzhan's train station and from Khabarovsk station are more frequent, but slightly more expensive ($2.50). You can also take a tour to here from Khabarovsk with either Intour-Khabarovsk or Dalgeo Tours – see Travel Agencies in the Khabarovsk section.

KHABAROVSK
ХАБАРОВСК
☎ 4212 • pop 617,800
🕙 Moscow + 0700

After the monotonous taiga of eastern Siberia and its severe wilderness towns, the big city of Khabarovsk comes as a welcome relief. Lying at the broad confluence of the Amur River and its tributary, the Ussuri, the capital of Khabarovsky Kray almost has the air of a coastal resort.

The main street, ulitsa Muravyova-Amurskogo, is a lively, tree-lined boulevard with some very attractive 19th-century brick architecture. You will see Asian faces among the crowds here – hardly surprising considering you're only 25km from China. Still Khabarovsk is distinctly European in atmosphere, and the closest you're likely to get to Asian culture – other than in the Chinese and Japanese restaurants – is at the city's admirable Regional History Museum.

History

Khabarovsk was founded in 1858 as a military post by the governor general of Eastern Siberia, Count Nikolay Muravyov (later Muravyov-Amursky), during his campaign to take the Amur back from the Manchus. It was named after the man who got Russia into trouble with the Manchus in the first place, the 17th-century Russian explorer Yerofey Khabarov.

Until the Trans-Siberian arrived from Vladivostok in 1897, Khabarovsk remained a garrison, a fur-trading post and an Amur River landing. During the Civil War, it was occupied by Japanese troops for most of

1920. The final Bolshevik victory in the Far East was at Volochaevka, 45km to the west.

In 1969, Soviet and Chinese soldiers fought a bloody hand-to-hand battle over Damansky Island which lies in the Ussuri River. The fighting stopped just short of all-out war but it did set in motion a huge military build-up. Since 1984, the tensions between the two have eased, and there's now substantial cross-border trade. Damansky and several other islands were handed back to the Chinese in 1991.

The Japanese are also back – this time for business and pleasure. They make up four-fifths of all foreign visitors here and their presence in town is reflected in the Japanese-style hotels and the restaurants that specialise in sushi. South Koreans are also arriving in large numbers, opening many businesses in the city.

Khabarovskians are 80% native Russian-speakers, with small Korean and communities from the Caucasus. The only indigenous people here in any numbers are the Nanai, whose capital is Troitskoe, three hours down the Amur.

Orientation & Information

The train station is 3.5km north-east of the Amur waterfront along the broad Amursky bulvar. Running more or less parallel down to the river is the city's busiest street, ulitsa Muravyova-Amurskogo, which becomes ulitsa Karla Marxa east of the parade square, ploshchad Lenina. South of ulitsa Muravyova-Amurskogo are Ussuriysky bulvar, then ulitsa Lenina.

There are numerous maps of Khabarovsk available – try the bookshop Knizhny Mir, at ulitsa Pushkina 56, where several are pinned up for examination.

There is a rash of currency exchange offices across the city. The exchange bureau at Hotel Intourist, open 9.30am to 10pm daily, changes travellers cheques. Sebrbank on Amursky bulvar across from the train station generally has the best rates. It's open 9.30am to 7pm weekdays, 10am to 5pm Saturday and 10am to 2pm Sunday.

The main post office, at ulitsa Muravyova-Amurskogo 28, open 8am to 8pm weekdays, and 9am to 6pm on weekends. The main telephone office is at ulitsa Pushkina 52, two doors along from Hotel Tsentralnaya; it's open 8.30am to 10pm daily.

The Internet Tsentr (☎ 32 23 14), ulitsa Muravyova-Amurskogo 44, is open 8am to 10.30pm daily; rates are around $1 an hour.

The Chinese Consulate is located at Lenin Stadium 1.

Travel Agencies Intour-Khabarovsk (☎ 38 73 17, fax 33 87 74, ⓔ int115@intour.khv .ru), Hotel Intourist, Amursky bulvar 2, has plenty of experience in dealing with foreigners – usually large groups with planned itineraries. We found the staff to be friendly, offering an impressive range of tours in the area and longer Trans-Siberian packages. You can book individual rail and plane tickets here for a commission of around $3. The 2½-hour city tour with a guide and car is $30.

Another helpful travel agency offering a similar range of services is Dalgeo Tours (☎ 74 77 84, fax 32 67 02, ⓔ dalgeo@dgt .khv.ru, Ⓦ www.dalgeotours.khv.ru) at 34A ulitsa Dzerzhinskogo. It can arrange homestays for $35 per person, with breakfast.

Ulitsa Muravyova-Amurskogo

A stroll along ulitsa Muravyova-Amurskogo is the best way to admire the graceful **architecture** that survived the Civil War. Start at ploshchad Lenina, where the fountains are a magnet for locals relaxing of an evening, and where old VI still looks down from in front of a handsome red-brick building.

The striking old **duma**, or local parliament building, which is at ulitsa Muravyova-Amurskogo 17, became the House of Pioneers (Dom Pionerov) in Soviet times. It now houses one of the best souvenir shops and downstairs has a gallery for local artists.

A statue of Mercury stands on top of the **Tsentralnaya Gastronom** *(ulitsa Muravyova-Amurskogo 9)*. This attractive 1895 mint-green Style Moderne building houses a glamorous food store and decent cafe.

At ulitsa Muravyova-Amurskogo 1 is the intricate red-brick facade of the **Far Eastern State Research Library** (1900–1902). Komsomolskaya ploshchad is dominated by a monument to the Bolshevik heroes of the Civil War. Across the square, on the corner of ulitsa Shevchenko, is the headquarters of the **Amur Steamship Company**, with its round, church-like tower. The square used to be the location of Khabarovsk's biggest cathedral, long since destroyed; a replica is currently being built on the northern side.

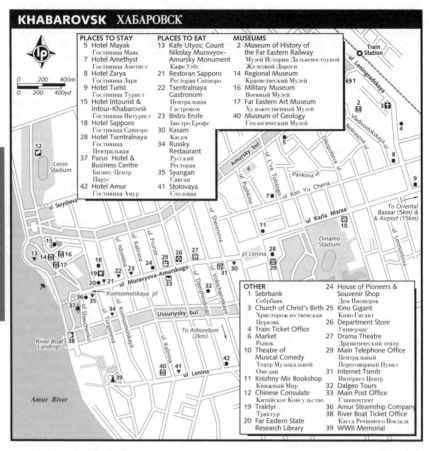

KHABAROVSK ХАБАРОВСК

PLACES TO STAY
5 Hotel Mayak
 Гостиница Маяк
7 Hotel Amethyst
 Гостиница Аметист
8 Hotel Zarya
 Гостиница Заря
9 Hotel Turist
 Гостиница Турист
15 Hotel Intourist &
 Intour-Khabarovsk
 Гостиница Интурист
18 Hotel Sapporo
 Гостиница Саппоро
28 Hotel Tsentralnaya
 Гостиница
 Центральная
37 Parus Hotel &
 Business Centre
 Бизнес-Центр
 Парус
42 Hotel Amur
 Гостиница Амур

PLACES TO EAT
13 Kafe Utyos; Count
 Nikolay Muravyov-
 Amursky Monument
 Кафе Утёс
21 Restoran Sapporo
 Ресторан Саппоро
22 Tsentralnaya
 Gastronom
 Центральном
 Гастроном
23 Bistro Erofe
 Бистро Ерофе
30 Kasam
 Касам
34 Russky
 Restaurant
 Русский
 Ресторан
35 Syangan
 Сянган
41 Stolovaya
 Столовая

MUSEUMS
2 Museum of History of
 the Far Eastern Railway
 Музей Истории Дальневосточной
 Железной Дороги
14 Regional Museum
 Краеведческий Музей
16 Military Museum
 Военный Музей
17 Far Eastern Art Museum
 Художественный Музей
40 Museum of Geology
 Геологический Музей

OTHER
1 Sebrbank
 Себрбанк
3 Church of Christ's Birth
 Христорождественская
 Церковь
4 Train Ticket Office
6 Market
 Рынок
10 Theatre of
 Musical Comedy
 Театр Музыкальной
 Омедии
11 Knizhny Mir Bookshop
 Книжный Мир
12 Chinese Consulate
 Китайское Консульство
19 Traktyr
 Трактыр
20 Far Eastern State
 Research Library
24 House of Pioneers &
 Souvenir Shop
 Дом Пионеров
25 Kino Gigant
 Кино Гигант
26 Department Store
 Универмаг
27 Drama Theatre
 Драматический театр
29 Main Telephone Office
 Центральный
 Переговорный Пункт
31 Internet Tsentr
 Интернет Центр
32 Dalgeo Tours
33 Main Post Office
 Главпочтамт
36 Amur Steamship Company
38 River Boat Ticket Office
 Касса Речного Вокзала
39 WWII Memorial

The Waterfront & River Trips

Steps from Komsomolskaya ploshchad lead to the **waterfront** and a strip of beach. South is a string of summertime food stalls and the landing stages for the suburban river boats. Farther on, as you climb the steps back up to ulitsa Lenina, you'll encounter Khabarovsk's bombastic **WWII memorial**.

A pleasant **city park** stretches for 1.5km downriver (north). On the promontory is a cliff-top **tower** in which a troupe of WWI Austro-Hungarian POW musicians was shot dead for refusing to play the Russian Imperial anthem. It now houses Kafe Utyos (see Places to Eat).

Opposite the tower is a statue of **Count Nikolay Muravyov-Amursky**. Muravyov's remains actually lie in the Montparnasse cemetery in Paris, the city in which he died in 1881. The **monument** at the foot of the cliff below the tower marks the spot where the city's founders first stepped ashore.

For short, local ferry trips on the Amur, check the schedules at the landings *(prichal)* by the beach. Good choices might be the trip downstream to Green Island (Ostrov Zelyony) from landing No 5, upstream to Vladimirovka from landing No 2 or around the back channels to Priamurskaya from landing No 3. Boats run May to October.

Museums

The excellent **Regional Museum** (*Kraevedchesky muzey;* ☎ 38 93 54, *ul Shevchenko 11; admission $2.60; open 10am-6pm Tues-Sun)* was founded in 1894. It includes displays on the natural history of the Far East (with the obligatory stuffed Amur or Siberian tiger), fascinating artefacts and costumes of the indigenous peoples, an archaeology section, and a recent history section with a striking 360° panorama depicting the 1922 Civil War battle at Volochaevka.

The **Far Eastern Art Museum** *(Khudozhestvenny muzey;* ☎ *32 83 38, ul Shevchenko 7; admission $3; open 10am-5pm Tues-Sun)* next door has a patchy assortment of religious icons, Japanese porcelain and some 19th-century Russian paintings on the upper floor. The lower floors are given over to displays of ethnic handicrafts, a contemporary gallery and a good souvenir shop.

Across the road, highlight of the **Military Museum** *(Voenny muzey;* ☎ *32 63 50, ul Shevchenko 20; admission $1; open 10am-5pm Tues-Sun)* for Trans-Siberian travellers is the luxury officers-only rail carriage dating from 1926 in the courtyard at the back, along with the tanks and rockets. Ask nicely, and the guards may let you peek inside.

Another must-see for train buffs is the small but interesting **Museum of History of the Far Eastern Railway** *(☎ 38 95 13, ul Vladivostokskaya 40; admission free; open 8.30am-5.30pm Mon-Fri)*. Call ahead and the helpful curator will give you a guided tour of the displays that include some evocative photographs, maps and models. The museum is about five minutes' walk south of the station.

There's also a **Museum of Geology** *(Geologichesky muzey;* ☎ *21 53 70, ul Lenina 15; admission $1; open 10am-6pm Tues-Sun)*, but it was closed when we visited and may not be reopening.

Other Attractions

Among the few churches that survived the Soviet years is the **Church of Christ's Birth** *(Khristorozhdestvenskaya tserkov;* ☎ *38 06 71, ul Leningradskaya 65)*. Its simple wooden construction hides a kaleidoscopic interior of coloured glass and glitzy icons. Services, with mesmeric hymn-singing, are held 7am to 9am and 5pm to 7pm daily, though this schedule tends to change on church holidays.

The **Arboretum** *(Dendrary; ul Volochaevskaya; open 9am-6pm daily)* is a 12-hectare botanical garden with samples of all the trees and shrubs of the Russian Far East. It's about 2km south of the city; Tram Nos 1, 2 and 6 run down here from the station.

Places to Stay

Budget Khabarovsk has a number of less expensive accommodation options.

Hotel Mayak (☎ 32 51 31, ul Kooperativnaya 11) Singles/doubles $8/12.50. The run-down apartment block in which this cheap hotel is housed was being upgraded when we visited. The rooms – all with shared bathrooms – are basic but clean and the staff friendly. There's no hot water in July. From the station, walk 400m along Amursky bulvar, and turn left immediately after No 48.

Hotel Turist (☎ 31 03 27, fax 78 36 40, ul Karla Marxa 67) Singles/doubles $16/20. This is a typical 1970s Soviet hotel, but its boxy rooms are well maintained with quite decent facilities.

Hotel Zarya (☎ 32 70 75, fax 31 01 03, ul Kim Yu Chena 81/16. Singles/doubles $17/24). This converted block of flats has reasonably spacious rooms. There are also cheaper ones available should you be able to persuade the friendly staff to let you have Russian prices.

A couple more moderately upgraded Soviet-era bastions are *Hotel Tsentralnaya (☎ 32 47 59, fax 31 41 88, ul Pushkina 52)* with singles and doubles for $22, and *Hotel Amur (☎ 21 39 53, fax 22 12 23, ul Lenina 29)* where singles/doubles are $30/60. Both get busy with tour groups and business travellers so advance booking is advised.

Mid-Range & Top End The boutique-style *Hotel Amethyst (☎ 32 54 81, fax 32 46 99,* e *amethyst@hotel.kht.ru, ul L'va Tolstogo 5A)* has just 16 spacious and nicely decorated rooms. Rooms are $60 for singles and $100 for doubles. The staff are great and there's a pleasant cafe and sauna ($6 per hour).

Hotel Intourist (☎ 38 73 13, fax 32 65 07, e *int115@intour.khv.ru,* w *www.intour.khv.ru, Amursky bul 2)* Singles/doubles with breakfast from $70/78. The Intourist is huge and offers plenty of services. It accommodates most package tourists who hit town. The rooms aren't too bad and many have great views of the Amur.

Hotel Sapporo (☎ 30 67 45, fax 30 44 18, e *sapporo@gin.ru, ul Komsomolskaya 79)*

Singles/doubles $85/100. The rooms here are straight out of a Japanese business hotel, to suit the requirements of visitors from across the Sea of Japan – thus standards are high and you'll need to book well in advance. The sauna ($5 for two hours) is recommended

Parus (☎ *32 72 70, fax 32 57 07,* e *guest@ parus.vic.ru, ul Shevchenko 5)* Singles/ doubles $100/130. Connected to a business centre, this is about as luxurious as you're going to get. There's a nicely decorated and equally pricey bar as well as a restaurant.

Places to Eat

Restaurants Cosy, although slightly kitsch, *Russky Restaurant* (☎ *30 65 87, Ussuriysky bul 9)* has great Russian food with mains for $3. Try the speciality – sturgeon sizzling on a hot stone plate. It's open noon to midnight every day, with some good live music performances as accompaniment.

Syangan (☎ *31 13 28, ul Muravyova-Amurskogo 2)* Mains around $5. Open noon-midnight daily. Top Chinese restaurant in town, the kind of place where the big round tables, if they're not hosting tour groups, are occupied by giggling office girls or gangsters in the midst of a deal.

Restoran Sapporo (☎ *33 51 75, ul Muravyova-Amurskogo 3)* Mains $10-15. It's the 3rd-floor Japanese restaurant that's the draw here – the sushi and other Japanese specialities aren't bad, with the lunchtime set menu for $11 being the best value. On the 2nd floor, there's an old-fashioned *Russian restaurant* (☎ *38 80 82)* where the locals get drunk and dance to Brezhnev-era hits. More up-to-date music sets the tone at the ground-floor *disco* ($4) that's open 9pm to 5am Friday and Saturday.

Hotel Intourist has a couple of decent places to eat: on the 11th floor is *Unikhab* (☎ *38 73 15),* a swish Japanese restaurant with a reasonably priced menu of standards such as sushi and tempura. In the basement is *Korea House* (☎ *38 72 34),* which serves, surprisingly enough, Korean cuisine; traditional rice dishes start at $3.

Cafes, Snacks & Self-Catering There are lots of cheap places for snacks along ulitsa Muravyova-Amurskogo, including outdoor kiosks serving *shashlyk* and pastries. Try *Bistro Erofe* (*ul Muravyova-Amurskogo 11)* or *Kasam* (*ul Muravyova-Amurskogo 50)*;

Kasam has an English menu with photos and does very nice bliny. For a cheap but filling meal an OK *stolovaya* (*ul Lenina 17)* is open 8am to 10am for breakfast and 11am to 5pm for lunch Monday to Friday.

Kafe Utyos (*ul Shevchenko 15)*. Mains $2-3. Open daily noon-midnight. One of the nicest places for a drink or snack is this cafe in the tower in the park overlooking the river.

For Trans-Siberian supplies, *Tsentralnaya Gastronom* (*ul Muravyova-Amurskogo 9; open 8am-10pm daily)* has practically all you could want in sumptuous surroundings; upstairs is a cute self-service cafe.

For fresh produce try the *market* (*8am-7pm daily)* on Amursky bulvar between ulitsa L'va Tolstogo and ulitsa Pushkina.

Entertainment

Apart from the disco in Restoran Sapporo at weekends, the bar/restaurant/casino *B52* at the Hotel Tsentralnaya tends to attract a late-night crowd.

Traktyr (*ul Komsomolskaya 19)* is a simple but popular bar serving the local brew Amur Pivo.

For more highbrow entertainment you'll need to brush up your Russian to appreciate the dramatic offerings at the *Drama Theatre* (*Teatr Dramy;* ☎ *23 55 33, ul Dzerzhinskogo 44)* and the *Theatre of Musical Comedy* (*Teatr Muzkomedii;* ☎ *21 14 09, ul Karla Marxa 64)*. Or you can wrestle with dubbed dialogue at the movies at *Kino Gigant* (☎ *32 58 28, ul Muravyova-Amurskogo 19)*.

Shopping

The *Oriental Bazaar* (*veshchevoy rynok)* is one of the biggest traders markets in the Far East. From about 10am to early afternoon, hordes of Chinese and Russian traders fill this vacant lot with stalls of cheap merchandise. Admission is $0.15, payable at the cashier's window right of the main gate.

Take trolley No 1 to the ulitsa Vyborgskaya stop where cabs are usually waiting to take you the next 3km to the market for $2, or $0.50 per person if shared.

Getting There & Away

Train Apart from the *Rossiya*, which departs for Moscow ($155 kupe, 5½ days) and Irkutsk ($92, 2½ days) on even-numbered days, there's also the daily No 43 service to Moscow and the No 7 to Novosibirsk.

Heading east, Vladivostok ($26, 13 hours) is best reached on the daily No 6 *Okean* service, which has a good restaurant car.

There is a daily service (No 225) to Tynda/Neryungri on the BAM. Train No 67/68 runs to/from Komsomolsk-on-Amur, another BAM station, with connections to Sovetskaya Gavan and Port Vanino for the ferry across to Sakhalin Island.

Tickets can easily be purchased at the station or the quieter ticket office at ulitsa Leningradskaya 56B, open 8am to 8pm daily, where you'll pay a $1 booking fee.

Air Domestic flights using Khabarovsk airport (east of the city) include three a day to/from Moscow ($267, 8½ hours), two daily to Yuzhno-Sakhalinsk ($100, 1½ hours), four each week to Irkutsk ($107, three hours) and Yakutsk ($150, three hours), two a week to Vladivostok ($67, 1¾ hours) and a weekly service to Magadan ($143, 2½ hours).

Internationally, there are flights to Harbin ($157), Guau ($257), Seoul ($350 to $440) and Niigata ($215).

The foreign airlines all have offices on the upper floor of the airport's international terminal, a modern two-storey building to the far left of the main building. Intour-Khabarovsk at Hotel Intourist can also book seats and issue tickets.

All international flights are subject to a $25 departure tax to be paid in roubles at the terminal's information desk prior to checking in. Intourist passengers making domestic flights should check in at the old international terminal, which is the odd-looking building with the portico, next to the new one.

Boat Boats sail down the Amur to Fuyuan in northern China from Khabarovsk's river station (see Around Khabarovsk). Between May and October, hydrofoils run north on the Amur between Khabarovsk and Komsomolsk ($12, six hours) and Nikolaevsk ($46, 15 hours). The ticket office, open 8am to 12.30pm and 1.30pm to 4pm daily, is across from the green river-boat station.

Getting Around
There might be a bus from the airport, 9.5km east of the centre but, if not, a taxi to/from the Hotel Intourist costs around $8.

From the train station at the eastern end of Amursky bulvar, the easiest way into the

city centre, is on tram No 1, 2, 4 or 6, which crosses ulitsa Muravyova-Amurskogo along ulitsa Sheronova. Bus No 1 also heads down ulitsa Muravyova-Amurskogo.

AROUND KHABAROVSK
Fuyuan (China)
Фуюань
At 8.15am every second day from mid-May to mid-October, a hydrofoil departs from the river station at Khabarovsk for Fuyuan, a small town on the Chinese bank of the Amur River ($37 round trip, three hours). If you return on the hydrofoil the same day at 6pm, supposedly no visa is required for the visit. Anyone wishing to travel farther on into China needs a valid visa (check with the Chinese consulate if you need a visa). From Fuyuan take a bus to Jiamusi and then on to Harbin (see the Tarskaya to Beijing chapter).

Troitskoe & Sikachi-Alyan
Троицкое и Сикачи-Алян
Both Intour-Khabarovsk and Dalgeo Tours (see Travel Agencies earlier) can arrange trips to these Nanai villages on the Amur River. Troitskoe, 130km north-east of Khabarovsk, is the larger of the two and home to about 22,000 indigenous Nanai. A day trip to here with a one-way transfer by hydrofoil and a visit to the museum, lunch and a folkmusic concert is around $100 per person for a minimum of three people.

The main attractions at Sikachi-Alyan, 40km downriver from Khabarovsk, are the many 11th-century BC petroglyphs – aboriginal stone carvings on the basalt boulders found at the water's edge. Between June and October, the river is infested with swarms of mosquitoes that can easily bite through cotton, so wear something more protective, and cover your hands and face.

In the village there's also the recently opened **Ecological Tourist Complex** with small displays about Nanai culture and the occasional music performance by locals. Day trips here are around $70 per person, again for a minimum of three people.

VLADIVOSTOK
ВЛАДИВОСТОК
☎ 4232 • pop 730,000
⊕ Moscow time + 0700
Sprinkled across a series of peaks, peninsulas and islands, Vladivostok is one of the

most attractively sited cities in all of Russia. Golden Horn Bay (Bukhta Zolotoy Rog), is named after Istanbul's similar-looking natural harbour, is home to the Russian Pacific Fleet, which made Vladivostok firmly off limits to all foreigners (and most Russians) during Soviet times.

Once again open to everyone, the Trans-Siberian line's eastern terminus is a bustling commercial city of seedy charm, where you're as likely to rub shoulders with burly 'business men' in sushi bars as with off-duty sailors or battalions of Chinese, Japanese and Korean tourists. It's now possible to explore the early-20th-century fortifications that made this such a crucial garrison at the Far Eastern end of the Russian empire, clamber through a Soviet submarine or even

lounge on island beaches that were once the sole preserve of the navy.

Tour agencies offer an impressive range of outdoor adventures, including hiking trips, river rafting and the chance to observe Amur (Siberian) tigers. Prone to torrential rain storms and power cuts in the depths of winter, you don't always need to be out in the wilderness to experience the rough life in Vladivostok. Steadily, though, the old cosmopolitan flair is returning, as witnessed in the city's most fashionable cafes – all of which make this a fine place to end, or start, your Trans-Siberian adventure.

History

Founded in 1860, Vladivostok, which translates as Lord of the East, became a naval

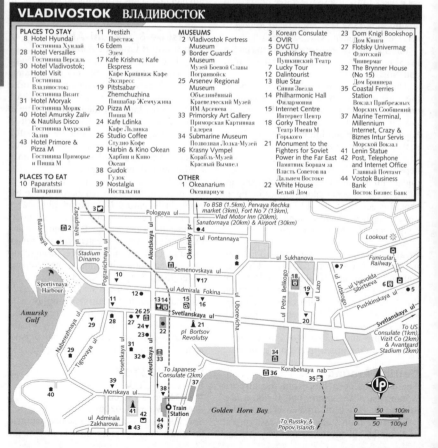

VLADIVOSTOK ВЛАДИВОСТОК

PLACES TO STAY
8 Hotel Hyundai
   Гостиница Хундай
28 Hotel Versailles
   Гостиница Версаль
30 Hotel Vladivostok;
   Hotel Visit
   Гостиница
   Владивосток;
   Гостиница Визит
31 Hotel Moryak
   Гостиница Моряк
40 Hotel Amursky Zaliv
   & Nautilus Disco
   Гостиница Амурский
   Залив
43 Hotel Primore &
   Pizza M
   Гостиница Приморье
   и Пицца М

PLACES TO EAT
10 Paparatstsi
   Папарацци

11 Prestizh
   Престиж
16 Edem
   Эдем
17 Kafe Krishna; Kafe
   Ekspress
   Кафе Кришнаж Кафе
   Экспресс
19 Pitstsabar
   Zhemchuzhina
   Пиццабар Жемчужина
20 Pizza M
   Пицца М
24 Kafe Ldinka
   Кафе Льдинка
26 Studio Coffee
   Студио Кофе
29 Harbin & Kino Okean
   Харбин и Кино
   Океан
38 Gudok
   Гудок
39 Nostalgia
   Ностальгия

MUSEUMS
2 Vladivostok Fortress
   Museum
9 Border Guards'
   Museum
   Музей Боевой Славы
   Пограничойск
25 Arseney Regional
   Museum
   Объединённый
   Краеведческий Музей
   ИМ Арсенева
33 Primorsky Art Gallery
   Приморская Картинная
   Галерея
34 Submarine Museum
   Подводная Лодка-Музей
36 Krasny Vympel
   Корабль-Музей
   Красный Вымпел

OTHER
1 Okeanarium
   Океанариум

3 Korean Consulate
4 OVIR
5 DVGTU
12 Pushkinsky Theatre
   Пушкинский Театр
12 Lucky Tour
12 Dalintourist
13 Blue Star
   Синяя Звезда
14 Philharmonic Hall
   Филармония
15 Internet Centre
   Интернет Центр
18 Gorky Theatre
   Театр Имени М
   Горького
21 Monument to the
   Fighters for Soviet
   Power in the Far East
   Памятник Борцам за
   Власть Советов на
   Дальнем Востоке
22 White House
   Белый Дом

23 Dom Knigi Bookshop
   Дом Книги
27 Flotsky Univermag
   Флотский
   Чивермаг
32 The Brynner House
   (No 15)
   Дом Бриннера
35 Coastal Ferries
   Station
   Вокзал Прибрежных
   Морских Сообщений
37 Marine Terminal,
   Millennium
   Internet, Crazy &
   Biznes Intur Servis
   Морской Вокзал
42 Post, Telephone
   and Internet Office
   Главный Почтамт
44 Vostok Business
   Bank
   Восток Бизнес Банк

base in 1872 when the residence of the governor general of Primorsky Oblast moved here from Nikolaevsk-on-Amur to the north.

Tsarevitch Nicholas II turned up in 1891 to inaugurate the new Trans-Siberian rail line. By the early 20th century, Vladivostok teemed with merchants, speculators and sailors of every nation in a manner more akin to Shanghai or Hong Kong than to Moscow. Korean and Chinese, many of whom had built the city, accounted for four out of every five of its citizens

After Port Arthur fell during the Russo-Japanese War of 1904–05, Vladivostok took on an even more crucial strategic role and, when the Bolsheviks seized power in European Russia in 1917, Japanese, Americans, French and English poured ashore here to support the tsarist counterattack. The city held out until 25 October 1922 when Soviet forces finally marched in and took control.

Stalin deported or shot most of the foreign population of the city, and further developed it as a port and ship-building centre. The northern suburb of Vtoraya Rechka became a transit centre for hundreds of thousands of prisoners waiting to be shipped to labour, and most likely perish, in the gold fields of Kolyma.

From 1958 to 1992 the city was entirely closed – during this period foreign Trans-Siberian travellers began or ended their journey in Nakhodka, 220km north-east of Vladivostok. The US consulate was one of the first to reopen in 1992 – 50 years after it had been forced to shut – signifying the continued strategic and trade importance of the city. Japanese and Korean cars are now vigorously traded (and driven!) here, along with all manner of other goods.

Orientation & Information

The train station is the heart of downtown Vladivostok on Aleutskaya ulitsa. Head north for 200m to reach the intersection with Svetlanskaya ulitsa, the city's main waterfront axis.

The majority of Vladivostok's hotels are west of Aleutskaya ulitsa, all within 10 minutes' walk of the station. Running north, Aleutskaya ulitsa feeds into other major roads to become the main highway out of the city, passing through the Sanatornaya region, where there are a few good but pricey hotels, and on to the airport.

Most bookshops stock up-to-date maps of the city. The best bookshop for English titles (there are only a few classic novels though) is Dom Knigi at Aleutskaya ulitsa 19.

There are currency-exchange desks in all the major hotels, at the Marine Terminal (Morskoy vokzal) and the Vostok Business Bank, nearby at Verkhneportovaya 1.

The main post office is on Aleutskaya ulitsa, opposite the train station. Envelopes, stamps, post boxes etc are on the first level (the stairs are on the left immediately as you enter the building), while on the ground level is the international telephone, fax and telegraph office, open 24 hours daily. There's an Internet service here too and plenty more around town: try Millennium Internet on the 2nd floor of the Marine Terminal and the Internet centre at Okeansky prospekt 1.

The *Vladivostok News* (**W** vn.vladnews .ru) is an online newspaper in English, with updates from Tuesday to Friday.

OVIR is at ulitsa Fontannaya 49. If you want to extend your visa here it will cost around $72. For details of consulates see the Facts for the Visitor chapter.

Travel Agencies The following agencies can arrange visas, train tickets, homestays and tours in and around Vladivostok. For details of tours that are offered farther afield see the boxed text 'Far Eastern Adventures' later in this chapter.

Dalintourist (☎ 22 29 49, fax 22 80 55,
  e dalint@mail.primorye.ru) ul Admirala
  Fokina 8
Vizit Co (☎/fax 26 91 72, **e** vizit@online
  .vladivostok.ru, **W** www.tour-vizit
  .vladivostok.ru) Svetlanskaya ul 147
Lucky Tour (☎ 22 33 33, fax 26 78 00,
  e vladivostok@luckytour.com,
  W www.luckytour.com) ul Sukhanova 20

City Centre and Waterfront

Although not quite on the same scale as Moscow's Yaroslavl Station, **Vladivostok Station**, originally built in 1912, is an equally exotic architectural concoction. The ceiling in the main hall is decorated with some bold murals that have benefited, like the rest of the building, from renovation.

Across the road stands an unusually animated Lenin who, curiously, as if he had known all along how things were going to turn out, points in the direction of Japan, whose business Vladivostok now so assiduously courts. Drop into the nearby **Post Office** and go upstairs to see some impressive Soviet-era mosaic murals on the walls.

Aleutskaya ulitsa is lined with once-grand buildings. The house at No 15 (the yellow building next door to the offices of the Far Eastern Shipping Company) was the childhood home of actor Yul Brynner, who was born in Vladivostok in 1920.

The centrepiece of **Ploshchad Bortsov Revolutsy** is the impressive **Monument to the Fighters for Soviet Power in the Far East**. The square, a focal point for performers and protestors of all kinds and Alexander Solzhenitsyn's first stop-off point on his internationally heralded return to Russia in 1994, hosts a big market every Friday. The monolithic slab at the square's western end is the **White House** (Bely dom), home to the regional administration.

Arsenev Regional Museum

The eclectic Arsenev Regional Museum *(Kraevedchesky muzey Arseneva; ☎ 41 11 73, Svetlanskaya ul 20; admission $1.50; open 9.30am-6pm Tues-Sun)*, named after a late 19th-century ethnographer, is worth a browse. The ground floor has the customary array of stuffed wildlife including a rare Amur leopard as well as two Amur (Siberian) tigers – one in a deadly scrap with a bear. The 2nd floor, has ethnographic and historical displays, including a small section on the Brynner family, while on the top floor there's more on the city's recent history and temporary art exhibitions. There's also an interesting antique and bric-a-brac store off the lobby selling old coins, badges, flags and the like.

Vladivostok Fortress Museum & Other Forts

Every day at noon, a giant gun is fired from the Vladivostok Fortress Museum *(Muzey Vladivostokskaya Krepost; ☎ 25 88 96, Batareynaya ul 4A; admission to fortress & museum $1.70; open 10am-6pm daily)*, one of only three places in Russia where this happens (the others are St Petersburg and Kaliningrad). Crowds of Oriental tourists gather for this big bang (ironic, given that these defences were originally intended to keep them out), so if you want to explore the renovated fort and its interesting museum in

peace it's recommended you turn up at a quieter time. You'll find the museum just up the hill from the aquarium.

The museum has models of the other forts around the city and across the nearby islands – most now in ruins but still impressive in their technical construction and locations. Turtsentr Briz (☎ 22 19 92, fax 22 84 43, e breze@mail.ru) runs tours to **Fort No 7**, 14km north of the city centre, including an English-speaking guide and exploration of the underground tunnels. To visit on your own take a bus along prospekt Stoletiya Vladivostok to the Zariya stop and then follow what looks like a dirt road uphill to the right. For information on the forts check w www.dvgu.ru/rus/region/culture/fort.

Submarine Museum

Having sunk 10 enemy ships during WWII, the S-56 submarine now serves as a museum *(Memornalnaya podvodnaya lodka S-56; ☎ 21 67 57, Korabelnaya nab; admission $1.30; open 10am-1pm, 2pm-8pm daily)*, and while the mainly photographic collection isn't too enthralling, clambering around inside is fun.

Opposite floats the *Krasny Vympel*, the Soviet Pacific Fleet's first ship launched in 1923, now also a missable museum.

Other Attractions

The best view of Golden Horn Bay is from the lookout at the top of ulitsa Sukhanova beside the buildings of the DVGTU (Far Eastern State Technical University). If you don't feel like climbing the hill (about 20 minutes from the waterfront), a **funicular railway** *(funikulyor; $0.10; open 7am-8pm daily)* runs from beside the elegantly restored Pushkinsky Theatre on ulitsa Pushkinskaya. Opposite here is the handsome main building of DVGTU.

Primorsky Art Gallery *(Primorskaya kartinnaya galereya; ☎ 41 11 95, Aleutskaya ul 12; admission $1; open 10am-1pm, 2pm-6.30pm Tues-Sat, 11am-5pm Sun)* is something of a surprise, with a large number of 17th-century Dutch paintings and some excellent works by Russian artists, including Repin and Vereshchagin.

The **Border Guards' Museum** *(Muzey boevoy slavy pogran-voysk; ☎ 21 20 74, Semenovskaya ul 17-19; admission $0.60; open 9am-1pm, 2pm-5pm Tues-Sat; closed* *last Fri of month)* is marginally interesting; the best part is using the high-definition binoculars on the top floor to spy on what's happening at the waterfront.

At the western end of Svetlanskaya ulitsa is a small **park** leading to a narrow strip of sandy beach at the edge of the chilly waters of the Amursky Gulf (Amursky zaliv). Not far north of the beach, past the sports stadium, is the **Okeanarium** *(Batareynaya ul 4; admission $1.50; open 10am-8pm Tues-Sun)*, a medium-sized aquarium with some interesting local species, shells, turtles and stuffed birds.

Harbour & Island Boat Tours

To catch ferries to the nearby Russky and Popov Islands, part of the archipelago that stretches south from Vladivostok towards North Korea, go to the coastal ferries station, 100m east along Korabelnaya naberezhnaya from the submarine museum. Many locals have *dachas* on these islands and there are secluded beaches where you can camp.

There are several services daily to Russky ($5.50, 30 minutes), but only one to Popov ($9, 1½ hours). Russky Island, once sole property of the Pacific Fleet, was said to have been stocked with sufficient firepower to blast Vladivostok to kingdom come. There are still parts that are off limits and if you want to explore safely it's best to arrange a trip here with one of the travel agencies mentioned earlier. They all run trips around the harbour, a great way to view the Russian Pacific Fleet, the container vessels and giant icebreakers up close.

Alternatively, try the fishing boats beside the Marine Terminal; if the skippers aren't busy they may be willing to take you for a harbour tour for around $20 an hour.

Places to Stay

One general word of caution about budget-to medium-priced hotels: each winter Vladivostok experiences severe energy shortages, which means that hot water is a rarity, and even cold water disappears on occasion. Keep your bathtub full and check with hotel administrators about saunas around town.

Homestays can be arranged through travel agencies for around $25 with breakfast.

Hotel Moryak (☎ 49 54 35, Posetskaya ul 38) Singles/doubles $8.50/13.50. You'll find basic rooms only at this no-frills budget option. There are some cheaper ones with shared bathrooms available, although foreigners are unlikely to score them.

Hotel Primore (☎ 41 14 22, fax 41 34 05, Posetskaya ul 20) Singles/doubles $30/40. This is the best mid-range deal, close to the train station. The newly renovated rooms are quite comfortable and the staff friendly.

Hotel Vladivostok (☎ 41 28 08, fax 41 20 21, ⓦ www.vladhotel.vl.ru, Naberezhnaya ul 10) Singles/doubles $27/40. The former flagship of the Soviet era, has reasonable enough rooms, with attached bathrooms, and half of them have great views over the Amursky Gulf.

Far Eastern Adventures

If you have time to spare before or after your Trans-Siberian trip, there are plenty of adventurous outdoor trips in the Russian Far East offered by travel agencies in Vladivostok (see Travel Agencies earlier). Among the popular options are:

- **Lake Khanka** – this 4000-sq-metre lake, about 235km north of Vladivostok is an ideal bird-watching spot, home to around 350 different species every summer. Its shallow waters – only around 4m in the deepest parts – are famous for its giant lotus-flower blooms.

- **Sikhote-Alin Nature Reserve** – the main draw of this 344,000-hectare forested reserve, headquartered in the coastal town of Ternei, a 10-hour ride north-east of Vladivostok, is the chance to find out about the Russian-American Siberian Tiger project. Chances of spotting tigers in this wilderness are very slim, but there'll be plenty of birds around Blagodtnoye Lake and seals on the coast.

- **White-water rafting** – day trips are run to the Partizanskaya River, a couple of hours' drive north of the city. This is a generally gentle run; more experienced rafters should look into the longer trips organised along the Kema River farther north with class-3 and the occasional class-4 rapids.

- **Gaivoron** – location of a Russian Academy of Sciences biological research reserve where studies are made of the rare Amur Tiger. Here you'll be able to see a few tigers who are being nursed because of injuries or illness. The institute is near Spassk, 210km north of Vladivostok on the way to Lake Khanka.

A couple of floors of Hotel Vladivostok are leased out to varous operating companies, including the 4th floor where you'll find *Hotel Visit (☎ 41 34 53, fax 41 06 13,* e *vizit@hotbox.ru)* Singles/doubles with breakfast $37/47. Here the refurbished rooms come with a few more comforts than in the main hotel (such as complimentary toiletries and minibars) but are otherwise pretty much the same.

Hotel Amursky Zaliv (☎ 22 55 20, fax 22 14 30, Naberezhnaya ul 9) Singles/doubles from $40/46. This rambling place dug into the cliff side (the top floor is at street level), is often overrun with noisy Chinese tour groups. The cheaper rooms are overpriced but the renovated ones with balconies overlooking the bay are not too bad.

Hotel Versailles (☎ 26 42 01, fax 26 51 24, Svetlanskaya ul 10) Singles/doubles $110/130. The palatial reception here is intimidating enough to send you scurrying if you're not packing a wallet full of credit cards. The rooms are quite sumptuous, and frequently booked out with the upmarket tour groups.

Hotel Hyundai (☎ 40 22 33, fax 40 70 08, w *www.htlhd.ru, Semenovskaya ul 29)* Double or twin rooms with breakfast $200. Offering plush accommodation and services to full international four-star specifications, the Hyundai is Vladivostok's top choice.

And if, after all your experiences crossing Russia, you're in need of a respite, may we suggest the *Vlad Motor Inn (☎ 33 13 51, fax 33 07 17,* w *www.vlad-inn.ru; ul Vosmaya 11, Sanatornaya)* Singles & doubles $157.50. This Canadian-Russian joint venture, 20km north of the centre, is far from convenient for sightseeing, but it is the closest you'll get to Western-style comfort without leaving the country. The rates include free airport transfers.

Places to Eat
Restaurants There's a variety of styles and prices among Vladivostok's dining options.

Nostalgia (☎ 41 05 13, ul Pervaya Morskaya 6/25) Mains $8. Open 8am-11pm daily. Excellent traditional Russian cuisine can be enjoyed at this long-established restaurant and cafe. The small dining room, heavy with crimson carpet, feels like a jewel box and reverberates to live music in the evening.

Gudok (☎ 41 29 98, Aleutskaya ul 2A) Mains around $10. Open noon-1am daily. At the northern end of Vladivostok Station this grandly decorated dining room offers a wide range of dishes including Russian favourites. The atmosphere again is enhanced (or marred, depending on your tastes) by the cabaret-style live music.

Pitstsabar Zhemchuzhina and *Pizza M (both Svetlanskaya ul 51A)* are two modern pizzerias around the corner from each other near the Gorky Theatre. Pizzas at both cost from $4, with those at Zhemchuzhina (meaning Pearl) reckoned to taste better. There's another branch of *Pizza M* attached to the Hotel Primore.

Harbin (☎ 41 34 98, Naberezhnaya ul 3) Mains around $5. Open noon-midnight daily. The Chinese food comes recommended at this attractive restaurant with good service and views over the Amursky Gulf, above the Okean cinema.

Edem (☎ 26 19 90, ul Admirala Fokina 22) Mains from $7. Open 11am-midnight Sun-Thur, 11am-2am Fri & Sat. The sushi and sashimi is pricey but fresh at Vladivostok's top Japanese restaurant. The atmosphere in the cellar-like space is a little on the weird side, with a pool table tucked away at the back and gangsters taking long lunch breaks.

For top-quality meals ($10 to $25-plus for a main course), try elegant *Versal (☎ 26 93 92)* at Hotel Versailles or *Tsarsky (☎ 40 73 24)* at the Hotel Hyundai. The restaurant at the Vlad-Motor Inn in Sanatornaya is also highly recommended – see Places to Stay.

Cafes The relaxed, modern *Studio Coffee (☎ 41 28 82, Svetlanskaya ul 18)* is about as trendy as it gets in Vladivostok and is open 24 hours. It does a good range of drinks, including alcohol, cakes and snack-type meals such as spaghetti with meatballs ($3) and salads for around $1.

Paparatstsi (☎ 22 86 67, ul Admirala Fokina 5) Mains $3. Open 9am-2am daily. The media theme here is translated into pleasing contemporary decor – there are even a few English-language novels to flick through as well as local glossy mags. The food's not bad either.

Kafe Ldinka (Aleutskaya ul 21). Mains $1.50. Open 10am-10pm daily. Bit of a throwback to Soviet times in terms of decor, but still a good cafe to linger over drinks, ice cream or a bowl of *pelmeni*.

Kafe Krishna *(Okeansky prosp 10/12)* Mains $1.50. Open 11am-7pm daily. There's cheap vegetarian food of the lentil variety at this Hare Krishna-run joint with the trademark Indian vibe. Next door, but with the same address, is the modern Russian *Kafe Ekspress (☎ 22 55 77)* where the service is indeed zippy.

Self-Catering Open 24 hours every day, ***Prestizh*** *(Svetlanskaya ul 1)* is a Western-style supermarket with a good bakery. For fresh fruit and vegetables, there are daily *stalls* along ulitsa Posetskaya behind the post office, the daily *market* at Pervaya Rechka (take tram No 7 from in front of the train station, and go north for six stops) and the *waterfront market* every Friday at ploshchad Bortsov Revolutsy.

Entertainment
Gorky Theatre *(Teatr Gorkogo; ☎ 26 48 91, Svetlanskaya ul 49)* is the city's main venue for drama. For classical music try the ***Philharmonic Hall*** *(Filarmoniya; ☎ 26 08 21, Svetlanskaya ul 15)*.

Kino Okean *(☎ 41 42 92, Naberezhnaya ul 3)* This modern multiplex cinema shows dubbed recent US releases. Tickets range from $1 to $3 depending on time of day and seat.

The popular local football team Luch plays at ***Stadium Dinamo*** *(Pogranichnaya ul)* on Wednesday at around 5.30pm, September to May. Tickets are $2 and, if the match is less than thrilling, the view from the stands across the Amursky Gulf is fine compensation. There are also speedway races at *Avantgard stadium (Svetlanskaya ul)* on Monday and Friday evenings.

Clubs & Bars The city's best club, ***BSB*** *(☎ 300 800, Kransogo Znameni prospekt 67)* presents a good mix of contemporary music, and on some Saturdays there are also live rock bands. The crowd here is studenty and relaxed.

Other options (but be prepared for a concentrated assault of Russian high-energy disco) include: ***Nautilus***, at Hotel Amersky Zaliv, a cavernous place packed with teenagers; cosy and louche ***Blue Star*** *(Sinyaya zvezda; Svetlanskaya ul 13)*; and *Crazy (4th*

floor, Morskoi Vokzal), where the only crazy things we could discern were the price of drinks and the quality of dancing.

For a quiet drink try either ***Studio Coffee*** or ***Paparatstsi*** (see Places to Eat), or visit the ritzy ***Sky Bar*** on the 12th floor of the Hotel Hyundai.

Shopping
Nostalgia *(ul Pervaya Morskaya 6/25)* has the best range of traditional handicrafts but it's pricey. There's no shortage of other places hawking the usual range of lacquered boxes, matryoshka dolls, painted trays and jewellery. A wander around ***GUM*** *(Svetlanskaya ul 35)* is recommended, more for the art deco elegance of the building than for the quality of its stock.

For souvenirs of Soviet Russia try the ***Arsenev Regional Museum*** or the ***Flotsky Univermag*** *(Svetlanskaya ul 11)*, an army and navy supplies store selling buttons, badges and other bits of military insignia.

Getting There & Away
Train Vladivostok is the eastern terminus for train No 1/2, the *Rossiya*. At the time of research, the train left on odd-numbered days at around 4.30pm local time, but be sure to check the schedule carefully, as this may change. Kupe tickets to Moscow are $120 and to Irkutsk $83.

Other trains west include the daily No 5 *Okean* overnight to Khabarovsk ($26) and No 7 *Sibir* to Novosibirsk ($111); and the No 53, which departs on odd-numbered days to Kharkiv (Kharkov), in Ukraine, and which has *platskartny* carriages should you wish to save money. The daily No 251 to Sovgavan ($15) is the service you'll need to catch if you're heading north for Port Vanino on the Pacific coast and ships to Sakhalin Island or, westbound, to Tynda and onwards along the BAM.

On Monday and Thursday the No 185 also connects Vladivostok with Harbin in the Heilongjiang province of northern China, from where there are daily connections to Beijing. A one-way sleeper ticket to Harbin costs $35. The train crosses the border at the Chinese town of Suifenhe and also stops at Mudanjiang.

Tickets Tickets for long-distance trains are sold in the office beside the main platform.

The Chief Conductor's Story

For the last 20 years Oleg Andreyevich has spent his working week travelling back and forth across Russia. I ask him whether he ever gets tired of it.

'No. This is the best route in Russia. I've no desire to change to another one', replies the jolly Trans-Siberian veteran.

Oleg is a chief conductor on the *Rossiya*. When I caught up with him, his train had just arrived at Vladivostok 13 hours late and he and his crew of 28 *provodniks* and *provodnitsas* plus one mechanic had just three hours to get ready for the return journey to Moscow.

'We work 13 days straight and then have two weeks off', Oleg tells me. For this the average salary for a conductor is 700 roubles a month – less than $25.

When I ask how working for the railway today compares to Soviet times, Oleg, laughs ruefully and echoes what many other conductors have told me along the journey: the system ain't what it used to be. The long delay on his train is put down to track work, but it's also true that such delays have become much more common since the timetable was changed in June 2001.

What does he like about the job? Surprisingly, he says the independence. His favourite station? Slyudyanka where Lake Baikal laps within metres of the rails. 'There's lots of good fish on sale there.'

Any memorable incidents on the train? 'Every trip has a story! Well, it's always the foreigners who manage to miss the train when they step off at some brief halt to get an ice cream or pirozhki.'

Remembering only too well how the train left without me at Ilanskaya (see the boxed text 'Arrested in Siberia' in the Krasnoyarsk to Irkutsk & Lake Baikal chapter), I decide this is the best point at which to end our interview.

Simon Richmond

Go downstairs from the main entrance, turn left and go back into the building. In the unlikely event there are long queues here you can also buy tickets in the Service Centre (open 9am to noon and 1pm to 5.45pm Monday to Friday), at the southern end of the building, for a commission of $2.75. The major travel agents will also happily buy tickets for you for similar fees.

Air There are flights three times daily to/from Moscow ($300, nine hours), twice daily to Khabarovsk ($60, 1¼ hours), and daily to Irkutsk ($122, four hours) and Yuzhno-Sakhalinsk ($110, 1¾ hours). Flights go three times a week to Petropavlovsk-Kamchatsky ($140, four hours) and once a week to Magadan ($175) and Yakutsk ($127).

Vladivostok Air flies twice a week to Niigata ($270), Osaka ($380) and Toyama ($300) in Japan, Seoul ($220) and Pusan ($220) in South Korea and Harbin ($90) in China. Korean Air has two flights a week to/from Seoul ($280).

Boat Biznes Intur Servis (☎ 49 74 03, ℮ bis @ints.vtc.ru, ⓦ www.bisintour.com), 3rd floor, Moskoy Vokzal, 1 Okeansky pr, handles bookings for the ferries between Vladivostok and the Japanese port of Fushiki from March to October. Only once or twice a season are there also sailings to Niigata in Japan and Pusan in South Korea. For full details see the Getting There & Away chapter.

Getting Around

To/From the Airport There is no cheap direct connection between the airport and the city centre. Instead, take any suburban train from the central station three stops to Vtoraya Rechka (Second River). There's a bus station 150m east of the railway along the main street, ulitsa Russkaya. From there take the infrequent bus No 101, the express airport service ($3, 45 minutes). Count on about two hours for the whole journey. Coming from the airport it's the reverse procedure. From the platform at Vtoraya Rechka you get a first sight of the city to the south, so you know which direction train you should catch. Alternatively, a taxi or car transfer arranged through a travel agency will cost around $35.

Public Transport Trolleybuses and trams are free and within the centre you'll probably only need to use the trams. From in front of the train station, tram Nos 4 and 5 run north then swing east onto Svetlanskaya ulitsa, to the head of the bay; tram No 7 stays on Aleutskaya ulitsa, running north past the market.

For local ferry information see Harbour & Boat Trips earlier in the chapter.

TRANS-MONGOLIAN

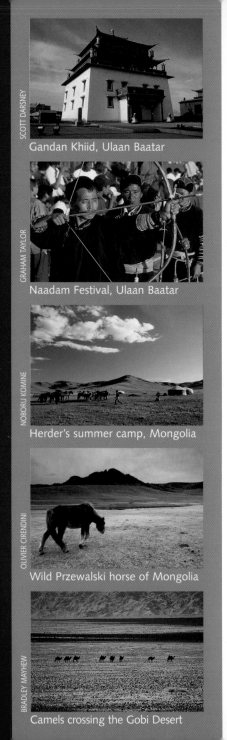

SCOTT DARSNEY

Gandan Khiid, Ulaan Baatar

GRAHAM TAYLOR

Naadam Festival, Ulaan Baatar

NOBORU KOMINE

Herder's summer camp, Mongolia

OLIVIER CIRENDINI

Wild Przewalski horse of Mongolia

BRADLEY MAYHEW

Camels crossing the Gobi Desert

TRANS-MONGOLIAN
Did you know?

- Mongolia is one of the highest countries in the world. The Trans-Mongolian Railway passes by the Khangai Nuruu range, the highest peak of which reaches 3905m. On the northern slope of these mountains is the source of the Selenge Gol, Mongolia's largest river, which flows north into Lake Baikal.

- The southern third of Mongolia is dominated by the Gobi Desert, most of which is desert steppe. Except for a small sliver of true barren desert in the far south, the Gobi has sufficient grass to support scattered herds of grazing animals.

- Despite its small population and a nomadic subsistence economy, increased herding is posing a serious threat to the previously abundant grasslands and hence the unique wildlife of the country.

- More Mongolians live outside of Mongolia than in it – about 3½ million live in China and about a million in Russia.

- The life of a nomad is inextricably linked with the environment and animals. For each of Mongolia's 2.4 million people, there is about one horse, 1½ cows or yaks, four goats and six sheep (plus one camel for every six humans).

- After decades of suppression under the communists, Mongolia is now experiencing a revival of interest in Buddhism with as many as 150 monasteries reopening.

- At its height in the 13th century, the Mongolian empire spread from Korea to Hungary, making it the largest the world has known. During this time – known as the Yuan dynasty – the Mongols ruled from Beijing.

Zaudinsky to Beijing

The Trans-Mongolian follows the well-worn route of the ancient tea caravans that travelled between Beijing and Moscow in the 18th and 19th centuries. In those days, travellers and traders made this 7865km journey in no less than 40 days. Since the Trans-Mongolian railroad began operating in the mid-1950s, the journey now takes about 5½ days.

The Route

The Trans-Mongolian line branches off from the main Trans-Siberian route at Zaudinsky, about 13km east of Ulan Ude. Mongolia and China each have their own kilometre markers. In Mongolia, the markers measure the distance to the Russian-Mongolian border, so 0km is the border town of Naushki. Once into China, the markers measure the distance to Beijing.

Zaudinsky to Naushki
Between Ulan Ude and the Russia-Mongolia border, the train passes through the semi-autonomous ethnic republic of Buryatia. Once a nomadic people practising shamanism and Tibetan Buddhism, the Buryats are close relatives of the Mongols.

At **Zaudinsky** (5655km), the branch line turns south and continues to follow the Selenga River, crossing at around 5701km. The river valley is verdant and lush. The scenery here is characterised by herds grazing and people fishing against a backdrop of green hills and a wide, lazy river. The dilapidated little villages are nonetheless charming for their bright window shutters painted with colourful patterns and their flourishing gardens that explode with fruits and flowers.

After you pass the town of **Zagustay** (5769km), the train follows the shores of Gusinoye Ozero, or Goose Lake. The landscape around the lake is more woodsy, thick with the pine and birch that are prevalent farther north.

The train crosses the Selenga again at 5885km before stopping at **Naushki** (5902/0km), a small, modern town that serves as the Russian border post.

Sükhbaatar to Zamyn-Üüd
Sükhbaatar (21km) is Mongolia's chief border town. Set at the junction of the Selenga and Orkhon Rivers, Sükhbaatar is the capital of the Selenge *aimag* (province). It is a quiet town of 20,000 people that was founded in the 1940s and named after the revolutionary hero Damdin Sükhbaatar (see the boxed text 'Sükhbaatar, Axe Hero' later in this chapter).

Entering Mongolia brings a rapid change of scenery; the forests thin out into the lush green pastures of the fertile Selenge Gol (Selenga River) basin. When you cross the river at 63km you may spot cranes, heron and other waterfowl in the marshy areas on the west side of the train.

With a population of 95,500, **Darkhan** (123km) is Mongolia's second-largest city. This modern, sterile city was built in 1961 to take pressure off of a rapidly expanding Ulaan Baatar. Thanks to a little advance urban planning, the industrial smokestacks are on the southern side of town and the relentless northern winds carry the pollution away from residential areas. Clustered around the train station is the old town, including Kharagiin Khiid, an increasingly active monastery housed in a pretty log cabin. The train stops for about 15 minutes, so you can get out and admire the sheep heads and other local specialities being sold on the platform.

The scenery south of Darkhan is lovely, especially on the western side of the train. As the landscape becomes less verdant, *ger*

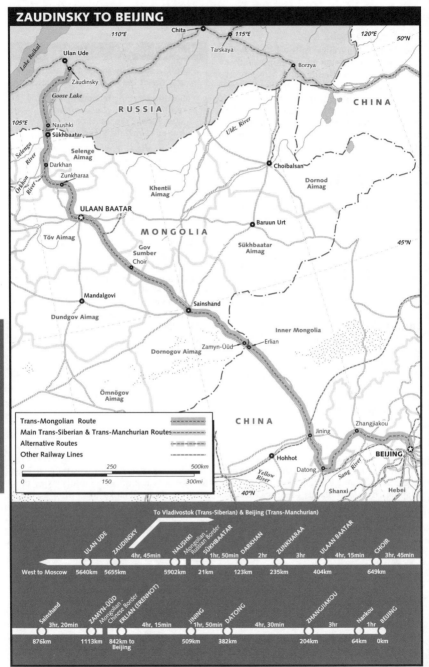

ZAUDINSKY TO BEIJING

Border Crossings

Russia-Mongolia

Crossing the border between Russia and Mongolia is facilitated by the fact that these countries' railway systems both use the Soviet gauge, so no bogie-changing is required. Customs procedures, however, are particularly rigorous here, so the crossing still requires several hours. Officials take their time searching the compartments of the Mongolian and Russian traders.

In **Naushki**, travellers must fill out customs forms in duplicate and Russian border guards collect passports. When you get your passport back you can get off the train. You can change money here if you happen to be crossing the border on weekdays; otherwise, vendors will probably accept dollars. There's a farmers market just outside the train station (walk to the southern end of the platform and cross the street).

The process is repeated by Mongolian officials in **Sükhbaatar**. These officials take their job seriously; they will study each passport diligently and examine the faces of each passenger. ('Smile, please', commanded one stern Mongolian border guard, when I apparently did not appear to be as cheerful as the photo in my passport.)

Mongolia-China

The border crossing is equally tedious no matter which direction you are travelling. Most trains cross this border at night, which pretty much guarantees that you will not get much sleep. In **Zamyn-Üüd**, Mongolian customs officials and border guards do their thing. Customs officials reserve most of their energy for Chinese and Mongolian traders. This process can take up to two hours.

In **Erlian**, Chinese customs and passport officials repeat the process (or start it, if you are travelling west). You must fill out customs forms and departure/arrival cards. The Erlian station is usually quite lively, even at night. Once your passport is returned, catch some fresh air and explore the station. Blinking lights and piped-in music give travellers an appropriate welcome or send-off as they enter/depart China. The duty-free shop, bank and food stalls are usually open. If you do get off, you will not have a chance to get back on the train for about two hours while the train's bogies are changed.

The railway systems of Mongolia and the former Soviet Union operate on a 5-foot gauge, which is slightly wider than the standard gauge used in the rest of the world. Before the train can continue its journey, it must make a stop at the bogie-changing shed, where the carriages are raised and the bogies are replaced with the appropriate size. If you wish to watch the bogie-changing operations, stay on the train until it leaves the platform and gets to the shed. You may be able to watch and take photos of the operation. You can then walk or take a rickshaw back to the station.

dot the wide grassy expanses, giving a glimpse of the grasslands to come farther south. Birch and pine trees cluster on the hills in the distance. You spend 10 minutes in **Züünkharaa** (231km), where trains loaded with tree trunks and processed wood stop en route from Siberia and northern Mongolia.

North of Ulaan Baatar, the rolling hills are covered with wildflowers and grazing animals, making for exquisite scenery. Around 384km, you will be able to catch views of Ulaan Baatar as the train descends into the valley.

The train stops in **Ulaan Baatar** (404km), the sprawling Mongolian capital, for 30 minutes. A collection of steam engines is about 1km east of the station, where the tracks cross under the highway.

South of Ulaan Baatar, the line winds through gently swelling hills of the **Bogdkhan Uul** mountain range. You'll notice that the trees eventually disappear. The landscape becomes a 180-degree panorama of uninterrupted steppe: green-brown earth, blue sky and little else. The only features to interrupt the landscape are wandering camels, grazing horses and occasional gers.

The train stops for 15 minutes at **Choir** (649km), a town of 13,300 on the edge of the Gobi Desert. A statue of the first Mongolian cosmonaut stands majestically in front of the train station. Prior to 1992, this grim town was home to the biggest Soviet military air base in Mongolia. Since the Russians left, many of the buildings sit empty and vandalised, lending the site the

Dealing with Bureaucracy: Mongolia-style

We board the Trans-Mongolian in Irkutsk, direction Beijing. Our compartment is near inaccessible, packed to the brim with strange merchandise: felt hats, leather jackets, jars of pickles, cartons of cigarettes, bottles of vodka, boxes of chocolates. It feels like we are in a warehouse. All these disparate goods belong to our new travel companions, a Mongolian merchant couple, who clearly know the meaning of the word 'business'. After proudly showing us their passports covered in Russian and Chinese stamps, they concede to make us a little space in the compartment.

Throughout the entire journey, the woman does not stop climbing onto her bunk, moving around the cartons, pulling them out, emptying them, transferring the contents from one package to another. As we approach the border, the agitated bustle intensifies throughout the carriage. Other 'business' passengers are hurriedly exchanging boxes of goods and the corridor is transformed by frenetic activity – quite surreal!

At 7pm the train stops at the border post. For some minutes now the compartment has been remarkably calm, and the Mongolians sit quietly as though nothing has gone on at all. Everyone is preparing psychologically for the crossing of the border.

Indeed, immense patience will be necessary; we will spend seven hours inside the compartment, the train stationary. The border crossing can give rise to all kinds of difficulties, but our travelling companions seem experienced in preventing any possible hitch. The young woman explains to us in broken English that they must present themselves to customs, due to all the merchandise they have purchased.

We sit, dumbfounded, as she prepares herself. Having reapplied her lipstick, she adjusts the plunging neckline of her dress. She slips on under her skirt a pair of knickerbockers, into which she slides a carton of cigarettes. Her actions are precise, meticulous; she has clearly done this before. Next, a box of Mon Cheri (this brand must have exotic connotations in Mongolia) astutely placed against her right hip, quickly joined by a flask of vodka. Then comes the final touch: a roll of banknotes tucked swiftly into her bra.

Her husband encourages her throughout these shrewd preparations, assuring us that 'she knows what she's doing'. He also confers upon us two cartons of cigarettes, which we store in our own baggage (and which he will reclaim later!). The woman then sprinkles a fine trail of sand in the doorway – may the gods be merciful – and disappears.

She returns half an hour later; from the huge smile on her face, we see that the transaction has been a great success. Welcome to Mongolia!

Caroline Guilleminot, Moscow to Beijing, May 1995

air of a ghost town. In order to promote economic growth, Choir formed an autonomous municipality called Gov-Sümber and declared itself a Free Trade Zone, but so far that declaration has had little effect.

The train continues south and enters the Dornogov aimag. This is classic Gobi country: flat, arid and sparsely populated. In a good year, the aimag sprouts short grass, which sustains a limited number of sheep, goats and camels for their ethnic Khalkh owners. In a bad year, the wells go dry, the grass turns brown and the animals die. Unless there is a sudden demand for sand, Dornogov's economic future will continue to be based on the railway to China. From the train, the view of this desolate landscape is impressive. Any small bodies of water (such as at 729km on the western side of the tracks) attract wildlife, and you will probably spot herds of horses, sheep and goats.

The capital of Dornogov is **Sainshand** (876km), which ironically means 'Good Pond'. The city, where the train stops for about 15 minutes, was established in 1931. Interesting sights nearby include natural and volcanic rock formations and – go figure – sand dunes.

The bleak, moon-like landscape continues to the Chinese border. The Mongolian border town is **Zamyn-Üüd** (1113km), where you will commence border procedures.

Erlian to Beijing

From the Chinese border post of **Erlian** (842km), the train takes about 13 hours to get to Beijing. For the first several hours, it continues through the Gobi, now in the Chinese province of Inner Mongolia. This so-called autonomous region, however, enjoys little or no autonomy. Mongolians make up only about 15% of the total population of this region. Since 1949 the Chinese have done their best to assimilate the Mongolians, even though they have been permitted to keep their written and spoken language. Physically, Inner Mongolia looks very much like Outer Mongolia (as the Chinese refer to the independent nation of Mongolia): flat, dusty and dry. In China, this region of grassy steppe is called the 'Grasslands'.

The Trans-Mongolian line continues south through green hills and valleys, potentially with brief stops at **Jining** (498km) and **Fengzhan** (415km). You'll get your first glimpse of the Great Wall as the line passes through it at about 385km. This is now Shanxi province, one of the earliest centres of Chinese civilisation. After Qin Shihuang unified the Chinese states in 221 BC, the northern part of Shanxi became the key defensive bulwark against nomadic tribes from the north. Despite the Great Wall, they still managed to break through and use Shanxi as a base for their conquest of the Middle Kingdom.

The ancient capital of this region was the city of **Datong** (371km), which today is a crowded, polluted and industrial metropolis of 2.7 million people. The train halts here for 10 minutes. Datong's main attraction is the nearby Yungang Buddhist Caves, which are cut into the southern cliffs of Wuzhou Mountain, 16km west of the city. Inside the caves are 50,000 statues, which were carved between AD 460 and 494. The local Datong Locomotive Factory produced steam engines for the main train lines until 1989. A museum that is maintained by the factory houses several steam locomotives. After wandering through the factory, visitors can enjoy a ride in the cabin of one of the locomotives.

From Datong, the train line turns east, and the brown earth gradually grows greener. Around 300km the train enters Hebei province, primarily a coal-mining region. Topographically, Hebei is characterised by its mountainous tableland where the Great Wall runs. There are good views of the Wall

A traditional Mongolian *ger.*

on the eastern side of the tracks between 295km and 275km.

The train stops for about 15 minutes in **Zhangjiakou** (193km). Formerly known as Khaalga, which means 'door' or 'gate' in Mongolian, this town used to be the place where the ancient tea caravans crossed the Great Wall. Now it is a large industrial city.

From here the terrain becomes increasingly mountainous and the scenery is quite dramatic. At 99km the train crosses the San Gan River. At 95km, the mountains provide a spectacular backdrop to the vibrant blue waterway. Now agricultural production is much more prevalent. Farms and orchards surrounded by mountains make for a visually stimulating ride.

Because of the steep mountain ascent, the train requires a banking engine; the train stops briefly at **Kanzuang** (82km) to attach/detach it (depending on which direction you are travelling). Between 80km and 50km, the train goes through a series of thrilling tunnels cutting through the mountains. Keep your eyes open, because each time the train emerges into the daylight, another fabulous view of the Great Wall and the surrounding mountains is revealed. The first is at **Badaling** (73km), immediately after the long 2km tunnel. The train then makes another, longer stop at **Qinglongqiao** (70km), where you can get out and take photos from the platform.

The final stop is at **Nankou** (53km), where the rear engine is attached/detached. About an hour later, the train pulls into **Beijing**.

ULAAN BAATAR
УЛААИ БААТАР
☎ 976-11 • pop 800,000
Despite the predominance of Soviet architecture, Ulaan Baatar – known to expats (but certainly not locals!) as UB – maintains

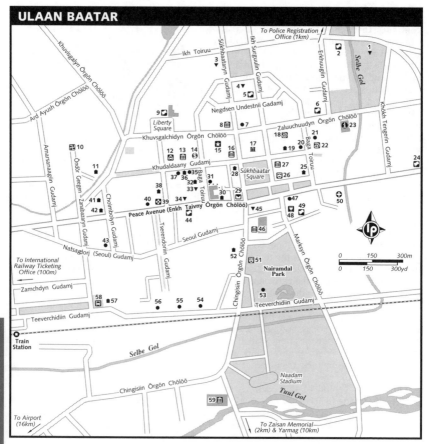

ULAAN BAATAR

the easy-going atmosphere of a provincial capital. It is not unusual to see women wearing traditional dress or men on horseback around the generally serene Sükhbaatar Square. Modernisation is kicking in, however. New Japanese models are replacing the old Soviet cars and young Mongolians are frequently seen jabbering away on their mobile phones.

Built along the Tuul Gol and in the valleys of the Four Holy Peaks, Ulaan Baatar is literally surrounded by some wonderful opportunities for outdoor enthusiasts. Hiking, biking and horse riding are all possible within an hour of the capital. It is also a pleasant place to visit and to base oneself for trips into the surrounding valleys, steppe or desert.

History

The first recorded capital city of the Mongolian empire, Örgöö, was established in 1639 at the Da Khüree monastery, about 420km from Ulaan Baatar. The monastery was the residence of the five-year-old Zanabazar, who had been proclaimed the head of Buddhism in Mongolia. In keeping with the nomadic lifestyle, the capital was moved frequently to various locations along the Orkhon (with a name change accompanying each move).

The capital was finally established in its present location in 1778. The town grew quickly as a religious, commercial and administrative centre. Its architecture, however, remained predominantly ger, and thus the capital earned the name 'City of Felt'.

ULAAN BAATAR

PLACES TO STAY
11 Gana's
    Ганаагийн Дэн Буудал
19 Tuushin Hotel
    Туушин Зочид Буудал
25 Ulaan Baatar Hotel; UB Tour
    Улаан Баатар Зочид Буудал;
    УБ Тур
28 Hotel Urge
    Өргөө Зочид Буудал
30 Nassan's
    Насангийн Дэн Буудал
32 UB Guesthouse
    Улаанбаатар Дэн Буудал
36 Center Hotel; Millie's Café
    Центр Зочид Буудал: Миллис
    Кафе
38 Bold's
    Болдын Дэн Буудал
41 Genex Hotel
    Женекс Зочид Буудал
42 Kharaa Hotel
    Хараа Зочид Буудал
52 Bayangol Hotel; Juulchin
    Баянгол Зочид Буудал
57 Idre's
    Идрээгийн Зэн Буудал

PLACES TO EAT
1   Abtai Sain Khaani Örgöö
    Абтай Сайн Хааны Өргөө
3   Chinggis Beer Co
    Чингис Пиво Ко
4   Chinggis Restaurant
    Чингис Ресторан
33 Amtat Bulag
    Амтат Булег
34 Chez Bernard
    Шей Бернард
45 City Coffee; Khanbrau Biergarten
    Сити Кофе: Хаан Брой

OTHER
2   US Embassy
    Элчин Ям Америкийн Нэгдсэн
5   German Embassy
    Элчин Ям Герман

6   Chinese Embassy
    Элчин Ям Хятад
7   Egshiglen National Musical
    Instrument Shop
    Эгшиглэн Үндэсний Газар
8   Museum of Natural History
    Байгалын Түүхийн Музей
9   Diplomatic Services Corps;
    Canadian Consulate; French
    Embassy
    Дипломат үйлчилгээний газар
10 Gandantegchinlen Khiid
    Гандантэгчинлэн Хийд
12 Taxi Stand
13 Zanabazar Museum of Fine Arts
    Занабазар Уран Зэргийн Музей
14 Trade & Development Bank
    Худалдаа Хөгжлийн Банк
15 Police Headquarters
    Цагдаагийн Газар
16 National Museum of
    Mongolian History
    Үндэсний Түүхийн Музей
17 Government House
    Засгийн Газрын Ордон
18 Internet@Copy Centre
    Каннон Интернэт Төв
20 Santis Language School
    Галаад Хэл Сургалтын Сантис
    Сургууль
21 Khan's Ger
    Хааны Гэр
22 Internet House Café
    Интернэт Хаус Кафе
23 Cultural Information Resource
    Centre
    Соёл Мэдээллийн Төв
24 UK Embassy
    Элчин Ям Их Британи
26 State Opera & Ballet Theatre
    Дуурь Бужгийн Академик
    Театр
27 Palace of Culture; Mongolian
    National Modern Art Gallery
    Соёлын Төв Ордон; Үндэсний
    Уран Зургийн Галлерей

29 Post Office
    Төв Шуудан
31 MIAT Airlines VBFN
    МИАТ Монголын Иргэний
    Агаарын Тээвэр
35 Federation for the Preservation
    of Mahayana Tradition
    Махаян уламжпалыг
    Хамгаалах Холбоо
37 Scrolls Bookshop
39 State Department Store
    Их Дэлгүүр
40 Nomadic Expeditions
    Номадик Экспедишн Компани
43 Aeroflot Office
44 Russian Embassy
    Оросын Элчин Ям
46 Monastery-Museum of Choijin
    Lama
    Чойжин Ламын Хийд-Музей
47 Ministry of External Relations
    Гадаад Арилшааны Ям
48 River Sounds
    Ривер Саундс Клуб
49 Japanese Embassy
50 Yonsei Friendship Hospital
    Енсэй Эмнэлэг
51 Tumen Ekh Ensemble Palace
    Түмэн Эх Чуула
53 National Recreation Center;
    Blue Sky Travel
    Үндэсний Соел Амралтын
    Хүрээлэн: Блю скай травэл
54 Karakorum Expeditions
    Хархорин Экспедишн
55 Circus
    Улсын Цирк
56 Merkuri Market & Dalai Market
    Меркури Худалдааны: Дэлай
    Ээж Хунсний Зах
58 Bus Station
    Автобусны Буудал
59 Winter Palace of Bogd Khaan &
    Museum
    Богд Хааны Өвлийн Ордон:
    Богдын Музей

ZAUDINSKY TO BEIJING

Further name changes accompanied various invasions by the Russians and the Chinese. Finally, in 1924 the city was renamed Ulaan Baatar (Red Hero) and declared the official capital of an independent Mongolia.

Orientation
The train station is in the south-western corner of the city about 1km from the centre. Most of the city spreads from east to west along the main road, Enkh Taivny Örgön Chölöö, also known as Peace Ave. The centre is Sükhbaatar Square.

Information
Tourist Offices Ulaan Baatar lacks a central tourist information office, but does have a Cultural Information Resource Centre (CIRC; ☎ 316 022, fax 315 358, Ⓦ www .mongolart.mn) in the Youth Palace, Zaluuchuudyn Örgön Chölöö. Several English-language publications such as *UB Guide* and *Welcome to Mongolia* are available at hotels and cafes around town.

Money Cash advances in US dollars are available at the Trade & Development Bank

(☎ 327 020), on the corner of Khudaldaany Gudamj and Baga Toiruu. TDB will also cash US travellers cheques for US dollars or for tögrög. There are no ATMs in Ulaan Baatar.

Post & Communications The Central Post Office is on the south-western corner of Sükhbaatar Square and it is open 24 hours. Ulaan Baatar has Internet cafes on almost every corner. Larger cafes with good connections include:

Internet@Copy Centre (☎ 323 236,
  🅴 blueskytrav@yahoo.com) Khuvsgalchidyn Örgön Chölöö
Internet House Café (☎ 9911 5986,
  🅴 byambaa@mongol.net) Youth Federation Building, Baga Toiruu

Travel Agencies Ulaan Baatar has no shortage of local tour operators and youth hostels which can help organise excursions or obtain train tickets.

Blue Sky Travel (☎/fax 312 067,
  🅴 blueskytrav@mgicnet.mn) National Recreation Centre, Nairamdal Park
Juulchin (☎ 328 428, fax 320 246,
  🅆 www.mol.mn/juulchin) Bayangol Hotel, 5B Chingisiin Örgön Chölöö
Karakorum Expeditions (☎/fax 315 655,
  🅆 www.gomongolia.com) Jiguur Grand Hotel, 5 Teeverchidiin Gudamj
Nomadic Expeditions (☎ 313 396,
  🅴 mongolia@nomadicexpeditions.com) 76 Peace Ave, west of State Department Store

UB Tour (☎ 324 740, fax 324 730,
  🅴 ubtour@mongol.net) Ulaan Baatar Hotel, 4th floor, 14 Sükhbaatar Square

Bookshops To stock up on reading material, head to Scrolls bookshop (☎ 9915 0656) on Khudaldaany Gudamj. The business centre on the 4th floor of the Ulaan Baatar Hotel also has used books and some not-too-current affairs magazines.

Medical Services The Yonsei Friendship Hospital (☎ 310 945), built by the South Koreans, provides the best medical service. If your situation is not an emergency, consider seeking medical help in Beijing, where the range and quality of service available is much better.

Around Sükhbaatar Square
The geographic and cultural centre of Ulaan Baatar is **Sükhbaatar Square**, named after the Mongolian revolutionary hero and first leader of independent Mongolia, Damdin Sükhbaatar. His words are engraved at the base of the statue in the centre of the square: 'If we, the whole people, unite in our common effort and will, there will be nothing in the world that we cannot achieve...' His remains are kept in the **mausoleum** at the northern end.

The massive building behind the mausoleum is **Government House**. To the northeast is the **Palace of Culture**, the **Mongolian**

Sükhbaatar, Axe Hero

Despite an impoverished background, Damdin Sükh (meaning 'axe') learned to read and write and excelled at horsemanship as a child. In 1911 he was conscripted to the army, where he developed nationalist convictions and gathered a loyal following of like-minded soldiers. His courageous performance combating the Chinese, earned him the moniker *baatar*, or hero.

When his unit was disbanded by the Chinese in 1919, Sükhbaatar used his network to form a nationalist army. He eventually joined forces with the revolutionary Khorloogiyn Choibalsan, who had close contact with the communist movement in Russia. With the assistance of the Soviet Red Army, they succeeded in defeating both the Chinese and the White Russians. On 11 July 1921, Sükhbaatar declared the People's Government of Mongolia.

Sükhbaatar was known as the 'people's warrior', a hero who rose from the most oppressed and remained their champion to his end. He is also considered to be a true Mongol, as exemplified by the 1922 Naadam festival, which celebrated the first anniversary of the revolution. According to one account, the skilled horseman and new governor delighted the crowds when, riding down the field at full gallop, he leaned from his saddle to pick up silver coins from the ground.

The following year – at the age of 30 – Sükhbaatar died of undetermined causes. Still visible astride his horse at the centre of Ulaan Baatar, he lives on in Mongolian history as an unrivalled national hero.

NOBORU KOMINE

A herder family outside its *ger*.

Gandantegchinlen (Gandan) Khiid, Ulaan Baatar, was built in 1838.

NOBORU KOMINE

BRADLEY MAYHEW

Youthful jockey at Naadam, UB.

OLIVIER CIRENDINI

Gandan Khiid monastery survived the communist period.

FELICITY VOLK

Mongolian horsemen parade at the opening of the Naadam festival.

BRADLEY MAYHEW

Mongolian tuba player.

Dragons and mythical beasts top the Forbidden City, Beijing.

Imperial lion, Forbidden City.

Card players near Beihai Park.

Boat on the northern shore of Kunming Lake, Beijing.

Kite-flying is an activity for the whole family in Tiananmen Square.

Entrance hall, Forbidden City.

A typical street scene in the capital during the late-19th century. Ulaan Baatar received its present name in 1924 as the capital of the newly declared Mongolian People's Republic.

National Modern Art Gallery and several other cultural institutions.

On the north-western corner of the square is the **National Museum of Mongolian History** (☎ *325 656, fax 326 802, Cnr Khudaldaany Gudamj & Sükhbaataryn Gudamj; admission T2000; open 10am-4.30pm Thur-Mon & 10am-2.30pm Tues)*. The museum contains exhibits on ancient burial sites, ethnic folk art and culture, Buddhist ceremonial objects and the Mongol horde. Exhibits have captions in English.

One block north, animals and stuffed birds abound at the **Museum of Natural History** *(State Central Museum; ☎ 321 716, ☎ 318 179, Cnr Khuvsgalchdyn Örgön Chölöö & Sükhbaataryn Gudamj; admission T3000; open 10am-4.30pm daily in summer, Wed-Sun in winter)*. This is the best look you will get at dinosaur fossils and skeletons, for which the Gobi is famous. The museum houses two impressive complete skeletons of a *Tarbosaurus* and a *Saurolophus*, as well as petrified dinosaur eggs and fossils. The *Guide to the Natural History Museum* in English is free.

Other Museums

Mongolia's eighth living Buddha and last king, Jebtzun Damba Hutagt VIII, lived for 20 years in the **Winter Palace of Bogd Khaan** *(☎ 342 195, Chinggisiin Örgön Chölöö; admission T2000; open 10am-5pm daily in summer, closed Wed-Thur in winter)*. The grounds house six temples; the white building on the right is the Palace itself. It contains an odd collection of gifts received from foreign dignitaries and an extraordinary array of stuffed animals. Take bus No 7 or 19.

Other worthwhile museums include the **Zanabazar Museum of Fine Arts**, across from the Center Hotel, and the **Monastery-Museum of Choijin Lama**, which is south of Sükhbaatar Square.

Gandantegchinlen Khiid
Гандантэгчинлэн Хийд

The largest and most important monastery in Mongolia is Gandantegchinlen Khiid *(Gandan Khiid; Öndör Geegen Zanabazaryn Gudamj; admission free, open 9am-9pm daily)*. The name translates roughly as 'the great place of complete joy'. Built in the mid-19th century, the place miraculously survived the communist purges of the 1930s (although the huge gold and bronze statue of Avalokitesvara did not; it was sent to Leningrad and melted down for bullets). Today there are over 150 monks in residence here.

The Naadam Festival Наадам

Naadam, meaning 'festival' or 'holiday', is Mongolia's main traditional cultural and sporting extravaganza. The largest and most exciting celebration is held every year in Ulaan Baatar on 11–13 July. The communists renamed it People's Revolution Day and fixed the dates to the anniversary of the Mongolian Revolution in 1921. The traditions, however, date back hundreds of years to the days when tribes would assemble to celebrate hunting or warring victories. Other smaller versions of the Naadam festivities are held in villages around the country on different dates throughout the summer.

Competitions of the three 'manliest' sports – wrestling, archery and horse racing – are held on the first and second days. In the evening, traditional artists and local rock groups perform free concerts at Sükhbaatar Square. Few events take place on the third day, which is more of a recovery day for celebrants nursing hangovers. All three days are official holidays and most shops and offices are closed.

Day one starts around 9am with a colourful ceremony at Sükhbaatar Square. Uniformed soldiers, military bands and traditionally dressed warriors parade around the square and then to the Naadam Stadium. Later in the morning at the stadium, the official opening ceremony ($12) includes more music and more pageantry featuring the athletes. These ceremonies are probably the highlight of the Naadam festival for foreign spectators (except for the big wrestling fans). Athletic competitions take place throughout both days, so it is possible to get a taste of each of the three 'manly' sports. The closing ceremony ($8) is held in the evening of the second day after the wrestling tournament is completed.

Tickets for the various events are normally available at the stadium. Travel agencies and guesthouses also help their guests obtain tickets. The schedule and prices vary from year to year, so you may wish to check details in one of the English-language publications or with a travel agency.

Naadam's Legendary Roots

Ancient oral histories, such as *Mongolian Heroic Stories*, include a legend from a primitive time in Mongolia. The story describes the struggles of a hero against a hideous monster with fifteen heads. He fights against the monster to save his motherland and to free his bride. Although it's a fight to the death, it is more like a contest, or struggle for supremacy, between hero and monster in the form of the three manly games. The hero ultimately defeats the monster in wrestling, horseracing and distance shooting. This story can offer us an impression that the earliest games perhaps started from personal arguments and disputes between people in early times. Later, they possibly evolved into pure entertainment…

There was a celebration of such games when the first states formed in the territory of Mongolia around the year 2 or 3 BC. The state of Hunnu at that time celebrated with games before starting or after winning wars. They also enjoyed the games when they elevated kings or sacrificed offerings to the sky. Hunnus also respected their foreign missions, welcoming and honouring them with holiday games. They hung balls of animal skin from a stick, placing them in a line at a distance. They would then shoot at them with precision, challenging other marksmen. The other traditional way to compete in archery was to hang many sheepskins from a stick and shoot four or five arrows [at them] while riding a swift horse. It was not only a military art but also a test of luck.

Later, during the time of the Great Empire under Chinggis Khaan in the 13th century, the games were elevated to a state of great entertainment and celebration. Once while young Timujin (Chinggis Khaan) was returning home from a war, he encountered a tribal ruler who wanted to test his military training. The tribal ruler especially wanted to observe his archery skills. 'Temujin, you look like a sky gifted son, but I do not know your military training. I will stick this flag in a 100-bow place (about 1500 metres). If you can shoot it, I will follow you.' Then Chuu, a sharp archer and warrior of Chinggis Khaan, shot it with a solitary arrow; and the tribe followed Chinggis.

N Enkhbayar, *Ger Magazine*, January 2000

Wrestling

The first round of wrestling starts at the stadium after the opening ceremony (around noon). The initial rounds on day one and the final rounds on day two are the most exciting matches. Ticket

SJ

prices range from $3 for a seat in the sun at the far end of the stadium to $8 for a shady spot with a closer view. Tickets are available at the stadium throughout both days.

Mongolian wrestling has no time limits; a match ends only when a wrestler falls (or any body part other than feet or hands touches the ground). It also has no weight divisions, so the biggest wrestlers (and they are big!) are often the best.

The highlight of the match is the 'eagle dance', which is performed beforehand by contestants to pay respect to the judges, and again afterwards by the winner. The loser must walk under the right arm of the winner, symbolising peace between the wrestlers. Another special feature of wrestling is the uniform, complete with heavy boots, tiny tight briefs and open midriff-baring vests.

Archery

Archery is held in an open stadium next to the main stadium. No tickets are required to view the competition. The sport of archery originated in the 11th century and modern day competitors still don traditional garb to compete. Archers use a bent composite bow made of layered horn, bark and wood. Arrows are usually made from willow branches and vulture feathers.

The target is a line of up to 20 or 30 colourful rings on the ground. Male contestants stand 75m from the target while female contestants stand 60m from it. After each shot, the judges emit a shout and raise their arms to indicate the quality of the shot. The winner who hits the targets the most times is declared the best archer, or *mergen*.

Horse Racing

Horse racing is held in the village of Yarmag, about 10km from Ulaan Baatar along the main road to the airport. Take a bus (T200) heading to Buyant-Ukhaa from Chingisiin Örgön Chölöö (the road to the Naadam Stadium) or catch a taxi (T4000). The races do not require tickets.

Horse racing has six categories, based the age of the horse and distance of the race. Jockeys – boys and girls between five and 13 – are decked out in colourful, traditional outfits. Before the race, they parade their horses in front of the judges to show respect, and the audience often sings traditional songs.

The races take place not on a track, but on the open steppe. From the finish line, spectators wait breathlessly as contestants speed across the hillside in a cloud of dust. The winning horses and riders are then the subject of laudatory poems and songs performed by the crowds. The five winning riders must drink some special *airag*, which is then sprinkled on the riders' heads and horses' backs.

The courtyard on the right contains two temples, the **Ochirdary Süm** and the smaller **Golden Dedenpovaran Süm**. If you come in the morning you can witness the fascinating ceremonies that take place here. The main path leads to the **Migjid Janraisig Süm** containing a 25m, 20-tonne statue that was built in the early 1990s to replace the original.

Cycling

Poor roads and heavy traffic can make conditions for cycling dangerous in the city, but it is a great way to explore the nearby countryside. A pleasant, easily accessible ride is along the Tuul Gol, south of the city. Head south past the Naadam Stadium and turn left to follow the river. Mountain bikes are available for hire at Karakorum Expeditions (see Travel Agencies earlier in this chapter), where you can also get more suggestions for cycling routes.

Places to Stay

Touts often linger at the station when international trains arrive to offer rooms in guesthouses and private homes. They may offer some good options, but be sure to check the location before you commit.

Budget Private, budget guesthouses are popping up around Ulaan Baatar like marmots in the Gobi. Many are in apartment buildings and can be difficult to find; however, most will send someone to meet your train if you call or email ahead.

Nassan's (☎ 9919 7466, e *nassan2037@yahoo.com, Baga Toiruu*) Dorm beds $3-5. Nassan has perhaps the most convenient location of the cheaper places, just a block away from Sükhbaatar Square.

UB Guesthouse (☎ 311 037, ☎ 9119 9859, w *www.ubguest.com, Baga Toiruu 10*) Dorm beds with breakfast $4. This well-run Korean place moved to a new location just across the street from Nassan's. The building looks sketchy, but the location is convenient.

Bold's (☎ 9919 6232, e *bold777@hotmail.com, Behind State Department Store, bldg 1, entrance 1, 2nd floor, apt 8*) Dorm beds $4. The place is a bit cramped, but Bold will buy train tickets for no commission.

Gana's (☎/fax 367 343, e *ganasger@magicnet.mn, Near Gandan Khiid, house no 22*) Beds in 6-bed ger/20-bed dorm $5/3. Gana's is one of the most popular spots for backpackers, probably because it fits so many people into its ramshackle house in the ger suburb. The facilities are more basic than most.

Idre's (☎ 316 749, ☎ 9916 6049, e *idre9@hotmail.com, South-east of bus station, bldg 23, entrance 2, apt 44*) Dorm beds/double $4/15. Idre invites you to roll out a mattress on the floor; that is unless you are lucky enough to score the one private double room available.

Mid-Range Places in the middle range are not particularly good value, but they normally include breakfast.

PO-ed (In More Ways Than One)

My father is fond of saying 'It's better to get pissed off than pissed on'. My wife Maggie had the rare opportunity for a double-header – both in one night – on a night train heading north out of Ulaan Baatar. We were sharing our four-person soft-sleeper compartment with a young Mongolian couple and their two-year-old daughter. As the sun set, they put their daughter to sleep and without a word to us, promptly left the compartment. We didn't think much about it until we were awakened by the couple returning rip-roaring drunk around 1am. Not only were they loud enough to wake (and keep) us up, they also managed to awaken their daughter. (The little I know about kids this age is that they can sleep through practically anything…drunk parents apparently excepted!) Finally around 2am, all three passed out and we fell back to sleep to the rhythmic clackety-clack of the train.

About an hour later, I was awakened once again, this time by Maggie shouting 'He's $£@!& pissing on me!' Sure enough, I looked to my left and the guy was urinating off his top bunk straight down onto Maggie's bed. When his wife finally came out of her stupor, she pulled him down to sleep on the pee-soaked lower bunk while Maggie switched to his upper. How many times do you get pissed on and pissed off in one night?

Jerry Gross, Beijing to Ulaan Baatar to Erdenet, July 2001

Center Hotel (☎ 328 731, fax 318 427, [e] centerhotel@mongol.net, 18 Khudaldaany Gudamj) Singles/doubles/deluxe $40/50/60-80. By far the best value in this range, the Center Hotel has comfortable rooms, a convenient location and easy access to Millie's cafe on its second floor.

Hotel Urge (Hotel Örgöö; ☎ 313 772, fax 312 712, 4 Khudaldamy Gudamj) Singles/doubles/suites $25/40/60. Down the street, this hotel (pronounced Ur-guh) is convenient and has an eager staff, both of which almost make up for the dilapidated and charmless environs.

Kharaa Hotel (☎ 313 733, 6 Choimbolyn Gudamj, north of Peace Ave) Doubles $25-45. The place has a deserted, almost-eerie atmosphere. Rooms are clean but small.

Genex Hotel (☎ 326 763, ☎/fax 323 827, [w] www.generalimpex.mn, 10 Choimbolyn St) Singles/doubles $48/80, without bath $35/50. Near the Kharaa, this hotel has a more modern, comfortable feel.

Top End These hotels provide the quality and services you would expect, but they usually tack on 20% in charges to the final bill. Prices include breakfast.

Bayangol Hotel (☎ 312 255, fax 326 880, [e] bayangol@magicnet.mn, 28 Chingisiin Örgön Chölöö) Singles/doubles from $70/90. This hotel, popular with Western tourists, offers a good position and a wide range of services.

Tuushin Hotel (☎ 323 162, fax 325 903, [e] tuushot@magicnet.mn, 2 Amaryn Gudamj) Singles/doubles from $66/88. Again, central and bright, spacious rooms make this one of UB's better hotels. A few cheaper singles with shared bathrooms are also available.

Ulaan Baatar Hotel (☎ 320 237, fax 324 485, [e] ubhotel@magicnet.mn, 14 Sükhbaatar Square) Singles/doubles from $70/104. The UB Hotel is the old Party hotel from the communist days of the city. Facilities are decent and you definitely can't beat the location.

Places to Eat

The days of food shortages in Mongolia are long gone, although you still would not confuse Mongolian food with *haute cuisine*. Nonetheless, the restaurants around UB offer a decent variety.

Restaurants & Cafes Chinese food and coffee are certainly an odd combination, but *City Coffee (☎ 328 077, Chinginssin Örgön Chölöö)* excels at both. Coffee costs from T1500, and meals from T3000 and it's open 9am-midnight daily.

Chez Bernard (☎ 324 622, Peace Ave) Mains T3000. Bernard's speciality is definitely French pastries, but the sandwiches and breakfasts are also good here.

Khanbrau Biergarten (☎ 324 064, Chingisiin Örgön Chölöö) Mains T3000. Open 11am-midnight daily. As the name implies, Khanbrau's main attractions are its pilsners and its open-air seating, but the food is not bad either. Try the Mongolian grill stick (T3600).

Chinggis Beer Co (☎ 325 820, 10 Sükhbaatar Gudamj) Mains T3000. Open 11am-midnight daily. This German-run microbrewery also serves Asian and international food.

Millie's (☎ 328 264, Center Hotel, Khudaldaany Gudamj) Mains T4000-6000. Open 9am-7pm Mon-Sat, 10am-3pm Sun. You may forget you are in Mongolia as you drink milkshakes and eat burgers at this favourite spot of UB expats. Don't miss Sunday brunch.

Abtai Sain Khaani Örgöö (☎ 453 129, Khökh Tengerin Gudamj) Dinner including cultural show T11,000. Open 11am-9pm daily. Situated in Mongolia's biggest ger, this place caters to visitors on organised tours who want to taste some good – as opposed to authentic – Mongolian food. Reservations are required.

Chinggis Restaurant (☎ 321 257, Baga Toiruu) Lunch/dinner T7000/8000. Open 11am-9pm daily. The buffet includes a salad bar (possibly the most vegetables you will see in one place in Mongolia) and decent *teppanyaki*, which is meat grilled on a sizzling hotplate. The price for dinner includes a show.

The restaurants at *Bayangol Hotel* and *Ulaan Baatar Hotel* are appealing (albeit expensive) places to try Mongolian food. Another cheaper, less touristy place is *Amtat Bulag* on Baga Toiruu.

Fast Food & Self-Catering For fast Mongolian fare, it is not difficult to find cheap, tasty *buuz* (steamed meat dumplings) or *khuushuur* (fried mutton pancake) at kiosks and canteens around town. Look for the signs that read *Guanz*.

To stock up for your train ride or a trip to the countryside, you can visit the ground floor of the *State Department Store*. For the widest selection of meats, cheeses and produce, go to *Merkuri Market* and *Dalai Market*, which are both off Seoulyn Gudamj not far from the State Circus. They are jointly known as the circus market.

Entertainment

For information on current shows, contact CIRC (see Tourist Offices earlier in this chapter).

Tumen Ekh Ensemble Palace (☎ 327 379, Nairamdal Park) Show 6pm daily. Admission T6000. The show usually includes examples of *khoomi*, the unique Mongolian throat-singing, contortionists to make your eyes water and recitals featuring the horse-head violin.

State Opera & Ballet Theatre (☎ 322 854, Sükhbaatar Square) Admission T5500. Productions include many of the classics, as well as works by Mongolia's most famous poet and playwright Natsagdorj.

River Sounds (☎ 320 497, Marksyn Örgön Chölöö) Open 9.30pm-1.30am. This club hosts live jazz and rock bands several nights a week.

The best places to sit outside on a summer evening and enjoy a frosty *pivo* (beer) are *Khanbrau Biergarten* and *Chinggis Beer Co* (see Places to Eat earlier).

Shopping

Shopping is a bit disappointing in Ulaan Baatar. Crafts are expensive, made solely for tourists. Souvenir shops are in major hotels, museums and tourist attractions. There are a few other places to find souvenirs.

Khan's Ger (☎ 328 410, Baga Toiruu, next to Youth Federation Bldg) Khan has one of the city's best selection of handicrafts, although they are not too cheap.

State Department Store (☎ 324 311, Peace Ave) Open 9am-8pm Mon-Sat, 10am-6pm Sun. The 'big shop', as it is commonly called, has a decent collection of souvenirs on the 4th floor, as well as traditional clothes on the 3rd floor.

Egshiglen National Musical Instrument Shop (☎ 312 732, Khuvsgalchdyn Örgön Chölöö) Opposite the Museum of Natural

History, this is the place to get your *morin khuur* (horse-head fiddle).

Getting There & Away

Train The Trans-Mongolian passes through Ulaan Baatar on Sunday heading towards Beijing. One additional train per week originates in Ulaan Baatar on Sunday, taking 30 hours to reach Beijing.

You have more options if you are heading to Russia. The Trans-Mongolian passes through on Thursday en route to Moscow. Two trains a week (Tuesday and Friday) originate in Ulaan Baatar and go all the way to Moscow. The daily trains to Irkutsk stop in every town along the way and the trip takes 36 hours.

Tickets International train tickets are available at the International Railway Ticketing

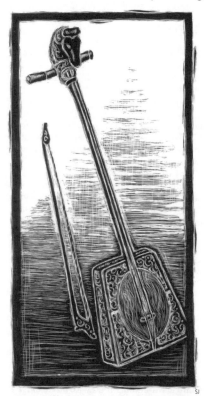

The horse-head fiddle or *morin khor* has two horse-hair strings and a carved horse's head.

Office (☎ 944 868), Zamchydn Gudamj, at the foreigners' booking office. The tickets for Moscow-Beijing trains don't go on sale until the day before departure. Be sure to arrive early and be prepared to fight for your place in line.

UB Tour or Juulchin (see Travel Agencies) will book your ticket for a small fee, which can avoid untold hassles.

Air The Mongolian airline MIAT (☎ 320 221) operates international flights to Berlin, Moscow, Irkutsk, Hohot, Beijing, Seoul and Osaka, as well as domestic flights to the aimag capitals. The office is at the southern end of Baga Toiruu. Foreign airlines operate flights to Beijing (Air China, ☎ 328 838); Moscow, Irkutsk and Ulan Ude (Aeroflot, ☎ 320 720); and Seoul (Air Korea, ☎ 326 643). One-way/return flights from Ulaan Baatar to Beijing are about Y2260/3500.

Bus The long-distance bus station is at the southern end of Öndör Geegen Zanabazaryn Gudamj. Minivans travel at least once or twice a week to most of the Mongolian provinces (except for three provinces in the far west). Long-distance journeys should be booked at least a day in advance, if possible. For shorter journeys, to places such as Baganuur, Darkhan and Zuunmod, the buses depart hourly and tickets are sold on the bus.

Getting Around

From the train station to the city centre is about 20 minutes' walk. Taking a taxi in Ulaan Baatar is also quite easy and cheap. The going rate is T300 per kilometre. Many taxis do not have meters, but the driver will probably wait for payment from you instead of telling you how much it costs. A private car might also stop to pick you up, but the charge should be the same. The taxi stand is across the street from the Center Hotel.

AROUND ULAAN BAATAR

Mongolia's real attraction lies in the still untouched beauty of the countryside, its exhilarating wide open spaces and rich nomadic culture. Fortunately, these aspects are within reach on day trips or overnights from Ulaan Baatar.

Manzshir Khiid
Манзшир Хийд

Forty-six kilometres from Ulaan Baatar, Manzshir Khiid *(admission T1000, plus T500 for a car)* was a monastery – established in 1733 – that once contained more than 20 temples and housed 350 monks. The main temple has been restored and now functions as a museum, but the other temples remain in ruins, as they were left after the purges in the 1930s.

The monastery itself is not as impressive as Gandan Khiid in UB, but the setting is exquisite. Hidden away in the Bogdkhan Uul Strictly Protected Area, the monastery overlooks a beautiful valley of pine, birch and cedar trees, dotted with granite boulders. Behind the main temple, you are able to climb up the rocks to discover some **Buddhist rock paintings**.

You can catch a bus or a taxi straight to Manzshir Khiid from Ulaan Baatar. Alternatively, you can go straight to the nearby town of Zuunmod and then walk to the monastery through the Bogdkhan Uul Strictly Protected Area (7km). Walk along the main road heading north-east out of Zuunmod. You can also walk from Manzshir Khiid back to Ulaan Baatar via Tsetseegun Uul (46km).

Tsetseegun Uul
Цэцээгүн Уул

Of the Four Holy Peaks that surround Ulaan Baatar, the most magnificent is Tsetseegun Uul (2256m). The Siberian larch forest and abundance of bird and animal life make this a great place to escape the city.

The easiest way to explore Tsetseegun Uul is to hike from Manzshir Khiid. Even if you do not enter the monastery/museum, you will have to pay the T1000 admission fee for Bogdkhan Uul Strictly Protected Area. The trail is reasonably marked, but you should also use a compass. This hike takes about 10 hours, so be prepared to camp and bring all the food and water you will need for at least two days.

From the monastery, follow the stream east until it nearly disappears, then turn north. About three hours' walking should bring you out over a ridge into a broad boggy meadow, which you will have to cross. If you walked due north, the twin rocky outcrops of the summit should be right in front of you. When you start to see Ulaan Baatar in the distance, you are on the highest ridge and close to the two large *ovoo* (sacred pyramid-shaped collection of stones) on the summit.

From the ovoo you can return to Manzshir or descend to Ulaan Baatar. Finding the most direct route to Ulaan Baatar is difficult, since you must estimate your location by your visual reference to the city. Once you reach the southern fringe of the city you can hitch or catch a taxi to the centre. Beware of hiking too close to the Presidential Palace in the Ikh Tenger Valley, as the guards can be up-tight about perceived 'trespassers'.

Terelj
Тэрэлж

Terelj, about 80km north-east of Ulaan Baatar, is part of the Gorkhi-Terelj National Park. At 1600m, this area is cool and the alpine scenery spectacular. There are many opportunities for hiking, rock climbing, swimming (in icy water), rafting and horse riding. The park has a daily T1000 entry fee, plus T3000 for each car, which is payable at the entrance to the park.

One potential destination for hiking or horse riding is **Gunjiin Sün**, a Manchurian-influenced temple surrounded by forests. From the main ger camp area, Gunjiin Sün is about 30km as the crow flies, but it is easier to find if you take the longer route along the Baruun Bayan Gol. Other pictur-esque routes are along the Terelj and Tuul Rivers towards Khentii Nuruu. Horses can be hired at any ger camp for about $5 per hour or $15 to $20 per day.

Most of the ger camps in Terelj offer identical facilities and prices – about $40, which includes with three hearty meals, or $10 without food. Some of the more se-cluded camps are *Tsolmon (☎ 322 870)* and *Miraj (☎ 325 188)*.

Buses go from Ulaan Baatar bus station to Terelj every day at 3pm, returning at 8am. An easier option is to hire a taxi, which costs about $25 one way.

TRANS-MANCHURIAN

Summer Palace, Beijing

Within the Forbidden City, Beijing

Imperial lion, Forbidden City

TRANS-MANCHURIAN
Did you know?

- Known in Mandarin as 'three north-east provinces', the region called Manchuria comprises the present-day Chinese provinces of Jilin, Heilonjiang and Liaoning. It is dominated by the Great Manchurian Plain, a vast agricultural plain crossed by the Sonhua and Liao Rivers.

- With an extreme continental climate like Siberia to the north, Manchuria is renowned for long, severe winters when temperatures routinely drop to -40°C.

- Economic development has come to Manchuria at the expense of clean air and water, pristine forests and biological diversity. Desertification caused by overgrazing and irrigation has been an ongoing problem in parts of the country.

- The three densely populated provinces that comprise Manchuria are among China's most important agricultural and industrial regions as well as being rich in natural resources such as timber, coal, iron and oil.

- The Manchurian region was traditionally inhabited by nomadic tribes such as Tungus, Eastern Turks and Khitan. The Manchus – who eventually founded the Qing dynasty in 1644 – were descended from the Jurchen, a tribe of pastoral nomads that settled in the Songhua valley.

- The Zhalong Nature Reserve, west of Harbin, is the breeding ground of the rare, endangered red-crowned crane, which ironically is a symbol of longevity in the Chinese culture.

- The architecture of cities like Tianjin reflects the history of occupation of Manchuria – militarily and economically – by Russia, Japan, Belgium, Austro-Hungary, Germany and Italy.

Tarskaya to Beijing

The segment of this route from the junction at Tarskaya, Russia, to Shenyang, China, was laid by the Russians between 1897 and 1903 as part of the East Chinese Railway line to Vladivostok and Dalian (Port Arthur). Now that the Manchurian region remains under solid Chinese control, trains no longer go directly through Manchuria to Vladivostok or directly from Russia to Dalian. But once a week, the *Vostok* makes the trip in each direction over the Trans-Manchurian route, taking about six days to travel between Moscow and Beijing. This is the longer route to Beijing, and arguably the less interesting. However, it does give its passengers a glimpse of the desolate beauty of the steppe while allowing them to skip the hassle of obtaining a Mongolian visa.

Highlights

- See the region that was the birthplace of the Manchus, the safe haven of the Russians and the industrial stronghold of the Japanese in the early 20th century.

- Don your long underwear and come to a winter wonderland at Harbin's Ice Lantern Festival.

- Admire the Russian spires, scalloped turrets and cobblestone streets in the Daoliqu section of Harbin.

- Get up close and personal with the rare and majestic Siberian tiger at the Siberian Tiger Park.

The Route

The Trans-Manchurian branches off from the main Trans-Siberian line at Tarskaya, 12km east of Karymskaya (6293km). In Russia, the kilometre markers continue to show the distance to Moscow. Once in China, they show the distance to Harbin; south of Harbin they show the distance to Beijing.

Tarskaya to Zabaikalsk

From Tarskaya, the train crosses the Ingoda River and heads south-east into the 'grasslands', or the steppe. The trees become more sparse and the landscape is dominated by green hills and more green hills.

After stopping for 10 minutes in **Olovyannaya** (6444km), the train crosses the Onon River, which is a tributary of the Ingoda. This area is said to be the birthplace of Chinggis Khaan (born 'Temujin' in 1162).

The train makes another 10-minute stop at **Borzya** (6543km). This area is sparsely populated, and you will see little development until you arrive at the Russian border post of **Zabaikalsk** (6666km). For details on the border crossing, refer to the boxed text later in this section.

Manzhouli to Beijing

The Chinese border post is **Manzhouli** (935km to Harbin), which was established in 1901 as a stop for the train. This town is growing at a phenomenal rate because of the cross-border trade with its northern neighbour. The Russians have played a major role throughout Manzhouli's history, including developing the open-pit coal mine at nearby **Zalainuo'er**, which the train passes just outside of Manzhouli. On the southern side of the tracks you will see the coal-processing plant, as well as the steam engines at work hauling coal.

This region of China is Inner Mongolia, the main feature of which is the vast grasslands that surround Manzhouli in verdant splendour. Thirty-nine kilometres south of the city is **Dalai Hu** (Dalai Lake), Inner Mongolia's largest lake.

The northernmost major town in Inner Mongolia is **Hailaer** (749km), where the train stops for about 10 minutes. Around 650km, the train starts to climb into the Greater Hinggan mountain range. It may make stops at towns such as **Mianduhe** (634km), **Yilick Ede** (574km) and **Xinganling** (564km). From here the train descends on the eastern side of the range.

Shortly after the 15-minute halt at **Boketu** (539km), the train leaves Inner Mongolia and enters the province of Heilongjiang, meaning 'Black Dragon River'. Known in Russian as the Amur River, the region's namesake marks the border with Russia in north-eastern China.

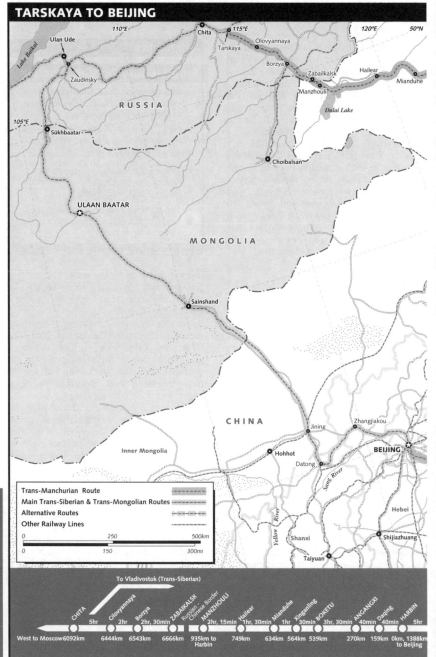

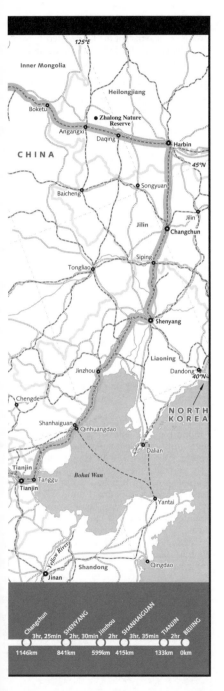

The train makes another 15-minute stop at **Angangxi** (270km), then heads eastward through an area of wetlands, part of which has been designated as the Zhalong Nature

Russia-China Border Crossing

Russian border guards and customs officials do their thing in **Zabaikalsk**. This process can take several hours, especially as the customs officials take their time searching the bags and compartments of Chinese traders.

The railway systems of Mongolia and the former Soviet Union operate on a 5-foot gauge, which is slightly wider than the standard gauge used in the rest of the world. Before the train can continue its journey, it must make a stop at the bogie-changing shed, where the carriages are raised and the bogies are replaced with the appropriate size. If you wish to watch the bogie-changing operations, stay on the train until it leaves the platform and gets to the shed.

After completing these procedures (which usually takes several hours), the train moves on to the Chinese border post of **Manzhouli**, where the passport and customs procedures are repeated by Chinese officials (more efficiently, however). Once you are cleared for entry, you can explore the new train station, check out the Friendship Store across the street and admire the steam locomotives still at work in the shunting yards.

If you are not on the *Vostok*, the process of crossing this border is much more difficult. The daily train from Chita arrives in the morning at Zabaikalsk station. From there, you can take a taxi ($2) to the border, where you will see hundreds of buses and minivans queuing to cross. For another $2 one of these vehicles will take you along. Try to get on a vehicle as close to the front as possible, and settle in for a long, slow wait.

Once through the gate, everyone in your vehicle should pile out, collect their luggage for inspection by Russian customs and go through Russian passport control. You can board your vehicle again only after all of its passengers have passed through. The process is the same (but much quicker) at Chinese customs and passport control. If you are lucky, you will make it to Manzhouli station before the departure of your onward train. Trains to Harbin (15 hours) depart daily at 11am and 4pm.

Reserve. The wetlands of the reserve lie strategically on a bird-migration path, which extends from the Russian Arctic down into South-East Asia. Some 236 different species of bird can be found here, including the rare red-crowned crane. This nearly extinct bird, ironically has long been a symbol of longevity and good luck in the Chinese culture.

The train makes a brief stop in **Daqing** (159km) at the centre of a large oil field. You will notice many oil rigs pumping crude oil out of the ground.

An industrial city of nine million people and the capital of Heilongjiang province, **Harbin** (0km/1388km from Beijing) is a 15-minute stop. For more information, see the section on Harbin later in this chapter. As the train leaves the city, the view of the skyline on the eastern side of the tracks gives a sense of its size.

The Last Emperor

In 1908, Emperor Puyi was the hand-chosen successor to the Empress Dowager Cixi, who had ruled an increasingly chaotic China – directly or indirectly – for 52 years. Cixi's logical successor would have been the emperor Kuang Hsü, but he died mysteriously just one day before the empress, sparking rumours that she poisoned him to keep him off the throne. Instead, the dowager's three-year-old grandnephew inherited the empire on the verge of revolution.

The young Emperor Puyi did not last long on the throne. The Manchu regent's increasingly anti-Chinese policies and teasing talk of constitutional monarchy were replaced in 1911 by Sun Yatsen's Provisional Republican Government, thus ending 267 years of Manchu rule. The last emperor, however, was not gone for good.

Between 1931 and 1932, the Japanese took control of Manchuria, renaming it Manchukuo. Seeing a chance to regain his childhood glory and to rule his homeland of Manchuria, Puyi cooperated with the Japanese and was thus appointed chief executive of the Japanese puppet state. In 1934, he took the title 'K'ang-te', meaning 'prosperity and virtue'. In reality, Puyi was at the mercy of the Japanese. In this way, the last emperor ruled Manchuria until the Japanese were defeated in 1945.

South of Harbin, the train enters the Jilin province, also part of the historic territory of the Manchus. The Japanese industrialised this region when they shaped it into the puppet state of Manchukuo (1931–45). The provincial capital is **Changchun** (1146km), where the train stops for 10 minutes. It is home to China's first car-manufacturing plant (as well as 6.8 million people).

From here, the train heads southward and enters Liaoning, once the southernmost province of Manchuria. **Shenyang** (841km) was a Mongol trading centre from the 11th century, becoming the capital of the Manchu empire in the 17th century. The founder of the Qing dynasty, Huang Taiji, is buried here in an impressive tomb. With the Manchu conquest of Beijing in 1644, Shenyang became a secondary capital under the Manchu name of Mukden, and a centre of the ginseng trade. Today it is a massive industrial city of 6.7 million people. The train stops here for 15 minutes.

After a brief stop in **Jinzhou** (599km), the line roughly follows the coast and enters the province of Hebei. The northern part of this province, spanned by the Great Wall, is characterised by scenic, mountainous tableland.

You will get a great view as the train passes through the Great Wall just north of **Shanhaiguan** (415km). Four kilometres from Shanhaiguan's centre, the Great Wall meets the sea.

The last stop before Beijing is **Tianjin** (133km), now a sprawling municipality of eight million people and a major industrial centre. During the 19th century this port city attracted the interest of almost every European nation that had a ship to put to sea. The evidence is that Tianjin is a living museum of early-20th-century European architecture. You will have 10 minutes to stroll around its modern train station.

Ninety minutes later, the train pulls into **Beijing** (0km). See that chapter for further information.

HARBIN
☎ 86-451 • pop 9.15 million

At the end of the 19th century, Harbin was a quiet village on the Songhua River. However, when the Russians negotiated the contract to construct the East Chinese Railway line through Manchuria, Harbin's role was changed forever. Even though the Japanese gained control of the new railway with the Russian defeat in the Russo-Japanese War, Russian refugees flocked to Harbin in 1917, fleeing the Bolsheviks. The Russians would continue to have an influence over the town's development until the end of WWII, when the region was finally handed over to the Kuomintang.

Remnants of Russian influence are still visible. Most evident is the graceful architecture that still stands in the Daoliqu market area. Nowadays, improving relations with Russia have also resulted in flourishing trade and cross-border tourism. Russian tourists – known to the Chinese as 'the hairy ones' – journey to Harbin to load up on cheap consumer goods.

Outside of Daoliqu, Harbin is a vast industrial city of over nine million people, where it is easy to get lost amid the giant, glitzy buildings and the fast pace and pollution of city life.

Orientation

The main train station is in the dead centre of Harbin, surrounded by a cluster of hotels. The Daoliqu area, which also contains a few hotels and many of the city's attractions, is about 3km north-west of the train station. At the northern end of its main thoroughfare, Zhongyang Dajie, Stalin Park is on the shores of the wide Songhua River. The river marks the northern boundary of the city centre.

Information

The China International Travel Service (CITS; ☎ 366 1159, fax 366 1190) has an extremely helpful international department that assists with train and airline tickets. It is on the 11th floor of the Hushi Building, across the street from the train station.

Most large hotels will change US dollars. You will also find many banks, such as the Bank of China and the CITIC Bank, on Zhongyang Dajie in Daoliqu.

The main post office is on the corner of Dongda Zhijie and Fendou Lu, with the main telephone office a few blocks north on Fendou Lu. The post office also has branches on Zhongyang Dajie and next door to the train station.

Heilongjiang Information Harbor (☎ 457 8002) is a giant, bustling Internet cafe at 129 Zhongyang Dajie.

Dalian

The original East Chinese Railway line continued from Shenyang about 250km south to the peninsula of Lüshun (Port Arthur). After securing the peninsula from the Japanese in 1898, the Russians intended to construct a port here as an alternative to icy Vladivostok. Russian troops accompanied the railroad construction workers, effectively resulting in Russian control of north-eastern China.

However, before construction of the port was complete, the town passed back into Japanese hands with the Russian defeat in the Russo-Japanese War. The Japanese completed construction in 1930, and the Russians regained control after WWII.

Today Dalian (firmly back under Chinese control) has the largest harbour in the north-east, and is also one of the most prosperous cities in China. Its relaxed atmosphere is enhanced by colourful old trams and exquisite architecture. Close to the sea, the weather is relatively warm and particularly pleasant in summer. However, the Trans-Manchurian route today heads to the south-west, bypassing this seaside town, chugging along directly to Beijing.

Daoliqu

Wandering around the old market area of Daoliqu is one of the highlights of Harbin. The Russian spires, scalloped turrets and cobblestone streets lend Harbin an old-world atmosphere that is unique in China. Thirteen buildings in this area have been designated as historical 'preserved buildings'; each is marked with a plaque with a brief history of the structure. Ironically, during Harbin's early years, this part of the city was known as 'Chinese town'; now, the pedestrian thoroughfare of Zhongyang Dajie is lined with Western shops and outdoor cafes (many of which actually serve coffee!).

Church of St Sophia

Two blocks east of Zhongyang Dajie is the majestic Church of St Sophia (Shèng Suofeiyà Jiàotáng), one of the many Orthodox churches built by the Russians. It is one of the few, however, that has been restored since being ransacked during the Cultural Revolution. The church sits on a delightful open square in the city centre.

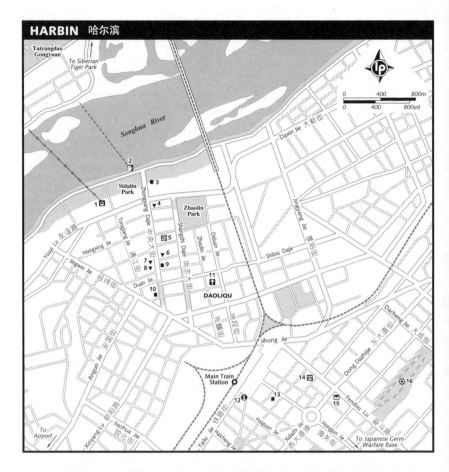

HARBIN 哈尔滨

HARBIN 哈尔滨

PLACES TO STAY
- 3 Gloria Inn; Coffee House
  松花江凯莱商务酒店;
  咖啡店
- 9 Modern Hotel
  马迭尔宾馆
- 10 Zhong Da Hotel
  中大大酒店
- 13 PSB Hostel
  公安局招待所

PLACES TO EAT
- 4 Russian Tea House
- 6 Portman Bar
  波特曼西餐厅

- 7 Third Grocery Store
- 8 Huamei Western Restaurant
  华梅西餐厅

OTHER
- 1 Cable Car
  览车
- 2 Ferries to Sun Island Park
  太阳岛游览船
- 5 Heilongjiang Information Harbor
  网吧

- 11 Church of St Sophia; Harbin Construction Arts Museum
  圣索菲亚教堂
- 12 CITS; Hushi Building
  中国国际旅行社
- 14 Telephone Office
  电信局
- 15 Main Post Office
  总邮局
- 16 Children's Park; Children's Railway
  儿童公园

The church's exquisite interior houses **Harbin Construction Arts Museum** (☎ 468 6904; North-eastern cnr of Zhaolin Jie & Toulong Jie; admission Y10; open 8.30am-5.30pm daily). The small museum is mainly a photographic exhibit of the history of the city and it also has models of some of Harbin's architectural showpieces (both past and present).

Parks

On the southern shore of the Songhua River is a tree-lined promenade that's dotted with sculptures and recreational facilities, known as **Stalin Park** (Sidàlín Gongyuàn). You can enjoy a cup of tea on the veranda of one of Daoliqu's 'preserved buildings', a historic **teahouse** that overlooks the river.

From here, ferries cross the river to **Sun Island Park** (Tàiyángdao Gongyuán), which features landscaped gardens, forested areas and water parks. Buy ferry tickets for Y1 from the dock directly north of the Flood Control Monument. You can also take a cable car (Y20/30 one way/return) from the foot of Tongjiang Jie, one block west.

Just south-east of the centre, the **Children's Park** (Értóng Gongyuán) houses a replica of the Harbin-Beijing line known as the Children's Railway. Its 2km of track are plied by a miniature diesel pulling seven cars. Engineers, ticket collectors and rail guards are all kids. Take bus No 8 from the southern end of Zhongyang Dajie to Fendou Lu.

Japanese Germ Warfare Base

The extreme horrors of war are on display at the Japanese Germ Warfare Experimental Base (Riben Xìjun Shíyàn Jidì; ☎ 680 4104, Cnr of Xinjiang Dajie & Xingjian Jie; Bus No 338; admission Y10; open 8.30am-4.30pm daily).

During 1939 the Japanese army set up a top-secret research centre, where Japanese medical experts experimented on prisoners of war. Over 4000 people were infected with bubonic plague, injected with syphilis or roasted alive in furnaces. When the Soviets took Harbin in 1945 the Japanese blew the place up, but a tenacious Japanese journalist dug up the story in the 1980s. The exhibition consists of only two small rooms plus a nearby vestige of the original base. The captions are in Chinese only. The museum is 20km south of the city, so it's a long haul.

Ice Lantern Festival

Ironically, Harbin's peak tourist season is the middle of winter, when visitors flock here to participate in the Ice Lantern Festival. It is held every year from 5 January to 15 February in Zhaolin Park. Fanciful sculptures are produced in the shapes of animals, plants, buildings and legendary figures. At night the sculptures are illuminated from the inside with coloured lights, creating a true winter wonderland.

Places to Stay

During the Ice Lantern Festival, prices are at least 20% higher than those listed here. At this time, accommodation is very difficult to find, so plan well in advance.

PSB Hostel (☎ 642-8560 8000, Hongjun Jie) Dorm beds/doubles Y38/120. Run by the local police, this is the only hostel that is technically legally open to foreigners. It is clean, friendly and conveniently around the corner from the train station.

Zhong Da Hotel (☎ 463 8888, ☎ 463 9988, 40 Zhongyang Dajie) Doubles Y240. Rooms are slightly run down, but this is the cheapest place to stay in the Daoliqu area.

Modern Hotel (☎ 461 5846, fax 461 4997, 89 Zhongyang Dajie) Doubles Y336. Housed in one of Daoliqu's historic buildings dating from 1906, the Modern Hotel defies its name. The hotel does maintain a rather majestic character, and the ongoing renovations may bring it up to date. Rooms are comfortable and the location is unbeatable.

Overlooking Stalin Park the **Songhua-jiang Gloria Inn** (☎ 463 8855, fax 463 8533, W www.giharbin.com) has comfortable rooms and an excellent restaurant. Doubles are Y339, but prices go up dramatically during the peak seasons.

Places to Eat

Harbin's culinary trademark is sausage, lengths of which hang in shop windows up and down Zhongyang Dajie. The street is also lined with **bakeries**, **cafes** and **kiosks**, which present no shortage of eating options.

Third Grocery Store (Tsentralny Univermag; 118 Zhongyang Dajie) Dishes Y1-5. Open 9am-9pm. Chinese customers queue up for the fresh dumplings, spicy sausage and tasty noodles being sold here. This is also a good place to stock up on supplies for train journeys.

Siberian Tiger Park

To study, breed, release and ultimately save the Siberian tiger is the mission of the **Siberian Tiger Park** (*Dongbei Hu Linyuán;* ☎ *409 0098; Bus No 85; admission Y50; open 10am-5pm daily*). The idea is to breed the tigers and eventually reintroduce them into the wild, thus replenishing their natural populations. It seems, however, that the reintroduction of these animals into the wild is a long way off.

Conservationists stress the need for minimal contact with humans, so the tigers develop a healthy fear of potential poachers. Logically, the breeding grounds should emulate, as much as possible, the wild environment where they will live after release. The Siberian Tiger Park in Harbin is anything but that. The tigers pay no heed to bus loads of tourists driving through their sanctuary snapping photos, and they are reportedly fed cows and chickens and other farm animals. It has been argued that such conditions will produce tigers who have a taste for livestock and who associate people and vehicles with feeding time.

Despite its less than convincing methods, nobody can fault the lofty goals of the Siberian Tiger Park. It is currently home to over 70 cats, including a whole slew of playful cubs. For visitors, it allows an up-close look at these strikingly beautiful animals, some of whom are living in captivity.

The admission fee includes a 20-minute bus tour of the sanctuary, where you will likely see others in their 'natural' habitat.

Tiger, tiger, burning bright, in the forest of the night
What immortal hand or eye could frame thy fearful symmetry?

William Blake's well-known stanza only begins to capture the fierce dignity of the Siberian tiger. Also known as the Amur or Manchurian tiger, the majestic Siberian tiger is indigenous to the Russian Far East, north-eastern China and North Korea. They are concentrated in the remaining forests along the Ussuri River.

The Siberian tiger is one of the world's five surviving subspecies of tiger. They are the biggest of the big cats, with an adult male growing to about 3.3m and weighing as much as 300kg. Females are no pussy cats either, averaging about 2.6m long and weighing 100kg to 150kg. Siberian tigers are lighter in colour than other breeds, enabling them to go undetected in the snow and grass. Their fur is paler orange with lighter brown stripes, while they have white chests, bellies and collars. A tiger may be difficult to spot, but its surly growls can be heard 2km away!

Contrary to what you might see in the park, tigers in the wild are loners. Awesome predators, tigers hunt at night, using their keen sense of smell (they even have scent receptors on their tongues) and agile movements to catch prey including red deer, wild boar and the occasional brown bear. An

---

Portman Bar (☎ *468 6888, 63 Xi 6 Dao Jie*) Mains from Y30. This restaurant has a comfortable, pub atmosphere and serves tasty Western food.

Russian Tea House (☎ *456 3207, 57 Xi Toudao Jie*) Mains from Y20. Housed in a historic building dating from 1914, this quaint restaurant serves Russian coffee and food.

Huamei Western Restaurant (☎ *467 5574, 112 Zhongyang Dajie*) Mains Y20-30. In this case, 'Western' means 'Russian', but the food and atmosphere are pleasant.

Coffee House (☎ *463 8855, 257 Zhongyang Dajie*) Mains Y35-50. Open 6.30am-midnight. This restaurant in the Gloria Inn

has an excellent selection of delicious Asian and Western dishes.

Getting There & Away

Train tickets are very hard to come by. CITS and travel agencies claim that they must be booked one week in advance during summer and three days in advance in less busy seasons. You can get tickets on shorter notice if you are flexible, resourceful and not easily frustrated. The international department of CITS is the best place to start.

On the Trans-Manchurian route, two trains daily go north to Manzhouli on the Russian border ($13 hard seat, 15 hours), and three express trains south to Beijing (Y450/290

Siberian Tiger Park

adult male might eat as much as 45kg of meat in one sitting (approximately 400 burgers)! Not surprisingly, after gorging on such a meal, tigers like to take a long nap in the shade. Some Siberian tigers are known to winter at the beach, where they lay in wait for deer that come to feed on salt and seaweed.

Unfortunately, the Siberian tiger is also one of the rarest breeds of tiger. Estimates of the world's total tiger population in the wild range from 5000 to 7000 cats. India's 3000 to 4000 Bengal tigers are the most plentiful. The Siberian tiger population is estimated at roughly 400 in the wild.

Still, that is an improvement. After WWII, it was presumed that less than 50 cats survived in the region. In 1947, the Soviet Union introduced a tiger protection program with habitat preservation. Moreover, the tense relationship between the Soviet Union and China placed the border region off limits to human settlement. As a result, the tiger made a significant recovery, reaching as many as 500 in the wild by the 1980s.

The fall of the communist regime, however, has made the tiger vulnerable again. A wildlife mafia moved into the area and incidences of poaching quickly increased. Tiger parts, especially bones, are a highly valued commodity in traditional Asian medicine. In addition, unregulated logging has cleared away large stretches of their forest habitat. Tigers require a lot of roaming space (up to 1000 sq km for an adult male). As human communities spread out, they encroach upon the territory of the tigers. The fear of lost livestock leads some farmers to take lethal action against the predators. This precarious situation prompted the World Wildlife Fund to place the Siberian tiger on its most endangered species list.

In the late 1990s, the Russian government took steps to protect the tiger, including more public education, farmer compensation and habitat protection. A special antipoaching unit, with real powers of enforcement, was formed to break up the wildlife mafias. The city of Vladivostok now hosts Tiger Day in early autumn, as a way to raise awareness and celebrate the native felines. The Chinese are doing their part as well, although it's likely to be too late. It is estimated that less than 20 Siberian tigers still reside in Manchuria. The Chinese government banned the use of tiger parts in medicines and has also launched a public education campaign. It remains to be seen if these efforts can save the Siberian tiger.

Getting There & Away

The Siberian Tiger Park is north of the city centre across the river. Bus No 85 drops you along the main highway, from where it's a 1.5km walk to the entrance. Alternatively, for Y170 you can hire a taxi that will wait at the park and bring you back to the city.

soft/hard sleeper, 13 hours). The *Vostok* passes once a week, on Thursday heading to Beijing and on Sunday to Moscow.

If you want to go to Vladivostok, you can take the daily train to Suifenhe on the Russian border. From there you should cross into Russia and catch another train onward.

Getting Around

The easiest way to get around Harbin is by using taxis. The charge is about Y1.20 per kilometre with a Y8 minimum.

Trolleybus and minibus Nos 101 and 103 regularly travel between Stalin Park and the train station.

TARSKAYA TO BEIJING

Beijing

☎ 86-10 • pop 12.16 million

You will start or finish your journey here if you travel on either the Trans-Mongolian or the Trans-Manchurian lines. Although it is perhaps not representative of China as a whole, the capital is where the country's cogs and wheels are turned; furthermore, Beijing is home to 13 million Chinese people, so it must be representative of something. It is worthwhile to spend several days here to get a taste of China's rich culture, a glimpse at its vast history and a first-hand view of the dynamism of modern Beijing.

HISTORY

Beijing has been a centre of cultural and political life in China since the 13th century, when Chinggis Khaan descended on the city (then known as Yanjing, which is now the name of a popular Beijing beer). His grandson, Kublai Khan, renamed the city Khanbaliq, or Khan's town. From here, he ruled the largest empire in world history.

Although the capital was moved for a brief period, Yongle (of the Ming dynasty) re-established Beijing as the capital in the 1400s and spent millions of *taels* of silver to refurbish the city. Yongle is known as the architect of modern Beijing, building the Forbidden City and the Temple of Heaven, as well as developing the bustling commercial streets outside the inner city. The Qing dynasty expanded the construction of temples, palaces and pagodas.

Many of these architectural achievements were destroyed during the Cultural Revolution, but repair and reconstruction have been ongoing since the early 1980s. Even more striking, the new development in Beijing is overwhelming, including posh hotels, shopping malls and super highways. It shows no sign of stopping, especially as the city makes preparations to host the 2008 Olympics.

ORIENTATION

The centre of Beijing is the Forbidden City, with the major avenues surrounding it in a grid pattern. Jianguomenwai Dajie, the most important east-west avenue, running just south of the Forbidden City, has many hotels and facilities. The east-west line of the metro follows this major road. The main

Highlights

- Marvel at the grandeur and expanse of the Great Wall of China.
- Explore the hidden *hutong* of Beijing's oldest neighbourhoods.
- Escape to the peace and solitude of the Lama and Confucius temples.
- Feast on Peking duck and other local specialities.
- Get lost in a maze of courtyards and pavilions at the Forbidden City.

train station, Beijing Zhan, is one block south of Jianguomenwai Dajie (3km southeast of the Forbidden City) and is accessible by the metro circle line.

INFORMATION
Tourist Offices

The main branch of Beijing Tourism Group (BTG; Beijing Luxíngshè), formerly known as the China International Travel Service (CITS; Zhongguó Guójì Luxíngshè) is at the Beijing Tourist Building (☎ 6515 8562, fax 6515 8603), 28 Jianguomenwai Dajie, between the New Otani and Gloria Plaza Hotels. Besides providing general tourist information about the city, the helpful staff sell air tickets and train tickets for the Trans-Manchurian and Trans-Mongolian.

Money

CITIC at the International Building, 19 Jianguomenwai Dajie, adjacent to the Friendship Store, will cash travellers cheques for US dollars or advance cash on major international credit cards. The Bank of China at Xindong'an Plaza – on Wangfujing Dajie near the Foreign Languages Bookstore – offers many of the same services. American Express (☎ 6505 2888, fax 6505 4972) has an office in the China World Trade Center, 1 Jianguomenwai Dajie.

ATMs with international access are situated at Xindong'an Plaza on Wangfujing Dajie; Sanlitun Lu (one block north of Dongzhimen Wai Dajie); and the China World Trade Center.

Post & Communications

The international post office is on the Second Ring Road, not far from the Friendship Store. It is open 8am to 6pm Monday to Friday. Poste Restante is open 9am to 5pm and there is a Y1.50 charge for each letter received by the office.

Email & Internet Access The following are a few places you can send or receive email and surf the Web.

Qian Yi Internet Café (☎ 6705 1722, fax 6705 1632, W www.qianyi-wb.com) Old Railway Station shopping mall, Tiananmen Square. Open 9.30am to 10pm daily.
Internet Café (☎ 6317 6945) 161 Tie Shu Jie (down the road from the Far East Hotel). Open 24 hours.
Sparkice Internet Café (☎ 6505 2288) 2nd floor, China World Trade Center, 1 Jianguomenwai Dajie. Open 10am to 10pm daily.

Bookshops

The Foreign Languages Bookstore is at 235 Wanfujing Dajie.

The Friendship Store, 17 Jianguomenwai Dajie, also has a book and magazine section that is a gold mine for travellers looking for reading material to keep them occupied on long trips.

Medical Services

The Beijing Union Medical Hospital (Xiéhé Yiyuàn; ☎ 6433 3960), 2 Jiangtai Lu, is a Chinese hospital that caters for foreigners.

THE FORBIDDEN CITY

The largest and best-preserved cluster of ancient buildings in China is the Forbidden City *(Zìjìn Chéng; Metro: Tian'anmen-dong; admission Y40, plus Y30 to rent audio guide; open 8.30am-5pm daily).* It was home to two dynasties of emperors, the Ming and the Qing, who rarely strayed from this pleasure dome, although it was off limits to everyone else (thus, the name).

The Chinese authorities refer to this complex as the Palace Museum *(Gùgong)*. Renting the cassette for the self-guided tour (available in many languages) is definitely worth the extra Y30; it is narrated by Roger Moore of James Bond fame. Entrance tickets and cassette rental are available at the south gate of the Forbidden City. Continue through Tiananmen and proceed northward until you cannot go any further without paying. (The booth in the centre of this plaza sells tickets to Tiananmen, *not* to the Forbidden City.)

The basic layout of Beijing city was established between 1406 and 1420. However,

The Forbidden City, called Gu Gong (in Chinese), was the imperial palace during the Ming and Qing dynasties.

BEIJING

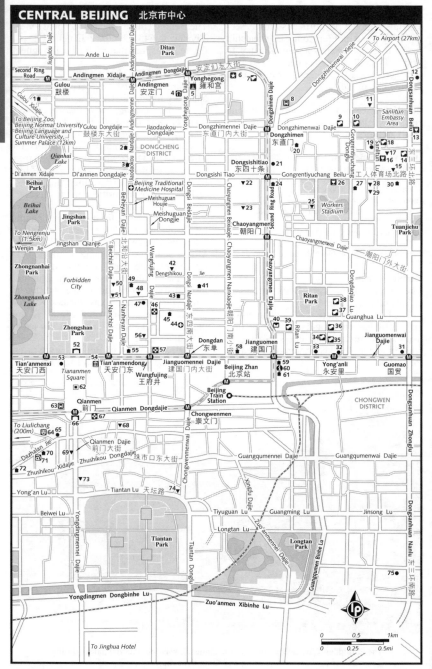

BEIJING

CENTRAL BEIJING 北京市中心

PLACES TO STAY
1 Bamboo Garden Hotel
   竹园宾馆
2 Youhao Hotel
   友好宾馆
3 Lusongyuan Hotel
   侣松园宾馆
20 Red House
24 Swissôtel
   瑞士酒店
27 City Hotel
30 Zhaolong Hotel & International Youth Hostel
   兆龙青年旅舍
41 Haoyuan Guesthouse
   好园宾馆
43 Novotel Peace Hotel
   北京诺富特和平宾馆
45 Central Academy of Arts Dormitory
49 Fangyuan Hotel
   芳园宾馆
55 Grand Hotel Beijing; Palace View
   贵宾楼饭店
58 Beijing International Hotel; Juulchin
59 New Otani Hotel
   长富宫
61 Gloria Plaza Hotel
70 Far East Hotel & International Youth Hostel
   远东饭店
72 Far East Hotel; Internet Cafe

PLACES TO EAT
11 Green Tea House
   紫云茗
15 1001 Nights
17 Serve the People
22 Red Capital Club
   新红资
23 Red Capital Club
25 Metro Café
   美特糕
28 The Den
29 Hidden Tree; Jam House; Monkey Business
   隐蔽的树
42 Green Angel Vegetarian Restaurant
   绿天食饭店

48 Dong'anmen Night Market
   东华门夜市
50 The Courtyard
   四合院
51 The Courtyard
56 Datianshujing Hutong
68 Lichun Roast Duck Restaurant
   利纯烤鸭店
69 First Floor Restaurant
   第一楼饭店
73 Gongdelin Vegetarian Restaurant
   功德林素菜馆
74 Beijing Noodle King

OTHER
4 Confucian Temple & Imperial College
   孔庙
5 Lama Temple
   雍和宫
6 PSB
   公安局外事科
7 Russian Embassy
   苏联大使馆
8 Dongzhimen Long-Distance Bus Station
   东直门长途汽车站
9 Australian & Canadian Embassies
   澳大利亚大使馆; 加拿大大使管
10 German Embassy
12 Lufthansa Center; Beijing International Medical Centre
   凯宾斯基饭店; 燕莎商城
13 CD Café
14 French Embassy
16 Public Space
18 Dutch Embassy
19 Jenny Lou's
21 Poly Plaza
   保利大厦
26 Havana Café
31 China World Trade Center; American Express; Sparkice Internet Café
   中国大饭店

32 Xiushui Silk Market
   秀水市场
33 Friendship Store; CITIC
   友谊商店;国际大厦
34 Mongolian Embassy
35 Irish Embassy
36 US Embassy
37 UK Embassy
38 New Zealand Embassy
39 Japanese Embassy
40 International Post & Communications
   国际邮电局
44 Beijing Union Medical Hospital
   北京协和山院
46 Xingdong'an Plaza; Bank of China
   新东安市场; 中国银行
47 Foreign Languages Bookstore
   外文书店
52 Tiananmen
   天安门
53 Great Hall of the People
   人民大会堂
54 Chinese Revolution History Museum
   中国历史博物馆
57 Oriental Plaza
   东方广场
60 Beijing Tourist Building (BTG, formerly CITS)
   旅游大厦
62 Mao Zedong Mausoleum; Monument to the People's Heroes
   毛主席纪念堂; 人民英雄纪念碑
63 Qianmen Tour Bus Station
64 Zhengyici Theatre
   正乙祠大戏楼
65 Ruifuxian
66 Qianmen
   前门
67 Old Railway Station Shopping Mall; Qian Yi Internet Café
71 Internet Café
75 Dirt Market
   潘家园市场

BEIJING

most of the buildings you see now are post-18th century, as are many restored structures around Beijing. The largely wooden palace was frequently a victim of destructive blazes, resulting from accidental fires and arson attempts by eunuchs and officials who hoped to profit from rebuilding. The palace complex is huge (800 buildings, 9000 rooms) and under constant renovation. The **ceremonial buildings** lie along the north-south access in the centre of the complex. However, the highlight of the Forbidden City may be exploring the delightful **courtyards** and **pavilions** (and mini-museums within them) on either side of the main drag.

AROUND TIANANMEN SQUARE

The vast cement expanse just south of the Forbidden City is the world's largest square and the centre of Chinese political life, Tiananmen Square *(Metro: Tian'anmendong or Qianmen)*. A forum for major rallies during the Cultural Revolution, the square is better known in the West as the place where army tanks and soldiers shot down pro-democracy demonstrators in 1989. More recently, followers of the Falun Gong religious movement held almost-daily protests here after China's ban of the movement in 1999. On a normal day, however, the buzz about Tiananmen Square consists mainly of excited tourists snapping photos, easy-going locals flying kites and endless announcements droning over loudspeakers.

On 1 October 1949, Mao Zedong proclaimed the Peoples' Republic of China from **Tiananmen** *(Gate of Heavenly Peace; admission Y15; open 8.30am-4.30pm daily)*. Now the gate (at the northern end of the square) prominently features his portrait, while the slogans read 'Long Live the People's Republic of China' and 'Long Live the Unity of the Peoples of the World'.

At the southern end, **Qianmen** *(Front Gate)* is a remnant of the wall that guarded the ancient Inner City as early as the 15th century. It actually consists of two gates: the Arrow Tower to the south and the Main Gate to the north.

On the site of the old Outer Palace Gate, the **Monument to the People's Heroes** is a 36m obelisk that bears bas-relief depictions of key revolutionary events.

One million people gathered at Tiananmen Square to pay their respects when Mao

died in 1976. Since 1977, throngs of Chinese (and some foreigners) continue to bring flowers and view the body at the **Mao Zedong Mausoleum** *(admission free; open 8.30am-11.30am daily)*, just behind the Monument to the People's Heroes. Most Chinese continue to respect and revere this leader, despite the atrocities carried out during his rule. The official Party line is that Mao was 70% right and 30% wrong in his ruling. Appropriately, a visit to the 'Maosoleum' is about 70% solemnity and 30% absurdity, especially considering the well-stocked gift shop, which does a brisk trade in Chairman Mao thermometers and alarm clocks. You must leave your bags across the street at the bag-check (Y10).

The National People's Congress, China's rubber-stamp legislature, sits on the western side of the square in the **Great Hall of the People** *(admission Y15; open 9am-2pm when Congress not in session)*. Many of the halls are named after provinces and regions of China and decorated appropriately.

On the eastern side of the square is the **Chinese Revolution History Museum** *(open 8.30am-3.30pm Tues-Sun)*. It actually contains two separate museums. The **Museum of History** *(admission Y5 plus Y40 to rent audio guide)* has artefacts and cultural relics from ancient history to 1919; less than half of the exhibits have English explanations. The **Museum of the Revolution** *(admission Y3)* has five distinct sections covering 1919 to 1949, with English explanations throughout. Apparently, China's history since 1949 has been tricky to document (no wonder, as it has been regularly revised according to the prevailing political situation).

SUMMER PALACE

One of Beijing's most popular tourist destinations is the Summer Palace *(Yíhéyuán; admission Y8; open 7am-5pm daily)*. As a result, this immense park with Qing architecture is often overcrowded during the summer months, especially on weekends. The admission fee is not all-inclusive.

Much of the park is occupied by **Kunming Lake**, where you can rent a rowing boat in summer or ice skate in winter. Empress Dowager Cixi rebuilt the park in 1888 with money supposedly intended for the creation of a modern navy. (At least she restored the still-immobile marble boat for

The Great Proletarian Cultural Revolution

The Great Proletarian Cultural Revolution (1966–70) was Mao Zedong's ill-fated attempt to revive China's revolutionary spirit. The resulting loss of culture, productivity and human life would become the greatest tragedy of 20th-century China.

The movement was rooted in the rejection of traditional Chinese culture. Mao also sought to redress the social inequalities that had developed since the founding of the PRC. The greatest offenders were those of the new bureaucratic ruling class, members of the Communist Party. This ideology set the stage for communist China's bloodiest struggle for revolution and reform.

In late 1965, a minor literary critic wrote a scathing review of a popular play *The Dismissal of Hai Rui from Office*. Although set in the Ming dynasty, the play was a clear critique of Mao's economic policy during the Great Leap Forward and his intolerance of dissenting opinions from Party officials. With the help of his wife, Mao set out to purge artistic and political circles of antisocialist elements.

Mao Zedong (1883–1976). The Mao badge still sells like hotcakes.

In response to Mao's call for criticism of the Party, students at Beijing University posted signs attacking the university administration. The criticism quickly degenerated into persecution and outright destruction. Known as the Red Guards, student rebel groups went on rampages through the country: schools were closed; intellectuals and artists were harassed, arrested and even killed; all scientific, literary and artistic output ceased; monasteries and temples were ransacked.

By early 1967, Mao recognised that he had lost control of the Great Proletarian Revolution, which was gradually deteriorating into anarchy. He called on the People's Liberation Army (PLA) – headed by Lin Biao – to restore order, instructing the army to break up any 'counter-revolutionary organisations'. This label was allowed a broad definition, resulting in bloody battles with Red Guards and workers' groups.

Throughout 1968, the PLA implemented its own reign of terror. Red Guards, intellectuals and others who were remotely suspect were arrested or executed. The culpable were sentenced to hard labour and self-criticism.

The outcome of this upheaval and destruction was a political order that was practically identical to the one China started with in 1966. The social consequences, however, were enormous, with as many as 400,000 lives lost, not to mention the destruction of culture and the bitter legacy of distrust.

---

lakeside dining.) The park also contains several **temples** with elaborate artwork and good views of the lake.

The palace was used as a summer home for residents of the Forbidden City. The main building is the **Hall of Benevolence and Longevity**, near the lake towards the eastern gate, which is where the emperor handled state affairs and received visitors. The 700m **Long Corridor** along the northern shore is decorated with mythical scenes. Visitors can also see exhibitions specific to the Empress Dowager Cixi, including her furniture and memorabilia.

The Summer Palace is about 12km northwest of the centre of Beijing. The easiest way to get there is to take bus No 375 from Xizhimen metro.

TEMPLES
Temple of Heaven Park

China's finest example of Ming architecture is the Temple of Heaven *(Tiāntán; admission Y15, plus Y20 to structures on the grounds; open 8.30am-4.30pm daily)*, in Tiantan Park. This complex functioned as a stage for the solemn rites performed by the Son of Heaven, who came here to pray for good harvests, seek divine clearance and atone for the sins of the people.

The design and position of the park, as well as the shape and colour of structures within, have symbolic significance for the ancient interplay between heaven and earth. The **Round Altar**, for example, possesses an obsessive symmetry revolving around the heavenly number nine (nine

BEIJING

The Great Wall

Stretching 7200km from the Bo Sea in the east to the Gobi Desert in the west, the Great Wall of China is truly a wonder, due to both its breathtaking beauty and its ancient architectural achievement.

History credits the 'original' construction of the Great Wall to Emperor Qin Shihuang (221–207 BC), China's First Sovereign Emperor. He accomplished this feat by reconstructing and linking the ruins of older walls, which had been built by the vassal states under the Zhou dynasty in the 7th century BC. The result was a magnificent 4800km stretch of wall, which was meant to keep out the marauding nomads in the north. The effort required hundreds of thousands of workers, many of them political prisoners. Over the course of 10 years, an estimated one million people died; legend has it that the bodies of deceased workers were among the building materials used.

By the collapse of the Qin, the Great Wall had already started to crumble due to years of neglect. Emperor Han Wu-Di once again undertook to rebuild the existing wall, and to extend it 480km farther west into the Gobi Desert. During this period, the wall served mainly as an elevated highway, along which men and equipment could be transported across mountainous terrain. Furthermore, the Hans established a system of smoke signals, by which they could warn each other of enemy attacks. Thus, the wall protected traders and explorers who were travelling the ancient caravan routes between China and Europe.

The wall that you visit today is largely a product of the Ming dynasty (1368–1644). The Ming wall was taller, longer and more ornate than any of its earlier incarnations. It was also stronger, due in part to the advanced brick technology the Ming workers used.

Several sections of the Great Wall have been recently revamped for the benefit of tourists. But to truly appreciate the magnificence of this ancient structure it is well worth the effort to explore the untouched, crumbling ruins at a less-visited section. The hikes detailed under 'Walking the Wild Wall' are based on William Lindesay's book, *Hiking on History: Exploring Beijing's Great Wall on Foot*.

Badaling

The majority of visitors see the Great Wall *(admission Y25)* at Badaling, 70km north-west of Beijing. This section of the wall has been totally restored, complete with guardrail and cable car. The admission fee includes a 15-minute film at the Great Wall Circle Vision Theatre and entrance into the China Great Wall Museum. Badaling is usually jam-packed with tourists sporting 'I climbed the Great Wall' T-shirts.

Tours to Badaling are run by CITS, CTS, most hotels and just about everyone else in the tourist industry. Inexpensive Chinese tours usually add a visit to the Ming Tombs. Big tour buses leave from the south-western corner of Tiananmen Square between 6.30am and 10am (Y50). From the southern end of the square (west of McDonald's), smaller buses go to the same destinations between 8am and 9.30am. The trips take about nine hours in total.

Simatai

In contrast to the over-restored wall at Badaling, the 19km section of the wall at Simatai remains in a crumbling condition. The air of historical authenticity, however, is minimised by the loudspeaker announcements and cable-car lines. The Simatai section of the wall dates from the Ming dynasty. Its most interesting features include the 135 **watchtowers** along the way and the **obstacle walls**, used as defences against enemies who had already scaled the Great Wall.

Simatai is not for the faint-hearted. It is very steep, and one narrow section of the footpath has a 500m drop. At least these treacherous passes serve their original purpose of keeping out the riffraff!

Simatai is 110km north-east of Beijing. From Dongzhimen bus station, take a minibus to Miyun (Y6), where you can hire a *miandi* 'bread taxi', yellow microbuses now banned in the centre of Beijing, to Simatai for Y70 return. Alternatively, you can pay Y30 for the one-way trip and try to catch a tour bus from Simatai back to Beijing (about Y30). The Jinghua Hotel also offers a tour for Y60 return.

The Great Wall

Walking the Wild Wall

Long sections of the Great Wall stride across the region's lofty mountain ranges well away from the heavily touristed areas. This 'Wild Wall' is lonely, unspoilt, overgrown and crumbling. There are no tickets, no signposts, no touts, no coach parks and no garbage. Trekking along narrow footpaths winding uphill from these tiny villages is, for some, the ultimate China experience.

Huanghua to Zhuangdaokou Pass (4km, three-hour loop) One hundred metres south of where the wall meets the road, a well-trodden path leaves the roadside and follows the left side of a creek. After 300m, the path veers towards the wall and fades among the terraces. Head towards the second watchtower.

Second Watchtower The first, lower tower has collapsed. To get to the second tower, make your way to an arched entrance just past the tower itself. As you pass through the archway, straight ahead is an engraved tablet, which details construction this length of the wall in 1579.

The tower has three windows along its northern and southern faces. Locals describe the towers by counting the number of openings along one face, referring to them as eyes, which makes this a three-eyed tower. It once had a wooden roof that supported a second storey, but its central area is now open to the sky.

Derelict Tower The next crumbling tower provides magnificent panoramic views. Looking east, the Huanghua Reservoir is in the foreground. Beyond, four towers dot the wall on its lower slopes, while a battle platform is visible near the summit. The stretch known as Gaping Jaw is in the far distance.

Looking north, a few seemingly solitary watchtowers are in the vicinity of Fenghuangtuo Mountain (1530m). The connecting walls are small in scale and inferior in quality. Looking south, you can see the town of Huanghua and a wide river valley leading towards Huanghuazhen.

Stone Ceiling Tower Larger slabs of igneous rock have been incorporated into the ceiling of this tower. Normally, rock was used only in foundations, with bricks employed throughout the upper levels. Given that the slabs are so large, their presence is difficult to explain; hoisting such heavy slabs into position would have required considerable manpower.

Leave the tower via the western door and follow the wall as it drops through a thick conifer plantation. After 200m and another three-eyed tower, the ramparts cross a valley where a pass existed.

Zhuangdaokou Pass This passageway through the wall, about 2.5m wide, is a brick archway founded on large igneous blocks. The striking engraved tablets on either side of the doorway record the name of the official who laid the tablets in 1577, and the ancient name of the pass, Suppress Captives Pass. Zhuangdaokou was originally fortified in 1404, during the early years of the Ming dynasty.

Zhuangdaokou Pass to Zhuangdaokou Village From the archway, turn south and follow the path downhill. It is about 500m to the village of Zhuangdaokou, a tiny settlement nestled within the walls of ancient barracks. The path is as old as the pass itself, linking the barracks with the wall. As you enter the village, the barracks are the large walled structure on the left.

Follow your nose through the narrow alleyways (note the Cultural Revolution slogans in yellow) to the southern edge of the village, turn left at the bank of the stream, and follow the main road for 1km to a T-junction. Buses for Huairou and Changping leave from here.

Huanghua to Gaping Jaw (4km, Four-Hour Loop) From Shuang Long Zhu Jin Jia (Pair of Dragons Playing with a Pearl) restaurant, walk north for 50m and cross the top of the dam holding back the Huanghua Reservoir. From the far end of the dam, climb up the footpath on the northern side and enter the first tower through one of its north-facing windows. Follow the wall as it climbs sharply to the second and third towers.

The Great Wall

Perfectly Preserved Tower A gradual 200m climb takes you to the fourth tower, which is in exceptionally good condition. On the floor is an engraving dating from the Longqing period (1567–72). Outside the eastern door, a flight of stairs cuts down into the ramparts leading to a perfectly preserved granite archway.

Battle Platform & Panorama Point Exiting the tower, the ramparts climb to a short steep section featuring small observation platforms in front of a large battle platform. This platform, close to the summit, commands a strategic position for cannon fire to the valley below.

From the battle platform, the wall climbs to the summit and then turns north to a tower that provides fine views. Looking north, you can see the distinctive shape of a section of the wall called Gaping Jaw. Looking east, the wall streaks up the Huanghua ridge towards the summit. From the south, the ridge profile looks like a camel's back and is called 'The Camel's Back which Breaks the Wind'.

Ming-Renovated Tower The colour of the top courses of bricks, especially on the southern face of the tower, appears to differ from the rest. Inside, some parts of the brickwork have been repaired with mortar of a different colour. These features suggest that the tower was rebuilt during the later Ming period.

Tablet Tower About 100m downhill is another four-eyed tower. The second chamber on the southern side houses an engraved tablet from 1570. Just before the tower, steps lead from the wall

KH

rings of stone, each ring composed of multiples of nine stones etc). The altar's most mystifying feature is its ability to amplify voices emanating from the centre of the upper terrace.

Just north of the round altar is the **Imperial Vault of Heaven**, which is surrounded by the **Echo Wall**. Sixty-five metres in diameter, the wall allows a whisper to travel clearly from one end to the other.

The crown of the whole complex is the **Hall of Prayer for Good Harvests**. Amazingly, this temple's wooden pillars support the ceiling without nails or cement!

Lama Temple

You'll find colourful frescoes and rich architectural detail are also on display at the exquisite Lama Temple *(Yonghé Gong; Metro: Yonghegong; admission Y15; open 9am-4pm daily)*. The five main halls and 10 exhibition rooms contain countless serene and smiling Buddhas, the most notable of which is the 18m statue of the **Maitreya Buddha** sculpted from a single piece of sandalwood.

The Lama Temple was once the official residence of Count Yin Zhen, who later became emperor and moved to the Forbidden City. In 1744 the buildings were converted to a lamasery. The temple somehow miraculously survived the Cultural Revolution and was 'restocked' with novice monks from Inner Mongolia in the 1980s. Today it is the most important Tibetan Buddhist temple in China (outside of Tibet itself).

The Great Wall

through an archway and down the gully. This easy route back reaches the valley via a small water-pumping station. For a longer walk, exit through the north door and walk around the Gaping Jaw and its steep eastern limb, Sawtooth Slope. The slope is extremely steep and slippery, with parts of the wall crumbling under your feet (or butt) as you walk (or slide).

Barracks to the Main Road Both routes end at the pumping station. From there, walk 50m south-west to the barracks. The barracks once housed up to 200 men stationed to guard this section of the wall, taking advantage of a sheltered position and a water source.

Walk south on the stony track that swings gradually to the west, crossing a concrete waterway after about 600m. Near the pump house, avoid the fork that heads up the bank to the right. Continue on the main track through the walnut and chestnut orchards. The track swings right and eventually hits the road by the post office. Head north to the bridge for transport to Huairou.

Getting There & Away

There is no direct bus to Huanghua, so you must take a public bus or minibus to Huairou from Dongzhimen long-distance bus station in Beijing. Both buses and minivans leave frequently and take just over an hour to get to Huairou (Y5). The bus driver will tell you where to get off if you tell him your intended destination. From Huairou take a minibus directly to Huanghua (Y4) or hire a *miandi* for Y60 return.

KH

Confucian Temple & Imperial College

Just a short distance down the *hutong*, or narrow alley, opposite the entrance to the Lama Temple is the Confucian Temple and Imperial College *(Kong Miào, Guózijian;* W *www.capitalmuseum.com,* ☎ *8401 1977, 13 Guozidian; Metro: Yonghegong; admission Y1; open 8.30am-5pm daily)*. The un-kempt grounds and undisturbed peace are a pleasant contrast to just about every other sight in Beijing. The **steles** in the temple courtyard record the names of those successful in the civil service examinations (possibly the world's first) of the imperial court. The Imperial College was where the emperor annually expounded the Confucian classics to an audience of thousands of kneeling students and professors. It is now the Capital Library.

PLACES TO STAY

Beijing's most atmospheric places to stay are courtyard hotels: they are in Beijing's hutong neighbourhoods and offer a glimpse of more traditional China. It is also worth noting that many places to stay have two standards. All facilities are listed according to their cheapest accommodation available.

Budget

Zhaolong Hotel & International Youth Hostel (☎ *6597 2299, fax 6597 2288,* W *www .zhaolonghotel.com.cn, 2 Gongti Beilu)* Metro: Dongsishitiao. Dorm beds HI members/non-members Y50/60, doubles Y600. Just around

BEIJING

the corner from Beijing's premier nightlife area, this youth hostel is one of the best options available in the city for the budget travellers. The hotel section is also good value and provides all the standard amenities of a hotel.

Red House (☎ 6416 7500, **W** www.red house.com.cn, 10 Taipingzhuang Dajie, Dongzhimenwai) Metro: Dongzhimen. Dorm beds/suites Y70/300. Convenient to the metro, the Red House offers suites that include kitchenettes.

Far East Hotel & International Youth Hostel (☎ 6301 8811, fax 6301 8233, **e** courtyard@dong.com, 90 Tieshuxie Jie, Qianmen Wai) Metro: Hepingmen. Dorm beds HI members/nonmembers Y50/60, doubles with/without bath Y300/160. The Far East has a great location in a vibrant hutong south of Tiananmen Square (at the western end of Dazhalan Jie). The newly opened hostel is set in a colourful courtyard across from the hotel.

Lusongyuan Hotel (☎ 6401 1116, ☎ 6404 0436, fax 6403 0418, 22 Banchang Hutong) Bus No 104 from Beijing train station. Dorm beds/singles/doubles Y100/220/510. Built during the Qing dynasty, this atmospheric courtyard hotel is decorated with traditional Qing and Ming furniture. Hotel guests can rent bicycles here to explore the nearby courtyard complex of Qing Prince Zeng Gelin.

Central Academy of Arts Dormitory (☎ 6513 0926, 8th floor, 5 Xiaowei Hutong) Metro: Wangfujing. Doubles without bath Y120. What this dormitory lacks in style, it makes up for with its location just a block from lively Wangfujing Dajie. Rooms are basic and bathrooms even more so.

Jinghua Hotel (☎ 6722 2211, Nansanhuan Zhonglu, Yongdingmenwai) Bus No 2 or 17 from Qianmen. Dorm beds/doubles Y40/180. Despite being far from the city centre, this hostel was once *the* place for backpackers in Beijing. Although it offers good facilities, the more central options are worth their slightly higher prices.

Mid-Range

Bamboo Garden Hotel (☎ 6403 2229, fax 6401 2633, 24 Xiaoshiqiao Hutong) Metro: Gulou. Singles/doubles/deluxe Y300/380/580. Once the home of the Empress Dowager Cixi's eunuchs, this courtyard hotel is

decorated with traditional Chinese rock gardens and bamboo groves.

Youhao Hotel (☎ 6403 1114, fax 6401 4603, 7 Houyuansi) Bus No 104 from Beijing train station. Singles/doubles Y296/392. This nice but slightly run-down courtyard hotel was at one time the residence of Chiang Kaishek.

Haoyuan Guesthouse (☎/fax 6512 5557, **W** www.women.org.cn/womenorg/hao/index .htm, 53 Shijia Hutong) Metro: Dongdan. Doubles Y400. The All-China Women's Federation owns and operates this quiet, comfortable courtyard hotel, where it offers efficient service to guests in a convenient position.

Fangyuan Hotel (☎ 6525 6331 or 6525 7047, fax 6513 8549, **e** hotel@cbw.com) Metro: Tian'anmendong or Wangfujing. Singles/doubles/suites with breakfast Y126/198/342. The rooms are drab, but good value, considering the air-con, private bath and television.

Top End

Note that top-end hotels will probably tack a 15% service charge onto these prices.

Novotel Peace Hotel (☎ 6512 8833, fax 6512 6863, **e** novotelp@163bj.com, 3 Jinyu Hutong) Metro: Wangfujing. Doubles US$88. Considering its convenient location and the moderate prices for rooms, the Peace Hotel is one of Beijing's better value high-end hotels.

City Hotel Beijing (☎ 6500 7799, fax 6500 7668, 4 Gongti Donglu) Metro: Dongsishitiao. Doubles Y900. Also good value, the City Hotel is midway between Sanlitun and the metro circle line.

Swissôtel (☎ 6501 2288, fax 6501 2501, **e** emailus.beijing@swissotel.com, 2 Chaoyangmen Dajie) Metro: Dongsishitiao. Standard/deluxe US$140/180. Besides its swimming pool and gym, the distinguishing feature of the Swissôtel is its position: not far from Sanlitun, but also very convenient to the metro circle line.

Grand Hotel Beijing (☎ 6513 0057, fax 6513 0050, **e** sales@mail.grandhotelbeijing .com.cn, 35 Dong Chang'an Jie) Metro: Wanfujing. Doubles from US$120. Perhaps Beijing's swankiest hotel, the Grand Hotel has decked out its rooms in an East-meets-West theme. Its central location allows for fabulous views of the Forbidden City.

PLACES TO EAT
Chinese Restaurants
Gongdelin Vegetarian Restaurant (☎ 6511 2542, 158 Qianmen Dajie) Metro: Qianmen. Dinner Y40-60. Open 8.30am-10.30pm. This restaurant makes up for its drab appearance with its colourfully descriptive names and tasty vegetarian food.

Green Angel Vegetarian Restaurant (☎ 6524 2349, 57 Dengshikou Dajie) Dinner Y80-100. The bright interior of this restaurant features famous vegetarians such as Socrates, Einstein, Darwin and Paul Newman. Specialities include Peking 'duck' and sweet and sour 'pork', all made exclusively from soybean products and vegetables.

Liqun Roast Duck Restaurant (☎ 6702 5681, 11 Beixiangfeng Hutong Zhengyi Lu Nankou) Metro: Qianmen. Dinner Y40-60. Open 10am-10pm daily. Squeezed into a traditional courtyard, this homey restaurant is the best place to sample Peking duck (Y68). From Qianmen metro, go east on Qianmen Dongdajie. Walk south along Zhengyi Lu as far as you can, then turn right into the alley and follow the signs. Reservations are required.

Nengrenju (☎ 6601 2560, 5 Taipingqiao, Baitasi, Xicheng) Metro: Fuchengmen. Dinner Y20-40. Nengrenju is a great place to try Mongolian hotpot (which, by the way, is much better in Beijing than anywhere in Mongolia). Originally prepared in the helmets of Mongol warriors, today the custom is for patrons to cook their own dinner in a brass pot with a flame inside.

Non-Chinese Restaurants
If you need a break from Chinese food, you can get it in Beijing.

Metro Café (☎ 6552 7828, 6 Gongti Xilu) Metro: Dongsishitiao. Mains Y40-60. This pleasant cafe offers an impressive selection of fresh pastas and home-made sauces.

Hidden Tree (☎ 6509 3642, 12 Sanlitun Nanlu) Metro: Dongsishitiao. Mains Y30-50. Open 7pm-2am. This pub offers decent bistro fare and pizza and, more importantly, Beijing's widest selection of imported beers.

The Den (☎ 6509 3833, 4 Gongti Donglu) Metro: Dongsishitiao. Brunch Y80. Nightclub 10pm-2am daily, brunch 10.30am-3.30pm weekends. Also a popular nightspot, The Den serves a delicious and hardy Western brunch on weekends.

1,001 Nights (☎ 6532 4050, Gongti Beilu) Metro: Dongsishitiao. Mains Y20-40. Open 11am-2am. This place across from the Zhaolong Hotel is a good option for tasty Middle Eastern food, especially if you get hungry late at night.

Serve the People (☎ 6415 3242, Sanlitun Jiuba Jie) Metro: Dongsishitiao. Mains Y30-50. Open noon-10.30pm. Indeed, serve them Thai food.

Fusion
For upmarket dining, Beijing does have a few exceptional restaurants that serve Chinese-influenced food with a modern twist. Reservations are necessary.

The Courtyard (☎ 6526 8881, 95 Donghuamen Dajie) Metro: Tiananmen Dong. Dinner Y200. Open 6pm-10.30pm. This chic restaurant boasts a stunning view of the Forbidden City. You may also visit the modern art gallery downstairs and the cosy cigar room upstairs.

Red Capital Club (☎ 6402 7150 daytime, ☎ 8401 8886 evenings & weekends, 66 Dongsi Jiu Tiao) Metro: Dongsishitiao. Dinner Y200. This meticulously restored courtyard restaurant serves dishes that each come with their own elaborate myth. Look for the red doors with no sign.

Green Tea House (☎ 6468 5903, 54 Tayuancun, Sanlitun) Metro: Dongsishitiao. Dinner Y200. Open for lunch and dinner, this tiny teahouse is lavishly decorated. Its refined dishes – truly works of art – are delightful to look at and to eat.

Fast Food & Self-Catering
Some of the best and cheapest places to sample local cuisine are the food stalls and local markets.

Dong'anmen Night Market (Dong'anmen Dajie) Metro: Wangfujing. Dishes Y4-8. Open 6pm-9pm daily. The stalls west of Wangfujing Dajie sell typical street food like *zóngzi* (sticky rice in lotus leaves) and *jianbi* (Chinese crepes), as well as more exotic fare, which you may not care to sample.

One block south, *Datianshujing Hutong* has another night market that is filled with aromatic food stalls. This alleyway has been revamped to look like an ancient Chinese village, and an open-air stage often hosts Chinese opera and other traditional performances. Look for the colourful gate leading into the hutong, which is usually packed with Chinese patrons in the evenings.

The Old Railway Station shopping mall, in the south-eastern corner of Tiananmen Square, has a *food court* in its basement, which is a convenient place to stop for a quick, cheap lunch.

First Floor Restaurant (☎ 6303 0268, 83 Qianmen Dajie) Metro: Qianmen. Dishes Y6-10. This centrally located place is good for tasty soup buns and bamboo steamers.

Beijing Noodle King (☎ 6705 6705, 29 Chongwenmenwai Dajie) Dishes Y6-10. As its name suggests, this is the place to try *zhajiang mian* – thick noodles with vegetables and served with a black bean sauce.

At Beijing's supermarkets you will find everything you need for long train journeys. The *Friendship Store (Youyì Shangdiàn)* has a good selection of groceries. Tiny *Jenny Lou's* on Sanlitun's Jiuba Jie is not exactly a supermarket, but it somehow manages to carry all the groceries you might be looking for. More expensive, the *Lufthansa Center* has a great supermarket in the basement packed with imported goods.

ENTERTAINMENT
Opera & Acrobatics

There are several venues to see traditional Chinese performing arts in Beijing.

Poly Plaza (☎ 6500 1188 ext 5127, 14 Dongzhimen Zandajie) Metro: Dongsishitiao. Admission Y80. Performances 7.15pm nightly. Over 2000 years old, acrobatics was one of the few art forms condoned by Mao. See such awe-inspiring acts as 'Swallowing Knives' and 'Jumping through Hoops'.

Zhengyici Theatre (☎ 6303 3104, 220 Xiheyan Dajie, Hepingmen Wai) Metro: Qianmen. Admission Y50. Performances 7.30pm nightly. This ornately decorated theatre is a wonderful place to experience classical Beijing Opera. Most operas have their roots in fairy tales and the legends of classical literature.

Bars & Clubs

Most bars and clubs are open daily from about 7pm, unless otherwise specified.

Palace View (☎ 6515 7788, 35 Dong Chang'an Jie) Open 6pm-10pm daily. As its name suggests, this bar that is in the Grand Hotel enjoys fabulous views of the Forbidden City.

Beijing Opera is a mixture of singing, dancing, speaking, mime and acrobatics.

The Sanlitun area is considered the centre of expat life in Beijing. It includes Sanlitun Lu, known to locals as 'Bar Street'; Sanlitun Nanlu, a narrow alleyway to the west; and the area around the City Hotel near the corner of Gongti Donglu and Gongti Beilu. The streets are lined with outdoor cafes in the summer. Both *Hidden Tree* and *The Den* are two popular bars in this area (see Places to Eat earlier in the chapter).

Public Space (☎ 6416 0759, 50 Sanlitun Lu) Metro: Dongsishitiao. Open 11am-2am. Also an option if you need a late dinner, Public Space attracts a hip crowd for drinks and dancing.

Jam House (☎ 6592 6290, Sanlitun Nanlu) Metro: Dongsishitiao. The principal attractions are the rooftop cafe and the live music downstairs.

Havana Café (☎ 6586 6166, Gongti Beilu) Metro: Dongsishitiao. Adept *salseros* pack the dance floor at this Latin club at the north gate of the Workers Stadium. If you need a break from the action, head to the sangria bar out the back.

CD Café (☎ *6501 8877 ext 3032, Dongsanhuan Lu)* Cover Y20. Open Tues-Sun, performances 9.30pm. This almost-swanky joint is a great place to check out Beijing's jazz music scene.

SHOPPING

Beijing has a huge selection of arts, crafts and antiques, including jewellery, furniture, and carpets. Be aware that many items for sale are not 'genuine'. You need a certificate to take genuine antiques out of China; the item should bear a red wax seal, which allows the owner to export it. The best Beijing bargains include silk and cashmere, brand-name clothing (often fake), and pirated CDs and DVDs. While prices are fixed in the department stores, bargaining is expected – even encouraged – everywhere else.

Wangfujing Metro: Wangfujing. This lively pedestrian way is two blocks east of the Forbidden City. Its name, meaning 'Well of Princely Palaces' derives from the 15th century, when this area was the site of several palaces occupied by 10 Ming princes. The royal palaces have since been destroyed to make way for the palaces of the people. The Oriental Plaza at the southern end and Xindong'an Plaza at the northern end are massive shopping malls that dominate this street.

Dazhalan Metro: Qianmen. A colourful hutong off Qianmen Dajie, Dazhalan is a heady jumble of silk shops, tea and herbal medicine shops, theatres and restaurants. Also known as 'Silk Street', it is a hangover from when specialised products were sold in particular areas. Good places to buy silk include *Ruifuxian* (☎ *6303 2808, 5 Dazhalan)* and the *Beijing Silk Shop* (☎ *6301 6658, 5 Zhubaoshi, Qianmen Dajie).*

Liulichang Metro: Hepingmen. Just west of Dazhalan, this tree-lined street has been designed to look like an ancient Chinese village, and it is a pleasant place to stroll and take photos. Liulichang, meaning 'glazed-tile factory', is crowded with shops selling Chinese paintings, calligraphy materials, art books and ceramics.

Dirt Market (*Panjiayuan)* Open dawn-2pm Sat & Sun. This weekend market is a great place to shop for arts, crafts and antiques. Its stalls are packed with carved furniture, hand-painted teapots, bronze Buddhas, Ming vases and Tibetan carpets.

On the outskirts, Mao paraphernalia and colourful kites are spread out over the ground. Come early and bargain hard.

For brand-name clothing, visit *Xiushui Silk Market* (*Jianguomenwai Dajie)*, which is between the Friendship Store and the Jianguo Hotel.

GETTING THERE & AWAY

The Trans-Mongolian departs from Beijing once a week (Wednesday), with additional weekly trains to Ulaan Baatar (Tuesday, 30 hours). The Trans-Manchurian also departs from Beijing once a week (Saturday). Two express trains per day go to Harbin (14 hours). In summer, tickets are very hard to come by. Even domestic tickets should be booked a week in advance (although it is possible to get them on shorter notice, with some luck). BTG and other travel agencies buy up blocks of tickets, so call around to see who has what available.

See the Getting There & Away chapter for more information and lists of travel agencies.

GETTING AROUND

The Trans-Mongolian and Trans-Manchurian trains both arrive at the Beijing main train station, which is a stop on the circle metro line (Beijing Zhan). A taxi from Beijing train station to the city centre or to the Sanlitun area should be less than Y20 if you can find a driver who will use the meter.

The airport is 27km from the city centre. A service desk inside the airport terminal sells tickets for buses (Y16) into town. Buses leave every half-hour between 5.30am and 7pm, and include routes to Beijing train station, Xidan metro and the China Art Gallery north of Wangfujing Dajie. A taxi should cost only about Y85 from the airport to the centre (including the Y15 road toll).

In general the metro is a hassle-free way to get around the centre of Beijing. It operates from 5.30am to 10.30pm and the fare is a flat Y3. Signs are in English and easy to understand. Stations are marked by a blue sign with the capital 'D'. Unfortunately, the hours of operation and two meagre lines limit its effectiveness under many circumstances.

Taxis are also a cost-effective means of getting around the city. The standard per-kilometre charge ranges from Y1.20 to Y2, with a Y10 minimum. Make sure your driver turns on the meter, especially coming from the airport or the train station. Most taxi drivers do not speak English (although they may be listening to English language tapes in preparation for the 2008 Olympics). Nor will they understand you if you try to pronounce your destination in Chinese. Your best bet is to have somebody write down your destination so you can show it to your taxi driver.

To get around the city in true Beijing style, consider riding a bicycle, which can be rented from many hotels, especially those in the budget range. Alternatively, the Dazhalan Bicycle Rental Shop (☎ 6303 5303) is just inside the gate at the western end of the Dazhalan Jie.

Language

Russian

Just about everyone in Russia speaks Russian, though there are also dozens of other languages spoken by ethnic minorities. Russian and most of the other languages are written in variants of the Cyrillic alphabet. It's easy to find English-speakers in the big cities but not so easy in small towns (sometimes not even in tourist hotels).

For a more detailed guide to the language, get a copy of Lonely Planet's *Russian phrasebook*.

Useful Words & Phrases

Two words you're sure to use are Здравствуйте (*zdrastvuyte*), the universal 'hello' (but if you say it a second time in one day to the same person, they'll think you forgot you already saw them!), and Пожалуйста (*pazhalsta*), the multipurpose word for 'please' (commonly included in all polite requests), 'you're welcome', 'pardon me', 'after you', 'here you are' and more.

Good morning.
dobrae utra Доброе утро.
Good afternoon.
dobry den' Добрый день.
Good evening.
dobry vecher Добрый вечер.
Goodbye.
da svidaniya До свидания.
Goodbye (informal).
paka Пока.
How are you?
kak dela? Как дела?
Yes.
dat Да.
No.
net Нет.

What's your name?
kak vas zavut? Как вас зовут?
My name is ...
menya zavut ... Меня зовут ...
Thank you (very much).
(bal'shoe) spasiba
(Большое) спасибо.
Pardon me.
prastite, pazhalsta
Простите, пожалуйста.

No problem/Never mind.
nichevo (literally, 'nothing')
Ничего.
Do you speak English?
vy gavarite pa angliski?
Вы говорите по-английски?
Please write it down.
zapishite, pazhalsta
Запишите, пожалуйста.
I don't understand.
ya ne panimayu
Я не понимаю.
Can you help me please?
pamagite, pazhalsta
Помогите, пожалуйста.
I need ...
mne nuzhna ...
Мне нужно ...
How much is it?
skol'ka stoit?
Сколько стоит?
Do you have ...?
u vas est'...?
У вас есть ...?
Where is ...?
gde ...?
Где ...?

hotel
gastinitsa гостиница
room
nomer номер
telephone
telefon телефон
toilet
tualet туалет
(Men)
muzhskoy Мужской (М)
(Women)
zhenskiy Женский (Ж)

How much is a room?
skol'ka stoit nomer?
Сколько стоит номер?
Do you have a cheaper room?
u vas net nichevo padeshevle?
У вас нет ничего подешевле?

Train Talk

I want to go to ...
ya khachu ekhat' v ...
Я хочу ехать в ...

The Cyrillic Alphabet

А а	a	as in 'path'
Б б	b	as in 'bit'
В в	v	as the 'v' in 'vet'
Г г	g	as in 'get'
Д д	d	as in 'day'
Е е	ye	as the 'ye' in 'yet'
	yö	as the 'yea' in 'yearn' (in Mongolian only)
Ё ё	yo	as in 'yonder'
Ж ж	j	as the 's' in 'pleasure'
З з	z	as in 'zoo'
И и	i	as in 'litre'
Й й	i	as in 'litre'
К к	k	as in 'king'
Л л	l	as in 'lamp'
М м	m	as in 'my'
Н н	n	as in 'not'
О о	o	as in British 'hot'
Ө ө	ö	long, as the 'u' in 'fur'
П п	p	as in 'put'
Р р	r	as in 'rub'
С с	s	as in 'sit'
Т т	t	as in 'ton'
У у	u	as the 'ou' in 'source'
Y y	ü	as the 'o' in 'who'
Ф ф	f	as in 'fun'
Х х	kh	as the 'ch' in Scottish *loch*
Ц ц	ts	as in 'hits'
Ч ч	ch	as in 'chip'
Ш ш	sh	as in 'shoe'
Щ щ	shch	as 'sh ch' in 'fresh chips'
Ь ь	'	* 'soft' sign (see below)
Ы ы	y	as the 'i' in 'ill'
Ъ ъ		* 'hard' sign (see below)
Э э	e	as in 'den'
Ю ю	yu	as the word 'you'
	yü	as 'yu' or as 'yo' (in Mongolian only)
Я я	ya	as the 'ya' in 'yard'

* The letters ь and ъ never occur alone, but simply affect the pronunciation of the previous letter – ь makes the preceding consonant sound as if there is a short 'y' after it; ъ prevents the preceding consonant being pronounced as if there is a 'y' after it, but it's quite rare to see this letter.

When is the next train?
kagda sleduyushiy poest?
Когда следующий поезд?

When does it leave?
kagda atpravlyaetsya?
Когда отправляется?
Are there SV/kupe/platskartny tickets on train no ... to ...?
est' bilety dlya es ve/dlya kupe/f platskarte na poest nomer ... na ...?
Есть билеты для СВ/для купе/ в плацкарте на поезд номер ... до ...?
I'd like to buy an SV/kupe/platstkartny ticket for train no ... to ...
ya khatel (m)/khatela (f) by kupit' bilet dlya es ve/dlya kupe/f platskarte na poest nomer ... na ...
Я хотел/хотела бы купить билет для СВ/для купе/в плацкарте на поезд номер ... до ...
Which platform does the train leave from?
s kakoy platformy atkhodit poest?
С какой платформы отходит поезд?
Please tell me why I can't buy a ticket.
skazhyte, pazhalsta, pachemu ya ne magu kupit' bileta!
Скажите, пожалуйста, почему я не могу купить билета!
There's no train today.
sevodnya ne budet paezda
Сегодня не будет поезда.
The train is full. (lit: All tickets are sold.)
fse bilety na etat poest prodany
Все билеты на этот поезд проданы.
There are no SV/kupe/platskartny tickets left for the train.
bilety dlya es ve/dlya kupe/f platskarte uzhe fse raspradalis'
Билеты для СВ/для купе/в плацкарте уже все распродались.
Tickets for that service aren't on sale until ...
bilety na etat gorat budut na pradazhe s ...
Билеты на этот город будут на продаже с ...
You're at the wrong ticket window. Please go to window ...
vy staite ne f tom meste
abrashyaytes' k akoshku ...!
Вы стоите не в том месте.
Обращайтесь к окошку ...!

train station
zheleznadarozhnyy vagzal
железнодорожный (ж. д.) вокзал
ticket/tickets
bilet/bilety　　　билет/билеты

one-way
  v adin kanets,   в один конец,
  ediny   единый
return, round-trip
  tuda i abratna,   туда и обратно,
  abratny   обратный
baggage
  bagazh   багаж
arrival
  pribytie   прибытие
departure
  atpravlenie   отправление

Time, Days & Numbers

When?
  kagda?   Когда?
today
  sevodnya   сегодня
yesterday
  vchera   вчера
tomorrow
  zaftra   завтра
day after tomorrow
  poslezaftra   послезавтра

Monday
  panedel'nik   понедельник
Tuesday
  ftornik   вторник
Wednesday
  sreda   среда
Thursday
  chetverk   четверг
Friday
  pyatnitsa   пятница
Saturday
  subota   суббота
Sunday
  vaskresen'e   воскресенье

January
  janvar'   январь
February
  fevral'   февраль
March
  mart   март
April
  aprel'   апрель
May
  may   май
June
  iyun'   июнь
July
  iyul'   июль
August
  avgust   август

Emergencies – Russian	
I'm ill.	
ya bolin (m)	Я болен.
ya bal'na (f)	Я больна.
I need a doctor.	
mne nuzhin vrach	Мне нужен врач.
hospital	
bal'nitsa	больница
police	
militsiya	милиция
Help!	
na pomashch'!/	На помощь!/
pamagiti!	Помогите!
Thief!	
vor!	Вор!

September
  sentabr'   сентябрь
October
  aktabr'   октябрь
November
  nayabr'   ноябрь
December
  dekabr'   декабрь

How many?
  skol'ka   Сколько?

0	*nol'*	ноль
1	*adin*	один
2	*dva*	два
3	*tri*	три
4	*chityri*	четыре
5	*pyat'*	пять
6	*shest'*	шесть
7	*sem'*	семь
8	*vosem'*	восемь
9	*devit'*	девять
10	*desit'*	десять
11	*adinatsat'*	одиннадцать
12	*dvenatsat'*	двенадцать
13	*trunatsat'*	тринадцать
20	*dvatsat'*	двадцать
21	*dvatsat' adin*	двадцать один
30	*tritsat'*	тридцать
40	*sorak*	сорок
50	*pyat'desyat*	пятьдесят
60	*shest'desyat*	шестьдесят
70	*sem'desyat*	семьдесят
80	*vosemdesyat*	восемьдесят
90	*divyanosta*	девяносто
100	*sto*	сто
200	*dvesti*	двести
1000	*tysyacha*	тысяча

Chinese

The Chinese spoken in Manchuria is the dialect spoken in Beijing. It is the official language of the PRC and is usually referred to in the west as 'Mandarin' – the Chinese call it *putonghua* (common speech).

For a more detailed guide to the language, get a copy of Lonely Planet's *Mandarin phrasebook*.

Pronunciation

Chinese is a tone language. This means that variations in pitch within syllables are used to determine word meaning. For example, in Mandarin the word *ma* can have several different meanings, depending on which tone is used:

high tone: *mā*, 'mother'
rising tone: *má*, 'hemp' or 'numb'
falling-rising tone: *mǎ*, 'horse'
falling tone: *mà*, 'scold' or 'swear'

In pinyin, apostrophes are occasionally used to separate syllables, eg, *ping'an* prevents the word being pronounced as *pin'gan*. The English 'v' sound doesn't occur in Chinese. For beginners, the trickiest sounds are **c**, **q** and **x** because their pronunciation isn't remotely similar to English.

c	as the 'ts' in 'bits'
ch	as in 'church', but with the tongue curled back
h	guttural, a bit like the 'ch' of 'loch'
q	as the 'ch' in 'chicken'
r	as the 's' in 'pleasure'
sh	as in 'ship', but with the tongue curled back
x	as the 'sh' in 'ship'
z	as the 'ds' in 'suds'
zh	as the 'j' in 'judge' but with the tongue curled back

Useful Words & Phrases

Hello.
   nǐ hǎo 你好
Goodbye.
   zàijiàn 再见
Thank you.
   xièxie 谢谢
You're welcome.
   búkèqi 不客气
I'm sorry.
   duìbùqǐ 对不起

May I ask your name?
   nín guìxìng? 您贵姓?
My (sur)name is ...
   wǒ xìng ... 我姓 ...
Where are you from?
   nǐ shì cōng 你是从 ...
   nǎr láide? 哪儿来的?
I'm from ...
   wǒ shì cōng ... láide 我是从 ... 来的
No. (don't have)
   méi yǒu 没有
No. (not so)
   búshì 不是
No, I don't want it.
   búyào 不要
I don't understand.
   wǒ tīngbudǒng 我听不懂
Could you speak more slowly please?
   qīng nǐ shuō màn 请你说慢
   yīdiǎn, hǎo ma? 一点，好吗?

In Town

How much is it?
   duōshǎo qián? 多少钱?
That's too expensive.
   tài guìle 太贵了
Bank of China
   zhōngguó yínháng 中国银行
change money
   huàn qián 换钱
telephone
   diànhuà 电话
Where is the ...?
   ... zài nǎlǐ? ... 在哪里?
hotel
   lǚguǎn 旅馆
tourist hotel
   bīnguǎn/fàdiàn/ 宾馆/饭店/
   jiǔdiàn 酒店
Is there a room vacant?
   yǒu méiyǒu kōng 有没有空房间?
   fángjiān?
Yes, there is/No, there isn't.
   yǒu/méiyǒu 有/没有
single room
   dānrénfáng 单人房
twin room
   shuāngrénfáng 双人房
toilet (restroom)
   cèsuǒ? 厕所
Men/Women 男/女
toilet paper
   wèishēng zhǐ 卫生纸
bathroom (washroom)
   xǐshǒu jiān 洗手间

21	*èrshíyī*	二十一
100	*yìbǎii*	一百
200	*liǎngbǎi*	两百
1000	*yìqiān*	一千

Emergencies – Chinese

I'm sick.
　wǒ shēng bìng 　我生病
Help!
　jiùmìng a! 　救命啊
Thief!
　xiǎo tōu! 　小偷
emergency
　jǐnjí qíngkuàng 　紧急情况
hospital
　yīyuàn 　医院
police
　jǐngchá 　警察
foreign affairs police
　wàishì jǐngchá 　外事警察

Train Talk

train station
　huǒchē zhàn 　火车站
ticket office
　shòupiào chù 　售票处
I want to go to ...
　wǒ yào qù ... 　我要去 ...
buy a ticket
　mǎi piào 　买票
one ticket
　yìzhāng piào 　一张票
two tickets
　liǎngzhāng piào 　两张票
hard-seat
　yìngxí/yìngzuò 　硬席/硬座
soft-seat
　ruǎnxí/ruǎnzuò 　软席/软座
hard-sleeper
　yìngwò 　硬卧
soft-sleeper
　ruǎnwò 　软卧

Numbers

0	*líng*	零
1	*yī/yāoo*	一/幺
2	*èr/liǎng*	二/两
3	*sān*	三
4	*sì*	四
5	*wǔ*	五
6	*liù*	六
7	*qī*	七
8	*bā*	八
9	*jiǔ*	九
10	*shí*	十
11	*shíyī*	十一
12	*shí'èr*	十二
20	*èrshí*	二十

Mongolian

The official national language is Mongolian, a member of the Ural-Altaic family of languages, which includes Finnish, Turkish, Kazak, Uzbek and Korean. Since 1944, the Russian Cyrillic alphabet has been used to write Mongolian. The only difference between Mongolian and Russian Cyrillic is that the Mongolian version has two additional characters, for a total of 35. See the Cyrillic alphabet chart in the Russian section of this chapter.

Double vowels indicate that the vowel is stressed. The Mongolian letters ө and γ are not found in Russian Cyrillic. For pronunciation guidelines, see the Cyrillic alphabet chart in the Russian section of this chapter.

For a more detailed look at the language, get a copy of Lonely Planet's *Mongolian phrasebook*.

Useful Words & Phrases

Hello, how are you?
　*sain baina **uu**?*
　Сайн байна уу?
Fine – and you?
　*sain ta sain baina **uu**?*
　Сайн. Та сайн байна уу?
Goodbye.
　*bayart**ai***
　Баяртай.
What's your name?
　tany nerig khen gedeg ve?
　Таны нэрийг хэн гэдэг вэ?
My name is ...
　*min**ii** neriig ... gedeg*
　Миний нэрийг ... гэдэг.
Yes.
　*t**ii**m*
　Тийм.
No.
　*üg**üi***
　Үгүй.
Thanks.
　*bayarlal**aa***
　Баярлалаа.
I'm sorry/Excuse me.
　*uuchl**aa**rai*
　Уучлаарай.

Emergencies – Mongolian

Help!
   tuslaarai!
   Туслаарай!
Call a doctor!
   emch duudaarai!
   Эмч дуудаарай!
I'm ill.
   minii biye övdöj baina
   Миний бие өвдөж байна.

Do you speak English?
   ta angilar yairdag uu?
   Та англиар ярьдаг уу?
I don't understand.
   bi oilgokhgüi baina
   Би ойлгохгүй байна.
What times does the train leave/arrive?
   galt tereg kheden tsagt yavdag/irdeg ve?
   Галт тэрэг хэдэн цагт явдаг/ирдэг вэ?

hotel
   zochid buudal
   зочид буудал
Do you have any rooms available?
   tanaid sul öröö baina uu?
   Танайд сул өрөө байна уу?
I'd like a single room.
   bi neg khünii öröö avmaar baina
   Би нэг хүний өрөө авмаар байна.
I'd like a double room.
   bi khoyor khünii öröö avmaar baina
   Би хоёр хүний өрөө авмаар байна.
What's the price per night/week?
   ene öröö khonogt/doloo khonogt yamar üntei ve?
   Энэ өрөө хоногт/долоо хоногт ямар үнэтэй вэ?
Where's the toilet?
   biye zasakh gazar khaana baidag ve?
   Бие засах газар хаана байдаг вэ?
Do you have a (town) map?
   tanaid (khotyn) zurag baina uu?
   Танайд (хотын) зураг байна уу?

Glossary

You may encounter some of the following words and abbreviations during your travels in Russia, China and Mongolia. See the special food and drink section for words that will help you while dining.

RUSSIA

aeroport – airport
apteka – pharmacy
avtobus – bus
avtomat – automatic ticket machine
avtostantsiya – bus stop
avtovokzal – bus terminal

babushka – grandmother
BAM – Baikalo-Amurskaya Magistral (a Trans-Siberian rail route)
bankomat – automatic teller machine (ATM)
banya – bathhouse
bashnya – tower
benzin – petrol
biblioteka – library
bilet – ticket
biznesmen/biznesmenka – literally, a businessman/-woman, but often used to mean a small-time operator on the fringe of the law
bolnitsa – hospital
boyar – high-ranking noble
bulvar – boulevard

CIS – Commonwealth of Independent States; an alliance (proclaimed in 1991) of independent states comprising the former USSR republics, with the exception of the three Baltic countries

dacha – country cottage, summer house
datsan – Buddhist monastery
deklaratsia – customs declaration
detsky – child's, children's
dezhurnaya – woman looking after a particular floor of a hotel
dom – house
dorogoy – expensive
duma – parliament
dvorets – palace
dvorets kultury – literally 'culture palace'; a meeting, social, entertainment or education centre, usually for a group like railway workers, children etc

elektrichka – suburban train
etazh – floor (storey)

GAI (Gosudarstvennaya Avtomobilnaya Inspektsia) – State Automobile Inspectorate (traffic police)
gallereya – gallery
gavan – harbour
gazeta – newspaper
glavpochtamt – main post office
gora – mountain
gorod – city, town
gostinitsa – hotel
gostiny dvor – trading arcade
granitsa – border
Gulag (Glavnoe Upravlenie Lagerey) – Main Administration for Camps; the Soviet network of concentration camps
GUM (Gosudarstvenny Univermag) – State Department Store

inostranets – foreigner
Intourist – the old Soviet State Committee for Tourism, now hived off, split up and in competition with hundreds of other travel agencies
izba – traditional single-storey wooden cottage

kamera khraneniya – left-luggage office
karta – map
kassa – ticket office, cashier's desk
kemping – camping ground, often with small cabins as well as tent sites
KGB (Komitet Gosydarstvennoy Bezopasnosti) – Committee of State Security
kholm – hill
khram – church
kino – cinema
kladbishche – cemetery
klyuch – key
kniga – book (plural *knigi*)
Komsomol – Communist Youth League
komnaty otdykha – literally 'rest rooms'; cheap lodgings in Siberian railway stations
kopek – kopeck; the smallest, worthless unit of Russian currency
kray – territory
krazha – theft
kreml – kremlin, a town's fortified stronghold
krugovoy – round trip
kupe – compartment (on a train)

kvartira – flat, apartment
kvitantsia – receipt

lavra – senior monastery
les – forest
lyux – a *lyux* room in a hotel is a kind of suite, with a sitting room in addition to the bedroom and bathroom

Mafia – anyone who has anything to do with crime, from genuine gangsters to victims of their protection rackets; also applied to anyone who's successful at anything (no-one believes they could have done it legally)
magazin – shop
manezh – riding school
marka – postage stamp or brand, trademark
marshrut – route
marshrutki, marshrutnoe taxi – minibus that runs along a fixed route
mashina – car
matryoshka – set of painted wooden dolls within dolls
mavzoley – mausoleum
mestnoe vremya – local time
mesto – place, seat
mezhdugorodnyy – intercity
mezhdunarodnaya kassa – international ticket office
militsia – police
more – sea
morskoy vokzal – sea terminal
Moskovskoe vremya – Moscow time
most – bridge
muzey – museum; also some palaces, art galleries and nonworking churches
muzhskoy – men's (toilet)

naberezhnaya – embankment
nomenklatura – literally 'list of nominees'; the old government and Communist Party elite
novy – new

oblast – region
obmen valyuty – currency exchange
okrug – district
ostanovka – bus stop
ostrov – island
OVIR (Otdel Viz I Registratsii) – Department of Visas & Registration
ozero – lake

pamyatnik – monument, statue
Paskha – Easter

passazhirskiy poezd – intercity stopping train
pereryv – break (when shops, ticket offices, restaurants etc close for an hour or two during the day; this always happens just as you arrive)
pereulok – lane
peshchera – cave
plan goroda – city map
ploshchad – square
plyazh – beach
pochta, pochtamt – post office
poezd – train
poliklinika – medical centre
posolstvo – embassy
prichal – landing, pier
prigorodny poezd – suburban train
prodazha – sale
proezd – passage
propusk – permit, pass
prospekt – avenue
provodnik (m), **provodnitsa** (f) – carriage attendant on a train

rayon – district
rechnoy vokzal – river terminal
reka – river
remont, na remont – closed for repairs (a sign you see all too often)
Rozhdestvo – Christmas
rubl – rouble
ruchnoy – handmade
rynok – market

sad – garden
samolyot – aeroplane
samovar – urn with an inner tube filled with hot charcoal used for heating water for tea
sanitarny den – literally 'sanitary day'; the monthly day on which a shop, museum, restaurant, hotel dining room etc shuts down for cleaning
schyot – bill
selo – village
sever – north
shlagbaum – checkpoint, barrier
shosse – highway
shtuka – piece (many produce items are sold by the piece)
skhema transporta – transport map
skoryy poezd – literally, fast train; a long-distance train
sobor – cathedral
Sodruzhestvo Nezavisimykh Gosudarstv (SNG) – Commonwealth of Independent States (CIS)

soviet – council
spravka – certificate
stary – old
suvenir – souvenir

taiga – northern pine, fir, spruce and larch forest
talon – bus ticket, coupon
teatr – theatre
traktir – tavern
tramvay – tram
troyka – vehicle drawn by three horses
tserkov – church
tsirk – circus
TsUM (Tsentralny Univermag) – name of department store
tualet – toilet
tuda i obratno – 'there and back', return ticket

ulitsa – street
univermag, universalnyy magazin – department store
valyuta – foreign currency
velosiped – bicycle
vkhod – way in, entrance
vodny vokzal – ferry terminal
vokzal – station
vorovstvo – theft
vostok – east
vrach – doctor
vykhod – way out, exit
vykhodnoy den – day off (Saturday, Sunday and holidays)
yezhednevno – every day
yug – south

zakaz – reservation
zal – hall, room
zaliv – gulf, bay
zamok – castle, fortress
zapad – west
zapovednik – (nature) reserve
zheleznodorozhnyy vokzal – train station
zhenskiy – women's (toilet)
zheton – token (for metro etc)

CHINA
bei – north
binguan – tourist hotel

CAAC – Civil Aviation Administration of China, which controls most of China's domestic and foreign airlines
CCP – Chinese Communist Party, founded in Shanghai in 1921

CITS – China International Travel Service
CTS – China Travel Service
cün – village

dajie – avenue
danwei – work unit, the cornerstone of China's social structure
dong – east

fandian – a hotel or restaurant
fen – one tenth of a jiao, in Chinese currency

Gang of Four – members of a clique headed by Mao's wife Jiang Qing, who were blamed for the disastrous Cultural Revolution
gongyuan – park

hu – lake
hutong – narrow alleyway

jiao – one-tenth of a yuan, in Chinese currency
jie – street
jiudiàn – hotel

kuài – a colloquial term for the currency, yuan
Kuomintang – Chiang Kaishek's Nationalist Party, the dominant political force after the fall of the Qing dynasy; now Taiwan's major political party

lu – road

Manchus – non-Chinese ethnic group from Manchuria (present-day north-east China) which took over China and established the Qing dynasty (AD 1644–1911)
miandi – 'bread taxi', yellow microbuses now banned in Beijing

nan – south

Peking – the spelling of 'Beijing' before the Communists adopted the Pinyin romanisation system in 1958
Pinyin – the system of writing the Chinese language in the roman alphabet adopted by the Communist Party in 1958
PLA – People's Liberation Army
Politburo – the 25-member supreme policy-making authority of the CCP
PRC – People's Republic of China
PSB – Public Security Bureau; the arm of the police force that deals with foreigners

Red Guards – a pro-Mao faction who persecuted rightists during the Cultural Revolution

renminbi – literally 'people's money', the formal name for the currency of China; shortened to RMB

siheyuan – traditional courtyard house

stele – stone slab or column decorated with figures or inscription

tael – unit of weight, one tael equals 37.5g and there are 16 tael to the catty

xi – west

yuan – the Chinese unit of currency, also referred to as RMB

MONGOLIA

aimag – province or state within Mongolia

airag – fermented horse's milk

arat – herdsman

arkhi – the common word to describe home-made vodka

bag – village, a subdivision of a sum

Bogd Gegen – hereditary line of reincarnated Buddhist leaders of Mongolia, the third highest in the Buddhist hierarchy, which started with Zanabazar

Bogd Khaan (Holy King) – title given to the 8th Bogd Gegen (1869-1924)

del – the all-purpose, traditional coat or dress worn by men and women

delgüür – shop

dorno – east

ger – traditional, circular felt yurt

gol – river

guanz – canteen or cheap restaurant

gudamj – street

hard seat – used to describe the standard seat in 2nd-class train carriages

hashaa – fenced-in ger, often found in suburbs

Inner Mongolia – a separate province within China

izba – traditional single-storey wooden house

Jebtzun Damba – also known as Bogd Gegen, a hereditary line of reincarnated spiritual leaders of Mongolia. The first was Zanabazar and the eighth was the Bogd Khan

Kazakh – Turkic ethnic group from Central Asia, also found in the west of Mongolia; people from Kazakhstan

khaan – a king or chief

khagan – great khaan

khaganate – pre-Mongol empire

Khalkh – the major ethnic group living in Mongolia

khiid – Buddhist monastery

khoomi – traditional form of Mongolian singing, commonly referred to as throat singing

khorol – traditional Mongolian game similar to checkers (draughts)

khot – city

kumiss – the Russian word for *airag*

lama – Tibetan Buddhist monk or priest

Lamaism – properly known as Vajramana, or Tibetan Buddhism

Living Buddha – common term for reincarnations of Buddhas; Buddhist spiritual leader in Mongolia

morin khuur – horse-head fiddle

MPRP – Mongolian People's Revolutionary Party

Naadam – game; the Naadam festival

nuruu – mountain range

ömnö – south

örgön chölöö – avenue

örnöd – west

Outer Mongolia – northern Mongolia as it was called during Manchurian rule (the term is not currently used to describe Mongolia)

ovoo – shamanistic collection of stones, wood or other offerings to the gods, usually placed in high places

shagai – traditional Mongolian dice game

stupa – Buddhist religious monument composed of a solid hemisphere topped by a spire, containing relics of the Buddha; also known as a pagoda, or *suburgan* in Mongolian

sum – administrative unit smaller than an aimag; a district

süm – Buddhist temple

takhi – a wild horse; also known as Przewalski's horse

tögrög – unit of currency in Mongolia

töv – central
Tsagaan Sar – 'white moon' or 'white month'; a festival to celebrate the start of the lunar year

ulaan – red
umard – north
uul – mountain
urtyn-duu – traditional singing style

yurt – Russian word for ger

zakh – market
zud – particularly bad winter, as experienced in 1999/2000

Food & Drink

RUSSIA
антрекот *(antrikot)* – entrecote, boned sirloin steak

баранина *(baranina)* – mutton
бефстроганов *(befstroganof)* – beef Stroganoff, beef slices in a rich sauce
бифштекс *(bifshteks)* – 'steak', usually a glorified hamburger filling
блины *(bliny)*, **блинчики** *(blinchiki)* – pancakes with sweet or savoury fillings
борщ *(borshch)* – beetroot soup with vegetables and meat
буфет *(bufyet)* – snack bar selling cheap cold meats, boiled eggs, salads, bread, pastries etc
булочная *(bulachnaya)* – bakery
бутерброд *(butirbrod)* – open sandwich

чай *(chai)* – tea

фрукты *(frukti)* – fruit

говядина *(gavyadina)* – beef
гастроном *(gastronom)* – speciality food shop
грибы *(griby)* – mushrooms

икра *(ikra)* – caviar

кафе *(kafe)* – cafe
каша *(kasha)* – buckwheat porridge
кефир *(kyifir)* – yogurt-like sour milk, served as a drink
хлеб *(khlep)* – bread
кофе *(kofe)* – coffee
компот *(kampot)* – fruit in syrup

коньяк *(kan'yak)* – brandy
котлета *(katlety)* – usually a croquette of ground meat
котлета по-киевски *(katlety pakiefski)* – chicken Kiev, fried boneless chicken breast stuffed with garlic butter
курица *(kuritsa)* – chicken
квас *(kvas)* – kvas, beer-like drink

лапша *(lapsha)* – chicken noodle soup

масло *(masla)* – butter
минеральная вода *(mineral'naya vada)* – mineral water
молоко *(malako)* – milk
мороженое *(marozhenae)* – ice cream
мясо *(myasa)* – meat

обед *(abyed)* – lunch
окрошка *(akroshka)* – cold or hot soup made from cucumbers, sour cream, potatoes, egg, meat and *kvas*
омлет *(amlet)* – omelette
омул *(omul)* – salmon-like fish from Lake Baikal
овощи *(ovashchi)* – vegetables

пельмени *(pilmyeni)* – small dumplings usually filled with meat
пирожное *(pirozhnaya)* – pastries
пиво *(piva)* – beer
плов *(plov)* – *pilaf*, rice with diced mutton and vegetables
птица *(ptitsa)* – poultry
перец *(perets)* pepper

ресторан *(restoran)* – restaurant
рис *(ris)* – rice
рыба *(riba)* – fish

сахар *(sakhar)* – sugar
салат *(sulat)* – salad
сыр *(syr)* – cheese
шампанское *(shampanskaya)* – sparkling wine
шашлык *(shashlyk)* – skewered and grilled mutton or other meat
щи *(shchi)* – cabbage soup or sauerkraut (many varieties)
сырники *(syrniki)* – fritters of cottage cheese, flour and egg
сметана *(smitana)* – sour cream
сок *(sok)* – juice
соль *(sol)* – salt
солянка *(salyanka)* – thick meat or fish soup with salted cucumbers and other vegetables

свинина *(sfinyna)* – pork
столовая *(stalovaya)* – canteen, cafeteria
ужин *(uzhin)* – supper

вода *(vada)* – water
вареники *(varyeniki)* – Ukrainian dumplings, with a variety of possible fillings
яйцо *(yaytsa)* – egg
   всмятку *(fsmyatku)* – soft-boiled
   крутое *(krutoye)* – hard-boiled
   яйчница *(yuichnitsa)* – fried

завтрак *(zaftrak)* – breakfast
закуски *(zakuski)* – appetisers, often grouped into: **холодные** *(kholodnye)* – cold; **горячие** *(goryachiye)* – hot

CHINA
bāozi 包子 – steamed meat bun
běijīng kǎoyā 北京烤鸭 – Beijing Duck
chá 茶 – tea
dànhuā tāng 蛋花汤 – egg & vegetable soup
dòufǔ cài tāng 豆腐菜汤 – bean curd & vegetable soup
gōngbào jūdīng 宫爆鸡丁 – spicy hot chicken with peanuts
guǒzhī 果汁 – fruit juice
jiǎozi 饺子 – dumplings
jiàng bào jī dīng 酱爆鸡丁 – stir-fried chicken with bamboo shoots
jīdàn chǎofàn 鸡蛋炒饭 – fried rice with egg
kuàng quán shuǐ 矿泉水 – mineral water
mántou 馒头 – steamed bun
mǐfàn 米饭 – steamed white rice
mǐfěn 米粉 – rice noodles
mógū dòufǔ 蘑菇豆腐 – bean curd & mushrooms
pújiǔ 啤酒 – beer
qīng tāng 清汤 – clear soup
qīngjiāo niúròu piàn 青椒牛肉片 – beef with green peppers
qīngxiāng shā wǔ jī 清香沙捂鸡 – chicken wrapped in lotus leaf
sān měi dòufu 三美豆腐 – bean curd & Chinese cabbage
shíjǐn chǎofàn 什锦炒饭 – fried rice
shūcài chǎomiàn 蔬菜炒面 – fried noodles with vegetables
sùchǎo qīngcài 素炒青菜 – fried green vegetables
sùshāo qiézi 素烧茄子 – fried eggplant

xīhóngshì chǎo jīdàn 西红柿炒鸡蛋 – fried tomatoes & eggs
yuán bào lǐjī 元爆里脊 – stir-fried pork with coriander
zhàcài ròusī miàn 榨菜肉丝面 – noodles, pork & mustard greens

MONGOLIA
байцаан зууш *(baitsaan zuush)* – cabbage salad
банштай шөл *(banshtai shöl)* – dumpling soup
банштай цай *(banshtai tsai)* – dumplings in tea
бантан *(bantan)* – cream soup
бифштекс *(bifshteks)* – patty
будаатай *(budaatai)* – with rice
бууз *(buuz)* – steamed mutton dumplings

гоймонтай шөл *(goimontai shöl)* – noodle soup
гурилтай шөл *(guriltai shöl)* – noodle soup

хонины мах *(khoniny makh)* – mutton
хуйцай *(khuitsai)* – vegetable & meatball soup
хууурга *(khuurga)* – meat in sauce
хуушуур *(khuushuur)* – fried meat pancake
луувангийн зууш *(luuvangiin zuush)* – carrot salad

мах *(makh)* – meat

ногоон зууш *(nogoon zuush)* – vegetable salad
нийслел зууш *(niislel zuush)* – potato salad
ногоотой *(nogootoi)* – with vegetables

рашаан ус *(rashaan us)* – mineral water

шар айраг *(shar airag)* – beer
шарсан өндөг *(sharsan öndög)* – fried egg
шарсан тахиа *(sharsan takhia)* – fried chicken
шницель *(shnitsel)* – schnitzel
шөл *(shöl)* – soup
сосиск *(sosisk)* – sausage
сүүтей цай *(süütei tsai)* – Mongolian milk tea

талх *(talkh)* – bread
цай *(tsai)* – tea
цөцгий *(tsötsgii)* – sour cream
цуйван *(tsuivan)* – fried noodles with meat

загас *(zagas)* – fish
зайдас *(zaidas)* – sausage

LONELY PLANET

You already know that Lonely Planet produces more than this one guidebook, but you might not be aware of the other products we have on this region. Here is a selection of titles that you may want to check out as well:

Mongolia
ISBN 1 86450 064 6
US$17.99 • UK£11.99

Cantonese phrasebook
ISBN 0 86442 645 3
US$6.95 • UK£4.50

Mongolian phrasebook
ISBN 0 86442 308 X
US$5.95 • UK£3.50

Beijing
ISBN 1 74059 281 6
US$15.99 • UK£9.99

China
ISBN 1 74059 117 8
US$29.99 • UK£17.99

Mandarin phrasebook
ISBN 0 86442 652 6
US$7.95 • UK£4.50

Moscow
ISBN 1 86450 054 9
US$15.99 • UK£9.99

Eastern Europe
ISBN 1 86450 149 9
US$24.99 • UK£14.99

Eastern Europe phrasebook
ISBN 1 86450 227 4
US$8.99 • UK£4.99

St Petersburg
ISBN 1 86450 325 4
US$15.99 • UK£9.99

Russia, Ukraine & Belarus
ISBN 0 86442 713 1
US$27.95 • UK£16.99

Russian phrasebook
ISBN 1 86450 106 5
US$7.95 • UK£4.50

Available wherever books are sold

LONELY PLANET

ON THE ROAD

Travel Guides explore cities, regions and countries, and supply information on transport, restaurants and accommodation, covering all budgets. They come with reliable, easy-to-use maps, practical advice, cultural and historical facts and a rundown on attractions both on and off the beaten track. There are over 200 titles in this classic series, covering nearly every country in the world.

 Lonely Planet Upgrades extend the shelf life of existing travel guides by detailing any changes that may affect travel in a region since a book has been published. Upgrades can be downloaded for free from **www.lonelyplanet.com/upgrades**

For travellers with more time than money, **Shoestring** guides offer dependable, first-hand information with hundreds of detailed maps, plus insider tips for stretching money as far as possible. Covering entire continents in most cases, the six-volume shoestring guides are known around the world as 'backpackers bibles'.

For the discerning short-term visitor, **Condensed** guides highlight the best a destination has to offer in a full-colour, pocket-sized format designed for quick access. They include everything from top sights and walking tours to opinionated reviews of where to eat, stay, shop and have fun.

CitySync lets travellers use their Palm™ or Visor™ hand-held computers to guide them through a city with handy tips on transport, history, cultural life, major sights, and shopping and entertainment options. It can also quickly search and sort hundreds of reviews of hotels, restaurants and attractions, and pinpoint their location on scrollable street maps. CitySync can be downloaded from **www.citysync.com**

MAPS & ATLASES

Lonely Planet's **City Maps** feature downtown and metropolitan maps, as well as transit routes and walking tours. The maps come complete with an index of streets, a listing of sights and a plastic coat for extra durability.

Road Atlases are an essential navigation tool for serious travellers. Cross-referenced with the guidebooks, they also feature distance and climate charts and a complete site index.

LONELY PLANET

ESSENTIALS

Read This First books help new travellers to hit the road with confidence. These invaluable predeparture guides give step-by-step advice on preparing for a trip, budgeting, arranging a visa, planning an itinerary and staying safe while still getting off the beaten track.

Healthy Travel pocket guides offer a regional rundown on disease hot spots and practical advice on predeparture health measures, staying well on the road and what to do in emergencies. The guides come with a user-friendly design and helpful diagrams and tables.

Lonely Planet's **Phrasebooks** cover the essential words and phrases travellers need when they're strangers in a strange land. They come in a pocket-sized format with colour tabs for quick reference, extensive vocabulary lists, easy-to-follow pronunciation keys and two-way dictionaries.

Miffed by blurry photos of the Taj Mahal? Tired of the classic 'top of the head cut off' shot? **Travel Photography: A Guide to Taking Better Pictures** will help you turn ordinary holiday snaps into striking images and give you the know-how to capture every scene, from frenetic festivals to peaceful beach sunrises.

Lonely Planet's **Travel Journal** is a lightweight but sturdy travel diary for jotting down all those on-the-road observations and significant travel moments. It comes with a handy time-zone wheel, a world map and useful travel information.

Lonely Planet's **eKno** is an all-in-one communication service developed especially for travellers. It offers low-cost international calls and free email and voicemail so that you can keep in touch while on the road. Check it out on **www.ekno.lonelyplanet.com**

FOOD & RESTAURANT GUIDES

Lonely Planet's **Out to Eat** guides recommend the brightest and best places to eat and drink in top international cities. These gourmet companions are arranged by neighbourhood, packed with dependable maps, garnished with scene-setting photos and served with quirky features.

For people who live to eat, drink and travel, **World Food** guides explore the culinary culture of each country. Entertaining and adventurous, each guide is packed with detail on staples and specialities, regional cuisine and local markets, as well as sumptuous recipes, comprehensive culinary dictionaries and lavish photos good enough to eat.

LONELY PLANET

OUTDOOR GUIDES

For those who believe the best way to see the world is on foot, Lonely Planet's **Walking Guides** detail everything from family strolls to difficult treks, with 'when to go and how to do it' advice supplemented by reliable maps and essential travel information.

Cycling Guides map a destination's best bike tours, long and short, in day-by-day detail. They contain all the information a cyclist needs, including advice on bike maintenance, places to eat and stay, innovative maps with detailed cues to the rides, and elevation charts.

The **Watching Wildlife** series is perfect for travellers who want authoritative information but don't want to tote a heavy field guide. Packed with advice on where, when and how to view a region's wildlife, each title features photos of over 300 species and contains engaging comments on the local flora and fauna.

With underwater colour photos throughout, **Pisces Books** explore the world's best diving and snorkelling areas. Each book contains listings of diving services and dive resorts, detailed information on depth, visibility and difficulty of dives, and a roundup of the marine life you're likely to see through your mask.

OFF THE ROAD

Journeys, the travel literature series written by renowned travel authors, capture the spirit of a place or illuminate a culture with a journalist's attention to detail and a novelist's flair for words. These are tales to soak up while you're actually on the road or dip into as an at-home armchair indulgence.

The range of lavishly illustrated **Pictorial** books is just the ticket for both travellers and dreamers. Off-beat tales and vivid photographs bring the adventure of travel to your doorstep long before the journey begins and long after it is over.

Lonely Planet **Videos** encourage the same independent, tough-minded approach as the guidebooks. Currently airing throughout the world, this award-winning series features innovative footage and an original soundtrack.

Yes, we know, work is tough, so do a little bit of deskside dreaming with the spiral-bound Lonely Planet **Diary** or a Lonely Planet **Wall Calendar**, filled with great photos from around the world.

TRAVELLERS NETWORK

Lonely Planet Online. Lonely Planet's award-winning Web site has insider information on hundreds of destinations, from Amsterdam to Zimbabwe, complete with interactive maps and relevant links. The site also offers the latest travel news, recent reports from travellers on the road, guidebook upgrades, a travel links site, an online book-buying option and a lively travellers bulletin board. It can be viewed at **www.lonelyplanet.com** or AOL keyword: lp.

Comet, our free monthly email newsletter, is loaded with travel news, advice, dispatches from authors, raging debates, travel competitions and letters from readers. To subscribe, click on the newsletters link on the front page of our Web site or go to: **www.lonelyplanet.com/comet/**.

Planet Talk is a free quarterly print newsletter, full of travel advice, tips from fellow travellers, author articles, news about forthcoming Lonely Planet events and a complete list of Lonely Planet books and other products. It provides an antidote to the being-at-home blues and helps you dream about and plan your next trip. To join our mailing list contact any Lonely Planet office or email us at: talk2us@lonelyplanet.com.au.

Lonely Planet Guides by Region

Lonely Planet is known worldwide for publishing practical, reliable and no-nonsense travel information in our guides and on our Web site. The Lonely Planet list covers just about every accessible part of the world. Currently there are 16 series: Travel guides, Shoestring guides, Condensed guides, Phrasebooks, Read This First, Healthy Travel, Walking guides, Cycling guides, Watching Wildlife guides, Pisces Diving & Snorkeling guides, City Maps, Road Atlases, Out to Eat, World Food, Journeys travel literature and Pictorials.

AFRICA Africa on a shoestring • Botswana • Cairo • Cairo City Map • Cape Town • Cape Town City Map • East Africa • Egypt • Egyptian Arabic phrasebook • Ethiopia, Eritrea & Djibouti • Ethiopian Amharic phrasebook • The Gambia & Senegal • Healthy Travel Africa • Kenya • Malawi • Morocco • Moroccan Arabic phrasebook • Mozambique • Namibia • Read This First: Africa • South Africa, Lesotho & Swaziland • Southern Africa • Southern Africa Road Atlas • Swahili phrasebook • Tanzania, Zanzibar & Pemba • Trekking in East Africa • Tunisia • Watching Wildlife East Africa • Watching Wildlife Southern Africa • West Africa • World Food Morocco • Zambia • Zimbabwe, Botswana & Namibia
Travel Literature: Mali Blues: Traveling to an African Beat • The Rainbird: A Central African Journey • Songs to an African Sunset: A Zimbabwean Story

AUSTRALIA & THE PACIFIC Aboriginal Australia & the Torres Strait Islands •Auckland • Australia • Australian phrasebook • Australia Road Atlas • Cycling Australia • Cycling New Zealand • Fiji • Fijian phrasebook • Healthy Travel Australia, NZ & the Pacific • Islands of Australia's Great Barrier Reef • Melbourne • Melbourne City Map • Micronesia • New Caledonia • New South Wales • New Zealand • Northern Territory • Outback Australia • Out to Eat – Melbourne • Out to Eat – Sydney • Papua New Guinea • Pidgin phrasebook • Queensland • Rarotonga & the Cook Islands • Samoa • Solomon Islands • South Australia • South Pacific • South Pacific phrasebook • Sydney • Sydney City Map • Sydney Condensed • Tahiti & French Polynesia • Tasmania • Tonga • Tramping in New Zealand • Vanuatu • Victoria • Walking in Australia • Watching Wildlife Australia • Western Australia
Travel Literature: Islands in the Clouds: Travels in the Highlands of New Guinea • Kiwi Tracks: A New Zealand Journey • Sean & David's Long Drive

CENTRAL AMERICA & THE CARIBBEAN Bahamas, Turks & Caicos • Baja California • Belize, Guatemala & Yucatán • Bermuda • Central America on a shoestring • Costa Rica • Costa Rica Spanish phrasebook • Cuba • Cycling Cuba • Dominican Republic & Haiti • Eastern Caribbean • Guatemala • Havana • Healthy Travel Central & South America • Jamaica • Mexico • Mexico City • Panama • Puerto Rico • Read This First: Central & South America • Virgin Islands • World Food Caribbean • World Food Mexico • Yucatán
Travel Literature: Green Dreams: Travels in Central America

EUROPE Amsterdam • Amsterdam City Map • Amsterdam Condensed • Andalucía • Athens • Austria • Baltic States phrasebook • Barcelona • Barcelona City Map • Belgium & Luxembourg • Berlin • Berlin City Map • Britain • British phrasebook • Brussels, Bruges & Antwerp • Brussels City Map • Budapest • Budapest City Map • Canary Islands • Catalunya & the Costa Brava • Central Europe • Central Europe phrasebook • Copenhagen • Corfu & the Ionians • Corsica • Crete • Crete Condensed • Croatia • Cycling Britain • Cycling France • Cyprus • Czech & Slovak Republics • Czech phrasebook • Denmark • Dublin • Dublin City Map • Dublin Condensed • Eastern Europe • Eastern Europe phrasebook • Edinburgh • Edinburgh City Map • England • Estonia, Latvia & Lithuania • Europe on a shoestring • Europe phrasebook • Finland • Florence • Florence City Map • France • Frankfurt City Map • Frankfurt Condensed • French phrasebook • Georgia, Armenia & Azerbaijan • Germany • German phrasebook • Greece • Greek Islands • Greek phrasebook • Hungary • Iceland, Greenland & the Faroe Islands • Ireland • Italian phrasebook • Italy • Kraków • Lisbon • The Loire • London • London City Map • London Condensed • Madrid • Madrid City Map • Malta • Mediterranean Europe • Milan, Turin & Genoa • Moscow • Munich • Netherlands • Normandy • Norway • Out to Eat – London • Out to Eat – Paris • Paris • Paris City Map • Paris Condensed • Poland • Polish phrasebook • Portugal • Portuguese phrasebook • Prague • Prague City Map • Provence & the Côte d'Azur • Read This First: Europe • Rhodes & the Dodecanese • Romania & Moldova • Rome • Rome City Map • Rome Condensed • Russia, Ukraine & Belarus • Russian phrasebook • Scandinavian & Baltic Europe • Scandinavian phrasebook • Scotland • Sicily • Slovenia • South-West France • Spain • Spanish phrasebook • Stockholm • St Petersburg • St Petersburg City Map • Sweden • Switzerland • Tuscany • Ukrainian phrasebook • Venice • Vienna • Wales • Walking in Britain • Walking in France • Walking in Ireland • Walking in Italy • Walking in Scotland • Walking in Spain • Walking in Switzerland • Western Europe • World Food France • World Food Greece • World Food Ireland • World Food Italy • World Food Spain **Travel Literature:** After Yugoslavia • Love and War in the Apennines • The Olive Grove: Travels in Greece • On the Shores of the Mediterranean • Round Ireland in Low Gear • A Small Place in Italy

Lonely Planet Mail Order

Lonely Planet products are distributed worldwide. They are also available by mail order from Lonely Planet, so if you have difficulty finding a title please write to us. North and South American residents should write to 150 Linden St, Oakland, CA 94607, USA; European and African residents should write to 10a Spring Place, London NW5 3BH, UK; and residents of other countries to Locked Bag 1, Footscray, Victoria 3011, Australia.

INDIAN SUBCONTINENT & THE INDIAN OCEAN Bangladesh • Bengali phrasebook • Bhutan • Delhi • Goa • Healthy Travel Asia & India • Hindi & Urdu phrasebook • India • India & Bangladesh City Map • Indian Himalaya • Karakoram Highway • Kathmandu City Map • Kerala • Madagascar • Maldives • Mauritius, Réunion & Seychelles • Mumbai (Bombay) • Nepal • Nepali phrasebook • North India • Pakistan • Rajasthan • Read This First: Asia & India • South India • Sri Lanka • Sri Lanka phrasebook • Tibet • Tibetan phrasebook • Trekking in the Indian Himalaya • Trekking in the Karakoram & Hindukush • Trekking in the Nepal Himalaya • World Food India **Travel Literature:** The Age of Kali: Indian Travels and Encounters • Hello Goodnight: A Life of Goa • In Rajasthan • Maverick in Madagascar • A Season in Heaven: True Tales from the Road to Kathmandu • Shopping for Buddhas • A Short Walk in the Hindu Kush • Slowly Down the Ganges

MIDDLE EAST & CENTRAL ASIA Bahrain, Kuwait & Qatar • Central Asia • Central Asia phrasebook • Dubai • Farsi (Persian) phrasebook • Hebrew phrasebook • Iran • Israel & the Palestinian Territories • Istanbul • Istanbul City Map • Istanbul to Cairo • Istanbul to Kathmandu • Jerusalem • Jerusalem City Map • Jordan • Lebanon • Middle East • Oman & the United Arab Emirates • Syria • Turkey • Turkish phrasebook • World Food Turkey • Yemen **Travel Literature:** Black on Black: Iran Revisited • Breaking Ranks: Turbulent Travels in the Promised Land • The Gates of Damascus • Kingdom of the Film Stars: Journey into Jordan

NORTH AMERICA Alaska • Boston • Boston City Map • Boston Condensed • British Columbia • California & Nevada • California Condensed • Canada • Chicago • Chicago City Map • Chicago Condensed • Florida • Georgia & the Carolinas • Great Lakes • Hawaii • Hiking in Alaska • Hiking in the USA • Honolulu & Oahu City Map • Las Vegas • Los Angeles • Los Angeles City Map • Louisiana & the Deep South • Miami • Miami City Map • Montreal • New England • New Orleans • New Orleans City Map • New York City • New York City City Map • New York City Condensed • New York, New Jersey & Pennsylvania • Oahu • Out to Eat – San Francisco • Pacific Northwest • Rocky Mountains • San Diego & Tijuana • San Francisco • San Francisco City Map • Seattle • Seattle City Map • Southwest • Texas • Toronto • USA • USA phrasebook • Vancouver • Vancouver City Map • Virginia & the Capital Region • Washington, DC • Washington, DC City Map • World Food New Orleans **Travel Literature:** Caught Inside: A Surfer's Year on the California Coast • Drive Thru America

NORTH-EAST ASIA Beijing • Beijing City Map • Cantonese phrasebook • China • Hiking in Japan • Hong Kong & Macau • Hong Kong City Map • Hong Kong Condensed • Japan • Japanese phrasebook • Korea • Korean phrasebook • Kyoto • Mandarin phrasebook • Mongolia • Mongolian phrasebook • Seoul • Shanghai • South-West China • Taiwan • Tokyo • Tokyo Condensed • World Food Hong Kong • World Food Japan **Travel Literature:** In Xanadu: A Quest • Lost Japan

SOUTH AMERICA Argentina, Uruguay & Paraguay • Bolivia • Brazil • Brazilian phrasebook • Buenos Aires • Buenos Aires City Map • Chile & Easter Island • Colombia • Ecuador & the Galapagos Islands • Healthy Travel Central & South America • Latin American Spanish phrasebook • Peru • Quechua phrasebook • Read This First: Central & South America • Rio de Janeiro • Rio de Janeiro City Map • Santiago de Chile • South America on a shoestring • Trekking in the Patagonian Andes • Venezuela **Travel Literature:** Full Circle: A South American Journey

SOUTH-EAST ASIA Bali & Lombok • Bangkok • Bangkok City Map • Burmese phrasebook • Cambodia • Cycling Vietnam, Laos & Cambodia • East Timor phrasebook • Hanoi • Healthy Travel Asia & India • Hill Tribes phrasebook • Ho Chi Minh City (Saigon) • Indonesia • Indonesian phrasebook • Indonesia's Eastern Islands • Java • Lao phrasebook • Laos • Malay phrasebook • Malaysia, Singapore & Brunei • Myanmar (Burma) • Philippines • Pilipino (Tagalog) phrasebook • Read This First: Asia & India • Singapore • Singapore City Map • South-East Asia on a shoestring • South-East Asia phrasebook • Thailand • Thailand's Islands & Beaches • Thailand, Vietnam, Laos & Cambodia Road Atlas • Thai phrasebook • Vietnam • Vietnamese phrasebook • World Food Indonesia • World Food Thailand • World Food Vietnam

ALSO AVAILABLE: Antarctica • The Arctic • The Blue Man: Tales of Travel, Love and Coffee • Brief Encounters: Stories of Love, Sex & Travel • Buddhist Stupas in Asia: The Shape of Perfection • Chasing Rickshaws • The Last Grain Race • Lonely Planet ... On the Edge: Adventurous Escapades from Around the World • Lonely Planet Unpacked • Lonely Planet Unpacked Again • Not the Only Planet: Science Fiction Travel Stories • Ports of Call: A Journey by Sea • Sacred India • Travel Photography: A Guide to Taking Better Pictures • Travel with Children • Tuvalu: Portrait of an Island Nation

Index

Abbreviations

C – China   M – Mongolia   R – Russia

Text

A

accommodation 49-51
  on the train 49
Achinsk (R) 164
activities 47-8, 245, 264, see also individual entries
Afghanistan War (1979–89) 170
air travel 57-62
  airports & airlines 57
  departure taxes 59
  to the region 59-61
  tickets 57-9
  within the region 61-2
Akademgorodok (R) 135, 183, 187
Akikan Valley (R) 224
Alexander II 113, 115
Alexander III 115, 116, 123, 138, 222
Altay Mountains (R) 185
Altay people 185
Amazar (R) 229
Amur leopard 230, 244
Amur River (R) 200, 229, 236, 241
Amur tiger, see Siberian tiger
Amursky Gulf (R) 230, 245
Angangxi (C) 267
Angara 120, 205, 222, 225
Angara River (R) 190, 222, 225
animals 203, 209-20, 230, 244, 245, 251, 252, 263
Arctic Circle 192, 197
Arzamas (R) 145
Assumption Cathedral, Vladimir (R) 151
AYam (Amur-Yakutsk Mainline) 191

B

Babushkin, Ivan 225
Bada (R) 228
Badaling (C) 253, 280
baggage, see luggage
Baikal Nature Reserve (R) 225
Baikal seal 206, 220
Baikal 205, 222, 225

Bold indicates maps.

Baikal-Amur Mainline (BAM) 129-30, 190-1, 208, 229
  museum, Severobaikalsk 208
  museum, Tynda 190
Baikalsh River (R) 219
Baikalskoe (R) 224
Baikalsky Range (R) 224
Balyezino (R) 145
Bamovskaya (R) 191, 229
banya 47, 97-8, 184
Barabinsk (R) 163
bargaining, see tipping & bargaining
Barguzin National Reserve (R) 207
Baruun Bayan River (M) 264
Bay of Ayaya (R) 224
beaches 47, 205
bears 214-15, 230
Beijing (C) 253, 268, 274-88, **276**
  accommodation 283-4
  attractions 275-85
  bars & clubs 286-8
  email & Internet access 275
  entertainment 286-7
  food 285-6
  Forbidden City 274, 275, 278
  history 274
  information 274-5
  Kunming Lake 278
  opera & acrobatics 286
  shopping 287-8
  Summer Palace 278-9
  Temple of Heaven 279
  temples 279, 282-3
  Tiananmen Square 278
  tourist offices 274
  travel to/from 288
  travel within 287-8
Belogorsk (R) 229
Bidzhan River(R) 235
Bikin (R) 229
Bikin River (R) 229
Bira River (R) 235
birds 215-19, 245, 263, 268
  crow family 219
  Lake Baikal 219-20
  raptors 218-219
  waterbirds 216-17

waterside 217-18
bird-watching 163, 245, 268
Birobidzhan (R) 229, 235-6
Blagodtnoye Lake (R) 245
Blagoveshchensk (R) 229
Bloody Sunday (1905) 72, 123
Bo Sea 280
boat travel 66-7
Bogdkhan Uul Mountains (M) 251
Bogdkhan Uul Strictly Protected Area (M) 263
Bogolyubovo (R) 145, 151
Bogotol (R) 164
Boketu (C) 265
Bolshevik Revolution (1917) 72, 79, 124, 166, 198, 243, 269
Bolshie Koty (R) 207
Bolshoi Ballet 100
bookings 14-18, 173
  Trans-Manchurian 14
  Trans-Mongolian 14
  Trans-Siberian 14
books 31-3, see also literature
  guidebooks 32
  history & politics 32-3
  travel 32
border crossings 62
  Asia 63-6
  Europe 63
  Finland & the Baltics 63, 64
  Mongolia-China 251
  Russia-China 267
  Russia-Mongolia 251, 252
Borzya 265
Boxer Rebellion 121
Bratsk (R) 190
Bratsk Sea (R) 190
Brynner, Yul 244
Buddhism
  China 279, 282
  Mongolia 142, 254, 257, 260, 263-4
  Russia 230, 231-2, 234-5, 249
Bukhta Peschanaya (R) 207
Buryat people 135, 198, 225, 230, 231, 232, 249
bus travel to the region 63-6
business hours 45-6

Bold indicates maps.

Bold indicates maps.

Boxed Text

MAP LEGEND

CITY ROUTES

Freeway _____ Freeway	⊐⊐⊐⊐ _____ Unsealed Road
Highway _____ Primary Road	_____ One Way Street
Road _____ Secondary Road	_____ Pedestrian Street
Street _____ Street	⊞⊞⊞⊞ _____ Stepped Street
Lane _____ Lane	⊐)= = _____ Tunnel
_____ On/Off Ramp	_____ Footbridge

REGIONAL ROUTES

_____ Tollway, Freeway
_____ Primary Road
_____ Secondary Road
_____ Minor Road

BOUNDARIES

▬ ▪ ▬ ▪ _____ International
▬ ▪ ▪ ▬ _____ State
▬ ▬ ▬ _____ Disputed
▬ ▬ _____ Fortified Wall

HYDROGRAPHY

_____ River, Creek	_____ Dry Lake; Salt Lake
_____ Canal	_____ Spring; Rapids
_____ Lake	_____ Waterfalls

TRANSPORT ROUTES & STATIONS

_____ Train	_____ Ferry
_____ Underground Train	_____ Walking Trail
_____ Metro	_____ Walking Tour
_____ Tramway	_____ Path
_____ Funicular Railway	_____ Pier or Jetty

AREA FEATURES

_____ Building	_____ Market	_____ Beach	_____ Campus
_____ Park, Gardens	_____ Sports Ground	_____ Cemetery	_____ Plaza

POPULATION SYMBOLS

✪ CAPITAL _____ National Capital	● CITY _____ City	● Village _____ Village
◉ CAPITAL _____ State Capital	● Town _____ Town	_____ Urban Area

MAP SYMBOLS

▪ _____ Place to Stay	▼ _____ Place to Eat	● _____ Point of Interest

✈ _____ Airport	⊞ _____ Church	⊙ _____ Mosque	⊠ _____ Ruins
⊛ _____ Bank	⊞ _____ Cinema	⊞ _____ Museum, Gallery	⊠ _____ Shopping Centre
⊡ _____ Bus Terminal	⊡ _____ Embassy	⟓ _____ Nature Park	⊞ _____ Stately Home
⊠ _____ Camping	⊕ _____ Fountain	⊞ _____ Police Station	⊠ _____ Synagogue
⊞ _____ Castle	⊕ _____ Hospital	⊠ _____ Post Office	⊞ _____ Temple
⊟ _____ Cathedral	⊡ _____ Internet Cafe	⊟ _____ Pub or Bar	❶ _____ Tourist Information
⊕ _____ Cave	⚑ _____ Monument	⊙ _____ Public Toilet	⊞ _____ Zoo

Note: not all symbols displayed above appear in this book

LONELY PLANET OFFICES

Australia
Locked Bag 1, Footscray, Victoria 3011
☎ 03 8379 8000 fax 03 8379 8111
email: talk2us@lonelyplanet.com.au

UK
10a Spring Place, London NW5 3BH
☎ 020 7428 4800 fax 020 7428 4828
email: go@lonelyplanet.co.uk

USA
150 Linden St, Oakland, CA 94607
☎ 510 893 8555 TOLL FREE: 800 275 8555
fax 510 893 8572
email: info@lonelyplanet.com

France
1 rue du Dahomey, 75011 Paris
☎ 01 55 25 33 00 fax 01 55 25 33 01
email: bip@lonelyplanet.fr
www.lonelyplanet.fr

World Wide Web: www.lonelyplanet.com *or* AOL keyword: lp
Lonely Planet Images: lpi@lonelyplanet.com.au